INTRODUCTION.

PREFATORY NOTE.—Owing to the numerous amendments recently adopted to the Constitution of the state, a new edition, bringing down to date both the text of the Constitution and the decisions construing its provisions, appears to be a necessity. While each election has added to it many new and radical features, many of them extremely detailed in character and partaking more the nature of legislative acts than provisions of a constitution, still the people at the last general election defeated a proposition for a constitutional convention to revise the Constitution. This attitude is largely due to the fact that the Constitution can be amended about as readily as a legislative act can be passed, and the habit of avoiding all constitutional questions by putting legislation in the form of constitutional amendments is growing at a rate calculated to alarm those who would desire to see the Constitution of the state a permanent instrument of fundamental principles and provisions. The more detailed the Constitution becomes, the more often will it require amendment, and it has already been amended over one hundred times. This condition will continue as long as legislative detail is retained in the Constitution. The present condition can only be considered transitory, and must eventually be remedied by a general revision in which all legislative matters shall be eliminated.

In preparing this volume, the aim has been to present in the most convenient form the decisions of our own courts, only referring to the decisions of other courts on subjects which our own have left untouched. While the main subject is the present Constitution of this state, the book also contains the former Constitution, the Constitution of the United States, and the treaty of Guadalupe Hidalgo.

Important features.—Some important features of the present edition are the following: (1) A table showing all

TABLE OF CONTENTS.

(iii)

SAN FRANCISCO
THE FILMER BROTHERS ELECTROTYPE COMPANY
TYPOGRAPHERS AND STEREOTYPERS

INTRODUCTION.

PREFATORY NOTE.—Owing to the numerous amendments recently adopted to the Constitution of the state, a new edition, bringing down to date both the text of the Constitution and the decisions construing its provisions, appears to be a necessity. While each election has added to it many new and radical features, many of them extremely detailed in character and partaking more the nature of legislative acts than provisions of a constitution, still the people at the last general election defeated a proposition for a constitutional convention to revise the Constitution. This attitude is largely due to the fact that the Constitution can be amended about as readily as a legislative act can be passed, and the habit of avoiding all constitutional questions by putting legislation in the form of constitutional amendments is growing at a rate calculated to alarm those who would desire to see the Constitution of the state a permanent instrument of fundamental principles and provisions. The more detailed the Constitution becomes, the more often will it require amendment, and it has already been amended over one hundred times. This condition will continue as long as legislative detail is retained in the Constitution. The present condition can only be considered transitory, and must eventually be remedied by a general revision in which all legislative matters shall be eliminated.

In preparing this volume, the aim has been to present in the most convenient form the decisions of our own courts, only referring to the decisions of other courts on subjects which our own have left untouched. While the main subject is the present Constitution of this state, the book also contains the former Constitution, the Constitution of the United States, and the treaty of Guadalupe Hidalgo.

Important features.—Some important features of the present edition are the following: (1) A table showing all

statutes of this state which have been declared unconstitutional in whole or in part. There are over one hundred and thirty such statutes scattered through the statute books. (2) A table of all California citations to either of the California Constitutions. This will permit a hasty examination of all decisions citing any particular section of the Constitution. (3) A table of parallel sections in the Constitutions of 1849 and 1879, which will also prove a useful feature. (4) Reference to all citations in the decisions of the federal courts regarding the Constitution of California. (5) The present text of the Constitution printed separately for ready reference. (6) References to decisions of the Railroad Commission of the state of California dealing with constitutional questions.

Annotations.—As to the form of the annotations, the aim has been to present in the most condensed form the principles of the decisions, rather than any statement of the facts of the cases. In other words, we have attempted something more than a mere digest, or syllabi of the decisions.

HISTORY OF THE CONSTITUTION.—California was admitted into the Union of states September 9, 1850. The first Constitution was adopted in convention October 10, 1849, ratified by the people November 13, 1849, proclaimed December 20, 1849. This Constitution was amended in 1857 and 1871, and the article on the judicial department was revised in 1862.

The present Constitution was adopted in convention March 3, 1879, ratified by the people May 7, 1879, and went into effect July 4, 1879, so far as it related to election of officers, etc., and January 1, 1880, for all other purposes. Various amendments have been made to it from time to time, but no systematic revision of it has been effected.

CONSTITUTIONAL CONSTRUCTION.—The Constitution of this state, unlike the federal Constitution, is not to be considered as a grant of power, but rather as a limita-

tion upon the powers of the legislature. (People v. Coleman, 4 Cal. 46, 60 Am. Dec. 581; People v. Jewett, 6 Cal. 291; State v. Rogers, 13 Cal. 159; People v. Twelfth District Court, 17 Cal. 547; Bourland v. Hildreth, 26 Cal. 161; Ex parte McCarthy, 29 Cal. 395.)

It is, however, to be considered as a grant of power to the other branches of the government. (People v. Jewett, 6 Cal. 291.)

Words and phrases.—Where a word, having a technical, as well as a popular, meaning, is used in the Constitution, the courts will accord to it its popular meaning, unless the nature of the subject indicates, or the context suggests, that it is used in its technical sense. (Weill v. Kenfield, 54 Cal. 111; Oakland Pav. Co. v. Hilton, 69 Cal. 479, 11 Pac. 3; Oakland Pav. Co. v. Tompkins, 72 Cal. 5, 1 Am. St. Rep. 17, 12 Pac. 801; Miller v. Dunn, 72 Cal. 462, 1 Am. St. Rep. 67, 14 Pac. 27; People v. Eddy, 43 Cal. 331, 13 Am. Rep. 143.)

Prospective construction.—Provisions of the Constitution are to be considered prospective and not retrospective unless a contrary intention clearly appears. (Gurnee v. Superior Court, 58 Cal. 88.)

Reasonable construction.—A construction should be adopted which tends to certainty, security, and substantial justice, in preference to that which involves uncertainty, insecurity, and inevitable injustice. (San Gabriel Land etc. Co. v. Witmer Bros. Co., 96 Cal. 623, 18 L. R. A. 465, 29 Pac. 500, 31 Pac. 588.)

But where a provision is plain and unambiguous, it cannot be changed by the courts to avoid what may seem to be an absurdity or injustice. (Moran v. Ross, 79 Cal. 549, 21 Pac. 958.)

All the provisions of the Constitution must be read together, and effect given to all of them. They must receive a practical common-sense construction, and be considered with reference to the prior state of the law, and the mis-

chief intended to be remedied.   (People v. Stephens, 62 Cal.
209; French v. Teschemaker, 24 Cal. 518.)

> Construction of inconsistent provisions or amendments of Con-
> stitution. See note, 18 Ann. Cas. 725.

**MEANS OF CONSTRUCTION—Debates of the conven-
tion.**—The debates of the constitutional convention may be
referred to for the purpose of construing the provisions of
the Constitution.   (People v. Chapman, 61 Cal. 262; People
v. Stephens, 62 Cal. 209; Isola v. Weber, 13 Misc. Rep. 100,
34 N. Y. Supp. 77; Higgins v. Prater, 91 Ky. 6, 14 S. W.
910; State v. Doron, 5 Nev. 399; Bank of Woodland v.
Pierce, 144 Cal. 434, 77 Pac. 1012.)

> Proceedings of constitutional convention as aid in construing Con-
> stitution. See notes, 10 Ann. Cas. 1146; 6 R. C. L., § 65, p. 67.

Judicial decisions.—Where a provision of the former Constitution, which has received a judicial construction, is cop-
ied into the new Constitution, it will be presumed that it
was adopted in view of that construction.   (Sharon v.
Sharon, 67 Cal. 185, 7 Pac. 456, 635, 8 Pac. 709; Thomason
v. Ruggles, 69 Cal. 465, 11 Pac. 20; Lord v. Dunster, 79 Cal.
477, 21 Pac. 865; People v. Freeman, 80 Cal. 233, 13 Am.
St. Rep. 122, 22 Pac. 173; People v. O'Brien, 96 Cal. 171, 31
Pac. 45; Morton v. Broderick, 118 Cal. 474, 50 Pac. 644;
Ex parte Ahern, 103 Cal. 412, 37 Pac. 390; People v. Edwards, 93 Cal. 153, 28 Pac. 831; Palache v. Hunt, 64 Cal.
473, 2 Pac. 245.)

The mere fact that a change is made in the phraseology
of such provision by subsequent revision will not be deemed
a change in the law, unless such phraseology evidently purports an intention to make a change.   (Hyatt v. Allen, 54
Cal. 353.)

The same rule applies to provisions of the Constitution
borrowed from the Constitutions of other states, and where
such provisions have received judicial construction in such
states, they are to be deemed to have been adopted in view
of such construction.   (People v. Coleman, 4 Cal. 46, 60
Am. Dec. 581; People v. Webb, 38 Cal. 467; Ex parte Liddell, 93 Cal. 633, 29 Pac. 251.)

The exposition of the Constitution by the highest court in existence under it, with regard to laws passed while it was in force, should be accepted by all succeeding courts, without regard to their own views as to the correctness of the doctrine. (Staude v. Board of Election Commrs., 61 Cal. 313; Emery v. Reed, 65 Cal. 351, 4 Pac. 200; Davis v. Superior Court, 63 Cal. 581. See, also, Ferris v. Coover, 11 Cal. 175.)

Legislative construction.—Legislative construction of a constitutional provision is a method of interpretation. (Moran v. Ross, 79 Cal. 159, 21 Pac. 547; San Luis Obispo County v. Darke, 76 Cal. 92, 18 Pac. 118; Lord v. Dunster, 79 Cal. 477, 21 Pac. 865; Washington v. Page, 4 Cal. 388; Bank of Woodland v. Pierce, 144 Cal. 434, 77 Pac. 1012.)

But this does not mean that the hasty and inconsiderate legislation of three winters shall be conclusive of the constitutionality of such legislation. (People v. Wells, 2 Cal. 198, 208.)

The fact that ever since the adoption of the Constitution all executive officers other than the governor and lieutenant-governor have been installed in office on the first Monday after the first day of January is entitled to great weight in the construction of the meaning of the Constitution. (People v. Nye, 9 Cal. App. 148, 98 Pac. 241.)

Universal practice of assessors may be looked to in aid of the construction of provisions of the Constitution relating to taxation. (Bank of Woodland v. Pierce, 144 Cal. 434, 77 Pac. 1012.)

POWER TO DECLARE STATUTES UNCONSTITUTIONAL.—A government with no limits but its own discretion is not a constitutional government, in the true sense of the term. (Billings v. Hall, 7 Cal. 1.)

The Constitution is a law, and must be construed by someone, and the judiciary possesses the power to construe it in all cases not expressly, or by necessary implication, reserved to the other departments. (Nougues v. Douglass, 7 Cal. 65; People v. Brooks, 16 Cal. 11.)

But where the right to determine the extent and effect of a restriction in the Constitution is expressly or by necessary implication confided to the legislature, the judiciary has no right to interfere with the legislative construction. (Nougues v. Douglass, 7 Cal. 65.)

In declaring a statute unconstitutional, the court cannot interfere with the exercise of the political power of the legislature. (Nougues v. Douglass, 7 Cal. 65.)

The courts can declare a statute unconstitutional only when the question arises as a pure matter of law unmixed with matters of fact. (Stevenson v. Colgan, 91 Cal. 649, 25 Am. St. Rep. 230, 14 L. R. A. 459, 27 Pac. 1089.)

Therefore, the constitutionality of a statute can be determined only from the facts appearing upon the face of the law, taken in connection with matters of which the court can take judicial notice. (Bourn v. Hart, 93 Cal. 321, 27 Am. St. Rep. 203, 15 L. R. A. 431, 28 Pac. 951; Stevenson v. Colgan, 91 Cal. 649, 25 Am. St. Rep. 230, 14 L. R. A. 459, 27 Pac. 1089; Conlin v. Board of Supervisors, 99 Cal. 17, 37 Am. St. Rep. 17, 21 L. R. A. 474, 33 Pac. 753; Fowler v. Peirce, 2 Cal. 165.)

But, while the courts may declare statutes unconstitutional, they have no power to avoid the effects of nonaction on the part of the legislature. (Myers v. English, 9 Cal. 341.)

> Power to declare statutes void. See 6 R. C. L., §§ 67–76, pp. 70–78.
>
> Extrinsic evidence to impeach statutes. See notes, 13 Am. Rep. 648; 51 Am. Rep. 616.

Presumption of constitutionality.—An act of the legislature is presumed to be constitutional. (In re Madera Irr. Dist., 92 Cal. 296, 27 Am. St. Rep. 106, 14 L. R. A. 755, 28 Pac. 272, 675; People v. Hayne, 83 Cal. 111, 17 Am. St. Rep. 217, 7 L. R. A. 348, 23 Pac. 1; In re Finley, 1 Cal. App. 198, 81 Pac. 1041; In re Bunkers, 1 Cal. App. 61, 81 Pac. 748; Title etc. Restoration Co. v. Kerrigan, 150 Cal. 289, 119 Am. St. Rep. 199, 8 L. R. A. (N. S.) 682, 88 Pac. 356; In re Spencer, 149 Cal. 396, 117 Am. St. Rep. 137, 9 Ann. Cas. 1105, 86

Pac. 896; Southern Cal. Lumber Co. v. Peters, 3 Cal. App. 478, 86 Pac. 816.)

A statute will not be declared unconstitutional, except when the conflict between it and the Constitution is palpable and incapable of reconciliation. (Stockton etc. R. R. Co. v. Common Council of Stockton, 41 Cal. 147; People v. Sassovich, 29 Cal. 480.)

Where there is a reasonable doubt as to its constitutionality, its constitutionality should be affirmed. (University of California v. Bernard, 57 Cal. 612; Bourland v. Hildreth, 26 Cal. 161.)

An act is to be so construed, if possible, as to make it constitutional. (French v. Teschemaker, 24 Cal. 518.)

Presumptions as to constitutionality. See 6 R. C. L., §§ 98–103, pp. 97–104.

Conflict with the Constitution.—In passing upon the constitutionality of a statute, the court is not required to imagine some possible contingency in which its provisions might conflict with the Constitution. (Woodward v. Fruitvale Sanitary Dist., 99 Cal. 554, 34 Pac. 239.)

In order to declare a statute unconstitutional, it is not necessary to find in the Constitution some specific inhibition which has been disregarded, or some express command which has been disobeyed; but if the statute is contrary to the first principles of the social compact, it is void. (Britton v. Board of Election Commrs., 129 Cal. 337, 51 L. R. A. 115, 61 Pac. 1115.)

Nor is it necessary to find some specific inhibition which, in precise language, refers to the particular law. (People v. Lynch, 51 Cal. 15, 21 Am. Rep. 677.)

But the courts cannot declare a law void upon the ground that it is contrary to the "spirit and policy of the Constitution," unless it is at variance with some express or clearly implied provision of that instrument. (Cohen v. Wright, 22 Cal. 293; Pattison v. Board of Suprs. of Yuba Co., 13 Cal. 175.)

When statutes will be declared void because conflicting with the Constitution. See note, 48 Am. Dec. 269.

Conflict with another statute.—The constitutionality of one act cannot be tested by the provisions of another. (Reed v. Omnibus R. R. Co., 33 Cal. 212.)

Motives.—The motives which induce legislative action are not a subject of judicial inquiry, and a legislative act cannot be declared unconstitutional because, in the opinion of the court, it was or might have been the result of improper considerations. (People v. Glenn Co., 100 Cal. 419, 38 Am. St. Rep. 305, 35 Pac. 302; People v. Bigler, 5 Cal. 23.)

The motives of the authors of a statute are equally immaterial. (Stockton etc. R. R. Co. v. Common Council of Stockton, 41 Cal. 147.)

> Judicial inquiry into motives prompting enactment of legislative ordinance. See note, Ann. Cas. 1912A, 716.
>
> Expediency, justice and policy of legislation. See 6 R. C. L., §§ 104–110, pp. 104–111.

Beneficial character.—In determining the constitutionality of a statute, its beneficial character cannot be considered. (Marsh v. Hanly, 111 Cal. 368, 43 Pac. 975.)

On the other hand, in construing the Constitution, the courts are bound to suppose that any inconveniences involved in the application of its provisions were considered in its formation, and accepted as less intolerable than those avoided, or as compensated by countervailing advantages. (People v. Pendegast, 96 Cal. 289, 31 Pac. 103.)

Impracticable statute.—A statute may also be declared void if it is impracticable. Thus an act providing for the appointment of three disinterested freeholders in the city and county of San Francisco to form an assessment district, which might include the entire city and county, and to assess the lands of the district for certain improvements, is void as impracticable, since it would be impossible to select disinterested commissioners. (Montgomery Avenue Case, 54 Cal. 579.)

> Long acquiescence in validity of statute as affecting its constitutionality. See notes, 16 Ann. Cas. 877; Ann. Cas. 1912A, 505.

EFFECT OF UNCONSTITUTIONALITY—Separable provisions.—The mere fact that certain provisions of a statute are in conflict with the Constitution does not necessarily render the entire act void. Where the court can see that an act, after eliminating all unconstitutional features, is still such an act as it may be presumed the legislature would have passed had it known such parts were void, the remainder may stand. (Dwyer v. Parker, 115 Cal. 544, 47 Pac. 372.)

If the different parts are severable and independent of each other, and the constitutional provisions are capable of being carried into effect after the unconstitutional part has been eliminated, and it is clear that it was the intent of the legislature to enact these provisions irrespective of the other, the unconstitutional provisions will be disregarded, and the statute read as if such provisions were not there. (Hale v. McGettigan, 114 Cal. 112, 45 Pac. 1049; Lathrop v. Mills, 19 Cal. 513; French v. Teschemaker, 24 Cal. 518; Mills v. Sargent, 36 Cal. 379; Christy v. Board of Supervisors, 39 Cal. 3; McCabe v. Jefferds, 122 Cal. 302, 54 Pac. 897; Rood v. McCargar, 49 Cal. 117; Johnson v. Tautphaus, 127 Cal. 605, 60 Pac. 172; People v. Whyler, 41 Cal. 351; McGowan v. McDonald, 111 Cal. 57, 52 Am. St. Rep. 149, 43 Pac. 418; Cahen v. Wells, 132 Cal. 447, 64 Pac. 699; In re Hallawell, 8 Cal. App. 563, 97 Pac. 320; In re Spencer, 149 Cal. 396, 117 Am. St. Rep. 137, 9 Ann. Cas. 1105, 86 Pac. 896.)

Inseparable provisions.—Where the constitutional and unconstitutional provisions of a statute are so inseparably blended together as to make it clear that either clause would not have been enacted without the other, the whole act is void. (San Francisco v. Spring Valley Water Works, 48 Cal. 493; Reed v. Omnibus R. R. Co., 33 Cal. 212; Orange Co. v. Harris, 97 Cal. 600, 32 Pac. 594; Wills v. Austin, 53 Cal. 152; Purdy v. Sinton, 56 Cal. 133; People v. Perry, 79 Cal. 105, 21 Pac. 423; Marsh v. Hanly, 111 Cal. 368, 43 Pac. 975; Lathrop v. Mills, 19 Cal. 513; Pioche v. Paul, 22 Cal. 105.)

If a provision be unconstitutional it cannot be given effect in part, if the result of giving it such partial effect would be to accomplish a purpose which the law-making power never intended, or where the legislative intent is doubtful. (Robert v. Police Court, 148 Cal. 131, 82 Pac. 838.)

Contracts and other statutes.—No repeal by implication can result from a provision in a subsequent statute, when that provision is itself devoid of constitutional force. (McAllister v. Hamlin, 83 Cal. 361, 23 Pac. 357.)

A contract entered into in view of an act later held unconstitutional is not made under a mistake of law. (Cooley v. Calaveras Co., 121 Cal. 482, 53 Pac. 1075.)

But a contract entered into by a public board or officer by sole authority of an unconstitutional statute is void, and not subject to ratification. (Phelan v. San Francisco, 6 Cal. 531.)

The legislature may refer to an unconstitutional act to indicate its will in respect to a constitutional purpose. (People v. Bircham, 12 Cal. 50.)

An unconstitutional act cannot have the effect to repeal prior acts on the same subject, though assuming to do so. (In re Clary, 149 Cal. 732, 87 Pac. 580.)

Liability for acts done under unconstitutional statute. See note, 64 Am. Dec. 51.

TABLE OF CASES CITED.

(xv)

CONTENTS

OF

CONSTITUTION OF 1879.

ARTICLE I.

DECLARATION OF RIGHTS.

ARTICLE II.

RIGHT OF SUFFRAGE.

ARTICLE III.

DISTRIBUTION OF POWERS.

ARTICLE IV.

LEGISLATIVE DEPARTMENT.

ARTICLE V.

EXECUTIVE DEPARTMENT.

ARTICLE VI.

JUDICIAL DEPARTMENT.

ARTICLE VII.

PARDONING POWER.

ARTICLE VIII.

MILITIA.

ARTICLE IX.

EDUCATION.

ARTICLE X.

STATE INSTITUTIONS AND PUBLIC BUILDINGS.

ARTICLE XI.

CITIES, COUNTIES, AND TOWNS.

ARTICLE XII.

CORPORATIONS.

ARTICLE XIII.

REVENUE AND TAXATION.

ARTICLE XIV.

WATER AND WATER RIGHTS.

ARTICLE XV.

HARBOR FRONTAGES, ETC.

ARTICLE XVI.

STATE INDEBTEDNESS.

ARTICLE XXI.
BOUNDARY.

ARTICLE XXII.
SCHEDULE.

ARTICLE XXIII.
RECALL OF PUBLIC OFFICIALS.

CONSTITUTION

STATE OF CALIFORNIA.

PREAMBLE AND DECLARATION OF RIGHTS.

PREAMBLE.

We, the people of the state of California, grateful to Almighty God for our freedom, in order to secure and perpetuate its blessings, do establish this Constitution.

ARTICLE I.

DECLARATION OF RIGHTS.

Section 1. All men are by nature free and independent, and have certain inalienable rights, among which are those of enjoying and defending life and liberty; acquiring, possessing, and protecting property; and pursuing and obtaining safety and happiness.

Sec. 2. All political power is inherent in the people. Government is instituted for the protection, security, and benefit of the people, and they have the right to alter or perform the same whenever the public good may require it.

Sec. 3. The state of California is an inseparable part of the American Union, and the Constitution of the United States is the supreme law of the land.

Sec. 4. The free exercise and enjoyment of religious profession and worship, without discrimination or preference, shall forever be guaranteed in this state; and no person shall be rendered incompetent to be a witness or juror on account of his opinions on matters of religious belief; but the liberty of conscience hereby secured shall not be so construed as to excuse acts of licentiousness, or justify practices inconsistent with the peace or safety of this state.

Constitution—1   (1)

Sec. 5. The privilege of the writ of habeas corpus shall not be suspended unless when, in cases of rebellion or invasion, the public safety may require its suspension.

Sec. 6. All persons shall be bailable by sufficient sureties, unless for capital offenses when the proof is evident or the presumption great. Excessive bail shall not be required; nor excessive fines imposed; nor shall cruel or unusual punishments be inflicted. Witnesses shall not be unreasonably detained, nor confined in any room where criminals are actually imprisoned.

Sec. 7. The right of trial by jury shall be secured to all, and remain inviolate; but in civil actions three-fourths of the jury may render a verdict. A trial by jury may be waived in all criminal cases not amounting to felony, by the consent of both parties, expressed in open court, and in civil actions by the consent of the parties, signified in such manner as may be prescribed by law. In civil actions and cases of misdemeanor, the jury may consist of twelve, or of any number less than twelve upon which the parties may agree in open court.

Sec. 8. Offenses heretofore required to be prosecuted by indictment shall be prosecuted by information, after examination and commitment by a magistrate, or by indictment, with or without such examination and commitment, as may be prescribed by law. A grand jury shall be drawn and summoned at least once a year in each county.

Sec. 9. Every citizen may freely speak, write, and publish his sentiments on all subjects, being responsible for the abuse of that right; and no law shall be passed to restrain or abridge the liberty of speech or of the press. In all criminal prosecutions for libels, the truth may be given in evidence to the jury; and if it shall appear to the jury that the matter charged as libelous is true, and was published with good motives, and for justifiable ends, the party shall be acquitted; and the jury shall have the right to determine the law and the fact. Indictments found, or information laid, for publications in newspapers, shall be tried in the county where such newspapers have their publication office,

or in the county where the party alleged to be libeled resided at the time of the alleged publication, unless the place of trial shall be changed for good cause.

Sec. 10. The people shall have the right to freely assemble together to consult for the common good, to instruct their representatives, and to petition the legislature for redress of grievances.

Sec. 11. All laws of a general nature shall have a uniform operation.

Sec. 12. The military shall be subordinate to the civil power. No standing army shall be kept up by this state in time of peace, and no soldier shall, in time of peace, be quartered in any house without the consent of the owner; nor in time of war, except in the manner prescribed by law.

Sec. 13. In criminal prosecutions, in any court whatever, the party accused shall have the right to a speedy and public trial; to have the process of the court to compel the attendance of witnesses in his behalf, and to appear and defend, in person and with counsel. No person shall be twice put in jeopardy for the same offense; nor be compelled, in any criminal case, to be a witness against himself; nor be deprived of life, liberty or property without due process of law. The legislature shall have power to provide for the taking, in the presence of the party accused and his counsel, of depositions of witnesses, in criminal cases other than cases of homicide, when there is reason to believe that the witness, from inability or other cause, will not attend at the trial.

Sec. 14. Private property shall not be taken or damaged for public use without just compensation having first been made to, or paid into court for, the owner, and no right of way shall be appropriated to the use of any corporation other than municipal until full compensation therefor be first made in money or ascertained and paid into court for the owner, irrespective of any benefits from any improvement proposed by such corporation, which compensation shall be ascertained by a jury, unless a jury be waived, as in other civil cases in a court of record, as shall be pre-

scribed by law. The taking of private property for a railroad run by steam or electric power for logging or lumbering purposes shall be deemed a taking for a public use, and any person, firm, company or corporation taking private property under the law of eminent domain for such purposes shall thereupon and thereby become a common carrier. [Amendment adopted October 10, 1911.]

Sec. 15. No person shall be imprisoned for debt in any civil action, on mesne or final process, unless in cases of fraud, nor in civil actions for torts, except in cases of willful injury to person or property; and no person shall be imprisoned for a militia fine in time of peace.

Sec. 16. No bill of attainder, ex post facto law, or law impairing the obligations of contracts, shall ever be passed.

Sec. 17. Foreigners, of the white race, or of African descent, eligible to become citizens of the United States under the naturalization laws thereof, while bona fide residents of this state, shall have the same rights in respect to the acquisition, possession, enjoyment, transmission, and inheritance of all property, other than real estate, as native-born citizens; provided, that such aliens owning real estate at the time of the adoption of this amendment may remain such owners; and provided, further, that the legislature may, by statute, provide for the disposition of real estate which shall hereafter be acquired by such aliens by descent or devise. [Amendment adopted November 6, 1894.]

Sec. 18. Neither slavery nor involuntary servitude, unless for the punishment of crime, shall ever be tolerated in this state.

Sec. 19. The right of the people to be secure in their persons, houses, papers and effects, against unreasonable seizures and searches, shall not be violated; and no warrant shall issue but on probable cause, supported by oath or affirmation, particularly describing the place to be searched and the person and things to be seized.

Sec. 20. Treason against the state shall consist only in levying war against it, adhering to its enemies, or giving them aid and comfort. No person shall be convicted of

treason unless on the evidence of two witnesses to the same overt act, or confession in open court.

Sec. 21.   No special privileges or immunities shall ever be granted which may not be altered, revoked, or repealed by the legislature, nor shall any citizen, or class of citizens, be granted privileges or immunities which, upon the same terms, shall not be granted to all citizens.

Sec. 22.   The provisions of this Constitution are mandatory and prohibitory, unless by express words they are declared to be otherwise.

Sec. 23.   This enumeration of rights shall not be construed to impair or deny others retained by the people.

Sec. 24.   No property qualification shall ever be required for any person to vote or hold office.

Sec. 25.   The people shall have the right to fish upon and from public lands of the state and in the waters thereof, excepting upon lands set aside for fish hatcheries, and no land owned by the state shall ever be sold or transferred without reserving in the people the absolute right to fish thereupon, and no law shall ever be passed making it a crime for the people to enter upon the public lands within this state for the purpose of fishing in any water containing fish that have been planted therein by the state; provided, that the legislature may by statute, provide for the season when and the conditions under which the different species of fish may be taken.   [New section adopted November 8, 1910.]

Sec. 26a.   Should an amendment to the Constitution of the state of California by adding to article I two new sections to be numbered respectively section 26 and section 27, as proposed by initiative petition filed with and certified to the secretary of state, and relating to intoxicating liquors, be enacted at the general election held on Nov. 3, 1914, then the force and effect of said section 26 shall be suspended until Feb. 15, 1915, at which time it shall have full force and effect except that, as to the manufacture and transportation of intoxicating liquors for delivery at points outside of the

state of California only, the force and effect thereof shall
be suspended until Jan. 1, 1916, at which time such manufacture and transportation also shall wholly cease and on
and after said date said section 26 shall in all respects have
full force and effect. (Amendment adopted November 3,
1914.)

NOTE.—The proposed amendment referred to in this amendment
was not adopted, so that this section never became operative, although
adopted.

ARTICLE II.
RIGHT OF SUFFRAGE.

Section 1. Every native citizen of the United States,
every person who shall have acquired the rights of citizenship under or by virtue of the treaty of Queretaro, and
every naturalized citizen thereof, who shall have become
such ninety days prior to any election, of the age of twenty-
one years, who shall have been resident of the state one year
next preceding the election, and of the county in which he
or she claims his or her vote ninety days, and in the election
precinct thirty days, shall be entitled to vote at all elections
which are now or may hereafter be authorized by law; provided, no native of China, no idiot, no insane person, no person convicted of any infamous crime, no person hereafter
convicted of the embezzlement or misappropriation of public money, and no person who shall not be able to read the
Constitution in the English language and write his or her
name, shall ever exercise the privileges of an elector in this
state; provided, that the provisions of this amendment relative to an educational qualification shall not apply to any
person prevented by a physical disability from complying
with its requisitions, nor to any person who now has the
right to vote, nor to any person who shall be sixty years of
age and upward at the time this amendment shall take effect. [Amendment adopted October 10, 1911.]

Sec. 2. Electors shall in all cases, except treason, felony,
or breach of the peace, be privileged from arrest on the

days of election, during their attendance at such election, going to and returning therefrom.

Sec. 2½. The legislature shall have the power to enact laws relative to the election of delegates to conventions of political parties; and the legislature shall enact laws providing for the direct nomination of candidates for public office, by electors, political parties, or organizations of electors without conventions, at elections to be known and designated as primary elections; also to determine the tests and conditions upon which electors, political parties, or organizations of electors may participate in any such primary election. It shall also be lawful for the legislature to prescribe that any such primary election shall be mandatory and obligatory. The legislature shall also have the power to establish the rates of compensation for primary election officers serving at such primary elections in any city, or city and county, or county, or other subdivision of a designated population, without making such compensation uniform, and for such purpose such law may declare the population of any city, city and county, county or political subdivision; provided, however, that until the legislature shall enact a direct primary election law under the provisions of this section, the present primary election law shall remain in force and effect. [Amendment adopted November 3, 1908.]

Sec. 3. No elector shall be obliged to perform militia duty on the day of election, except in time of war or public danger.

Sec. 4. For the purpose of voting, no person shall be deemed to have gained or lost a residence by reason of his presence or absence while employed in the service of the United States; nor while engaged in the navigation of the waters of this state, or of the United States, or of the high seas; nor while a student at any seminary of learning; nor while kept in any almshouse or other asylum, at public expense; nor while confined in any public prison.

Sec. 5. All elections by the people shall be by ballot or by such other method as may be prescribed by law; provided, that secrecy in voting be preserved. [Amendment adopted November 3, 1896.]

Sec. 6. The inhibitions of this Constitution to the con-trary notwithstanding, the legislature shall have power to provide that in different parts of the state different methods may be employed for receiving and registering the will of the people as expressed at elections, and may provide that mechanical devices may be used within designated subdivisions of the state at the option of the local authority indicated by the legislature for that purpose. [New section adopted November 4, 1902.]

ARTICLE III.

DISTRIBUTION OF POWERS.

Section 1. The powers of the government of the state of California shall be divided into three separate departments —the legislative, executive, and judicial; and no person charged with the exercise of powers properly belonging to one of these departments shall exercise any functions appertaining to either of the others, except as in this Constitution expressly directed or permitted.

ARTICLE IV.

LEGISLATIVE DEPARTMENT.

Section 1. The legislative power of the state shall be vested in a Senate and Assembly which shall be designated "The Legislature of the State of California," but the people reserve to themselves the power to propose laws and amendments to the Constitution, and to adopt or reject the same, at the polls independent of the legislature, and also reserve the power, at their own option, to so adopt or reject any act, or section or part of any act, passed by the legislature. The enacting clause of every law shall be "The people of the State of California do enact as follows":

The first power reserved to the people shall be known as the initiative. Upon the presentation to the secretary of state of a petition certified as herein provided to have been signed by qualified electors, equal in number to eight per cent of all the votes cast for all candidates for governor at the last preceding general election, at which a governor was

elected, proposing a law or amendment to the Constitution, set forth in full in said petition, the secretary of state shall submit the said proposed law or amendment to the Constitution to the electors at the next succeeding general election occurring subsequent to ninety days after the presentation aforesaid of said petition, or at any special election called by the governor in his discretion prior to such general election. All such initiative petitions shall have printed across the top thereof in twelve point black-face type the following: "Initiative measure to be submitted directly to the electors."

Upon the presentation to the secretary of state, at any time not less than ten days before the commencement of any regular session of the legislature, of a petition certified as herein provided to have been signed by qualified electors of the state equal in number to five per cent of all the votes cast for all candidates for governor at the last preceding general election, at which a governor was elected, proposing a law set forth in full in said petition, the secretary of state shall transmit the same to the legislature as soon as it convenes and organizes. The law proposed by such petition shall be either enacted or rejected without change or amendment by the legislature, within forty days from the time it is received by the legislature. If any law proposed by such petition shall be enacted by the legislature it shall be subject to referendum, as hereinafter provided. If any law so petitioned for be rejected, or if no action is taken upon it by the legislature, within said forty days, the secretary of state shall submit it to the people for approval or rejection at the next ensuing general election. The legislature may reject any measure so proposed by initiative petition and propose a different one on the same subject by a yea and nay vote upon separate roll-call, and in such event both measures shall be submitted by the secretary of state to the electors for approval or rejection at the next ensuing general election or at a prior special election called by the governor, in his discretion, for such purpose. All said initiative petitions last above described shall have printed in

twelve point black-face type the following: "Initiative measure to be presented to the legislature."

The second power reserved to the people shall be known as the referendum. No act passed by the legislature shall go into effect until ninety days after the final adjournment of the session of the legislature which passed such act, except acts calling elections, acts providing for tax levies or appropriations for the usual current expenses of the state, and urgency measures necessary for the immediate preservation of the public peace, health or safety, passed by a two-thirds vote of all the members elected to each house. Whenever it is deemed necessary for the immediate preservation of the public peace, health or safety that a law shall go into immediate effect, a statement of the facts constituting such necessity shall be set forth in one section of the act, which section shall be passed only upon a yea and nay vote, upon a separate roll-call thereon; provided, however, that no measure creating or abolishing any office or changing the salary, term or duties of any officer, or granting any franchise or special privilege, or creating any vested right or interest, shall be construed to be an urgency measure. Any law so passed by the legislature and declared to be an urgency measure shall go into immediate effect.

Upon the presentation to the secretary of state within ninety days after the final adjournment of the legislature of a petition certified as herein provided, to have been signed by qualified electors equal in number to five per cent of all the votes cast for all candidates for governor at the last preceding general election at which a governor was elected, asking that any act or section or part of any act of the legislature be submitted to the electors for their approval or rejection, the secretary of state shall submit to the electors for their approval or rejection, such act, or section or part of such act, at the next succeeding general election, occurring at any time subsequent to thirty days after the filing of said petition or at any special election which may be called by the governor, in his discretion, prior to such regular election, and no such act or section or part of such shall go into effect until and unless approved by a majority of

the qualified electors voting thereon; but if a referendum petition is filed against any section or part of any act the remainder of such act shall not be delayed from going into effect.

Any act, law or amendment to the Constitution submitted to the people by either initiative or referendum petition and approved by a majority of the votes cast thereon, at any election, shall take effect five days after the date of the official declaration of the vote by the secretary of state. No act, law or amendment to the Constitution, initiated or adopted by the people, shall be subject to the veto power of the governor, and no act, law or amendment to the Constitution, adopted by the people at the polls under the initiative provisions of this section, shall be amended or repealed except by a vote of the electors, unless otherwise provided in said initiative measure; but acts and laws adopted by the people under the referendum provisions of this section may be amended by the legislature at any subsequent session thereof. If any provision or provisions of two or more measures, approved by the electors at the same election, conflict, the provision or provisions of the measure receiving the highest affirmative vote shall prevail. Until otherwise provided by law, all measures submitted to a vote of the electors, under the provisions of this section, shall be printed, and together with arguments for and against each such measure by the proponents and opponents thereof, shall be mailed to each elector in the same manner as now provided by law as to amendments to the Constitution, proposed by the legislature; and the persons to prepare and present such arguments shall, until otherwise provided by law, be selected by the presiding officer of the Senate.

If for any reason any initiative or referendum measure, proposed by petition as herein provided, be not submitted at the election specified in this section, such failure shall not prevent its submission at a succeeding general election, and no law or amendment to the Constitution, proposed by the legislature, shall be submitted at any election unless at the same election there shall be submitted all measures pro-

posed by petition of the electors, if any be so proposed, as herein provided.

Any initiative or referendum petition may be presented in sections, but each section shall contain a full and correct copy of the title and text of the proposed measure. Each signer shall add to his signature his place of residence, giving the street and number if such exist. His election precinct shall also appear on the paper after his name. The number of signatures attached to each section shall be at the pleasure of the person soliciting signatures to the same. Any qualified elector of the state shall be competent to solicit said signatures within the county or city and county of which he is an elector. Each section of the petition shall bear the name of the county or city and county in which it is circulated, and only qualified electors of such county or city and county shall be competent to sign such section. Each section shall have attached thereto the affidavit of the person soliciting signatures to the same, stating his own qualifications and that all the signatures to the attached section were made in his presence and that to the best of his knowledge and belief each signature to the section is the genuine signature of the person whose name it purports to be, and no other affidavit thereto shall be required. The affidavit of any person soliciting signatures hereunder shall be verified free of charge by any officer authorized to administer oaths. Such petitions so verified shall be prima facie evidence that the signatures thereon are genuine and that the persons signing the same are qualified electors. Unless and until it be otherwise proven upon official investigation, it shall be presumed that the petition presented contains the signatures of the requisite number of qualified electors.

Each section of the petition shall be filed with the clerk or registrar of voters of the county or city and county in which it was circulated, but all said sections circulated in any county or city and county shall be filed at the same time. Within twenty days after the filing of such petition in his office the said clerk, or registrar of voters, shall determine from the records of registration what number of qualified electors have signed the same, and if necessary the

board of supervisors shall allow said clerk or registrar additional assistants for the purpose of examining such petition and provide for their compensation. The said clerk
or registrar, upon the completion of such examination, shall
forthwith attach to said petition, except the signatures
thereto appended, his certificate, properly dated, showing
the result of said examination and shall forthwith transmit
said petition, together with his said certificate, to the secretary of state and also file a copy of said certificate in his
office. Within forty days from the transmission of the said
petition and certificate by the clerk or registrar to the secretary of state, a supplemental petition identical with the
original as to the body of the petition but containing supplemental names, may be filed with the clerk or registrar of
voters, as aforesaid. The clerk or registrar of voters shall
within ten days after the filing of such supplemental petition make like examination thereof as of the original petition, and upon the completion of such examination shall
forthwith attach to said petition his certificate, properly
dated, showing the result of said examination, and shall
forthwith transmit a copy of said supplemental petition,
except the signatures thereto appended, together with his
certificate, to the secretary of state.

When the secretary of state shall have received from one
or more county clerks or registrars of voters a petition certified as herein provided to have been signed by the requisite number of qualified electors, he shall forthwith transmit
to the county clerk or registrar of voters of every county or
city and county in the state his certificate showing such
fact. A petition shall be deemed to be filed with the secretary of state upon the date of the receipt by him of a certificate or certificates showing said petition to be signed by the
requisite number of electors of the state. Any county clerk
or registrar of voters shall, upon receipt of such copy, file
the same for record in his office. The duties herein imposed
upon the clerk or registrar of voters shall be performed by
such registrar of voters in all cases where the office of registrar of voters exists.

The initiative and referendum powers of the people are hereby further reserved to the electors of each county, city and county, city and town of the state, to be exercised under such procedure as may be provided by law. Until otherwise provided by law, the legislative body of any such county, city and county, city or town may provide for the manner of exercising the initiative and referendum powers herein reserved to such counties, cities and counties, cities and towns, but, shall not require more than fifteen per cent of the electors thereof to propose any initiative measure nor more than ten per cent of the electors thereof to order the referendum. Nothing contained in this section shall be construed as affecting or limiting the present or future powers of cities or cities and counties having charters adopted under the provisions of section eight of article XI of this Constitution. In the submission to the electors of any measure under this section, all officers shall be guided by the general laws of this state, except as is herein otherwise provided. This section is self-executing, but legislation may be enacted to facilitate its operation, but in no way limiting or restricting either the provisions of this section or the powers herein reserved. [Amendment adopted October 10, 1911.]

Sec. 2. The sessions of the legislature shall be biennial, unless the governor shall, in the interim, convene the legislature, by proclamation, in extraordinary session. All sessions, other than extraordinary, shall commence at 12 o'clock M., on the first Monday after the first day of January next succeeding the election of its members, and shall continue in session for a period not exceeding thirty days thereafter; whereupon a recess of both houses must be taken for not less than thirty days. On the reassembling of the legislature, no bill shall be introduced in either house without the consent of three-fourths of the members thereof, nor shall more than two bills be introduced by any one member after such reassembling. [Amendment adopted October 10, 1911.]

Sec. 3. Members of the assembly shall be elected in the year eighteen hundred and seventy-nine, at the time and in the manner now provided by law. The second election of

members of the assembly, after the adoption of this Constitution, shall be on the first Tuesday after the first Monday in November, eighteen hundred and eighty. Thereafter members of the assembly shall be chosen biennially, and their term of office shall be two years; and each election shall be on the first Tuesday after the first Monday in November, unless otherwise ordered by the legislature.

Sec. 4. Senators shall be chosen for the term of four years, at the same time and place as members of the assembly, and no person shall be a member of. the senate or assembly who has not been a citizen and inhabitant of the state three years, and of the district for which he shall be chosen one year, next before his election.

Sec. 5. The senate shall consist of forty members, and the assembly of eighty members, to be elected by districts, numbered as hereinafter provided. The seats of the twenty senators elected in the year eighteen hundred and eighty-two from the odd-numbered districts shall be vacated at the expiration of the second year, so that one-half of the senators shall be elected every two years; provided, that all the senators elected at the first election under this Constitution shall hold office for the term of three years.

Sec. 6. For the purpose of choosing members of the legislature, the state shall be divided into forty senatorial and eighty assembly districts, as nearly equal in population as may be, and composed of contiguous territory, to be called senatorial and assembly districts. Each senatorial district shall choose one senator, and each assembly district shall choose one member of assembly. The senatorial districts shall be numbered from one to forty, inclusive, in numerical order, and the assembly districts shall be numbered from one to eighty in the same order, commencing at the northern boundary of the state and ending at the southern boundary thereof. In the formation of such districts no county, or city and county, shall be divided, unless it contains sufficient population within itself to form two or more districts, nor shall a part of any county, or of any city and county, be united with any other county or city and county,

in forming any district. The census taken under the direction of the Congress of the United States in the year one thousand eight hundred and eighty, and every ten years thereafter, shall be the basis of fixing and adjusting the legislative districts; and the legislature shall, at its first session after each census, adjust such districts and reapportion the representation so as to preserve them as near equal in population as may be. But in making such adjustment no persons who are not eligible to become citizens of the United States, under the naturalization laws, shall be counted as forming a part of the population of any district. Until such districting as herein provided for shall be made, senators and assemblymen shall be elected by the districts according to the apportionment now provided for by law.

Sec. 7. Each house shall choose its officers, and judge of the qualifications, elections, and returns of its members.

Sec. 8. A majority of each house shall constitute a quorum to do business, but a smaller number may adjourn from day to day, and may compel the attendance of absent members in such manner and under such penalties as each house may provide.

Sec. 9. Each house shall determine the rule of its proceeding, and may, with the concurrence of two-thirds of all the members elected, expel a member.

Sec. 10. Each house shall keep a journal of its proceedings, and publish the same; and the yeas and nays of the members of either house, on any question, shall, at the desire of any three members present, be entered on the journal.

Sec. 11. Members of the legislature shall, in all cases, except treason, felony, and breach of the peace, be privileged from arrest, and shall not be subject to any civil process during the session of the legislature, nor for fifteen days next before the commencement and after the termination of each session.

Sec. 12. When vacancies occur in either house, the governor, or the person exercising the functions of the governor, shall issue writs of election to fill such vacancies.

Sec. 13.   The doors of each house shall be open, except on such occasions as, in the opinion of the house, may require secrecy.

Sec. 14.   Neither house shall, without the consent of the other, adjourn for more than three days, nor to any place other than that in which they may be sitting.   Nor shall the members of either house draw pay for any recess or adjournment for a longer time than three days.

Sec. 15.   No law shall be passed except by bill.   Nor shall any bill be put upon its final passage until the same, with the amendments thereto, shall have been printed for the use of the members; nor shall any bill become a law unless the same be read on three several days in each house, unless, in case of urgency, two-thirds of the house where such bill may be pending, shall, by a vote of yeas and nays, dispense with this provision.   Any bill may originate in either house, but may be amended or rejected by the other; and on the final passage of all bills they shall be read at length, and the vote shall be by yeas and nays upon each bill separately, and shall be entered on the journal, and no bill shall become a law without the concurrence of a majority of the members elected to each house.

Sec. 16.   Every bill which may have passed the legislature shall, before it becomes a law, be presented to the governor.   If he approve it, he shall sign it; but if not, he shall return it, with his objections, to the house in which it originated, which shall enter such objections upon the journal and proceed to reconsider it.   If after such reconsideration, it again pass both houses, by yeas and nays, two-thirds of the members elected to each house voting therefor, it shall become a law, notwithstanding the governor's objections. If any bill shall not be returned within ten days after it shall have been presented to him (Sundays excepted), the same shall become a law in like manner as if he had signed it, unless the legislature, by adjournment, prevents such return, in which case it shall not become a law, unless the governor, within thirty days after such adjournment (Sundays excepted), shall sign and deposit the same in the office

of the secretary of state, in which case it shall become a law in like manner as if it had been signed by him before adjournment. If any bill presented to the governor contains several items of appropriation of money, he may object to one or more items, while approving other portions of the bill. In such case he shall append to the bill at the time of signing it a statement of the items to which he objects, and the reasons therefor, and the appropriation so objected to shall not take effect unless passed over the governor's veto, as hereinbefore provided. If the legislature be in session, the governor shall transmit to the house in which the bill originated a copy of such statement, and the items so objected to shall be separately reconsideerd in the same manner as bills which have been disapproved by the governor. [Amendment adopted November 3, 1908.]

Sec. 17.   The assembly shall have the sole power of impeachment, and all impeachments shall be tried by the senate. When sitting for that purpose, the senators shall be upon oath or affirmation and no person shall be convicted without the concurrence of two-thirds of the members elected.

Sec. 18.   The governor, lieutenant-governor, secretary of state, controller, treasurer, attorney general, surveyor-general, chief justice and associate justices of the supreme court, judges of the district courts of appeal, and judges of the superior courts, shall be liable to impeachment for any misdemeanor in office; but judgment in such cases shall extend only to removal from office and disqualification to hold any office of honor, trust, or profit under the state; but the party convicted or acquitted shall nevertheless be liable to indictment, trial and punishment according to law. All other civil officers shall be tried for misdemeanor in office in such manner as the legislature may provide. [Amendment adopted October 10, 1911.]

Sec. 19.   No senator or member of assembly shall, during the term for which he shall have been elected, be appointed to any civil office of profit under this state which shall have been created, or the emoluments of which have been in-

creased, during such term, except such offices as may be filled by election by the people.

Sec. 20. No person holding any lucrative office under the United States, or any other power, shall be eligible to any civil office of profit under this state; provided, that officers in the militia who receive no annual salary, local officers, or postmasters whose compensation does not exceed five hundred dollars per annum shall not be deemed to hold lucrative offices.

Sec. 21. No person convicted of the embezzlement or defalcation of the public funds of the United States, or of any state, or of any county or municipality therein, shall ever be eligible to any office of honor, trust, or profit under this state, and the legislature shall provide, by law, for the punishment of embezzlement or defalcation as a felony.

Sec. 22. No money shall be drawn from the treasury but in consequence of appropriations made by law, and upon warrants duly drawn thereon by the controller; and no money shall ever be appropriated or drawn from the state treasury for the purpose or benefit of any corporation, association, asylum, hospital, or any other institution not under the exclusive management and control of the state as a state institution, nor shall any grant or donation of property ever be made thereto by the state, provided, that notwithstanding anything contained in this or any other section of this Constitution, the legislature shall have the power to grant aid to the institutions conducted for the support and maintenance of minor orphans, or half-orphans, or abandoned children, or aged persons in indigent circumstances—such aid to be granted by a uniform rule, and proportioned to the number of inmates of such respective institutions; provided, further, that the state shall have at any time the right to inquire into the management of such institution; provided, further, that whenever any county, or city and county, or city, or town, shall provide for the support of minor orphans, or half-orphans, or abandoned children, or aged persons in indigent circumstances, such county, city and county, city, or town shall be entitled to

receive the same pro rata appropriations as may be granted
to such institutions under church or other control. An accurate statement of the receipts and expenditures of public
moneys shall be attached to and published with the laws at
every regular session of the legislature; provided, however,
that for the purpose of raising five million dollars ($5,-
000,000), to be used in establishing, maintaining, and supporting in the city and county of San Francisco, state of
California, an exposition in commemoration of the completion of the Panama canal, to be known as the Panama-Pacific International Exposition, the state board of equalization shall, for the fiscal year beginning July 1, 1911, and for
each fiscal year thereafter, to and including the fiscal year
beginning July 1, 1914, fix, establish, and levy such an ad
valorem rate of taxation, as when levied upon all the taxable property in the state, after making due allowance for
delinquency, shall produce for each of such fiscal years a
sum of one million two hundred and fifty thousand dollars
($1,250,000). The said taxes shall be levied, assessed, and
collected upon every kind and character of property in the
state of California not exempt from taxation under the law,
and subject to taxation on the first day of July, 1910, and
in the same manner, and by the same method, as other state
taxes were levied, assessed, and collected under the law, as
the same existed on the first day of July, 1910. The state
board of equalization shall each year, at the time it determines the amount of revenue required for other state purposes, determine, fix, and include the rate of tax necessary
to raise the revenue herein provided for.

There is hereby created in the state treasury a fund to be
known as the Panama-Pacific International Exposition fund,
and all moneys collected pursuant to this provision, after
deducting the proportionate share of the expense for the
collection of the same, shall be paid into the state treasury,
and credited to such fund. All moneys so paid into such
fund are hereby appropriated, without reference to fiscal
years, for the use, establishment, maintenance, and support
of said Panama-Pacific International Exposition. No tax,

license fee, or charge of any kind or character shall ever be levied or assessed or charged against any property of said Panama-Pacific International Exposition, or against any property used as exhibit therein, while being used or exhibited in connection therewith.

There is hereby created a commission to be known as the Panama-Pacific International Exposition Commission of the state of California, which shall consist of the governor of said state and four other members to be appointed by the governor, by and with the advice and consent of the senate of said state. The governor shall have the power to fill all vacancies occurring at any time in said commission. The members of said commission shall receive no compensation and shall hold office until such exposition shall have been closed and its affairs settled. Said four members of said commission shall be selected from different sections of the state, and the appointment thereof shall be made by the governor of the state during the month of February, 1911. The commission hereby created shall have the exclusive charge and control of all moneys paid into the Panama-Pacific International Exposition fund; and provided, further, that the legislature shall pass all laws necessary to carry out the provisions of this act, including the times and the manner in which and the terms and conditions upon which moneys shall be drawn from the state treasury by said commission; where contracts and vouchers shall be filed; to whom and how often reports shall be made; what disposition shall be made of any sum left unexpended or received from the sale of any property of buildings purchased or constructed by said commission for the use of said exposition, or of any disposition of any building or improvement constructed by said commission out of said fund, and to provide for the transfer to the general fund of the state of California of any portion of said Panama-Pacific International Exposition fund unused.

The commission herein created is authorized and directed to make such proper contracts with the Panama-Pacific International Exposition Company, a corporation organized under the laws of the state of California on the 22d day of

· March, 1910, as will entitle the state of California to share proportionately with the contributors to the said Panama-Pacific International Exposition in the returns from the holding of said exposition at the city and county of San Francisco. [Amendment adopted November 8, 1910.]

Sec. 23. The members of the legislature shall receive for their services the sum of one thousand dollars each for each regular session, to be paid at such times during the session as may be provided by law, and the sum of ten dollars each for each day while in attendance at a special or extraordinary session, for a number of days not exceeding thirty; and mileage to be fixed by law, all paid out of the state treasury; such mileage shall not exceed ten cents per mile; and each member shall be allowed contingent expenses not exceeding twenty-five dollars per member for each regular biennial session. The legislature may also provide for additional help; but in no case shall the total expense for officers, employees and attaches exceed the sum of five hundred dollars per day for either house, at any regular or biennial session, nor the sum of two hundred dollars per day for either house at any special or extraordinary session, nor shall the pay of any officer, employee or attaché be increased after he is elected or appointed. [Amendment adopted November 3, 1908.]

Sec. 23a. The legislature may also provide for the employment of help; but in no case shall the total expense for officers, employees and attaches exceed the sum of five hundred dollars per day for either house, at any regular or biennial session, nor the sum of two hundred dollars per day for either house at any special or extraordinary session, nor shall the pay of any officer, employee or attaché be increased after he is elected or appointed. [New section adopted November 3, 1908.]

Sec. 24. Every act shall embrace but one subject, which subject shall be expressed in its title. But if any subject shall be embraced in an act which shall not be expressed in its title, such act shall be void only as to so much thereof as shall not be expressed in its title. No law shall be re-

vised or amended by reference to its title; but in such case the act revised or section amended shall be re-enacted and published at length as revised or amended; and all laws of the state of California, and all official writings, and the executive, legislative, and judicial proceedings, shall be conducted, preserved, and published in no other than the English language.

Sec. 25. The legislature shall not pass local or special laws in any of the following enumerated cases, that is to say:

First—Regulating the jurisdiction and duties of justices of the peace, police judges, and of constables.

Second—For the punishment of crimes and misdemeanors.

Third—Regulating the practice of courts of justice.

Fourth—Providing for changing the venue in civil or criminal actions.

Fifth—Granting divorces.

Sixth—Changing the names of persons or places.

Seventh—Authorizing the laying out, opening, altering, maintaining, or vacating roads, highways, streets, alleys, town plots, parks, cemeteries, graveyards, or public grounds not owned by the state.

Eighth—Summoning and impaneling grand and petit juries, and providing for their compensation.

Ninth—Regulating county and township business, or the election of county and township officers.

Tenth—For the assessment or collection of taxes.

Eleventh—Providing for conducting elections or designating the places of voting, except on the organization of new counties.

Twelfth—Affecting estates of deceased persons, minors, or other persons under legal disabilities.

Thirteenth—Extending the time for the collection of taxes.

Fourteenth—Giving effect to invalid deeds, wills, or other instruments.

Fifteenth—Refunding money paid into the state treasury.

Sixteenth—Releasing or extinguishing, in whole or in part, the indebtedness, liability, or obligation of any cor-

poration or person to this state, or to any municipal corporation therein.

Seventeenth—Declaring any person of age, or authorizing any minor to sell, lease or encumber his or her property.

Eighteenth—Legalizing, except as against the state, the unauthorized or invalid act of any officer.

Nineteenth—Granting to any corporation, association, or individual any special or exclusive right, privilege or immunity.

Twentieth—Exempting property from taxation.

Twenty-first—Changing county seats.

Twenty-second—Restoring to citizenship persons convicted of infamous crimes.

Twenty-third—Regulating the rate of interest on money.

Twenty-fourth—Authorizing the creation, extension, or impairing of liens.

Twenty-fifth—Chartering or licensing ferries, bridges, or roads.

Twenty-sixth—Remitting fines, penalties, or forfeitures.

Twenty-seventh—Providing for the management of common schools.

Twenty-eighth—Creating offices, or prescribing the powers and duties of officers in counties, cities, cities and counties, township, election or school districts.

Twenty-ninth—Affecting the fees or salary of any officer.

Thirtieth—Changing the law of descent or succession.

Thirty-first—Authorizing the adoption or legitimation of children.

Thirty-second—For limitation of civil or criminal actions.

Thirty-third—In all other cases where a general law can be made applicable.

Sec. 25½. The legislature may provide for the division of the state into fish and game districts, and may enact such laws for the protection of fish and game therein as it may deem appropriate to the respective districts. [New section adopted November 4, 1902.]

Sec. 26. The legislature shall have no power to authorize lotteries or gift enterprises for any purpose and shall

pass laws to prohibit the sale in this state of lottery or gift enterprise tickets or tickets in any scheme in the nature of a lottery. The legislature shall pass laws to prohibit the fictitious buying and selling of the shares of the capital stock of corporations in any stock board, stock exchange or stock market under the control of any corporation or association. All contracts for the purchase or sale of shares of the capital stock of any corporation or association without any intention on the part of one party to deliver and of the other party to receive the shares, and contemplating merely the payment of differences between the contract and market prices on divers days, shall be void, and neither party to any such contract shall be entitled to recover any damages for failure to perform the same, or any money paid thereon, in any court of this state. [Amendment adopted November 3, 1908.]

Sec. 27. When a congressional district shall be composed of two or more counties, it shall not be separated by any county belonging to another district. No county, or city and county, shall be divided in forming a congressional district so as to attach one portion of a county, or city and county, to another county, or city and county, except in cases where one county, or city and county, has more population than the ratio required for one or more congressmen; but the legislature may divide any county, or city and county, into as many congressional districts as it may be entitled to by law. Any county, or city and county containing a population greater than the number required for one congressional district, shall be formed into one or more congressional districts, according to the population thereof, and any residue, after forming such district or districts, shall be attached, by compact adjoining assembly districts, to a contiguous county or counties, and form a congressional district. In dividing a county, or city and county, into congressional districts, no assembly district shall be divided so as to form a part of more than one congressional district, and every such congressional district shall be composed of compact contiguous assembly districts.

Sec. 28. In all elections by the legislature the members thereof shall vote viva voce, and the vote shall be entered on the journal.

Sec. 29. The general appropriation bill shall contain no item or items of appropriation other than such as are required to pay the salaries of the state officers, the expenses of the government, and of the institutions under the exclusive control and management of the state.

Sec. 30. Neither the legislature, nor any county, city and county, township, school district, or other municipal corporation, shall ever make an appropriation, or pay from any public fund whatever, or grant anything to or in aid of any religious sect, church, creed, or sectarian purpose, or help to support or sustain any school, college, university, hospital, or other institution controlled by any religious creed, church, or sectarian denomination whatever; nor shall any grant or donation of personal property or real estate ever be made by the state, or any city, city and county, town, or other municipal corporation, for any religious creed, church, or sectarian purpose, whatever; provided, that nothing in this section shall prevent the legislature granting aid pursuant to section 22 of this article.

Sec. 31. The legislature shall have no power to give or to lend, or to authorize the giving or lending, of the credit of the state, or of any county, city and county, city, township, or other political corporation or subdivision of the state now existing, or that may be hereafter established, in aid of or to any person, association, or corporation, whether municipal or otherwise, or to pledge the credit thereof, in any manner whatever, for the payment of the liabilities of any individual, association, municipal or other corporation whatever; nor shall it have power to make any gift, or authorize the making of any gift, of any public money or thing of value to any individual, municipal or other corporation whatever; provided, that nothing in this section (shall prevent the legislature granting aid pursuant to section 22 of this article; and it shall not have power to authorize the state or any political subdivision thereof, to

subscribe for stock, or to become a stockholder in any corporation) shall prevent the legislature granting aid pursuant to section 22 of this article; and it shall not have power to authorize the state, or any political subdivision thereof, to subscribe for stock, or to become a stockholder in any corporation whatever; provided, further, that irrigation districts for the purpose of acquiring the control of any entire international water system necessary for its use and purposes, a part of which is situated in the United States, and a part thereof in a foreign country, may in the manner authorized by law, acquire the stock of any foreign corporation which is the owner of, or which holds the title to the part of such system situated in a foreign country. [Amendment adopted November 3, 1914.]

NOTE.—The repetition of the words indicated by parentheses in the above section occurred in the resolution by which the amendment of the above section was proposed to the people. As no change could be made thereafter the section was voted on and adopted in the above form.

Sec. 32. The legislature shall have no power to grant, or authorize any county or municipal authority to grant, any extra compensation or allowance to any public officer, agent, servant, or contractor, after service has been rendered, or a contract has been entered into and performed, in whole or in part, nor to pay, or to authorize the payment of, any claim hereafter created against the state, or any county or municipality of the state, under any agreement or contract made without express authority of law; and all such unauthorized agreements or contracts shall be null and void.

Sec. 33. The legislature shall pass laws for the regulation and limitation of the charges for services performed and commodities furnished by telegraph and gas corporations, and the charges by corporations or individuals for storage and wharfage, in which there is a public use; and where laws shall provide for the selection of any person or officer to regulate and limit such rates, no such person or officer shall be selected by any corporation or individual

interested in the business to be regulated, and no person shall be selected who is an officer or stockholder in any such corporation.

Sec. 34.   No bill making an appropriation of money, except the general appropriation bill, shall contain more than one item of appropriation, and that for one single and certain purpose, to be therein expressed.

Sec. 35.   Any person who seeks to influence the vote of a member of the legislature by bribery, promise of reward, intimidation, or any other dishonest means, shall be guilty of lobbying, which is hereby declared a felony; and it shall be the duty of the legislature to provide, by law, for the punishment of this crime. Any member of the legislature who shall be influenced, in his vote or action upon any matter pending before the legislature, by any reward, or promise of future reward, shall be deemed guilty of a felony, and upon conviction thereof, in addition to such punishment as may be provided by law, shall be disfranchised and forever disqualified from holding any office or public trust. Any person may be compelled to testify in any lawful investigation or judicial proceeding against any person who may be charged with having committed the offense of bribery or corrupt solicitation, or with having been influenced in his vote or action, as a member of the legislature, by reward, or promise of future reward, and shall not be permitted to withhold his testimony upon the ground that it may criminate himself, or subject him to public infamy; but such testimony shall not afterward be used against him in any judicial proceeding, except for perjury in giving such testimony.

Sec. 36.   The legislature shall have power to establish a system of state highways or to declare any road a state highway, and to pass all laws necessary or proper to construct and maintain the same, and to extend aid for the construction and maintenance in whole or in part of any county highway.   [New section adopted November 4, 1902.]

ARTICLE V.

EXECUTIVE DEPARTMENT.

Section 1. The supreme executive power of this state shall be vested in a chief magistrate, who shall be styled the governor of the state of California.

Sec. 2. The governor shall be elected by the qualified electors at the time and places of voting for members of the Assembly, and shall hold his office four years from and after the first Monday after the first day of January subsequent to his election, and until his successor is elected and qualified.

Sec. 3. No person shall be eligible to the office of governor who has not been a citizen of the United States and a resident of this state five years next preceding his election and attained the age of twenty-five years at the time of such election.

Sec. 4. The returns of every election for governor shall be sealed up and transmitted to the seat of government, directed to the speaker of the assembly, who shall, during the first week of the session, open and publish them in the presence of both houses of the legislature. The person having the highest number of votes shall be governor; but, in case any two or more have an equal and the highest number of votes, the legislature shall, by joint vote of both houses, choose one of such persons so having an equal and the highest number of votes for governor.

Sec. 5. The governor shall be commander-in-chief of the militia, the army and navy of this state.

Sec. 6. He shall transact all executive business with the officers of government, civil and military, and may require information, in writing, from the officers of the executive department upon any subject relating to the duties of their respective offices.

Sec. 7. He shall see that the laws are faithfully executed.

Sec. 8. When any office shall, from any cause, become vacant, and no mode is provided by the Constitution and law for filling such vacancy, the governor shall have power

to fill such vacancy by granting a commission, which shall expire at the end of the next session of the legislature, or the next election by the people.

Sec. 9. He may, on extraordinary occasions, convene the legislature by proclamation, stating the purposes for which he has convened it, and when so convened it shall have no power to legislate on any subjects other than those specified in the proclamation, but may provide for the expenses of the session, and other matters incidental thereto.

Sec. 10. He shall communicate, by message to the legislature, at every session, the condition of the state, and recommend such matters as he shall deem expedient.

Sec. 11. In case of a disagreement between the two houses with respect to the time of adjournment, the governor shall have power to adjourn the legislature to such time as he may think proper; provided, it be not beyond the time fixed for the meeting of the next legislature.

Sec. 12. No person shall, while holding any office under the United States, or this state, exercise the office of governor, except as hereinafter expressly provided.

Sec. 13. There shall be a seal of this state, which shall be kept by the governor, and used by him officially, and shall be called "The Great Seal of the State of California."

Sec. 14. All grants and commissions shall be in the name and by the authority of the people of the state of California, sealed with the great seal of the state, signed by the governor, and countersigned by the secretary of state.

Sec. 15. A lieutenant-governor shall be elected at the same time and place, and in the same manner, as the governor, and his term of office and his qualifications shall be the same. He shall be president of the senate, but shall only have a casting vote therein. [Amendment adopted November 8, 1898.]

Sec. 16. In case of the impeachment of the governor, or his removal from office, death, inability to discharge the powers and duties of his office, resignation, or absence from the state, the powers and duties of the office shall devolve upon the lieutenant-governor for the residue of the term,

or until the disability shall cease. And should the lieuten-ant-governor be impeached, displaced, resign, die, or be-come incapable of performing the duties of his office, or be absent from the state, the president pro tempore of the senate shall act as governor until the vacancy in the office of governor shall be filled at the next general election when members of the legislature shall be chosen, or until such disability of the lieutenant-governor shall cease. In case of a vacancy in the office of governor for any of the reasons above named, and neither the lieutenant-governor nor the president pro tempore of the senate succeed to the powers and duties of governor, then the powers and duties of such office shall devolve upon the speaker of the assembly, until the office of governor shall be filled at such general election. [Amendment adopted November 8, 1898.]

Sec. 17. A secretary of state, a controller, a treasurer, an attorney general, and a surveyor-general shall be elected at the same time and places, and in the same manner, as the governor and lieutenant-governor, and their terms of office shall be the same as that of the governor.

Sec. 18. The secretary of state shall keep a correct rec-ord of the official acts of the legislative and executive de-partments of the government, and shall, when required, lay the same, and all matters relative thereto, before either branch of the legislature, and shall perform such other duties as may be assigned him by law.

Sec. 19. The governor, lieutenant-governor, secretary of state, controller, treasurer, attorney general and surveyor-general shall, at stated times during their continuance in office, receive for their services a compensation which shall not be increased or diminished during the term for which they shall have been elected, which compensation is hereby fixed for the following officers, as follows: governor, ten thousand dollars per annum; lieutenant-governor, four thousand dollars, the secretary of state, controller, treas-urer, and surveyor-general, five thousand dollars each per annum, and the attorney general, six thousand dollars per annum, such compensation to be in full for all services by

them respectively rendered in any official capacity or employment whatsoever during their respective terms of office; provided, however, that the legislature may, by law, diminish the compensation of any or all of such officers, but in no case shall have the power to increase the same above the sums hereby fixed by this Constitution. No salary shall be authorized by law for clerical service in any office provided for in this article, exceeding eighteen hundred dollars per annum for each clerk employed. The legislature may, in its discretion, abolish the office of surveyor-general; and none of the officers hereinbefore named shall receive for their own use any fees or perquisites for the performance of any official duty. [Amendment adopted November 3, 1908.]

Sec. 20. United States senators shall be elected by the people of the state in the manner provided by law. [Amendment adopted November 3, 1914.]

ARTICLE VI.
JUDICIAL DEPARTMENT.

Section 1. The judicial power of the state shall be vested in the senate, sitting as a court of impeachment, in a supreme court, district courts of appeal, superior courts and such inferior courts as the legislature may establish in any incorporated city or town, township, county, or city and county. [Amendment adopted October 10, 1911.]

Sec. 2. The supreme court shall consist of a chief justice and six associate justices. The court may sit in departments and in bank, and shall always be open for the transaction of business. There shall be two departments, denominated, respectively, department one and department two. The chief justice shall assign three of the associate justices to each department, and such assignment may be changed by him from time to time. The associate justices shall be competent to sit in either department, and may interchange with each other by agreement among themselves, or as ordered by the chief justice. Each of the departments shall have the power to hear and determine

causes, and all questions arising therein, subject to the provisions hereinafter contained in relation to the court in bank. The presence of three justices shall be necessary to transact any business in either of the departments, except such as may be done at chambers, and the concurrence of three justices shall be necessary to pronounce a judgment. The chief justice shall apportion the business to the departments, and may, in his discretion, order any cause pending before the court to be heard and decided by the court in bank. The order may be made before or after judgment pronounced by a department; but where a cause has been allotted to one of the departments, and a judgment pronounced thereon, the order must be made within thirty days after such judgment, and concurred in by two associate justices, and if so made it shall have the effect to vacate and set aside the judgment. Any four justices may, either before or after judgment by a department, order a case to be heard in bank. If the order be not made within the time above limited, the judgment shall be final. No judgment by a department shall become final until the expiration of the period of thirty days aforesaid, unless approved by the chief justice, in writing, with the concurrence of two associate justices. The chief justice may convene the court in bank at any time, and shall be the presiding justice of the court when so convened. The concurrence of four justices present at the argument shall be necessary to pronounce a judgment in bank; but if four justices, so present, do not concur in a judgment, then all the justices qualified to sit in the cause shall hear the argument; but to render a judgment a concurrence of four judges shall be necessary. In the determination of causes, all decisions of the court, in bank or in department, shall be given in writing, and the grounds of the decision shall be stated. The chief justice may sit in either department, and shall preside when so sitting, but the justices assigned to each department shall select one of their number as presiding justice. In case of the absence of the chief justice from the place at which the court is held, or his inability to act, the associate justices shall select one of their own number

Constitution—3

to perform the duties and exercise the powers of the chief justice during such absence or inability to act.

Sec. 3. The chief justice and the associate justices shall be elected by the qualified electors of the state at large at the general state elections, at the time and places at which state officers are elected; and the term of office shall be twelve years from and after the first Monday after the first day of January next succeeding their election; provided, that the six associate justices elected at the first election shall, at their first meeting, so classify themselves, by lot, that two of them shall go out of office at the end of four years, two of them at the end of eight years, and two of them at the end of twelve years, and an entry of such classification shall be made in the minutes of the court in bank, signed by them, and a duplicate thereof shall be filed in the office of the secretary of state. If a vacancy occur in the office of a justice, the governor shall appoint a person to hold the office until the election and qualification of a justice to fill the vacancy, which election shall take place at the next succeeding general election, and the justice so elected shall hold the office for the remainder of the unexpired term. The first election of the justices shall be at the first general election after the adoption and ratification of this Constitution.

Sec. 4. The supreme court shall have appellate jurisdiction on appeal from the superior courts in all cases in equity, except such as arise in justices' courts; also, in all cases at law which involve the title or possession of real estate, or the legality of any tax, impost, assessment, toll, or municipal fine, or in which the demand, exclusive of interest, or the value of the property in controversy, amounts to two thousand dollars; also, in all such probate matters as may be provided by law; also, on questions of law alone, in all criminal cases where judgment of death has been rendered; the said court shall also have appellate jurisdiction in all cases, matters and proceedings pending before a district court of appeal, which shall be ordered by the supreme court to be transferred to itself for hearing and decision, as hereinafter provided. The said court shall also have

power to issue writs of mandamus, certiorari, prohibition, and habeas corpus, and all other writs necessary or proper to the complete exercise of its appellate jurisdiction. Each of the justices shall have power to issue writs of habeas corpus to any part of the state, upon petition by or on behalf of any person held in actual custody, and may make such writs returnable before himself or the supreme court, or before any district court of appeal, or before any judge thereof, or before any superior court in the state, or before any judge thereof.

The state is hereby divided into three appellate districts, in each of which there shall be a district court of appeal consisting of three justices. The first district shall embrace the following counties: San Francisco, Marin, Contra Costa, Alameda, San Mateo, Santa Clara, Fresno, Santa Cruz, Monterey, and San Benito.

The second district shall embrace the following counties: Tulare, Kings, San Luis Obispo, Kern, Inyo, Santa Barbara, Ventura, Los Angeles, San Bernardino, Orange, Riverside and San Diego.

The third district shall embrace the following counties: Del Norte, Siskiyou, Modoc, Humboldt, Trinity, Shasta, Lassen, Tehama, Plumas, Mendocino, Lake, Colusa, Glenn, Butte, Sierra, Sutter, Yuba, Nevada, Sonoma, Napa, Yolo, Placer, Solano, Sacramento, El Dorado, San Joaquin, Amador, Calaveras, Stanislaus, Mariposa, Madera, Merced, Tuolumne, Alpine and Mono.

The supreme court, by orders entered in its minutes, may from time to time remove one or more counties from one appellate district to another, but no county not contiguous to another county of a district shall be added to such district.

Said district courts of appeal shall hold their regular sessions respectively at San Francisco, Los Angeles, and Sacramento, and they shall always be open for the transaction of business.

The district courts of appeal shall have appellate jurisdiction on appeal from the superior courts in all cases at law in which the demand, exclusive of interest, or the value

of the property in controversy, amounts to three hundred dollars, and does not amount to two thousand dollars; also, in all cases of forcible and unlawful entry and detainer (except such as arise in justices' courts), in proceedings in insolvency, and in actions to prevent or abate a nuisance; in proceedings of mandamus, certiorari and prohibition, usurpation of office, contesting elections and eminent domain, and in such other special proceedings as may be provided by law (excepting cases in which appellate jurisdiction is given to the supreme court); also on questions of law alone, in all criminal cases prosecuted by indictment or information in a court of record, excepting criminal cases where judgment of death has been rendered. The said courts shall also have appellate jurisdiction in all cases, matters, and proceedings pending before the supreme court which shall be ordered by the supreme court to be transferred to a district court of appeal for hearing and decision. The said courts shall also have power to issue writs of mandamus, certiorari, prohibition and habeas corpus, and all other writs necessary or proper to the complete exercise of their appellate jurisdiction. Each of the justices thereof shall have power to issue writs of habeas corpus to any part of his appellate district upon petition by or on behalf of any person held in actual custody, and may make such writs returnable before himself or the district court of appeal of his district, or before any superior court within his district, or before any judge thereof.

The supreme court shall have power to order any cause pending before the supreme court to be heard and determined by a district court of appeal, and to order any cause pending before a district court of appeal to be heard and determined by the supreme court. The order last mentioned may be made before judgment has been pronounced by a district court of appeal, or within thirty days after such judgment shall have become final therein. The judgments of the district courts of appeal shall become final therein upon the expiration of thirty days after the same shall have been pronounced.

The supreme court shall have power to order causes pending before a district court of appeal for one district to be transferred to the district court of appeal of another district for hearing and decision.

The justices of the district courts of appeal shall be elected by the qualified electors within their respective districts, at the general state elections at the times and places at which justices of the supreme court are elected. Their terms of office and salaries shall be the same as those of justices of the supreme court, and their salaries shall be paid by the state. Upon the ratification by the people of this amendment the governor shall appoint nine persons to serve as justices of the district courts of appeal until the first Monday after the first day of January in the year 1907; provided, that not more than six of said persons shall be members of the same political party. At the election in the year 1906 nine of such justices shall be elected as above provided, and the justices of each district court of appeal shall so classify themselves by lot that one of them shall go out of office at the end of four years, one of them at the end of eight years, and one of them at the end of twelve years; an entry of such classification shall be made in the minutes of the court, signed by the three justices thereof, and a duplicate thereof filed in the office of the secretary of state. If any vacancy occur in the office of a justice of the district courts of appeal, the governor shall appoint a person to hold office until the election and qualification of a justice to fill the vacancy; such election shall take place at the next succeeding general state election as aforesaid; the justice then elected shall hold the office for the unexpired term.

One of the justices of each of the district courts of appeal shall be the presiding justice thereof, and as such shall be appointed or elected as the case may be. The presence of three justices shall be necessary for the transaction of any business by such court, except such as may be done at chambers, and the concurrence of three justices shall be necessary to pronounce a judgment.

Whenever any justice of the supreme court is for any reason disqualified or unable to act in a cause pending before

it, the remaining justices may select one of the justices of the district court of appeal to act pro tempore in the place of the justice so disqualified or unable to act.

Whenever any justice of a district court of appeal is for any reason disqualified or unable to act in any cause pending before it, the supreme court may appoint a justice of the district court of appeal of another district, or a judge of a superior court who has not acted in the cause in the court below, to act pro tempore in the place of the justice so disqualified or unable to act.

No appeal taken to the supreme court or to a district court of appeal shall be dismissed for the reason only that the same was not taken to the proper court, but the cause shall be transferred to the proper court upon such terms as to costs or otherwise as may be just, and shall be proceeded with therein as if regularly appealed thereto.

All statutes now in force allowing, providing for, or regulating appeals to the supreme court shall apply to appeals to the district courts of appeal so far as such statutes are not inconsistent with this article and until the legislature shall otherwise provide.

The supreme court shall make and adopt rules not inconsistent with law for the government of the supreme court and of the district courts of appeal and of the officers thereof, and for regulating the practice in said courts. [Amendment adopted November 8, 1904.]

Sec. 4½. No judgment shall be set aside, or new trial granted, in any case, on the ground of misdirection of the jury, or of the improper admission or rejection of evidence, or for any error as to any matter of pleading, or for any error as to any matter of procedure, unless, after an examination of the entire cause, including the evidence, the court shall be of the opinion that the error complained of has resulted in a miscarriage of justice. [Amendment adopted November 3, 1914.]

Sec. 5. The superior court shall have original jurisdiction in all cases in equity, and in all cases at law which involve the title or possession of real property, or the legal-

ity of any tax, impost, assessment, toll, or municipal fine, and in all other cases in which the demand, exclusive of interest or the value of the property in controversy amounts to three hundred dollars, and in all criminal cases amounting to felony, and cases of misdemeanor not otherwise provided for; of actions of forcible entry and detainer; of proceedings in insolvency; of actions to prevent or abate a nuisance; of all matters of probate; of divorce and for annulment of marriage; and of all such special cases and proceedings as are not otherwise provided for; and said court shall have the power of naturalization, and to issue papers therefor. They shall have appellate jurisdiction in such cases arising in inferior courts in their respective counties as may be prescribed by law. They shall be always open (legal holidays and nonjudicial days excepted), and their process shall extend to all parts of the state; provided, that all actions for the recovery of the possession of, quieting the title to, or for the enforcement of liens upon real estate, shall be commenced in the county in which the real estate, or any part thereof, affected by such action or actions, is situated. Said courts, and their judges, shall have power to issue writs of mandamus, certiorari, prohibition, quo warranto, and habeas corpus, on petition by or on behalf of any person in actual custody, in their respective counties. Injunctions and writs of prohibition may be issued and served on legal holidays and nonjudicial days. [Amendment adopted October 10, 1911.]

Sec. 6. There shall be in each of the organized counties, or cities and counties, of the state, a superior court, for each of which at least one judge shall be elected by the qualified electors of the county, or city and county, at the general state election; provided, that until otherwise ordered by the legislature, only one judge shall be elected for the counties of Yuba and Sutter, and that in the city and county of San Francisco there shall be elected twelve judges of the superior court, any one or more of whom may hold court. There may be as many sessions of said court, at the same time, as there are judges thereof. The said judges shall choose, from their own number, a presiding judge, who may be removed at

their pleasure. He shall distribute the business of the court among the judges thereof, and prescribe the order of business. The judgments, orders, and proceedings of any session of the superior court held by any one or more of the judges of said courts, respectively, shall be equally effectual as if all the judges of said respective courts presided at such session. In each of the counties of Sacramento, San Joaquin, Los Angeles, Sonoma, Santa Clara, and Alameda there shall be elected two such judges. The term of office of judges of the superior courts shall be six years from and after the first Monday of January, next succeeding their election; provided, that the twelve judges of the superior court elected in the city and county of San Francisco, at the first election held under this Constitution, shall at their first meeting so classify themselves, by lot, that four of them shall go out of office at the end of two years, and four of them shall go out of office at the end of four years, and four of them shall go out of office at the end of six years, and an entry of such classification shall be made in the minutes of the court, signed by them, and a duplicate thereof filed in the office of the secretary of state. The first election of judges of the superior courts shall take place at the first general election held after the adoption and ratification of this Constitution. If a vacancy occur in the office of judge of the superior court, the governor shall appoint a person to hold the office until the election and qualification of a judge to fill the vacancy, which election shall take place at the next succeeding general election, and the judge so elected shall hold office for the remainder of the unexpired term.

Sec. 7. In any county, or city and county, other than the city and county of San Francisco, in which there shall be more than one judge of the superior court, the judges of such court may hold as many sessions of said court at the same time as there are judges thereof, and shall apportion the business among themselves as equally as may be.

Sec. 8. A judge of any superior court may hold a superior court in any county, at the request of a judge of the

superior court thereof, and upon the request of the governor it shall be his duty so to do. But a cause in the superior court may be tried by a judge pro tempore, who must be a member of the bar, agreed upon in writing by the parties litigant, or their attorneys of record, and sworn to try the cause, and the person so selected shall be empowered to act in such capacity in all further proceedings in any suit or proceedings tried before him until the final determination thereof. There may be as many sessions of a superior court at the same time as there are judges thereof, including any judge or judges acting upon request, or any judge or judges pro tempore. The judgment, orders, acts and proceedings of any session of any superior court held by one or more judges acting upon request, or judge or judges pro tempore, shall be equally effective as if the judge or all of the judges of such court presided at such session. [Amendment adopted November 8, 1910.]

Sec. 9. The legislature shall have no power to grant leave of absence to any judicial officer; and any such officer who shall absent himself from the state for more than sixty consecutive days shall be deemed to have forfeited his office. The legislature of the state may, at any time, two-thirds of the members of the senate and two-thirds of the members of the assembly voting therefor, increase or diminish the number of judges of the superior court in any county, or city or county, in the state; provided, that no such reduction shall affect any judge who has been elected.

Sec. 10. Justices of the supreme court, and of the district courts of appeal, and judges of the superior courts may be removed by concurrent resolution of both houses of the legislature adopted by a two-thirds vote of each house. All other judicial officers, except justices of the peace, may be removed by the senate on the recommendation of the governor; but no removal shall be made by virtue of this section unless the cause thereof be entered on the journal, nor unless the party complained of has been served with a copy of the complaint against him and shall have had an opportunity of being heard in his defense. On the question of

removal the ayes and noes shall be entered on the journal. [Amendment adopted November 8, 1904.]

Sec. 11.   The legislature shall determine the number of each of the inferior courts in incorporated cities or towns, and in townships, counties, or cities and counties, according to the population thereof and the number of judges or justices thereof, and shall fix by law the powers, duties and responsibilities of each of such courts and of the judges or justices thereof; provided, such powers shall not in any case trench upon the jurisdiction of the several courts of record, except that the legislature shall provide that said courts shall have concurrent jurisdiction with the superior courts in cases of forcible entry and detainer, where the rental value does not exceed twenty-five dollars per month, and where the whole amount of damages claimed does not exceed two hundred dollars, and in cases to enforce and foreclose liens on personal property when neither the amount of liens nor the value of the property amounts to three hundred dollars.   [Amendment adopted October 10, 1911.]

Sec. 12.   The supreme court, the district courts of appeal, the superior courts, and such other courts as the legislature shall prescribe, shall be courts of record.   [Amendment adopted November 8, 1904.]

Sec. 13.   The legislature shall fix by law the jurisdiction of any inferior courts which may be established in pursuance of section 1 of this article, and shall fix by law the powers, duties, and responsibilities of the judges thereof.

Sec. 14.   The county clerks shall be ex-officio clerks of the courts of record in and for their respective counties, or cities and counties.   The legislature may also provide for the appointment, by the several superior courts, of one or more commissioners in their respective counties, or cities and counties, with authority to perform chamber business of the judges of the superior courts, to take depositions, and perform such other business connected with the administration of justice as may be prescribed by law.   [Amendment adopted October 10, 1911.]

Sec. 15. No judicial officer, except court commissioners, shall receive to his own use any fees or perquisites of office; provided, that justices of the peace now holding office shall receive to their own use such fees as are now allowed by law during the terms for which they have been elected. [Amendment adopted October 10, 1911.]

Sec. 16. The legislature shall provide for the speedy publication of such opinions of the supreme court and of the district courts of appeal as the supreme court may deem expedient, and all opinions shall be free for publication by any person. [Amendment adopted November 8, 1904.]

Sec. 17. The justices of the supreme court and of the district courts of appeal, and the judges of the superior courts, shall severally, at stated times during their continuance in office, receive for their service such compensation as is or shall be provided by law. The salaries of the judges of the superior court, in all counties having but one judge, and in all counties in which the terms of the judges of the superior court expire at the same time, shall not hereafter be increased or diminished after their election, nor during the term for which they shall have been elected. Upon the adoption of this amendment the salaries then established by law shall be paid uniformly to the justices and judges then in office. The salaries of the justices of the supreme court and of the district courts of appeal shall be paid by the state. One-half of the salary of each superior court judge shall be paid by the state; and the other half thereof shall be paid by the county for which he is elected. On and after the first day of January, A. D. one thousand nine hundred and seven, the justices of the supreme court shall each receive an annual salary of eight thousand dollars, and the justices of the several district courts of appeal shall each receive an annual salary of seven thousand dollars; the said salaries to be payable monthly. [Amendment adopted November 6, 1906.]

Sec. 18. The justices of the supreme court, and of the district courts of appeal, and the judges of the superior courts shall be ineligible to any other office or public em-

ployment than a judicial office or employment during the term for which they shall have been elected. [Amendment adopted November 8, 1904.]

Sec. 19. Judges shall not charge juries with respect to matters of fact, but may state the testimony and declare the law.

Sec. 20. The style of process shall be "The People of the State of California," and all prosecutions shall be conducted in their name and by their authority.

Sec. 21. The supreme court shall appoint a clerk of the supreme court; provided, however, that any person elected to the office of clerk of the supreme court before the adoption hereof, shall continue to hold such office until the expiration of the term for which he may have been elected. Said court may also appoint a reporter and not more than three assistant reporters of the decisions of the supreme court and of the district courts of appeal. Each of the district courts of appeal shall appoint its own clerk. All the officers herein mentioned shall hold office and be removable at the pleasure of the courts by which they are severally appointed, and they shall receive such compensation as shall be prescribed by law, and discharge such duties as shall be prescribed by law, or by the rules or orders of the courts by which they are severally appointed. [Amendment adopted October 10, 1911.]

Sec. 22. No judge of a court of record shall practice law in any court of this state during his continuance in office.

Sec. 23. No one shall be eligible to the office of a justice of the supreme court, or of a district court of appeal, or of a judge of a superior court, unless he shall have been admitted to practice before the supreme court of the state. [Amendment adopted November 8, 1904.]

Sec. 24. No judge of the supreme court nor of a district court of appeal, nor of a superior court, shall draw or receive any monthly salary unless he shall make and subscribe an affidavit before an officer entitled to administer oaths, that no cause in his court remains pending and undecided, that has been submitted for decision for a period of ninety

days. In the determination of causes all decisions of the supreme court and of the district courts of appeal shall be given in writing, and the grounds of the decisions shall be stated. When the justices of a district court of appeal are unable to concur in a judgment, they shall give their several opinions in writing and cause copies thereof to be forwarded to the supreme court. [Amendment adopted November 8, 1904.]

Sec. 25. The present supreme court commission shall be abolished at the expiration of its present term of office, and no supreme court commission shall be created or provided for after January 1, A. D. 1905. [New section adopted November 8, 1904.]

ARTICLE VII.

PARDONING POWER.

Section 1. The governor shall have the power to grant reprieves, pardons, and commutations of sentence, after conviction, for all offenses except treason and cases of impeachment, upon such conditions, and with such restrictions and limitations, as he may think proper, subject to such regulations as may be provided by law relative to the manner of applying for pardons. Upon conviction for treason, the governor shall have power to suspend the execution of the sentence until the case shall be reported to the legislature at its next meeting, when the legislature shall either pardon, direct the execution of the sentence, or grant a further reprieve. The governor shall communicate to the legislature, at the beginning of every session, every case of reprieve or pardon granted, stating the name of the convict, the crime for which he was convicted, the sentence, its date, the date of the pardon or reprieve, and the reasons for granting the same. Neither the governor nor the legislature shall have power to grant pardons, or commutations of sentence, in any case where the convict has been twice convicted of a felony, unless upon the written recommendation of a majority of the judges of the supreme court.

ARTICLE VIII.

MILITIA.

Section 1. The legislature shall provide, by law, for organizing and disciplining the militia, in such manner as it may deem expedient, not incompatible with the Constitution and laws of the United States. Officers of the militia shall be elected or appointed in such manner as the legislature shall, from time to time, direct, and shall be commissioned by the governor. The governor shall have power to call forth the militia to execute the laws of the state, to suppress insurrections, and repel invasions.

Sec. 2. All military organizations provided for by this Constitution, or any law of this state, and receiving state support, shall, while under arms, either for ceremony or duty, carry no device, banner, or flag of any state or nation, except that of the United States or the state of California.

ARTICLE IX.

EDUCATION.

Section 1. A general diffusion of knowledge and intelligence being essential to the preservation of the rights and liberties of the people, the legislature shall encourage by all suitable means the promotion of intellectual, scientific, moral and agricultural improvement.

Sec. 2. A superintendent of public instruction shall, at each gubernatorial election after the adoption of this Constitution, be elected by the qualified electors of the state. He shall receive a salary equal to that of the secretary of state, and shall enter upon the duties of his office on the first Monday after the first day of January next succeeding his election.

Sec. 3. A superintendent of schools for each county shall be elected by the qualified electors thereof at each gubernatorial election; provided, that the legislature may authorize two or more counties to unite and elect one superintendent for the counties so uniting.

Sec. 4. The proceeds of all lands that have been or may be granted by the United States to this state for the support of common schools, which may be, or may have been, sold or disposed of, and the five hundred thousand acres of land granted to the new states under an act of Congress distributing the proceeds of the public lands among the several states of the Union, approved A. D. one thousand eight hundred and forty-one, and all estates of deceased persons who may have died without leaving a will or heir, and also such per cent as may be granted, or may have been granted, by Congress on the sale of lands in this state, shall be and remain a perpetual fund, the interest of which, together with all the rents of the unsold lands, and such other means as the legislature may provide, shall be inviolably appropriated to the support of common schools throughout the state.

Sec. 5. The legislature shall provide for a system of common schools; by which a free school shall be kept up and supported in each district at least six months in every year, after the first year in which a school has been established.

Sec. 6. The public school system shall include day and evening elementary schools, and such day and evening secondary schools, normal schools, and technical schools as may be established by the legislature, or by municipal or district authority. The entire revenue derived from the state school fund and from the general state school tax shall be applied exclusively to the support of day and evening elementary schools; but the legislature may authorize and cause to be levied a special state school tax for the support of day and evening secondary schools and technical schools, or either of such schools, included in the public school system, and all revenue derived from such special tax shall be applied exclusively to the support of the schools for which such special tax shall be levied. [Amendment adopted November 3, 1908.]

Sec. 7. The legislature shall provide for the appointment or election of a state board of education, and said board shall provide, compile, or cause to be compiled, and adopt,

a uniform series of text-books for use in the day and evening elementary schools throughout the state. The state board may cause such text-books, when adopted, to be printed and published by the superintendent of state printing, at the state printing office; and wherever and however such text-books may be printed and published, they shall be furnished and distributed by the state free of cost or any cost or any charge whatever, to all children attending the day and evening elementary schools of the state, under such conditions as the legislature shall prescribe. The text-books, so adopted, shall continue in use not less than four years, without any change or alteration whatsoever which will require or necessitate the furnishing of new books to such pupils, and said state board shall perform such other duties as may be prescribed by law. The legislature shall provide for a board of education in each county in the state. The county superintendents and the county boards of education shall have control of the examination of teachers and the granting of teachers' certificates within their respective jurisdictions. [Amendment adopted November 5, 1912.]

Sec. 8. No public money shall ever be appropriated for the support of any sectarian or denominational school, or any school not under the exclusive control of the officers of the public schools; nor shall any sectarian or denominational doctrine be taught, or instruction thereon be permitted, directly or indirectly, in any of the common schools of this state.

Sec. 9. The University of California shall constitute a public trust, and its organization and government shall be perpetually continued in the form and character prescribed by the organic act creating the same, passed March twenty-third, eighteen hundred and sixty-eight (and the several acts amendatory thereof), subject only to such legislative control as may be necessary to insure compliance with the terms of its endowments and the proper investment and security of its funds. It shall be entirely independent of all political or sectarian influence, and kept free therefrom in the appointment of its regents, and in the administration of

its affairs; provided, that all the moneys derived from the sale of the public lands donated to this state by act of Congress, approved July second, eighteen hundred and sixty-two (and the several acts amendatory thereof), shall be invested as provided by said acts of Congress, and the interest of said moneys shall be inviolably appropriated to the endowment, support, and maintenance of at least one college of agriculture, where the leading objects shall be (without excluding other scientific and classical studies, and including military tactics) to teach such branches of learning as are related to scientific and practical agriculture and mechanic arts in accordance with, the requirements and conditions of said acts of Congress; and the legislature shall provide that if through neglect, misappropriation, or any other contingency, any portion of the funds so set apart shall be diminished or lost, the state shall replace such portion so lost or misappropriated, so that the principal thereof shall remain forever undiminished. No person shall be debarred admission to any of the collegiate departments of the university on account of sex.

Sec. 10. The trusts and estates created for the founding, endowment, and maintenance of the Leland Stanford Junior University, under and in accordance with "An act to advance learning," etc., approved March ninth, eighteen hundred and eighty-five, by the endowment grant executed by Leland Stanford and Jane Lathrop Stanford on the eleventh day of November, A. D. eighteen hundred and eighty-five, and recorded in liber 83 of Deeds, at page 23 et seq., records of Santa Clara county, and by the amendments of such grant, and by gifts, grants, bequests, and devises supplementary thereto, and by confirmatory grants, are permitted, approved, and confirmed. The board of trustees of the Leland Stanford Junior University, as such, or in the name of the institution, or by other intelligible designation of the trustees of the institution, may receive property, real or personal, and wherever situated, by gift, grant, devise, or bequest, for the benefit of the institution, or of any department thereof, and such property, unless otherwise provided, shall be held by the trustees of the Leland Stanford Junior

Constitution—4

University upon the trusts provided for in the grant founding the university, and amendments thereof, and grants,
bequests, and devises supplementary thereto. The legislature, by special act, may grant to the trustees of the Leland
Stanford Junior University corporate powers and privileges,
but it shall not thereby alter their tenure, or limit their
powers or obligations as trustees. All property now or
hereafter held in trust for the founding, maintenance, or
benefit of the Leland Stanford Junior University, or of any
department thereof, may be exempted by special act from
state taxation, and all personal property so held, the Palo
Alto farm as described in the endowment grant to the trustees of the university, and all other real property so held
and used by the university for educational purposes exclusively, may be similarly exempted from county and municipal taxation; provided, that residents of California shall be
charged no fees for tuition unless such fees be authorized
by act of the legislature. [New section adopted November
6, 1900.]

Sec. 11.   All property now or hereafter belonging to "The
California School of Mechanical Arts," an institution
founded and endowed by the late James Lick to educate
males and females in the practical arts of life, and incorporated under the laws of the state of California, November twenty-third, eighteen hundred and eighty-five, having
its school buildings located in the city and county of San
Francisco, shall be exempt from taxation. The trustees of
said institution must annually report their proceedings and
financial accounts to the governor. The legislature may
modify, suspend, and revive at will the exemption from
taxation herein given. [New section adopted November 6,
1900.]

Sec. 12.   All property now or hereafter belonging to the
"California Academy of Sciences," an institution for the advancement of science and maintenance of a free museum,
and chiefly endowed by the late James Lick, and incorporated under the laws of the state of California, January
sixteenth, eighteen hundred and seventy-one, having its
buildings located in the city and county of San Francisco,

shall be exempt from taxation. The trustees of said institution must annually report their proceedings and financial accounts to the governor. The legislature may modify, suspend, and revive at will the exemption from taxation herein given. [New section adopted November 8, 1904.]

Sec. 13. All property now or hereafter belonging to the Cogswell Polytechnical College, an institution for the advancement of learning, incorporated under the laws of the state of California, and having its buildings located in the city and county of San Francisco, shall be exempt from taxation. The trustees of said institution must annually report their proceedings and financial accounts to the governor. The legislature may modify, suspend, and revive at will the exemption from taxation herein given. [New section adopted November 6, 1906.]

ARTICLE X.

STATE INSTITUTIONS AND PUBLIC BUILDINGS.

Section 1. There shall be a state board of prison directors, to consist of five persons, to be appointed by the governor, with the advice and consent of the senate, who shall hold office for ten years, except that the first appointed shall, in such manner as the legislature may direct, be so classified that the term of one person so appointed shall expire at the end of each two years during the first ten years, and vacancies occurring shall be filled in like manner. The appointee to vacancy occurring before the expiration of a term shall hold office only for the unexpired term of his predecessor. The governor shall have the power to remove either of the directors for misconduct, incompetency, or neglect of duty, after an opportunity to be heard upon written charges.

Sec. 2. The board of directors shall have the charge and superintendence of the state prisons, and shall possess such powers and perform such duties, in respect to other penal and reformatory institutions of this state, as the legislature may prescribe.

Sec. 3. The board shall appoint the warden and clerk, and determine the other necessary officers of the prisons. The board shall have power to remove the wardens and clerks for misconduct, incompetency, or neglect of duty. All other officers and employees of the prisons shall be appointed by the warden thereof, and be removed at his pleasure.

Sec. 4. The members of the board shall receive no compensation, other than reasonable traveling and other expenses incurred while engaged in the performance of official duties, to be audited as the legislature may direct.

Sec. 5. The legislature shall pass such laws as may be necessary to further define and regulate the powers and duties of the board, wardens, and clerks, and to carry into effect the provisions of this article.

Sec. 6. After the first day of January, eighteen hundred and eighty-two, the labor of convicts shall not be let out by contract to any person, copartnership, company, or corporation, and the legislature shall, by law, provide for the working of convicts for the benefit of the state.

ARTICLE XI.
COUNTIES, CITIES, AND TOWNS.

Section 1. The several counties, as they now exist, are hereby recognized as legal subdivisions of this state.

Sec. 2. No county seat shall be removed unless two-thirds of the qualified electors of the county, voting on the proposition at a general election, shall vote in favor of such removal. A proposition of removal shall not be submitted in the same county more than once in four years.

Sec. 3. The legislature, by general and uniform laws, may provide for the alteration of county boundary lines, and for the formation of new counties; provided, however, that no new county shall be established which shall reduce any county to a population of less than twenty thousand; nor shall a new county be formed containing a less popula-

tion than eight thousand; nor shall any line thereof pass within five miles of the exterior boundary of the city or town in which the county seat of any county proposed to be divided is situated. Every county which shall be enlarged or created from territory taken from any other county or counties, shall be liable for a just proportion of the existing debts and liabilities of the county or counties from which such territory shall be taken. [Amendment adopted November 8, 1910.]

Sec. 4. The legislature shall establish a system of county governments, which shall be uniform throughout the state; and by general laws shall provide for township organizations, under which any county may organize whenever a majority of the qualified electors of such county, voting at a general election, shall so determine; and whenever a county shall adopt township organization, the assessment and collection of the revenue shall be made, and the business of such county and the local affairs of the several townships therein shall be managed and transacted, in the manner prescribed by such general laws.

Sec. 5. The legislature, by general and uniform laws, shall provide for the election or appointment, in the several counties, of boards of supervisors, sheriffs, county clerks, district attorneys, and such other county, township, and municipal officers as public convenience may require, and shall prescribe their duties and fix their terms of office. It shall regulate the compensation of all such officers, in proportion to duties, and may also establish fees to be charged and collected by such officers for services performed in their respective offices, in the manner and for the uses provided by law, and for this purpose may classify the counties by population; and it shall provide for the strict accountability of county and township officers for all fees which may be collected by them, and for all public and municipal moneys which may be paid to them, or officially come into their possession. It may regulate the compensation of grand and trial jurors in all courts within the classes of counties herein permitted to be made; such compensation, however, shall

not, in any class, exceed the sum of three dollars per day and mileage. [Amendment adopted November 3, 1908.]

Sec. 6. Corporations for municipal purposes shall not be created by special laws; but the legislature shall, by general laws, provide for the incorporation, organization, and classification, in proportion to population, of cities and towns, which laws may be altered, amended, or repealed; and the legislature may, by general laws, provide for the performance by county officers of certain of the municipal functions of cities and towns so incorporated, whenever a majority of the electors of any such city or town voting at a general or special election shall so determine. Cities and towns heretofore organized or incorporated may become organized under the general laws passed for that purpose, whenever a majority of the electors voting at a general election shall so determine, and shall organize in conformity therewith. Cities and towns hereafter organized under charters framed and adopted by authority of this Constitution are hereby empowered, and cities and towns heretofore organized by authority of this Constitution may amend their charters in the manner authorized by this Constitution so as to become likewise empowered hereunder, to make and enforce all laws and regulations in respect to municipal affairs, subject only to the restrictions and limitations provided in their several charters, and in respect to other matters they shall be subject to and controlled by general laws. Cities and towns heretofore or hereafter organized by authority of this Constitution may, by charter provision or amendment, provide for the performance by county officers of certain of their municipal functions, whenever the discharge of such municipal functions by county officers is authorized by general laws or by the provisions of a county charter framed and adopted by authority of this Constitution. [Amendment adopted November 3, 1914.]

Sec. 7. City and county governments may be merged and consolidated into one municipal government, with one set of officers, and may be incorporated under general laws providing for the incorporation and organization of corpora-

tions for municipal purposes. The provisions of this Constitution applicable to cities, and also those applicable to counties, so far as not inconsistent or prohibited to cities, shall be applicable to such consolidated government. [Amendment adopted November 6, 1894.]

Sec. 7½. Any county may frame a charter for its own government consistent with and subject to the Constitution (or, having framed such a charter, may frame a new one), and relating to matters authorized by provisions of the Constitution, by causing a board of fifteen freeholders, who have been for at least five years qualified electors thereof, to be elected by the qualified electors of said county, at a general or special election. Said board of freeholders may be so elected in pursuance of an ordinance adopted by the vote of three-fifths of all the members of the board of supervisors of such county, declaring that the public interest requires the election of such board for the purpose of preparing and proposing a charter for said county, or in pursuance of a petition of qualified electors of said county as hereinafter provided. Such petition, signed by fifteen per centum of the qualified electors of said county, computed upon the total number of votes cast therein for all candidates for governor at the last preceding general election at which a governor was elected, praying for the election of a board of fifteen freeholders to prepare and propose a charter for said county, may be filed in the office of the county clerk. It shall be the duty of said county clerk, within twenty days after the filing of said petition, to examine the same, and to ascertain from the record of the registration of electors of the county, whether said petition is signed by the requisite number of qualified electors. If required by said clerk, the board of supervisors shall authorize him to employ persons specially to assist him in the work of examining such petition, and shall provide for their compensation. Upon the completion of such examination, said clerk shall forthwith attach to said petition his certificate, properly dated, showing the result thereof, and if, by said certificate, it shall appear that said petition is signed by the requisite number of qualified electors, said clerk shall immediately present said

petition to the board of supervisors, if it be in session, otherwise at its next regular meeting after the date of such certificate. Upon the adoption of such ordinance, or the presentation of such petition, said board of supervisors shall order the holding of a special election for the purpose of electing such board of freeholders, which said special election shall be held not less than twenty days nor more than sixty days after the adoption of the ordinance aforesaid or the presentation of said petition to said board of supervisors; provided, that if a general election shall occur in said county not less than twenty days nor more than sixty days after the adoption of the ordinance aforesaid, or such presentation of said petition to said board of supervisors, said board of freeholders may be elected at such general election. Candidates for election as members of said board of freeholders shall be nominated by petition, substantially in the same manner as may be provided by general law for the nomination, by petition of electors, of candidates for county offices, to be voted for at general elections. It shall be the duty of said board of freeholders, within one hundred and twenty days after the result of such election shall have been declared by said board of supervisors, to prepare and propose a charter for said county, which shall be signed in duplicate by the members of said board of freeholders, or a majority of them, and be filed, one copy in the office of the county clerk of said county and the other in the office of the county recorder thereof. Said board of supervisors shall thereupon cause said proposed charter to be published for at least ten times in a daily newspaper of general circulation, printed, published and circulated in said county; provided, that in any county where no such daily newspaper is printed, published and circulated, such proposed charter shall be published for at least three times in at least one weekly newspaper, of general circulation, printed, published and circulated in such county; and provided, that in any county where neither such daily nor such weekly newspaper is printed, published and circulated, a copy of such proposed charter shall be posted by the county clerk in three public places in

said county, and on or near the entrance to at least one public schoolhouse in each school district in said county, and the first publication or the posting of such proposed charter shall be made within fifteen days after the filing of a copy thereof, as aforesaid, in the office of the county clerk. Said proposed charter shall be submitted by said board of supervisors to the qualified electors of said county at a special election held not less than thirty days nor more than sixty days after the completion of such publication, or after such posting; provided, that if a general election shall occur in said county, not less than thirty days nor more than sixty days after the completion of such publication, or after such posting, then such proposed charter may be so submitted at such general election. If a majority of said qualified electors, voting thereon at such general or special election, shall vote in favor of such proposed charter it shall be deemed to be ratified, and shall be forthwith submitted to the legislature, if it be in regular session, otherwise at its next regular session, or it may be submitted to the legislature in extraordinary session, for its approval or rejection as a whole, without power of alteration or amendment. Such approval may be made by concurrent resolution, and if approved by a majority vote of the members elected to each house, such charter shall become the charter of such county and shall become the organic law thereof relative to the matters therein provided, and supersede any existing charter framed under the provisions of this section, and all amendments thereof, and shall supersede all laws inconsistent with such charter relative to the matters provided in such charter. A copy of such charter, certified and authenticated by the chairman and clerk of the board of supervisors under the seal of said board and attested by the county clerk of said county, setting forth the submission of such charter to the electors of said county, and its ratification by them, shall, after the approval of such charter by the legislature, be made in duplicate, and filed, one in the office of the secretary of state and the other, after being recorded in the office of the recorder of said county, shall be filed in the office of the county clerk thereof, and thereafter all courts shall take judicial notice of said charter.

The charter, so ratified, may be amended by proposals therefor submitted by the board of supervisors of the county to the qualified electors thereof at a general or special election held not less than thirty days nor more than sixty days after the publication of such proposals for ten times in a daily newspaper of general circulation, printed, published and circulated in said county; provided, that in any county where no such daily newspaper is printed, published and circulated, such proposed charter shall be published for at least three times in at least one weekly newspaper, of general circulation, printed, published, and circulated in such county; provided, that in any county where neither such daily nor such weekly newspaper is printed, published and circulated, a copy of such proposed charter shall be posted by the county clerk in three public places in said county, and on or near the entrance to at least one public schoolhouse in each school district in said county. If a majority of such qualified electors voting thereon, at such general or special election, shall vote in favor of any such proposed amendment or amendments, or any amendment or amendments proposed by petition as hereinafter provided, such amendment or amendments shall be deemed to be ratified, and shall be forthwith submitted to the legislature, if it be in regular session, otherwise at its next regular session, or may be submitted to the legislature in extraordinary session, for approval or rejection as a whole, without power of alteration or amendment, and if approved by the legislature, as herein provided for the approval of the charter, such charter shall be amended accordingly. A copy of such amendment or amendments shall, after the approval thereof by the legislature, be made in duplicate, and shall be authenticated, certified, recorded and filed as herein provided for the charter, and with like force and effect. Whenever a petition signed by ten per centum of the qualified electors of any county, computed upon the total number of votes cast in said county for all candidates for governor at the last general election, at which a governor was elected, is filed in the office of the county clerk of said county, petitioning the board of supervisors thereof to submit any pro-

posed amendment or amendments to the charter of such county, which amendment or amendments shall be set forth in full in such petition, to the qualified electors thereof, such petition shall forthwith be examined and certified by the county clerk, and if signed by the requisite number of qualified electors of such county, shall be presented to the said board of supervisors, by the said county clerk, as hereinbefore provided for petitions for the election of boards of freeholders. Upon the presentation of said peti-tion to said board of supervisors, said board must sub-mit the amendment or amendments set forth therein to the qualified electors of said county, at a general or spe-cial election held not less than thirty days nor more than sixty days after the publication or posting of such pro-posed amendment or amendments in the same manner as hereinbefore provided in the case of the submission of any proposed amendment or amendments to such charter, pro-posed and submitted by the board of supervisors. In sub-mitting any such charter, or amendments thereto, any alter-native article or proposition may be presented for the choice of the electors, and may be voted on separately without prejudice to others.

Every special election held under the provisions of this section, for the election of boards of freeholders or for the submission of proposed charters, or any amendment or amendments thereto, shall be called by the board of super-visors, by ordinance, which shall specify the purpose and time of such election and shall establish the election pre-cincts and designate the polling places therein, and the names of the election officers for each such precinct. Such ordinance, prior to such election, shall be published five times in a daily newspaper, or twice in a weekly newspaper, if there be no such daily newspaper, printed, published and circulated in said county; provided, that if no such daily or weekly newspaper be printed or published in such county, then a copy of such ordinance shall be posted by the county clerk in three public places in such county and in or near the entrance to at least one public schoolhouse in each school district therein. In all other respects, every such

election shall be held and conducted, the returns thereof canvassed and the result thereof declared by the board of supervisors in the same manner as provided by law for general elections. Whenever boards of freeholders shall be elected, or any such proposed charter, or amendment or amendments thereto, submitted, at a general election, the general laws applicable to the election of county officers and the submission of propositions to the vote of electors, shall be followed in so far as the same may be applicable thereto.

It shall be competent, in all charters, framed under the authority given by this section to provide, in addition to any other provisions allowable by this Constitution, and the same shall provide, for the following matters:

1. For boards of supervisors and for the Constitution, regulation and government thereof, for the times at which and the terms for which the members of said board shall be elected, for the number of members, not less than three, that shall constitute such boards, for their compensation and for their election, either by the electors of the counties at large or by districts; provided, that in any event said board shall consist of one member for each district, who must be a qualified elector thereof; and

2. For sheriffs, county clerks, treasurers, recorders, license collectors, tax collectors, public administrators, coroners, surveyors, district attorneys, auditors, assessors and superintendents of schools, for the election or appointment of said officers, or any of them, for the times at which and the terms for which, said officers shall be elected or appointed, and for their compensation, or for the fixing of such compensation by boards of supervisors, and, if appointed, for the manner of their appointment; and

3. For the number of justices of the peace and constables for each township, or for the number of such judges and other officers of such inferior courts as may be provided by the Constitution or general law, for the election or appointment of said officers, for the times at which and the terms for which said officers shall be elected or appointed, and for their compensation, or for the fixing of such compensation

by boards of supervisors, and if appointed, for the manner of their appointment; and

4. For the powers and duties of boards of supervisors and all other county officers, for their removal and for the consolidation and segregation of county offices, and for the manner of filling all vacancies occurring therein; provided, that the provisions of such charters relating to the powers and duties of boards of supervisors and all other county officers shall be subject to and controlled by general laws; and

4½. For the assumption and discharge by county officers of certain of the municipal functions of the cities and towns within the county, whenever, in the case of cities and towns incorporated under general laws, the discharge by county officers of such municipal functions is authorized by general law, or whenever, in the case of cities and towns organized under section eight of this article, the discharge by county officers of such municipal functions is authorized by provisions of the charters, or by amendments thereto, of such cities or towns.

5. For the fixing and regulation by boards of supervisors, by ordinance, of the appointment and number of assistants, deputies, clerks, attachés and other persons to be employed, from time to time, in the several offices of the county, and for the prescribing and regulating by such boards of the powers, duties, qualifications and compensation of such persons, the times at which, and terms for which they shall be appointed, and the manner of their appointment and removal; and

6. For the compensation of such fish and game wardens, probation and other officers as may be provided by general law, or for the fixing of such compensation by boards of supervisors.

All elective officers of counties, and of townships, of road districts and of highway construction divisions therein shall be nominated and elected in the manner provided by general laws for the nomination and election of such officers.

All charters framed under the authority given by this section, in addition to the matters herein above specified, may provide as follows:

For officers other than those required by the Constitution and laws of the state, or for the creation of any or all of such offices by boards of supervisors, for the election or appointment of persons to fill such offices for the manner of such appointment, for the times at which and the terms for which such persons shall be so elected or appointed, and for their compensation, or for the fixing of such compensation by boards of supervisors.

For offices hereafter created by this Constitution or by general law, for the election or appointment of persons to fill such offices, for the manner of such appointment, for the times at which and the terms for which such persons shall be so elected or appointed, and for their compensation, or for the fixing of such compensation by boards of supervisors.

For the formation, in such counties, of road districts for the care, maintenance, repair, inspection and supervision only of roads, highways and bridges; and for the formation, in such counties, of highway construction divisions for the construction only of roads, highways and bridges; for the inclusion in any such district or division, of the whole or any part of any incorporated city or town, upon ordinance passed by such incorporated city or town authorizing the same, and upon the assent to such inclusion by a majority of the qualified electors of such incorporated city or town, or portion thereof, proposed to be so included, at an election held for that purpose; for the organization, government, powers and jurisdiction of such districts and divisions, and for raising revenue therein, for such purposes, by taxation, upon the assent of a majority of the qualified electors of such districts or divisions, voting at an election to be held for that purpose; for the incurring of indebtedness therefor by such counties, districts or divisions for such purposes respectively, by the issuance and sale, by the counties, of bonds of such counties, districts or divisions, and the expenditure of the proceeds of the sale of such bonds, and for levying and collecting taxes against the property of the counties, districts or divisions, as the case may be, for the payment of the principal and interest of such in-

debtedness at maturity; provided, that any such indebtedness shall not be incurred without the assent of two-thirds of the qualified electors of the county, district or division, as the case may be, voting at an election to be held for that purpose, nor unless before or at the time of incurring such indebtedness provision shall be made for the collection of an annual tax sufficient to pay the interest on such indebtedness as it falls due, and also for a sinking fund for the payment of the principal thereof on or before maturity, which shall not exceed forty years from the time of contracting the same, and the procedure for voting, issuing and selling such bonds shall, except in so far as the same shall be prescribed in such charters, conform to general laws for the authorizing and incurring by counties of bonded indebtedness, so far as applicable; provided, further, that provisions in such charters for the construction, care, maintenance, repair, inspection and supervision of roads, highways and bridges for which aid from the state is granted, shall be subject to such regulations and conditions as may be imposed by the legislature.

Whenever any county has framed and adopted a charter, and the same shall have been approved by the legislature, as herein provided, the general laws adopted by the legislature in pursuance of sections 4 and 5 of this article, shall, as to such county, be superseded by said charter as to matters for which, under this section it is competent to make provision in such charter, and for which provision is made therein, except as herein otherwise expressly provided; and except that any such charter shall not affect the tenure of office of the elective officers of the county, or of any district, township or division thereof, in office at the time such charter goes into effect, and such officers shall continue to hold their respective offices until the expiration of the term for which they shall have been elected, unless sooner removed in the manner provided by law.

The charter of any county, adopted under the authority of this section, may be surrendered and annulled with the assent of two-thirds of the qualified electors of such county, voting at a special election, held for that purpose, and to

be ordered and called by the board of supervisors of the
county upon receiving a written petition, signed and certified as hereinabove provided for the purposes of the adoption of charters, requesting said board to submit the question of the surrender and annulment of such charter to the
qualified electors of such county, and, in the event of the
surrender and annulment of any such charter, such county
shall thereafter be governed under general laws in force
for the government of counties.

The provisions of this section shall not be applicable to
any county that is consolidated with any city. [Amend-
ment adopted November 3, 1914.]

Sec. 8.   Any city or city and county containing a population of more than three thousand five hundred inhabitants, as ascertained by the last preceding census taken
under the authority of the Congress of the United States or
of the legislature of California, may frame a charter for its
own government, consistent with and subject to this Constitution; and any city, or city and county having adopted
a charter may adopt a new one.   Any such charter shall be
framed by a board of fifteen freeholders chosen by the electors of such city at any general or special election, but no
person shall be eligible as a candidate for such board unless
he shall have been, for the five years next preceding, an
elector of said city.   An election for choosing freeholders
may be called by a two-thirds vote of the legislative body
of such city, and, on presentation of a petition signed by
not less than fifteen per cent of the registered electors of
such city, the legislative body shall call such election at any
time not less than thirty nor more than sixty days from
date of the filing of the petition.   Any such petition shall
be verified by the authority having charge of the registration records of such city or city and county and the
expenses of such verification, shall be provided by the legislative body thereof.   Candidates for the office of freeholders shall be nominated either in such manner as may be
provided for the nomination of officers of the municipal government or by petition, substantially in the same manner
as may be provided by general laws for the nomination by

petition of electors of candidates for public offices to be
voted for at general elections. The board of freeholders
shall, within one hundred and twenty days after the result
of the election is declared, prepare and propose a charter
for the government of such city; but the said period of one
hundred and twenty days may with the consent of the legislative body of such city be extended by such board not
exceeding a total of sixty days. The charter so prepared
shall be signed by a majority of the board of freeholders
and filed in the office of the clerk of the legislative body of
said city. The legislative body of said city shall within
fifteen days after such filing cause such charter to be published once in the official paper of said city; (or in case
there be no such paper, in a paper of general circulation);
and shall cause copies of such charter to be printed in convenient pamphlet form, and shall, until the date fixed for
the election upon such charter, advertise in one or more
papers of general circulation published in said city a notice
that such copies may be had upon application therefor.
Such charter shall be submitted to the electors of such city
at a date to be fixed by the board of freeholders, before
such filing and designated on such charter, either at a special election held not less than sixty days from the completion of the publication of such charter as above provided,
or at the general election next following the expiration of
said sixty days. If a majority of the qualified voters voting thereon at such general or special election shall vote in
favor of such proposed charter, it shall be deemed to be ratified, and shall be submitted to the legislature, if then in
session, or at the next regular or special session of the legislature. The legislature shall by concurrent resolution approve or reject such charter as a whole, without power of
alteration or amendment; and if approved by a majority of
the members elected to each house it shall become the organic law of such city or city and county, and supersede
any existing charter and all laws inconsistent therewith.
One copy of the charter so ratified and approved shall be
filed with the secretary of state, one with the recorder of
the county in which such city is located, and one in the

Constitution—5

archives of the city; and thereafter the courts shall take judicial notice of the provisions of such charter. The charter of any city or city and county may be amended by proposals therefor submitted by the legislative body of the city on its own motion or on petition signed by fifteen per cent of the registered electors, or both. Such proposals shall be submitted to the electors only during the six months next preceding a regular session of the legislature or thereafter and before the final adjournment of that session and at either a special election called for that purpose or at any general or special election. Petitions for the submission of any amendment shall be filed with the legislative body of the city or city and county not less than sixty days prior to the general election next preceding a regular session of the legislature. The signatures on such petitions shall be verified by the authority having charge of the registration records of such city or city and county, and the expenses of such verification shall be provided by the legislative body thereof. If such petitions have a sufficient number of signatures the legislative body of the city or city and county shall so submit the amendment or amendments so proposed to the electors. Amendments proposed by the legislative body and amendments proposed by petition of the electors may be submitted at the same election. The amendments so submitted shall be advertised in the same manner as herein provided for the advertisement of a proposed charter, and the election thereon held at a date to be fixed by the legislative body of such city, not less than forty and not more than sixty days after the completion of the advertising in the official paper. If a majority of the qualified voters voting on any such amendment vote in favor thereof it shall be deemed ratified, and shall be submitted to the legislature at the regular session next following such election; and approved or rejected without power of alteration in the same manner as herein provided for the approval or rejection of a charter. In submitting any such charter or amendment separate propositions, whether alternative or conflicting, or one included within the other, may be submitted at the same time to be voted on by the electors sepa-

rately, and, as between those so related, if more than one
receive a majority of the votes, the proposition receiving
the larger number of votes shall control as to all matters in
conflict.   It shall be competent in any charter framed under
the authority of this section to provide that the municipality governed thereunder may make and enforce all laws
and regulations in respect to municipal affairs, subject only
to the restrictions and limitations provided in their several
charters and in respect to other matters they shall be subject to general laws.   It shall be competent in any charter
to provide for the division of the city or city and county
governed thereby into boroughs or districts, and to provide
that each such borough or district may exercise such general or special municipal powers, and to be administered in
such manner, as may be provided for each such borough or
district in the charter of the city or city and county.

The percentages of the registered electors herein required for the election of freeholders or the submission of
amendments to charters shall be calculated upon the total
vote cast in the city or city and county at the last preceding general state election; and the qualified electors shall
be those whose names appear upon the registration records
of the same or preceding year.   The election laws of such
city or city and county shall, so far as applicable, govern
all elections held under the authority of this section.
[Amendment adopted November 3, 1914.]

Sec. 8a.   The charter of the city and county of San Francisco may be amended, in addition to the method and the
times provided in section 8 of article XI of the Constitution,
in the following particulars:

(a) Authorizing the city and county of San Francisco, a
municipal corporation, by its legislative authority, to incur
a bonded indebtedness in an amount not exceeding five
million dollars, and to issue municipal bonds therefor, and
to grant and turn over to the Panama-Pacific International
Exposition Company (a corporation organized under the
laws of the state of California March 22, 1910) the proceeds
of said bonds, the same to be used and disbursed by said
exposition company for the purpose of an exposition to be

held in the city and county of San Francisco to celebrate the completion of the Panama Canal; said bonds, so issued, to be of such form and to be redeemable, registered and converted in such manner and amounts, and at such times not later than forty years from the date of their issue, as such legislative authority shall determine; the interest on said bonds to not exceed five per centum per annum, and said bonds to be exempt from all taxes for state and municipal purposes, and to be sold for not less than par at such times and places, and in such manner, as shall be determined by said legislative authority; the proceeds of said bonds, when sold, to be payable immediately by the treasurer of said city and county to the treasurer of said Panama-Pacific International Exposition Company, upon the demand of said treasurer of said exposition company, without the necessity of the approval of such demand by other authority, the same to be used and disbursed by said Panama-Pacific International Exposition Company for the purposes of such exposition, under the direction and control of such exposition company;

(b) Providing that any bonded indebtedness incurred for the purposes aforesaid shall be exclusive of the bonded indebtedness of the said city and county limited by section nine of article XII of said charter;

(c) Granting to said Panama-Pacific International Exposition Company the exclusive possession and use, together with the management and control, of that portion of Golden Gate Park in the city and county of San Francisco westerly from Twentieth avenue, as extended, for such exposition purposes, such possession and use, also management and control, to terminate not later than one year after the closing of such exposition;

(d) Granting to said Panama-Pacific International Exposition Company the exclusive possession and use, together with the management and control, for such exposition purposes, of any lands held by the board of education of the city and county of San Francisco, and by the city and county of San Francisco, not in actual use, such possession

and use, also management and control, to terminate not later than one year after the closing of such exposition;

(e) Authorizing said Panama-Pacific International Exposition Company to temporarily close streets in the city and county of San Francisco westerly from Twentieth avenue, for such exposition purposes, and to have the exclusive possession and use, together with the management and control, of said streets for such exposition purposes, such possession and use, also management and control of said streets, to terminate not later than one year after the closing of such exposition.

Proposals to amend the charter of the city and county of San Francisco in the foregoing particulars may be submitted by the legislative authority of said city and county to the electors of said city and county, at any general or special election (and a special election may be called therefor) held in said city and county, after the publication of such proposals in a newspaper of general circulation in said city and county, for such time as shall be determined by said legislative authority. Upon the ratification of any such proposed amendment by a majority of the electors of said city and county voting at such election on such proposed amendment, said proposed amendment receiving such majority vote shall become operative immediately as an amendment to said charter, without the necessity of approval thereof by the legislature.

Any act of the legislative authority of the city and county of San Francisco, in submitting to the electors of said city and county, at any general or special election, proposals to amend the charter of said city and county in the foregoing particulars, including any notice by publication or otherwise of such proposals, and of such election, and the holding of such election, in accordance with the provisions hereof, before the adoption of this amendment, are hereby validated in all respects as if performed subsequent to the adoption of this amendment. The disbursement of all funds obtained from said bonds shall be accounted for by said Panama-Pacific International Exposition Company by an itemized statement thereof to be filed with the auditor of

the city and county of San Francisco. [New section adopted November 8, 1910.]

Sec. 8½. It shall be competent, in all charters framed under the authority given by section 8 of this article, to provide, in addition to those provisions allowable by this Constitution and by the laws of the state as follows:

1. For the constitution, regulation, government, and jurisdiction of police courts, and for the manner in which, the times at which, and the terms for which the judges of such courts shall be elected or appointed, and for the qualifications and compensation of said judges and of their clerks and attachès; and for the establishment, constitution, regulation, government and jurisdiction of municipal courts, with such civil and criminal jurisdiction as by law may be conferred upon inferior courts; and for the manner in which, the times at which, and the terms for which the judges of such courts shall be elected or appointed, and for the qualifications and compensation of said judges and of their clerks and attaches; provided, such municipal courts shall never be deprived of the jurisdiction given inferior courts created by general law.

In any city or any city and county, when such municipal court has been established, there shall be no other court inferior to the superior court; and pending actions, trials, and all pending business of inferior courts within the territory of such city or city and county, upon the establishment of any such municipal court, shall be and become pending in such municipal court, and all records of such inferior courts shall thereupon be and become the records of such municipal court.

2. For the manner in which, the times of which, and the terms for which the members of boards of education shall be elected or appointed, for their qualifications, compensation and removal, and for the number which shall constitute any one of such boards.

3. For the manner in which, the times at which and the terms for which the members of the boards of police commissioners shall be elected or appointed; and for the con-

stitution, regulation, compensation, and government of such boards and of the municipal police force.

4. For the manner in which and the times at which any municipal election shall be held and the result thereof determined; for the manner in which, the times at which, and the terms for which the members of all boards of election shall be elected or appointed, and for the constitution, regulation, compensation and government of such boards, and of their clerks and attachés, and for all expenses incident to the holding of any election.

It shall be competent in any charter framed in accordance with the provisions of this section, or section 8 of this article, for any city or consolidated city and county, and plenary authority is hereby granted, subject only to the restrictions of this article, to provide therein or by amendment thereto, the manner in which, the method by which, the times at which, and the terms for which the several county and municipal officers and employees whose compensation is paid by such city or city and county, excepting judges of the superior court, shall be elected or appointed, and for their recall and removal, and for their compensation, and for the number of deputies, clerks and other employees that each shall have, and for the compensation, method of appointment, qualifications, tenure of office and removal of such deputies, clerks and other employees. All provisions of any charter of any such city or consolidated city and county, heretofore adopted, and amendments thereto, which are in accordance herewith, are hereby confirmed and declared valid.

5. It shall be competent in any charter or amendment thereof, which shall hereafter be framed under the authority given by section 8 of this article, by any city having a population in excess of fifty thousand ascertained as prescribed by said section 8, to provide for the separation of said city from the county of which it has theretofore been a part and the formation of said city into a consolidated city and county to be governed by such charter, and to have combined powers of a city and county, as provided in this Constitution for consolidated city and county govern-

ment, and further to prescribe in said charter the date for
the beginning of the official existence of said consolidated
city and county.

It shall also be competent for any such city, not having
already consolidated as a city and county to hereafter
frame, in the manner prescribed in section 8 of this article,
a charter providing for a city and county government, in
which charter there shall be prescribed territorial boundaries which may include contiguous territory not included
in such city, which territory, however, must be included in
the county within which such city is located.

If no additional territory is proposed to be added, then,
upon the consent to the separation of any such city from
the county in which it is located, being given by a majority
of the qualified electors voting thereon in such county and
upon the ratification of such charter by a majority of the
qualified electors voting thereon in such city, and the approval thereof by the legislature, as prescribed in section 8
of this article, said charter shall be deemed adopted and
upon the date fixed therein said city shall be and become a
consolidated city and county.

If additional territory which consists wholly of only one
incorporated city or town, or which consists wholly of unincorporated territory, is proposed to be added, then, upon
the consent to such separation of such territory and of the
city initiating the consolidation proposal being given by a
majority of the qualified electors voting thereon in the
county in which the city proposing such separation is located, and upon the ratification of such charter by a majority of the qualified electors voting thereon in such city so
proposing the separation, and also upon the approval of the
proposal hereinafter set forth, by a majority of the qualified
electors voting thereon in the whole of such additional territory, and the approval of said charter by the legislature,
as prescribed in section 8 of this article, said charter shall
be deemed adopted, the indebtedness hereinafter referred
to shall be deemed to have been assumed, and upon the date
fixed in said charter such territory and such city shall be
and become one consolidated city and county.

The proposal to be submitted to the territory proposed to be added shall be substantially in the following form and submitted as one indivisible question:

"Shall the territory (herein designate in general terms the territory to be added) consolidate with the city of (herein insert name of the city initiating the proposition to form a city and county government) in a consolidated city and county government, and shall the charter as prepared by the city of (herein insert the name of the city initiating such proposition) be adopted as the charter of the consolidated city and county, and shall the said added territory become subject to taxation along with the entire territory of the proposed city and county, in accordance with the assessable valuation of the property of the said territory, for the following indebtedness of said city (herein insert name of the city initiating such proposition) to wit: (herein insert in general terms reference to any debts to be assumed, and if none insert 'none')."

If additional territory is proposed to be added, which includes unincorporated territory, and one or more incorporated cities or towns, or which includes more than one incorporated city or town, the consent of any such incorporated city or town shall be obtained by a majority vote of the qualified electors thereof voting upon a proposal substantially as follows:

"Shall (herein insert the name of the city or town to be included in such additional territory) be included in a district to be hereafter defined by the city of (herein insert the name of the city initiating the proposition to form a city and county government) which district shall, within two years from the date of this election, vote upon a proposal submitted as one indivisible question that such district to be then described and set forth shall consolidate with (herein insert name of the city initiating said consolidation proposition) in a consolidated city and county government, and also that a certain charter, to be prepared by the city of (herein insert name of the city initiating such proposition) be adopted as the charter of such consolidated city and county, and that such district become subject to taxa-

tion along with the entire territory of the proposed city and county in accordance with the assessable valuation of the property of said district for the following indebtedness of said city of (herein insert name of the city initiating such proposition) to wit: (herein insert in general terms, reference to any debts to be assumed and if none insert 'none')."

Any and all incorporated cities or towns to which the foregoing proposal shall have been submitted and a majority of whose qualified electors voting thereon shall have voted in favor thereof, together with such unincorporated territory as the city initiating such consolidation proposal may desire to have included, the whole to form an area contiguous to said city, shall be created into a district by such city, and the proposal substantially as above prescribed to be used when the territory proposed to be added consists wholly of only one incorporated city or town, or wholly of unincorporated territory, shall, within two years, be submitted to the voters of said entire district as one indivisible question.

Upon consent to the separation of such district and of the city initiating the consolidation proposal being given by a majority of the qualified electors voting thereon in the county in which the city proposing such separation is located, and upon the ratification of such charter by a majority of the qualified electors voting thereon in such city, and upon the approval of the proposal hereinbefore set forth by a majority of the qualified electors voting thereon in the whole of said district so proposed to be added, and upon the approval of said charter by the legislature, as prescribed in section 8 of this article, said charter shall be deemed adopted, the said indebtedness referred to in said proposal shall be deemed to have been assumed, and upon the date fixed in said charter, such district and such city shall be and become one consolidated city and county.

6. It shall be competent for any consolidated city and county now existing, or which shall hereafter be organized, to annex territory contiguous to such consolidated city and county, unincorporated or otherwise, whether situated wholly in one county, or parts thereof be situate in differ-

ent counties, said annexed territory to be an integral part of such city and county, provided that such annexation of territory shall only include any part of the territory which was at the time of the original consolidation of the annexing city and county, within the county from which such annexing city and county was formed, together with territory which was concurrently, or has since such consolidation been joined in a county government with the area of the original county not included in such consolidated city and county.

If additional territory, which consists wholly of only one incorporated city, city and county or town, or which consists wholly of unincorporated territory, is proposed to be annexed to any consolidated city and county now existing or which shall hereafter be organized, then, upon the consent to any such annexation being given by a majority of the qualified electors voting thereon in any county or counties in which any such additional territory is located, and upon the approval of such annexation proposal by a majority of the qualified electors voting thereon in such city and county, and also upon the approval of the proposal hereinafter set forth by a majority of the qualified electors voting thereon in the whole of such territory proposed to be annexed, the indebtedness hereinafter referred to shall be deemed to have been assumed, and at the time stated in such proposal, such additional territory and such city and county shall be and become one consolidated city and county, to be governed by the charter of the city and county proposing such annexation, and any subsequent amendment thereto.

The proposal to be submitted to the territory proposed to be annexed, shall be substantially in the following form and submitted as one indivisible question:

"Shall the territory (herein designate in general terms the territory to be annexed) consolidate with the city and county of (herein insert the name of the city and county initiating the annexation proposal) in a consolidated city and county government, said consolidation to take effect (herein insert date when such consolidation shall take effect) and shall the said annexed territory become subject to taxation,

as an integral part of the city and county so formed, in accordance with the assessable valuation of property of said territory for the following indebtedness of said city and county of (herein insert name of the city and county) to wit: (herein insert in general terms, reference to any debts to be assumed and if none insert 'none')."

If additional territory including unincorporated territory and one or more incorporated cities, cities and counties, or towns, or including more than one incorporated city, city and county, or town, is proposed to be annexed to any consolidated city and county now existing or which shall hereafter be organized, the consent of each such incorporated city, city and county, or town, shall be obtained by a majority vote of the qualified electors of any such incorporated city, city and county, or town, voting upon a proposal substantially as follows:

"Shall (herein insert name of the city, city and county, or town, to be included in such annexed territory) be included in a district to be hereafter defined by the city and county of (herein insert the name of the city and county initiating the annexation proposal) which district shall within two years from the date of this election vote upon a proposal submitted as one indivisible question, that such district to be then described and set forth shall consolidate with (herein insert name of the city and county initiating the annexation proposal) in a consolidated city and county government, and that such district become subject to taxation, along with the entire territory of the proposed city and county in accordance with the assessable valuation of the property of said district for the following indebtedness of said city and county of (herein insert name of the city and county initiating the annexation proposal) to wit: (herein insert in general terms, reference to any debts to be assumed and if none insert 'none')."

Any and all incorporated cities, cities and counties, or towns, to which the foregoing proposal shall have been submitted, and a majority of whose qualified electors voting thereon shall have voted in favor thereof, together with such unincorporated territory as the city and county initi-

ating such annexation proposal may desire to have included, the whole to form an area contiguous to said city and county, shall be created into a district by said city and county, and the proposal substantially in the form above set forth to be used when the territory proposed to be added consists wholly of only one incorporated city, city and county, or town, or wholly of unincorporated territory, shall, within said two years, be submitted to the voters of said entire district as one indivisible question.

Upon consent to any such annexation being given by a majority of the qualified electors voting thereon in any county or counties in which any such territory proposed to be annexed to said city and county is located, and upon the approval of any such annexation proposal by a majority of the qualified electors voting thereon in such city and county proposing such annexation, and also upon the approval of the proposal hereinbefore set forth by a majority of the qualified electors voting thereon in the whole of the district so proposed to be annexed, then, the said indebtedness referred to in said proposal shall be deemed to have been assumed, and upon the date stated in such annexation proposal such district and such city and county shall be and become one consolidated city and county, to be governed by the charter of the city and county proposing such annexation, and any subsequent amendment thereto.

Whenever any proposal is submitted to the electors of any county, territory, district, city, city and county, or town, as above provided, there shall be published, for at least five successive publications, in a newspaper of general circulation printed and published in any such county, territory, district, city, city and county, or town, the last publication to be not less than twenty days prior to any such election, a particular description of any territory or district to be separated, added, or annexed, together with a particular description of any debts to be assumed, as above referred to, unless such particular description is contained in the said proposal so submitted. In addition to said description, such territory shall also be designated in such notice by some appropriate name or other words of identifi-

cation, by which such territory may be referred to and indicated upon the ballots to be used at any election at which the question of annexation or consolidation of additional territory is submitted as herein provided. If there be no such newspaper so printed and published in any such county, territory, district, city, city and county, or town, then such publication may be made in any newspaper of general circulation printed and published in the nearest county, city, city and county, or town where there may be such a newspaper so printed and published.

If, by the adoption of any charter, or by annexation, any incorporated municipality becomes a portion of a city and county, its property, debts and liabilities of every description shall be and become the property, debts and liabilities of such city and county.

Every city and county which shall be formed, or the territory of which shall be enlarged as herein provided from territory taken from any county or counties, shall be liable for a just proportion of the debts and liabilities and be entitled to a just proportion of the property and assets of such county or counties, existing at the time such territory is so taken.

The provisions of this Constitution applicable to cities, and cities and counties, and also those applicable to counties, so far as not inconsistent or prohibited to cities, or cities and counties, shall be applicable to such consolidated city and county government; and no provision of subdivision five or six of this section shall be construed as a restriction upon the plenary authority of any city or city and county having a freeholders' charter, as provided for in this Constitution, to determine in said charter any and all matters elsewhere in this Constitution authorized and not inconsistent herewith.

The legislature shall provide for the formation of one or more counties from the portion or portions of a county or counties remaining after the formation of or annexation to a consolidated city and county, or for the transfer of such portion or portions of such original county or counties to adjoining counties. But such transfer to an adjoining

county shall only be made after approval by a majority vote of the qualified electors voting thereon in such territory proposed to be so transferred.

The provisions of section 2 of this article, and also those provisions of section 3 of this article which refer to the passing of any county line within five miles of the exterior boundary of a city or town in which a county seat of any county proposed to be divided is situated, shall not apply to the formation of, nor to the extension of the territory of such consolidated cities and counties, nor to the formation of new counties, nor to the annexation of existing counties, as herein specified.

Any city and county formed under this section shall have the right, if it so desires, to be designated by the official name of the city initiating the consolidation as it existed immediately prior to its adoption of a charter providing for a consolidated city and county government, except that such city and county shall be known under the style of a city and county.

It shall be competent in any charter framed for a consolidated city and county, or by amendment thereof, to provide for the establishment of a borough system of government for the whole or any part of the territory of said city and county, by which one or more districts may be created therein, which districts shall be known as boroughs and which shall exercise such municipal powers as may be granted thereto by such charter, and for the organization, regulation, government and jurisdiction of such boroughs.

No property in any territory hereafter consolidated with or annexed to any city or city and county shall be taxed for the payment of any indebtedness of such city or city and county outstanding at the date of such consolidation or annexation and for the payment of which the property in such territory was not, prior to such consolidation or annexation, subject to such taxation, unless there shall have been submitted to the qualified electors of such territory the proposition regarding the assumption of indebtedness as hereinbefore set forth and the same shall have been approved by a majority of such electors voting thereon.

7. In all cases of annexation of unincorporated territory to an incorporated city, or the consolidation of two or more incorporated cities, assumption of existing bonded indebtedness by such unincorporated territory or by either of the cities so consolidating may be made by a majority vote of the qualified electors voting thereon in the territory or city which shall assume an existing bonded indebtedness. This provision shall apply whether annexation or consolidation is effected under this section or any other section of this Constitution, and the provisions of section 18 of this article shall not be a prohibition thereof.

The legislature shall enact such general laws as may be necessary to carry out the provisions of this section and such general or special laws as may be necessary to carry out the provisions of subdivisions 5 and 6 of this section, including any such general or special act as may be necessary to permit a consolidated city and county to submit a new charter to take effect at the time that any consolidation, by reason of annexation to such consolidated city and county, takes effect, and, also, any such general law or special act as may be necessary to provide for any period after such consolidation, by reason of such annexation, takes effect, and prior to the adoption and approval of any such new charter. [Amendment adopted November 3, 1914.]

Sec. 9.   The compensation of any county, city, town, or municipal officer shall not be increased after his election or during his term of office; nor shall the term of any such officer be extended beyond the period for which he is elected or appointed.

Sec. 10.   [Repealed November 8, 1910.]

Sec. 11.   Any county, city, town, or township may make and enforce within its limits all such local, police, sanitary, and other regulations as are not in conflict with general laws.

Sec. 12.   The legislature shall have no power to impose taxes upon counties, cities, towns or other public or municipal corporations, or upon the inhabitants or property thereof, for county, city, town, or other municipal purposes,

but may, by general laws, vest in the corporate authorities thereof the power to assess and collect taxes for such purposes.

Sec. 13.   The legislature shall not delegate to any special commission, private corporation, company, association or individual any power to make, control, appropriate, supervise or in any way interfere with any county, city, town or municipal improvement, money, property, or effects, whether held in trust or otherwise, or to levy taxes or assessments or perform any municipal function whatever, except that the legislature shall have power to provide for the supervision, regulation and conduct, in such manner as it may determine, of the affairs of irrigation districts, reclamation districts or drainage districts, organized or existing under any law of this state.   [Amendment adopted November 3, 1914.]

Sec. 13½.   Any county, city and county, city, town, municipality, irrigation district, or other public corporation, issuing bonds under the laws of the state, is hereby authorized and empowered to make said bonds and the interest thereon payable at any place or places within or outside of the United States, and in any money, domestic or foreign, designated in said bonds.   [Amendment adopted November 3, 1914.]

Sec. 14.   The legislature may by general and uniform laws provide for the inspection, measurement and graduation of merchandise, manufactured articles and commodities, and may provide for the appointment of such officers as may be necessary for such inspection, measurement and graduation. [Amendment adopted October 10, 1911.]

Sec. 15.   Private property shall not be taken or sold for the payment of the corporate debt of any political or municipal corporation.

Sec. 16.   All moneys, assessments, and taxes belonging to or collected for the use of any county, city, town, or other public or municipal corporation, coming into the hands of any officer thereof, shall immediately be deposited with the treasurer, or other legal depositary, to the credit of such

Constitution—6

city, town, or other corporation, respectively, for the benefit of the funds to which they respectively belong.

Sec. 16½. All moneys belonging to the state, or to any county or municipality within this state, may be deposited in any national bank or banks within this state, or in any bank or banks organized under the laws of this state, in such manner and under such conditions as may be provided by law; provided, that such bank or banks in which such moneys are deposited shall furnish as security for such deposits, bonds of the United States, or of this state or of any county, municipality or school district within this state, or of any irrigation district within this state, to be approved by the officer or officers designated by law, to an amount in value of at least ten per cent in excess of the amount of such deposit; and provided, that such bank or banks shall pay a reasonable rate of interest, not less than two per cent per annum on the daily balances therein deposited; and provided, that no deposit shall at any one time exceed fifty per cent of the paid-up capital stock of such depositary bank or banks; and provided, further, that no officer shall deposit at one time more than twenty per cent of such public moneys available for deposit in any bank while there are other qualified banks requesting such deposits. [Amended November 5, 1912.]

Sec. 17. The making of profit out of county, city, town, or other public money, or using the same for any purpose not authorized by law, by any officer having the possession or control thereof, shall be a felony, and shall be prosecuted and punished as prescribed by law.

Sec. 18. No county, city, town, township, board of education or school district, shall incur any indebtedness or liability in any manner or for any purpose exceeding in any year the income and revenue provided for such year, without the assent of two-thirds of the qualified electors thereof, voting at an election to be held for that purpose, nor unless before or at the time of incurring such indebtedness provision shall be made for the collection of an annual tax sufficient to pay the interest on such indebtedness as it falls due,

and also provision to constitute a sinking fund for the
payment of the principal thereof on or before maturity,
which shall not exceed forty years from the time of contracting the same; provided, however, that the city and
county of San Francisco may at any time pay the unpaid
claims, with interest thereon at the rate of five per cent
per annum, for materials furnished to and work done for
said city and county during the forty-first, forty-second,
forty-third, forty-fourth, and fiftieth fiscal years, and for
unpaid teachers' salaries for the fiftieth fiscal year, out of
the income and revenue of any succeeding year or years, the
amount to be paid in full of said claims not to exceed in the
aggregate the sum of five hundred thousand dollars, and
that no statute of limitations shall apply in any manner to
these claims; and provided, further, that the city of Vallejo,
of Solano county, may pay its existing indebtedness, incurred in the construction of its waterworks, whenever two-
thirds of the electors thereof, voting at an election held
for that purpose, shall so decide, and that no statute of
limitations shall apply in any manner. Any indebtedness
or liability incurred contrary to this provision, with the exceptions hereinbefore recited, shall be void. The city and
county of San Francisco, the city of San Jose, and the town
of Santa Clara may make provision for a sinking fund, to
pay the principal of any indebtedness incurred, or to be
hereafter incurred by it, to commence at a time after the
incurring of such indebtedness of no more than a period of
one-fourth of the time of maturity of such indebtedness,
which shall not exceed seventy-five years from the time of
contracting the same. Any indebtedness incurred contrary
to any provision of this section shall be void; and provided,
further, that the county of Alameda may, upon the assent of
two-thirds of the qualified electors thereof voting at an election to be held for that purpose, incur a bonded indebtedness of not to exceed one million dollars, and the legislative
authority of said county of Alameda shall issue bonds therefor and grant and turn over to the Panama-Pacific International Exposition Company, a corporation organized under
the laws of the state of California, March 22, 1910, the pro-

ceeds of said bonds for stock in said company or under such other terms and conditions as said legislative authority may determine, the same to be used and disbursed by said exposition company for the purpose of an exposition to be held in the city and county of San Francisco to celebrate the completion of the Panama canal; said bonds, so issued, to be of such form and to be redeemable, registered and converted in such manner and amounts, and at such times not later than forty years from the date of their issue as the legislative authority of said county of Alameda shall determine; the interest on said bonds not to exceed five per centum per annum, and said bonds to be exempted from all taxes for state, county and municipal purposes, and to be sold for not less than par at such times and places, and in such manner, as shall be determined by said legislative authority; the proceeds of said bonds, when sold, to be payable immediately upon such terms or conditions as said legislative body may determine, to the treasurer of said Panama-Pacific International Exposition Company, upon demands of said treasurer of said exposition company, without the necessity of the approval of such demands by other authority, than said legislative authority of Alameda county, the same to be used and disbursed by said Panama-Pacific International Exposition Company for the purposes of such exposition, under the direction and control of said exposition company; and the legislative authority of said county of Alameda is hereby empowered and directed to levy a special tax on all taxable property in said county each year after the issue of said bonds to raise an amount to pay the interest on said bonds as the same become due, and to create a sinking fund to pay the principal thereof when the same shall become due. [Amendment adopted November 3, 1914.]

Sec. 19. Any municipal corporation may establish and operate public works for supplying its inhabitants with light, water, power, heat, transportation, telephone service or other means of communication. Such works may be acquired by original construction or by the purchase of existing works, including their franchises, or both. Persons or corporations may establish and operate works for supplying

the inhabitants with such services upon such conditions and under such regulations as the muncipality may prescribe under its organic law, on condition that the municipal government shall have the right to regulate the charges thereof. A municipal corporation may furnish such services to inhabitants outside its boundaries; provided, that it shall not furnish any service to the inhabitants of any other municipality owning or operating works supplying the same service to such inhabitants, without the consent of such other municipality, expressed by ordinance. [Amendment adopted October 10, 1911.]

ARTICLE XII.
CORPORATIONS.

Section 1. Corporations may be formed under general laws, but shall not be created by special act. All laws now in force in the state concerning corporations, and all laws that may be hereafter passed pursuant to this section, may be altered from time to time or repealed.

Sec. 2. Dues from corporations shall be secured by such individual liability of the corporators and other means as may be prescribed by law.

Sec. 3. Each stockholder of a corporation, or joint-stock association, shall be individually and personally liable for such proportion of all its debts and liabilities contracted or incurred, during the time he was a stockholder, as the amount of stock or shares owned by him bears to the whole of the subscribed capital stock, or shares of the corporation or association. The directors or trustees of corporations and joint-stock associations shall be jointly and severally liable to the creditors and stockholders for all moneys embezzled or misappropriated by the officers of such corporation or joint-stock association, during the term of office of such director or trustee.

Nothing in the preceding paragraph of this section shall be held to apply to any exposition company organized to promote and carry on any international exposition or world's fair within the state of California, and the liability

of stockholders in any such exposition company shall be and the same is hereby limited to an amount not exceeding the par value of the stock of said corporation subscribed for by such stockholders. [Amendment adopted November 3, 1908.]

Sec. 4.   The term "corporation," as used in this article, shall be construed to include all associations and joint-stock companies having any of the powers or privileges of corporations not possessed by individuals or partnerships, and all corporations shall have the right to sue and be subject to be sued, in all courts, in like cases as natural persons.

Sec. 5.   The legislature shall have no power to pass any act granting any charter for banking purposes, but corporations or associations may be formed for such purposes under general laws, and the legislature shall provide for the classification of cities and towns by population for the purpose of regulating the business of banking.   No corporation, association, or individual shall issue or put in circulation, as money, anything but the lawful money of the United States. [Amendment adopted November 8, 1910.]

Sec. 6.   All existing charters, grants, franchises, special or exclusive privileges, under which an actual and bona fide organization shall not have taken place, and business been commenced in good faith, at the time of the adoption of this Constitution, shall thereafter have no validity.

Sec. 7.   The legislature shall not extend any franchise or charter, nor remit the forfeiture of any franchise or charter of any quasi-public corporation now existing or which shall hereafter exist under the laws of this state.   The term of existence of any other corporation now or hereafter existing under the laws of this state, may be extended at any time prior to the expiration of its corporate existence, for a period not exceeding fifty years from the date of such extension, by the vote or written consent of stockholders representing two-thirds of its capital stock or of two-thirds of the members thereof.   A certificate of such vote or consent shall be signed and sworn to by the president and secretary, and by a majority of the directors of the corporation and

filed and certified in the manner and upon payment of fees required by law for filing and certifying articles of incorporation, and thereupon the terms of the corporation shall be extended for the period specified in such certificate, and such corporation shall thereafter pay all annual or other fees required by law to be paid by corporations. [Amendment adopted November 3, 1908.]

Sec. 8. The exercise of the right of eminent domain shall never be so abridged or construed as to prevent the legislature from taking the property and franchises of incorporated companies and subjecting them to public use the same as the property of individuals, and the exercise of the police power of the state shall never be so abridged or construed as to permit corporations to conduct their business in such manner as to infringe the rights of individuals or the general well-being of the state.

Sec. 9. No corporation shall engage in any business other than that expressly authorized in its charter or the law under which it may have been or may hereafter be organized; nor shall it hold for a longer period than five years any real estate except such as may be necessary for carrying on its business.

Sec. 10. The legislature shall not pass any laws permitting the leasing or alienation of any franchise, so as to relieve the franchise or property held thereunder from the liabilities of the lessor or grantor, lessee or grantee, contracted or incurred in the operation, use, or enjoyment of such franchise or any of its privileges.

Sec. 11. No corporation shall issue stock or bonds, except for money paid, labor done, or property actually received, and all fictitious increase of stock or indebtedness shall be void. The stock and bonded indebtedness of corporations shall not be increased, except in pursuance of general law, nor without the consent of the persons holding the larger amount in value of the stock, at a meeting called for that purpose, giving sixty days' public notice, as may be provided by law.

Sec. 12. In all elections for directors or managers of corporations every stockholder shall have the right to vote, in

person or by proxy, the number of shares of stock owned by him, for as many persons as there are directors or managers to be elected, or to cumulate said shares and give one candidate as many votes as the number of directors multiplied by the number of his shares of stock shall equal, or to distribute them, on the same principle, among as many candidates as he shall think fit; and such directors or managers shall not be elected in any other manner, except that members of co-operative societies formed for agricultural, mercantile, and manufacturing purposes may vote on all questions affecting such societies in manner prescribed by law.

Sec. 13. The state shall not, in any manner, loan its credit, nor shall it subscribe to or be interested in the stock of any company, association, or corporation.

Sec. 14. Every corporation other than religious, educational, or benevolent, organized or doing business in this state, shall have and maintain an office or place in this state for the transaction of its business, where transfers of stock shall be made, and in which shall be kept, for inspection by every person having an interest therein, and legislative committees, books in which shall be recorded the amount of capital stock subscribed, and by whom; the names of the owners of its stock, and the amounts owned by them, respectively; the amount of stock paid in, and by whom; the transfers of stock; the amount of its assets and liabilities, and the names and places of residence of its officers.

Sec. 15. No corporation organized outside the limits of this state shall be allowed to transact business within this state on more favorable conditions than are prescribed by law to similar corporations organized under the laws of this state.

Sec. 16. A corporation or association may be sued in the county where the contract is made or is to be performed, or where the obligation or liability arises or the breach occurs; or in the county where the principal place of business of such corporation is situated, subject to the power of the court to change the place of trial as in other cases.

Sec. 17. All railroad, canal, and other transportation companies are declared to be common carriers, and subject

to legislative control. Any association or corporation, organized for the purpose under the laws of this state, shall have the right to connect at the state line with railroads of other states. Every railroad company shall have the right with its road to intersect, connect with, or cross any other railroad, and shall receive and transport each the other's passengers, tonnage, and cars, without delay or discrimination.

Sec. 18. No president, director, officer, agent, or employee of any railroad or canal company shall be interested directly or indirectly, in the furnishing of material or supplies to such company, nor in the business of transportation as a common carrier of freight or passengers over the works owned, leased, controlled, or worked by such company, except such interest in the business of transportation as lawfully flows from the ownership of stock therein.

Sec. 19. No railroad or other transportation company shall grant free passes, or passes or tickets at a discount, to any person holding any office of honor, trust, or profit in this state; and the acceptance of any such pass or ticket by a member of the legislature, or any public officer, other than railroad commissioner, shall work a forfeiture of his office.

Sec. 20. No railroad or other transportation company shall raise any rate of charge for the transportation of freight or passengers or any charge connected therewith or incidental thereto, under any circumstances whatsoever, except upon a showing before the railroad commission provided for in this Constitution, that such increase is justified, and the decision of the said commission upon the showing so made shall not be subject to review by any court except upon the question whether such decision of the commission will result in confiscation of property. [Amendment adopted October 10, 1911.]

Sec. 21. No discrimination in charges or facilities for transportation shall be made by any railroad or other transportation company between places or persons, or in the facilities for the transportation of the same classes of freight or passengers within this state. It shall be unlawful for any

railroad or other transportation company to charge or receive any greater compensation in the aggregate for the transportation of passengers or of like kind of property for a shorter than for a longer distance over the same line or route in the same direction, the shorter being included within the longer distance, or to charge any greater compensation as a through rate than the aggregate of the inter. mediate rates; provided, however, that upon application to the railroad commission provided for in this Constitution such company may, in special cases, after investigation, be authorized by such commission to charge less for longer than for shorter distances for the transportation of persons or property and the railroad commission may from time to time prescribe the extent to which such company may be relieved from the prohibition to charge less for the longer · than for the shorter haul. The railroad commission shall have power to authorize the issuance of excursion and commutation tickets at special rates. Nothing herein contained shall be construed to prevent the railroad commission from ordering and compelling any railroad or other transportation company to make reparation to any shipper on account of the rates charged to said shipper being excessive or discriminatory, provided no discrimination will result from such reparation. [Amendment adopted October 10, 1911.]

Sec. 22. There is hereby created a railroad commission which shall consist of five members and which shall be known as the railroad commission of the state of California. The commission shall be appointed by the governor from the state at large; provided, that the legislature, in its discretion, may divide the state into districts for the purpose of such appointments, said districts to be as nearly equal in population as practicable; and provided, further, that the three commissioners in office at the time this section takes effect shall serve out the term for which they were elected, and that two additional commissioners shall be appointed by the governor immediately after the adoption of this section, to hold office during the same term. Upon the expiration of said term, the term of office of each commissioner thereafter shall be six years, except the commissioners first appointed

hereunder after such expiration, one of whom shall be appointed to hold office until January 1, 1917, two until January 1, 1919, and two until January 1, 1921. Whenever a vacancy in the office of commissioner shall occur, the governor shall forthwith appoint a qualified person to fill the same for the unexpired term. Commissioners appointed for regular terms shall at the beginning of the term for which they are appointed, and those appointed to fill vacancies, shall, immediately upon their appointment, enter upon the duties of their offices. The legislature shall fix the salaries of the commissioners, but pending such action the salaries of the commissioners, their officers and employees shall remain as now fixed by law. The legislature shall have the power, by a two-thirds vote of all members elected to each house, to remove any one or more of said commissioners from office for dereliction of duty or corruption or incompetency. All of said commissioners shall be qualified electors of this state, and no person in the employ of or holding any official relation to any person, firm or corporation, which said person, firm or corporation is subject to regulation by said railroad commission and no person owning stock or bonds of any such corporation or who is in any manner pecuniarily interested therein, shall be appointed to or hold the office of railroad commissioner. No vacancy in the commission shall impair the right of the remaining commissioners to exercise all the powers of the commission. The act of a majority of the commissioners when in session as a board shall be deemed to be the act of commission; but any investigation, inquiry or hearing which the commission has power to undertake or to hold may be undertaken or held by or before any commissioner designated for the purpose by the commission, and every order made by a commissioner so designated, pursuant to such inquiry, investigation or hearing, when approved or confirmed by the commission ordered filed in its office, shall be deemed to be the order of the commission.

Said commission shall have the power to establish rates of charges for the transportation of passengers and freight by railroads and other transportation companies, and no rail-

road or other transportation company shall charge or demand or collect or receive a greater or less or different compensation for such transportation of passengers or freight, or for any service in connection therewith, between the points named in any tariff of rates, established by said commission, than the rates, fares and charges which are specified in such tariff. The commission have the further power to examine books, records and papers of all railroad and other transportation companies; to hear and determine complaints against railroad and other transportation companies; to issue subpoenas and all necessary process and send for persons and papers; and the commission and each of the commissioners shall have the power to administer oaths, take testimony and punish for contempt in the same manner and to the same extent as courts of record; the commission may prescribe a uniform system of accounts to be kept by all railroad and other transportation companies.

No provision of this Constitution shall be construed as a limitation upon the authority of the legislature to confer upon the railroad commission additional powers of the same kind or different from those conferred herein which are not inconsistent with the powers conferred upon the railroad commission in this Constitution, and the authority of the legislature to confer such additional powers is expressly declared to be plenary and unlimited by any provision of this Constitution.

The provisions of this section shall not be construed to repeal in whole or in part any existing law not inconsistent herewith, and the "Railroad Commission Act" of this state approved February 10, 1911, shall be construed with reference to this constitutional provision and any other constitutional provision becoming operative concurrently herewith. And the said act shall have the same force and effect as if the same had been passed after the adoption of this provision of the Constitution and of all other provisions adopted concurrently herewith, except that the three commissioners referred to in said act shall be held and construed to be the five commissioners provided for herein. [Amendment adopted October 10, 1911.]

Sec. 23. Every private corporation, and every individual or association of individuals, owning, operating, managing, or controlling any commercial railroad, interurban railroad, street railroad, canal, pipe-line, plant, or equipment, or any part of such railroad, canal, pipe-line, plant, or equipment within this state for the transportation or conveyance of passengers, or express matter, or freight of any kind, including crude oil, or for the transmission of telephone or telegraph messages, or for the production, generation, transmission, delivery or furnishing of heat, light, water or power or for the furnishing of storage or wharfage facilities, either directly or indirectly, to or for the public, and every common carrier, is hereby declared to be a public utility subject to such control and regulation by the railroad commission as may be provided by the legislature, and every class of private corporations, individuals, or associations of individuals hereafter declared by the legislature to be public utilities shall likewise be subject to such control and regulation. The railroad commission shall have and exercise such power and jurisdiction to supervise and regulate public utilities, in the state of California, and to fix the rates to be charged for commodities furnished, or services rendered by public utilities as shall be conferred upon it by the legislature, and the right of the legislature to confer powers upon the railroad commission respecting public utilities is hereby declared to be plenary and to be unlimited by any provision of this Constitution. From and after the passage by the legislature of laws conferring powers upon the railroad commission respecting public utilities, all powers respecting such public utilities vested in boards of supervisors, or municipal councils, or other governing bodies of the several counties, cities and counties, cities and towns, in this state, or in any commission created by law and existing at the time of the passage of such laws, shall cease so far as such powers shall conflict with the powers so conferred upon the railroad commission; provided, however, that this section shall not affect such powers of control over public utilities as relate to the making and enforcement of local, police, sanitary and other regulations, other than the fixing of rates,

vested in any city and county or incorporated city or town as, at an election to be held pursuant to law, a majority of the qualified electors of such city and county, or incorporated city or town, voting thereon, shall vote to retain, and until such election such powers shall continue unimpaired; but if the vote so taken shall not favor the continuation of such powers they shall thereafter vest in the railroad commission as provided by law; and provided, further, that where any such city and county, or incorporated city or town, shall have elected to continue any of its powers to make and enforce such local, police, sanitary and other regulations, other than the fixing of rates, it may, by vote of a majority of its qualified electors voting thereon, thereafter surrender such powers to the railroad commission in the manner prescribed by the legislature; and provided, further, that this section shall not affect the right of any city and county or incorporated city or town, to grant franchises for public utilities upon the terms and conditions and in the manner prescribed by law. Nothing in this section shall be construed as a limitation upon any power conferred upon the railroad commission by any provision of this Constitution now existing or adopted concurrently herewith [Amendment adopted November 3, 1914.]

Sec. 23a. The railroad commission shall have and exercise such power and jurisdiction as shall be conferred upon it by the legislature to fix the just compensation to be paid for the taking of any property of a public utility in eminent domain proceedings by the state or any county, city and county, incorporated city or town, or municipal water district, and the right of the legislature to confer such powers upon the railroad commission is hereby declared to be plenary and to be unlimited by any provision of this Constitution. All acts of the legislature heretofore adopted, which are in accordance herewith, are hereby confirmed and declared valid. [New section adopted November 3, 1914.]

Sec. 24. The legislature shall pass all laws necessary for the enforcement of the provisions of this article.

ARTICLE XIII.

REVENUE AND TAXATION.

Section 1. All property in the state except as otherwise in this Constitution provided, not exempt under the laws of the United States, shall be taxed in proportion to its value, to be ascertained as provided by law, or as hereinafter provided. The word "property," as used in this article and section, is hereby declared to include moneys, credits, bonds, stocks, dues, franchises, and all other matters and things, real, personal, and mixed, capable of private ownership; provided, that a mortgage, deed of trust, contract, or other obligation by which a debt is secured when land is pledged as security for the payment thereof, together with the money represented by such debt, shall not be considered property subject to taxation; and further provided, that property used for free public libraries and free museums, growing crops, property used exclusively for public schools, and such as may belong to the United States, this state, or to any county, city and county, or municipal corporation within this state shall be exempt from taxation, except such lands and the improvements thereon located outside of the county, city and county, or municipal corporation owning the same as were subject to taxation at the time of the acquisition of the same by said county, city and county, or municipal corporation; provided, that no improvements of any character whatever constructed by any county, city and county or municipal corporation shall be subject to taxation. All lands or improvements thereon, belonging to any county, city and county, or municipal corporation, not exempt from taxation, shall be assessed by the assessor of the county, city and county, or municipal corporation in which said lands or improvements are located, and said assessment shall be subject to review, equalization and adjustment by the state board of equalization. The legislature may provide, except in the case of credits secured by mortgage or trust deed, for a deduction from credits of debts due to bona fide residents of this state. [Amendment adopted November 3, 1914.]

Sec. 1¼. The property to the amount of one thousand dollars of every resident in this state who has served in the army, navy, marine corps, or revenue marine service of the United States in time of war, and received an honorable discharge therefrom; or lacking such amount of property in his own name, so much of the property of the wife of any such person as shall be necessary to equal said amount; and property to the amount of one thousand dollars of the widow resident in this state, or if there be no such widow, of the widowed mother resident in this state, of every person who has so served and has died either during his term of service or after receiving honorable discharge from said service; and the property to the amount of one thousand dollars of pensioned widows, fathers, and mothers, resident in this state, of soldiers, sailors, and marines who served in the army, navy, or marine corps, or revenue marine service of the United States, shall be exempt from taxation; provided, that this exemption shall not apply to any person named herein owning property of the value of five thousand dollars or more, or where the wife of such soldier or sailor owns property of the value of five thousand dollars or more. No exemption shall be made under the provisions of this act of the property of a person who is not a legal resident of this state. [New section adopted October 10, 1911.]

Sec. 1½. All buildings, and so much of the real property on which they are situated as may be required for the convenient use and occupation of said buildings, when the same are used solely and exclusively for religious worship shall be free from taxation; provided, that no building so used which may be rented for religious purposes and rent received by the owner therefor, shall be exempt from taxation. [New section adopted November 6, 1900.]

Sec. 1¾. All bonds hereafter issued by the state of California, or by any county, city and county, municipal corporation, or district (including school, reclamation, and irrigation districts) within said state, shall be free and exempt from taxation. [New section adopted November 4, 1902.]

Sec. 1a. Any educational institution of collegiate grade, within the state of California, not conducted for profit, shall

hold exempt from taxation its buildings and equipment, its grounds within which its buildings are located, not exceeding one hundred acres in area, its securities and income used exclusively for the purposes of education. [New section adopted November 3, 1914.]

Sec. 2. Land, and the improvements thereon, shall be separately assessed. Cultivated and uncultivated land, of the same quality, and similarly situated, shall be assessed at the same value.

Sec. 3. Every tract of land containing more than six hundred and forty acres, and which has been sectionized by the United States government, shall be assessed, for the purposes of taxation, by sections or fractions of sections. The legislature shall provide by law for the assessment, in small tracts, of all lands not sectionized by the United States government.

Sec. 4. All vessels of more than fifty tons burden registered at any port in this state and engaged in the transportation of freight or passengers, shall be exempt from taxation except for state purposes, until and including the first day of January, nineteen hundred thirty-five. [New section adopted November 3, 1914.]

Sec. 5. [Repealed November 6, 1906.]

Sec. 6. The power of taxation shall never be surrendered or suspended by any grant or contract to which the state shall be a party.

Sec. 7. The legislature shall have the power to provide by law for the payment of all taxes on real property by installments.

Sec. 8. The legislature shall by law require each taxpayer in this state to make and deliver to the county assessor, annually, a statement, under oath, setting forth specifically all the real and personal property owned by such taxpayer, or in his possession, or under his control, at twelve o'clock meridian on the first Monday of March.

Sec. 9. A state board of equalization, consisting of one member from each congressional district in this state, as the

same existed in eighteen hundred and seventy-nine, shall be
elected by the qualified electors of their respective districts,
at the general election to be held in the year one thousand
eight hundred and eighty-six, and at each gubernatorial
election thereafter, whose term of office shall be for four
years; whose duty it shall be to equalize the valuation of
the taxable property in the several counties of the state for
the purposes of taxation. The controller of state shall be
ex-officio a member of the board. The boards of supervisors
of the several counties of the state shall constitute boards of
equalization for their respective counties, whose duty it
shall be to equalize the valuation of the taxable property in
the county for the purpose of taxation; provided, such state
and county boards of equalization are hereby authorized and
empowered, under such rules of notice as the county boards
may prescribe as to county assessments, and under such
rules of notice as the state board may prescribe as to the
action of the state board, to increase or lower the entire
assessment-roll, or any assessment contained therein, so as
to equalize the assessment of the property contained in said
assessment-roll, and make the assessment conform to the
true value in money of the property contained in said roll;
provided, that no board of equalization shall raise any mortgage, deed of trust, contract or other obligation by which a
debt is secured, money, or solvent credits, above its face
value. The present state board of equalization shall continue in office until their successors, as herein provided for,
shall be elected and shall qualify. The legislature shall
have power to redistrict the state into four districts, as
nearly equal in population as practicable, and to provide for
the elections of members of said board of equalization.
[Amendment adopted November 4, 1884.]

Sec. 10. All property, except as otherwise in this Constitution provided, shall be assessed in the county, city,
city and county, town or township, or district in which it is
situated, in the manner prescribed by law. [Amendment
adopted November 8, 1910.]

Sec. 10½. The personal property of every householder
to the amount of one hundred dollars, the articles to be se-

lected by each householder, shall be exempt from taxation. [New section adopted November 8, 1904.]

Sec. 11. Income taxes may be assessed to and collected from persons, corporations, joint-stock associations, or companies resident or doing business in this state, or any one or more of them, in such cases and amounts, and in such manner, as shall be prescribed by law.

Sec. 12. No poll tax or head tax for any purpose whatsoever shall be levied or collected in the state of California. [New section adopted November 3, 1914.]

Sec. 12¾. Fruit and nut bearing trees under the age of four years from the time of planting in orchard form, and grape vines under the age of three years from the time of planting in vineyard form, shall be exempt from taxation, and nothing in this article shall be construed as subjecting such trees and grape vines to taxation. [New section adopted November 6, 1894.]

Sec. 13. The legislature shall pass all laws necessary to carry out the provisions of this article.

Sec. 14. Taxes levied, assessed and collected as hereinafter provided upon railroads, including street railways, whether operated in one or more counties; sleeping-car, dining-car, drawing-room car and palace-car companies, refrigerator, oil, stock, fruit, and other car-loaning and other car companies operating upon railroads in this state; companies doing express business on any railroad, steamboat, vessel or stage line in this state; telegraph companies; telephone companies; companies engaged in the transmission or sale of gas or electricity; insurance companies; banks, banking associations, savings and loan societies, and trust companies; and taxes upon all franchises of every kind and nature, shall be entirely and exclusively for state purposes, and shall be levied, assessed and collected in the manner hereinafter provided. The word "companies" as used in this section shall include persons, partnerships, joint stock associations, companies, and corporations.

(a) All railroad companies, including street railways, whether operated in one or more counties; all sleeping-car,

dining-car, drawing-room car, and palace-car companies, all refrigerator, oil, stock, fruit, and other car-loaning and other car companies, operating upon the railroads in this state; all companies doing express business on any railroad, steamboat, vessel or stage line in this state; all telegraph and telephone companies; and all companies engaged in the transmission or sale of gas or electricity shall annually pay to the state a tax upon their franchises, roadways, roadbeds, rails, rolling stock, poles, wires, pipes, canals, conduits, rights of way, and other property, or any part thereof used exclusively in the operation of their business in this state, computed as follows: Said tax shall be equal to the percentages hereinafter fixed upon the gross receipts from operation of such companies, and each thereof within this state. When such companies are operating partly within and partly without this state, the gross receipts within this state shall be deemed to be all receipts on business beginning and ending within this state, and a proportion, based upon the proportion of the mileage within this state to the entire mileage over which such business is done, of receipts on all business passing through, into, or out of this state.

The percentages above mentioned shall be as follows: On all railroad companies, including street railways, four per cent; on all sleeping-car, dining-car, drawing-room car, palace-car companies, refrigerator, oil, stock, fruit, and other car-loaning and other car companies, three per cent; on all companies doing express business on any railroad, steamboat, vessel or stage line, two per cent; on all telegraph and telephone companies, three and one-half per cent; on all companies engaged in the transmission or sale of gas or electricity, four per cent. Such taxes shall be in lieu of all other taxes and licenses, state, county and municipal, upon the property above enumerated of such companies except as otherwise in this section provided; provided, that nothing herein shall be construed to release any such company from the payment of any amount agreed to be paid or required by law to be paid for any special privilege or franchise granted by any of the municipal authorities of this state.

(b) Every insurance company or association doing business in this state shall annually pay to the state a tax of one and one-half per cent upon the amount of the gross premiums received upon its business done in this state, less return premiums and reinsurance in companies or associations authorized to do business in this state; provided, that there shall be deducted from said one and one-half per cent upon the gross premiums the amount of any county and municipal taxes paid by such companies on real estate owned by them in this state. This tax shall be in lieu of all other taxes and licenses, state, county and municipal, upon the property of such companies, except county and municipal taxes on real estate, and except as otherwise in this section provided; provided, that when by the laws of any other state or country, any taxes, fines, penalties, licenses, fees, deposits of money, or of securities, or other obligations or prohibitions, are imposed on insurance companies of this state, doing business in such other state or country, or upon their agents therein, in excess of such taxes, fines, penalties, licenses, fees, deposits of money, or of securities, or other obligations or prohibitions, imposed upon insurance companies of such other state or country, so long as such laws continue in force, the same obligations and prohibitions of whatsoever kind may be imposed by the legislature upon insurance companies of such other state or country doing business in this state.

(c) The shares of capital stock of all banks, organized under the laws of this state, or of the United States, or of any other state and located in this state, shall be assessed and taxed to the owners or holders thereof by the state board of equalization, in the manner to be prescribed by law, the city or town where the bank is located and not elsewhere. There shall be levied and assessed upon such shares of capital stock an annual tax, payable to the state, of one per centum upon the value thereof. The value of each share of stock in each bank, except such as are in liquidation, shall be taken to be the amount paid in thereon, together with its pro rata of the accumulated surplus and undivided profits. The value of each share of stock in each

bank which is in liquidation shall be taken to be its pro rata
of the actual assets of such bank. This tax shall be in lieu
of all other taxes and licenses, state, county and municipal,
upon such shares of stock and upon the property of such
banks, except county and municipal taxes on real estate and
except as otherwise in this section provided. In determining the value of the capital stock of any bank there shall be
deducted from the value, as defined above, the value, as assessed for county taxes, of any real estate, other than mortgage interests therein, owned by such bank and taxed for
county purposes. The banks shall be liable to the state for
this tax and the same shall be paid to the state by them on
behalf of the stockholders in the manner and at the time
prescribed by law, and they shall have a lien upon the
shares of stock and upon any dividends declared thereon to
secure the amount so paid.

. The moneyed capital, reserve, surplus, undivided profits
and all other property belonging to unincorporated banks
or bankers of this state, or held by any bank located in this
state which has no shares of capital stock, or employed in
this state by any branches, agencies, or other representatives of any banks doing business outside of the state of
California, shall be likewise assessed and taxed to such
banks or bankers by the said board of equalization, in the
manner to be provided by law and taxed at the same rate
that is levied upon the shares of capital stock of incorporated banks, as provided in the first paragraph of this subdivision. The value of said property shall be determined by
taking the entire property invested in such business, together with all the reserve, surplus, and undivided profits,
at their full cash value, and deducting therefrom the value
as assessed for county taxes of any real estate, other than
mortgage interests therein, owned by such bank and taxed
for county purposes. Such taxes shall be in lieu of all other
taxes and licenses, state, county and municipal, upon the
property of the banks and bankers, mentioned in this paragraph, except county and municipal taxes on real estate
and except as otherwise in this section provided. It is the
intention of this paragraph that all moneyed capital and

property of the banks and bankers mentioned in this paragraph shall be assessed and taxed at the same rate as an incorporated bank, provided for in the first paragraph of this subdivision. In determining the value of the moneyed capital and property of the banks and bankers mentioned in this subdivision, the said state board of equalization shall include and assess to such banks all property and everything of value owned or held by them, which go to make up the value of the capital stock of such banks and bankers, if the same were incorporated and had shares of capitaı stock.

The word "banks" as used in this subdivision shall include banking association, savings and loan societies and trust companies, but shall not include building and loan associations.

(d) All franchises, other than those expressly provided for in this section, shall be assessed at their actual cash value, in the manner to be provided by law, and shall be taxed at the rate of one per centum each year, and the taxes collected thereon shall be exclusively for the benefit of the state.

(e) Out of the revenues from the taxes provided for in this section, together with all other state revenues, there shall be first set apart the moneys to be applied by the state to the support of the public school system and the State University. In the event that the above-named revenues are at any time deemed insufficient to meet the annual expenditures of the state, including the above-named expenditures for educational purposes, there may be levied, in the manner to be provided by law, a tax, for state purposes, on all the property in the state including the classes of property enumerated in this section, sufficient to meet the deficiency. All property enumerated in subdivisions a, b, and d of this section shall be subject to taxation, in the manner provided by law, to pay the principal and interest of any bonded indebtedness created and outstanding by any city, city and county, county, town, township or district, before the adoption of this section. The taxes so paid for principal and interest on such bonded indebtedness shall be de-

ducted from the total amount paid in taxes for state purposes.

(f) All the provisions of this section shall be self-executing and the legislature shall pass all laws necessary to carry this section into effect, and shall provide for a valuation and assessment of the property, enumerated in this section, and shall prescribe the duties of the state board of equalization and any other officers in connection with the administration thereof. The rates of taxation fixed in this section shall remain in force until changed by the legislature, two-thirds of all the members elected to each of the two houses voting in favor thereof. The taxes herein provided for shall become a lien on the first Monday in March of each year after the adoption of this section and shall become due and payable on the first Monday in July thereafter. The gross receipts and gross premiums herein mentioned shall be computed for the year ending the thirty-first day of December prior to the levy of such taxes and the value of any property mentioned herein shall be fixed as of the first Monday in March. Nothing herein contained shall affect any tax levied or assessed prior to the adoption of this section; and all laws in relation to such taxes in force at the time of the adoption of this section shall remain in force until changed by the legislature. Until the year 1918 the state shall reimburse any and all counties which sustain loss of revenue by the withdrawal of railroad property from county taxation for the net loss in county revenue occasioned by the withdrawal of railroad property from county taxation. The legislature shall provide for reimbursement from the general funds of any county to districts therein where loss is occasioned in such districts by the withdrawal from local taxation of property taxed for state purposes only.

(g) No injunction shall ever issue in any suit, action or proceeding in any court against this state or against any officer thereof to prevent or enjoin the collection of any tax levied under the provisions of this section; but after payment action may be maintained to recover any tax illegally collected in such manner and at such time as may now or

hereafter be provided by law. [New section adopted November 8, 1910.]

NOTE.—The rates fixed in the above section were changed by the legislature in 1913 (act approved February 3, 1913), and in 1915 (act approved January 28, 1915).

ARTICLE XIV.
WATER AND WATER RIGHTS.

Section 1. The use of all water now appropriated, or that may hereafter be appropriated, for sale, rental, or distribution, is hereby declared to be a public use, and subject to the regulation and control of the state, in the manner to be prescribed by law; provided, that the rates or compensation to be collected by any person, company, or corporation in this state for the use of water supplied to any city and county, or city, or town, or the inhabitants thereof, shall be fixed, annually, by the board of supervisors, or city and county, or city, or town council, or other governing body of such city and county, or city, or town, by ordinance or otherwise, in the manner that other ordinances or legislative acts or resolutions are passed by such body, and shall continue in force for one year and no longer. Such ordinances or resolutions shall be passed in the month of February of each year, and take effect on the first day of July thereafter. Any board or body failing to pass the necessary ordinances or resolutions fixing water rates, where necessary, within such time, shall be subject to peremptory process to compel action, at the suit of any party interested, and shall be liable to such further processes and penalties as the legislature may prescribe. Any person, company, or corporations collecting water rates in any city and county, or city, or town in this state, otherwise than as so established, shall forfeit the franchises and waterworks of such person, company, or corporation to the city and county, or city, or town, where the same are collected, for the public use.

Sec. 2. The right to collect rates or compensation for the use of water supplied to any county, city and county, or

town, or the inhabitants thereof, is a franchise, and cannot be exercised except by authority of and in the manner prescribed by law.

ARTICLE XV.

HARBOR FRONTAGE, ETC.

Section 1. The right of eminent domain is hereby declared to exist in the state to all frontages on the navigable waters of this state.

Sec. 2. No individual, partnership, or corporation, claiming or possessing the frontage or tidal lands of a harbor, bay, inlet, estuary, or other navigable water in this state, shall be permitted to exclude the right of way to such water whenever it is required for any public purpose, nor to destroy or obstruct the free navigation of such water; and the legislature shall enact such laws as will give the most liberal construction to this provision, so that access to the navigable waters of this state shall be always attainable for the people thereof.

Sec. 3. All tide-lands within two miles of any incorporated city or town in this state, and fronting on the waters of any harbor, estuary, bay, or inlet, used for the purposes of navigation, shall be withheld from grant or sale to private persons, partnerships, or corporations.

ARTICLE XVI.

STATE INDEBTEDNESS.

Section 1. The legislature shall not, in any manner, create any debt or debts, liability or liabilities, which shall, singly or in the aggregate with any previous debts or liabilities, exceed the sum of three hundred thousand dollars, except in case of war to repel invasion or suppress insurrection, unless the same shall be authorized by law for some single object or work to be distinctly specified therein, which law shall provide ways and means, exclusive of loans, for the payment of the interest of such debt or liability as it falls due, and also to pay and discharge the principal of such debt or liability within seventy-five years of the time

of the contracting thereof, and shall be irrepealable until the principal and interest thereon shall be paid and discharged and such law may make provision for a sinking fund to pay the principal of such debt or liability to commence at a time after the incurring of such debt or liability of not more than a period of one-fourth of the time of maturity of such debt or liability; but no such law shall take effect until, at a general election, it shall have been submitted to the people and shall have received a majority of all the votes cast for and against it at such election; and all moneys raised by authority of such law shall be applied only to the specific object therein stated or to the payment of the debt thereby created, and such law shall be published in at least one newspaper in each county, or city and county, if one be published therein, throughout the state, for three months next preceding the election at which it is submitted to the people. The legislature may, at any time after the approval of such law by the people, if no debt shall have been contracted in pursuance thereof, repeal the same. [Amendment adopted November 3, 1908.]

ARTICLE XVII.
LAND AND HOMESTEAD EXEMPTION.

Section 1. The legislature shall protect, by law, from forced sale, a certain portion of the homestead and other property of all heads of families.

Sec. 2. The holding of large tracts of land, uncultivated and unimproved, by individuals or corporations, is against the public interest, and should be discouraged by all means not inconsistent with the rights of private property.

Sec. 3. Lands belonging to this state, which are suitable for cultivation, shall be granted only to actual settlers, and in quantities not exceeding three hundred and twenty acres to each settler, under such conditions as shall be prescribed by law.

ARTICLE XVIII.

AMENDING AND REVISING THE CONSTITUTION.

Section 1. Any amendment or amendments to this Constitution may be proposed in the senate or assembly, and
if two-thirds of all the members elected to each of the two
houses shall vote in favor thereof, such proposed amendment or amendments shall be entered in their journals, with
the yeas and nays taken thereon; and it shall be the duty
of the legislature to submit such proposed amendment or
amendments to the people in such manner, and at such time,
and after such publication as may be deemed expedient.
Should more amendments than one be submitted at the same
election, they shall be so prepared and distinguished, by
numbers or otherwise, that each can be voted on separately.
If the people shall approve and ratify such amendment or
amendments, or any of them, by a majority of the qualified
electors voting thereon, such amendment or amendments
shall become a part of this Constitution.

Sec. 2. Whenever two-thirds of the members elected to
each branch of the legislature shall deem it necessary to
revise this Constitution, they shall recommend to the electors to vote, at the next general election, for or against a
convention for that purpose, and if a majority of the electors voting at such election on the proposition for a convention shall vote in favor thereof, the legislature shall,
at its next session, provide by law for calling the same.
The convention shall consist of a number of delegates not
to exceed that of both branches of the legislature, who
shall be chosen in the same manner, and have the same
qualifications, as members of the legislature. The delegates
so elected shall meet within three months after their election, at such place as the legislature may direct. At a
special election to be provided for by law, the Constitution
that may be agreed upon by such convention shall be submitted to the people for their ratification or rejection, in
such manner as the convention may determine. The returns of such election shall, in such manner as the convention shall direct, be certified to the executive of the state,

who shall call to his assistance the controller, treasurer, and secretary of state, and compare the returns so certified to him; and it shall be the duty of the executive to declare, by his proclamation, such Constitution as may have been ratified by a majority of all the votes cast at such special election, to be the Constitution of the state of California.

ARTICLE XIX.
CHINESE.

Section 1. The legislature shall prescribe all necessary regulations for the protection of the state, and the counties, cities, and towns thereof, from the burdens and evils arising from the presence of aliens who are or may become vagrants, paupers, mendicants, criminals, or invalids afflicted with contagious or infectious diseases, and from aliens otherwise dangerous or detrimental to the well-being or peace of the state, and to impose conditions upon which such persons may reside in the state, and to provide the means and mode of their removal from the state, upon failure or refusal to comply with such conditions; provided, that nothing contained in this section shall be construed to impair or limit the power of the legislature to pass such police laws or other regulations as it may deem necessary.

Sec. 2. No corporation now existing or hereafter formed under the laws of this state shall, after the adoption of this Constitution, employ, directly or indirectly, in any capacity, any Chinese or Mongolian. The legislature shall pass such laws as may be necessary to enforce this provision.

Sec. 3. No Chinese shall be employed on any state, county, municipal, or other public work, except in punishment for crime.

Sec. 4. The presence of foreigners ineligible to become citizens of the United States is declared to be dangerous to the well-being of the state, and the legislature shall discourage their immigration by all the means within its power. Asiatic coolieism is a form of human slavery, and is forever prohibited in this state, and all contracts for coolie labor

shall be void. All companies or corporations, whether formed in this country or any foreign country, for the importation of such labor, shall be subject to such penalties as the legislature may prescribe. The legislature shall delegate all necessary power to the incorporated cities and towns of this state for the removal of Chinese without the limits of such cities and towns, or for their location within prescribed portions of those limits, and it shall also provide the necessary legislation to prohibit the introduction into this state of Chinese after the adoption of this Constitution. This section shall be enforced by appropriate legislation.

ARTICLE XX.
MISCELLANEOUS SUBJECTS.

Section 1. The city of Sacramento is hereby declared to be the seat of government of this state, and shall so remain until changed by law; but no law changing the seat of government shall be valid or binding unless the same be approved and ratified by a majority of the qualified electors of the state voting therefor at a general state election, under such regulations and provisions as the legislature, by a two-thirds vote of each house, may provide, submitting the question of change to the people.

Sec. 2. Any citizen of this state who shall, after the adoption of this Constitution, fight a duel with deadly weapons, or send or accept a challenge to fight a duel with deadly weapons either within this state or out of it, or who shall act as second, or knowingly aid or assist in any manner those thus offending, shall not be allowed to hold any office of profit, or to enjoy the right of suffrage under this Constitution.

Sec. 3. Members of the legislature, and all officers, executive and judicial, except such inferior officers as may be by law exempted, shall, before they enter upon the duties of their respective offices, take and subscribe the following oath or affirmation:

"I do solemnly swear (or affirm, as the case may be) that I will support the Constitution of the United States and the

Constitution of the state of California, and that I will faithfully discharge the duties of the office of ——— according to the best of my ability."

And no other oath, declaration, or test shall be required as a qualification for any office or public trust.

Sec. 4. All officers or commissioners whose election or appointment is not provided for by this Constitution, and all officers or commissioners whose offices or duties may hereafter be created by law, shall be elected by the people, or appointed, as the legislature may direct.

Sec. 5. The fiscal year shall commence on the first day of July.

Sec. 6. Suits may be brought against the state in such manner and in such courts as shall be directed by law.

Sec. 7. No contract of marriage, if otherwise duly made, shall be invalidated for want of conformity to the requirement of any religious sect.

Sec. 8. All property, real and personal, owned by either husband or wife, before marriage, and that acquired by either of them afterward by gift, devise, or descent, shall be their separate property.

Sec. 9. No perpetuities shall be allowed except for eleemosynary purposes.

Sec. 10. Every person shall be disqualified from holding any office of profit in this state who shall have been convicted of having given or offered a bribe to procure his election or appointment.

Sec. 11. Laws shall be made to exclude from office, serving on juries, and from the right of suffrage, persons convicted of bribery, perjury, forgery, malfeasance in office, or other high crimes. The privilege of free suffrage shall be supported by laws regulating elections, and prohibiting, under adequate penalties, all undue influence thereon from power, bribery, tumult, or other improper practice.

Sec. 12. Absence from this state, on business of the state or of the United States, shall not affect the question of residence of any person.

Sec. 13. A plurality of the votes given at any election shall constitute a choice where not otherwise directed in this Constitution; provided, that it shall be competent in all charters of cities, counties or cities and counties framed under the authority of this Constitution to provide the manner in which their respective elective officers may be elected and to prescribe a higher proportion of the vote therefor; and provided, also, that it shall be competent for the legislature by general law to provide the manner in which officers of municipalities organized or incorporated under general laws may be elected and to prescribe a higher proportion of the vote therefor. [Amendment adopted October 10, 1911.]

Sec. 14. The legislature shall provide, by law, for the maintenance and efficiency of a state board of health.

Sec. 15. Mechanics, materialmen, artisans, and laborers of every class shall have a lien upon the property upon which they have bestowed labor or furnished material, for the value of such labor done and material furnished and the legislature shall provide, by law, for the speedy and efficient enforcement of such liens.

Sec. 16. When the term of any officer or commissioner is not provided for in this Constitution, the term of such officer or commissioner may be declared by law; and if not so declared, such officer or commissioner shall hold his position as such officer or commissioner during the pleasure of the authority making the appointment; but in no case shall such term exceed four years; provided, however, that in the case of any officer or employee of any municipality governed under a legally adopted charter, the provisions of such charter with reference to the tenure of office or the dismissal from office of any such officer or employee, shall control; and provided, further, that the term of office of any person heretofore or hereafter appointed to hold office or employment during good behavior under civil service laws of the state or of any political division thereof shall not be limited by this section. [Amendment adopted October 10, 1911.]

Sec. 17. The time of service of all laborers or workmen or mechanics employed upon any public works of the state of California, or of any county, city and county, city, town, district, township, or any other political subdivision thereof, whether said work is done by contract or otherwise, shall be limited and restricted to eight hours in any one calendar day, except in cases of extraordinary emergency caused by fire, flood, or danger to life and property, or except to work upon public, military, or naval works or defenses in time of war, and the legislature shall provide by law that a stipulation to this effect shall be incorporated in all contracts for public work, and prescribe proper penalties for the speedy and efficient enforcement of said law. [Amendment adopted November 4, 1902.]

Sec. 17½. The legislature may, by appropriate legislation, provide for the establishment of a minimum wage for women and minors and may provide for the comfort, health, safety and general welfare of any and all employees. No provision of this Constitution shall be construed as a limitation upon the authority of the legislature to confer upon any commission now or hereafter created, such power and authority as the legislature may deem requisite to carry out the provisions of this section. [New section adopted November 3, 1914.]

Sec. 18. No person shall, on account of sex, be disqualified from entering upon or pursuing any lawful business, vocation, or profession.

Sec. 19. Nothing in this Constitution shall prevent the legislature from providing by law, for the payment of the expenses of the convention framing this Constitution, including the per diem of the delegates for the full term thereof.

Sec. 20. Elections of the officers provided by this Constitution, except at the election in the year eighteen hundred and seventy-nine, shall be held on the even-numbered years next before the expiration of their respective terms. The terms of such officers shall commence on the first Monday after the first day of January next following their election.

Constitution—8

Sec. 21. The legislature may by appropriate legislation create and enforce a liability on the part of all employers to compensate their employees for any injury incurred by the said employees in the course of their employment, irrespective of the fault of either party. The legislature may provide for the settlement of any disputes arising under the legislation contemplated by this section by arbitration, or by an industrial accident board, by the courts or by either, any or all of these agencies, anything in this Constitution to the contrary notwithstanding. [Amendment adopted October 10, 1911.]

ARTICLE XXI.
BOUNDARY.

Section 1. The boundary of the state of California shall be as follows: Commencing at the point of intersection of the forty-second degree of north latitude with the one hundred and twentieth degree of longitude west from Greenwich, and running south on the line of said one hundred and twentieth degree of west longitude until it intersects the thirty-ninth degree of north latitude; thence running in a straight line, in a southeasterly direction to the River Colorado, at a point where it intersects the thirty-fifth degree of north latitude; thence down the middle of the channel of said river to the boundary line between the United States and Mexico, as established by the treaty of May thirtieth, one thousand eight hundred and forty-eight; thence running west and along said boundary line to the Pacific Ocean, and extending therein three English miles; thence running in a northwesterly direction and following the direction of the Pacific coast to the forty-second degree of north latitude; thence on the line of said forty-second degree of north latitude to the place of beginning. Also, including all the islands, harbors, and bays along and adjacent to the coast.

ARTICLE XXII.

SCHEDULE.

That no inconvenience may arise from the alterations and amendments in the Constitution of this state, and to carry the same into complete effect, it is hereby ordained and declared:

Section 1: That all laws in force at the adoption of this Constitution, not inconsistent therewith, shall remain in full force and effect until altered or repealed by the legislature; and all rights, actions, prosecutions, claims, and contracts of the state, counties, individuals, or bodies corporate, not inconsistent therewith, shall continue to be as valid as if this Constitution had not been adopted. The provisions of all laws which are inconsistent with this Constitution shall cease upon the adoption thereof, except that all laws which are inconsistent with such provisions of this Constitution as require legislation to enforce them shall remain in full force until the first day of July, eighteen hundred and eighty, unless sooner altered or repealed by the legislature.

Sec. 2. That all recognizances, obligations, and all other instruments entered into or executed before the adoption of this Constitution, to this state, or to any subdivision thereof, or any municipality therein, and all fines, taxes, penalties, and forfeitures due or owing to this state, or any subdivision or municipality thereof, and all writs, prosecutions, actions, and causes of action, except as herein otherwise provided, shall continue and remain unaffected by the adoption of this Constitution. All indictments or information which shall have been found, or may hereafter be found, for any crime or offense committed before this Constitution takes effect, may be proceeded upon as if no change had taken place, except as otherwise provided in this Constitution.

Sec. 3. All courts now existing, save justices' and police courts, are hereby abolished, and all records, books, papers, and proceedings from such courts, as are abolished by this Constitution, shall be transferred, on the first day of Janu-

ary, eighteen hundred and eighty, to the courts provided for in this Constitution; and the courts to which the same are thus transferred shall have the same power and jurisdiction over them as if they had been in the first instance commenced, filed, or lodged therein.

Sec. 4.   The superintendent of printing of the state of California, shall, at least thirty days before the first Wednesday in May, A. D. eighteen hundred and seventy-nine, cause to be printed at the state printing office, in pamphlet form, simply stitched, as many copies of this Constitution as there are registered voters in this state, and mail one copy thereof to the postoffice address of each registered voter; provided, any copies not called for ten days after reaching their delivery office, shall be subject to general distribution by the several postmasters of the state.   The governor shall issue his proclamation, giving notice of the election for the adoption or rejection of this Constitution, at least thirty days before the said first Wednesday of May, eighteen hundred and seventy-nine, and the boards of supervisors of the several counties shall cause said proclamation to be made public in their respective counties, and general notice of said election to be given at least fifteen days next before said election.

Sec. 5.   The superintendent of printing of the state of California shall, at least twenty days before said election, cause to be printed and delivered to the clerk of each county in this state five times the number of properly prepared ballots for said election that there are voters in said respective counties, with the words printed thereon: "For the New Constitution."   He shall likewise cause to be so printed and delivered to said clerks five times the number of properly prepared ballots for said election that there are voters in said respective counties with the words printed thereon: "Against the New Constitution."   The secretary of state is hereby authorized and required to furnish the superintendent of state printing a sufficient quantity of legal ballot paper, now on hand, to carry out the provisions of this section.

Sec. 6. The clerks of the several counties in the state shall, at least five days before said election, cause to be delivered to the inspectors of elections, at each election precinct or polling place, in their respective counties, suitable registers, poll books, forms of return, and an equal number of the aforesaid ballots, which number, in the aggregate, must be ten times greater than the number of voters in the said election precincts or polling places. The returns of the number of votes cast at the presidential election in the year eighteen hundred and seventy-six shall serve as a basis of calculation for this and the preceding section; provided, that the duties in this and the preceding section imposed upon the clerks of the respective counties shall, in the city and county of San Francisco, be performed by the registrar of voters for said city and county.

Sec. 7. Every citizen of the United States, entitled by law to vote for members of the assembly in this state, shall be entitled to vote for the adoption or rejection of this Constitution.

Sec. 8. The officers of the several counties of this state, whose duty it is, under the law, to receive and canvass the returns from the several precincts of their respective counties, as well as of the city and county of San Francisco, shall meet at the usual places of meeting for such purposes on the first Monday after said election. If, at the time of meeting, the returns from each precinct in the county in which the polls were opened have been received, the board must then and there proceed to canvass the returns; but if all the returns have not been received, the canvass must be postponed from time to time until all the returns are received, or until the second Monday after said election, when they shall proceed to make out returns of the votes cast for and against the new Constitution; and the proceedings of said board shall be the same as those prescribed for like boards in the case of an election for governor. Upon the completion of said canvass and returns, the said boards shall immediately certify the same, in the usual form, to the governor of the state of California.

Sec. 9. The governor of the state of California shall, as soon as the returns of said election shall be received by him, or within thirty days after said election, in the presence and with the assistance of the controller, treasurer, and secretary of state, open and compute all the returns received of votes cast for and against the new Constitution. If, by such examination and computation, it is ascertained that a majority of the whole number of votes cast at such election is in favor of such new Constitution, the executive of this state shall, by his proclamation, declare such new Constitution to be the Constitution of the state of California, and that it shall take effect and be in force on the days hereinafter specified.

Sec. 10. In order that future elections in this state shall conform to the requirements of this Constitution, the terms of all officers elected at the first election under the same shall be, respectively, one year shorter than the terms as fixed by law or by this Constitution; and the successors of all such officers shall be elected at the last election before the expiration of the terms as in this section provided. The first officers chosen after the adoption of this Constitution shall be elected at the time and in the manner now provided by law. Judicial officers and the superintendent of public instruction shall be elected at the time and in the manner that state officers are elected.

Sec. 11. All laws relative to the present judicial system of the state shall be applicable to the judicial system created by this Constitution until changed by legislation.

Sec. 12. This Constitution shall take effect and be in force on and after the fourth day of July, eighteen hundred and seventy-nine, at twelve o'clock meridian, so far as the same relates to the election of all officers, the commencement of their terms of office, and the meeting of the legislature. In all other respects, and for all other purposes, this Constitution shall take effect on the first day of January, eighteen hundred and eighty, at twelve o'clock meridian.

ARTICLE XXIII.
RECALL OF PUBLIC OFFICIALS.

Section 1. Every elective public officer of the state of California may be removed from office at any time by the electors entitled to vote for a successor of such incumbent, through the procedure and in the manner herein provided for, which procedure shall be known as the recall, and is in addition to any other method of removal provided by law.

The procedure hereunder to effect the removal of an incumbent of an elective public office shall be as follows: A petition signed by electors entitled to vote for a successor of the incumbent sought to be removed, equal in number to at least twelve per cent of the entire vote cast at the last preceding election for all candidates for the office, which the incumbent sought to be removed occupies (provided that if the officer sought to be removed is a state officer who is elected in any political subdivision of the state, said petition shall be signed by electors entitled to vote for a successor to the incumbent sought to be removed, equal in number to at least twenty per cent of the entire vote cast at the last preceding election for all candidates for the office which the incumbent sought to be removed occupies) demanding an election of a successor to the officer named in said petition, shall be addressed to the secretary of state and filed with the clerk, or registrar of voters, of the county or city and county in which the petition was circulated; provided, that if the officer sought to be removed was elected in the state at large such petition shall be circulated in not less than five counties of the state, and shall be signed in each of such counties by electors equal in number to not less than one per cent of the entire vote cast, in each of said counties, at said election, as above estimated. Such petition shall contain a general statement of the grounds on which the removal is sought, which statement is intended solely for the information of the electors, and the sufficiency of which shall not be open to review.

When such petition is certified as is herein provided to the secretary of state, he shall forthwith submit the said

petition, together with a certificate of its sufficiency, to the governor, who shall thereupon order and fix a date for holding the election, not less than sixty days nor more than eighty days from the date of such certificate of the secretary of state.

The governor shall make or cause to be made publication of notice for the holding of such election, and officers charged by law with duties concerning elections shall make all arrangements for such election and the same shall be conducted, returned, and the result thereof declared, in all respects as are other state elections. On the official ballot at such election shall be printed, in not more than two hundred words, the reasons set forth in the petition for demanding his recall. And in not more than three hundred words there shall also be printed, if desired by him, the officer's justification of his course in office. Proceedings for the recall of any officer shall be deemed to be pending from the date of the filing with any county, or city and county clerk, or registrar of voters, of any recall petition against such officer; and if such officer shall resign at any time subsequent to the filing thereof, the recall election shall be held notwithstanding such resignation, and the vacancy caused by such resignation, or from any other cause, shall be filled as provided by law, but the person appointed to fill such vacancy shall hold his office only until the person elected at the said recall election shall qualify.

Any person may be nominated for the office which is to be filled at any recall election by a petition signed by electors, qualified to vote at such recall election, equal in number to at least one per cent of the total number of votes cast at the last preceding election for all candidates for the office which the incumbent sought to be removed occupies. Each such nominating petition shall be filed with the secretary of state not less than twenty-five days before such recall election.

There shall be printed on the recall ballot, as to every officer whose recall is to be voted on thereat, the following question: "Shall (name of person against whom the recall petition is filed) be recalled from the office of

(title of office)?" following which question shall be the
words "Yes" and "No" on separate lines, with a blank space
at the right of each, in which the voter shall indicate,
by stamping a cross (X), his vote for or against such
recall. On such ballots, under each such question, there
shall also be printed the names of those persons who
have been nominated as candidates to succeed the person
recalled, in case he shall be removed from office by said
recall election; but no vote cast shall be counted for any
candidate for said office unless the voter also voted on said
question of the recall of the person sought to be recalled
from said office. The name of the person against whom the
petition is filed shall not appear on the ballot as a candidate
for the office. If a majority of those voting on said question of the recall of any incumbent from office shall vote
"No," said incumbent shall continue in said office. If a
majority shall vote "Yes," said incumbent shall thereupon
be deemed removed from such office upon the qualification
of his successor. The canvassers shall canvass all votes for
candidates for said office and declare the result in like manner as in a regular election. If the vote at any such recall
election shall recall the officer, then the candidate who has
received the highest number of votes for the office shall be
thereby declared elected for the remainder of the term. In
case the person who received the highest number of votes
shall fail to qualify within ten days after receiving the certificate of election, the office shall be deemed vacant and
shall be filled according to law.

Any recall petition may be presented in sections, but each
section shall contain a full and accurate copy of the title
and text of the petition. Each signer shall add to his signature his place of residence, giving the street and number,
if such exist. His election precinct shall also appear on the
paper after his name. The number of signatures appended
to each section shall be at the pleasure of the person soliciting signatures to the same. Any qualified elector of the
state shall be competent to solicit such signatures within
the county, or city and county, of which he is an elector.
Each section of the petition shall bear the name of the

county, or city and county, in which it is circulated, and only qualified electors of such county or city and county shall be competent to sign such section. Each section shall have attached thereto the affidavit of the person soliciting signatures to the same stating his qualifications and that all the signatures to the attached section were made in his presence and that to the best of his knowledge and belief each signature to the section is the genuine signature of the person whose name it purports to be; and no other affidavit, thereto shall be required. The affidavit of any person soliciting signatures hereunder shall be verified free of charge by any officer authorized to administer an oath. Such petition so verified shall be prima facie evidence that the signatures thereto appended are genuine and that the persons signing the same are qualified electors. Unless and until it is otherwise proven upon official investigation, it shall be presumed that the petition presented contains the signatures of the requisite number of electors. Each section of the petition shall be filed with the clerk, or registrar of voters, of the county or city and county in which it was circulated; but all such sections circulated in any county or city and county shall be filed at the same time. Within twenty days after the date of filing such petition, the clerk, or registrar of voters, shall finally determine from the records of registration what number of qualified electors have signed the same; and, if necessary, the board of supervisors shall allow such clerk or registrar additional assistants for the purpose of examining such petition and provide for their compensation. The said clerk or registrar, upon the completion of such examination, shall forthwith attach to such petition his certificate, properly dated, showing the result of such examination, and submit said petition, except as to the signatures appended thereto, to the secretary of state and file a copy of said certificate in his office. Within forty days from the transmission of the said petition and certificate by the clerk or registrar of voters to the secretary of state, a supplemental petition, identical with the original as to the body of the petition but containing supplemental names, may be filed with the clerk or regis-

trar of voters, as aforesaid. The clerk or registrar of voters shall within ten days after the filing of such supplemental petition make like examination thereof as of the original petition, and upon the conclusion of such examination shall forthwith attach to such petition his certificate, properly dated, showing the result of such examination, and shall forthwith transmit such supplemental petition, except as to the signatures thereon, together with his said certificate, to the secretary of state.

When the secretary of state shall have received from one or more county clerks, or registrars of voters, a petition certified as herein provided to have been signed by the requisite number of qualified electors, he shall forthwith transmit to the county clerk or registrar of voters of every county or city and county in the state a certificate showing such fact; and such clerk or registrar of voters shall thereupon file said certificate for record in his office.

A petition shall be deemed to be filed with the secretary of state upon the date of the receipt by him of a certificate or certificates showing the said petition to be signed by the requisite number of electors of the state.

No recall petition shall be circulated or filed against any officer until he has actually held his office for at least six months; save and except it may be filed against any member of the state legislature at any time after five days from the convening and organizing of the legislature after his election.

If at any recall election the incumbent whose removal is sought is not recalled, he shall be repaid from the state treasury any amount legally expended by him as expenses of such election, and the legislature shall provide appropriation for such purpose, and no proceedings for another recall election of said incumbent shall be initiated within six months after such election.

If the governor is sought to be removed under the provisions of this article, the duties herein imposed upon him shall be performed by the lieutenant-governor; and if the secretary of state is sought to be removed, the duties herein imposed upon him shall be performed by the state con-

troller; and the duties herein imposed upon the clerk or registrar of voters, shall be performed by such registrar of voters in all cases where the office of registrar of voters exists.

The recall shall also be exercised by the electors of each county, city and county, city and town of the state, with reference to the elective officers thereof, under such procedure as shall be provided by law.

Until otherwise provided by law, the legislative body of any such county, city and county, city or town may provide for the manner of exercising such recall powers in such counties, cities and counties, cities and towns, but shall not require any such recall petition to be signed by electors more in number than twenty-five per cent of the entire vote cast at the last preceding election for all candidates for the office which the incumbent sought to be removed occupies. Nothing herein contained shall be construed as affecting or limiting the present or future powers of cities or counties or cities and counties having charters adopted under the authority given by the Constitution.

In the submission to the electors of any petition proposed under this article all officers shall be guided by the general laws of the state, except as otherwise herein provided.

This article is self-executing, but legislation may be enacted to facilitate its operation, but in no way limiting or restricting the provisions of this article or the powers herein reserved.   [New article; adopted October 10, 1911.]

J. P. HOGE, President.

Attest: EDWIN F. SMITH, Secretary.

MEMBERS OF THE CONSTITUTIONAL CONVENTION OF 1879.

A. R. Andrews,
James J. Ayres,
Clitus Barbour,
Edward Barry,
James N. Barton,
C. J. Beerstecher,
Isaac S. Belcher,
Peter Bell,
Marion Biggs,
E. T. Blackmer,
Josiah Boucher,
Joseph C. Brown,
Saml. B. Burt,
James Caples,
Aug. H. Chapman,
J. M. Charles,
John D. Condon,
C. W. Cross,
Hamlet Davis,
Jas. E. Dean,
P. T. Dowling,
Luke D. Doyle,
W. L. Dudley,
Jonathan M. Dudley,
Presley Dunlap,
John A. Eagon,
Henry Edgerton,
Thomas H. Estey,
M. M. Estee,
Edward Evey,
Simon J. Farrell,
J. A. Filcher,
Jacob Richard Freud,
Abraham Clark Freeman,
J. B. Garvey,
B. B. Glascock,
Joseph C. Gorman,
W. P. Grace,
William J. Graves,
V. A. Gregg,
Jno. S. Hager,
John B. Hall,
J. E. Hale,
Thomas Harrison,
Joel A. Harvey,
T. D. Heiskell,
Conrad Herold,

D. W. Herrington,
S. G. Hilborn,
J. R. W. Hitchcock,
Sam A. Holmes,
Volney E. Howard,
W. J. Howard,
W. F. Huestis,
Wm. Procter Hughey,
G. W. Hunter,
Daniel Inman,
George A. Johnson,
L. F. Jones,
Peter J. Joyce,
John J. Kenny,
J. M. Kelley,
James H. Keyes,
C. R. Kleine,
T. H. Laine,
R. M. Lampson,
H. W. La Rue,
Henry Larkin,
David Lewis,
R. Lavigne,
J. F. Lindow,
Jno. Mansfield,
J. West Martin,
Edward Martin,
John G. McCallum,
Rush McComas,
Thomas McConnell,
John McCoy,
Thomas B. McFarland,
John Fleming McNutt,
Wm. S. Moffatt,
L. D. Morse,
Hiram Mills,
W. W. Moreland,
James E. Murphy,
Edmond Nason,
Thorwald Klaudius Nelson,
Henry Neunaber,
Chas. C. O'Donnell,
George Ohleyer,
James O'Sullivan,
A. P. Overton,
James Martin Porter,

William H. Prouty,
M. R. C. Pulliam,
Patrick Reddy,
Chas. F. Reed,
Jas. S. Reynolds,
Jno. M. Rhodes,
Chas. S. Ringgold,
Horace C. Rolfe,
Geo. W. Schell,
J. Schomp,
James McM. Shafter,
Rufus Shoemaker,
Benj. Shurtleff,
E. O. Smith,
H. W. Smith,
Geo. Venable Smith,
E. P. Soule,
John C. Stedman,
Geo. Steele,
D. C. Stevenson,
Chas. V. Stuart,
W. J. Sweasey,
Charles Swenson,
R. S. Swing,
D. S. Terry,
S. B. Thompson,
W. J. Tinnin,
F. O. Townsend,
P. B. Tully,
H. K. Turner,
Daniel Tuttle,
A. P. Vacquerel,
Walter Van Dyke,
Wm. Van Voorhies,
Jno. Walker,
Hugh Walker,
Byron Waters,
J. V. Webster,
Joseph R. Weller,
Patrick M. Wellin,
John P. West,
Wm. F. White,
John T. Wickes,
H. C. Wilson,
Jos. W. Winans,
N. G. Wyatt.

NOTE.—The following were also members of the convention, but did not sign the Constitution, being absent on the day when it was adopted: Barnes, Wm. H. L.; Berry, J.; Boggs, H. C.; Campbell, A., Jr.; Casserly, Eugene; Cowden, D. H.; Crouch, Robert; Fawcett, Eugene; Finney, Chas. G., Jr.; Miller, John F.; Noel, Alonzo E.; Wilson, Samuel M.

CONSTITUTION

STATE OF CALIFORNIA.

ADOPTED IN CONVENTION, AT SACRAMENTO, MARCH 3, A. D.
1879; RATIFIED BY A VOTE OF THE PEOPLE ON WEDNES-
DAY, MAY 7, 1879.

PREAMBLE AND DECLARATION OF RIGHTS.

PREAMBLE.

We, the people of the state of California, grateful to
Almighty God for our freedom, in order to secure and perpetuate its blessings, do establish this Constitution.

STATE OF CALIFORNIA.—The names "The State of California"
and "The People of the State of California" describe the same party,
and a statute which requires a bond to be given in one name is satisfied by a bond given in the other. (People v. Love, 19 Cal. 676.)

FORM OF GOVERNMENT.—Our system is not a pure democracy,
but a representative republican government. (Hobart v. Butte
County Supervisors, 17 Cal. 23.)

(127)

ARTICLE I.

DECLARATION OF RIGHTS.

Inalienable rights.

Section 1. All men are by nature free and independent, and have certain inalienable rights, among which are those of enjoying and defending life and liberty; acquiring, possessing, and protecting property; and pursuing and obtaining safety and happiness.

PROPERTY.—The right of acquiring, possessing, and protecting property is one of the primary objects of government, is guaranteed by the Constitution, and cannot be impaired by the legislature. (Billings v. Hall, 7 Cal. 1.)

The right of protecting property is not the mere right to protect it by individual force, but the right to protect it by the law of the land, and the force of the body politic. (Billings v. Hall, 7 Cal. 1.)

The right of property antedates all Constitutions. This right is invaded if the owner is not at liberty to contract with others respecting the use to which he may subject his property, or the manner in which he may enjoy it. (Stimson Mill Co. v. Braun, 136 Cal. 122, 89 Am. St. Rep. 116, 57 L. R. A. 726, 68 Pac. 481.)

A statute declaring that all contracts for the construction of buildings, with certain exceptions, must provide for the payment of the contract price in money, is in violation of this section. (Stimson Mill Co. v. Braun, 136 Cal. 122, 89 Am. St. Rep. 116, 57 L. R. A. 726, 68 Pac. 481.)

The right to acquire property is the right to use the proper means to attain the end; and the use of such means cannot be prohibited by the legislature, unless the peace and safety of the state require it. (Ex parte Newman, 9 Cal. 502.)

An act requiring a party to pay for improvements put upon his land by a trespasser, against his will, is void. (Billings v. Hall, 7 Cal. 1.)

So an act altering or destroying the nature or tenure of estates is void. (Dewey v. Lambier, 7 Cal. 347.)

The provision of section 1203 of the Code of Civil Procedure that a failure to comply with the section by filing a good and sufficient bond with the building contract in an amount equal to at least twenty-five per cent of the contract price shall render "the owner and contractor jointly and severally liable in damages to any and all materialmen, and subcontractors entitled to liens upon property affected by said contract," is an unreasonable restraint upon the owner of the property in the use thereof, and is an unreasonable restriction upon the power to make contracts, and is, therefore, unconstitutional. (Gibbs v. Tally, 133 Cal. 373, 60 L. R. A. 815, 65 Pac. 970; San Francisco Lumber Co. v. Bibb, 139 Cal. 192, 72 Pac. 964; Montague & Co. v. Furness, 145 Cal. 205, 78 Pac. 640.)

An act authorizing the probate court to order a sale of the property of a decedent, when it is for the best interest of the estate, is valid. (Estate of Porter, 129 Cal. 86, 79 Am. St. Rep. 78, 61 Pac. 659.)

But such an act cannot affect estates of decedents who died before the passage of the act. (Brenham v. Story, 39 Cal. 179; Estate of Packer, 125 Cal. 396, 73 Am. St. Rep. 58, 58 Pac. 59; Estate of Freud, 131 Cal. 667, 82 Am. St. Rep. 407, 63 Pac. 1080.)

An ordinance requiring street-car transfers to be issued and delivered within the street-cars from which the transfer is made, and received only within the car to which it is made, and forbidding any person to whom a transfer is issued to give away, transfer, or sell the same, is not in violation of this section. (Ex parte Lorenzen, 128 Cal. 431, 79 Am. St. Rep. 47, 50 L. R. A. 55, 61 Pac. 68.)

An act requiring litigants to take the oath of allegiance is not in violation of this section. (Cohen v. Wright, 22 Cal. 293.)

An act making it unlawful to buy or sell quail is not in violation of this section. (Ex parte Kenneke, 136 Cal. 527, 89 Am. St. Rep. 177, 69 Pac. 261.)

A statute exempting a municipal corporation from liability for damages for injuries sustained by any person on its graded streets, but making the officers of the city liable therefor, is valid. (Parsons v. San Francisco, 23 Cal. 462.)

The act of 1907, page 122, prohibiting waste from artesian wells does not unconstitutionally interfere with private property. (Ex parte Elam, 6 Cal. App. 233, 91 Pac. 811.)

An ordinance providing for the destruction of dogs not licensed is not an unconstitutional interference with property. (In re Ackerman, 6 Cal. App. 5, 91 Pac. 429.)

A provision in the specifications for public street work that no unnaturalized alien should be employed in the work, except with the permission of the highway commission, is invalid. (City Street Imp. Co. v. Kroh, 158 Cal. 308, 110 Pac. 933.)

Section 384 of the Penal Code, subdivision 3, declaring it a misdemeanor to willfully and negligently build a fire on one's own land for the purposes of burning brush, etc., is violative of the federal and state Constitutions as an unreasonable and oppressive interference with the right to use and enjoy property. (In re McCapes, 157 Cal. 26, 106 Pac. 229.)

The provision of the mechanic's lien law allowing an attorney's fee to plaintiff but not to defendant is in violation of this provision. (Builders' Supply Depot v. O'Connor, 150 Cal. 265, 119 Am. St. Rep. 193, 11 Ann. Cas. 712, 17 L. R. A. (N. S.) 909, 88 Pac. 982.)

The right of property includes the right to dispose of such property in such manner as the owner pleases, and to sell it for such price as he can obtain in fair barter. (Ex parte Quarg, 149 Cal. 79, 117 Am. St. Rep. 115, 9 Ann. Cas. 747, 5 L. R. A. (N. S.) 183, 84 Pac. 766.)

The mechanic's lien law is not unconstitutional because it abridges the right of contract in respect to one's property. (Stimson Mill Co. v. Nolan, 5 Cal. App. 754, 91 Pac. 262.)

The provision of section 1203 of the Code of Civil Procedure that a failure to comply with the section by filing a good and sufficient bond with the building contract in an amount equal to at least twenty-five per cent of the contract price shall render "the owner and contractor jointly and severally liable in damages to any and all materialmen, and subcontractors entitled to liens upon property affected by said contract," is an unreasonable restraint upon the owner of the property in the use thereof, and is an unreasonable restriction upon the power to make contracts, and is, therefore, unconstitutional. (Martin v. McCabe, 21 Cal. App. 658, 132 Pac. 606.)

Business.—The legislature cannot forbid the lawful pursuit of a lawful occupation on one day of the week any more than it can forbid it altogether. (Ex parte Newman, 9 Cal. 502. But see Ex parte Andrews, 18 Cal. 678.)

But this provision does not prevent the legislature from prohibiting the conducting of offensive trades within the limits of a city. (Ex parte Shrader, 33 Cal. 279.)

So an ordinance making it unlawful for any person to conduct a laundry within certain limits without a certificate from the health officer as to its sanitary condition, and a certificate from the fire wardens as to the condition of the heating appliances, and forbidding the operation of any laundry between 10 P. M. and 6 A. M., or on Sunday, is valid. (Ex parte Moynier, 65 Cal. 33, 2 Pac. 728.)

An ordinance making it unlawful to play any instrument, etc., in any saloon, etc., after midnight, and for any female to be in any saloon, etc., after midnight, does not violate this provision. (Ex parte Smith & Keating, 38 Cal. 702.)

A statute limiting the compensation of employment agencies is invalid. (Ex parte Dickey, 144 Cal. 234, 103 Am. St. Rep. 82, 1 Ann. Cas. 428, 66 L. R. A. 928, 77 Pac. 924.)

When a lawful business is of a beneficial character, and not dangerous to the public, it cannot be subjected to police regulation. (Ex parte Dickey, 144 Cal. 234, 103 Am. St. Rep. 82, 1 Ann. Cas. 428, 66 L. R. A. 928, 77 Pac. 924.)

It is always a judicial question whether any particular regulation of the constitutional right of the citizen to engage in an innocent and useful business is a valid exercise of the legislative power. (Ex parte Hayden, 147 Cal. 649, 109 Am. St. Rep. 183, 1 L. R. A. (N. S.) 184, 82 Pac. 315.)

An act making it unlawful to issue trading stamps and coupons is unconstitutional. (Ex parte Drexel, 147 Cal. 763, 3 Ann. Cas. 878, 2 L. R. A. (N. S.) 588, 82 Pac. 429.)

The legislature has the constitutional right to modify the common law by taking away the revocable nature of the license granted by a ticket to a place of public amusement. (Greenberg v. Western Turf Assn., 148 Cal. 126, 113 Am. St. Rep. 216, 82 Pac. 684.)

An act forbidding the employment of women for more than eight hours a day does not conflict with this section so far as it applies to women employed in hotels. (Matter of Application of Miller, 162 Cal. 687, 124 Pac. 427; affirmed in Miller v. Wilson, 236 U. S. 373, 59 L. Ed. 628, 35 Sup. Ct. Rep. 342.)

> Constitutionality of statutes restricting contracts and business. See note, 21 L. R. A. 789.

Sunday laws.—In Ex parte Newman, 9 Cal. 502, it was held that an act making it unlawful to transact any business upon the Sabbath, except certain designated ones, was in violation of this provision, on the ground that the legislature can no more forbid the lawful pursuit of a lawful occupation on one day of the week than it can forbid it altogether. This decision was overruled in Ex parte Andrews, 18 Cal. 678, and Ex parte Bird, 19 Cal. 130.

An act making it a misdemeanor to keep open a barber-shop on Sundays or other holidays is in violation of this section. (Ex parte Jentzsch, 112 Cal. 468, 32 L. R. A. 664, 44 Pac. 803.)

Life, liberty, etc.—A law imposing the death penalty upon a person undergoing a life sentence, who, with malice aforethought, commits an assault upon another with a deadly weapon, or by any means likely to produce bodily injury, is valid. (In re Finley, 1 Cal. App. 198, 81 Pac. 1041.)

> Right of privacy, when and how may be enforced. See note, 89 Am. St. Rep. 844.

> Right to life, liberty and the pursuit of happiness. See 6 R. C. L., §§ 243–250, pp. 258–266.

Political power.

Sec. 2. All political power is inherent in the people. Government is instituted for the protection, security, and

benefit of the people, and they have the right to alter or reform the same whenever the public good may require it.

THE PEOPLE.—The people are such as are born upon the soil, and such foreigners as may elect to assume the obligations of citizens by naturalization. Those who are not of the people have no share in political power; and, therefore, an alien is not eligible to an office in this state. (Walther v. Rabolt, 30 Cal. 185.)

Relation to the American Union.

Sec. 3.   The state of California is an inseparable part of the American Union, and the Constitution of the United States is the supreme law of the land.

AMERICAN UNION.—The United States Constitution is the supreme law of the land. (U. S. Const., art. VI, sec. 2; Prigg v. Commonwealth, 16 Pet. 590, 628, 10 L. Ed. 1080, 1094; New Jersey v. Wilson, 7 Cranch, 164, 3 L. Ed. 303; Terrett v. Taylor, 9 Cranch, 43, 3 L. Ed. 650; Von Hoffman v. Quincy, 4 Wall. 535, 18 L. Ed. 403; Taylor v. Taintor, 16 Wall. 366, 21 L. Ed. 287; Ex parte Romaine, 23 Cal. 585.)

The object of the United States Constitution was to establish a government which, to the extent of its powers, should be supreme within its sphere of action. (Dobbins v. Commrs. of Erie Co., 16 Pet. 435, 10 L. Ed. 1022; Ableman v. Booth, 21 How. 506, 520; 16 L. Ed. 169, 175; Cohens v. Virginia, 6 Wheat. 264, 5 L. Ed. 257; United States v. Rhodes, 1 Abb. U. S. 28, 44, Fed. Cas. No. 16,151; McCulloch v. Maryland, 4 Wheat. 316, 4 L. Ed. 579.)

The Constitution of the United States is a part of the organic law of each state. (Taylor v. Taintor, 16 Wall. 366, 21 L. Ed. 287; Ex parte Romaine, 23 Cal. 585.)

This section does not have the effect to make the various provisions of the Constitution of the United States a part of our state Constitution. (People v. Nolan, 144 Cal. 75, 77 Pac. 774.)

Religious freedom.

Sec. 4.   The free exercise and enjoyment of religious profession and worship, without discrimination or preference, shall be forever guaranteed in this state; and no person shall be rendered incompetent to be a witness or juror on account of his opinions on matters of religious belief; but the liberty of conscience hereby secured shall not be so construed as to excuse acts of licentiousness, or justify practices inconsistent with the peace or safety of this state.

SUNDAY LAWS.—In Ex parte Newman, 9 Cal. 502, it was held that an act making it unlawful to transact any business upon the

Sabbath, except certain designated ones, was in violation of this provision. In reaching this conclusion, the following principles were laid down:

Our constitutional theory regards all religions, as such, as equally entitled to protection and equally unentitled to preference. Where there is no ground or necessity upon which a principle can rest but a religious one, then the Constitution steps in and says that it shall not be enforced by authority of law.

When the citizen is compelled by the legislature to do any affirmative act, or to refrain from doing anything, merely because it violates a religious principle or observance, the act is unconstitutional.

This provision does not mean to guarantee merely toleration, but religious liberty in its largest sense, and a perfect equality, without distinction, between religious sects. An enforced observance of a day held sacred by one of these sects is a discrimination in favor of that sect, and a violation of the religious freedom of the others.

This decision, however, has been overruled by later cases: Ex parte Andrews, 18 Cal. 678; Ex parte Bird, 19 Cal. 130; Ex parte Burke, 59 Cal. 6, 43 Am. Rep. 231.

WITNESSES.—This section means that a witness is competent without respect to his religious sentiments or convictions—the law leaving his competency to legal sanctions, or, at least, to considerations independent of religious sentiments and convictions. (Fuller v. Fuller, 17 Cal. 605.)

> Religious belief as affecting competency of witness. See notes, 92 Am. Dec. 473; 12 Ann. Cas. 155.

> Right to religious freedom. See 6 R. C. L., § 237, p. 251.

Habeas corpus.

Sec. 5. The privilege of the writ of habeas corpus shall not be suspended unless when, in cases of rebellion or invasion, the public safety may require its suspension.

HABEAS CORPUS.—This right is to be exercised in a reasonable manner. The writ should not issue to run out of the county, unless for good cause shown—as the absence, disability, or refusal to act of the local judge—or other reason showing that the object and reason of the law requires its issuance. Nor should it issue from the supreme court in any case, except under the same circumstances. (Ex parte Ellis, 11 Cal. 222.)

The writ of habeas corpus will not issue when the restraint is not real, but merely nominal and permissive. (In re Gow, 139 Cal. 242, 73 Pac. 145.)

As to what courts may issue writs of habeas corpus, see article VI, sections 4, 5; People v. Turner, 1 Cal. 143, 52 Am. Dec. 295; Ex parte Perkins, 2 Cal. 424; People v. Booker, 51 Cal. 317; Tyler v. Houghton, 25 Cal. 26.

> Nature and purpose of writ of habeas corpus. See note, 87 Am. St. Rep. 168.

When refusal of writ of habeas corpus is justifiable. See note, 67 Am. Dec. 395.

Authority of state courts in habeas corpus. See note, 37 Am. Dec. 200.

Suspension of writ during insurrection or rebellion necessitating government by martial law. See note, 98 Am. St. Rep. 776.

Suspension of writ. See note, 45 L. R. A. 832.

Original jurisdiction of state court of last resort to issue writ of habeas corpus. See note, Ann. Cas. 1913A, 156.

Right to bail—Rights of witnesses.

Sec. 6. All persons shall be bailable by sufficient sureties, unless for capital offenses when the proof is evident or the presumption great. Excessive bail shall not be required, nor excessive fines imposed; nor shall cruel or unusual punishments be inflicted. Witnesses shall not be unreasonably detained, nor confined in any room where criminals are actually imprisoned.

BAIL.—Admission to bail in capital cases, where the proof is evident or the presumption great, may be made, under our Constitution, matter of discretion, and may be forbidden by the legislature. In all other cases the admission to bail is a right of the accused, which no judge or court can properly refuse. (People v. Tinder, 19 Cal. 539, 81 Am. Dec. 77.)

An act making admission to bail matter of discretion in all cases where the punishment is death, unless the proof is evident or the presumption great, is in conflict with this section. (People v. Tinder, 19 Cal. 539, 81 Am. Dec. 77.)

This section does not prevent the court from ordering the defendant into custody as soon as the trial is commenced. (People v. Williams, 59 Cal. 674.)

This provision applies only to cases in which the party has not been already convicted. (Ex parte Voll, 41 Cal. 29.)

A person arrested for felony must, in order to procure bail, be taken before the magistrate who issued the warrant, or some other magistrate in the same county. (Ex parte Hung Sin, 54 Cal. 102.)

The court should not refuse to accept on bail a surety who is a nonresident of the county unless there is some circumstance that would reasonably excite suspicion as to such surety, or unless it would be difficult to investigate his financial standing. (Ex parte Ruef, 8 Cal. App. 468, 97 Pac. 89.)

Sureties on a bail bond may qualify with property real or personal in the county or elsewhere. (Ex parte Ruef, 8 Cal. App. 468, 97 Pac. 89.)

A court has no power to refuse friends and relatives of the accused as bail for the sole reason that they are such. (Ex parte Ruef, 8 Cal. App. 468, 97 Pac. 89.)

Unless there is an affirmative showing of danger to the safety of an accused person or to society in allowing him to be admitted to bail, he is entitled to be admitted to bail until a hearing and examination can be had. (In re Henley, 18 Cal. App. 1, 121 Pac. 933.)

> Admission to bail after indictment for murder. See notes, 81 Am. Dec. 87; 39 L. R. A. (N. S.) 752.

> Bail as matter of right or of discretion. See notes, 1 Ann. Cas. 12; 9 Ann. Cas. 619.

> Right to bail. See 3 R. C. L., §§ 3-21, pp. 5-21.

WITNESSES.—A person detained as a witness ninety days, and after several continuances not satisfactorily accounted for, is entitled to his discharge under this section. (Ex parte Dressler, 67 Cal. 257, 7 Pac. 645.)

PUNISHMENT.—"Cruel and unusual punishments" are punishments of a barbarous character and unknown to the common law. (State v. McCauley, 15 Cal. 429.)

A statute authorizing the leasing out of convicts is not in violation of this provision. (State v. McCauley, 15 Cal. 429.)

A law making an offense punishable "by imprisonment in the state prison not exceeding five years, or in the county jail not exceeding six months, or both," is valid. (People v. Perini, 94 Cal. 573, 29 Pac. 1027.)

An act imposing merely a minimum penalty is not unconstitutional. (In re Hallawell, 8 Cal. App. 563, 97 Pac. 320.)

Imprisonment in the county jail or state prison is not unusual nor cruel. (In re O'Shea, 11 Cal. App. 568, 105 Pac. 776.)

Cruel and unusual punishments are punishments of a barbarous nature unknown to the common law, being such as disgraced the civilization of former ages and made one shudder with horror to read of them. (In re O'Shea, 11 Cal. App. 568, 105 Pac. 776.)

The death penalty, imposed by section 246 of the Penal Code, upon a person undergoing a life sentence who commits an assault with a deadly weapon, is not a cruel or unusual punishment forbidden by the Constitution. (People v. Oppenheimer, 156 Cal. 733, 106 Pac. 74.)

This section removes the danger that persons may be imprisoned for an unlimited period for nonpayment of a fine for contempt. (Ex parte Karlson, 160 Cal. 378, Ann. Cas. 1912D, 1334, 117 Pac. 447.)

> Power to imprison until fine paid. See note, 12 Am. St. Rep. 202.

> Cruel and unusual punishment. See notes, 19 Ann. Cas. 725; 35 L. R. A. 561; 8 R. C. L., §§ 271-279, pp. 262-269.

Trial by jury.

Sec. 7. The right of trial by jury shall be secured to all, and remain inviolate; but in civil actions three-fourths of the jury may render a verdict. A trial by jury may be waived in all criminal cases, not amounting to felony, by the consent of both parties, expressed in open court, and in

civil actions by the consent of the parties, signified in such
manner as may be prescribed by law. In civil actions, and
cases of misdemeanor, the jury may consist of twelve, or of
any number less than twelve upon which the parties may
agree in open court.

TRIAL BY JURY.—This section only gives a right to a trial by
jury in cases where the right existed at common law. (Cassidy v.
Sullivan, 64 Cal. 266, 28 Pac. 234; Koppikus v. State Capitol Commrs.,
16 Cal. 248; Woods v. Varnum, 85 Cal. 639, 24 Pac. 843; Vallejo etc.
R. R. Co. v. Reed Orchard Co., 169 Cal. 545, 147 Pac. 238.)

It cannot be demanded as of right in an equity case, but only in
criminal and civil cases in which an issue of fact is joined. (Koppikus v. State Capitol Commrs., 16 Cal. 248.)

The right does not exist in actions for divorce (Cassidy v. Sullivan, 64 Cal. 266, 28 Pac. 234); condemnation proceedings (Koppikus
v. State Capitol Commrs., 16 Cal. 248); proceedings for the removal of
public officers (Woods v. Varnum, 85 Cal. 639, 24 Pac. 843); or in
cases of equity jurisdiction. (Pacific Ry. Co. v. Wade, 91 Cal. 449,
25 Am. St. Rep. 201, 13 L. R. A. 754, 27 Pac. 768.)

A party is not entitled to a jury trial in an action brought to abate
a nuisance, and for an injunction to prevent it, although damages
are also prayed for. (McCarthy v. Gaston Ridge Mill etc. Co., 144
Cal. 542, 78 Pac. 7.)

As to the right to a jury trial in an action to quiet title, where the
defendant is in possession, see Hyde v. Redding, 74 Cal. 493, 16 Pac.
380; Angus v. Craven, 132 Cal. 691, 64 Pac. 1091, and cases there
cited.

An act providing for the removal of officers for extortion, and providing generally that the practice governing other civil actions shall
apply thereto, does not deprive the defendant of a jury trial. (Ryan
v. Johnson, 5 Cal. 86.)

The refusal to allow a jury is mere error and cannot be reviewed by
writ of review. (Goodman v. Superior Court, 8 Cal. App. 232, 96 Pac.
395.)

Both in criminal cases not amounting to felony, and in civil actions, the right of trial by jury may be waived. (Goodman v. Superior Court, 8 Cal. App. 232, 96 Pac. 395.)

The granting of a nonsuit is not violation of the constitutional
right to a jury trial where it already appears that plaintiff is guilty
of contributory negligence. (Bohn v. Pacific Electric Ry. Co., 5 Cal.
App. 622, 91 Pac. 115.)

Section 1192 of the Penal Code, conferring upon the court the power
to determine the degree of a crime upon a plea of guilty, is not unconstitutional as infringing upon the right of trial by jury. (People
v. Chew Lan Ong, 141 Cal. 550, 99 Am. St. Rep. 88, 75 Pac. 186.)

The power of the court to grant a new trial for insufficiency of the
evidence, or for excessive damages, does not violate the right of trial
by jury. (Ingraham v. Weidler, 139 Cal. 588, 73 Pac. 415; Estate of
Bainbridge, 169 Cal. 166, 146 Pac. 427.)

Conditions and restrictions which may be imposed by the legislature upon trial by jury. See note, 98 Am. St. Rep. 538.

In what cases legislature may dispense with trial by jury. See
note, 48 Am. Dec. 185.

General scope of constitutional provisions guaranteeing right of
trial by jury. See note, 1 Ann. Cas. 703.

Validity of court rule regulating right to jury trial. See note,
Ann. Cas. 1914B, 1184.

Right of accused to trial by jury. See 8 R. C. L., § 19, p. 67.

Petty offenses.—This provision does not prohibit the legislature
from providing for summary proceedings without a jury in cases of
such petty offenses as were enumerated in the English statutes at the
time of the separation of the American colonies from England, or in
cases where the offenses are intrinsically of the same nature and degree. (Ex parte Wong You Ting, 106 Cal. 296, 39 Pac. 627; In re
Fife, 110 Cal. 8, 42 Pac. 299.)

But where the offense falls within the legal or common-law notion
of crime or misdemeanor, and is embraced in the criminal code of the
state, the constitutional right of trial by jury cannot be evaded.
(Taylor v. Reynolds, 92 Cal. 573, 28 Pac. 688; Ex parte Wong You
Ting, 106 Cal. 296, 39 Pac. 627.)

A jury is not a necessary constituent part of a court for the trial
of a misdemeanor. (Wittman v. Police Court, 145 Cal. 474, 78 Pac.
1052.)

Whether jury in criminal case may be more or less than twelve.
See note, Ann. Cas. 1914A, 872; 43 L. R. A. 34.

Vicinage.—By the common law, the trial of all crimes is required
to be by a jury selected from the vicinage or county where the crime
is alleged to have been committed; and the same right is secured by
this section. Therefore, section 1033 of the Penal Code, allowing
a criminal action to be removed to another county without the consent of the defendant, is unconstitutional. (People v. Powell, 87 Cal.
348, 11 L. R. A. 75, 25 Pac. 481.)

Jurors.—A law taking away the challenge to a juror for implied
bias, on the ground that the juror has formed or expressed an un-
qualified opinion as to the guilt of the accused, is constitutional.
(People v. Ah Lee Doon, 97 Cal. 171, 31 Pac. 933.)

The court may, in its discretion, permit a separation of the jurors
during the impaneling of the jury and the subsequent progress of the
trial. (People v. Chaves, 122 Cal. 134, 54 Pac. 596.)

Waiver of jury trial.—The legislature alone, and not the court,
can determine what shall constitute a waiver of a jury trial. (Exline
v. Smith, 5 Cal. 112.)

The right to a jury trial is not waived by going to trial after it
has been denied, and the denial of it may be reviewed upon an appeal
from the judgment. (In re Robinson, 106 Cal. 493, 39 Pac. 862.)

A plea of guilty is a waiver of a jury trial. (People v. Lennox, 67
Cal. 113, 7 Pac. 260.) Also a failure to demand it in a civil case

before the trial begins. (Polack v. Gurnee, 66 Cal. 266, 5 Pac. 229, 610.)

The legislature alone can determine what shall constitute a waiver of a jury trial, and a jury may be waived only in one of the three modes prescribed by section 631 of the Code of Civil Procedure. (People v. Metropolitan Surety Co., 164 Cal. 174, Ann. Cas. 1914B, 1181, 128 Pac. 324.)

Waiver of jury trial in criminal cases. See notes, 1 Ann. Cas. 597; 9 Ann. Cas. 1183.

Failure of defendant in criminal case to demand jury as waiver of jury trial. See note, 9 Ann. Cas. 263.

Refusal of, how reviewed.—The denial of a jury trial may be reviewed upon an appeal from a judgment (In re Robinson, 106 Cal. 493, 39 Pac. 862), but cannot be reached by a writ of habeas corpus. (Ex parte Miller, 82 Cal. 454, 22 Pac. 1113.)

Refusal of a court to allow a jury trial cannot be reviewed by certiorari. (Wittman v. Police Court, 145 Cal. 474, 78 Pac. 1052.)

Offenses, how prosecuted.

Sec. 8.   Offenses heretofore required to be prosecuted by indictment shall be prosecuted by information, after examination and commitment by a magistrate, or by indictment, with or without such examination and commitment, as may be prescribed by law. A grand jury shall be drawn and summoned at least once a year in each county.

INDICTMENT AND INFORMATION.—A crime committed before the adoption of the new Constitution may, after such adoption, be prosecuted by information. (People v. Campbell, 59 Cal. 243, 43 Am. Rep. 257.)

As to the distinction between an indictment and a presentment, see In re Grosbois, 109 Cal. 445, 42 Pac. 444.

Under this provision a presentment by the grand jury for a misdemeanor is unauthorized. (In re Grosbois, 109 Cal. 445, 42 Pac. 444.)

This section does not prohibit a prosecution by indictment of any criminal offense, including a misdemeanor. (Ex parte McCarthy, 53 Cal. 412.)

A defendant cannot be put upon trial under an information until after examination and commitment by a magistrate. (Ex parte Nicholas, 91 Cal. 640, 28 Pac. 47.)

The Constitution has left the form of the indictment to the legislature. (People v. Kelly, 6 Cal. 210.)

The provision of this section for proceeding in criminal cases by information is not in conflict with the Constitution of the United States, as not being "due process of law." (Kalloch v. Superior Court, 56 Cal. 229.)

A conviction upon an information for murder is not illegal as violating the fourteenth amendment to the Constitution of the United

States prohibiting any state from depriving "any person of life, liberty or property without due process of law." (Hurtado v. California, 110 U. S. 516, 4 Sup. Ct. Rep. 292, 28 L. Ed. 232; McNulty v. California, 149 U. S. 645, 37 L. Ed. 882, 13 Sup. Ct. Rep. 959.)

A person indicted several times for the same offense is entitled to his release on nominal bail on the duplicate indictments. (Ex parte Ruef, 7 Cal. App. 750, 96 Pac. 24.)

Bail must not be exacted for the purpose of punishing the defendant. (Ex parte Ruef, 7 Cal. App. 750, 96 Pac. 24.)

The discretion of the trial court in fixing bail will not be interfered with, unless it clearly appears that the court has abused its discretion, and that the bail demanded is per se unreasonably great and clearly disproportionate to the offense involved. (Ex parte Ruef, 7 Cal. App. 750, 96 Pac. 24.)

It is within the power of the state to abolish the grand jury and authorize the procedure to punish crimes by information. (People v. Lewis, 9 Cal. App. 279, 98 Pac. 1078.)

When a defendant before the impaneling of a grand jury has been given an opportunity to examine the prospective grand jurors touching their qualifications, the court may refuse to permit him to go over the same ground on a motion to set aside the indictment. (Borello v. Superior Court, 8 Cal. App. 215, 96 Pac. 404.)

A person who has not been held to answer, but who may be accused of a public offense and who may be indicted by the grand jury, is not entitled to examine the individual grand jurors before they are impaneled and sworn touching their qualifications to inquire into and act upon his case. (Borello v. Superior Court, 8 Cal. App. 215, 96 Pac. 404.)

When an information has been filed, prohibition will not lie on the ground that the defendant has not had a preliminary examination. (Western Meat Co. v. Superior Court, 9 Cal. App. 538, 99 Pac. 976.)

Upon the filing of an information the presumption arises that the accused has been given the preliminary hearing by a magistrate. (Western Meat Co. v. Superior Court, 9 Cal. App. 538, 99 Pac. 976.)

An information may be filed by the district attorney, although the grand jury is in session. (People v. Lewis, 9 Cal. App. 279, 98 Pac. 1078.)

A grand jury does not lack jurisdiction to find an indictment merely because some of its members are disqualified. (Kitts v. Superior Court, 5 Cal. App. 462, 90 Pac. 977.)

A member of the grand jury who lacks the qualifications provided by law, is a de facto officer and the acts of the jury are not invalidated. (Kitts v. Superior Court, 5 Cal. App. 462, 90 Pac. 977.)

An indictment can be set aside by reason of the disqualification of jurors only for the reasons specified by the Penal Code. (Kitts v. Superior Court, 5 Cal. App. 462, 90 Pac. 977.)

When a person is indicted by a grand jury he has no opportunity to question the qualifications of the jurors, except by motion to set aside the indictment. (Kitts v. Superior Court, 5 Cal. App. 462, 90 Pac. 977.)

Section 1008 of the Penal Code, which permits an indictment to be amended by the district attorney as to mere matters of form, is constitutional. (People v. Anthony, 20 Cal. App. 586, 129 Pac. 968.)

Constitutionality of statutes permitting amendment of indictments. See note, 3 Ann. Cas. 558.

The phrase, "offenses heretofore required to be prosecuted by indictment," in this section, re-enacted the rule of the old Constitution that capital or other infamous crimes must be prosecuted by indictment, and the same offenses as were required under it to be prosecuted by indictment are still required to be so prosecuted except where the new procedure permits in addition to indictment, proceeding by information after examination and commitment by a magistrate. (In re Westenberg, 167 Cal. 309, 139 Pac. 674.)

Under this section a prosecution for criminal libel is not required to be by indictment. (Matter of Application of Westenberg, 167 Cal. 309, 139 Pac. 674.)

Under this section of Constitution of 1849 the only offenses required to be prosecuted by indictment were capital or other infamous crimes, and criminal libel was not among them. (In re Westenberg, 167 Cal. 309, 139 Pac. 674.)

Liberty of speech and freedom of the press—Trials for libel.

Sec. 9. Every citizen may freely speak, write and publish his sentiments on all subjects, being responsible for the abuse of that right; and no law shall be passed to restrain or abridge the liberty of speech or of the press. In all criminal prosecutions for libels, the truth may be given in evidence to the jury; and if it shall appear to the jury that the matter charged as libelous is true, and was published with good motives and for justifiable ends, the party shall be acquitted; and the jury shall have the right to determine the law and the fact. Indictments found, or information laid, for publication in newspapers shall be tried in the county where such newspapers have their publication office, or in the county where the party alleged to be libeled resided at the time of the alleged publication, unless the place of trial shall be changed for good cause.

LIBERTY OF THE PRESS.—This provision does not make all publications in a newspaper privileged. (Gilman v. McClatchy, 111 Cal. 606, 44 Pac. 241.)

The liberty of the press is not more under the protection of the Constitution than the liberty of speech, and the publishers of a newspaper can defend an action for libel only upon precisely the same grounds upon which any other individual could defend an action for slander. (Edwards v. San Jose etc. Publishing Soc., 99 Cal. 431, 37 Am. St. Rep. 70, 34 Pac. 128.)

A court has power to punish as a contempt a publication charging a judge with "deliberate lying about the law," etc., in a case before him. (Ex parte Barry, 85 Cal. 603, 20 Am. St. Rep. 248, 25 Pac. 256.)

Under this section a court has no power to forbid the representation upon the theatrical stage of the facts of a criminal case, pending the trial of such case. (Dailey v. Superior Court, 112 Cal. 94, 53 Am. St. Rep. 160, 32 L. R. A. 273, 44 Pac. 458.)

It is proper for the court to inform the jury as to the rules of evidence, and the law applicable to the case, and to tell them that they should go contrary to the instructions of the court only when they have a deep and confident conviction that the court is wrong, and that they are right. (People v. Seeley, 139 Cal. 118, 72 Pac. 834.)

The last sentence of this section applies to the case of a person who causes a libel to be published in a newspaper, as well as to a publication by the publishers and proprietors alone. (In re Kowalsky, 73 Cal. 120, 14 Pac. 399.)

> Infringing liberty of the press. See note, 78 Am. St. Rep. 260.
>
> Constitutional liberty of speech and press. See notes, 15 Ann. Cas. 3; 6 R. C. L., §§ 239–242a, pp. 253–258.
>
> Venue of action for libel or slander. See note, 6 Ann. Cas. 513.

"Good cause," within the meaning of the last sentence of this section, is that set forth in section 1033 of the Penal Code. The provision is not self-executing and confers no enlarged discretion upon the court. (Older v. Superior Court, 157 Cal. 770, 109 Pac. 478.)

The provisions of this section and of section 251 of the Penal Code that in the trial of a case of criminal libel the jury shall have the right to determine the law and the fact does not take away from the court the right to rule upon the admissibility of evidence during the trial. (People v. Pryal, 25 Cal. App. 779, 147 Pac. 114.)

> General rules applicable to libel and slander. See note, 4 Am. Dec. 348.
>
> Justification in actions for libel or slander. See note, 91 Am. St. Rep. 285.
>
> Province of court and jury in prosecutions for libel. See note, 13 Am. St. Rep. 625.
>
> Jury as judge of law and fact. See note, 42 Am. St. Rep. 290.
>
> Truth alone as complete defense in civil action for libel. See note, 17 Ann. Cas. 761.

Popular assemblies.

Sec. 10. The people shall have the right to freely assemble together to consult for the common good, to instruct their representatives, and to petition the legislature for redress of grievances.

RIGHT TO FREELY ASSEMBLE.—This section does not prevent the legislature from forbidding unlawful assemblies. As to what are such assemblies, see People v. Most, 128 N. Y. 108, 26 Am. St. Rep.

458, 27 N. E. 970; Rex v. Birt, 5 Car. & P. 154; Regina v. Neale, 9 Car. & P. 431; Beatty v. Gillbanks, 9 Q. B. Div. 308.

> Right to assemble and petition government. See 6 R. C. L., § 236, p. 250.

Uniformity of laws.

Sec. 11. All laws of a general nature shall have a uniform operation.

UNIFORMITY OF LAWS.—This provision does not affect laws in force at the adoption of the Constitution; and, therefore, while section 204 of the Code of Civil Procedure, relating to the impaneling of grand jurors, might have been void under this provision, a mere amendment to that section, making it applicable to the present judicial system, does not make it unconstitutional. (People v. Durrant, 116 Cal. 179, 48 Pac. 75.)

General Principles.—The word "uniform" does not mean "universal." (People v. Twelfth District Court, 17 Cal. 547; Hellman v. Shoulters, 114 Cal. 136, 44 Pac. 915, 45 Pac. 1057; In re Zhizhuzza, 147 Cal. 328, 81 Pac. 955.)

All that is necessary to constitute uniformity is that the law shall operate uniformly upon all persons in the same category, and upon rights and things in the same relation. (People v. Henshaw, 76 Cal. 436, 18 Pac. 413; People v. Twelfth District Court, 17 Cal. 547; Ex parte Halsted, 89 Cal. 471, 26 Pac. 961; Wigmore v. Buell, 122 Cal. 144, 54 Pac. 600.)

A statute is uniform in its operation if it applies alike to all persons or objects within a class founded upon some natural, intrinsic, or constitutional distinction. (Vail v. San Diego Co., 126 Cal. 35, 58 Pac. 392; Solano Co. v. McCudden, 120 Cal. 648, 53 Pac. 213; Cody v. Murphey, 89 Cal. 522, 26 Pac. 1081; Kahn v. Sutro, 114 Cal. 316, 33 L. R. A. 620, 46 Pac. 87; Murphy v. Pacific Bank, 119 Cal. 334, 51 Pac. 317; Ruperich v. Baehr, 142 Cal. 190, 75 Pac. 782.)

The meaning of this provision is that the legislature shall not grant to any citizen or class of citizens privileges or immunities which upon the same terms shall not equally belong to all citizens. (Ex parte Smith & Keating, 38 Cal. 702; Miller v. Kister, 68 Cal. 142, 8 Pac. 813; People v. Henshaw, 76 Cal. 436, 18 Pac. 413; Brooks v. Hyde, 37 Cal. 366.)

The operation of a law is none the less uniform because it operates differently upon different classes, provided there is a reasonable basis for the lack of uniformity, and the corporation license tax act is not invalid because failure of payment by a California corporation results in a forfeiture of its charter, while nonpayment by a foreign corporation results in a forfeiture of its right to do business within the state. (Kaiser Land & Fruit Co. v. Curry, 155 Cal. 638, 103 Pac. 341.)

This provision has no application to municipal ordinances. (In re Zhizhuzza, 147 Cal. 328, 81 Pac. 955.)

This section of Constitution of 1849 did not prohibit the granting of rights of way along waters, roads and highways to telegraph com-

panies. (Western Union Telegraph Co. v. Hopkins, 160 Cal. 106, 116 Pac. 557.)

This section of the Constitution of 1849 did not forbid special legislation nor the conferring of special powers upon municipalities by their charters, even when there was a general law upon the same subject matter. (Vallejo Ferry Co. v. Lang & McPherson, 161 Cal. 672, 120 Pac. 421.)

Quaere, as to whether section 629 of the Civil Code, making it the duty of certain public service corporations to furnish gas, electricity, steam or heat, on demand, is constitutional. (Thompson v. San Francisco Gas etc. Co., 18 Cal. App. 30, 121 Pac. 937.)

Special laws.—It is only laws of a general nature that are required to have a uniform operation, and this section does not forbid special laws. (People v. Central Pac. R. R. Co., 43 Cal. 398; Brooks v. Hyde, 37 Cal. 366; Addison v. Saulnier, 19 Cal. 82; People v. Twelfth District Court, 17 Cal. 547.)

Particular acts held not to be uniform.—In conformity with these principles, the following statutes have been held void as not uniform in their operation:

A provision of the County Government Act that, in counties of a certain designated population, county licenses collected in cities shall be paid into the treasuries of such cities for street improvements (San Luis Obispo Co. v. Graves, 84 Cal. 71, 23 Pac. 1032); an act authorizing a named street railway company to operate a street railway on designated streets (Omnibus R. R. Co. v. Baldwin, 57 Cal. 160); a a provision of the Insolvency Act, giving a right of appeal in cases of contempt—a right not given in other cases of contempt (Ex parte Clancy, 90 Cal. 553, 27 Pac. 411); a law requiring cities of two designated classes to make an effort to agree with the owners of land sought to be condemned, before instituting condemnation proceedings (City of Pasadena v. Stimson, 91 Cal. 238, 27 Pac. 604); a provision of the County Government Act of 1883, that the boards of supervisors of counties of certain designated classes may allow county officers a deputy whenever in the opinion of such board the salaries of such officers are insufficient (Dougherty v. Austin, 94 Cal. 601, 16 L. R. A. 161, 28 Pac. 834, 29 Pac. 1092); the provision of the Australian ballot law for the voting of straight tickets by stamping the ticket opposite the name of the political party to be printed at the head of the ticket (Eaton v. Brown, 96 Cal. 371, 31 Am. St. Rep. 225, 17 L. R. A. 697, 31 Pac. 250); an act providing that in cities having boards of education, the city treasurers are to have the custody of the state and county school money appropriated to the city (Bruch v. Colombet, 104 Cal. 347, 38 Pac. 45); a provision in the County Government Act that, in counties of one particular class only, witnesses in criminal cases shall be paid the same fees as jurors, in the discretion of the judge (Turner v. Siskiyou Co., 109 Cal. 332, 42 Pac. 434); a provision of the County Government Act that, in all counties of one particular class, certain additional fees shall be collected for filing the inventory in estates of deceased persons (Bloss v. Lewis, 109 Cal. 493, 41 Pac. 1081); the Primary Election Law of 1895, being confined in its operation to counties of the first and second

class (Marsh v. Hanly, 111 Cal. 368, 43 Pac. 975); a law giving the
district attorney supervisory control over fees of justices of the peace
and constables in criminal cases (Dwyer v. Parker, 115 Cal. 544, 47
Pac. 372); an act fixing different rates of liability upon stockholders
in different corporations (French v. Teschemaker, 24 Cal. 518); the
provision of the County Government Act that no supplies, etc., shall
be purchased for the county from any person who has not had a
business in the county for a year prior to the purchase (Van Harlingen v. Doyle, 134 Cal. 53, 54 L. R. A. 771, 66 Pac. 44); the provision of section 1197 of the Political Code forbidding the name of a
nominee to be placed upon the ballot more than once (Murphy v.
Curry, 137 Cal. 479, 59 L. R. A. 97, 70 Pac. 461); a statute providing
that all county printing must be let to persons who have been established in business in the county for more than one year (Van Harlingen v. Doyle, 134 Cal. 53, 54 L. R. A. 771, 66 Pac. 44); the act of
March 21, 1905, regarding rates of interest on chattel mortgages, and
fixing a different penalty for its violation when committed by corporations than when committed by individuals (Ex parte Sohncke, 148
Cal. 262, 113 Am. St. Rep. 236, 7 Ann. Cas. 475, 2 L. R. A. (N. S.)
813, 82 Pac. 956); a law regulating the rate of interest on chattel
mortgages on certain classes of property (Ex parte Sohncke, 148
Cal. 262, 113 Am. St. Rep. 236, 7 Ann. Cas. 475, 2 L. R. A. (N. S.)
813, 82 Pac. 956).

Particular acts held valid.—On the other hand, the following acts
have been held not to be obnoxious to the provision of this section,
and valid:

An act whose object it is to legalize the assessment of taxes in San
Francisco, since it is not a general, but a special, law (San Francisco
v. Spring Valley Water Works, 54 Cal. 571); an act establishing different fee bills for separate counties, not being of a general nature
(Ryan v Johnson, 5 Cal. 86); an act to remedy the failure of the tax
collector to publish the names of the owners, etc., it being not a general, but a special, law (Moore v. Patch, 12 Cal. 265); the provision
of the County Government Act of 1893, empowering certain of the
county officers in counties of one class to appoint a certain number of
deputies, whose salaries are fixed by the act and made payable out of
the county treasury, although in other counties the principal must
pay the salaries of his deputies (Tulare Co. v. May, 118 Cal. 303, 50
Pac. 427, overruling Welsh v. Bramlet, 98 Cal. 219, 33 Pac. 66, and
Walser v. Austin, 104 Cal. 128, 37 Pac. 869); an act subjecting trespassing animals to attachment without the affidavit required in other
cases of attachment (Wigmore v. Buell, 122 Cal. 144, 54 Pac. 600); a
law providing that assessors in counties of one particular class shall
pay all percentage for the collection of poll taxes into the county
treasury (Summerland v. Bicknell, 111 Cal. 567, 44 Pac. 232); an act
providing for police courts in all cities of a designated population,
and providing that it shall go into effect upon the expiration of the
term of office of the present police judges of such cities (People v.
Henshaw, 76 Cal. 436, 18 Pac. 413); an act providing for the commitment of minor criminals to nonsectarian charitable corporations at
the expense of the county (Boys' and Girls' Aid Society v. Reis, 71

Cal. 627, 12 Pac. 796); an ordinance prohibiting public laundries in
designated parts of a city (In re Hang Kie, 69 Cal. 149, 10 Pac. 327);
an ordinance making it unlawful for any person to conduct a laundry
within certain limits without a certificate from the fire wardens as to
the condition of the heating appliances, and forbidding the operation
of any laundry between 10 P. M. and 6 A. M., or on Sunday (Ex parte
Moynier, 65 Cal. 33, 2 Pac. 728); an act making it unlawful to keep
open any place of business on Sundays, except barber-shops, bath-
houses and hairdressing saloons (Ex parte Burke, 59 Cal. 6, 43 Am.
Rep. 231); the Revenue Act of 1853, since the legislature may discriminate in the imposition of taxes on certain classes of persons,
occupations or species of property, taxing some and exempting others
(People v. Coleman, 4 Cal. 46, 60 Am. Dec. 581); an act prohibiting
all persons, except innkeepers and the like, from keeping open their
places of business on Sundays for the transaction of business (Ex
parte Andrews, 18 Cal. 678); a statute establishing a limitation upon
actions for the recovery of lands in San Francisco under the Van Ness
Ordinance (Brooks v. Hyde, 37 Cal. 366); an ordinance making it unlawful to play upon any musical instrument in any saloon, etc., after
midnight, and for any female to be in any saloon, etc., after midnight
(Ex parte Smith & Keating, 38 Cal. 702); an act giving to laborers
working upon mines only a lien for their wages (Quale v. Moon, 48
Cal. 478); a state revenue law making different provisions in the different counties with regard to the enforcement of the payment of
delinquent taxes (People v. Central Pac. R. R. Co., 43 Cal. 398); the
provisions of section 1373 of the Political Code, making the county
in which the indictment was found chargeable with the support of
insane criminals (Napa State Hospital v. Yuba County, 138 Cal. 378,
71 Pac. 450); an act providing that in divorce suits the final decree
shall not be entered until the expiration of one year from the filing
of the decision (Deyoe v. Superior Court, 140 Cal. 476, 98 Am. St.
Rep. 73, 74 Pac. 28); the act regulating the practice of medicine and
surgery (Ex parte Gerino, 143 Cal. 412, 66 L. R. A. 249, 77 Pac. 166);
the case of Abeel v. Clark, 84 Cal. 226, 24 Pac. 383, approved as to
the constitutionality of an "act to encourage and provide for general
vaccination in the state of California" (French v. Davidson, 143 Cal.
658, 77 Pac. 663); an act making it unlawful to buy or sell quail (Ex
parte Kenneke, 136 Cal. 527, 89 Am. St. Rep. 177, 69 Pac. 261); the
act providing for the application of the salaries of public officers to
the payment of their debts (Ruperich v. Baehr, 142 Cal. 190, 75 Pac.
782); the act in regard to the practice of architecture (Ex parte
McManus, 151 Cal. 331, 90 Pac. 702); the provision of the child labor
law permitting the employment of children in certain cases where
they can "read English at sight and write simple English sentences"
(In re Spencer, 149 Cal. 396, 117 Am. St. Rep. 137, 9 Ann. Cas. 1105,
86 Pac. 896); section 246 of the Penal Code, providing the death penalty for any person undergoing a life sentence who commits an assault
with a deadly weapon (People v. Finley, 153 Cal. 59, 94 Pac. 248;
People v. Carson, 155 Cal. 164, 99 Pac. 970); the act of 1905, creating the "Sacramento Drainage District," as the subject matter of the
act required a special law (People v. Sacramento Drainage District,

155 Cal. 373, 103 Pac. 207); "an act to prohibit the sale of intoxicating liquors within a certain distance of any camp or assembly of men, numbering twenty-five or more, engaged upon the construction, repair or operation of any public work, improvement, or utility" (Stats. 1909, p. 722) (Ex parte King, 157 Cal. 161, 106 Pac. 578); "an act to amend section 4243 of the Political Code of the state of California, relating to the compensation and expenses of officers in counties of the fourteenth class" (Stats. 1900, p. 322) (Crockett v. Mathews, 157 Cal. 153, 106 Pac. 575); an act to provide for laying out, opening, extending, widening, etc., any street, etc. (Stats. 1889, p. 70) (Clute v. Turner, 157 Cal. 73, 106 Pac. 240); section 710 of the Code of Civil Procedure, providing for the garnishment of the salaries of certain public officers at the instance of their judgment creditors (Lawson v. Lawson, 158 Cal. 446, 111 Pac. 354); a law prohibiting waste of water from artesian wells (Ex parte Elam, 6 Cal. App. 233, 91 Pac. 811); an ordinance prohibiting the wholesale liquor business within a designated area in a municipality (Grumbach v. Lelande, 154 Cal. 679, 98 Pac. 1059); the act of 1909, regulating loan brokers and limiting rates of interest (Eaker v. Bryant, 24 Cal. App. 87, 140 Pac. 310); section 172a of the Penal Code, prohibiting the selling of liquor near university grounds of any university of more than one thousand students (Matter of Petition of Burke, 160 Cal. 300, 116 Pac. 755); an act forbidding the employment of women for more than eight hours a day in certain places (Matter of Application of Miller, 162 Cal. 687, 124 Pac. 427; affirmed in Miller v. Wilson, 236 U. S. 373, 59 L. Ed. 628, 35 Sup. Ct. Rep. 342); an act providing for the payment by the state, county or city of the premium on official bonds of all state, county or city officers (except notaries public) when given by surety companies (County of San Luis Obispo v. Murphy, 162 Cal. 588, Ann. Cas. 1913D, 712, 123 Pac. 808; County of San Luis Obispo v. Smith, 21 Cal. App. 55, 130 Pac. 838); an act authorizing the respective counties and municipalities of the state to appoint sealers of weights and measures (Scott v. Boyle, 164 Cal. 321, 128 Pac. 941); sections 1670 and 1671 of the Political Code, as they existed prior to the amendments of 1909, exempting the property in a union high school district from taxation for the support of a county high school (Wood v. County of Calaveras, 164 .Cal. 398, 129 Pac. 283); an act relating to the responsibility of employers for injuries to or death of employees (Pritchard v. Whitney Estate Co., 164 Cal. 564, 129 Pac. 989); an act concerning actions for libel and slander which allows either party prevailing in such actions to recover as costs one hundred dollars to cover counsel fees (Engel v. Ehret, 21 Cal. App. 112, 130 Pac. 1197); the Tenement House Act regulating the construction of buildings intended for human habitation and providing that such buildings shall not be occupied until the issuance of certain certificates by the health and building departments (Matter of Stoltenberg, 21 Cal. App. 722, 132 Pac. 841); the Medical Practice Act of 1911 (Bohannon v. Board of Medical Examiners, 24 Cal. App. 215, 140 Pac. 1089); section 636½ of Penal Code prohibiting the use of certain kinds of nets in fishing (Matter of Application of Mascolo, 25 Cal. App. 92, 142 Pac. 903).

As to the uniform operation of the County Government Act, which goes into effect at different times as to different counties, see Freman v. Marshall, 137 Cal. 159, 69 Pac. 986.

What is a general law. See note, 21 Am. St. Rep. 780.

Inhibition of local or special law where general law can be made applicable. See note, 93 Am. St. Rep. 106.

Discrimination in favor of soldiers or veterans. See note, 82 Am. St. Rep. 529, 117 Am. St. Rep. 891.

Fourteenth amendment considered with relation to special privileges, burdens and restrictions. See note, 25 Am. St. Rep. 870.

Equal privileges and immunities. See note, 14 L. R. A. 579.

Military power.

Sec. 12. The military shall be subordinate to the civil power. No standing army shall be kept up by this state in time of peace, and no soldier shall, in time of peace, be quartered in any house without the consent of the owner; nor in time of war, except in the manner prescribed by law.

Personal and property rights.

Sec. 13. In criminal prosecutions, in any court whatever, the party accused shall have the right to a speedy and public trial; to have the process of the court to compel the attendance of witnesses in his behalf, and to appear and defend, in person and with counsel. No person shall be twice put in jeopardy for the same offense; nor be compelled, in any criminal case, to be a witness against himself; nor be deprived of life, liberty, or property without due process of law. The legislature shall have power to provide for the taking, in the presence of the party accused and his counsel, of depositions of witnesses in criminal cases, other than cases of homicide, when there is reason to believe that the witness, from inability or other cause, will not attend at the trial.

SPEEDY TRIAL.—Section 1382 of the Penal Code is mandatory, and the court has no discretion to deny the defendant a speedy trial as provided by that section. (People v. Morino, 85 Cal. 515, 24 Pac. 892; In re Ford, 160 Cal. 334, 116 Pac. 757; Ford v. Superior Court, 17 Cal. App. 1, 118 Pac. 96.)

An accused person held in custody an unreasonable length of time without trial will be discharged upon habeas corpus. (In re Begerow, 133 Cal. 349, 85 Am. St. Rep. 178, 56 L. R. A. 513, 65 Pac. 828; People v. Moran, 144 Cal. 48, 77 Pac. 777.)

When good cause is shown for the delay, a dismissal will not be ordered when the trial has been delayed more than sixty days. (People v. Moran, 144 Cal. 48, 77 Pac. 777.)

Pronouncing judgment is no part of the trial, and the constitutional right to a speedy trial is not violated by a delay of thirty-five days in pronouncing judgment. (People v. Stokes, 5 Cal. App. 205, 89 Pac. 997.)

> Right to speedy trial. See notes, 41 Am. Dec. 604; 17 Ann. Cas. 170; 8 R. C. L., §§ 24–28, pp. 70–75.

> Speedy trial of persons accused of crime, and what amounts to denial of. See note, 85 Am. St. Rep. 187.

PUBLIC TRIAL.—The word "public" is used in this section in opposition to the word "secret." (People v. Swafford, 65 Cal. 223, 3 Pac. 809.)

The trial should be public in the ordinary, common-sense acceptation of the term, the doors should be open, the public admitted with due regard to the size of the courtroom, the conveniences of the court, the right to exclude objectionable characters and youths of tender years, and to do other things which may facilitate the proper conduct of the trial. (People v. Hartman, 103 Cal. 242, 42 Am. St. Rep. 108, 37 Pac. 153.)

An order excluding from the courtroom all persons except the officers of the court and the defendant is in violation of this provision and is presumed to be prejudicial. (People v. Hartman, 103 Cal. 242, 42 Am. St. Rep. 108, 37 Pac. 153. But see People v. Swafford, 65 Cal. 223, 3 Pac. 809.)

Where a defendant during a trial becomes excited and indulges in profane and abusive language, thus creating commotion among the spectators and interrupting the trial, an order excluding from the courtroom everyone except the officers of the court, reporters of the press, friends of the defendant, and persons necessary for him to have on his trial, is proper. (People v. Kerrigan, 73 Cal. 222, 14 Pac. 849.)

The defendant may waive the right to a public trial. (People v. Tarbox, 115 Cal. 57, 46 Pac. 896.)

> Right to public trial and what are infringements of. See notes, 28 Am. St. Rep. 308; 8 R. C. L., §§ 29–31, pp. 75–81.

WITNESSES.—The legislature has power to limit the compulsory attendance of prisoners confined in the state prison to cases of necessity, the existence of which is to be determined by the court. (Willard v. Superior Court, 82 Cal. 456, 22 Pac. 1120.)

The defendant may waive his right to be confronted with the witnesses. (People v. Bird, 132 Cal. 261, 64 Pac. 259.)

A court cannot refuse to compel the attendance of witnesses from an adjoining county merely because the district attorney offers to allow their testimony on a former trial to be read. (People v. Bossert, 14 Cal. App. 111, 111 Pac. 15.)

A defendant is entitled to a reasonable time within which to procure the attendance of witnesses. (People v. Bossert, 14 Cal. App. 111, 111 Pac. 15.)

It is the duty of the court, when due diligence has been used, and it appears that the application is made in good faith, and the evidence is material, to continue the case for a reasonable time to obtain an absent witness. (People v. Fong Chung, 5 Cal. App. 587, 91 Pac. 105.)

> Right to compulsory process to secure attendance of witnesses. See 8 R. C. L., §§ 36–38, pp. 81, 82.
>
> Right to be confronted by witnesses. See notes, 129 Am. St. Rep. 24; 8 R. C. L., §§ 41–47, pp. 84–89.

Subdivision 3, section 686, Penal Code, as amended in 1911, admitting the testimony of a witness, who cannot, with due diligence be found within the state, given at a former trial in the presence of the defendant, who has cross-examined the witness or had an opportunity to do so, is not in conflict with this section. (People v. Wilson, 26 Cal. App. 336, 146 Pac. 1048.)

RIGHT TO APPEAR AND DEFEND.—This provision only gives the defendant the right to appear and defend in person and with counsel, and does not give him the right to appear by counsel when he is himself absent. Therefore, when a defendant in a criminal case escapes after conviction, and pending an appeal, the appeal will not be heard in his absence, but will be dismissed. (People v. Redinger, 55 Cal. 290, 36 Am. Rep. 32.)

When a person, with the consent and acquiescence of the defendant, appears as attorney for the defendant, although another attorney has theretofore appeared, and there is no formal substitution, the defendant cannot be heard to complain that he has been deprived of the right to counsel. (People v. Garnett, 9 Cal. App. 194, 98 Pac. 247.)

To require a prisoner during the progress of his trial to appear and remain with chains upon his limbs, without evident necessity as a means of securing his presence for judgment, is in violation of this section. (People v. Harrington, 42 Cal. 165, 10 Am. Rep. 296.)

> Right to be free from shackles. See 8 R. C. L., § 22, p. 68.

A view of the premises without the presence of the defendant is in violation of this section. (People v. Bush, 68 Cal. 623, 10 Pac. 169.)

JEOPARDY.—When a person is placed on trial upon a valid indictment, before a competent court and jury, he is in jeopardy. (People v. Cage, 48 Cal. 323, 17 Am. Rep. 436; Ex parte Hartman, 44 Cal. 32; People v. Webb, 38 Cal. 467; Ex parte Fenton, 77 Cal. 183, 19 Pac. 267; People v. Smalling, 94 Cal. 112, 29 Pac. 421.)

After he has thus been put in jeopardy, he cannot be again tried for the same offense unless the jury is discharged from rendering a verdict by a legal necessity, or by his consent; or, in case a verdict is rendered, it be set aside at his instance. (People v. Webb, 38 Cal. 467; People v. Smalling, 94 Cal. 112, 29 Pac. 421.)

This is true although the judgment is arrested by the court (Ex parte Hartman, 44 Cal. 32); or an acquittal is obtained by reason of an erroneous instruction (People v. Webb, 38 Cal. 467; People v. Roberts, 114 Cal. 67, 45 Pac. 1016; People v. Horn, 70 Cal. 17, 11 Pac. 470); or the action is dismissed by the court on the ground that he is,

in the opinion of the court, guilty of a more serious offense (People v. Ny Sam Chung, 94 Cal. 304, 28 Am. St. Rep. 129, 29 Pac. 642).

Where the court is prohibited from pronouncing judgment upon the defendant because the indictment is invalid, jeopardy does not attach. (People v. Terrill, 133 Cal. 120, 65 Pac. 303.)

To hold a person guilty of the crime of offering a bribe, and by the same act guilty of the crime of being an accomplice to the crime of receiving a bribe, would not be allowable. (People v. Bunkers, 2 Cal. App. 197, 84 Pac. 364, 370.)

A dismissal of a charge on motion of the district attorney is not a bar to another prosecution. (People v. Kerrick, 144 Cal. 46, 77 Pac. 711.)

When a defendant is acquitted because of a variance between the proof and the indictment, and the variance is such that a conviction is legally impossible, he has not been in jeopardy. (People v. Mc-Nealy, 17 Cal. 332; People v. Oreileus, 79 Cal. 178, 21 Pac. 724.)

A judgment rendered upon a plea of which the court has no jurisdiction does not place the defendant in jeopardy so far as that plea is concerned. (People v. Woods, 84 Cal. 441, 23 Pac. 1119; People v. Hamberg, 84 Cal. 468, 24 Pac. 298.)

Subdivision 6 of section 1238 of the Penal Code, allowing the people to appeal from an order of the court directing the jury to find for the defendant, is void, since the defendant has been in jeopardy. (People v. Horn, 70 Cal. 17, 11 Pac. 470.)

The fact that the defendant has been held to answer by a justice of the peace and discharged does not prevent him from again being held to answer. (Ex parte Cahill, 52 Cal. 463.)

If a demurrer is sustained to an information, without leave to amend, it is a bar to another prosecution. (People v. Jordan, 63 Cal. 219.)

Where an information is dismissed because it charges the commission of an offense subsequent to the date of its filing, a plea of once in jeopardy will not prevail. (People v. Larson, 68 Cal. 18, 8 Pac. 517.)

A discharge upon preliminary examination does not place the defendant in jeopardy. (Ex parte Fenton, 77 Cal. 183, 19 Pac. 267.)

Discharge of jury.—If the jury is discharged without the consent of the defendant, except in case of unavoidable accident or necessity, the defendant cannot be again prosecuted. (People v. Cage, 48 Cal. 323, 17 Am. Rep. 436.)

Inability of the jury to agree after a reasonable time for deliberation is an unavoidable necessity. (People v. Cage, 48 Cal. 323, 17 Am. Rep. 436; People v. Smalling, 94 Cal. 112, 29 Pac. 421; People v. James, 97 Cal. 400, 32 Pac. 317; People v. Disperati, 11 Cal. App. 469, 105 Pac. 617.)

The fact of such necessity cannot be impeached by extrinsic evidence, and such discharge may be made in the absence of the defendant, if his presence is waived by his counsel. (People v. Smalling, 94 Cal. 112, 29 Pac. 421.)

Even if the court instructed the jury to acquit, a plea of once in jeopardy will not prevail if the jury is discharged for failure to agree. (People v. James, 97 Cal. 400, 32 Pac. 317.)

The court cannot discharge the jury merely upon a report of the sheriff that the jury cannot agree. (People v. Cage, 48 Cal. 323, 17 Am. Rep. 436.)

Where the jury is discharged for failure to agree, it is not necessary that the record should show that it satisfactorily appeared to the judge that there was no reasonable probability that the jury could agree. (People v. Greene, 100 Cal. 140, 34 Pac. 630.)

Where the defendant flees during the trial and the jury is discharged, a plea of once in jeopardy has no merit. (People v. Higgins, 59 Cal. 357.)

Where the jury is discharged with the consent of the defendant, a plea of once in jeopardy will not prevail. (People v. Curtis, 76 Cal. 57, 17 Pac. 941.)

The same is true if the jury is discharged on account of the sickness of one of the jurors. (People v. Ross, 85 Cal. 383, 24 Pac. 789.)

But if a defendant is indicted for manslaughter, the court cannot lawfully discharge the jury because it is of the opinion that he is guilty of murder. (People v. Hunckeler, 48 Cal. 331.)

Nor can the jury be lawfully discharged because it has found a verdict convicting the defendant of a crime not included in the charge. (People v. Arnett, 129 Cal. 306, 61 Pac. 930.)

Different offenses.—Where the legislature has forbidden the sale of opium, unless a record of the sale is kept, and a city ordinance forbids the sale without a prescription of a physician, a prosecution under each of these provisions is no violation of this provision. (Ex parte Hong Shen, 98 Cal. 681, 33 Pac. 799.)

A prosecution for fraudulently procuring a note of one of the joint makers is not a bar to a prosecution for fraudulently procuring the joint note of the two makers. (People v. Cummings, 123 Cal. 269, 55 Pac. 898.)

An acquittal upon a charge of libel in the publication of a charge in a newspaper is a bar to a prosecution for the publication of another charge in the same issue and against the same individual, although the charges are not the same. (People v. Stephens, 79 Cal. 428, 4 L. R. A. 845, 21 Pac. 856.)

A charge of altering the brands of cattle is not included in a charge of grand larceny of the same cattle, in which evidence was given of the same alteration of brands. (People v. Kerrick, 144 Cal. 46, 77 Pac. 711.)

Lesser offense.—A conviction of a lesser offense than that charged is an acquittal of the higher. (People v. Apgar, 35 Cal. 389; People v. Ny Sam Chung, 94 Cal. 304, 28 Am. St. Rep. 129, 29 Pac. 642; People v. Gordon, 99 Cal. 227, 33 Pac. 901.)

Where a defendant is charged with assault with a deadly weapon, and is convicted of battery, and the judgment is reversed, a plea of once in jeopardy will not lie, as assault does not include battery. (People v. Helbing, 61 Cal. 620.)

A defendant tried for murder, and convicted of murder in the second degree, who has the judgment vacated and a new trial granted, may be subsequently convicted of murder in the first degree. (People v. Keefer, 65 Cal. 232, 3 Pac. 818.)

A conviction of an assault, under an information charging an assault with intent to murder, is a bar to a prosecution for mayhem committed during the assault. (People v. Defoor, 100 Cal. 150, 34 Pac. 642.)

A verdict of manslaughter is the equivalent of a verdict of not guilty of murder, and the defendant, after such verdict, cannot be again tried upon the charge of murder. (People v. Muhlner, 115 Cal. 303, 47 Pac. 128.)

A conviction for petit larceny committed in connection with a burglary is not a bar to a prosecution for burglary. (People v. Devlin, 143 Cal. 128, 76 Pac. 900.)

New trials and appeals.—Where a new trial is ordered for insufficiency of the evidence, a plea of once in jeopardy has no merit. (People v. Hardisson, 61 Cal. 378.)

Where a judgment of conviction is reversed because of a defective information, and the action is dismissed and a new information filed for the same offense, the defendant cannot plead once in jeopardy. (People v. Schmidt, 64 Cal. 260, 30 Pac. 814; People v. Eppinger, 109 Cal. 294, 41 Pac. 1037; People v. Clark, 67 Cal. 99, 7 Pac. 178; People v. Mooney, 132 Cal. 13, 63 Pac. 1070.)

The same is true where the judgment is reversed because the verdict fails to find the degree of the crime. (People v. Travers, 73 Cal. 580, 15 Pac. 293; People v. Lee Yune Chong, 94 Cal. 379, 29 Pac. 776.)

Also where the judgment is reversed for failure to file the information within the time prescribed by the statute. (People v. Wickham, 116 Cal. 384, 48 Pac. 329.)

Also where the judgment is reversed for failure to find upon a plea of once in jeopardy. (People v. Tucker, 117 Cal. 229, 49 Pac. 134.)

Where the defendant has not asked for a new trial, the supreme court in reversing the judgment may nevertheless grant it. (People v. Travers, 77 Cal. 176, 19 Pac. 268; People v. Lee Yune Chong, 94 Cal. 379, 29 Pac. 776.)

New trial as former jeopardy. See 8 R. C. L., §§ 152–156, pp. 160–164.

Practice.—The question of jeopardy can only arise after an issue has been made of once in jeopardy. (People v. Lee Yune Chong, 94 Cal. 379, 29 Pac. 776.)

The defendant is entitled to a special verdict upon a plea of once in jeopardy. (People v. Tucker, 115 Cal. 337, 47 Pac. 111.)

Where the jury on the first trial found for the people on the plea of once in jeopardy, but failed to agree as to the plea of not guilty, the former plea need not be again submitted to the jury on a second trial. (People v. Smith, 121 Cal. 355, 53 Pac. 802.)

Former acquittal or conviction as defense. See note, 11 Am. St. Rep. 228.

Identity of offenses in plea of former jeopardy. See note, 92 Am. St. Rep. 89.

Effect of granting new trial after conviction. See note, 14 Am. Rep. 751.

Granting new trial after conviction for manslaughter does not permit subsequent conviction for a greater crime. See note, 12 Am. Rep. 473.

Granting of new trial, whether may subject defendant to conviction for higher offense. See note, 4 Am. St. Rep. 117.

Waiver or estoppel to plead former jeopardy. See note, 135 Am. St. Rep. 70.

Former jeopardy in general. See 8 R. C. L., §§ 114–156, pp. 134–164.

Examination before magistrate as former jeopardy. See note, 18 Ann. Cas. 993.

Former jeopardy notwithstanding order of mistrial. See notes, 1 Ann. Cas. 118; 10 Ann. Cas. 1086; Ann. Cas. 1914B, 774.

Conviction for lesser offense on trial for greater as bar to prosecution for greater on new trial. See notes, 4 Ann. Cas. 778; 16 Ann. Cas. 1206; Ann. Cas. 1912C, 668.

WITNESS AGAINST SELF.—A proceeding to remove a public officer for misconduct in office, no matter in what form the statutes may clothe it, is in its nature a criminal case. (Thurston v. Clark, 107 Cal. 285, 40 Pac. 435.)

Sections 1458 to 1461 of the Code of Civil Procedure are not penal in their nature. (Levy v. Superior Court, 105 Cal. 600, 29 L. R. A. 811, 38 Pac. 965.)

Where the examination of the defendant is confined entirely to the instrument which he is charged with forging, he cannot be cross-examined in reference to the forgery of another instrument. (People v. Baird, 104 Cal. 462, 38 Pac. 310.)

Where a defendant testifies that he drew the pistol merely to scare the deceased and had had no quarrel with him on that day, it is proper on cross-examination to ask him whether or not he had a quarrel with the deceased a few moments before the shooting, and as to what kind of a pistol he had, and why he cocked it. (People v. Brown, 76 Cal. 573, 18 Pac. 678.)

Where a defendant in his cross-examination voluntarily makes a statement concerning matters not embraced in his examination in chief, he may be cross-examined for the purpose of making such statements more clear. (People v. Sutton, 73 Cal. 243, 15 Pac. 86.)

The fact that the defendant has been compelled to testify concerning the offense is merely a defense to the indictment, and does not affect the jurisdiction of the court. (Rebstock v. Superior Court, 146 Cal. 308, 80 Pac. 65.)

It is sufficient, to bring a person within the immunity of this provision, that there is a law creating the offense under which the witness may be prosecuted, and which does not secure him against use, in a criminal prosecution, of the evidence that he may give; and in such case he cannot be compelled to answer in any collateral proceeding as to acts constituting such offense. (Ex parte Clarke, 103 Cal. 352, 37 Pac. 230.)

Where the statute gives the witness complete immunity from prosecution for the offense with reference to which his testimony is given,

he cannot refuse to answer. (Ex parte Cohen, 104 Cal. 524, 43 Am. St. Rep. 127, 26 L. R. A. 423, 38 Pac. 364.)

A law can absolutely secure a party against use in a criminal prosecution of the evidence he may give, only by a provision that, if he submits to the examination and answers the questions, he shall be exempt from any criminal prosecution for the offense to which the inquiry relates. (Ex parte Clarke, 103 Cal. 352, 37 Pac. 230.)

The mere fact that an answer might disgrace the witness is not ground for refusal to answer; and where an act provides that the testimony shall not be used against him in any criminal prosecution, he cannot refuse to answer under this provision. (Ex parte Rowe, 7 Cal. 184.)

It is for the court and not for the witness to determine whether or not the answer will incriminate the witness. (In re Rogers, 129 Cal. 468, 62 Pac. 47.)

A defendant in a criminal prosecution, who has become a witness in his own behalf, cannot be cross-examined as to any facts or matters not testified to by him on his examination in chief. (People v. O'Brien, 66 Cal. 602, 6 Pac. 695.)

When a defendant offers himself as a witness he is subject to the same rules of cross-examination as any other witness. (People v. Maughs, 8 Cal. App. 107, 96 Pac. 407.)

Where a person, suspected of being concerned in a crime, is taken before the grand jury, before any formal charge is made against him, and is sworn and examined concerning his actions before and at the time of the crime, without being informed of his constitutional right to decline to be a witness against himself, nor warned that his statements might be used against him, the testimony so given by him cannot be used against him. (People v. O'Bryan, 165 Cal. 55, 130 Pac. 1042.)

A person is not compelled to be a witness against himself in violation of this section, when doctors are allowed to give their opinions of his sanity in a criminal trial, which opinions are based upon their examinations, to which he voluntarily submitted. (People v. Bundy, 168 Cal. 777, 145 Pac. 537.)

Section 367c of the Penal Code, which requires the driver of a motor vehicle who has injured a person or vehicle to give to the injured person the number of his vehicle, his name and address, and the name of the owner of such vehicle, does not offend this provision. (People v. Diller, 24 Cal. App. 799, 142 Pac. 797.)

> Privilege of witness as to incriminating testimony. See notes, 21 Am. Dec. 55; 75 Am. St. Rep. 318.
>
> Waiver of privilege of witness by voluntarily testifying in own behalf. See notes, 19 Am. Rep. 348; 2 Ann. Cas. 247; 11 Ann. Cas. 822.
>
> Compelling accused to perform acts, exhibit himself, or to submit to physical examination. See note, 94 Am. St. Rep. 336.
>
> Witness or court as proper one to decide whether answer to question asked will tend to degrade or incriminate witness. See notes, 5 Ann. Cas. 41; 11 Ann. Cas. 1079; 12 Ann. Cas. 661.
>
> Immunity from self-incrimination. See 8 R. C. L., §§ 32–35, pp. 77–81.

DUE PROCESS OF LAW—Property.—The right to practice law is not "property" within the meaning of this section. (Cohen v. Wright, 22 Cal. 293.)

The right to a salary attached to a public office is not property. (Pennie v. Reis, 80 Cal. 266, 22 Pac. 176; Clarke v. Reis, 87 Cal. 543, 25 Pac. 759.)

Title by prescription is property which is protected by this provision. (Sharp v. Blankenship, 59 Cal. 288.)

A vested right in a pension fund is property within the meaning of this provision. (Kavanagh v. Board of Police Pension Fund Commrs., 134 Cal. 50, 66 Pac. 36.)

The question whether an act deprives persons of property without due process of law is a federal question, upon which the decisions of the United States are the controlling authority. (Brookes v. City of Oakland, 160 Cal. 423, 117 Pac. 433.)

What is "due process."—"Due process of law" means such an exertion of the powers of the government as the settled maxims of law permit and sanction, and under such safeguards for the protection of individual rights as those maxims prescribe for the class of cases to which the one in question belongs. (Ex parte Ah Fook, 49 Cal. 402; Wulzen v. Board of Supervisors, 101 Cal. 15, 40 Am. St. Rep. 17, 35 Pac. 353.)

The words "due process of law" were intended to convey the same meaning as the words "the law of the land" in Magna Charta, and mean public laws binding all the members of the community under similar circumstances, and not partial or private laws affecting the rights of individuals. (Kalloch v. Superior Court, 56 Cal. 229.)

Due process of law requires a trial governed by the established rules of evidence, and a procedure suitable and proper to the nature of the case, and sanctioned by the established usage and customs of the courts. (San Jose Ranch Co. v. San Jose Land etc. Co., 126 Cal. 322, 58 Pac. 824.)

Police power.—In the exercise of the police power certain kinds of property, when held or used so as to be injurious to the general public, may be seized and destroyed. (Collins v. Lean, 68 Cal. 284, 9 Pac. 173.)

An act defining pure wine, prohibiting the use of deleterious substitutes, and forbidding the sale of impure wine, does not deprive one of property without due process of law. (Ex parte Kohler, 74 Cal. 38, 15 Pac. 436.)

Where the exercise of the police power is permissible, the provision of the Constitution declaring that private property shall not be taken without due process of law is inapplicable. (Ex parte Elam, 6 Cal. App. 233, 91 Pac. 811.)

An ordinance prohibiting the sale of liquors is not unconstitutional because it deprives one of the right to dispose of large quantities of liquor which he had on hand at the time the ordinance was passed. (Ex parte Young, 154 Cal. 317, 22 L. R. A. (N. S.) 330, 97 Pac. 822.)

Where an ordinance, fixing the limits within which a disagreeable business may be exercised, has in fact some relation to public health and is appropriate and adapted to that end, it cannot be urged that

the ordinance deprives the owner of his property without due process of law. (Ex parte Lacey, 108 Cal. 326, 49 Am. St. Rep. 93, 38 L. R. A. 640, 41 Pac. 411.)

Particular statutes.—The provision of the Constitution allowing prosecutions by information affords due process of law. (Kalloch v. Superior Court, 56 Cal. 229.)

The provision of section 971 of the Penal Code as to charging an accessory before the fact as a principal does not deprive him of life, liberty or property without due process of law. (People v. Nolan, 144 Cal. 75, 77 Pac. 774.)

The expulsion of a member of the legislature without a hearing does not deprive him of property without due process of law. (French v. Senate, 146 Cal. 604, 2 Ann. Cas. 756, 69 L. R. A. 556, 80 Pac. 1031.)

The legislature has power to provide that a deed in a street assessment matter shall be conclusive evidence of the regularity of all required steps other than those necessary to constitute due process of law or to comply with the Constitution. (Chase v. Trout, 146 Cal. 350, 80 Pac. 81.)

The statute prescribing an increased punishment for a second offense does not deprive a defendant of liberty without due process of law. (People v. Coleman, 145 Cal. 609, 79 Pac. 283.)

A law imposing the death penalty upon a person undergoing a life sentence, who, with malice aforethought, commits an assault upon another with a deadly weapon, or by any means likely to produce bodily injury, is valid. (In re Finley, 1 Cal. App. 198, 81 Pac. 1041.)

An act making the issuance of bonds conclusive evidence of the validity of the lien is void; but an act making the issuance conclusive evidence of the regularity of the proceedings not essential to the jurisdiction of the officers to create the lien is valid. (Ramish v. Hartwell, 126 Cal. 443, 58 Pac. 920.)

This provision does not prohibit a summary proceeding by the state to collect taxes, without the intervention of a court. (High v. Shoemaker, 22 Cal. 363.)

The act of 1875, providing for a judicial proceeding to authorize the sale of the homestead upon the insanity of either spouse, by the sane spouse alone, is valid, in so far as it relates to a homestead upon the community property acquired subsequent to the passage of the act. (Rider v. Regan, 114 Cal. 667, 46 Pac. 820.)

A law authorizing the court to strike out the pleading of a defendant for failure to sign a deposition or as a punishment for a contempt of court is invalid. (Foley v. Foley, 120 Cal. 33, 65 Am. St. Rep. 147, 52 Pac. 122.)

To enter judgment against a defendant for failure to deposit his share of the per diem of the reporter is taking property without due process of law. (Meacham v. Bear Valley Irr. Co., 145 Cal. 606, 68 L. R. A. 600, 79 Pac. 281.)

A statute providing that no case shall be reversed for error, unless it appears that a different result would have been probable if the error had not occurred, is void as depriving parties of due process of law. (San Jose Ranch Co. v. San Jose etc. Land Co., 126 Cal. 322, 58 Pac. 824.)

An act divesting the title of the purchaser of property from a mortgagor by a foreclosure suit in which the mortgagor alone is defendant is void. (Skinner v. Buck, 29 Cal. 253.)

An act extending the corporate limits of a town so as to include lands used solely for agricultural purposes was upheld in Santa Rosa v. Coulter, 58 Cal. 537.

The act of 1907, page 122, prohibiting waste from artesian wells does not unconstitutionally interfere with private property. (Ex parte Elam, 6 Cal. App. 233, 91 Pac. 811.)

The mechanic's lien law is not unconstitutional because it takes property without due process of law. (Stimson Mill Co. v. Nolan, 5 Cal. App. 754, 91 Pac. 262.)

The amendments to the Code of Civil Procedure providing for a new and alternative method of appeal do not violate the "due process of law" clauses of the state and federal Constitutions in failing to require service of notices of appeal upon respondents. (Estate of McPhee, 154 Cal. 385, 97 Pac. 878.)

The amendment to the Code of Civil Procedure relative to the method of preparing the record to be used on appeal is not unconstitutional in not providing for service of the notice filed with the clerk that the appellant intends to appeal and requiring that a transcript be made up. (Estate of McPhee, 154 Cal. 385, 97 Pac. 878.)

The legislature has power to permit execution to issue on a judgment after the expiration of the five years' limitation in effect when the judgment was rendered, provided the judgment had not become barred at the time of the amendment. (Weldon v. Rogers, 151 Cal. 432, 90 Pac. 1062.)

The legislature may extend the time within which an action may be brought at any time before the action is barred. (Weldon v. Rogers, 151 Cal. 432, 90 Pac. 1062.)

The legislature has power to make a tax deed conclusive evidence that after a sale to the state the tax collector stamped all subsequent bills "sold for taxes" and the date of the sale. (Bank of Lemoore v. Fulgham, 151 Cal. 234, 90 Pac. 936.)

It is not within the power of the legislature to take away the right of redemption from a tax sale which existed at the time of the sale. (Johnson v. Taylor, 150 Cal. 201, 119 Am. St. Rep. 181, 10 L. R. A. (N. S.) 818, 88 Pac. 903.)

Section 526 of the Code of Civil Procedure does not prevent the issuance of an injunction to restrain the board of public works of a city from enforcing assessments levied for the condemnation of land for street purposes, where plaintiffs claimed they were being deprived of their property without due process of law. (Pierce v. City of Los Angeles, 159 Cal. 516, 114 Pac. 818.)

Section 3897 of the Political Code, concerning the sale of property purchased by the state, does not deprive of property without due process of law (Merchants' Trust Co. v. Wright, 161 Cal. 149, 118 Pac. 517); an act providing for the discontinuance of a public lane leading from one public road to another by the board of supervisors without a hearing does not deprive the abutting owner of his property without due process of law. (Swift v. Board of Supervisors, 16 Cal. App. 72, 116 Pac. 317.)

The provision of the act of 1889 providing for the laying out, opening, extending, widening, straightening or closing up city streets, directing the city council to determine objections made to the report of the commissioners and to the assessments, and that a time must be set for the hearing thereof, of which reasonable notice must be given, constitutes due process of law. (United Real Estate etc. Co. v. Barnes, 159 Cal. 242, 113 Pac. 167.)

Where property is sold for taxes to the state and the owner does not redeem, there is no constitutional objection to the state acquiring the title free from all equities, which it can sell and convey to the highest bidder for cash and which will be good as against the former owner. (Chapman v. Zobelein, 19 Cal. App. 132, 124 Pac. 1021.)

The State Banking Act of 1909, in authorizing the summary seizure by the superintendent of banks of the property and business of a bank whenever he has reason to conclude that it is in an unsound condition, without action brought or judicial warrant for the taking, does not violate the due process of law clause of the Constitution. (State Savings etc. Bank v. Anderson, 165 Cal. 437, 132 Pac. 755.)

Notice.—A judgment obtained without service of summons on, or voluntary appearance by, the defendant does not constitute due process of law. (Baker v. O'Riordan, 65 Cal. 368, 4 Pac. 232; Belcher v. Chambers, 53 Cal. 635; De La Montanya v. De La Montanya, 112 Cal. 101, 53 Am. St. Rep. 165, 32 L. R. A. 82, 44 Pac. 345.)

A law authorizing the commitment of a person to an insane asylum without notice is void. (Matter of Lambert, 134 Cal. 626, 86 Am. St. Rep. 296, 55 L. R. A. 856, 66 Pac. 851.)

The shortness of the period of constructive notice to nonresident heirs of the probate of a will does not deprive them of due process of law, since they are allowed to contest the will within a year after probate. (Estate of Davis, 136 Cal. 590, 69 Pac. 412.)

An ex parte order for alimony is void. (Baker v. Baker, 136 Cal. 302, 68 Pac. 971.)

The fact that the street bond act does not in terms give a lienholder an opportunity to object does not render it unconstitutional. (German Sav. etc. Soc. v. Ramish, 138 Cal. 120, 69 Pac. 89, 70 Pac. 1067.)

An act authorizing a personal judgment against a defendant concealing himself within the state, for whom the court has appointed an attorney with privilege to the defendant to come in within six months, is valid. (Ware v. Robinson, 9 Cal. 107.)

Sections 1206 and 1207 of the Penal Code must be construed as requiring that both debtor and creditor are to have notice of claims for wages, otherwise they would deprive the debtor of his property without due process of law. (Taylor v. Hill, 115 Cal. 143, 44 Pac. 336, 46 Pac. 922.)

Whether a notice of not more than ten days is valid, query? (Boorman v. Santa Barbara, 65 Cal. 313, 4 Pac. 31.)

A general notice of an intended improvement, before it has been determined either finally or conditionally what land will be affected does not constitute due process of law. (Boorman v. Santa Barbara, 65 Cal. 313, 4 Pac. 31.)

An act authorizing an assessment for street improvements without notice to the parties to be assessed is void. (Boorman v. Santa Barbara, 65 Cal. 313, 4 Pac. 31.)

Notice by posting constitutes due process of law. (Davies v. Los Angeles, 86 Cal. 37, 24 Pac. 771.)

Section 720 of the Code of Civil Procedure, allowing the judgment creditor to institute an action against an alleged debtor of the judgment debtor, is not unconstitutional on the ground that no notice is given to the judgment debtor. (High v. Bank of Commerce, 95 Cal. 386, 29 Am. St. Rep. 121, 30 Pac. 556.)

In matters of taxation and assessment, the state is not bound to accord personal service of process upon the citizen. (Wulzen v. Board of Supervisors, 101 Cal. 15, 40 Am. St. Rep. 17, 35 Pac. 353.)

An assessment without giving an opportunity to the taxpayer to show that the assessment is not proportionate to the benefits is unconstitutional. (Lower Kings River Rec. Dist. No. 531 v. Phillips, 108 Cal. 306, 39 Pac. 630, 41 Pac. 335.)

In a proceeding for the sale of the homestead of an insane person, publication for three weeks in a newspaper, and personal service upon the nearest male relative of the insane spouse to be found in the state, or, if none, then upon the public administrator, whose duty it is to appear for such insane spouse, constitutes due process of law. (Rider v. Regan, 114 Cal. 667, 46 Pac. 820.)

Heirs and devisees are not deprived of their property without due process of law by an order setting aside a homestead in probate without notice to them. (Otto v. Long, 144 Cal. 144, 77 Pac. 885.)

A statute allowing an execution to issue against the "joint property" of persons sued, when only one of the defendants has been served, is unconstitutional. (Tay v. Hawley, 39 Cal. 93.)

An act allowing a peace officer to seize all nets, etc., used in catching fish in violation of the game laws, and to destroy them without notice, or to sell them upon notice posted anywhere in the county for five days, is in violation of this provision. (Hey Sing Ieck v. Anderson, 57 Cal. 251, 40 Am. Rep. 115.)

To take property from the possession of a person without a hearing, and compel him to prove title to regain it, is taking property without due process of law. (Havemeyer v. Superior Court, 84 Cal. 327, 18 Am. St. Rep. 192, 10 L. R. A. 627, 24 Pac. 121.)

A forfeiture of the charter and property of a subordinate grove by the grand grove, without sufficient charges to show jurisdiction over the subject matter, and without sufficient notice, is in violation of this provision. (Grand Grove etc. v. Garibaldi Grove, 130 Cal. 116, 80 Am. St. Rep. 80, 62 Pac. 486.)

An order of the probate court made without notice, compelling an attorney of an executrix to repay a fee paid to him by her, is in violation of this provision. (Tomsky v. Superior Court, 131 Cal. 620, 63 Pac. 1020.)

Due process of law does not require that the defendant should have notice of a motion for the issuance of execution. (Harrier v. Bassford, 145 Cal. 529, 78 Pac. 1038.)

The inheritance tax act does not deprive the heir of his property without due process of law, since he is given an opportunity to be

heard. (Trippet v. State, 149 Cal. 521, 8 L. R. A. (N. S.) 1210, 86 Pac. 1084.)

An act providing that when a foreign corporation doing business in this state fails to appoint an agent upon whom process may be served process may be served on the secretary of state is valid. (Olender v. Crystalline Min. Co., 149 Cal. 482, 86 Pac. 1082.)

A statute allowing the filing of a memorandum of costs on appeal without opportunity to the adverse party to have the same taxed would be unconstitutional. (Bell v. Superior Court, 150 Cal. 31, 87 Pac. 1031.)

The act for the establishment of titles in San Francisco in cases where the records were destroyed by fire does not deprive anyone of property without due process of law. (Title etc. Restoration Co. v. Kerrigan, 150 Cal. 289, 119 Am. St. Rep. 199, 8 L. R. A. (N. S.) 682, 88 Pac. 356.)

The legislature may prescribe moral and unprecedented methods of procedure, provided they afford the parties affected substantial securities against arbitrary and unjust spoliation. (Title etc. Restoration Co. v. Kerrigan, 150 Cal. 289, 119 Am. St. Rep. 199, 8 L. R. A. (N. S.) 682, 88 Pac. 356.)

The provisions of the Code of Civil Procedure providing for the dissolution of corporations without personal notice to creditors is not invalid. (Crossman v. Vivienda Water Co., 150 Cal. 575, 89 Pac. 335.)

The "Torrens Law" does not deprive unknown owners of property without due process of law. (Robinson v. Kerrigan, 151 Cal. 40, 121 Am. St. Rep. 90, 12 Ann. Cas. 829, 90 Pac. 129.)

The provisions for the probate of wills is not unconstitutional because the notice of ten days is insufficient to reach nonresident heirs, since they are allowed one year after probate within which to contest the probate. (Tracy v. Muir, 151 Cal. 363, 121 Am. St. Rep. 117, 90 Pac. 832.)

The probate act does not deprive the nonresident of his property without due process of law because it provides a different notice to residents than to nonresidents. (Tracy v. Muir, 151 Cal. 363, 121 Am. St. Rep. 117, 90 Pac. 832.)

The legislature is, primarily, the judge of the necessity which will warrant a substituted instead of a personal service of process. (Hoffman v. Superior Court, 151 Cal. 386, 90 Pac. 939.)

The "McEnerney Act," for the establishment of titles where the records have been destroyed, is not unconstitutional because it does not require the plaintiff to show the efforts made by him to discover possible claimants to the property. (Hoffman v. Superior Court, 151 Cal. 386, 90 Pac. 939.)

Section 1582 of the Code of Civil Procedure, authorizing an action to foreclose a mortgage against the estate of a deceased person to be brought against the personal representative alone, is not unconstitutional in depriving the heirs of property without due process of law. (McCaughey v. Lyall, 152 Cal. 615, 93 Pac. 681.)

The fact that, under section 2 of the act of March 31, 1897, as amended in 1911, providing for the organization and government of irrigation districts and for the acquisition or construction thereby of works for irrigation, and providing for the distribution of water for

irrigation, it is unnecessary to the jurisdiction of the board of supervisors that the notice of the time of presentation of the petition for the organization of the proposed district should be signed by all the petitioners therefor and that some might sign in behalf of all, does not make the act unconstitutional as not constituting due process of law. (Imperial Water Co. v. Supervisors, 162 Cal. 14, 120 Pac. 780.)

In any action against known defendants, personal service of summons is essential whenever it can be had, and publication of same as against nonresidents or absentees must not be less than two months. (King v. Pauly, 159 Cal. 549, 115 Pac. 210.)

The act of February 13, 1911, providing that the city council of any city may create sewer districts within it and fix their boundaries, is unconstitutional, because it contains no provision for any notice or hearing upon the question of the limits of the districts, and because no opportunity is afforded a property owner to be heard upon the question whether the proposed sewer will benefit his property. (Brookes v. City of Oakland, 160 Cal. 423, 117 Pac. 433.)

Liens.—The mechanics' lien law of 1868 is not unconstitutional on the ground that it attempts to appoint agents for private persons; nor that it confiscates property; nor as to the notice required of owners as to responsibility for improvements; nor that it attempts to take away vested rights, or to clothe private persons with power to divest citizens of their property. (Hicks v. Murray, 43 Cal. 515.)

Giving a laborer a lien upon a threshing machine in the lawful possession of a person holding under the owner does not deprive the latter of property without due process of law. (Lambert v. Davis, 116 Cal. 292, 48 Pac. 123.)

An act authorizing the creation of a lien upon land by virtue of a contract for the improvement of the street adjacent thereto, entered into with one who is only the reputed owner of the land, is void. (Santa Cruz Rock etc. Co. v. Lyons, 117 Cal. 212, 59 Am. St. Rep. 174, 48 Pac. 1097.)

Curative Acts.—The legislature has power to pass curative acts by which the various acts and proceedings of the officers and boards charged with the levying and assessing of taxes are rendered valid, notwithstanding that errors and irregularities have intervened. But where the officer or tribunal has no jurisdiction, the act is void, and cannot be cured. (People v. Goldtree, 44 Cal. 323.)

An act to validate a judgment of a court void for want of jurisdiction is void. (Pryor v. Downey, 50 Cal. 388, 19 Am. Rep. 656.)

An act attempting to validate a void assessment is in violation of this provision. (Brady v. King, 53 Cal. 44; People v. Lynch, 51 Cal. 15, 21 Am. Rep. 677; People v. Goldtree, 44 Cal. 323; Schumacker v. Toberman, 56 Cal. 508; Taylor v. Palmer, 31 Cal. 240; People v. McCune, 57 Cal. 153.)

An act attempting to legalize a sale of property for a void tax is unconstitutional. (Harper v. Rowe, 53 Cal. 233; Wills v. Austin, 53 Cal. 152; Houghton v. Austin, 47 Cal. 646.)

An act curing tax deeds not containing a recital of the time allowed for redemption is valid. (Baird v. Monroe, 150 Cal. 560, 89 Pac. 352.)

The legislature may validate past transactions wherein no vested rights are affected. (Redlands v. Brook, 151 Cal. 474, 91 Pac. 150.)

Assessments.—The so-called "front-foot" method of assessment for street improvements has been many times upheld in this state. (Hadley v. Dague, 130 Cal. 207, 62 Pac. 500; Cohen v. Alameda, 124 Cal. 504, 57 Pac. 377; Chambers v. Satterlee, 40 Cal. 497; Emery v. San Francisco Gas Co., 28 Cal. 345; Emery v. Bradford, 29 Cal. 75; Taylor v. Palmer, 31 Cal. 240; Whiting v. Quackenbush, 54 Cal. 306; Whiting v. Townsend, 57 Cal. 515; Lent v. Tillson, 72 Cal. 404; 14 Pac. 71; Jennings v. Le Breton, 80 Cal. 8, 21 Pac. 1127; San Francisco Pav. Co. v. Bates, 134 Cal. 39, 66 Pac. 2; Banaz v. Smith, 133 Cal. 102, 65 Pac. 309; Chapman v. Ames, 135 Cal. 246, 67 Pac. 1125; Belser v. Allman, 134 Cal. 399, 66 Pac. 492; Reid v. Clay, 134 Cal. 207, 66 Pac. 262; Alameda v. Cohen, 133 Cal. 5, 65 Pac. 127; German Sav. etc. Soc. v. Ramish, 138 Cal. 120, 69 Pac. 89, 70 Pac. 1067.)

Considerable doubt was cast upon the correctness of these decisions by the decision of the United States supreme court in Norwood v. Baker, 172 U. S. 269, 43 L. Ed. 443, 19 Sup. Ct. Rep. 187; but the doctrine of these cases has been since sustained by the decision of that court in Tonawanda v. Lyon, 181 U. S. 389, 45 L. Ed. 908, 21 Sup. Ct. Rep. 609.

An act authorizing the street superintendent to assess benefits, without prescribing the precise mode of assessment, is valid. (Harney v. Benson, 113 Cal. 314, 45 Pac. 687; Greenwood v. Morrison, 128 Cal. 350, 60 Pac. 971.)

An assessment is not invalid because the owner of the land is not given an opportunity to be heard before the assessment is made, if he is given that opportunity in an action to enforce the assessment. (Reclamation Dist. No. 108 v. Evans, 61 Cal. 104.)

An act permitting the owners of one-half of the land of a district to form an assessment district, without making any provision for a determination as to whether the other owners will be benefited by the improvement, is unconstitutional. (Moulton v. Parks, 64 Cal. 166, 30 Pac. 613; Brandenstein v. Hoke, 101 Cal. 131, 35 Pac. 562; People v. Reclamation Dist. No. 551, 117 Cal. 114, 48 Pac. 1016.)

The mode of assessment is a matter for the legislature, and the courts will not interfere on the ground of an improper apportionment or inequality of burden or benefit, unless there is a palpable violation of private rights. (Reclamation Dist. v. Hagar, 66 Cal. 54, 4 Pac. 945.)

It is sufficient if the parties interested are given an opportunity to be heard before the lien becomes final upon their property, and they are not entitled to be heard upon the question whether or not the improvement should be made. (Lent v. Tillson, 72 Cal. 404, 14 Pac. 71; Board of Directors v. Tregea, 88 Cal. 334, 26 Pac. 237.)

Where the limits of an assessment district are defined in the statute, notice need not be addressed to the persons affected by name. (Lent v. Tillson, 72 Cal. 404, 14 Pac. 71.)

An act for the protection of swamp lands, which provides for making assessments therefor a charge upon the lands benefited, and for a sale of such lands for such assessments, without any opportunity for a hearing of the land owner in regard to the assessment, and without

any suit or opportunity of defense, is invalid. (Hutson· v. Wood-bridge Protection Dist., 79 Cal. 90, 16 Pac. 549, 21 Pac. 435.)

The property of a land owner within an irrigation district is not taken from him without due process of law, if he is allowed a hear-ing at any time before the lien of an assessment for taxes levied thereon becomes final. (In re Madera Irr. Dist., 92 Cal. 296, 27 Am. St. Rep. 106, 14 L. R. A. 755, 28 Pac. 272, 675.)

The property of a land owner is not taken from him without due process of law under the Wright Act, since a hearing, upon notice, as to the facts on which the petition for the formation of the district is based, and as to the benefit to the land included therein, is pro-vided for. (Fallbrook Irr. Dist. v. Bradley, 164 U. S. 112, 41 L. Ed. 369, 17 Sup. Ct. Rep. 56.)

When the legal title of the property of irrigation districts is vested in the district only in trust for the land owners, the rights of such land owners are private property which cannot be taken without due process of law. (Merchants' Nat. Bank v. Escondido Irr. Dist., 144 Cal. 329, 77 Pac. 937.)

The "Wright Act" providing for irrigation districts is constitu-tional. (In re Central Irr. Dist., 117 Cal. 382, 49 Pac. 354, and cases there cited.)

The provision of the Street Improvement Bond Act of 1893, re-quiring the property owner, as a condition for the nonissuance of an assessment bond against his property, to present to the treasurer a certificate made by a searcher of records that he is the owner of record of the property, does not deprive him of property without due process of law. (Schaffer v. Smith, 169 Cal. 764, 147 Pac. 976.)

> What is due process of law. See notes, 24 Am. Dec. 538; 20 Am. St. Rep. 554; 122 Am. St. Rep. 904; 6 R. C. L., §§ 430–485, pp. 433–485.

DEPOSITIONS.—This section does not prevent the legislature from providing that depositions taken on the preliminary examination may be used on the trial. (People v. Oiler, 66 Cal. 101, 4 Pac. 1066.)

As to the power of the legislature to authorize the conditional ex-amination of witnesses, see Willard v. Superior Court, 82 Cal. 456, 22 Pac. 1120.

The provision of the Penal Code allowing depositions taken at the preliminary examination of a defendant charged with murder to be read in evidence for the prosecution upon the trial is not in conflict with this section. (People v. Sierp, 116 Cal. 249, 48 Pac. 88; People v. Cady, 117 Cal. 10, 48 Pac. 908; People v. Clark, 151 Cal. 200, 90 Pac. 549.)

Eminent domain.

Sec. 14.   Private property shall not be taken or damaged for public use without just compensation having first been made to, or paid into court for, the owner, and no right of way shall be appropriated to the use of any corporation other than municipal until full compensation therefor be

first made in money or ascertained and paid into court for
the owner, irrespective of any benefits from any improvement proposed by such corporation, which compensation
shall be ascertained by a jury, unless a jury be waived, as in
other civil cases in a court of record, as shall be prescribed
by law. The taking of private property for a railroad run
by steam or electric power for logging or lumbering purposes shall be deemed a taking for a public use, and any
person, firm, company or corporation taking private property under the law of eminent domain for such purposes
shall thereupon and thereby become a common carrier.
(Amendment approved October 10, 1911.)

[ORIGINAL SECTION.]

Sec. 14. Private property shall not be taken or damaged for
public use without just compensation having been first made to,
or paid into court, for the owner, and no right of way shall be
appropriated to the use of any corporation other than municipal
until full compensation therefor be first made in money or ascertained and paid into court for the owner, irrespective of any
benefit from any improvement proposed by such corporation, which
compensation shall be ascertained by a jury, unless a jury be
waived, as in other civil cases in a court of record, as shall be
prescribed by law.

PRIVATE PROPERTY FOR PUBLIC USE.—A municipal corporation has no power to take a lot to which it has no title, which is in
the actual possession of another, who claims to be the owner, although
he in fact is not, and appropriate it to the use of the public, without
paying compensation. (Gunter v. Geary, 1 Cal. 462.)

The property of a citizen cannot be taken from him for public use,
unless ample means of remuneration are provided. (McCann v. Sierra
County, 7 Cal. 121.)

The only constitutional limitation to the taking of private property
for public use is that compensation shall first be made. (Hercules
Water Co. v. Fernandez, 5 Cal. App. 726, 91 Pac. 401.)

A municipal corporation cannot take private property for public
use, without making compensation in advance or providing a fund out
of which compensation shall be made as soon as the amount to be
paid can be determined. (Colton v. Rossi, 9 Cal. 595.)

The legislature has no power to take the property of one person
and give it to another; nor can it be taken for public use, unless
compensation to the owner precede or accompany the taking. (Gillan
v. Hutchinson, 16 Cal. 153.)

An act directing the governor to take possession of the state prison
in the possession of a lessee, without making any provision for compensation, is void. (McCauley v. Weller, 12 Cal. 500.)

The act of 1863, providing for the widening of streets in San Francisco by agreement with the owners, does not deprive the owners.

of any right or privilege guaranteed by this section. (San Francisco v. Kiernan, 98 Cal. 614, 33 Pac. 720.)

Where property is sold for taxes to the state and the owner does not redeem, there is no constitutional objection to the state acquiring the title free from all equities, which it can sell and convey to the highest bidder for cash and which will be good as against the former owner. (Chapman v. Zobelein, 19 Cal. App. 132, 124 Pac. 1021.)

Property.—The right of a riparian owner cannot be taken away, except for public use on due compensation. (Lux v. Haggin, 69 Cal. 255, 372, 4 Pac. 919, 10 Pac. 674.)

This section does not apply to any mere diminution in value of abutting lands by the closing of a street in whole or in part, nor to any mere inconvenience to abutting owners thereby occasioned, if access to their land is not prevented. (Brown v. Board of Supervisors, 124 Cal. 274, 57 Pac. 82.)

Although the supervisors have authority to close a public street, the owner of adjoining property has an easement therein, of which he cannot be deprived without compensation. (Bigelow v. Ballerino, 111 Cal. 559, 44 Pac. 307.)

The right of the owner of a city lot to the use of the street adjacent thereto is property, and any act by which this right is impaired is to that extent a damage. (Eachus v. Los Angeles etc. Ry. Co., 103 Cal. 614, 42 Am. St. Rep. 149, 37 Pac. 750.)

The right of the owner of land abutting on a city street to access over it to and from his premises is a right of property of which he cannot be deprived without compensation. (Coates v. Atchison etc. Ry. Co., 1 Cal. App. 441, 82 Pac. 640.)

No compensation need be made for the vacation of a public street which has not been dedicated by the owners of the land. (Levee Dist. No. 9 v. Farmer, 101 Cal. 178, 23 L. R. A. 388, 35 Pac. 569.)

Section 17 of article XII of the Constitution, permitting one railroad to cross the tracks of another, is subject to the provision of this section that compensation must first be made. (Boca etc. R. R. Co. v. Sierra Valleys R. R. Co., 2 Cal. App. 546, 84 Pac. 298.)

Property appropriated to public use is private property. (Boca etc. R. R. Co. v. Sierra Valleys R. R. Co., 2 Cal. App. 546, 84 Pac. 298.)

Money is not that species of property which the sovereign authority can authorize to be taken in the exercise of the right of eminent domain. (Burnett v. Sacramento, 12 Cal. 76; Emery v. San Francisco Gas Co., 28 Cal. 345.)

The leasehold interest in convicts leased by the state is as much property as are lands held in fee. (People v. Brooks, 16 Cal. 11.)

A franchise for a street railroad is property capable of being benefited by the widening of the street. (Appeal of North Beach etc. R. R. Co., 32 Cal. 499.)

The legislature may grant the right to construct a railroad upon a public street without providing for compensation for the damage done to the owners of the adjacent property, provided the owners of the property are not the owners usque ad filum viae. (Carson v. Central R. R. Co., 35 Cal. 325.)

A person who owns lots fronting on a street dedicated by himself to the public use is entitled to damages if a railroad company lays its

track along the street, and thereby obstructs it for the use of teams
and vehicles, and if the value of the lot is diminished thereby.
(Southern Pac. R. R. Co. v. Reed, 41 Cal. 256.)

An act providing that a tax collector shall receive the fees allowed
by law, and pay a part of such fees into the treasury for the benefit
of the county, does not take private property for public use. (Ream
v. Siskiyou County, 36 Cal. 620.)

> Delegation of power of eminent domain. See note, 1 Ann. Cas.
> 537.

> Right of de facto corporation to exercise power of eminent do-
> main. See notes, 9 Ann. Cas. 594; Ann. Cas. 1913C, 271.

> Water apart from land as subject to law of eminent domain. See
> note, 13 Ann. Cas. 72.

Public use.—The formation of an irrigation district for the purpose
of reclaiming arid land is a public purpose for which private property may be taken. (Turlock Irr. Dist. v. Williams, 76 Cal. 360, 18
Pac. 379; Central Irr. Dist. v. De Lappe, 79 Cal. 351, 21 Pac. 825; Crall
v. Poso Irr. Dist., 87 Cal. 140, 26 Pac. 797.)

The legislature is the sole judge of the public necessity or advantage of a proposed improvement as a public use. (Gilmer v. Lime
Point, 18 Cal. 229.)

The words "public use" mean a use which concerns the whole community, as distinguished from a particular individual or a particular
number of individuals. But it is not necessary that each and every
individual member of society should have the same degree of interest
in this use, or be personally or directly affected by it, in order to
make it public. (Gilmer v. Lime Point, 18 Cal. 229.)

When the legislature specially designates a particular thing as a
public use, or delegates that function to a local board, the courts will
not interfere with this legislative discretion, but when the legislature
simply designates a general use as public, the courts must determine
whether the particular use is public. (Madera R. Co. v. Raymond
Granite Co., 3 Cal. App. 668, 87 Pac. 27.)

To condemn land within the state for a United States fort or other
military or naval purpose is to condemn land for a public use. (Gilmer v. Lime Point, 18 Cal. 229.)

The only test of the admissibility of the power of the state to condemn land for "public use" is that the particular object for which the
land is condemned tends to promote the general interest, in its relation to any legitimate object of government. (Gilmer v. Lime Point,
18 Cal. 229.)

The "public use" is left in large measure to legislative determination; and the legislative resolve, by which a tax is imposed or private
property taken, is such legislative determination. (Stockton etc. R.
R. Co. v. Common Council of Stockton, 41 Cal. 147; Contra Costa
R. Co. v. Moss, 23 Cal. 323.)

But the legislative determination that a certain business is a public
use is not conclusive of its character. (Consolidated Channel Co. v.
Central Pac. R. R. Co., 51 Cal. 269.)

A railroad for the transportation of passengers and freight is a
public use. (San Francisco etc. R. R. Co. v. Caldwell, 31 Cal. 367;

Contra Costa etc. R. Co. v. Moss, 23 Cal. 323; Stockton etc. R. R. Co. v. Common Council of Stockton, 41 Cal. 147; Napa Valley R. R. Co. v. Board of Suprs., 30 Cal. 435.)

The taking of land by a drainage district for its ditch is a public use. (Laguna Drainage District v. Charles Martin Co., 144 Cal. 209, 77 Pac. 933.)

The formation of an irrigation district under the Wright Act for the purpose of reclaiming arid land is a public purpose for which private property may be taken. (Fallbrook Irr. Dist. v. Bradley, 164 U. S. 112, 41 L. Ed. 369, 17 Sup. Ct. Rep. 56.)

> What is taking property for public use. See notes, 16 Am. St. Rep. 610; 18 L. R. A. 166.
>
> Power of the legislature to determine what is a public use. See note, 88 Am. St. Rep. 926.
>
> Public use, and necessity for taking, whether a legislative or a judicial question. See note, 42 Am. St. Rep. 406.
>
> Uses for which power of eminent domain cannot be taken. See note, 102 Am. St. Rep. 809.
>
> Right to take lands already held for a public use. See notes, 24 Am. Rep. 551; 40 Am. Rep. 748.
>
> What constitutes public use for which property may be taken by eminent domain. See notes, 2 Ann. Cas. 50; 14 Ann. Cas. 903; Ann. Cas. 1912D, 1002.
>
> Irrigation as public use. See notes, 1 Ann. Cas. 304; 1 L. R. A. (N. S.) 208; 22 L. R. A. (N. S.) 162; 33 L. R. A. (N. S.) 807.

Private use.—The legislature cannot take private property for a private use, and it must declare the purpose to be one of public necessity or convenience. (Nickey v. Stearns Ranchos Co., 126 Cal. 150, 58 Pac. 459; Consolidated Channel Co. v. Central Pac. R. R. Co., 51 Cal. 269; Brenham v. Story, 39 Cal. 179; Sherman v. Buick, 32 Cal. 241, 91 Am. Dec. 577.)

Thus an act permitting a person to build a flume on the land of another to carry off the tailings from his mine is void. (Consolidated Channel Co. v. Central Pac. R. R. Co., 51 Cal. 269.)

Also an act giving a right to miners to enter upon private property, where no such right existed anterior to its passage. (Gillan v. Hutchinson, 16 Cal. 153.)

Also an act authorizing an administrator to sell real property belonging to the estate of his decedent, who died before the passage of the act, except in satisfaction of the liens of creditors, for the support of the family, or to pay the expenses of administration. (Brenham v. Story, 39 Cal. 179.)

The legislature has power to open so-called "private roads," from main roads to the residences or farms of individuals. The fact that they are called "private" is immaterial, since all roads are public. (Sherman v. Buick, 32 Cal. 241, 91 Am. Dec. 577; County of Madera v. Raymond Granite Co., 139 Cal. 128, 72 Pac. 915.)

> Right to condemn lands for private ways and roads. See note, 91 Am. Dec. 585.

Condemnation of property for private use. See note, 1 Ann. Cas. 188.

Right of railroad company to condemn land for spur to private establishment. See notes, 7 Ann. Cas. 835; 13 Ann. Cas. 1012; Ann. Cas. 1912D, 234.

Damaged.—The provision of this section against property being damaged for public use is not found in the Constitution of 1849. As to the meaning of the word "damaged" as used in this section, see Reardon v. San Francisco, 66 Cal. 492, 501-506, 56 Am. Rep. 109, 6 Pac. 317.

A mere infringement of the owner's personal pleasure or enjoyment, or merely rendering the property less desirable for certain purposes, or even causing personal annoyance and discomfort, does not constitute a damage within the meaning of this section. (Eachus v. Los Angeles etc. Ry. Co., 103 Cal. 614, 42 Am. St. Rep. 149, 37 Pac. 750.)

Digging and maintaining ditches and drains across private lands is a taking of property. (Nickey v. Stearns Ranchos Co., 126 Cal. 150, 58 Pac. 459.)

Drainage of land as public use within law of eminent domain. See notes, 20 Ann. Cas. 272; 49 L. R. A. 781; 1 L. R. A. (N. S.) 208; 22 L. R. A. (N. S.) 163.

·Where the damage is not the natural, certain and immediate consequences of an improvement, compensation need not be made in advance. (De Baker v. Southern Cal. Ry. Co., 106 Cal. 257, 46 Am. St. Rep. 237, 39 Pac. 610.)

Consequential damages to property from proper exercise of governmental power a taking. See note, 4 Ann. Cas. 1185.

Streets.—A city is liable for damages caused the owner of an abutting lot by excavating the street in front thereof, in pursuance of a contract let by the city for that purpose. (Eachus v. Los Angeles, 130 Cal. 492, 80 Am. St. Rep. 147, 62 Pac. 829; Reardon v. San Francisco, 66 Cal. 492, 56 Am. Rep. 109, 6 Pac. 317.)

The damage for which compensation must first be paid is damage other than such as is sustained in common with other abutters on the street, or the general public, that is a special injury received over and above such common injury. (McCray v. Manning, 22 Cal. App. 25, 133 Pac. 17.)

The fact that the ingress and egress to property will be affected during the time an improvement is being made does not constitute damage that must be compensated. (McCray v. Manning, 22 Cal. App. 25, 133 Pac. 17.)

Damages caused by the raising of a street to the official grade cannot be pleaded as a defense to an action brought to foreclose the lien for improving the street. (Hornung v. McCarthy, 126 Cal. 17, 58 Pac. 303.)

An owner of land abutting upon a street is entitled to compensation for any injury to his property, which he sustains over and above that sustained in common with other abutting owners, resulting from a change in the grade of the street. (Eachus v. Los Angeles Ry. Co.,

103 Cal. 614, 42 Am. St. Rep. 149, 37 Pac. 750; Jennings v. Le Roy, 63 Cal. 397.)

But a city is not responsible for the unauthorized act of its officers in raising the grade of a street and thus damaging adjoining property. (Sievers v. San Francisco, 115 Cal. 648, 56 Am. St. Rep. 153, 47 Pac. 687.)

An owner of property fronting on a public street in a municipality is entitled, in the absence of waiver by him, to recover from the city compensation for the injury done to his property by the grading of the street to a new grade, but no statute or charter provision effecting a waiver by the owner should bar the owner who has not presented his claim in accord with its terms in the absence of clear provision therein that such shall be the effect. (Sala v. City of Pasadena, 162 Cal. 714, 124 Pac. 539.)

To change the channel of a natural watercourse so as to increase the flow of water in another watercourse, to the injury of adjoining lands, is a violation of this section. (Rudel v. Los Angeles, 118 Cal. 281, 50 Pac. 400; Conniff v. San Francisco, 67 Cal. 45, 7 Pac. 41; Tyler v. Tehama Co., 109 Cal. 618, 42 Pac. 240. But see Green v. Swift, 47 Cal. 536; Larrabee v. Cloverdale, 131 Cal. 96, 63 Pac. 143.)

A municipal corporation is liable for damages caused by the construction of sewers, etc., in such a manner that the surface water of a large territory, which did not naturally flow in that direction, is gathered into a body and precipitated upon private property. (Stanford v. San Francisco, 111 Cal. 198, 43 Pac. 605.)

But a municipal corporation is not liable for damages caused by the prevention of the flow of surface water from the lot of a private owner, by reason of the raising of a street to the grade established by law, where such surface water does not run in a natural channel across the lot. (Corcoran v. Benicia, 96 Cal. 1, 31 Am. St. Rep. 171, 30 Pac. 798; Lampe v. San Francisco, 124 Cal. 546, 57 Pac. 461, 1001.)

A statute exempting a municipal corporation from liability for damages for injuries sustained by any person on its graded streets, but making the officers of the city liable therefor, is valid. (Parsons v. San Francisco, 23 Cal. 462.)

A contractor of the city is not liable under this provision for damage to private property caused by a public improvement. (De Baker v. Southern Cal. Ry. Co., 106 Cal. 257, 46 Am. St. Rep. 237, 39 Pac. 610.)

The street opening act (Stats. 1889, p. 70) is not violative of this section. The provisions of the law, so far as they pertain to the assessment of its lands in the district for special benefits, are referable to the sovereign power of taxation. (Clute v. Turner, 157 Cal. 73, 106 Pac. 240.)

Procedure.—Section 1254 of the Code of Civil Procedure, providing that the plaintiff in an action of eminent domain may enter into possession without first making compensation, is in violation of this section. (Steinhart v. Superior Court, 137 Cal. 575, 92 Am. St. Rep. 183, 59 L. R. A. 404, 70 Pac. 629; Beveridge v. Lewis, 137 Cal. 619, 92 Am. St. Rep. 188, 59 L. R. A. 581, 67 Pac. 1040, 70 Pac. 1083. But see Spring Valley Waterworks v. Drinkhouse, 95 Cal. 220, 30 Pac. 218.)

A statute allowing the plaintiff to take possession upon the filing of a bond is void. (Vilhac v. Stockton etc. R. R. Co., 53 Cal. 208; San Mateo Waterworks v. Sharpstein, 50 Cal. 284; Sanborn v. Belden, 51 Cal. 266. But see Fox v. Western Pac. R. R. Co., 31 Cal. 538.)

Section 1254 of the Code of Civil Procedure authorizing the plaintiff in eminent domain to be put into possession upon making a proper deposit in court is constitutional. (Heilbron v. Superior Court, 151 Cal. 271, 90 Pac. 706; Reed Orchard Co. v. Superior Court, 19 Cal. App. 648, 128 Pac. 9, 18.)

This provision contemplates and provides for a proceeding in court in all cases where private property is taken for a public use, and prohibits any other proceeding to that end; and the owner is entitled to a jury trial for the purpose of ascertaining the damages. (Weber v. Board of Suprs. Santa Clara Co., 59 Cal. 265; Trahern v. Board of Suprs. of San Joaquin Co., 59 Cal. 320.)

The means of compensation must be provided before the property is taken. (McCauley v. Weller, 12 Cal. 500.)

If failure be made in paying or providing such compensation, the party may retake possession of the property. (Colton v. Rossi, 9 Cal. 595.)

The state may select its own agents and agencies in exercising the power of eminent domain, and may select foreign corporations or governments. (Gilmer v. Lime Point, 18 Cal. 229.)

The provision for just compensation only requires that a certain and adequate remedy be provided by which the owner can obtain his compensation without unreasonable delay; and a law providing for a jury to determine the value, that the money be paid into the county treasury for the owner, to be paid to him when his ownership is ascertained, is valid. (Gilmer v. Lime Point, 18 Cal. 229.)

An act providing for a proposed alteration of a public road, and requiring persons claiming compensation for land to be taken to present their claims within a certain time, or be deemed as waiving all right to damages, is valid. (Potter v. Ames, 43 Cal. 75.)

It is competent for the legislature to prescribe the several steps to be pursued in the assertion of the right to compensation for land appropriated for public use, but the prescribed procedure must not destroy or substantially impair the right itself. (Potter v. Ames, 43 Cal. 75.)

The fact to be ascertained is the value of the land at the time it is taken, and testimony to prove the annual net profits is not admissible. (Stockton etc. R. Co. v. Galgiana, 49 Cal. 139.)

Compensation.—An ordinance fixing water rates must allow a just and reasonable compensation to the water company for the property used and the services furnished by it. (San Diego Water Co. v. San Diego, 118 Cal. 556, 62 Am. St. Rep. 261, 38 L. R. A. 460, 50 Pac. 633.)

In a condemnation proceeding the land owner is not liable for costs, but is entitled to recover his own costs from the plaintiff. (San Francisco v. Collins, 98 Cal. 259, 33 Pac. 56.)

No rule of court, however general its terms may be for the allowance of costs to a successful appellant, as rule XXIII of the supreme court, may contravene a privilege based upon the constitutional right

of the land owner. (San Joaquin etc. Irr. Co. v. Stevinson, 165 Cal. 540, 132 Pac. 1021.)

Where a railroad company, prior to the commencement of proceedings to condemn a right of way, but with a bona fide intent to commence such proceedings, erects structures thereon, it is not required to pay for the structures so erected in the condemnation proceeding. (Albion River R. R. Co. v. Hesser, 84 Cal. 435, 24 Pac. 288; San Francisco etc. R. R. Co. v. Taylor, 86 Cal. 246, 24 Pac. 1027.)

The provision of section 1249 of the Code of Civil Procedure that, for the purpose of assessing compensation and damages, the right thereto shall be deemed to have accrued at the date of the summons, is not in conflict with this provision. (California Southern R. R. Co. v. Kimball, 61 Cal. 90; Tehama Co. v. Bryan, 68 Cal. 57, 8 Pac. 673; Sacramento Terminal Co. v. McDougall, 19 Cal. App. 562, 126 Pac. 503.

Under the former Constitution, where the land taken is a part only of a tract, the difference between the value of the tract without the improvement and with it is the compensation to be made. (San Francisco etc. R. R. Co. v. Caldwell, 31 Cal. 367.)

Both the injury to the land and the benefit to it should be considered. (San Francisco etc. R. R. Co. v. Caldwell, 31 Cal. 367.)

Section 1249 of the Code of Civil Procedure, fixing the damages at the date of the summons, is constitutional. (Los Angeles v. Gager, 10 Cal. App. 378, 102 Pac. 17.)

The defendant is entitled to receive for a strip of land taken for an alley an amount equal to that for which it could have been sold in the open market, on the day of the summons, for cash, after reasonable time taken by the owner to make the sale. (Santa Ana v. Brunner, 132 Cal. 234, 64 Pac. 287.)

The provision of this section, providing for compensation, "irrespective of any benefit from any improvement proposed," is not limited to the land taken, but also to the land not taken, and the damages to the property not taken must be fixed, irrespective of any benefit which may result from the proposed improvement. (San Bernardino etc. Ry. Co. v. Haven, 94 Cal. 489, 29 Pac. 875.)

The provision of this section, prohibiting any deduction from the damages to land not taken of the amount of benefits accruing from the improvement to such land, only applies to "corporations other than municipal," and does not apply to individuals. (Moran v. Ross, 79 Cal. 549, 21 Pac. 958.)

In a proceeding by a railroad corporation to condemn land for its road, the compensation to be awarded the owner must be ascertained irrespective of any benefit that will accrue to the remainder of his land from the building of the road. (Pacific Coast Ry. Co. v. Porter, 74 Cal. 261, 15 Pac. 774.)

An act requiring commissioners, in assessing the value of lands sought to be taken by a railroad company, to make allowance for any benefit that will accrue to the person whose lands are taken, is valid. (San Francisco etc. R. R. Co. v. Caldwell, 31 Cal. 367.)

The increased cost of irrigation which would be caused by the building of a railroad is a legitimate subject of inquiry for the purpose of ascertaining the damage sustained by the owner. (San Bernardino etc. Ry. Co. v. Haven, 94 Cal. 489, 29 Pac. 875.)

The term "just compensation," used in this section, does not include reasonable disbursements made by the owner of the property for attorneys at the trial. (Pacific Gas etc. Co. v. Chubb, 24 Cal. App. 265, 141 Pac. 36.)

In the case of all public utilities the power of eminent domain has been vested by the legislature in the railroad commission with power to determine the public convenience and make an award for damages without the intervention of a jury. While this is constitutional, the commission must, in the exercise of its powers of eminent domain, make compensation for the taking of the property of a public utility and decree payment thereof in advance of the actual taking. (Pacific Telephone etc. Co. v. Eshleman, 166 Cal. 640, Ann. Cas. 1915C, 822, 50 L. R. A. (N. S.) 652, 137 Pac. 1119.)

An order of the railroad commission requiring a long-distance telephone company to connect physically with the lines of a local competing company and give the latter long-distance service involves the taking of the former's property, and it not having been compensated, the order is void. (Pacific Telephone etc. Co. v. Eshleman, 166 Cal. 640, Ann. Cas. 1915C, 822, 50 L. R. A. (N. S.) 652, 137 Pac. 1119.)

A county is not a municipal corporation within the meaning of this section. (County of San Mateo v. Coburn, 130 Cal. 631, 63 Pac. 78, 621.)

Compensation where lands are taken for right of way of a railroad. See note, 19 Am. St. Rep. 458.

Right to compensation for taking private right of way. See note, 19 Ann. Cas. 681.

Right to compensation for improvements placed upon land by condemnor without authority. See notes, 6 Ann. Cas. 382; 13 Ann. Cas. 980; Ann. Cas. 1912A, 244.

Right of land owner to compensation for improvements placed by him on land after institution of condemnation proceedings. See note, 17 Ann. Cas. 1033.

Price paid by condemnor for other property for use in same enterprise as evidence of value of land condemned. See notes, 20 Ann. Cas. 695; Ann. Cas. 1914A, 375.

Time with reference to which value of property taken by eminent domain is to be estimated. See note, 9 Ann. Cas. 115.

Offer to purchase by third person as evidence of value of property taken in eminent domain. See note, 5 Ann. Cas. 971.

Assessments.—An assessment upon a lot adjacent to a street to pay for improvements made on the street cannot be maintained when the lot has received only an injury by the work on the street; and therefore in no case can the owner be made personally liable for any deficiency after the lot has been exhausted. (Creighton v. Manson, 27 Cal. 613; Taylor v. Palmer, 31 Cal. 240; Gaffney v. Gough, 36 Cal. 104; Coniff v. Hastings, 36 Cal. 292. But see Walsh v. Mathews, 29 Cal. 123.)

Benefits for street improvements accrue to the land and not to the buildings. (Appeal of Piper, 32 Cal. 530.)

The so-called "front-foot" method of assessment for street improvements has been many times upheld in this state. (Chambers v. Satterlee, 40 Cal. 497; Hadley v. Dague, 130 Cal. 207, 62 Pac. 500; Cohen v. Alameda, 124 Cal. 504, 57 Pac. 377; Emery v. San Francisco Gas Co., 28 Cal. 345; Emery v. Bradford, 29 Cal. 75; Taylor v. Palmer, 31 Cal. 240; Whiting v. Quackenbush, 54 Cal. 306; Whiting v. Townsend, 57 Cal. 515; Lent v. Tillson, 72 Cal. 404, 14 Pac. 71; Jennings v. Le Breton, 80 Cal. 8, 21 Pac. 1127; San Francisco Pav. Co. v. Bates, 134 Cal. 39, 66 Pac. 2; Banaz v. Smith, 133 Cal. 102, 65 Pac. 309.)

Considerable doubt was cast upon the correctness of these decisions by the decision of the United States supreme court in Norwood v. Baker, 172 U. S. 269, 43 L. Ed. 443, 19 Sup. Ct. Rep. 187, but the doctrine of these cases has been since sustained by the decision of that court in Tonawanda v. Lyon, 181 U. S. 389, 45 L. Ed. 908, 21 Sup. Ct. Rep. 609.

An assessment for a street improvement upon the front-foot system is an exercise of the power of taxation, and not of eminent domain. (Emery v. San Francisco Gas Co., 28 Cal. 345.)

Benefits may be assessed in the ratio of their value. (Appeal of Piper, 32 Cal. 530.)

An assessment upon an assessment district is valid. (Appeal of Piper, 32 Cal. 530.)

The street bond act, authorizing the imposition of a charge upon property for ten years is not invalid, as taking private property for public use. (German Sav. etc. Soc. v. Ramish, 138 Cal. 120, 69 Pac. 89, 70 Pac. 1067.)

> Deduction of benefits in assessing damages for land taken by eminent domain proceedings. See notes, 13 Ann. Cas. 603; 19 Ann. Cas. 859; Ann. Cas. 1914B, 478.

> Contingent advantage to owner as element of compensation. See note, Ann. Cas. 1914B, 512.

Jury.—The right of trial by jury in cases of eminent domain did not exist prior to the new Constitution. (Koppikus v. State Capitol Commrs., 16 Cal. 248; People v. Blake, 19 Cal. 579.)

A property owner whose property is damaged by a public improvement is entitled to a jury trial for the purpose of ascertaining the damages, and he cannot be deprived of this constitutional guaranty by the decision of a city council that he is not damaged. (Wilcox v. Engebretsen, 160 Cal. 288, 116 Pac. 750.)

This section gives to the defendants in a condemnation suit the absolute right to a jury trial of the issuance of compensation; but the legislature is left free to provide as it may see fit for the method of trial of other issues. (Vallejo etc. R. R. Co. v. Reed Orchard Co., 169 Cal. 545, 147 Pac. 238.)

> Right to trial by jury in eminent domain proceedings. See note, 18 Ann. Cas. 680.

Police power.—The police power will not authorize the state to take private property for public use without compensation, when such property can be condemned and paid for. (People v. Elk River Mill etc. Co., 107 Cal. 221, 48 Am. St. Rep. 125, 40 Pac. 531.)

This provision does not prevent the legislature from prohibiting the conducting of offensive trades within the limits of a city. (Ex parte Shrader, 33 Cal. 279.)

A person having on hand large quantities of wine at the time of its enactment is not deprived of his property without just compensation by a county ordinance which prohibits the sale of liquors within the county. (Ex parte Young, 154 Cal. 317, 22 L. R. A. (N. S.) 330, 97 Pac. 822.)

The restriction of a municipal ordinance which undertakes to absolutely forbid the erection and maintenance of billboards for advertising purposes is, if not a taking pro tanto of the property, a damaging thereof, for which the owner is entitled to compensation. (Varney & Green v. Williams, 155 Cal. 318, 132 Am. St. Rep. 88, 21 L. R. A. (N. S.) 741, 100 Pac. 867.)

Imprisonment in civil cases.

Sec. 15. No person shall be imprisoned for debt in any civil action, on mesne or final process, unless in cases of fraud, nor in civil actions for torts, except in cases of willful injury to person or property; and no person shall be imprisoned for a militia fine in time of peace.

IMPRISONMENT FOR DEBT.—An assault and battery is not a case of fraud within the meaning of this provision. (Ex parte Prader, 6 Cal. 239.)

In a suit to recover money received by a person as agent, such agent cannot be arrested without showing some fraudulent conduct on his part, or a demand on him by the principal and a refusal to pay. (In re Holdforth, 1 Cal. 438.)

The proceedings for the settlement of an estate are not a civil action within the meaning of this section. (Ex parte Smith, 53 Cal. 204.)

Nor is money in the hands of an executor a "debt" within the meaning of this section. (Ex parte Smith, 53 Cal. 204.)

To punish a person by imprisonment for failure to pay a debt to a receiver is in violation of this provision. (Knutte v. Superior Court, 134 Cal. 660, 66 Pac. 875.)

By this provision the right of a creditor to control and confine the person of his debtor by the process of arrest has been abolished, save in the cases of fraud. (In re Crane, 26 Cal. App. 22, 145 Pac. 733.)

The act of 1911 providing for the time of payment of wages is unconstitutional in that it in effect permits an imprisonment on mesne process for debt. (In re Crane, 26 Cal. App. 22, 145 Pac. 733.)

What statutes violate prohibitions against imprisonment for debt. See note, 37 Am. St. Rep. 758.

Provision against imprisonment for debt as applicable to imprisonment for failure to pay alimony. See note, Ann. Cas. 1913E, 1087.

Statute punishing frauds on innkeepers as within constitutional provision against imprisonment for debt. See note, 16 Ann. Cas. 1231.

Laws prohibited—Bills of attainder, ex post facto, etc.

Sec. 16. No bill of attainder, ex post facto law, or law impairing the obligation of contracts, shall ever be passed.

IMPAIRING OBLIGATION OF CONTRACTS—Contract.—A liquor license is not a contract within the meaning of this section, and may be revoked at any time. (Hevren v. Reed, 126 Cal. 219, 58 Pac. 536.)

No person has a vested right to an unenforced penalty; and if such a penalty is reduced to judgment, the judgment will be reversed upon appeal, if, pending the appeal, the statute imposing the penalty is repealed.. (Anderson v. Byrnes, 122 Cal. 272, 54 Pac. 821.)

As to whether or not the charter of a corporation is a contract within the meaning of this provision, see Spring Valley Waterworks v. Board of Suprs. of San Francisco, 61 Cal. 3.

A legislative grant of property to a municipal corporation is an executed contract, and as such within this clause. (Grogan v. San Francisco, 18 Cal. 590.)

The filing of the copy of the order of the supervisors declaring certain territory duly incorporated as a city in the office of the secretary of state, and the resulting incorporation of the city, is the equivalent of the passage of a law within the meaning of the provisions of the state and federal Constitutions forbidding the passage of a law impairing the obligation of a contract. (People v. Banning Co., 166 Cal. 635, 138 Pac. 101.)

The right to practice law is not a contract. (Cohen v. Wright, 22 Cal. 293.)

An act authorizing the contractor to sue for a street assessment is a contract. (Creighton v. Pragg, 21 Cal. 115.)

The remedy, so far as it affects substantial rights, is included in the term "obligation of contracts." (Welsh v. Cross, 146 Cal. 621, 106 Am. St. Rep. 63, 2 Ann. Cas. 796, 81 Pac. 229.)

A law giving a new remedy to determine whether land is suitable for cultivation does not impair the obligation of the contract of purchase. (Boggs v. Ganeard, 148 Cal. 711, 84 Pac. 195.)

Judicial decisions.—The decisions of state courts in regard to general rules of law, although they may affect contract rights, are not subject to the rule laid down by the federal courts that a judicial construction of a statute, so far as contract rights acquired under it are concerned, becomes a part of the statute, and that a change in such construction has the same effect on contracts as a legislative amendment. (Alferitz v. Borgwardt, 126 Cal. 201, 58 Pac. 460.)

The decision holding that a chattel mortgage vests the title in the mortgagee was not a judicial construction of section 1888 of the Civil Code, which was overlooked by the court, and does not fall within the rule of the federal courts that contract rights acquired under a judicial construction of a statute by a state court will be governed thereby, and cannot be affected by a subsequent change in such construction. (Alferitz v. Borgwardt, 126 Cal. 201, 58 Pac. 460.)

Decisions declaring that a conveyance absolute in form, but intended as security, did not pass the legal title, cannot be considered as forming part of a conveyance executed after such decisions and

before they were overruled. (Allen v. Allen, 95 Cal. 184, 16 L. R. A. 446, 30 Pac. 213.)

Impairment of obligation of contracts by judicial decision. See notes, 4 Ann. Cas. 93; 9 Ann. Cas. 1121; 6 R. C. L., § 324, p. 332.

Impairing the obligation.—Impairing the obligation of other things than contracts is not prohibited. (Robinson v. Magee, 9 Cal. 81, 70 Am. Dec. 638.)

A valid contract cannot be abrogated by the adoption of a new Constitution, any more than it can be by the enactment of a law by the legislature. (Ede v. Knight, 93 Cal. 159, 28 Pac. 860.)

An act destroying the legal remedy upon a contract impairs the obligation of the contract. (Bates v. Gregory, 89 Cal. 387, 26 Pac. 891; Robinson v. Magee, 9 Cal. 81, 70 Am. Dec. 638; Creighton v. Pragg, 21 Cal. 115; People v. Hays, 4 Cal. 127.)

The legislature may alter or change the remedy, provided the right is not materially affected; but whenever the remedy is so far altered as to impair, destroy, change, or render the right scarcely worth pursuing, the obligation of the contract upon which the right is founded is impaired. (Smith v. Morse, 2 Cal. 524.)

The Constitution does not inhibit all legislation in respect to contracts, but only forbids the impairing of their obligation. (Thornton v. Hooper, 14 Cal. 9.)

The legislature cannot, after the contract is made, change its terms, or authorize a performance different from that prescribed in the contract. (McGee v. San Jose, 68 Cal. 91, 8 Pac. 641.)

Contracts with state, counties and cities.—A state can no more impair the obligation of a contract made by it with an individual than a contract between two citizens. (Floyd v. Blanding, 54 Cal. 41.)

An act extinguishing the debts of a city is void. (Smith v. Morse, 2 Cal. 524.)

An act ratifying an ordinance of the city and county of San Francisco transferring all of the property of the city to the "Commissioners of the Sinking Fund," and thus placing it beyond the reach of the city's creditors, is void. (Smith v. Morse, 2 Cal. 524.)

When bonds of a city are issued and accepted by the creditors of the city under a statute requiring an annual levy of taxes in payment thereof, the contract is made as solemn and binding and as much beyond subsequent legislation as it would have been if made between private persons. (Meyer v. Brown, 65 Cal. 583, 26 Pac. 281; Bates v. Porter, 74 Cal. 224, 15 Pac. 732.)

Where creditors of a city, under the act of 1851, creating the board of fund commissioners of San Francisco, surrendered the old indebtedness and took a new security, bearing a different rate of interest, the act entered into the contract, and cannot be amended so as to impair or destroy the rights of the parties under the contract. (People v. Woods, 7 Cal. 579; People v. Bond, 10 Cal. 563.)

The act to authorize the funding of the floating debt of San Francisco is a contract, and its obligations cannot be impaired by amendments, but new provisions may be added, provided the rights of credi-

tors are not injuriously affected. (Thornton v. Hooper, 14 Cal. 9; Babcock v. Middleton, 20 Cal. 643.)

As a general rule, a provision, whether made by a state or a corporation, to meet its debts or engagements, may be regarded as only a means of executing its own policy or transacting its own business, and may be altered or repealed at pleasure. (San Francisco v. Beideman, 17 Cal. 443.)

An act providing for the payment of the debts of a county by refunding is not void, as the creditor had no remedy against the county which could be impaired. (Hunsaker v. Borden, 5 Cal. 288, 63 Am. Dec. 130.)

The legislature cannot divest the right of a party to have a county warrant paid when that right is complete, vested and determined. (Laforge v. Magee, 6 Cal. 650.)

A statute requiring all persons holding certain county warrants to present them for registry before a certain date or be forever barred from enforcing the payment thereof adds a new condition to the contract, and therefore impairs its obligation. (Robinson v. Magee, 9 Cal. 81, 70 Am. Dec. 638.)

This provision relates solely to contracts between individuals and not to contracts between individuals and the state, because the state cannot be sued. (Myers v. English, 9 Cal. 341. But see 23 Am. & Eng. Ency. of Law, 1st ed., 79.)

The provisions of the act for the organization of irrigation districts as to the extent of the liability of the land created a contract between the land owners and the state, which could not be impaired by future legislation. (Merchants' Nat. Bank v. Escondido Irr. Dist., 144 Cal. 329, 77 Pac. 937.)

An act authorizing a county to fund its outstanding warrants, which were not to draw interest, and to make the bonds given in exchange therefor bear interest, is not unconstitutional. (Chapman v. Morris, 28 Cal. 393.)

A law for the funding of the debts of a county is valid, for the county cannot be sued except by consent of the state, and that consent can be granted upon any terms the state sees fit to impose. (Sharp v. Contra Costa Co., 34 Cal. 284.)

But while the state and its legal subdivisions cannot be compelled to perform their contracts, the state cannot annul them. Therefore, an act creating funding commissioners and providing that no claim against the county shall be valid unless presented to and allowed by the commissioners is void. (Rose v. Estudillo, 39 Cal. 270.)

The legislature cannot require the creditors of a county to surrender their evidences of indebtedness, and accept new ones in different terms, but it may refuse to provide funds to pay any portion of the old indebtedness, unless the creditor will accept such new indebtedness. (People v. Morse, 43 Cal. 534.)

A municipality has no power to contract away the right of the state to supervise and regulate a public utility, unless the state has expressly given it this right, and the state, acting through the Railroad Commission, may constitutionally regulate a public utility, even though a contract as to rates and service is in force between the

utility and a municipality. (Ukiah v. The Snow Mountain Water & Power Co., 4 C. R. C. 293, 309.)

Retrospective statutes.—It is to be presumed that no statute is to operate retrospectively, unless the contrary clearly appears. (Pignaz v. Burnett, 119 Cal. 157, 51 Pac. 48.)

A retrospective statute is void only when it deprives a person of some vested right, secured either by some constitutional guaranty, or protected by the principles of natural justice. (Galland v. Lewis, 26 Cal. 46.)

A law making certain transfers presumptively fraudulent cannot be given a retrospective effect. (Cook v. Cockins, 117 Cal. 140, 48 Pac. 1025.)

Remedial statutes.—Remedial statutes, which are retrospective, but do not impair contracts or disturb absolute vested rights, and only go to confirm rights already existing, are valid. (Dentzel v. Waldie, 30 Cal. 138.)

The legislature may legalize defective and invalid assessments of taxes. (People v. Holladay, 25 Cal. 300.)

Particular statutes.—Where, upon the death of the ancestor, the heirs become at once vested with the full title to his real estate, subject only to certain liens or burdens, the legislature cannot, by a subsequent enactment, interfere with such vested right by authorizing a sale of the property by an executor or administrator solely for the benefit of the heirs. (Estate of Packer, 125 Cal. 396, 73 Am. St. Rep. 58, 58 Pac. 59.)

A law reducing the percentage payable upon redemption, passed after the sale, is void. (Thresher v. Atchison, 117 Cal. 73, 59 Am. St. Rep. 159, 48 Pac. 1020.)

A law imposing more onerous conditions upon the right to redeem from a tax sale than those which existed when the sale was made is void. (Teralta Land etc. Co. v. Shaffer, 116 Cal. 518, 58 Am. St. Rep. 194, 48 Pac. 613.)

The legislature may reduce the time within which a deed must be made by a tax collector, provided a reasonable time is allowed in which to obtain the deed. (Tuttle v. Block, 104 Cal. 443, 38 Pac. 109.)

To extend the time for redemption is to alter the substance of the contract. (Rollins v. Wright, 93 Cal. 395, 29 Pac. 58; Barnitz v. Beverly, 163 U. S. 118, 41 L. Ed. 93, 16 Sup. Ct. Rep. 1042; Haynes v. Tredway, 133 Cal. 400, 65 Pac. 892; Malone v. Roy, 134 Cal. 344, 66 Pac. 313.)

A statute passed after the making of a contract, giving a right of redemption from an execution sale, is unconstitutional. (People v. Hays, 4 Cal. 127.)

A law extending the time of redemption passed after judgment, but before levy or sale, cannot apply to a redemption from such sale. (Welsh v. Cross, 146 Cal. 621, 106 Am. St. Rep. 63, 2 Ann. Cas. 796, 81 Pac. 229, overruling Tuolumne Redemption Co. v. Sedgwick, 15 Cal. 515.)

A state cannot enact an insolvent law discharging the obligations of contracts made out of the state. (Lowenberg v. Levine, 93 Cal. 215, 16 L. R. A. 159, 28 Pac. 941.)

A law which shortens the time within which to file a notice of a mechanic's lien may constitutionally be made to apply to pending cases of uncompleted buildings; provided, an adequate and availing remedy be left to enforce the lien. (Kerckhoff-Cuzner Mill etc. Co. v. Olmstead, 85 Cal. 80, 24 Pac. 648.)

A law providing for the discharge of a debt contracted before its adoption is valid. (Porter v. Imus, 79 Cal. 183, 21 Pac. 729. But see 16 Am. & Eng. Ency. of Law, 2d ed., 640.)

The construction of section 4, article XIII, of the Constitution, so that it makes the mortgagee of a mortgage executed prior to the adoption of the Constitution primarily liable for the taxes, where the mortgage makes no provision on the subject, does not impair the obligation of the contract. (Hay v. Hill, 65 Cal. 383, 4 Pac. 378; McCoppin v. McCartney, 60 Cal. 367.)

To give section 5, article XIII, of the Constitution a retrospective operation, would be impairing the obligation of contracts. (Beekman v. Skaggs, 59 Cal. 541.)

The act, commonly known as the Water Lot Act, providing for the disposition of submerged lands and fixing a line which is to "remain a permanent waterfront," does not amount to a contract with the grantees of the land that the waterfront so fixed shall not be extended or otherwise changed. (Floyd v. Blanding, 54 Cal. 41.)

An act exempting property from execution after a debt is contracted is void. (Smith v. Morse, 2 Cal. 524.)

A law changing the time within which an action must be brought does not impair any vested right, for it only affects the remedy, and not the right. (Billings v. Hall, 7 Cal. 1.)

An act requiring a person to pay for improvements put upon his land by a trespasser against his will does not impair the obligation of any contract, as the individuals forming a government are not contractors with such government, within the meaning of this section. (Billings v. Hall, 7 Cal. 1.)

An act making void prior deeds, unless recorded in accordance therewith, does not impair vested rights. (Stafford v. Lick, 7 Cal. 479.)

After having made an appropriation in view of a contemplated contract to be based thereon, and such contract is made, and funds to meet the appropriation are received into the treasury, the legislature cannot deprive the party with whom the contract is made of such funds by repealing the appropriation. (People v. Brooks, 16 Cal. 11.)

An act making the assessment prima facie proof of the tax, and prohibiting the defendant from setting up any informality in the levy or assessment of the tax is valid, since it goes merely to the remedy. (People v. Seymour, 16 Cal. 332, 76 Am. Dec. 521.)

An act requiring litigants to take the oath of allegiance is valid. (Cohen v. Wright, 22 Cal. 293.)

The "Specific Contract Act" is not in violation of this section. (Galland v. Lewis, 26 Cal. 46; Otis v. Haseltine, 27 Cal. 80.)

An act validating powers of attorney theretofore made by married women for the sale of their separate property, and conveyances made by attorneys in fact thereunder, is valid. (Dentzel v. Waldie, 30 Cal. 138.)

The legislature may impose on debtors the obligation to pay interest after the passage of the act on debts already due. (Dunne v. Mastick, 50 Cal. 244.)

An ordinance providing that no liquor license shall be granted to any person who has conducted the business of selling liquors in any place where females are employed is valid. (Foster v. Board of Police Commrs., 102 Cal. 483, 41 Am. St. Rep. 194, 37 Pac. 763.)

The amendment of March 1, 1905, to section 3897 of the Political Code, dealing with the sale of property purchased by the state, is not open to constitutional objection, either on account of retroactive character or as impairing rights. (Buck v. Canty, 162 Cal. 226, 121 Pac. 924.)

The statute of June 3, 1906, extending the time of performance of certain acts to a time beyond the period of time fixed therefor, cannot have the effect of extending the period of redemption after judgment and execution sale. (Summers v. Hammell, 17 Cal. App. 493, 120 Pac. 63.)

The provision of section 11 of the act of 1909 that proceedings for a street improvement pending at the time of the passage of that act shall be continued under the provisions of that act is not unconstitutional because of the limitation of the right of abandonment under that act. (Title Insurance & Trust Co. v. Lusk, 15 Cal. App. 358, 115 Pac. 53.)

When statutes deemed to impair contracts. See note, 79 Am. Dec. 495.

Statutes making pre-existing contracts illegal. See note, 120 Am. St. Rep. 468.

Impairing obligation of contracts by franchise tax. See note, 131 Am. St. Rep. 878.

Impairing obligation of contracts by altering or repealing corporate charter. See note, 62 Am. St. Rep. 165.

Prohibiting revival of judgment as impairment of obligation of contracts. See note, 3 Ann. Cas. 1148.

Municipal ordinance as within purview of clause in federal Constitution against impairment of obligation of contracts. See note, 12 Ann. Cas. 503.

Impairment of ordinance granting privilege as impairment of contract obligation. See note, 3 Ann. Cas. 88.

Impairment of obligation. See 6 R. C. L., §§ 312–363, pp. 323–369.

Statute extending exemption from execution as impairing obligation of contract. See note, Ann. Cas. 1912B, 259.

EX POST FACTO LAWS.—A law changing the forms of procedure by which persons accused of crime are to be tried for offenses committed before the law was passed is not an ex post facto law. (People v. Mortimer, 46 Cal. 114.)

A crime committed before the adoption of the Constitution of 1879 may, after such adoption, be prosecuted by information. (People v. Campbell, 59 Cal. 243, 43 Am. Rep. 257.)

The section of the Penal Code which provides that one who has been convicted of petit larceny, who shall again commit the same offense, is to be deemed guilty of a felony, is not ex post facto, when applied to one who committed the first offense prior to the taking effect of the provision. (Ex parte Gutierrez, 45 Cal. 429.)

Where, after the commission of a crime, the crime is reduced by statute from a felony to a misdemeanor, such statute works a repeal of the former law, and such crime cannot be punished under either law. (People v. Tisdale, 57 Cal. 104.)

> What are ex post facto laws and when valid. See note, 37 Am. St. Rep. 582.
>
> Laws changing punishment as ex post facto. See note, 3 Ann. Cas. 77.
>
> Constitutional provision against ex post facto laws as applicable to judicial decisions. See note, Ann. Cas. 1914C, 228.
>
> Ex post facto and retrospective laws. See 6 R. C. L., §§ 276–291, pp. 290–305.

BILLS OF ATTAINDER.—A resolution expelling a member of the legislature is not a bill of attainder. (French v. Senate, 146 Cal. 604, 2 Ann. Cas. 756, 69 L. R. A. 556, 80 Pac. 1031.)

Rights of foreign residents.

Sec. 17. Foreigners of the white race, or of African descent, eligible to become citizens of the United States under the naturalization laws thereof, while bona fide residents of this state, shall have the same rights in respect to the acquisition, possession, enjoyment, transmission, and inheritance of all property, other than real estate, as native-born citizens; provided, that such aliens owning real estate at the time of the adoption of this amendment may remain such owners; and provided further, that the legislature may, by statute, provide for the disposition of real estate which shall hereafter be acquired by such aliens by descent or devise. (Amendment adopted November 6, 1894.)

[ORIGINAL SECTION.]

Sec. 17. Foreigners of the white race or of African descent, eligible to become citizens of the United States under the naturalization laws thereof, while bona fide residents of this state, shall have the same rights in respect to the acquisition, possession, enjoyment, transmission, and inheritance of property as native-born citizens.

ALIENS.—An alien is not eligible to an office in this state. (Walther v. Rabolt, 30 Cal. 185.)

By the common law, aliens could not acquire property by descent or other operation of law; and this section only removes this dis-

ability from those who are bona fide residents within the state. (Norris v. Hoyt, 18 Cal. 217.)

A nonresident alien may take and hold property acquired by purchase until office found. (Norris v. Hoyt, 18 Cal. 217.)

An act permitting nonresident aliens to inherit real and personal estate is valid. (State v. Rogers, 13 Cal. 159; Billings v. Hauver, 65 Cal. 593, 4 Pac. 639; Lyons v. State, 67 Cal. 380, 7 Pac. 763.)

This provision by implication excludes nonresident aliens from the rights mentioned in this section. (Siemssen v. Bofer, 6 Cal. 250.)

This section prohibits the legislature from depriving resident foreigners of any of the rights enjoyed by native-born citizens with respect to the acquisition, possession, enjoyment, transmission, or inheritance of property. (State v. Smith, 70 Cal. 153, 12 Pac. 121.)

A provision in the specifications for public street work that no unnaturalized alien should be employed in the work, except with the permission of the highway commission, is invalid. (City Street Imp. Co. v. Kroh, 158 Cal. 308, 110 Pac. 933.)

This section and section 671 of the Civil Code, allowing aliens to take, hold and dispose of property in this state, are not in conflict with article I, section 10 of the United States Constitution, declaring that "no state shall enter into any treaty, alliance or confederation." (Blythe v. Hinckley, 180 U. S. 333, 45 L. Ed. 557, 21 Sup. Ct. Rep. 390.)

> Power of aliens to hold lands. See note, 14 Am. Dec. 97.
>
> Rights of aliens to receive or transmit inheritance. See note, 12 Am. St. Rep. 93.
>
> Right of alien to act as executor or administrator. See notes 3 Ann. Cas. 988; Ann. Cas. 1912A, 747.
>
> Estoppel of grantor in deed to deny title of alien grantee on ground that latter cannot hold property. See note, 13 Ann. Cas. 532.
>
> Right of alien with respect to inheritance of real property as affected by treaty with foreign country. See note, Ann. Cas. 1912A, 1100.

Slavery prohibited.

Sec. 18. Neither slavery nor involuntary servitude, unless for the punishment of crime, shall ever be tolerated in this state.

SLAVERY.—Performance of work upon an assessment for repair of roads is not such involuntary servitude as is contemplated by this provision. (In re Dassler, 35 Kan. 678, 12 Pac. 130.)

On this subject, generally, see In re Turner, 1 Abb. U. S. 84, Fed. Cas. No. 14,247; Clark's Case, 1 Blackf. (Ind.) 122, 12 Am. Dec. 213; In re Sah Quah, 31 Fed. 327; U. S. Const., art. XIII.

Searches and seizures, restriction on.

Sec. 19. The right of the people to be secure in their persons, houses, papers, and effects, against unreasonable

seizures and searches, shall not be violated; and no warrant shall issue, but on probable cause, supported by oath or affirmation, particularly describing the place to be searched and the persons and things to be seized.

SEARCH-WARRANTS.—The legislature has power to authorize the issuance of a warrant to search the person of an individual in a proper case. (Collins v. Lean, 68 Cal. 284, 9 Pac. 173.)

Sections 1458 to 1461 of the Code of Civil Procedure do not violate this section. (Levy v. Superior Court, 105 Cal. 600, 29 L. R. A. 811, 38 Pac. 965.)

Under this section no person can be forced to surrender his private books and papers to another who does not own or have any interest in them, except upon convincing proof that they contain evidence which materially affects the rights in litigation of the person demanding them. (Kullman, Salz & Co. v. Superior Court, 15 Cal. App. 276, 114 Pac. 589; Funkenstein v. Superior Court, 23 Cal. App. 663, 139 Pac. 101.)

> History and purpose of search-warrants. See note, 40 Am. Dec. 666.
>
> Searches and seizures, what deemed unreasonable. See note, 32 Am. St. Rep. 643.
>
> Search of premises of private persons. See note, 101 Am. St. Rep. 328.
>
> Sufficiency of description of premises in search-warrant or affidavit therefor. See note, 17 Ann. Cas. 232.
>
> Validity of statutes authorizing seizure and destruction of gambling apparatus. See notes, 2 Ann. Cas. 936; 13 Ann. Cas. 454.

Treason defined.

Sec. 20. Treason against the state shall consist only in levying war against it, adhering to its enemies, or giving them aid and comfort. No person shall be convicted of treason unless on the evidence of two witnesses to the same overt act, or confession in open court.

TREASON.—The constitutional definition of treason in the United States Constitution cannot be restricted or extended by Congress. (United States v. Greathouse, 4 Sawy. 457, 2 Abb. U. S. 364, Fed. Cas. No. 15,254; United States v. Hanway, 2 Wall. Jr. 139, Fed. Cas. No. 15,299.)

As to treason against a state, see People v. Lynch, 11 Johns. (N. Y.) 549; Charge to Grand Jury, 1 Story, 614, Fed. Cas. No. 18,275.

The constitutional requirement of two witnesses, etc., does not apply to the preliminary examination by magistrate or grand jury. (United States v. Hanway, 2 Wall. Jr. 139, Fed. Cas. No. 15,299.)

Privileges and immunities of citizens.

Sec. 21. No special privileges or immunities shall ever be granted which may not be altered, revoked, or repealed by the legislature; nor shall any citizen, or class of citizens, be granted privileges or immunities which, upon the same terms, shall not be granted to all citizens.

EXCLUSIVE PRIVILEGES.—Under the former Constitution, it was held that exclusive privileges and franchises might be conferred by the legislature upon persons or corporations. (California State Tel. Co. v. Alta Tel. Co., 22 Cal. 398.) But this decision was overruled in San Francisco v. Spring Valley Waterworks, 48 Cal. 493, 517.

The legislature may deny to one man a privilege extended to another. The Constitution is violated only when a privilege extended to one is denied to another on substantially the same facts; and whether the facts of a particular case constitute a proper exception to the general law is for the legislature to determine. (People v. Twelfth District Court, 17 Cal. 547.)

The provision of the state dental law exempting from its operation persons practicing before its passage is not violative of this provision. (Ex parte Whitley, 144 Cal. 167, 1 Ann. Cas. 13, 77 Pac. 879.)

An ordinance prohibiting public laundries in designated parts of a city is not in violation of this section. (In re Hang Kie, 69 Cal. 149, 10 Pac. 327.)

An ordinance levying a license tax upon all sheep which are pastured in the county, except sheep listed as taxable property in the county, and upon which taxes are paid, is in violation of this section. (Lassen Co. v. Cone, 72 Cal. 387, 14 Pac. 100.)

But an ordinance requiring all persons engaged in the business of raising, grazing, herding, or pasturing sheep in the county to pay an annual license of fifty dollars for every thousand sheep is not in violation of this provision. (Ex parte Mirande, 73 Cal. 365, 14 Pac. 888.)

A law providing a special method of assessment and collection of taxes against railroads situated in more than one county is not in violation of this section. (People v. Central Pac. R. R. Co., 105 Cal. 576, 38 Pac. 905; overruling People v. Central Pac. R. R. Co., 83 Cal. 393, 23 Pac. 303, and affirmed in Central Pac. R. R. Co. v. People, 162 U. S. 91, 40 L. Ed. 903, 16 Sup. Ct. Rep. 776.)

An act making it a misdemeanor to keep open a barber-shop on Sundays or other holidays is in violation of this section. (Ex parte Jentzsch, 112 Cal. 468, 32 L. R. A. 664, 44 Pac. 803.)

The Primary Election Law of 1899, which prohibits the election of delegates to a convention of any political party not representing three per cent of the votes cast at the previous election, is void. (Britton v. Board of Election Commrs., 129 Cal. 337, 51 L. R. A. 115, 61 Pac. 1115. Per Henshaw, J., Van Dyke, J., and McFarland, J.)

The provision of the County Government Act that no supplies, etc., shall be purchased for the county from any person who has not had a business in the county for a year prior to the purchase is in viola-

tion of this section. (Van Harlingen v. Doyle, 134 Cal. 53, 54 L. R. A. 771, 66 Pac. 44.)

The act regulating the practice of medicine and surgery does not violate this section. (Ex parte Gerino, 143 Cal. 412, 66 L. R. A. 249, 77 Pac. 166.)

An act applying uniformly to all cities of a particular class is not in violation of this section. (Ex parte Jackson, 143 Cal. 564, 77 Pac. 457.)

The provision of section 1197 of the Political Code, forbidding the name of a nominee to be placed upon the ballot more than once, is in violation of this section. (Murphy v. Curry, 137 Cal. 479, 59 L. R. A. 97, 70 Pac. 461.)

A law regulating the rate of interest on chattel mortgages on certain classes of property is in violation of this provision. (Ex parte Sohncke, 148 Cal. 262, 113 Am. St. Rep. 236, 7 Ann. Cas. 475, 2 L. R. A. (N. S.) 813, 82 Pac. 956.)

The act in regard to the practice of architecture is not unconstitutional because it discriminates between certified architects and uncertified architects. (Ex parte McManus, 151 Cal. 331, 90 Pac. 702.)

An ordinance prohibiting the wholesale liquor business within a designated area in a municipality is not unreasonably or unjustly discriminatory, merely because saloons and restaurants where liquor is sold are permitted within such prohibited zone. (Grumbach v. Lelande, 154 Cal. 679, 98 Pac. 1059.)

An act regulating the hours of employment in underground mines and in smelting and reduction works does not violate this section. (In re Martin, 157 Cal. 51, 26 L. R. A. (N. S.) 242, 106 Pac. 235.)

A law prohibiting waste of water from artesian wells is not unconstitutional because not made applicable to surface water and pumps. (Ex parte Elam, 6 Cal. App. 233, 91 Pac. 811.)

The right or privilege granted by the act of 1907, providing for the change of the boundary line between Fresno and Kings county, to electors who have resided for ninety days preceding the election in the territory to be transferred to Kings county, which is not granted to other electors of that territory or to other electors of Fresno county, is not such a privilege as is forbidden by this section of the Constitution. (Wheeler v. Herbert, 152 Cal. 224, 92 Pac. 353.)

Under this section the amendment of November 23, 1907, to section 135 of the Code of Civil Procedure providing for the transaction of judicial business, except in certain cases, on special holidays, is unconstitutional in that it creates a class of litigants, without any rational or constitutional distinction to justify the classification. (Diepenbrock v. Superior Court, 153 Cal. 597, 95 Pac. 1121.)

The Insanity Act of 1897, providing for the recovery from the estates of insane persons the cost of their care and maintenance, is valid. (Napa State Hospital v. Dasso, 153 Cal. 698, 15 Ann. Cas. 910, 18 L. R. A. (N. S.) 643, 96 Pac. 355.)

An act providing for the payment by the state, county or city of the premium on official bonds of all state, county or city officers (except notaries public) when given by surety companies is not in violation of this section. (County of San Luis Obispo v. Murphy, 162 Cal. 588, Ann. Cas. 1913D, 712, 123 Pac. 808.)

An act forbidding the employment of women for more than eight hours a day in certain places is not in violation of this section. (Matter of Application of Miller, 162 Cal. 687, 124 Pac. 427; affirmed in Miller v. Wilson, 236 U. S. 373, 59 L. Ed. 628, 35 Sup. Ct. Rep. 342.)

The Employers' Liability Act, giving a right of action for damages to the widow, children, dependent parents, and dependent brothers and sisters of an employee killed by a fellow-servant's negligence, and not granting such a right to the husband, nephews and nieces or other collateral heirs of the person so killed, is not in violation of this section. (Pritchard v. Whitney Estate Co., 164 Cal. 564, 129 Pac. 989.)

The amendment of 1907 to section 1970 of the Civil Code extending the liability of an employer, for an injury resulting from the wrongful act or negligence of a coemployee engaged in another department of labor from that of the employee injured, or employed upon a machine, railroad train, switch-signal point, locomotive engine, or other appliance than that upon which the employee injured is employed is not in violation of this section. (Patton v. Los Angeles Pacific Co., 18 Cal. App. 522, 123 Pac. 613.)

The Tenement House Act regulating the construction of buildings intended for human habitation and providing that such buildings shall not be occupied until the issuance of certain certificates by the health and building departments is not in violation of this section. (Matter of Stoltenberg, 21 Cal. App. 722, 132 Pac. 841.)

The act of 1909 regulating loan brokers and limiting rates of interest does not violate this section. (Eaker v. Bryant, 24 Cal. App. 87, 140 Pac. 310.)

The provision of section 2289 of the Political Code that no child whose parents have not resided in this state for at least three years prior to the application for aid or whose parents have not become citizens of this state shall be deemed a minor orphan, half-orphan or abandoned child. (Sacramento O. etc. Home v. Chambers, 25 Cal. App. 536, 144 Pac. 317.)

> Constitutionality of statutes granting exclusive rights or privileges. See note, 1 Ann. Cas. 847.
>
> Special privileges. See 6 R. C. L., §§ 400–404, pp. 405–408.

Provisions of Constitution construed.

Sec. 22. The provisions of this Constitution are mandatory and prohibitory, unless by express words they are declared to be otherwise.

MANDATORY AND PROHIBITORY.—As to the meaning of this provision, see Matter of Maguire, 57 Cal. 604, 40 Am. Rep. 125.

Notwithstanding this section, where a provision of the Constitution is expressly made permissive, as by the use of the word "may," it will not be deemed mandatory. (Fresno Nat. Bank v. Superior Court, 83 Cal. 491, 24 Pac. 157.)

Section 5, article XI, of the Constitution, is mandatory. (Knight v. Martin, 128 Cal. 245, 60 Pac. 849; Dwyer v. Parker, 115 Cal. 544, 47 Pac. 372.)

Section 19, article XI, of the Constitution, is mandatory. (McDonald v. Patterson, 54 Cal. 245; Pereria v. Wallace, 129 Cal. 397, 62 Pac. 61.)

Under this provision it is held that the provision of section 11, article XII, requiring sixty days' notice of a meeting of stockholders to increase capital stock, is mandatory. (Navajo Mining etc. Co. v. Curry, 147 Cal. 581, 109 Am. St. Rep. 176, 82 Pac. 247.)

The Constitution provides simply a limitation upon the power of the legislature, which, otherwise, is supreme. (People v. Nye, 9 Cal. App. 148, 98 Pac. 241.)

The provision of section 1 of article XVII does not restrict the power of the legislature to give homesteads to the heads of families only. (Hohn v. Pauly, 11 Cal. App. 724, 106 Pac. 266.)

Where the Constitution makes no provision as to what shall constitute a vacancy in an office, the legislature may specify what constitutes a vacancy and provide for filling the same. (People v. Nye, 9 Cal. App. 148, 98 Pac. 241.)

The provisions of the Constitution which are mandatory and prohibitory are binding upon every department of the state government, legislative, executive, and judicial. (People v. California Fish Co., 166 Cal. 576, 138 Pac. 79.)

The declarations of this Constitution are all mandatory and prohibitory unless the contrary is expressly declared. (Cake v. City of Los Angeles, 164 Cal. 705, 130 Pac. 723.)

This section refers to the effect, not to the meaning, of the constitutional provisions, and declares that they are imperative and paramount, according to their true meaning, ascertained by the rules of construction otherwise applicable thereto. (Clark v. Los Angeles, 160 Cal. 30, 116 Pac. 722.)

Rights retained by the people.

Sec. 23. This enumeration of rights shall not be construed to impair or deny others retained by the people.

IMPLIED RIGHTS.—The Primary Election Law of 1899, which allows members of one political party to vote for delegates to the party convention of another party, is void. (Britton v. Board of Election Commrs., 129 Cal. 337, 51 L. R. A. 115, 61 Pac. 1115.)

Property qualification not required.

Sec. 24. No property qualification shall ever be required for any person to vote or hold office.

PROPERTY QUALIFICATION.—This section does not apply to a voter in a reclamation district. (People v. Reclamation Dist. No. 551, 117 Cal. 114, 48 Pac. 1016.)

The provision of the act creating the Sacramento Drainage District restricting the right to vote for drainage commissioners to the owners of real property within the district does no violence to the constitutional inhibition against requiring a property qualification for

voters. (People v. Sacramento Drainage District, 155 Cal. 373, 103 Pac. 207.)

The provisions of the Primary Election Law of 1909 requiring the payment of fees by candidates on filing their nomination papers is not the exaction of a property qualification to vote or hold office. The exaction of such fees is a valid exercise of the power of the legislature, under section 2½ of article II, to provide reasonable conditions for the exercise of the rights granted by the act. (Socialist Party v. Uhl, 155 Cal. 776, 103 Pac. 181.)

This section does not apply to the act relating to permanent road divisions, which restricts the right to sign the petition for the formation of a permanent road district to land owners residing within the district. (Potter v. Santa Barbara County, 160 Cal. 349, 116 Pac. 1101.)

Right to fish upon public lands.

Sec. 25. The people shall have the right to fish upon and from the public lands of the state and in the waters thereof, excepting upon lands set aside for fish hatcheries, and no land owned by the state shall ever be sold or transferred without reserving in the people the absolute right to fish thereupon; and no law shall ever be passed making it a crime for the people to enter upon the public lands within this state for the purpose of fishing in any water containing fish that have been planted therein by the state; provided, that the legislature may by statute, provide for the season when and the conditions under which the different species of fish may be taken. (New section added by amendment adopted November 8, 1910.)

RIGHT TO FISH.—The act of the legislature imposing a license tax of ten dollars a year for the privilege of fishing for profit in the waters of the state is valid, and does not violate this section. (Matter of Application of Parra, 24 Cal. App. 339, 141 Pac. 393.)

The principal object of this section is to reserve to the people the right to fish upon the public lands of the state and to require that grants of land by the state should not be made "without reserving to the people the absolute right to fish thereupon." (Matter of Application of Parra, 24 Cal. App. 339, 141 Pac. 393.)

Power of states to regulate taking of fish in tide waters. See note, 23 Am. St. Rep. 837.

Right of fishery. See note, 131 Am. St. Rep. 751.

Power of state to grant to private individual exclusive right to shell-fish within waters of state. See note, 16 Ann. Cas. 198.

Intoxicating liquor amendment.

Sec. 26a. Should an amendment to the Constitution of the state of California by adding to article I two new sections to be numbered respectively section 26 and section 27, as proposed by initiative petition filed with and certified to the secretary of state, and relating to intoxicating liquors, be enacted at the general election held on Nov. 3, 1914, then the force and effect of said section 26 shall be suspended until Feb. 15, 1915, at which time it shall have full force and effect except that, as to the manufacture and transportation of intoxicating liquors for delivery at points outside of the state of California only, the force and effect thereof shall be suspended until Jan. 1, 1916, at which time such manufacture and transportation also shall wholly cease and on and after said date said section 26 shall in all respects have full force and effect. (Amendment adopted November 3, 1914.)

NOTE.—The proposed amendment referred to in this amendment was not adopted, so that this section never became operative, although adopted.

ARTICLE II.

RIGHT OF SUFFRAGE.

Who are and who are not electors.

Section 1. Every native citizen of the United States, every person who shall have acquired the rights of citizenship under or by virtue of the treaty of Queretaro, and every naturalized citizen thereof, who shall have become such ninety days prior to any election, of the age of twenty-one years, who shall have been resident of the state one year next preceding the election, and of the county in which he or she claims his or her vote ninety days, and in the election precinct thirty days, shall be entitled to vote at all elections which are now or may hereafter be authorized by law; provided, no native of China, no idiot, no insane person, no person convicted of any infamous crime, no person hereafter convicted of the embezzlement or misappropriation of public money, and no person who shall not be able to read the Constitution in the English language and write his or her name, shall ever exercise the privileges of an elector in this state; provided, that the provisions of this amendment relative to an educational qualification shall not apply to any person prevented by a physical disability from complying with its requisitions, nor to any person who now has the right to vote, nor to any person who shall be sixty years of age and upwards at the time this amendment shall take effect. (Amendment approved October 10, 1911.)

[AMENDMENT OF 1894.]

Section 1. Every native male citizen of the United States, every male person who shall have acquired the right of citizenship under or by virtue of the treaty of Queretaro, and every male naturalized citizen thereof, who shall have become such ninety days prior to any election, of the age of twenty-one years, who shall have been resident of the state one year next preceding the elec-

tion, and of the county in which he claims his vote ninety days, and in the election precinct thirty days, shall be entitled to vote at all elections which are now or may hereafter be authorized by law; provided, no native of China, no idiot, no insane person, no person convicted of any infamous crime, no person hereafter convicted of the embezzlement or misappropriation of public money, and no person who shall not be able to read the Constitution in the English language and write his name, shall ever exercise the privileges of an elector in this state; provided, that the provisions of this amendment relative to an educational qualification shall not apply to any person prevented by a physical disability from complying with its requisitions, nor to any person who has the right to vote, nor to any person who shall be sixty years of age and upwards at the time this amendment shall take effect. (Amendment adopted November 6, 1894.)

[ORIGINAL SECTION.]

Section 1. Every native male citizen of the United States, every male person who shall have acquired the rights of citizenship under or by virtue of the treaty of Queretaro, and every male naturalized citizen thereof, who shall have become such ninety days prior to any election, of the age of twenty-one years, who shall have been a resident of the state one year next preceding the election, and of the county in which he claims his vote ninety days, and in the election precinct thirty days, shall be entitled to vote at all elections which are now or may hereafter be authorized by law; provided, no native of China, no idiot, insane person, or person convicted of any infamous crime, and no person hereafter convicted of the embezzlement or misappropriation of public money, shall ever exercise the privileges of an elector in this state.

RIGHT OF SUFFRAGE.—When Congress admitted California as a state, the constituent members of the state, in their aggregate capacity, became vested with the sovereign powers of government "according to the principles of the Constitution," and had the right to prescribe the qualifications of electors. (People v. De la Guerra, 40 Cal. 311.)

It was no violation of the ninth article of the treaty of Guadalupe Hidalgo that the qualifications of electors, as prescribed in the Constitution of California, were such as to exclude some of the inhabitants from certain political rights. (People v. De la Guerra, 40 Cal. 311.)

The elective franchise is not one of the privileges of citizens secured by the fourteenth amendment, nor is the power of the state to determine the class of inhabitants who may vote within her limits curtailed by that amendment; and the only limitation contained in the fifteenth amendment is that the state cannot discriminate on account of race, color, or previous condition of servitude; but the power of exclusion upon all other grounds, including that of sex, remains intact. (Van Valkenburg v. Brown, 43 Cal. 43, 13 Am. Rep. 136.)

The legislature cannot add any essential to the constitutional definition of an elector. (Bergevin v. Curtz, 127 Cal. 86, 59 Pac. 312.)

The courts of equity have power to see that the constitutional rights of suffrage are enjoyed. (Cerini v. De Long, 7 Cal. App. 398, 94 Pac. 582.)

A person may be an elector, although not a registered voter. (Bergevin v. Curtz, 127 Cal. 86, 59 Pac. 312.)

A woman who has lost her United States citizenship by marrying an alien is not entitled to vote. (Mackenzie v. Hare, 165 Cal. 776, Ann. Cas. 1915B, 261, 134 Pac. 713; affirmed in Mackenzie v. Hare, 239 U. S. 299.)

Registration is not a qualification of an elector, and cannot add to the qualifications fixed by the Constitution; but it is to be regarded as a reasonable regulation by the legislature for the purpose of ascertaining who are qualified electors in order to prevent illegal voting. (Bergevin v. Curtz, 127 Cal. 86, 59 Pac. 312.)

Registration of voters. See 9 R. C. L., §§ 52–55, pp. 1036–1040.

A primary election is an election "authorized by law," within the meaning of this section, and the provisions thereof, defining the qualifications of electors, are controlling in determining the right to vote at such elections, and such right can neither be enlarged nor curtailed by the legislature. (Spier v. Baker, 120 Cal. 370, 41 L. R. A. 196, 52 Pac. 659.)

A provision of the Primary Election Law that all native-born citizens, who since the last general election have become of legal age, and who have been legal residents of the county thirty days prior to the election, as well as all citizens who have become such by naturalization since the last general election, and who have been residents as aforesaid, shall be entitled to vote, is an enlargement of the constitutional right of suffrage and void. (Spier v. Baker, 120 Cal. 370, 41 L. R. A. 196, 52 Pac. 659.)

A provision of the Primary Election Law, that no person shall vote at primary elections whose name does not appear upon the last great register, or supplements thereto, curtails the right of suffrage, and is void. (Spier v. Baker, 120 Cal. 370, 41 L. R. A. 196, 52 Pac. 659.)

This section does not apply to a voter in a reclamation district. (People v. Reclamation Dist. No. 551, 117 Cal. 114, 48 Pac. 1016.)

The act to change the boundary line between Fresno and Kings county is not unconstitutional because it prescribes different qualifications for the electors who shall be entitled to vote at the election therein provided for than are prescribed by this section. (Wheeler v. Herbert, 152 Cal. 224, 92 Pac. 353.)

The provision of the Political Code that, when a voter erases the name of a candidate without substituting another, the vote must be counted for the candidate whose name is erased, unless the words "no vote" are written after the name erased, is not unconstitutional, as prescribing an educational qualification for the voter, or destroying the secrecy of the ballot. (Rutledge v. Crawford, 91 Cal. 526, 25 Am. St. Rep. 212, 13 L. R. A. 761, 27 Pac. 779.)

A person born in a foreign state, whose father was once a citizen of the United States, but renounced his allegiance before the birth of such person, is not a citizen of the United States. (Browne v. Dexter, 66 Cal. 39, 4 Pac. 913.)

The legislature has no power to authorize electors to give their votes at any place outside of the county or district in which they have had a legal residence for thirty days previous to the election. (Bourland v. Hildreth, 26 Cal. 161.)

An act providing for taking the votes of the electors of the state, who are in the military service of the United States, outside of the county of their legal residence, to be returned to the secretary of state, and counted in the counties of the legal residence of the electors, is void. (Bourland v. Hildreth, 26 Cal. 161; Day v. Jones, 31 Cal. 261.)

The Constitution does not vest in any person the right to sign a petition for the recall of an officer. (Davenport v. Los Angeles, 146 Cal. 508, 80 Pac. 684.)

> Power of legislature to define qualifications of voters. See note, 7 Ann. Cas. 665; 9 R. C. L., § 6, p. 982, § 41, p. 1024.

> What constitutes conviction of crime within constitutional provision denying right to vote to convicted person. See note, 15 Ann. Cas. 103.

> Right of suffrage. See 9 R. C. L., §§ 4–6, pp. 979–983.

> Right to vote and citizenship. See 9 R. C. L., § 40, p. 1023.

Privileges of electors.

Sec. 2. Electors shall in all cases, except treason, felony, or breach of the peace, be privileged from arrest on the days of election, during their attendance at such election, going to and returning therefrom.

> Civil liability for preventing exercise of right to vote. See note, 20 Ann. Cas. 1008.

Primary election.

Sec. 2½. The legislature shall have the power to enact laws relative to the election of delegates to conventions of political parties; and the legislature shall enact laws providing for the direct nomination of candidates for public office, by electors, political parties, or organizations of electors without conventions, at elections to be known and designated as primary elections; also to determine the tests and conditions upon which electors, political parties, or organizations of electors may participate in any such primary election. It shall also be lawful for the legislature to prescribe that any such primary election shall be mandatory and obligatory. The legislature shall also have the power to establish the rates of compensation for primary election offi-

cers serving at such primary elections in any city, or city and county, or county, or other subdivision of a designated population, without making such compensation uniform, and for such purpose such law may declare the population of any city, city and county, county or political subdivision. Provided, however, that until the legislature shall enact a direct primary election law under the provisions of this section, the present primary election law shall remain in force and effect. (Amendment adopted November 3, 1908.)

[AMENDMENT OF 1900.]

Sec. 2½. The legislature shall have the power to enact laws relative to the election of delegates to conventions of political parties at elections known and designated as primary elections. Also to determine the tests and conditions upon which electors, political parties, or organizations of voters, may participate in any such primary election, which tests or conditions may be different from the tests and conditions required and permitted at other elections authorized by law; or the legislature may delegate the power to determine such tests or conditions, at primary elections, to the various political parties participating therein. It shall also be lawful for the legislature to prescribe that any such primary election law shall be obligatory and mandatory in any city, or any city and county, or in any county, or in any political subdivision, of a designated population, and that such law shall be optional in any city, city and county, county, or political subdivision of a lesser population, and for such purpose such law may declare the population of any city, city and county, county, or political subdivision, and may also provide what, if any, compensation primary election officers in defined places or political subdivisions may receive, without making compensation either general or uniform. (Amendment adopted November 6, 1900.)

PRIMARY ELECTIONS.—Prior to the adoption of this amendment, three acts regulating primary elections were passed by the legislature, each of which was held invalid by the supreme court.

1. **Act of 1895.**—The first act on the subject was held invalid because it only applied to counties of the first and second class, and was therefore local and special. (Marsh v. Hanly, 111 Cal. 368, 43 Pac. 975.)

2. **Act of 1897.**—The second act on the subject was held invalid on the following grounds: (a) because it enlarged the right of suffrage; (b) because it restricted the right of suffrage; (c) because certain portions of it were not expressed in the title of the act; (d) because it was special, in that it discriminated in favor of and against certain classes and individuals. (Spier v. Baker, 120 Cal. 370, 41 L. R. A. 196, 52 Pac. 659.)

3. **Act of 1899.**—The third act on the subject was held invalid because it permitted members of one political party or of no party to vote for delegates to the party convention of another party, and thus

took away the rights of self-control and self-preservation from political parties. Three of the justices (Henshaw, J., Van Dyke, J., and McFarland, J.) also held it invalid because it prohibited the election of delegates to a convention of any political party not representing three per cent of the votes cast at the last election. (Britton v. Board of Election Commrs., 129 Cal. 337, 51 L. R. A. 115, 61 Pac. 1115.)

4. Act of 1901.—This section authorizes the. provision of the primary election law of 1901, requiring each person to take an oath that he has a bona fide present intention of supporting the nominees of the party. (Rebstock v. Superior Court, 146 Cal. 308, 80 Pac. 65.)

The Primary Election Law of 1909 is not violative of the Constitution by providing for an expression of a choice as to a candidate for United States senator at a primary. (Socialist Party v. Uhl, 155 Cal. 776, 103 Pac. 181.)

The Primary Election Law of 1909 is not invalid because it does not give to classes other than political organizations the right to participate in the first primary held under the act. (Socialist Party v. Uhl, 155 Cal. 776, 103 Pac. 181.)

The Constitution only requires that a primary election law should apply to general elections, and the primary election law of 1909 does not violate the Constitution by providing that its provisions as to primary elections shall not apply to the nomination of officers of municipalities whose charters provide a system of nominating candidates for such offices. (Socialist Party v. Uhl, 155 Cal. 776, 103 Pac. 181.)

The Constitution is not violated by the primary election law because the latter does not preserve secrecy in voting, because it arbitrarily classifies voters, because it impairs the right of citizens to assemble together and instruct their representatives, or because it invests state officers with judicial functions. (Katz v. Fitzgerald, 152 Cal. 433, 93 Pac. 112.)

The legislature may compel electors when registering to declare their party affiliations as a prerequisite to the right to vote at primary elections. (Schostag v. Cator, 151 Cal. 600, 91 Pac. 502.)

The legislature may partly prescribe the tests of the rights of electors to vote at primary elections, and may partly delegate such power to political parties. (Schostag v. Cator, 151 Cal. 600, 91 Pac. 502.)

The legislature had power to determine the tests and conditions upon which "electors," "political parties," or "organizations of electors" should participate in a primary election, and the tests and conditions provided in the primary election law of 1909 being reasonable and not arbitrary, those provisions of the act are not unconstitutional. (Socialist Party v. Uhl, 155 Cal. 776, 103 Pac. 181.)

Under this section the legislature may prescribe tests and conditions for candidates, as well as for electors, but it is not bound to make membership in a party a condition of the right to seek the nomination of that party. (Hart v. Jordan, 168 Cal. 321, 143 Pac. 537.)

Effect of tie vote at primary election. See note, Ann. Cas. 1913E, 745.

Primary elections. See 9 R. C. L., §§ 86–100, pp. 1072–1091.

Militia duty, privilege of electors.

Sec. 3. No elector shall be obliged to perform militia duty on the day of election, except in time of war or public danger.

Residence of voters, gained or lost.

Sec. 4. For the purpose of voting, no person shall be deemed to have gained or lost a residence by reason of his presence or absence while employed in the service of the United States, nor while engaged in the navigation of the waters of this state or of the United States, or of the high seas; nor while a student at any seminary of learning; nor while kept at any almshouse or other asylum, at public expense; nor while confined in any public prison.

RESIDENCE.—This provision does not preclude the gaining of a residence for the purpose of voting by soldiers, college students, or inhabitants of a veterans' home, upon proof of their intention to acquire a domicile in the county of which they are inhabitants. (Stewart v. Kyser, 105 Cal. 459, 39 Pac. 19; People v. Holden, 28 Cal. 123.)

Presence in the state more than six months and in the county more than thirty days, under orders as a soldier in the military service of the United States, does not of itself entitle a person to vote. (Devlin v. Anderson, 38 Cal. 92.)

This section does not authorize an act providing for the taking of the votes of electors of this state, in the military service of the United States, outside of the counties of their legal residences. (Bourland v. Hildreth, 26 Cal. 161; Day v. Jones, 31 Cal. 261.)

Election by ballot.

Sec. 5. All elections by the people shall be by ballot* or by such other method as may be prescribed by law; provided, that secrecy in voting be preserved. (All after* added by amendment adopted November 3, 1896.)

SECRECY OF THE BALLOT.—The provision of the primary election law of 1901, requiring the person voting to take an oath that he has a bona fide present intention of supporting the nominees of the party, does not violate the provision of this section securing the secrecy of the ballot. (Rebstock v. Superior Court, 146 Cal. 308, 80 Pac. 65.)

Voting machines.

Sec. 6. The inhibitions of this Constitution to the contrary notwithstanding, the legislature shall have power to

provide that in different parts of the state different methods may be employed for receiving and registering the will of the people as expressed at elections, and may provide that mechanical devices may be used within designated subdivisions of the state at the option of the local authority indicated by the legislature for that purpose. (Amendment adopted November 4, 1902.)

Use of voting machines at elections. See notes, 2 Ann. Cas. 840; 12 Ann. Cas. 474; 9 R. C. L., § 78, p. 1062.

ARTICLE III.

DISTRIBUTION OF POWERS.

Section 1. The powers of the government of the state of California shall be divided into three separate departments —the legislative, executive, and judicial; and no person charged with the exercise of powers properly belonging to one of these departments shall exercise any functions appertaining to either of the others, except as in this Constitution expressly directed or permitted.

DEPARTMENTS OF GOVERNMENT.—The departments mentioned in this section are the departments of the state government, and not the local governments thereafter to be created by the legislature. (People v. Provines, 34 Cal. 520; Staude v. Board of Election Commrs., 61 Cal. 313; Holley v. Orange Co., 106 Cal. 420, 39 Pac. 790. Burgoyne v. Board of Supervisors, 5 Cal. 9, and cases following it, overruled.)

This provision does not place either department above the law, nor make either independent of the other. (People v. Brooks, 16 Cal. 11.)

As to how far the several departments are independent of each other, see People v. Twelfth District Court, 17 Cal. 547.

Legislative department.—The distinction between a judicial and a legislative act is, that the former determines what the law is and what the rights of the parties are, with reference to transactions already had, and the latter prescribes what the law shall be in future cases arising under it. (People v. Board of Education, 54 Cal. 375.)

Legislative power prescribes rules of conduct for the government of the citizen or subject, while judicial power punishes and redresses wrongs growing out of rules previously established. The distinction lies between a rule and a sentence. (Ex parte Shrader, 33 Cal. 279; Smith v. Strother, 68 Cal. 194, 8 Pac. 852; Wulzen v. Board of Supervisors, 101 Cal. 15, 40 Am. St. Rep. 17, 35 Pac. 353.)

The legislature cannot exercise judicial functions. (Guy v. Hermance, 5 Cal. 73, 63 Am. Dec. 85.)

An act providing that no injunction shall issue against commissioners created by the act is an exercise of judicial functions, and void. (Guy v. Hermance, 5 Cal. 73, 63 Am. Dec. 85.)

The election of officers is political, and may be exercised by both the legislative and executive branches of the government. (People v. Langdon, 8 Cal. 1.)

To audit and allow the claim of a judgment creditor against a city is not the exercise of a judicial function. (People v. Board of Supervisors, 11 Cal. 206.)

The legislature may pass a special law directing a court to transfer an indictment for murder pending therein to another court for trial. (People v. Twelfth District Court, 17 Cal. 547.)

An act conferring upon boards of supervisors power to try a contest in relation to the office of county judge is void. (Stone v. Elkins, 24 Cal. 125.)

An act of the legislature granting a new trial, or reopening a judgment in an action between individuals, would be an assumption of judicial power; but an act allowing a judgment in favor of the state to be reopened would not be invalid. (People v. Frisbie, 26 Cal. 135.)

The legislature cannot by law fix the assessed value of property. (People v. Hastings, 29 Cal. 449.)

The legislature has no power to legalize existing pleadings substantially defective, without first requiring them to be amended. (People v. Mariposa Co., 31 Cal. 196.)

An act determining that certain trades are offensive is not an exercise of judicial power. (Ex parte Shrader, 33 Cal. 279.)

An act to validate a judgment of a court void for want of jurisdiction is void. (Pryor v. Downey, 50 Cal. 388, 19 Am. Rep. 656.)

The exercise by the legislature of visitorial or supervisorial power over corporations does not violate this section. (In re Bunkers, 1 Cal. App. 61, 81 Pac. 748.)

The provisions of the act regulating the practice of architecture that the board may adopt rules and regulations is not a delegation of legislative function. (Ex parte McManus, 151 Cal. 331, 90 Pac. 702.)

The legislative approval of a survey of a county line before the line was actually run is not a delegation of legislative power to the surveyor. (Trinity County v. Mendocino County, 151 Cal. 279, 90 Pac. 685.)

As to whether the sale of the property of a minor is a matter of judicial cognizance exclusively, see Paty v. Smith, 50 Cal. 153.

An act prescribing the contents of a complaint to foreclose a street assessment is not a usurpation of judicial functions. (Whiting v. Townsend, 57 Cal. 515.)

The action of a board of education, in adopting a series of readers for the public schools, in lieu of a series previously in use, is an exercise of legislative and not judicial power. (People v. Board of Education, 54 Cal. 375.)

Judicial department.—The legislature has no power to confer other than judicial functions upon the courts. (Burgoyne v. Board of Supervisors, 5 Cal. 9; Hardenburgh v. Kidd, 10 Cal. 402.)

An act authorizing the judges of the superior court to fix the salaries of the official reporters of the courts is void as imposing legislative functions upon the judiciary. (Smith v. Strother, 68 Cal. 194, 8 Pac. 852.)

But an act permitting the judge to fix the compensation of a shorthand reporter after the services are rendered does not confer legislative power upon the judiciary. (McAllister v. Hamlin, 83 Cal. 361, 23 Pac. 357; Stevens v. Truman, 127 Cal. 155, 59 Pac. 397.)

An act conferring upon district judges the power to appoint police commissioners is not in conflict with this section. (Staude v. Board of Election Commrs., 61 Cal. 313.)

A law providing for the change of names of corporations upon petition to the superior court is not unconstitutional as delegating legislative power to the judiciary. (Matter of La Societe Francaise etc., 123 Cal. 525, 56 Pac. 458, 787.)

The legislature cannot confer nonjudicial power upon the judges of a court as commissioners any more than upon the court itself. (Burgoyne v. Board of Supervisors, 5 Cal. 9.)

An act conferring upon the courts of sessions the entire management of the financial business of the counties is void. (Burgoyne v. Board of Supervisors, 5 Cal. 9; Phelan v. San Francisco, 6 Cal. 531; Phelan v. San Francisco, 20 Cal. 39.)

An act authorizing the trial judge to make the crime a felony or a misdemeanor is not an attempt to delegate legislative power. (In re O'Shea, 11 Cal. App. 568, 105 Pac. 776.)

The proceedings provided by the "Torrens Land Law" are judicial and not administrative. (Robinson v. Kerrigan, 151 Cal. 40, 121 Am. St. Rep. 90, 12 Ann. Cas. 829, 90 Pac. 129.)

The duties conferred on the county recorder by the "Torrens Land Law" are not judicial. (Robinson v. Kerrigan, 151 Cal. 40, 121 Am. St. Rep. 90, 12 Ann. Cas. 829, 90 Pac. 129.)

The "McEnerney Act" for the establishment of titles provides for a judicial proceeding and not an administrative proceeding. (Hoffman v. Superior Court, 151 Cal. 386, 90 Pac. 939.)

The corporation license tax act of March 29, 1905, is not unconstitutional as conferring judicial power upon the secretary of state. His determination of the class to which a corporation belongs, as provided in section 7 of the act, is a mere incident to the exercise of a purely ministerial function and is not binding on any corporation. (Kaiser Land & Fruit Co. v. Curry, 155 Cal. 638, 103 Pac. 341.)

The power of appointment of probation officers vested by the Juvenile Court Law (Stats. 1909, p. 213) in the superior court in the exercise of its jurisdiction as a juvenile court is not unconstitutional as vesting an executive function in judicial officers. (Nicholl v. Koster, 157 Cal. 416, 108 Pac. 302.)

The State Dental Law does not confer upon the board of dental examiners judicial functions by giving it authority to indorse reputable dental colleges. (Ex parte Whitley, 144 Cal. 167, 1 Ann. Cas. 13, 77 Pac. 879.)

An act providing that the court may prescribe by rule what shall be deemed a waiver of a jury trial is in violation of this section. (Exline v. Smith, 5 Cal. 112.)

The judiciary has power to examine into the action of the executive in surrendering a fugitive from justice. (In re Manchester, 5 Cal. 237.)

The legislature cannot confer upon the county judge power to call an election. (Dickey v. Hurlburt, 5 Cal. 343.)

An act conferring upon the county court power of incorporating towns is void. (People v. Nevada, 6 Cal. 143.)

The assessment of taxes is not a judicial, but a legislative, function. (Hardenburgh v. Kidd, 10 Cal. 402.)

The duties of a judge in a proceeding to condemn land are judicial. (Gilmer v. Lime Point, 18 Cal. 229.)

The legislature may declare the mayor of a city to be ex officio a justice of the peace. (Uridias v. Morrill, 22 Cal. 473.)

The chief justice of the supreme court is prohibited by this section from exercising the functions and duties of trustee of the state

library. (People v. Sanderson, 30 Cal. 160. But see People v. Provines, 34 Cal. 520.)

This section does not prohibit a police judge of a city from performing the duties of a police commissioner. (People v. Provines, 34 Cal. 520.)

The legislature may invest judicial officers with power to punish for contempt. (Crocker v. Conrey, 140 Cal. 213, 73 Pac. 1006.)

The legislature cannot invest ministerial officers with the power to punish individuals by fine and imprisonment. (Burns v. Superior Court, 140 Cal. 1, 73 Pac. 597.)

The power to remove a public officer for cause is not judicial in its character. (Matter of Carter, 141 Cal. 316, 74 Pac. 997.)

Executive department.—The power of appointment to office is not essentially an executive function, within the meaning of this section; and such power may be exercised by the members of the legislature, (People v. Freeman, 80 Cal. 233, 13 Am. St. Rep. 122, 22 Pac. 173; People v. Langdon, 8 Cal. 1.)

The power to levy a tax is purely legislative, and cannot be delegated to the county superintendent of schools, who is an executive officer. (McCabe v. Carpenter, 102 Cal. 469, 36 Pac. 836.)

A law requiring the auditor's certificate that there is sufficient money in the treasury before an appropriation is made is valid, and does not vest judicial functions in a ministerial officer. (Higgins v. San Diego Water Co., 118 Cal. 524, 45 Pac. 824, 50 Pac. 670; Pollok v. San Diego, 118 Cal. 593, 50 Pac. 769.)

A law conferring power upon city trustees to remove a municipal officer is valid. (Croly v. Board of Trustees of Sacramento, 119 Cal. 229, 51 Pac. 323.)

An act giving to horticultural commissioners power to determine whether any particular place is a nuisance, because infected with insect pests, does not confer judicial power on such commissioners. (Los Angeles v. Spencer, 126 Cal. 670, 77 Am. St. Rep. 217, 59 Pac. 202.)

A law authorizing the high school board to furnish the supervisors with an estimate of the amount of the tax required, but leaving it to the supervisors to fix the tax, is not invalid as delegating legislative power to an executive officer. (People v. Lodi High School Dist., 124 Cal. 694, 57 Pac. 660; McCabe v. Carpenter, 102 Cal. 469, 36 Pac. 836, distinguished.)

Division of powers of government between the several departments. See 6 R. C. L., §§ 144–181, pp. 144–182.

ARTICLE IV.

LEGISLATIVE DEPARTMENT.

Senate and assembly, and enacting clause—Initiative and referendum.

Section 1. The legislative power of this state shall be vested in a senate and assembly which shall be designated

"The legislature of the State of California," but the people reserve to themselves the power to propose laws and amendments to the Constitution, and to adopt or reject the same, at the polls independent of the legislature, and also reserve the power, at their own option, to so adopt or reject any act, or section or part of any act, passed by the legislature. The enacting clause of every law shall be "The people of the State of California do enact as follows:"

The first power reserved to the people shall be known as the initiative. Upon the presentation to the secretary of state of a petition certified as herein provided to have been signed by qualified electors, equal in number to eight per cent of all the votes cast for all candidates for governor at the last preceding general election, at which a governor was elected, proposing a law or amendment to the Constitution, set forth in full in said petition, the secretary of state shall submit the said proposed law or amendment to the Constitution to the electors at the next succeeding general election occurring subsequent to ninety days after the presentation aforesaid of said petition, or at any special election called by the governor in his discretion prior to such general election. All such initiative petitions shall have printed across the top thereof in twelve point black-face type the following: "Intiative measure to be submitted directly to the electors."

Upon the presentation to the secretary of state, at any time not less than ten days before the commencement of any regular session of the legislature, of a petition certified as herein provided to have been signed by qualified electors of the state equal in number to five per cent of all the votes cast for all candidates for governor at the last preceding general election, at which a governor was elected, proposing a law set forth in full in said petition, the secretary of state shall transmit the same to the legislature as soon as it convenes and organizes. The law proposed by such petition shall be either enacted or rejected without change or amendment by the legislature, within forty days from the time it is received by the legislature. If any law proposed by such petition shall be enacted by the legislature it shall be sub-

ject to referendum, as hereinafter provided. If any law so petitioned for be rejected, or if no action is taken upon it by the legislature within said forty days, the secretary of state shall submit it to the people for approval or rejection at the next ensuing general election. The legislature may reject any measure so proposed by initiative petition and propose a different one on the same subject by a yea and nay vote upon separate roll-call, and in such event both measures shall be submitted by the secretary of state to the electors for approval or rejection at the next ensuing general election or at a prior special election called by the governor, in his discretion, for such purpose. All said initiative petitions last above described shall have printed in twelve point black-face type the following: "Initiative measure to be presented to the legislature."

The second power reserved to the people shall be known as the referendum. No act passed by the legislature shall go into effect until ninety days after the final adjournment of the session of the legislature which passed such act, except acts calling elections, acts providing for tax levies or appropriations for the usual current expenses of the state, and urgency measures necessary for the immediate preservation of the public peace, health or safety, passed by a two-thirds vote of all the members elected to each house. Whenever it is deemed necessary for the immediate preservation of the public peace, health or safety that a law shall go into immediate effect, a statement of the facts constituting such necessity shall be set forth in one section of the act, which section shall be passed only upon a yea and nay vote, upon a separate roll-call thereon; provided, however, that no measure creating or abolishing any office or changing the salary, term or duties of any officer, or granting any franchise or special privilege, or creating any vested right or interest, shall be construed to be an urgency measure. Any law so passed by the legislature and declared to be an urgency measure shall go into immediate effect.

Upon the presentation to the secretary of state within ninety days after the final adjournment of the legislature of a petition certified as herein provided, to have been

signed by qualified electors equal in number to five per cent
of all the votes cast for all candidates for governor at the
last preceding general election at which a governor was
elected, asking that any act or section or part of any act
of the legislature, be submitted to the electors for their approval or rejection, the secretary of state shall submit to
the electors for their appproval or rejection, such act, or
section or part of such act, at the next succeeding general
election occurring at any time subsequent to thirty days
after the filing of said petition or at any special election
which may be called by the governor, in his discretion, prior
to such regular election, and no such act or section or part
of such act shall go into effect until and unless approved by
a majority of the qualified electors voting thereon; but if
a referendum petition is filed against any section or part
of any act the remainder of such act shall not be delayed
from going into effect.

Any act, law or amendment to the Constitution submitted
to the people by either initiative or referendum petition
and approved by a majority of the votes cast thereon, at
any election, shall take effect five days after the date of the
official declaration of the vote by the secretary of state. No
act, law or amendment to the Constitution, initiated or
adopted by the people, shall be subject to the veto power
of the governor, and no act, law or amendment to the Constitution, adopted by the people at the polls under the initiative provisions of this section, shall be amended or repealed except by a vote of the electors, unless otherwise
provided in said initiative measure; but acts and laws
adopted by the people under the referendum provisions of
this section may be amended by the legislature at any subsequent session thereof. If any provision or provisions of
two or more measures, approved by the electors at the same
election, conflict, the provision or provisions of the measure receiving the highest affirmative vote shall prevail. Until otherwise provided by law, all measures submitted to a
vote of the electors, under the provisions of this section,
shall be printed, and together with arguments for and
against each such measure by the proponents and opponents

thereof, shall be mailed to each elector in the same manner as now provided by law as to amendments to the Constitution, proposed by the legislature; and the persons to prepare and present such arguments shall, until otherwise provided by law, be selected by the presiding officer of the senate.

If for any reason any initiative or referendum measure, proposed by petition as herein provided, be not submitted at the election specified in this section, such failure shall not prevent its submission at a succeeding general election, and no law or amendment to the Constitution, proposed by the legislature, shall be submitted at any election unless at the same election there shall be submitted all measures proposed by petition of the electors, if any be so proposed, as herein provided.

Any initiative or referendum petition may be presented in sections, but each section shall contain a full and correct copy of the title and text of the proposed measure. Each signer shall add to his signature his place of residence, giving the street and number if such exist. His election precinct shall also appear on the paper after his name. The number of signatures attached to each section shall be at the pleasure of the person soliciting signatures to the same. Any qualified elector of the state shall be competent to solicit said signatures within the county or city and county of which he is an elector. Each section of the petition shall bear the name of the county or city and county in which it is circulated, and only qualified electors of such county or city and county shall be competent to sign such section. Each section shall have attached thereto the affidavit of the person soliciting signatures to the same, stating his own qualifications and that all the signatures to the attached section were made in his presence and that to the best of his knowledge and belief each signature to the section is the genuine signature of the person whose name it purports to be, and no other affidavit thereto shall be required. The affidavit of any person soliciting signatures hereunder shall be verified free of charge by any officer authorized to administer oaths. Such petitions so verified shall be prima facie evidence that the signatures thereon are genuine and

that the persons signing the same are qualified electors. Unless and until it be otherwise proven upon official investigation, it shall be presumed that the petition presented contains the signatures of the requisite number of qualified electors.

Each section of the petition shall be filed with the clerk or registrar of voters of the county or city and county in which it was circulated, but all said sections circulated in any county or city and county shall be filed at the same time. Within twenty days after the filing of such petition in his office the said clerk, or registrar of voters, shall determine from the records of registration what number of qualified electors have signed the same, and if necessary the board of supervisors shall allow said clerk or registrar additional assistants for the purpose of examining such petition and provide for their compensation. The said clerk or registrar, upon the completion of such examination, shall forthwith attach to said petition, except the signatures thereto appended, his certificate, properly dated, showing the result of said examination and shall forthwith transmit said petition, together with his said certificate, to the secretary of state and also file a copy of said certificate in his office. Within forty days from the transmission of the said petition and certificate by the clerk or registrar to the secretary of state, a supplemental petition identical with the original as to the body of the petition but containing supplemental names, may be filed with the clerk or registrar of voters, as aforesaid. The clerk or registrar of voters shall within ten days after the filing of such supplemental petition make the examination thereof, as of the original petition, and upon the completion of such examination shall forthwith attach to said petition his certificate, properly dated, showing the result of said examination, and shall forthwith transmit a copy of said supplemental petition, except the signatures thereto appended, together with his certificate, to the secretary of state.

When the secretary of state shall have received from one or more county clerks or registrars of voters a petition certified as herein provided to have been signed by the requi-

site number of qualified electors, he shall forthwith transmit to the county clerk or registrar of voters of every county or city and county in the state his certificate showing such fact. A petition shall be deemed to be filed with the secretary of state upon the date of the receipt by him of a certificate or certificates showing said petition to be signed by the requisite number of electors of the state. Any county clerk or registrar of voters shall, upon receipt of such copy, file the same for record in his office. The duties herein imposed upon the clerk or registrar of voters shall be performed by such registrar of voters in all cases where the office of registrar of voters exists.

The initiative and referendum powers of the people are hereby further reserved to the electors of each county, city and county, city and town of the state, to be exercised under such procedure as may be provided by law. Until otherwise provided by law, the legislative body of any such county, city and county, city or town may provide for the manner of exercising the initiative and referendum powers herein reserved to such counties, cities and counties, cities and towns, but shall not require more than fifteen per cent of the electors thereof to propose any initiative measure nor more than ten per cent of the electors thereof to order the referendum. Nothing contained in this section shall be construed as affecting or limiting the present or future powers of cities or cities and counties having charters adopted under the provisions of section eight of article eleven of this Constitution. In the submission to the electors of any measure under this section, all officers shall be guided by the general laws of this state, except as is herein otherwise provided. This section is self-executing, but legislation may be enacted to facilitate its operation, but in no way limiting or restricting either the provisions of this section or the powers herein reserved. (Amendment approved October 10, 1911.)

[ORIGINAL SECTION.]

Section 1. The legislative power of this state shall be vested in a senate and assembly, which shall be designated "The Legislature of the State of California," and the enacting clause of every law shall be as follows: "The People of the State of California, represented in Senate and Assembly, do enact as follows."

LEGISLATIVE POWER.—The legislature has the same unlimited power of legislation which resides in the British parliament, except when restrained and limited either by express words of the Constitution or by necessary implication; and its power cannot be restrained by any unnecessary implications. (Mitchell v. Winnek, 117 Cal. 520, 49 Pac. 579.)

The legislature is not synonymous with the law-making power and does not include the governor except as applied to the enactment of laws. (Brooks v. Fischer, 79 Cal. 173, 4 L. R. A. 429, 21 Pac. 652.)

The Constitution is not a grant of power, but a restriction upon the power of the legislature, and the legislature has the entire legislative power of the state not prohibited to the legislature or conferred upon some other body. (Sheehan v. Scott, 145 Cal. 684, 79 Pac. 350; Mendenhall v. Gray, 167 Cal. 233, 139 Pac. 67.)

All powers of any of the departments of the government, not disposed of or distributed by the Constitution, are left at the disposal of the legislature. (Ross v. Whitman, 6 Cal. 361.)

· The legislature is not controlled as to its powers or the mode of their exercise otherwise than by the restrictions of the Constitution. (Hobart v. Supervisors, 17 Cal. 23; People v. Seymour, 16 Cal. 332, 76 Am. Dec. 521.)

The legislature represents the independent sovereignty of the people of the state, and is supreme and unlimited in all legitimate subject matters of legislation, and is controlled only by such restrictions as are imposed by the organic law of the state. (Beals v. Amador Co., 35 Cal. 624.)

The legislature may accept a private bounty for the benefit of the state, although such bounty influences legislative action. (People v. Bigler, 5 Cal. 23.)

The legislature has full power to alienate the tide-lands of the state, subject only to the right of the public to use them for the purposes of navigation and fishing. (Oakland v. Oakland Water Front Co., 118 Cal. 160, 50 Pac. 277.)

The legislature may determine whether or not a certain improvement is of a public nature, and the courts will not interfere with this determination, unless it is palpably and entirely for private benefit. (In re Madera Irr. Dist., 92 Cal. 296, 27 Am. St. Rep. 106, 14 L. R. A. 755, 28 Pac. 272, 675; Hagar v. Supervisors, 47 Cal. 222.)

As to the validity of acts contrary to natural justice, see People v. Bigler, 5 Cal. 23.

Under this section of the Constitution of 1849 the legislature had the power to create municipal corporations at will, by special laws, and a given territory could be incorporated by it as a municipal corporation without the consent or the acceptance of the inhabitants thereof. (People v. California Fish Co., 166 Cal. 576, 138 Pac. 79.)

Exercise of power.—A legislative assembly has all the powers and privileges which are necessary to the proper exercise, in all respects, of its appropriate functions. (Ex parte McCarthy, 29 Cal. 395.)

The senate has power to summon witnesses to testify concerning a charge of bribery brought against its members. (Ex parte McCarthy, 29 Cal. 395.)

Constitution—14

The legislature may compel the attendance of all persons within the limits of their constituency, as witnesses, in regard to subjects on which they have power to act and into which they institute an investigation. (Ex parte McCarthy, 29 Cal. 395.)

Witnesses before either branch of the legislature may be compelled to testify by process of contempt. (Ex parte McCarthy, 29 Cal. 395.)

Appropriations.—Under this section appropriations for the erection of buildings, the construction of other improvements for state institutions, and the payment of the transportation of Civil War veterans to and from the Gettysburg reunion, cannot be paid prior to ninety days after the adjournment of the legislature. (McClure v. Nye, 22 Cal. App. 248, 133 Pac. 1145.)

Delegation of power.—The power to make laws cannot be delegated by the legislature to the people of the state, or to any portion of the people. (Ex parte Wall, 48 Cal. 279, 17 Am. Rep. 425.)

The legislature has no power to refer a statute to the people to decide by a popular vote whether it shall go into effect. (Ex parte Wall, 48 Cal. 279, 17 Am. Rep. 425.)

As to whether the legislature may confer upon the voters of a county directly the power to enact laws, questioned but not decided. (Ex parte Anderson, 134 Cal. 69, 86 Am. St. Rep. 236, 66 Pac. 194.)

There cannot be two equal, co-ordinate law-making powers within the same territory, each existing without any restrictions the one upon the other; and, therefore, a law empowering the voters of a county and also the board of supervisors of the county to enact and repeal laws on the same subjects is invalid. (Ex parte Anderson, 134 Cal. 69, 86 Am. St. Rep. 236, 66 Pac. 194.)

The legislature cannot delegate its general legislative functions, but it can authorize others to do those things which it cannot understandingly or advantageously do itself. Thus, it can delegate to the voters of a county power to select a county seat. (Upham v. Supervisors, 8 Cal. 378.)

Laws may be either absolute, dependent upon no contingency, or subject to conditions. They may take effect only upon the happening of events which are future and uncertain, and among others, the voluntary act of the parties upon whom they are designed to operate. (Blanding v. Burr, 13 Cal. 343.)

Thus, a provision of an act that the question of the issuance of bonds shall be submitted to the people is valid. (Blanding v. Burr, 13 Cal. 343.)

But while a statute may be conditional, so that its taking effect may depend upon a subsequent event which may be named in it, yet this event must be one which shall produce such a change of circumstances that the lawmakers, in their own judgment, can declare it wise that the law shall take effect when the event shall occur. (Ex parte Wall, 48 Cal. 279, 17 Am. Rep. 425.)

A county ordinance prohibiting the granting of a liquor license in any precinct in which a majority of the electors voted against the granting of liquor licenses therein, is not a delegation of legislative functions. (Denton v. Vann, 8 Cal. App. 677, 97 Pac. 675.)

The grant of power comprehends the exercise of all the sovereign authority of the state in matters which are properly the subject of legislation. (People v. Nye, 9 Cal. App. 148, 98 Pac. 241.)

A common council has no power to delegate its functions and in the absence of special authority has no power to submit a question to the electors for the purpose of ascertaining their desires. (Galindo v. Walter, 8 Cal. App. 234, 96 Pac. 505.)

The act regulating the practice of medicine and surgery does not delegate legislative functions. (Arwine v. Board of Medical Examiners, 151 Cal. 499, 91 Pac. 319.)

A freeholders' charter may incorporate the procedure known as the initiative and referendum so as to authorize the majority of the electors to participate directly in the enactment of local laws. (In re Pfahler, 150 Cal. 71, 11 Ann. Cas. 911, 11 L. R. A. (N. S.) 1092, 88 Pac. 270.)

An act authorizing the submission to the people of the question of a tax for an improvement is valid. (Pattison v. Yuba Co., 13 Cal. 175.)

The act providing for the annexation of territory to incorporated towns does not, in its provision for a vote by the people, comprise any unwarranted delegation of legislative power. (People v. Town of Ontario, 148 Cal. 625, 84 Pac. 205.)

The provision of the act creating the board of medical examiners permitting the board to revoke a license for "advertising of medical business in which grossly'improbable statements are made" is void. (Hewitt v. Board of Medical Examiners, 148 Cal. 590, 113 Am. St. Rep. 315, 7 Ann. Cas. 750, 3 L. R. A. (N. S.) 896, 84 Pac. 39.)

The legislature may delegate to the legislative authorities power to determine what shall constitute a public offense. (Denninger v. Recorder's Court, 145 Cal. 629, 79 Pac. 360.)

The legislature may make a local law depend for effect upon the will of all the voters of a locality, or of a majority, or upon the assent of a few, as in the case of removal of capitols, courthouses, etc., upon donations or other advantages received. (Hobart v. Supervisors, 17 Cal. 23. But see Dickey v. Hurlburt, 5 Cal. 343; by Heydenfeldt, J.)

The legislature cannot delegate its power to fix water rates. (Spring Valley Water Works v. San Francisco, 61 Cal. 3.)

An act which leaves it permissive with a board whether or not the work shall be done, and when and where taxes shall be levied for the same, is an unlawful delegation of legislative functions. (Per McKee, J., in People v. Parks, 58 Cal. 624, 641.)

An act authorizing a commissioner to require factories and workshops to provide mechanical contrivances to prevent the inhaling of dust, filaments and gases, when it appears to him that it can be to a great extent prevented by such contrivances, is an unlawful delegation of legislative functions. (Schaezlein v. Cabaniss, 135 Cal. 466, 87 Am. St. Rep. 122, 56 L. R. A. 733, 67 Pac. 755.)

An ordinance prohibiting the alteration or repair of any wooden building within certain designated fire limits, without permission of the fire wardens and approval of a majority of the committee on fire department and the mayor, is not an unlawful delegation of legislative functions. (Ex parte Fiske, 72 Cal. 125, 13 Pac. 310.)

An act providing for forming the county of Orange out of part of the county of Los Angeles, upon the assent of two-thirds of the qualified electors of the proposed new county, is not a delegation of legislative power. (People v. McFadden, 81 Cal. 489, 15 Am. St. Rep. 66, 22 Pac. 851.)

Municipal boards can delegate only duties ministerial in character, and not calling for the exercise of discretion. (Holley v. Orange Co., 106 Cal. 420, 39 Pac. 790.)

Powers conferred upon a municipal corporation, involving the exercise of judgment and discretion, are in the nature of public trusts, and cannot be delegated. (Scollay v. Butte Co., 67 Cal. 249, 7 Pac. 661.)

The legislature had power to enact the act of 1891, to establish law libraries, and to provide that counties might come within the provisions of the act, as the boards of supervisors of the respective counties might determine. (Board of Library Trustees v. Supervisors, 99 Cal. 571, 34 Pac. 244.)

A provision of the County Government Act of 1883, that the boards of supervisors of counties of certain designated classes may allow county officers a deputy whenever in the opinion of such board the salary of such officers is insufficient, is an unlawful delegation of legislative power. (Dougherty v. Austin, 94 Cal. 601, 16 L. R. A. 161, 28 Pac. 834, 29 Pac. 1092; People v. Johnson, 95 Cal. 471, 31 Pac. 611.)

An act providing that a board of harbor commissioners may impose penalties not exceeding five hundred dollars for the violation of the rules made by them is a delegation of legislative functions. (Harbor Commrs. v. Redwood Co., 88 Cal. 491, 22 Am. St. Rep. 321, 26 Pac. 375.)

The legislature cannot delegate to a board of medical examiners the power of declaring what acts shall constitute a misdemeanor. (Per Paterson, J., in Ex parte McNulty, 77 Cal. 164, 11 Am. St. Rep. 257, 19 Pac. 237.)

An act authorizing a commission to make certain quarantine regulations, and declaring that a violation of them shall be a misdemeanor, is an unlawful delegation of legislative power. (Ex parte Cox, 63 Cal. 21.)

An act creating a state board of equalization and providing that such board shall determine the rate of taxation, is not an unlawful delegation of legislative power. (Savings etc. Soc. v. Austin, 46 Cal. 415. But see Houghton v. Austin, 47 Cal. 646.)

An act which submits to a popular vote of the electors of a county the question whether certain territory shall be annexed thereto is valid. (People v. Nally, 49 Cal. 478.)

The so-called Wyllie or "Local Option Act" of April 4, 1911, is not invalid as involving a delegation of its legislative power by the legislature to the electors. (Ex parte Beck, 162 Cal. 701, 124 Pac. 543; Matter of Ellsworth, 165 Cal. 677, 133 Pac. 272.)

The legislature may provide either a state system for the inspection, measurement and graduation of merchandise and manufactured articles and commodities, administered by state officers, or a local system administered by the respective counties, cities, or cities and counties, through officers which they may appoint under the authority of the general statute. (Scott v. Boyle, 164 Cal. 321, 128 Pac. 941.)

Police power.—The legislature cannot, under the guise of police regulations, enact laws not pertaining to the public welfare, health or morals, and which impose onerous and unnecessary burdens upon business and property. (Ex parte Hayden, 147 Cal. 649, 109 Am. St. Rep. 183, 1 L. R. A. (N. S.) 184, 82 Pac. 315; Ex parte Drexel, 147 Cal. 763, 3 Ann. Cas. 878, 2 L. R. A. (N. S.) 588, 82 Pac. 429.)

An act designed to obtain for people of a certain locality an advantage cannot be upheld as a police regulation. (Hellman v. Los Angeles, 147 Cal. 653, 82 Pac. 313.)

Police regulations are not unconstitutional because they may incidentally operate to deprive individuals of their property without compensation, nor because they may create a monopoly. (In re Zhizhuzza, 147 Cal. 328, 81 Pac. 955.)

An act forbidding the issuance of trading stamps and coupons redeemable in "anything unidentified by or unselected by the purchaser at the time of the sale," is unconstitutional. (Ex parte Drexel, 147 Cal. 763, 3 Ann. Cas. 878, 2 L. R. A. (N. S.) 588, 82 Pac. 429.)

An act requiring all fruit shipped to be stamped with a statement truly designating the county and immediate locality in which such fruit is grown is not a reasonable exercise of the police power. (Ex parte Hayden, 147 Cal. 649, 109 Am. St. Rep. 183, 1 L. R. A. (N. S.) 184, 82 Pae. 315.)

The police power will not authorize the state to take private property for public use without compensation when such property can be condemned and paid for. (People v. Elk River etc. Co., 107 Cal. 221, 48 Am. St. Rep. 125, 40 Pac. 531.)

An act making it a misdemeanor to keep open a barber-shop on Sundays or other holidays is unreasonable. (Ex parte Jentzsch, 112 Cal. 468, 32 L. R. A. 664, 44 Pac. 803.)

The state has authority to regulate fisheries within its borders, and may provide the places as well as the times in which fish may be taken, and may make exclusive grants of fisheries in designated waters. (Heckman v. Swett, 107 Cal. 276, 40 Pac. 420.)

An act providing for a bounty on coyote scalps comes within the purview of the police power. (Ingram v. Colgan, 106 Cal. 113, 46 Am. St. Rep. 221, 28 L. R. A. 187, 38 Pac. 315, 39 Pac. 437.)

A law making it a felony to sell intoxicating liquor to an Indian is valid. (People v. Bray, 105 Cal. 344, 27 L. R. A. 158, 38 Pac. 731.)

It is within the police power of the state in the protection of the wild game of the state to prohibit the sale of the meat of any wild game within the state. (Ex parte Maier, 103 Cal. 476, 42 Am. St. Rep. 129, 37 Pac. 402.)

It is not competent for the legislature to vest in an adjoining proprietor the power to prevent his neighbor from building such structure on his own land as he pleases, provided it is not a nuisance; and it is not a nuisance merely because it obstructs the passage of light and air. But the legislature may regulate the erection of division walls on the division line. (Western etc. Co. v. Knickerbocker, 103 Cal. 111, 37 Pac. 192.)

An act to prohibit Chinese persons from coming into the state, and prescribing terms and conditions upon which those residing in the

state shall be permitted to remain and travel therein, is void. (Ex parte Ah Cue, 101 Cal. 197, 35 Pac. 556.)

The act of 1891, permitting the organization and creation of sanitary districts, is within the police power of the state. (Woodward v. Fruitvale Sanitary Dist., 99 Cal. 554, 34 Pac. 239.)

An act forbidding the sale of liquors within certain distances of certain named educational and reformatory institutions is a valid police regulation. (Ex parte McClain, 61 Cal. 436, 44 Am. Rep. 554.)

It is within the police power of the state to authorize the channel of a river to be turned or straightened. (Green v. Swift, 47 Cal. 536.)

The legislature has no power to declare that a physician is guilty of unprofessional conduct in advertising himself as a specialist in certain diseases, and punishable as for a misdemeanor. (Per Thornton, J., in Ex parte McNulty, 77 Cal. 164, 11 Am. St. Rep. 257, 19 Pac. 237.)

The legislature has power to organize agricultural societies. (People v. San Joaquin Valley Agr. Assn., 151 Cal. 797, 91 Pac. 740.)

The business of pawnbroker is the subject of police regulation. (Levinson v. Boas, 150 Cal. 185, 11 Ann. Cas. 661, 12 L. R. A. (N. S.) 575, 88 Pac. 825.)

The support of poor and destitute persons unable to care for themselves is a public purpose, clearly within the general legislative power. (Board of Directors v. Nye, 8 Cal. App. 527, 97 Pac. 208.)

The Tenement House Act regulating the construction of buildings intended for human habitation and providing that such buildings shall not be occupied until the issuance of certain certificates by the health and building departments is within the police power of the state. (Matter of Stoltenberg, 21 Cal. App. 722, 132 Pac. 841.)

An ordinance limiting the hours of labor in public laundries to the period between 7 A. M. and 6 P. M. is constitutional. (In re Wong Wing, 167 Cal. 109, 51 L. R. A. (N. S.) 361, 138 Pac. 695.)

> Police power and the fourteenth amendment. See note, 25 Am. St. Rep. 852, 888.
>
> Police power defined. See note, 53 Am. St. Rep. 572.
>
> Police power to regulate or prohibit sale or manufacture of goods. See note, 1 Am. St. Rep. 644.
>
> Building regulations. See note, 93 Am. St. Rep. 403.
>
> Validity of statute or ordinance regulating sewage disposal. See note, Ann. Cas. 1913D, 61.
>
> Validity of legislation for prevention of fraud in weights and measures. See note, Ann. Cas. 1912C, 251.
>
> Police power. See 6 R. C. L., §§ 182-231, pp. 183-245.

INITIATIVE AND REFERENDUM.—The validity of the initiative and referendum was upheld by the supreme court of the United States in the case of Pacific States Telegraph and Telephone Co. v. State of Oregon, 223 U. S. 118, 56 L. Ed. 377, 32 Sup. Ct. Rep. 224. Mr. Louis Bartlett prepared for the Commonwealth Club of California an exhaustive review of the authorities applicable to the question, and

with his permission and the permission of the club that review is here set forth:

"To the Commonwealth Club:

"Gentlemen:—The following cases discuss 'The republican form of government guaranteed to states by the United States Constitution.'

"1.

"Luther v. Borden, 7 How. 1, 12 L. Ed. 581.

"This involved determining which state government was in force in Rhode Island in 1842—the old charter government established when Rhode Island was an English colony, or a new government attempted to be established by some people of the state, acting without warrant of the existing law. It was held that 'What is the existing government' is a political question, to be settled by the political branch of the government; and in admitting the representatives of a state to Congress, the latter necessarily decides that the form of government is republican; and its 'decision is binding on every other department of the government and could not be questioned in a judicial tribunal.'

"The question of what is a republican form of government did not arise and was not discussed.

"2.

"Minor v. Happersett, 21 Wallace, 175, 88 U. S. 175, 23 L. Ed. 631.

"This was an action against a registrar of voters for refusing to register a woman—the state Constitution providing that 'every male citizen of the United States . . . shall be entitled to vote.' It was held that the right to vote is not conferred upon woman by the guaranty to every state of a republican form of government.

" 'The guaranty is of a republican form of government. No particular government is designated as republican, neither is the exact form to be guaranteed, in any manner especially designated. Here, as in other parts of the instrument, we are compelled to resort elsewhere to ascertain what was intended.

" 'The guaranty necessarily implies a duty on the part of the states themselves to provide such a government. All the states had governments when the Constitution was adopted. In all, the people participated to some extent, through their representatives elected in the manner specially provided. These governments the Constitution did not change. They were accepted precisely as they were, and it is, therefore, to be presumed that they were such as it was the duty of the states to provide. Thus we have unmistakable evidence of what was republican in form, within the meaning of that term as employed in the Constitution.

" 'As has been seen, all the citizens of the states were not invested with the right of suffrage. In all, save perhaps New Jersey, this right was only bestowed upon men, and not upon all of them. Under these circumstances it is certainly now too late to contend that a government is not republican, within the meaning of this guaranty in the Constitution, because women are not made voters.'

"This case concerns itself with the classes of people who can participate in the government and not with the method of their action, whether direct or representative.

"3.

"In re Pfahler, 150 Cal. 71 [11 Ann. Cas. 911, 11 L. R. A. (N. S.)
1092, 88 Pac. 270].

"The question was as to the constitutionality of a police regulation
of the city of Los Angeles, adopted as an ordinance under the initiative provisions of the charter:

"Held by majority of the court, McFarland dissenting, that the
federal guaranty of a republican form of government does not prohibit the direct exercise of legislative power by the people of a subdivision of a state in strictly local affairs, as this system existed
and was well known when the Constitution was adopted. 'It is apparent from this condition of affairs, existing continuously from the
moment of the adoption of the Constitution, that, if there is anything
therein inconsistent with a republican form of government, within the
meaning of these words as used in the federal Constitution, the constitutional guaranty was intended to apply only to the form of government for the state at large, and not at all to the local government
prescribed by the state for its municipalities and other subdivisions.'

"4.

"Kadderly v. City of Portland, 44 Or. 118, 74 Pac. 710, 75 Pac. 222.

"Held that the provision of the United States Constitution, guaranteeing to every state a republican form of government does not prevent a state Constitution from providing for the initiative and
referendum in laws of state-wide application. The initiative and
referendum amendment does not abolish or destroy the republican
form of government or substitute another in its place. The representative character of the government still remains. The people simply reserve to themselves a larger share of legislative power, but they
have not overthrown the republican form of government and substituted another in its place.'

"5.

"Kiernan v. City of Portland, 57 Or. 454, 37 L. R. A. (N. S.) 332, 112
Pac. 402, at page 404.

"In discussing the constitutional guaranty of a republican form of
government, the court said:

" 'To ascertain whether taking from the legislature and delegating
to the municipalities or to the localities affected, local self-government, or a right to enact, maintain, and alter their charters as the
legislature formerly did, and whether the taking from the legislature
the right to make special laws upon the subject violates this provision of the national Constitution makes it important that we first
ascertain what is meant by a republican form of government. It is
an expression which all assume to understand, yet, judging from the
many unsuccessful attempts of eminent statesmen and writers to
give it a clear meaning, it would seem the phrase is not susceptible
to being given a precise definition. Especially is this true when
sought to be applied to the Constitution of different states, concerning which Mr. James Madison, a member of the constitutional convention. said: " . . . If we resort for a criterion to the different
principles on which different forms of government are established, we

may define a republic to be, or may at least bestow that name on, a government which derives all its powers directly or indirectly from the great body of the people, and is administered by persons holding their office during pleasure for a limited period or during good behavior. It is essential to such government that it be derived from the great body of society and not from any inconsiderable portion of a favored class of it. . . . " The Federalist (Hamilton ed.), paper 39, p. 301. Another and more pointed definition appears in Chisholm v. Georgia, 2 Dall. 419–457, 1 L. Ed. 440, by Mr. Justice Wilson, member of the constitutional convention, who, but a short time after the adoption of the federal Constitution, in adverting to what is meant by a republican form of government, remarked, "As a citizen, I know the government of that state (Georgia) to be republican, and my short definition of such a government—one constructed on this principle, that the supreme power resides in the body of the people." From which it follows that the converse must be true; that is to say, any government in which the supreme power resides with the people is republican in form. See, also, Mr. Justice Wilson's remarks to the same effect reported in 5 Elliott's Debates, 160.

" 'Measured in the light of the above, it is difficult to conceive of any system of law-making coming nearer to the great body of the people of the entire state, or by those comprising the various municipalities, than that now in use here, and, being so, we are at a loss to understand how the adoption and use of this system can be held a departure from a republican form of government. It was to escape the oppression resulting from governments controlled by the select few, so often ruling under the assumption that "might makes right," that gave birth to republics. Monarchical rulers refuse to recognize their accountability to the people governed by them. In a republic the converse is the rule. The tenure of office may be for a short or a long period, or even for life, yet those in office are at all times answerable, either directly or indirectly to the people, and in proportion to their responsibility for those for whom they may be the public agents, and the nearer the power to enact laws and control public servants lies with the great body of the people, the more nearly does a government take unto itself the form of a republic,—not in name alone, but in fact. From this it follows that each republic may differ in its political system or in the political machinery by which it moves, but, so long as the ultimate control of its officials and affairs of state remain in its citizens, it will in the eye of all republics be recognized as a government of that class. Of this we have many examples in Central and South America. It becomes then a matter of degree, and the fear manifested by the briefs filed in this case would seem to indicate, not that we are drifting from the secure moorings of a republic, but that our state, by the direct system of legislation complained of, is becoming too democratic—advancing too rapidly toward a republic pure in form. This, it is true, counsel for petitioner does not concede, but under any interpretation of which the term is capable, or from any view thus far found expressed in the writings of the prominent statesmen who were members of the constitutional convention, or who figured in the early upbuilding of the nation, it follows that the system here assailed brings us nearer

to a state republican in form than before its adoption. Mr. Thomas Jefferson, in 1816, when discussing the term republic, defined and illustrated his view thereof as follows: "Indeed, it must be acknowledged that the term 'republic' is of very vague application in every language. Witness the self-styled republics of Holland, Switzerland, Genoa, Venice, Poland. Were I to assign to this term a precise and definite idea, I would say, purely and simply, it means a government by its citizens in mass, acting directly and not personally, according to the rules established by the majority, and that every other government is more or less republican, in proportion as it has in its composition more or less of this ingredient of the direct action of the citizens." Writings of Thomas Jefferson, vol. 15, p. 19. It is well known that at the time of the adoption of the federal Constitution there existed in some of the Atlantic states a system of local government, known as "New England towns," in which the people had the right to legislate upon various matters, and masses assembling at stated periods for that purpose; all of which was within the knowledge of those composing the constitutional convention. After observing that a direct republic under his definition would necessarily be restrained to narrow limits, such as in a New England township, and that the next step in use at that time was through the representative system, Mr. Jefferson pointed out that the farther the officials of state or nation are separated from the masses proportionately less does such state or government retain the elements of a republic; and on page 23 concludes: "On this view of the import of the term 'republic,' instead of saying, as has been said, that it may mean anything or nothing, we may say with truth and meaning that governments are more or less republican, as they have more or less of the element of popular election and control in their composition; and believing, as I do, that the mass of citizens is the safest depository of their own rights and, especially, that the evils flowing through duperies of the people are less injurious than those from the egoism of their agents, I am a friend to that composition of government which has in it the most of this ingredient." The observations quoted are in full accord with the recorded views of all of the writers and statesmen of that time, when the intention of the framers of our national Constitution was fully understood, in the light of which it seems inconceivable that a state, merely because it may evolve a system by which its citizens become a branch of its legislative department, co-ordinate with their representatives in the legislature, loses caste as a republic. The extent to which a legislature of any state may enact laws is, and always has been, one of degree, depending upon limitations prescribed by its Constitution; some Constitutions having few and others many limitations. But in all states, whatever may be the restriction placed upon their representatives, the people, either by constitutional amendment or by convention, called for that purpose, have had, and have, the power to directly legislate, and to change all or any laws so far as deemed proper—limited only by clear inhibitions of the national Constitution. Cooley Const. Lim. (6th ed.), 44.

"'An examination of our state Constitution, as first adopted, discloses many restrictions upon the law-making department, among

which is a provision to the effect that no amendment thereto should
be submitted to the people for ratification until after it passed two
successive sessions of the legislature. In course of time, an amend
ment under this provision was legally submitted and adopted by a
majority vote of the people, by which the people reserved the right
to change the Constitution, or any part thereof without awaiting this
legislative formality, the validity of which is not open to doubt. It
is not possible, indeed, it is not practicable, then, for the people further to restrict the power of their representatives to legislate upon
matters of public interest, and in so doing are they not, and even
under the old system were they not, directly legislating? This system of direct legislation has been in common use throughout the various state governments since their inception, but until the adoption
of the initiative and referendum amendments, no one was heard to
assert that an amendment to the Constitution of a state merely
because of depriving the legislature of some law-making power or
powers held by it at the adoption of the national Constitution was
void on the grounds of being inconsistent with a republican form of
government. The absurdity of such a contention, if made, would at
once be obvious.'

"6.

"Following the case of Luther v. Borden, it appears that when Congress, the political branch of the federal government, has admitted
the representatives of a state to Congress, it has by that fact decided
that the form of government of that state is republican.

"Congress has admitted the representatives of the state of Oklahoma, and by so doing has declared that its form of government is
republican. Its Constitution contains the following provisions concerning the initiative and referendum:

"Article V.
"Legislative Department.
"Initiative and Referendum.

"Section 1. The legislative authority of the state shall be vested
in a legislature, consisting of a Senate and a House of Representatives, but the people reserve to themselves the power to propose laws
and amendments to the Constitution and to enact or reject the same
at the polls independent of the legislature, and also reserve power
at their own option to approve or reject at the polls any act of the
legislature.

"Section 2. The first power reserved by the people is the initiative,
and eight per centum of the legal voters shall have the right to propose any legislative measure, and fifteen per centum of the legal
voters shall have the right to propose amendments to the Constitution
by petition, and every such petition shall include the full text of the
measure so proposed. The second power is the referendum, and it
may be ordered (except as to laws necessary for the immediate preservation of public peace, health or safety), either by petition signed
by five per centum of the legal voters or by the legislature, as other
bills are enacted. The ratio and per centum of legal voters hereinbefore stated shall be based upon the total general election for the
state office receiving the highest number of votes at such election.

"Section 7. The reservation of the powers of the initiative and referendum in this article shall not deprive the legislature of the right to repeal any laws, propose or pass any measure, which may be consistent with the Constitution of the state and the Constitution of the United States.

"7.

"Eckerson v. City of Des Moines, 137 Iowa, 452, 115 N. W. 177.

" 'The federal guaranty of a republican form of government applies only to states and does not affect their subdivisions.'

"8.

"Hopkins v. Duluth, 81 Minn. 189, 83 N. W. 536.

" 'Providing local self-government by the voters directly interested through a referendum is abstractly as well as concretely more republican, than through representatives of the people in the legislature.' And the state Constitution doing this provides a republican form of government.

"9.

"State v. Schluer, 59 Or. 18, 115 Pac. 1057.

"This is the most recent case decided in Oregon and concerns the construction and effect of initiative provisions of the Oregon Constitution, but does not consider whether they are consistent with a republican form of government.

"10.

"To sum up:

"(a) The political branch of the federal government has decided in admitting Oklahoma to the Union, that the initiative and referendum of state-wide application are not inconsistent with a republican form of government, guaranteed by the federal Constitution.

"(b) The supreme court of California has decided that the initiative and referendum in municipal affairs is consistent with a republican form of government.

"(c) The supreme court of Oregon has declared that the referendum and initiative of state-wide application are not repugnant to a republican form of government.

"Respectfully submitted,
"LOUIS BARTLETT."

Additional References.—Political Science Quarterly, Vol. XXVI, No. 1 (March, 1911)—"People's Rule in Oregon"—Haynes.

Journal of Accountancy, Vol. XII, No. 2 (June, 1911)—"Facts About the Oregon System"—Ford; "Direct Legislation, etc."—Walker; "Oregon System in Practice"—Owen; "Massachusetts Wants the Initiative and Referendum"—Johnson.

Congressional Record, 62d Congress, 1st Session (1911). Debates on Constitution of Arizona.

The People's Law, or Popular Participation in Law-Making; a Study in the Evolution of Democracy and Direct Law-Making. By Charles S. Lobinger, N. Y. The Macmillan Co., 1909, pp. xxi, 429. This work contains a copious bibliography.

Appellant's brief, State of Oregon v. Pacific States Telegraph and Telephone Co., Sup. Ct. Or., March term, 1908. Full argument for invalidity of initiative legislation.

Initiative and Referendum: Ex parte Wagner, 21 Okl. 33, 18 Ann. Cas. 197, 95 Pac. 435; Norris et al. v. Cross, 25 Okl. 287, 105 Pac. 1000; State v. Langworthy, 55 Or. 303, 104 Pac. 424; In re Initiative Petition No. 2, 26 Okl. 548, 109 Pac. 823; Haines v. City of Forest Grove, 54 Or. 443, 103 Pac. 775; State v. Pacific Tel. & Tel. Co., 53 Or. 162, 99 Pac. 427; Farrell v. City of Portland, 52 Or. 582, 98 Pac. 145; Southwestern Tel. & Tel. Co. v. City of Dallas (Tex.), 131 S. W. 80; State v. Roach, 230 Mo. 408, 139 Am. St. Rep. 639, 130 S. W. 689; Brazell v. Zeigler, 26 Okl. 826, 110 Pac. 1052.

Constitutionality of initiative and referendum provisions in either state Constitutions or municipal charters. See note, 11 Ann. Cas. 920.

Validity of statute other than local option law which takes effect only upon ratification by voters. See note, 20 Ann. Cas. 652.

Initiative: In re Initiative State Question, No. 10, 26 Okl. 554, 110 Pac. 647; Common Council v. Harrington, 160 Mich. 550, 125 N. W. 383.

Initiative, Referendum and Recall: Graham v. Roberts, 200 Mass. 152, 85 N. E. 1009; Booth v. McGuinness, 78 N. J. L. 346, 75 Atl. 455.

Recall: Hilzinger v. Gillman, 56 Wash. 228, 21 Ann. Cas. 305, 105 Pac. 471.

Referendum: Meyer et al. v. Town of Boonville, 162 Ind. 165, 70 N. E. 146; Ray v. Colby & Tenney et al., 5 Neb. Unof. 151, 97 N. W. 591; Board of Education of Sapulpa v. McMahan, 26 Okl. 588, 110 Pac. 907; State v. Russell, 124 Wis. 548, 102 N. W. 1052; North v. McMahan, 26 Okl. 502, 110 Pac. 1115; State v. Portland Ry. Light & Power Co., 56 Or. 32, 107 Pac. 958.

The Referendum as a "Republican Form of Government."—The Harvard Law Review has the following discussion in its issue for December, 1910:

"The referendum has frequently been attacked as a delegation of legislative power and hence contrary to the state institutions, which vest that power in the legislature. (For a discussion of this phase of the problem, see 7 Harv. L. Rev. 485; 16 Ibid. 218.) Notwithstanding this argument, a general statute to take effect only if approved by a majority of the voters was upheld in a recent Wisconsin case. State ex rel. Van Alstine v. Frear, 142 Wis. 320, 20 Ann. Cas. 633, 125 N. W. 961. (For a discussion of another point in the same case, see 24 Harv. L. Rev. 50.)

"In view of the comparative ease with which state Constitutions are amended, the relation to them of direct legislation is not of such great practical importance as its validity under the Constitution of the United States. An objection to the referendum, especially when coupled with the initiative, which has frequently been suggested [see McClain, Constitutional Law, 10; 56 Cent. L. J. 247. But see Southwestern Telegraph & Telephone Co. v. City of Dallas (Tex.), 131 S. W. 80], but is not discussed in the principal case, is that direct

legislation violates the clause of the federal Constitution which guarantees to each state a republican form of government. (U. S. Const., art. IV, sec. 4. The contention is that a republic is a representative democracy as distinguished from a direct or pure democracy. Hence, it becomes important to determine the true meaning of the word.

"The Latin, res publica, at least as late as the sixteenth century, was altogether colorless as to the form of government it designated. (See Calvin, Institutionum Christianae Religionis, lib. 4, cap. 20.) The compound aljective is not found in classical or mediaeval Latin. (It does not appear in Du Cange, Glossarium.) The noun 'republic' and the adjective 'republican' were used by Wilson [see Chisholm v. Georgia, 2 Dall. (U. S.) 419, 457, 1 L. Ed. 440, 457], the author of the clause in its final form (see 2 Gilpin, Madison Papers, 1141), and by other publicists (see 1 Madison, Letters and Other Writings, 350; 4 Ibid. 467; 10 Ford, Writings of Thomas Jefferson, 28) of the time in a sense broad enough to include direct democracy. The same thing is true of the use of the corresponding French words republique and republicain by Montesquieu (see L'Esprit des Lois, liv. 2, c. 1, 2) and apparently by Rousseau (see Contrat Social, liv. 3, c. 4), the writings of both of whom had a great influence on American political thought of that period. The political party which advocated keeping the government as close to the people as possible was called, shortly after the formation of the Constitution, the Republican Party. (See Hart, Formation of the Union, 155, 164.) On the other hand, Madison defines a republic as 'a government in which the scheme of representation takes place," and contrasts it with a pure democracy. (See The Federalist, No. 10.) Discussion of the clause under consideration in the constitutional convention indicates that it was directed against insurrection, invasion, and monarchical forms. (See 2 Gilpin, Madison Papers, 1139–1141.)

"The state governments in existence in 1787 must be taken as examples of the republican form, in the sense in which that phrase is used in the Constitution. [See Minor v. Happersett, 21 Wall. (U. S.) 162, 22 L. Ed. 627.] In spite of the fact that the referendum appears in the formation of some of the state Constitutions (see Lobingier, The People's Law, 163–187) and in spite of the existence of the New England town government (for an argument from this that the guaranty has no application to local government, see Eckerson v. Des Moines, 137 Iowa, 452, 115 N. W. 177), so close a student of political science as Hamilton believed that the state governments were then wholly representative. (See The Federalist, No. 63.) Another of the authors of The Federalist, however, points out that the Constitution does not forbid the substitution of other republican forms for those then existing. [See Ibid, No. 43, sec. 6 (Madison).] It seems, on the whole, that 'republican' in the Constitution is ambiguous, and that a positive construction that it had a meaning so narrow as to exclude direct legislation cannot be supported.

"But even if 'Republican Form of Government' does mean representative government, it might well be contended that a slight tincture of direct democracy would not destroy the representative character of a state government. (See State v. Pacific States Telephone & Telegraph Co., 53 Or. 162, 99 Pac. 427; Kadderly v. City of Port-

land, 44 Or. 118, 74 Pac. 710, 75 Pac. 222.) Furthermore, it is probable that the enforcement of the constitutional guaranty is a political
question for Congress and the President rather than for the judiciary.
[See Taylor v. Beckham, 178 U. S. 548, 578, 44 L. Ed. 1187, 20 Sup.
Ct. Rep. 1009; Luther v. Borden, 7 How. (U. S.) 1, 42, 12 L. Ed.
581.]"

Sessions of legislature.

Sec. 2. The sessions of the legislature shall be biennial,
unless the governor shall, in the interim, convene the legislature, by proclamation, in extraordinary session. All sessions, other than extraordinary, shall commence at 12
o'clock M., on the first Monday after the first day of January next succeeding the election of its members, and shall
continue in session for a period not exceeding thirty days
thereafter; whereupon a recess of both houses must be
taken for not less than thirty days. On the reassembling of
the legislature, no bill shall be introduced in either house
without the consent of three-fourths of the members thereof,
nor shall more than two bills be introduced by any one member after such reassembling. (Amendment approved October 10, 1911.)

[AMENDMENT OF 1908.]

Sec. 2. The sessions of the legislature shall commence at 12
o'clock M. on the first Monday after the first day of January next
succeeding the election of its members, and after the election held
in the year 1880, shall be biennial, unless the governor shall, in
the interim, convene the legislature by proclamation. No bill shall
be introduced in either house forty days after the commencement
of each session without the consent of three-fourths of the members thereof. (Amendment adopted November 3, 1908.)

[ORIGINAL SECTION.]

Sec. 2. The sessions of the legislature shall commence at 12
o'clock M. on the first Monday after the first day of January next
succeeding the election of its members, and, after the election
held in the year eighteen hundred and eighty, shall be biennial,
unless the governor shall, in the interim, convene the legislature by
proclamation. No pay shall be allowed to members for a longer
time than sixty days, except for the first session after the adoption of this Constitution, for which they may be allowed pay for
one hundred days. And no bill shall be introduced, in either
house, after the expiration of ninety days from the commencement
of the first session, nor after fifty days after the commencement
of each succeeding session, without the consent of two-thirds of
the members thereof.

SESSIONS.—After the legislature has adjourned sine die, the court has no power to carry into effect a mandate requiring legislative action, even if such mandate were otherwise proper. (French v. Senate, 146 Cal. 604, 2 Ann. Cas. 756, 69 L. R. A. 556, 80 Pac. 1031.)

The legislature cannot be convened upon the mandate of the judicial power. (French v. Senate, 146 Cal. 604, 2 Ann. Cas. 756, 69 L. R. A. 556, 80 Pac. 1031.)

INTRODUCTION OF BILLS.—After the fifty days within which bills may be introduced have expired, a bill previously introduced may be amended in the same manner as before, and several bills may be consolidated in the form of a substitute. (Hale v. McGettigan, 114 Cal. 112, 45 Pac. 1049.)

If the legislative journals are silent upon the observance of any constitutional requirement as to the passage of bills, it cannot be assumed that such requirement was omitted by the legislature. (Hale v. McGettigan, 114 Cal. 112, 45 Pac. 1049.)

Election and term of assemblymen.

Sec. 3.   Members of the assembly shall be elected in the year eighteen hundred and seventy-nine, at the time and in the manner now provided by law.   The second election of members of the assembly, after the adoption of this Constitution, shall be on the first Tuesday after the first Monday in November, eighteen hundred and eighty.   Thereafter, members of the assembly shall be chosen biennially, and their term of office shall be two years; and each election shall be on the first Tuesday after the first Monday in November, unless otherwise ordered by the legislature.

Election and term of senators.

Sec. 4.   Senators shall be chosen for the term of four years, at the same time and places as members of the assembly, and no person shall be a member of the senate or assembly who has not been a citizen and inhabitant of the state three years, and of the district for which he shall be chosen one year, next before his election.

MEMBERS.—A person properly qualified when elected to the senate does not forfeit his office by the redistricting of the state, leaving the person outside of the district which he represents. (People v. Markham, 96 Cal. 262, 31 Pac. 102.)

Number and classes of senators.

Sec. 5.   The senate shall consist of forty members, and the assembly of eighty members, to be elected by districts,

numbered as hereinafter provided. The seats of the twenty senators elected in the year eighteen hundred and eighty-two from the odd-numbered districts shall be vacated at the expiration of the second year, so that one-half of the senators shall be elected every two years; provided, that all the senators elected at the first election under this Constitution shall hold office for the term of three years.

TERM OF OFFICE.—The seats of the twenty senators elected in 1882, from the districts designated in the act of 1874 by odd numbers, became vacant at the expiration of the second year, and their successors were required to be elected from the same districts for the term of two years. (McPherson v. Bartlett, 65 Cal. 577, 4 Pac. 582.)

Senatorial and legislative districts.

Sec. 6. For the purpose of choosing members of the legislature, the state shall be divided into forty senatorial and eighty assembly districts,. as nearly equal in population as may be, and composed of contiguous territory, to be called senatorial and assembly districts. Each senatorial district shall choose one senator, and each assembly district shall choose one member of assembly. The senatorial districts shall be numbered from one to forty, inclusive, in numerical order, and the assembly districts shall be numbered from one to eighty, in the same order, commencing at the northern boundary of the state, and ending at the southern boundary thereof. In the formation of such districts, no county, or city and county, shall be divided, unless it contain sufficient population within itself to form two or more districts; nor shall a part of any county, or of any city and county, be united with any other county, or city and county, in forming any district. The census taken under the direction of the Congress of the United States, in the year one thousand eight hundred and eighty, and every ten years thereafter, shall be the basis of fixing and adjusting the legislative districts; and the legislature shall, at its first session after each census, adjust such districts and reapportion the representation so as to preserve them as near equal in population as may be. But in making such adjustment no persons who are not eligible to become citizens of the United States, under the naturalization laws, shall be counted as

forming a part of the population of any district. Until such districting as herein provided for shall be made, senators and assemblymen shall be elected by the districts according to the apportionment now provided for by law.

LEGISLATIVE DISTRICTS.—The legislature may join two counties in one assembly district. (People v. Hill, 7 Cal. 97.)

The term of members of the senate is not affected by the fact that after their election the state is so redistricted that some counties in the newly formed districts will have double representation and others will be deprived of their fair and equal representation. (People v. Pendegast, 96 Cal. 289, 31 Pac. 103.)

Where the first legislature whose duty it is to provide for the apportionment fails to do so, the duty devolves upon each succeeding legislature until it is performed. (People v. Rice, 135 N. Y. 473, 16 L. R. A. 836, 31 N. E. 921.)

The legislature cannot be compelled to make an apportionment. (In re State Census, 6 S. D. 540, 62 N. W. 129.)

The apportionment must be according to population, but mathematical exactness is not required. (People v. Thompson, 155 Ill. 451, 40 N. E. 307; Parker v. State, 133 Ind. 178, 18 L. R. A. 567, 32 N. E. 836, 33 N. E. 119; Prouty v. Stover, 11 Kan. 235; Board of Supervisors v. Blacker, 92 Mich. 638, 16 L. R. A. 432, 52 N. W. 951; People v. Broome, 65 Hun, 624, 20 N. Y. Supp. 470; People v. Board of Aldermen, 14 Misc. Rep. 105, 35 N. Y. Supp. 259; People v. Rice, 135 N. Y. 473, 16 L. R. A. 836, 31 N. E. 921; Matter of Baird, 142 N. Y. 523, 37 N. E. 619; Matter of Whitney, 75 Hun, 581, 27 N. Y. Supp. 657; State v. Dudley, 1 Ohio St. 437; State v. Cunningham, 81 Wis. 440, 15 L. R. A. 561, 51 N. W. 724.)

If the apportionment is made in the exercise of a fair and honest discretion so as to preserve, as nearly as may be, equality of representation, it cannot be overthrown because not mathematically equal; but if the apportionment does not give substantially just and equal representation to the people of each county, it cannot be sustained. (Ballentine v. Willey, 3 Idaho, 496, 95 Am. St. Rep. 17, 31 Pac. 994; Prouty v. Stover, 11 Kan. 235; People v. Thompson, 155 Ill. 451, 40 N. E. 307; People v. Broome, 65 Hun, 624, 20 N. Y. Supp. 470; People v. Rice, 135 N. Y. 473, 16 L. R. A. 836, 31 N. E. 921; Smith v. St. Lawrence Co., 148 N. Y. 187, 42 N. E. 592; State v Cunningham, 83 Wis. 90, 35 Am. St. Rep. 27, 17 L. R. A. 145, 53 N. W. 35.)

While this section provides that persons who are not eligible to become citizens of the United States shall not be counted in making the apportionment, an apportionment is not necessarily invalid because they are counted. (Matter of Whitney, 142 N. Y. 531, 37 N. E. 621; People v. Rice, 135 N. Y. 473, 16 L. R. A. 836, 31 N. E. 921; Matter of Whitney, 75 Hun, 581, 27 N. Y. Supp. 657.)

This section requires that the districts shall be composed of contiguous territory, and, while the legislature has some discretion in this matter, if it has been wholly ignored, the apportionment is void. (People v. Thompson, 155 Ill. 451, 40 N. E. 307; State v. Cunningham, 83 Wis. 90, 35 Am. St. Rep. 27, 17 L. R. A. 145, 53 N. W. 35.)

As to what territory is "contiguous," see Board of Supervisors v. Blacker, 92 Mich. 638, 16 L. R. A. 432, 52 N. W. 951; Parker v. State, 133 Ind. 178, 18 L. R. A. 567, 32 N. E. 836, 33 N. E. 119; People v. Thompson, 155 Ill. 451, 40 N. E. 307.

Under this section a county cannot be divided, unless it contains sufficient population to make two or more districts. (Board of Supervisors v. Blacker, 92 Mich. 638, 16 L. R. A. 432, 52 N. W. 951; State v. Cunningham, 81 Wis. 440, 15 L. R. A. 561, 51 N. W. 724; People v. Board of Aldermen, 89 Hun, 460, 35 N. Y. Supp. 817.)

Organization of legislature.

Sec. 7.   Each house shall choose its officers, and judge of the qualifications, elections, and returns of its members.

QUALIFICATIONS OF MEMBERS.—Whether a senator has been regularly elected is a question exclusively for the senate. (Opinion of Justices, 12 Fla. 686.)

The house is to judge of the election of its members and the returns are only prima facie evidence of election. (Chrisman v. Anderson, 2 Cong. El. Cas. 328; Spaulding v. Mead, 1 Cong. El. Cas. 157.)

The refusal of the executive of a state to grant a certificate of election will not prejudice the right to a seat. (Richard's Case, Clark & H. 95; Clement's Case, Cong. El. Cas. 1864–65, 366.)

The qualifications of members being fixed by the Constitution, additional ones cannot be required by the legislature. (Barney v. McCreery, 1 Cong. El. Cas. 167; Turney v. Marshall, 2 Cong. El. Cas. 167; Trumbull's Case, 2 Cong. El. Cas. 618.)

While the jurisdiction conferred by this provision upon the legislature is exclusive of the jurisdiction of the courts, the canvassers may be compelled by mandamus to conduct the canvass and declare the result, thus giving the person holding the certificate the prima facie right to the seat. (O'Ferrall v. Colby, 2 Minn. 180.)

As to the qualifications of members of inferior legislative bodies, see People v. Bingham, 82 Cal. 238, 22 Pac. 1039.

By this section the assembly is made the exclusive judge of the qualifications of its members, and the law providing for an official ballot cannot be held to have changed the intent of the people in adopting that constitutional provision that the assembly should be the sole and exclusive judge of the eligibility of those whose election is properly certified. (Allen v. Lelande, 164 Cal. 56, 127 Pac. 643.)

What number constitutes a quorum.

Sec. 8.   A majority of each house shall constitute a quorum to do business, but a smaller number may adjourn from day to day, and may compel the attendance of absent members in such manner, and under such penalties, as each house may provide.

QUORUM.—A rule providing that "on demand of any member, or at the suggestion of the speaker, the names of members sufficient to

make a quorum in the hall of the house who do not vote shall be noted by the clerk and recorded in the journal, and reported to the speaker with the names of the members voting, and be counted and announced in determining the presence of a quorum to do business," is a constitutional mode of ascertaining the presence of a quorum. (United States v. Ballin, 144 U. S. 1, 36 L. Ed. 321, 12 Sup. Ct. Rep. 507.)

Rules for their government—Expulsions.

Sec. 9.   Each house shall determine the rule of its proceeding, and may, with the concurrence of two-thirds of all the members elected, expel a member.

EXPULSION OF MEMBERS.—A member may be expelled for any misdemeanor which, though not punishable by statute, is inconsistent with the trust and duty of a member. (Smith's Case, 1 Hall Law J. 459.)

The power granted by this section to expel a member for bribery is not affected by the provision of section 35 of this article, making such bribery a felony. (French v. Senate, 146 Cal. 604, 2 Ann. Cas. 756, 69 L. R. A. 556, 80 Pac. 1031.)

A resolution of expulsion from the legislature has no effect upon the rights of the member expelled further than to terminate his right to sit as a member of the legislative body. (French v. Senate, 146 Cal. 604, 2 Ann. Cas. 756, 69 L. R. A. 556, 80 Pac. 1031.)

The power of the senate to expel a member is exclusive and the judiciary has no power to control the most arbitrary and unfair action of the legislative department in that regard. (French v. Senate, 146 Cal. 604, 2 Ann. Cas. 756, 69 L. R. A. 556, 80 Pac. 1031.)

As to the power to punish for contempt, see note to section 1 of this article.

> Power of legislature to expel members. See note, 2 Ann. Cas. 759.

Each house to keep a journal.

Sec. 10.   Each house shall keep a journal of its proceedings, and publish the same, and the yeas and nays of the members of either house, on any question, shall, at the desire of any three members present, be entered on the journal.

JOURNALS.—A journal is a public record of which courts may take judicial notice. (Brown v. Nash, 1 Wyo. 85.)

The journal cannot be kept secret unless the proceedings are secret. The holding of a secret session by either house is in its discretion. (Nugent's Case, 1 Am. L. J. (N. S.) 139, Fed. Cas. No. 10,375.)

The journals required by law to be kept are a record of the proceedings of the houses of the legislature, and so intended. They are, to all intents and purposes, records made in perpetuam memoriam

rei, there entered. (Oakland Pav. Co. v. Hilton, 69 Cal. 479, 11 Pac. 3.)

The decisions in the various states are conflicting as to how far, if at all, the journals of the legislature may be resorted to in order to determine whefher or not an act was properly passed; but in this state it is held that the validity of a statute, which has been duly certified, approved, enrolled, and deposited in the office of the secretary of state, cannot be impeached by a resort to the journals of the legislature. (Yolo Co. v. Colgan, 132 Cal. 265, 84 Am. St. Rep. 41, 64 Pac. 403; People v. Harlan, 133 Cal. 16, 65 Pac. 9.)

The court takes judicial notice of the proceedings had in the legislature and entered upon its journals. (French v. Senate, 146 Cal. 604, 2 Ann. Cas. 756, 69 L. R. A. 556, 80 Pac. 1031.)

This section does not require any entry on the journals of either house respecting the return to the legislature of a bill vetoed by the governor. (Parkinson v. Johnson, 160 Cal. 756, 117 Pac. 1057.)

Privilege of members.

Sec. 11. Members of the legislature shall, in all cases, except treason, felony, and breach of the peace, be privileged from arrest, and shall not be subject to any civil process during the session of the legislature, nor for fifteen days next before the commencement and after the termination of each session.

PRIVILEGE FROM ARREST.—Arrest implies corporate restraint. (Wooley v. Butler, 1 Bank. L. T. 35.)

This privilege extends to judicial as well as mesne process, and a person arrested is entitled to his discharge on the privilege afterward acquired. (Coxe v. McClenachan, 3 Dall. 478, 1 L. Ed. 687; Nones v. Edsall, 1 Wall. Jr. 189, Fed. Cas. No. 10,290.)

There is no privilege from the service or obligation of a subpoena in a criminal case. (United States v. Cooper, 4 Dall. 341, 1 L. Ed. 859, Fed. Cas. No. 14,861.)

Members are privileged not only from arrest, but also from a service of summons or other civil process while in attendance on their public duties. (Coxe v. McClenachan, 3 Dall. 478, 1 L. Ed. 687; Geyer v. Irwin, 4 Dall. 107, 1 L. Ed. 762; Nones v. Edsall, 1 Wall. Jr. 191, Fed. Cas. No. 10,290.)

Service of civil process upon members of the legislature. See note, 2 Ann. Cas. 615.

Vacancies, how filled.

Sec. 12. When vacancies occur in either house, the governor, or the person exercising the functions of the governor, shall issue writs of election to fill such vacancies.

VACANCIES may be created by death, resignation, or removal, or by the acceptance of an incompatible office. (People v. Carrique, 2

Hill (N. Y.), 93; Powell v. Wilson, 16 Tex. 60; Biencourt v. Parker, 27 Tex. 558.)

A resignation sent to the governor of a state is sufficient. (Edward's Case, Clark & H. 92; Mercer's Case, Clark & H. 44; Bledsoe's Case, Clark & H. 869.)

The executive may issue writs for a new election without waiting to be informed by the house that a vacancy exists. (Mercer's Case, Clark & H. 44.)

Open doors and secret sessions.

Sec. 13. The doors of each house shall be open, except on such ocasions as, in the opinion of the house, may require secrecy.

Adjournment, how long and where to.

Sec. 14. Neither house shall, without the consent of the other, adjourn for more than three days, nor to any place other than that in which they may be sitting. Nor shall the members of either house draw pay for any recess or adjournment for a longer time than three days.

ADJOURNMENT.—An adjournment of the house for more than three days without the concurrence of the senate does not ipso facto work a dissolution of the general assembly. (West Phil. Pass. R. R. Co. v. Union Pass. R. Co., 4 Leg. Gaz. 193, 29 Leg. Int. 196.)

Origin and passage of bills.

Sec. 15. No law shall be passed except by bill. Nor shall any bill be put upon its final passage until the same, with the amendments thereto, shall have been printed for the use of the members; nor shall any bill become a law unless the same be read on three several days in each house, unless, in case of urgency, two-thirds of the house where such bill may be pending shall, by a vote of yeas and nays, dispense with this provision. Any bill may originate in either house, but may be amended or rejected by the other; and on the final passage of all bills they shall be read at length, and the vote shall be by yeas and nays upon each bill separately, and shall be entered on the journal; and no bill shall become a law without the concurrence of a majority of the members elected to each house.

PASSAGE OF BILLS.—The word "read" is used in this section in its popular, and not in its technical, sense, and means read at length,

and not read as is usual in parliamentary bodies. (Weill v. Ken-field, 54 Cal. 111.)

It is not essential to the validity of a statute that it should affirma-tively appear from the legislative journals that every act required by the Constitution to be done in the enactment of a law has been done; nor will it be presumed, in the absence of a showing, that such acts were not done. (People v. Dunn, 80 Cal. 211, 13 Am. St. Rep. 118, 22 Pac. 140; Hale v. McGettigan, 114 Cal. 112, 45 Pac. 1049.)

If an act is properly enrolled and authenticated, and is deposited with the secretary of state, it is conclusive evidence of the legisla-tive will, and courts will not look into the journals of the legislature to see whether or how the bill passed. (People v. Burt, 43 Cal. 560; Yolo Co. v. Colgan, 132 Cal. 265, 84 Am. St. Rep. 81, 64 Pac. 403; People v. Harlan, 133 Cal. 16, 65 Pac. 9.)

A resolution adopted by a two-thirds vote, declaring that a number of specified bills "present cases of urgency," and that the provision of the Constitution "requiring that the bill be read on three separate days in each house is hereby dispensed with," is sufficient, and it is not objectionable on the ground that it includes more than one bill. (People v. Glenn Co., 100 Cal. 419, 38 Am. St. Rep. 305, 35 Pac. 302.)

The fact that several of the senators who voted to declare a bill a case of urgency afterward voted against the bill is immaterial. (People v. Glenn Co., 100 Cal. 419, 38 Am. St. Rep. 305, 35 Pac. 302.)

> What constitutes final passage of bill within constitutional pro-vision requiring vote on final passage to be by yeas and nays. See note, 16 Ann. Cas. 977.
>
> Necessity of signature of presiding officers to bills passed by legis-lature. See note, 4 Ann. Cas. 905.
>
> Legislative journals as evidence of due passage of statutes. See note, 58 Am. Dec. 574.
>
> Impeachment of act of legislature by reference to legislative journals. See notes, 9 Ann. Cas. 582; 20 Ann. Cas. 350.
>
> Judicial notice of contents of legislative journals on issues as to enactment of statute. See note, 20 Ann. Cas. 449.

Approval and return of bills—Passage over veto.

Sec. 16. Every bill which may have passed the legisla-ture shall, before it becomes a law, be presented to the gov-ernor. If he approve it, he shall sign it; but if not, he shall return it, with his objections, to the house in which it origi-nated, which shall enter such objections upon the journal and proceed to reconsider it. If after such reconsideration, it again pass both houses, by yeas and nays, two-thirds of the members elected to each house voting therefor, it shall become a law, notwithstanding the governor's objections. If any bill shall not be returned within ten days after it shall have been presented to him (Sundays excepted), the

same shall become a law in like manner as if he had signed it, unless the legislature, by adjournment, prevents such return, in which case it shall not become a law, unless the governor, within thirty days after such adjournment (Sundays excepted), shall sign and deposit the same in the office of the secretary of state, in which case it shall become a law in like manner as if it had been signed by him before adjournment. If any bill presented to the governor contains several items of appropriation of money, he may object to one or more items, while approving other portions of the bill. In such a case he shall append to the bill at the time of signing it, a statement of the items to which he objects, and the reasons therefor, and the appropriation so objected to shall not take effect unless passed over the governor's veto, as hereinbefore provided. If the legislature be in session, the governor shall transmit to the house in which the bill originated a copy of such statement, and the items so objected to shall be separately reconsidered in the same manner as bills which have been disapproved by the governor. (Amendment adopted November 3, 1908.)

[ORIGINAL SECTION.]

Sec. 16. Every bill which may have passed the legislature shall, before it becomes a law, be presented to the governor. If he approve it, he shall sign it; but if not, he shall return it, with his objections, to the house in which it originated, which shall enter such objections upon the journal and proceed to reconsider it. If, after such reconsideration, it again pass both houses, by yeas and nays, two-thirds of the members elected to each house voting therefor, it shall become a law, notwithstanding the governor's objections. If any bill shall not be returned within ten days after it shall have been presented to him (Sundays excepted), the same shall become a law in like manner as if he had signed it, unless the legislature, by adjournment, prevents such return, in which case it shall not become a law, unless the governor, within ten days after such adjournment (Sundays excepted), shall sign and deposit the same in the office of the secretary of state, in which case it shall become a law in like manner as if it had been signed by him before adjournment. If any bill presented to the governor contains several items of appropriation of money, he may object to one or more items, while approving other portions of the bill. In such case he shall append to the bill, at the time of signing it, a statement of the items to which he objects, and the reasons therefor, and the appropriation so objected to shall not take effect unless passed over the governor's veto, as hereinbefore provided. If the legislature be in session, the governor shall

transmit to the house in which the bill originated a copy of such statement, and the items so objected to shall be separately reconsidered in the same manner as bills which have been disapproved by the governor.

APPROVAL BY THE GOVERNOR.—The day upon which the bill is presented to the governor should be excluded. (Price v. Whitman, 8 Cal. 412; Iron Mountain Co. v. Haight, 39 Cal. 540.)

In People v. Whitman, 6 Cal. 659, it was held that only where the last day fell upon a Sunday should Sundays be excepted in making the computation; but this case was overruled in the case of Price v. Whitman, 8 Cal. 412, it having been decided upon an error in the printed copy of the Constitution, the word "Sundays" being used in the singular.

A law is not finally passed until it is approved by the governor and transmitted by him to the secretary of state. (Davis v. Whidden, 117 Cal. 618, 49 Pac. 766.)

Where inconsistent acts are approved on the same day, it is to be presumed that they were published in the chronological order of their approval; but the court will take judicial notice of the time of the approval of each act, and may resort to the office of the secretary of state to learn the exact time thereof. (Davis v. Whidden, 117 Cal. 618, 49 Pac. 766.)

Where an act purports to have been approved by the governor on the last day of the session, parol evidence is admissible to show that in fact it was approved on the succeeding day. (Fowler v. Peirce, 2 Cal. 165.)

Where a statute is declared to take effect from and after its passage, it takes effect at the very moment of its approval by the governor. (People v. Clark, 1 Cal. 406.)

An act approved by the governor after the adjournment of the legislature was void under the former Constitution. (Fowler v. Peirce, 2 Cal. 165.)

When exercising the powers of approving or disapproving bills, the governor is a special agent with limited powers, and can act only in the specified mode and can exercise only the granted powers. (Lukens v. Nye, 156 Cal. 498, 20 Ann. Cas. 158, 36 L. R. A. (N. S.) 244, 105 Pac. 593.)

Only the objections of the governor to a bill he has vetoed and returned to the legislature are required to be entered upon the journal of each house, and the time of the return of the bill need not be entered. (Parkinson v. Johnson, 160 Cal. 756, 117 Pac. 1057.)

> Power of executive to approve bill in part only. See note, 20 Ann. Cas. 162.
>
> Computation of time allowed executive to sign or reject bill passed by legislature. See note, 6 Ann. Cas. 717.
>
> Right of executive to withdraw approval of bill. See note, 13 Ann. Cas. 230.

Impeachments, presentment and trial of.

Sec. 17. The assembly shall have the sole power of impeachment, and all impeachments shall be tried by the sen-

ate. When sitting for that purpose, the senators shall be upon oath or affirmation, and no person shall be convicted without the concurrence of two-thirds of the members elected.

IMPEACHMENT.—A member of the house voting for the prosecution of an impeachment is not thereby rendered disqualified, if subsequently elected to the senate, from sitting on a trial thereof. (Addison's Trial, 21–28; Porter's Trial, 53.)

All the functions of the governor are entirely suspended during his trial. (Opinion of Judges, 3 Neb. 463.)

For an impeachment to be effectual, the articles must be presented to the senate, and a constitutional quorum of the entire membership must receive it. (Opinion of Justices, 12 Fla. 653.)

What officers liable to impeachment—Judgment on.

Sec. 18. The governor, lieutenant-governor, secretary of state, controller, treasurer, attorney general, surveyor-general, chief justice and associate justices of the supreme court, judges of the district court of appeal, and judges of the superior courts, shall be liable to impeachment for any misdemeanor in office; but judgment in such cases shall extend only to removal from office, and disqualification to hold any office of honor, trust, or profit under the state; but the party convicted or acquitted shall nevertheless be liable to indictment, trial, and punishment according to law. All other civil officers shall be tried for misdemeanor in office in such manner as the legislature may provide. (Amendment approved October 10, 1911.)

[ORIGINAL SECTION.]

Sec. 18. The governor, lieutenant-governor, secretary of state, controller, treasurer, attorney general, surveyor-general, chief justice and associate justices of the supreme court, and judges of the superior courts, shall be liable to impeachment for any misdemeanor in office; but judgment in such cases shall extend only to removal from office, and disqualification to hold any office of honor, trust, or profit under the state; but the party convicted or acquitted shall nevertheless be liable to indictment, trial, and punishment according to law. All other civil officers shall be tried for misdemeanor in office in such manner as the legislature may provide.

REMOVAL OF OFFICERS.—This section gives to the legislature power to provide for the removal of officers without a jury trial. (Woods v. Varnum, 85 Cal. 639, 24 Pac. 843.)

The supreme court has no jurisdiction of an appeal from a judgment in a proceeding under section 772 of the Penal Code for the re-

moval of public officers, the legislature not having provided for such jurisdiction. (In re Curtis, 108 Cal. 661, 41 Pac. 793.)

The act of 1853 entitled "An act to prevent extortion in office and to enforce official duty," held valid. (Matter of Marks, 45 Cal. 199.)

While the Constitution has provided for the impeachment of certain officers, it has left all other civil officers to be tried for misdemeanors in such manner as the legislature may provide. (Matter of Marks, 45 Cal. 199.)

A presiding judge is liable to impeachment for preventing an associate judge from delivering his opinion to a grand or petit jury upon a matter before the court. (Addison's Trial, 114, 151; Commonwealth v. Addison, 4 Dall. 225, 1 L. Ed. 810; Porter's Trial, 61.)

A public officer who refuses to enforce the law forbidding gambling is guilty of "misdemeanor in office." (Coffey v. Superior Court, 147 Cal. 525, 82 Pac. 75.)

Sections 758 and following of the Penal Code do not provide for the removal of public officers by indictment, and the people have no appeal from an order sustaining a demurrer to the accusation. (Matter of Burleigh, 145 Cal. 35, 78 Pac. 242.)

The legislature had plenary power to pass sections 758 et seq. of the Penal Code dealing with the removal of civil officers otherwise than by impeachment. (Matter of Accusation of Shepard, 161 Cal. 171, 118 Pac. 513.)

This section does not authorize the legislature to enlarge the appellate jurisdiction of the higher courts beyond the limits expressly laid down in another part of the Constitution, and section 770 of the Penal Code giving an apppeal to the supreme court from a judgment removing a public officer cannot be sustained under it. (People v. McKamy, 168 Cal. 531, 143 Pac. 752.)

Member ineligible to office created during the term.

Sec. 19. No senator or member of assembly shall, during the term for which he shall have been elected, be appointed to any civil office of profit under this state which shall have been created, or the emoluments of which have been increased, during such term, except such offices as may be filled by election by the people.

OFFICES.—This section does not inhibit the appointment of a member of the legislature to the office of harbor commissioner, which office was not created, nor the emoluments thereof increased, during his term of office—the method of filling, the duties and functions of the office alone being changed. (People v. Burns, 53 Cal. 660.)

This section does not disqualify a member of the legislature from holding an office, the emoluments of which are increased during his legislative term, but after his election to such office. (State v. Boyd, 21 Wis. 208.)

Who ineligible to office under state government—Proviso.

Sec. 20. No person holding any lucrative office under the United States, or any other power, shall be eligible to any civil office of profit under this state; provided, that officers in the militia, who receive no annual salary, local officers, or postmasters whose compensation does not exceed five hundred dollars per annum, shall not be deemed to hold lucrative offices.

OFFICE OF PROFIT.—The words "lucrative office" in the proviso of this section refer solely to the office under the United States; and if the salary of that office exceeds five hundred dollars per annum, its incumbent cannot hold any civil office of profit under the state, notwithstanding the profit of the state office is less than five hundred dollars per annum. (People v. Leonard, 73 Cal. 230, 14 Pac. 853.)

The federal office of surveyor-general is a "lucrative office," and the office of controller of state an "office of profit." (People v. Whitman, 10 Cal. 38.)

The office of school superintendent of a county is a civil office. (Crawford v. Dunbar, 52 Cal. 36.)

The office of inspector of customs in a collection district, to which there is annexed a salary of one thousand dollars per annum, is a lucrative office. (Crawford v. Dunbar, 52 Cal. 36.)

A retired army officer does not hold a lucrative "office" within the meaning of this section. (Reed v. Schon, 2 Cal. App. 55, 83 Pac. 77.)

To constitute a holding, the officer must be appointed and qualify by giving a bond and taking the oath of office; and one who has not so qualified under a federal appointment is eligible to office in this state. (People v. Whitman, 10 Cal. 38.)

This section applies to incumbents de facto of a lucrative office. (Crawford v. Dunbar, 52 Cal. 36.)

This section refers to the power to hold as well as to be elected to office; consequently, a person duly eligible and elected to a civil office of profit under the state cannot hold the office after he has accepted a lucrative federal office. (People v. Leonard, 73 Cal. 230, 14 Pac. 853.)

"Eligible" means capable of being chosen—the subject of selection or choice; and "compensation" means the income of the office, not its profits. (Searcy v. Grow, 15 Cal. 117.)

If a member at the time of his election hold a disqualifying office, it is sufficient that he qualify himself by a resignation of it before he is sworn in. (Commonwealth v. Pyle, 18 Pa. 519.)

The appointment to a second incompatible office is not absolutely void, but the first office is ipso facto vacated. (People v. Carrique, 2 Hill (N. Y.), 93; Biencourt v. Parker, 27 Tex. 558.)

A person holding two compatible offices is not precluded from holding the salaries of both. (Converse v. United States, 21 How. (U. S.) 463, 16 L. Ed. 192; Brown's Case, 9 Op. Atty. Gen. 508.)

Embezzlement or defalcation—Penalty for.

Sec. 21. No person convicted of the embezzlement or de-falcation of the public funds of the United States, or of any state, or of any county or municipality therein, shall ever be eligible to any office of honor, trust, or profit under this state, and the legislature shall provide, by law, for the punishment of embezzlement or defalcation as a felony.

Public moneys and accounts—Statement of receipts and expenditures—Panama-Pacific International Exposition.

Sec. 22. No money shall be drawn from the treasury but in consequence of appropriations made by law, and upon warrants duly drawn thereon by the controller; and no money shall ever be appropriated or drawn from the state treasury for the purpose or benefit of any corporation, asso-ciation, asylum, hospital, or any other institution not under the exclusive management and control of the state as a state institution, nor shall any grant or donation of property ever be made thereto by the state; provided, that notwithstand-ing anything contained in this or any other section of this Constitution, the legislature shall have the power to grant aid to the institutions conducted for the support and mainte-nance of minor orphans, or half orphans, or abandoned chil-dren, or aged persons in indigent circumstances—such aid to be granted by a uniform rule, and proportioned to the number of inmates of such respective institutions; provided, further, that the state shall have at any time the right to inquire into the management of such institution; provided, further, that whenever any county, or city and county, or city, or town, shall provide for the support of minor or-phans, or half orphans, or abandoned children, or aged persons in indigent circumstances, such county, city and county, city, or town shall be entitled to receive the same pro rata appropriations as may be granted to such institu-tions under church or other control. An accurate statement of the receipts and expenditures of public moneys shall be attached to and published with the laws at every regular session of the legislature.

Provided, however, that for the purpose of raising five million dollars ($5,000,000), to be used in establishing, main-

taining, and supporting in the city and county of San Francisco, state of California, an exposition in commemoration of the completion of the Panama canal, to be known as the Panama-Pacific International Exposition, the state board of equalization shall, for the fiscal year beginning July 1, 1911, and for each fiscal year thereafter, to and including the fiscal year beginning July 1, 1914, fix, establish, and levy such an ad valorem rate of taxation, as when levied upon all the taxable property in the state, after making due allowance for delinquency, shall produce for each of such fiscal years a sum of one million two hundred and fifty thousand dollars ($1,250,000). The said taxes shall be levied, assessed, and collected upon every kind and character of property in the state of California not exempt from taxation under the law, and subject to taxation on the 1st day of July, 1910, and in the same manner, and by the same method, as other state taxes were levied, assessed, and collected under the law, as the same existed on the 1st day of July, 1910. The state board of equalization shall each year, at the time it determines the amount or revenue required for other state purposes, determine, fix, and include the rate of tax necessary to raise the revenue herein provided for.

There is hereby created in the state treasury a fund to be known as the Panama-Pacific International Exposition fund, and all moneys collected pursuant to this provision, after deducting the proportionate share of the expense for the collection of the same, shall be paid into the state treasury, and credited to such fund. All moneys so paid into such fund are hereby appropriated, without reference to fiscal years, for the use, establishment, maintenance, and support of said Panama-Pacific International Exposition. No tax, license fee, or charge of any kind or character shall ever be levied or assessed or charged against any property of said Panama-Pacific International Exposition, or against any property used as exhibit therein, while being used or exhibited in connection therewith.

There is hereby created a commission to be known as the Panama-Pacific International Exposition Commission of the state of California, which shall consist of the governor of

said state and four other members to be appointed by the governor, by and with the advice and consent of the senate of said state. The governor shall have the power to fill all vacancies occurring at any time in said commission. The members of said commission shall receive no compensation and shall hold office until such exposition shall have been closed and its affairs settled. Said four members of said commission shall be selected from different sections of the state, and the appointment thereof shall be made by the governor of the state during the month of February, 1911. The commission hereby created shall have the exclusive charge and control of all moneys paid into the Panama-Pacific International Exposition fund; and provided further that the legislature shall pass all laws necessary to carry out the provisions of this act, including the times and the manner in which and the terms and conditions upon which money shall be drawn from the state treasury by said commission; where contracts and vouchers shall be filed; to whom and how often reports shall be made; what disposition shall be made of any sum left unexpended or received from the sale of any property or buildings purchased or constructed by said commission for the use of said exposition, or of any disposition of any building or improvement constructed by said commission out of said fund, and to provide for the transfer to the general fund of the state of California of any portion of said Panama-Pacific International Exposition fund unused.

The commission herein created is authorized and directed to make such proper contracts with the Panama-Pacific International Exposition Company, a corporation organized under the laws of the state of California on the 22d day of March, 1910, as will entitle the state of California to share proportionately with the contributors to the said Panama-Pacific International Exposition in the returns from the holding of said exposition at the city and county of San Francisco. (Amendment adopted November 8, 1910.)

[ORIGINAL SECTION.]

Sec. 22. No money shall be drawn from the treasury but in consequence of appropriations made by law, and upon warrants

duly drawn thereon by the controller; and no money shall ever be appropriated or drawn from the state treasury for the use or benefit of any corporation, association, asylum, hospital, or any other institution not under the exclusive management and control of the state as a state institution, nor shall any grant or donation of property ever be made thereto by the state; provided, that notwithstanding anything contained in this or any other section of this Constitution, the legislature shall have the power to grant aid to institutions conducted for the support and maintenance of minor orphans, or half orphans, or abandoned children, or aged persons in indigent circumstances—such aid to be granted by a uniform rule, and proportioned to the number of inmates of such respective institutions; provided further, that the state shall have, at any time, the right to inquire into the management of such institutions; provided further, that whenever any county, or city and county, or city, or town shall provide for the support of minor orphans, or half orphans, or abandoned children, or aged persons in indigent circumstances, such county, city and county, city, or town shall be entitled to receive the same pro rata appropriations as may be granted to such institutions under church or other control. An accurate statement of the receipts and expenditures of public moneys shall be attached to and published with the laws at every regular session of the legislature.

APPROPRIATIONS.—No money can be drawn from the treasury but in consequence of appropriations made by law. (Baggett v. Dunn, 69 Cal. 75, 10 Pac. 125.)

To an appropriation nothing more is requisite than a designation of the amount and fund out of which it shall be paid. It is not essential to its validity that funds to meet the same shall be at the time in the treasury. (People v. Brooks, 16 Cal. 11.)

This provision is designed only to secure to the legislative department the exclusive power of deciding to what purpose the public funds shall be devoted in each fiscal year, and no particular form of legislative words is required to make an appropriation valid. (Humbert v. Dunn, 84 Cal. 57, 24 Pac. 111.)

This provision does not prohibit the legislature from appropriating its funds in time of war to aid a corporation in the construction of a railroad to be used by the state for military purposes. (People v. Pacheco, 27 Cal. 175.)

There is no restriction as to the time for which appropriations may be made. (People v. Pacheco, 27 Cal. 175.)

The provision of this section giving counties, cities, and towns the same pro rata amounts granted by the legislature to private institutions is self-executing, and where the legislature grants such aid to private institutions, such counties, cities, and towns become entitled to the same aid. (Yolo Co. v. Dunn, 77 Cal. 133, 19 Pac. 262; San Francisco v. Dunn, 69 Cal. 73, 10 Pac. 191.)

An act appropriating three hundred thousand dollars to meet the expenses of erecting buildings and maintaining an exhibit of the products of the state at the World's Fair at Chicago, and providing that the appropriation should be expended under the exclusive charge of

a commission appointed by the governor, is not in conflict with this provision. (Daggett v. Colgan, 92 Cal. 53, 27 Am. St. Rep. 95, 14 L. R. A. 474, 28 Pac. 51.)

An act creating an office and providing that the officer "shall receive a salary of two thousand four hundred dollars per annum, payable monthly, . . . to be paid out of any money in the state treasury not otherwise appropriated," is sufficient to show an intention to appropriate such sum. (Humbert v. Dunn, 84 Cal. 57, 24 Pac. 111.)

An act providing for the commitment of minor criminals to nonsectarian charitable corporations, the expense of maintenance to be paid by the county, is not in violation of this section, since it only applies to the state treasury. (Boys' & Girls' Aid Soc. v. Reis, 71 Cal. 627, 12 Pac. 796.)

A law providing for the payment of a salary "out of any money in the general fund not otherwise appropriated," only applies to the money subject to appropriation by that legislature and not to some subsequent legislature. (Baggett v. Dunn, 69 Cal. 75, 10 Pac. 125.)

An act attempting retroactively to exempt resident nephews and nieces from the payment of unpaid taxes upon collateral inheritances is in violation of this section. (Estate of Stanford, 126 Cal. 112, 45 L. R. A. 788, 54 Pac. 259, 58 Pac. 462.)

The act of 1855, providing a fund for the indigent sick, has no application to a fund which comes to a county by operation of this section. (Power v. May, 123 Cal. 147, 55 Pac. 796.)

The act establishing the state agricultural society made it a state institution, and appropriation for it is not obnoxious to this provision. (Melvin v. State, 121 Cal. 16, 53 Pac. 416.)

The act of 1891, fixing a bounty on coyote scalps, did not make a specific appropriation out of the general fund for the payment of such bounties. (Ingram v. Colgan, 106 Cal. 113, 46 Am. St. Rep. 221, 28 L. R. A. 187, 38 Pac. 315, 39 Pac. 437.)

An act requiring the tax collector to pay a part of the fees allowed him by law into the county treasury does not violate this section— first, because the money had never been in the state treasury, and, second, because such act amounts to an appropriation. (Ream v. Siskiyou Co., 36 Cal. 620.)

The legislature has no power to appropriate money to agricultural societies not under the exclusive control of the state. (People v. San Joaquin Valley Agr. Assn., 151 Cal. 797, 91 Pac. 740.)

The Constitution does not expressly prohibit the legislature from converting a private corporation into a state institution and placing it under state control, provided the purposes sought are within the general legislative power, or under some duty or function of government. (Board v. Nye, 8 Cal. App. 527, 97 Pac. 208.)

An act appropriating one hundred thousand dollars for the support and maintenance of a mining bureau is not unconstitutional because it fails to state specifically on what fund the warrant is to be drawn, or that the money is appropriated out of any moneys in the treasury not otherwise appropriated. (Proll v. Dunn, 80 Cal. 220, 22 Pac. 143.)

Section 2283 of the Political Code, as amended in 1913, appropriating money to institutions and municipal corporations for the support of orphans or abandoned children, is expressly authorized by this

section. (Sacramento Orphanage etc. Home v. Chambers, 25 Cal. App. 536, 144 Pac. 317.)

Section 3669 of the Political Code, directing the state controller, in the event of a final judgment being recovered against the state treasurer for the amount of taxes illegally assessed by the state board of equalization and collected by the treasurer, to draw his warrant therefor upon the treasurer and directing the latter to pay it, is in violation of this section, forbidding the drawing of money from the treasury "but in consequence of appropriations made by law." (Westinghouse Electric Co. v. Chambers, 169 Cal. 131, 145 Pac. 1025.)

If section 270d of the Penal Code should be decided unconstitutional under this section, the constitutionality of section 270 would be unaffected by it, since it is wholly independent of section 270d. (In re Mitchell, 19 Cal. App. 567, 126 Pac. 856.)

Compensation of members and attachés.

Sec. 23. The members of the legislature shall receive for their services, the sum of one thousand dollars each for each regular session, to be paid at such times during the session as may be provided by law, and the sum of ten dollars each, for each day while-in attendance at a special or extraordinary session, for a number of days not exceeding thirty; and mileage to be fixed by law, all paid out of the state treasury; such mileage shall not exceed ten cents per mile; and each member shall be allowed contingent expenses not exceeding twenty-five dollars per member for each regular biennial session. The legislature may also provide for additional help; but in no case shall the total expense for officers, employees and attachés exceed the sum of five hundred dollars per day for either house, at any regular or biennial session, nor the sum of two hundred dollars per day for either house, at any special or extraordinary session, nor shall the pay of any officer, employee or attaché be increased after he is elected or appointed.   (Amendment adopted November 3, 1908.)

[ORIGINAL SECTION.]

Sec. 23. The members of the legislature shall receive for their services a per diem and mileage, to be fixed by law, and paid out of the public treasury; such per diem shall not exceed eight dollars, and such mileage shall not exceed ten cents per mile, and for contingent expenses not exceeding twenty-five dollars for each session. No increase in compensation or mileage shall take effect during the term for which the members of either house shall have been elected, and the pay of no attaché shall be increased after he is elected or appointed.

LEGISLATIVE EXPENSES.—This section, as amended in 1908, means that neither house of the legislature shall in any case provide for an expense for officers, employees and attachés to exceed the sum of five hundred dollars per day at any regular session, or two hundred dollars per day at any special or extraordinary session, and all post session expenses must be met out of these allowances. (Hilborn v. Nye, 15 Cal. App. 298, 114 Pac. 801.)

Officers, employees and attachés.

Sec. 23a. The legislature may also provide for the employment of help; but in no case shall the total expense for officers, employees and attachés exceed the sum of five hundred dollars per day for either house, at any regular or biennial session nor the sum of two hundred dollars per day for either house at any special or extraordinary session, nor shall the pay of any officer, employee or attaché be increased after he is elected or appointed. (Amendment adopted November 3, 1908.)

Title of laws—Revision and amendment—Publication of.

Sec. 24. Every act shall embrace but one subject, which subject shall be expressed in its title. But if any subject shall be embraced in an act which shall not be expressed in its title, such act shall be void only as to so much thereof as shall not be expressed in its title. No law shall be revised or amended by reference to its title; but in such case the act revised or section amended shall be re-enacted and published at length as revised or amended; and all laws of the state of California, and all official writings, and the executive, legislative, and judicial proceedings shall be conducted, preserved, and published in no other than the English language.

TITLE AND FORM OF ACTS—Construction.—A like provision of the former Constitution was held to be merely directory. (Washington v. Page, 4 Cal. 388; Pierpont v. Crouch, 10 Cal. 315; San Francisco v. Spring Valley W. W., 54 Cal. 571.)

But the provisions of this section are held to be mandatory. (Ex parte Liddell, 93 Cal. 633, 29 Pac. 251.)

It was by reason of the provision of section 22 of article I that this section was declared mandatory. (Law v. San Francisco, 144 Cal. 384, 77 Pac. 1014.)

A like provision of the San Francisco charter is held to be directory only. (Law v. San Francisco, 144 Cal. 384, 77 Pac. 1014.)

The title of an act cannot be used to restrain or control any positive provision of the act, but where the meaning of the body of the act is doubtful, the title may be resorted to as a means of ascertaining the intention of the legislature. (People v. Abbott, 16 Cal. 358; Barnes v. Jones, 51 Cal. 303; Matter of Boston Min. etc. Co., 51 Cal. 624; Harris v. Supervisors, 52 Cal. 553.)

The provisions of this section should be liberally construed, and the matter must be left largely to legislative discretion. (Ex parte Liddell, 93 Cal. 633, 29 Pac. 251; Abeel v. Clark, 84 Cal. 226, 24 Pac. 383.)

This section does not apply to municipal ordinances. (Ex parte Haskell, 112 Cal. 412, 32 L. R. A. 527, 44 Pac. 725.)

As to whether this section applies to the amendment of statutes enacted before the present Constitution, see People v. Parvin, 74 Cal. 549, 16 Pac. 490.

One subject.—Numerous provisions having one general object fairly indicated by the title may be united. (Ex parte Liddell, 93 Cal. 633, 29 Pac. 251; People v. Parks, 58 Cal. 624; Ex parte Kohler, 74 Cal. 38, 15 Pac. 436; De Witt v. San Francisco, 2 Cal. 289; Murphy v. Bondshu, 2 Cal. App. 249, 83 Pac. 278.)

The act of 1891, adding a new part to the Vrooman Act in relation to street improvement bonds, does not contain more than one subject. (Hellman v. Shoulters, 114 Cal. 136, 44 Pac. 915, 45 Pac. 1057.)

An act entitled: "An act to establish a uniform system of county and township governments," classifying the counties by population and fixing the compensation of the county officers, only contains one subject. (Longan v. Solano County, 65 Cal. 122, 3 Pac. 463.)

A resolution approving thirteen separate amendments to a city charter is not in violation of this section. (In re Pfahler, 150 Cal. 71, 11 Ann. Cas. 911, 11 L. R. A. (N. S.) 1092, 88 Pac. 270.)

The "Torrens Land Law" only embraces one subject. (Robinson v. Kerrigan, 151 Cal. 40, 12 Ann. Cas. 829, 121 Am. St. Rep. 90, 90 Pac. 129.)

The act of March 23, 1901 (Stats. 1901, p. 647), adding certain sections to the Political Code, re-enacting others, amending others, and repealing others, all relating to revenue and taxation, does not violate this provision. (Murphy v. Bondshu, 3 Cal. App. 249, 83 Pac. 278.)

The primary election law of 1909 is not unconstitutional for embracing in its title the subject of an advisory vote for United States senators, as the matter of such a vote is germane to the subject of a primary election. (Socialist Party v. Uhl, 155 Cal. 776, 103 Pac. 181.)

The act of March 19, 1878 (Stats. 1877-78, 339), does not contain more than one subject. (San Francisco v. Spring Valley W. W., 54 Cal. 571.)

If the act is made of incongruous parts, or to comprehend unconnected and dissimilar subjects to that expressed in the title, it cannot be upheld. (People v. Parks, 58 Cal. 624.)

The preservation of fish and game is a single subject of legislation. (Ah King v. Police Court, 139 Cal. 718, 73 Pac. 587.)

An act purporting in its title to add seven enumerated sections to the Penal Code "all relating to the prostituting of women" only em-

braces one subject. (People v. Duncan, 22 Cal. App. 430, 134 Pac. 797.)

An act entitled, "An act to add another section to the Code of Civil Procedure of the State of California, relating to incompetent persons," only contains one subject. (Matter of Coburn, 165 Cal. 202, 131 Pac. 352.)

An act entitled, "An act to provide for work upon public roads, etc., not within the territory of incorporated cities or towns; for the incidental establishment of grades thereof; for the construction therein or thereon of sidewalks, etc., for the issue of bonds representing the costs and expenses thereof; for a special fund derived in part by special assessment upon a district and for the establishment of such districts," only contains one subject. (McCray v. Manning, 22 Cal. App. 25, 133 Pac. 17.)

An act entitled "An act to amend section 1970 of the Civil Code of the state of California, relating to the responsibility of employers for injuries to or death of employees," only contains one subject. (Pritchard v. Whitney Estate Co., 164 Cal. 564, 129 Pac. 989.)

An act entitled "An act to amend sections 204, 205, 206 and 208 of the Code of Civil Procedure," only contains one subject. (Ross v. Aguirre, 191 U. S. 60, 48 L. Ed. 94, 24 Sup. Ct. Rep. 22.)

An act entitled "An act limiting the hours of labor of females employed in any manufacturing, mechanical or mercantile establishment, etc.; compelling each employer in any manufacturing, mechanical or mercantile establishment, etc., to provide seats for all female employees and to permit them to use such seats when they are not engaged in the active duties of their employment; and providing a penalty for failure, neglect or refusal of the employer to comply with the provisions of this act and for permitting or suffering any overseer, etc., to violate the provisions of this act," only contains one subject. (In re Miller, 162 Cal. 687, 124 Pac. 427; affirmed in Miller v. Wilson, 236 U. S. 373, 59 L. Ed. 628, 35 Sup. Ct. Rep. 342.)

The fact that the title of an act is broader than the act itself does not render the act obnoxious to this section. (Ex parte Mascolo, 25 Cal. App. 92, 142 Pac. 903.)

The title of the Street Law of 1907 does not contain more than one subject. (Hunt v. Manning, 24 Cal. App. 44, 140 Pac. 39.)

Title.—The purpose of this provision is to protect the members of the legislature as well as the public against fraud from deceitful and misleading titles. (Ex parte Liddell, 93 Cal. 633, 29 Pac. 251, Abeel v. Clark, 84 Cal. 226, 24 Pac. 383; Matter of Bonds of South San Joaquin I. Dist., 161 Cal. 345, 119 Pac. 198; Matter of Maginnis, 162 Cal. 200, 121 Pac. 723.)

If the title is of such a character as to mislead the public or the members of the legislature, as to the subjects embraced in it, it is void. (Wood v. Election Commrs., 58 Cal. 561.)

The words in a title "and for other purposes" do not validate provisions which are not germane to the particular subjects expressed in the title. (Spier v. Baker, 120 Cal. 370, 41 L. R. A. 196, 52 Pac. 659.)

It is not necessary that the title of an act should embrace an abstract or catalogue of its contents. (Abeel v. Clark, 84 Cal. 226, 24 Pac. 383; Ex parte Liddell, 93 Cal. 633, 29 Pac. 251; People v. Supe-

rior Court, 100 Cal. 105, 34 Pac. 492; People v. Linda Vista Irr. Dist., 128 Cal. 477, 61 Pac. 86; Hellman v. Shoulters, 114 Cal. 136, 44 Pac. 915, 45 Pac. 1057; Ex parte Hallawell, 155 Cal. 112, 99 Pac. 490.)

The title of an act is not misleading, because it purports to provide for a "general" vaccination, when in fact it only applies to children in the public schools. (Abeel v. Clark, 84 Cal. 226, 24 Pac. 383; French v. Davidson, 143 Cal. 658, 77 Pac. 663.)

If the act entitled, "An act to amend 'An act to protect stockholders and persons dealing with corporations in this state,' approved March 20, 1878," would, if passed as a new act, be invalid under the present Constitution, because of insufficiency of its title to express the subject, yet it is nevertheless valid, since the original act of 1878 was valid under the former Constitution, and since the amendatory act recites the original valid act, of which it is amendatory, and re-enacts the act as amended in full. (People v. Merritt, 18 Cal. App. 58, 122 Pac. 839.)

> Effect of provisions requiring statutes to embrace but one subject, which shall be expressed in the title. See note, 61 Am. Dec. 337.
>
> Sufficiency of title. See note, 64 Am. St. Rep. 70.
>
> When title embraces but one subject and what it may include. See note, 79 Am. St. Rep. 456.
>
> Construction of constitutional provisions relative to titles of statutes. See note, 1 Ann. Cas. 584.
>
> Validity of statute having title more comprehensive than act itself. See note, Ann. Cas. 1912A, 102.
>
> Validity of statute providing for penalty or punishment not mentioned in title. See note, Ann. Cas. 1912D, 157.

Particular acts held valid.—The titles of the following acts have been held sufficient: An act entitled, "An act to amend section 3581 of the Political Code" (People v. Parvin, 74 Cal. 549, 16 Pac. 490. But see Lewis v. Dunne, 134 Cal. 291, 86 Am. St. Rep. 257, 55 L. R. A. 833, 66 Pac. 478); a title expressing the object of the act to be "to amend section ——" of a named code "relating" to the particular object treated of in the body of the act (San Francisco etc. R. R. Co. v. State Board, 60 Cal. 12); an act entitled, "An act to prohibit the sophistication and adulteration of wine, and to prevent fraud in the manufacture and sale thereof," and defining pure wine, prohibiting the use of deleterious substitutes, and forbidding the sale of impure wine (Ex parte Kohler, 74 Cal. 38, 15 Pac. 436); an act entitled, "An act to amend an act entitled 'An act to establish a Penal Code,' approved February 14, 1872, by amending section 634, relating to fish and game" (People v. Dobbins, 73 Cal. 257, 14 Pac. 860); an act entitled, "An act to provide for laying out, etc., any street, etc., and to condemn and acquire any and all lands and property necessary or convenient for that purpose," and providing for the assessment of other lands to pay for lands condemned (Davies v. Los Angeles, 86 Cal. 37, 24 Pac. 771); an act entitled, "An act for the better protection of stockholders in corporations formed under the laws of the state of California for the purpose of carrying on and conducting the

business of mining," and providing a penalty for failure to make or
post an itemized account or balance-sheet (Francais v. Somps, 92 Cal.
503, 28 Pac. 592); an act entitled, "An act to establish a state reform
school for juvenile offenders, and to make an appropriation therefor,"
and providing for the commitment of juvenile offenders to such
schools (Ex parte Liddell, 93 Cal. 633, 29 Pac. 251); an act entitled,
"An act to provide for laying out, etc., any street, etc., in municipalities, and to condemn and acquire any and all land and property
necessary and convenient for that purpose," and validating former
proceedings for the widening of streets (San Francisco v. Kiernan,
98 Cal. 614, 33 Pac. 720); an act entitled, "An act creating a board
of bank commissioners, and prescribing their duties and powers," and
providing for winding up of banking corporations (People v. Superior
Court, 100 Cal. 105, 34 Pac. 492); an act entitled, "An act to create
the county of Kings, to define the boundaries thereof, and to provide
for its organization and election of officers, and to classify said
county," and providing for the collection of taxes levied before the
formation of the county but collected afterward (Kings County v.
Johnson, 104 Cal. 198, 37 Pac. 870); an act entitled, "An act to create
the office of commissioner of transportation, and to define its powers
and duties; to fix the maximum charges for transporting passengers
and freights on certain railroads, and to prevent extortion and unjust
discrimination thereon," and providing for the collection of fines
against a person evading the payment of his fare (Gieseke v. San
Joaquin County, 109 Cal. 489, 42 Pac. 446); an act entitled, "An act
to establish a uniform system of county and township governments,"
and classifying the counties by population, and fixing the compensation of the county officers (Longan v. Solano County, 65 Cal. 122,
3 Pac. 463); an act entitled, "An act to regulate fees in office," and
providing that the officer shall pay part of his fees into the treasury
(Beam v. Siskiyou Co., 36 Cal. 621); an act entitled, "An act to enable certain parties therein named to alienate and encumber homesteads," and providing for the alienation of the homestead by the
sane spouse, under order of the probate court (Jones v. Falvella, 126
Cal. 24, 58 Pac. 311); an act entitled, "An act to protect and promote
the horticultural interests of the state," and making the expense of
abating an insect pest nuisance from any property a lien thereon
(Los Angeles County v. Spencer, 126 Cal. 670, 77 Am. St. Rep. 217,
59 Pac: 202); a provision relating to city justices of the peace in an
act entitled, "An act to establish a uniform system of county and
township government" (People v. Cobb, 133 Cal. 74, 65 Pac. 325);
an act purporting in its title to add thirty-four enumerated sections
to the Political Code, "all relating to the establishment of a board
of state harbor commissioners for the bay of San Diego," and authorizing the commissioners to institute an action for the possession of
any portion of the entire bay of San Diego, of which they are given
the possession and control (People v. Mullender, 132 Cal. 217, 64 Pac.
299); the statutes of December 25, 1877, and March 30, 1878, in relation to highways in Los Angeles county (Southern Pac. Co. v.
Pomona, 144 Cal. 339, 77 Pac. 929); an act entitled, "An act in relation to foreign corporations," and providing for the designation of
agents, services of process and proof of corporate existence (Anglo-

Californian Bank v. Field, 146 Cal. 644, 80 Pac. 1080); an act entitled, "An act to provide for the establishment and quieting of title to real property in case of loss or destruction of public records" (Title etc. Restoration Co. v. Kerrigan, 150 Cal. 289, 119 Am. St. Rep. 199, 8 L. R. A. (N. S.) 682, 88 Pac. 356); the act of March 29, 1905, providing for a license tax on corporations (Kaiser Land & Fruit Co. v. Curry, 155 Cal. 638, 103 Pac. 341); an act to create a drainage district to be called "Sacramento Drainage District," etc. (People v. Sacramento Drainage District, 155 Cal. 373, 103 Pac. 207); "an act regulating the sale of poison in the state of California, and providing a penalty for the violation thereof" (Ex parte Hallawell, 155 Cal. 112, 99 Pac. 490); "An act creating a board of bank commissioners and prescribing their duties and powers" (People v. Bank of San Luis Obispo, 154 Cal. 194, 97 Pac. 306); "An act to add three new sections to the Code of Civil Procedure, to be known as sections numbers 941a, 941b and 941c of said code, respectively, providing a new and alternative method by which appeals may be taken from judgments, orders or decrees of the superior court of the state of California to the supreme court or district courts of appeal thereof" (Estate of McPhee, 154 Cal. 385, 97 Pac. 878); "An act to insure the better education of practitioners of dental surgery, and to regulate the practice of dentistry in the state of California, providing penalties for the violation hereof, and to repeal an act now in force relating to the same and known as "An act, . . . etc., approved March 12, 1885" (Ex parte Hornef, 154 Cal. 355, 97 Pac. 891); the act approved June 2, 1913, for the regulation of the practice of medicine and surgery, etc. (People v. Ah Fong, 25 Cal. App. 724, 145 Pac. 153); an act entitled, "An act to regulate the sale and use of poisons in the state of California, and providing for the violation thereof," which makes the mere possession of certain drugs, with certain exceptions, a crime (Matter of Yun Quong, 159 Cal. 508, Ann. Cas. 1912C, 969, 114 Pac. 835); an act entitled, "An act to provide for the organization and government of irrigation districts, and to provide for the acquisition or construction thereby of works for the irrigation of the lands embraced within such districts, and, also, to provide for the distribution of water for irrigation purposes," and providing for the institution and prosecution by the district of a proceeding brought to test the validity of an assessment (Matter of Bonds of the San Joaquin I. Dist., 161 Cal. 345, 119 Pac. 198); an act entitled, "An act limiting the hours of labor of females employed in any manufacturing, mechanical or mercantile establishment, etc.; compelling each employer in any manufacturing, mechanical or mercantile establishment, etc., to provide suitable seats for all female employees and to permit them to use such seats when they are not engaged in the active duties of their employment; and providing a penalty for failure, neglect or refusal of the employer to comply with the provisions of this act and for permitting or suffering any overseer, etc., to violate the provisions of this act," since it embraced but one general subject—the regulation of female employment (In re Miller, 162 Cal. 687, 124 Pac. 427; affirmed in Miller v. Wilson, 236 U. S. 373, 59 L. Ed. 628, 35 Sup. Ct. Rep. 342); an act entitled, "An act concerning dependent and delinquent minor children, providing

for their care, custody and maintenance, etc. (In re Maginnis, 162 Cal. 200, 121 Pac. 723); an act entitled, "An act to amend section 1970 of the Civil Code of the state of California, relating to the responsibility of employers for injuries to or death of employees" (Pritchard v. Whitney Estate Co., 164 Cal. 564, 129 Pac. 989); an act entitled, "An act to add another section to the Code of Civil Procedure of the state of California relating to incompetent persons" (Matter of Coburn, 165 Cal. 202, 131 Pac. 352); an act entitled, "An act to amend section sixty-one of the Civil Code, relating to the granting of divorces" (Estate of Elliott, 165 Cal. 339, 132 Pac. 439); an act entitled, "An act to amend 'An act to protect stockholders and persons dealing with corporations in this state,' approved March 20, 1878," notwithstanding the body of the act as amended is wholly penal in its provisions (People v. Merritt, 18 Cal. App. 58, 122 Pac. 839); an act entitled, "An act to prohibit the formation and existence of secret oath-bound fraternities in the public schools" (Bradford v. Board of Education, 18 Cal. App. 19, 121 Pac. 929); an act entitled, "An act concerning dependent and delinquent minor children, providing for their care, custody and maintenance until twenty-one years of age" (Moore v. Williams, 19 Cal. App. 600, 127 Pac. 509); an act entitled, "An act to regulate the use and operation of vehicles," etc. (In re Schuler, 167 Cal. 282, Ann. Cas. 1915C, 706, 139 Pac. 685); "An act to add a new section to the Penal Code of the state of California, to be numbered 636½, to prevent the use or possession of lompara nets, paranzella nets, trawl or drag nets, and providing the penalty therefor" (Ex parte Mascolo, 25 Cal. App. 92, 142 Pac. 903).

See, also, People v. King, 127 Cal. 570, 60 Pac. 35; Leake v. Colgan, 125 Cal. 413, 58 Pac. 69; Jennings v. Le Roy, 63 Cal. 397; People v. Henshaw, 76 Cal. 436, 18 Pac. 413; Pennie v. Reis, 80 Cal. 266, 22 Pac. 176; People v. Linda Vista Irr. Dist., 128 Cal. 477, 61 Pac. 86; Carpenter v. Furrey, 128 Cal. 665, 61 Pac. 369; Vernon etc. Dist. v. Board of Education, 125 Cal. 593, 58 Pac. 175; Ex parte Pfirrman, 134 Cal. 143, 66 Pac. 205; Jackson v. Baehr, 138 Cal. 266, 71 Pac. 167; In re Martin, 157 Cal. 51, 26 L. R. A. (N. S.) 242, 106 Pac. 235.

Validity of liquor law under constitutional provision as to title and subject matter of statutes. See note, 20 Ann. Cas. 323.

Particular acts held invalid.—The following acts have been held to violate this provision: An act whose title simply purports to repeal the statute concerning the publication of constitutional amendments, but in the body of the act also provides a new method of publishing such amendments (People v. Curry, 130 Cal. 82, 62 Pac. 516); an act amending the act for the formation of sanitary districts, and providing that sanitary boards may determine the qualification of persons authorized to sell liquors at retail, this subject not being germane to the title of the original act (In re Werner, 129 Cal. 567, 62 Pac. 97); an act entitled, "An act to establish fees," etc., and providing for the payment of one dollar for each one thousand dollars in excess of three thousand dollars of the appraised value of the estate upon filing the inventory, such payment being a tax and not a fee (Fatjo v. Pfister, 117 Cal. 83, 48 Pac. 1012); an act entitled, "An act to amend sec-

tions four thousand and four," and other sections "to establish a system of county governments, approved April 27, 1880," but referring to no particular code or statute (Leonard v. January, 56 Cal. 1); an act entitled, "An act to promote drainage," and providing for the control of debris from mining and other operations, the improvement and rectification of river channels, and the erection of embankments or dykes necessary for the protection of lands, towns or cities from inundation (People v. Parks, 58 Cal. 624; Doane v. Weil, 58 Cal. 334); an act the title of which provides only for the refunding of the indebtedness of cities, and the issuance of bonds therefor, and repealing an act for the incurring of indebtedness by municipal corporations (Los Angeles v. Hance, 122 Cal. 77, 54 Pac. 387); an act entitled, "An act to establish a uniform system of county and township governments" and providing for the salaries of official reporters of the superior courts (Pratt v. Browne, 135 Cal. 649, 67 Pac. 1082); an act entitled, "An act creating a board of commissioners of building and loan associations, and prescribing their duties and powers," and providing for withdrawals (Provident etc. Assn. v. Davis, 143 Cal. 253, 76 Pac. 1034); an act purporting in its title to deal with publications by certain public officers and in the body of the act providing for other classes of publications (Estate of Melone, 141 Cal. 331, 74 Pac. 991); an act entitled, "An act to establish a tax on collateral inheritances, bequests, and devises" and imposing such a tax on direct kindred (Estate of Winchester, 140 Cal. 468, 74 Pac. 10); an act to amend the fish and game law of 1911, by adding a new section thereto, and in fact materially changing and amending every section of the act of 1911 (In re Mascolo, 25 Cal. App. 92, 142 Pac. 903).

Amendments of codes.—An act entitled an act to amend a particular section of one of the codes sufficiently states the subject of the act. (People v. Oates, 142 Cal. 12, 75 Pac. 337.)

The fact that an act does not deal with the matter of crimes and punishments does not prevent it from being in the form of an amendment to the Penal Code, if its title shows its subject matter. (County of Butte v. Merrill, 141 Cal. 396, 74 Pac. 1036.)

An act entitled an act to add a new section to a named code relating to a named subject is sufficient to embrace all matters relating to such subject. (Deyoe v. Superior Court, 140 Cal. 476, 98 Am. St. Rep. 73, 74 Pac. 28.)

Section 146 of the Civil Code is not unconstitutional because the act of 1873–74 passing it was entitled, "An act to amend the Civil Code" (Zanone v. Sprague, 16 Cal. App. 333, 116 Pac. 989).

The fact that an act adds certain sections which relate to procedure to the Civil Code, instead of the Code of Civil Procedure, does not make it invalid. (Deyoe v. Superior Court, 140 Cal. 476, 98 Am. St. Rep. 73, 74 Pac. 28.)

An act entitled "An act to revise the Code of Civil Procedure of the state of California by amending certain sections, repealing others, and adding certain new sections," was held not to sufficiently state its subject in its title, for the reason that the "Code of Civil Procedure" does not state or express any subject. (Lewis v. Dunne, 134 Cal. 291, 86 Am. St. Rep. 257, 55 L. R. A. 833, 66 Pac. 478.)

That such terms as the "Code of Civil Procedure," "Criminal Code," "Probate Code," "Political Code," etc., do sufficiently state a subject, see Central etc. R. Co. v. State, 104 Ga. 831, 42 L. R. A. 518, 31 S. E. 531; Porter v. Thompson, 22 Iowa, 391; State v. Brassfield, 81 Mo. 151, 51 Am. Rep. 234; Woodruff v. Baldwin, 23 Kan. 491; Heller v. People, 2 Colo. App. 459, 31 Pac. 773; Johnson v. Harrison, 47 Minn. 575, 28 Am. St. Rep. 382, 50 N. W. 923; Marston v. Humes, 3 Wash. 267, 28 Pac. 520; Mathis v. State, 31 Fla. 291, 12 South. 681; Ex parte Thomas, 113 Ala. 1, 21 South. 369; Tribune etc. Co. v. Barnes, 7 N. D. 591, 75 N. W. 904; Murphey v. Menard, 11 Tex. 673.

If the adoption of section 1767 of the Code of Civil Procedure amended the existing law as declared in said code, it amended it by implication only, and this constitutional provision has no application to such implied amendments. (Matter of Coburn, 165 Cal. 202, 131 Pac. 352.)

Publishing at length.—A revised act must be construed as a new and original piece of legislation. (Donlon v. Jewett, 88 Cal. 530, 26 Pac. 370; In re Bunkers, 1 Cal. App. 61, 81 Pac. 748.)

This provision applies only to acts which are in terms revisory or amendatory of some former act; and it does not apply to an independent act, although it is inconsistent with some existing statute. (Pennie v. Reis, 80 Cal. 266, 22 Pac. 176; Jennings v. Le Roy, 63 Cal. 397; Baum v. Raphael, 57 Cal. 361; In re Bunkers, 1 Cal. App. 61, 81 Pac. 748.)

An act adding a new section to the Political Code, and by implication amending another section of the same code, was held to violate this provision, if considered as an amendment, since it did not republish the section of the code affected by it. (Earle v. Board of Education, 55 Cal. 489. But see Hellman v. Shoulters, 114 Cal. 136, 44 Pac. 915, 45 Pac. 1057; University of California v. Bernard, 57 Cal. 612.)

In amending a section the entire section must be re-enacted. (City of Los Angeles v. Lelande, 11 Cal. App. 302, 104 Pac. 717.)

This section does not apply to amendments by implication, nor to an act which merely adds new sections relating to a named subject, which leaves in full operation all the language of the statute which it purports to amend, and does not purport to amend any section of that act, but affects its operation only by implication from the sections added. (Hellman v. Shoulters, 114 Cal. 136, 44 Pac. 915, 45 Pac. 1057. But see Earle v. Board of Education, 55 Cal. 489.)

This section does not prevent a section amended from taking its place by its appropriate number in the original act. (Fletcher v. Prather, 102 Cal. 413, 36 Pac. 658.)

It is a sufficient compliance with this provision to republish the section of the act amended. (Estate of Campbell, 143 Cal. 623, 77 Pac. 674.)

Where a section of the code is "amended to read as follows," and the amended section is published at length, without any saving clause, the effect of the amendment is to repeal the section as it originally stood; and a section of the amendatory act merely providing that the amendment shall be applicable to certain counties does not operate as

a saving clause to continue the original section in force in other counties. (Huffman v. Hall, 102 Cal. 26, 36 Pac. 417.)

Under the provisions of this section the amendment of a statute operates as an absolute repeal of the statute or section amended, even if the amendment takes nothing away from the old law, but merely adds a proviso in certain cases. (Billings v. Harvey, 6 Cal. 381.)

An act adding five new sections to the Political Code is not within the mischief which this section was intended to prevent. (University of California v. Bernard, 57 Cal. 612.)

An act entitled "An act to revise the Code of Civil Procedure of the state of California by amending certain sections, repealing others, and adding certain new sections," and amending, repealing, or adding some five hundred sections of that code, and which did not set out and republish at length the entire Code of Civil Procedure, was held to violate this provision of the Constitution. (Lewis v. Dunne, 134 Cal. 291, 86 Am. St. Rep. 257, 55 L. R. A. 833, 66 Pac. 478.)

See, however, on the same subject the following cases: Portland v. Stock, 2 Or. 70; Dolan v. Barnard, 5 Or. 390; David v. Portland etc. Co., 14 Or. 98, 12 Pac. 174; Greencastle etc. Co. v. State, 28 Ind. 382; Town etc. v. Frieze, 33 Ind. 507; Smails v. White, 4 Neb. 353; Arnoult v. New Orleans, 11 La. Ann. 54; Tuskaloosa etc. Co. v. Olmsted, 41 Ala. 9.

The act of April 9, 1880, amending one hundred and eight sections of the Penal Code, repealing ten sections, and adding a new section thereto, is not a revision of the entire code, requiring a republication thereof. (People v. Oates, 142 Cal. 12, 75 Pac. 337.)

As to whether an act is an amendment or a revision of another act, see Beach v. Von Detten, 139 Cal. 462, 73 Pac. 187.

Under the provisions of this section the amendment of a statute operates as an absolute repeal of the statute or section amended. (Buck v. Canty, 162 Cal. 226, 121 Pac. 924.)

> Constitutionality of code amendments and revisions. See notes, 86 Am. St. Rep. 267; 55 L. R. A. 842.

English language.—If a libel in the Japanese and Chinese language is correctly translated into English in the complaint, a copy of the original libel need not be inserted in it. (Stevens v. Kobayshi, 20 Cal. App. 153, 128 Pac. 419.)

Local and special laws prohibited.

Sec. 25. The legislature shall not pass local or special laws in any of the following enumerated cases, that is to say:

First—Regulating the jurisdiction and duties of justices of the peace, police judges, and of constables.

Second—For the punishment of crimes and misdemeanors.

Third—Regulating the practice of courts of justice.

Fourth—Providing for changing the venue in civil or criminal actions.

Fifth—Granting divorces.

Sixth—Changing the names of persons or places.

Seventh—Authorizing the laying out, opening, altering, maintaining, or vacating roads, highways, streets, alleys, town plats, parks, cemeteries, graveyards, or public grounds not owned by the state.

Eighth—Summoning and impaneling grand and petit juries, and providing for their compensation.

Ninth—Regulating county and township business, or the election of county and township officers.

Tenth—For the assessment or collection of taxes.

Eleventh—Providing for conducting elections, or designating the places of voting, except on the organization of new counties.

Twelfth—Affecting the estates of deceased persons, minors, or other persons under legal disabilities.

Thirteenth—Extending the time for the collection of taxes.

Fourteenth—Giving effect to invalid deeds, wills, or other instruments.

Fifteenth—Refunding money paid into the state treasury.

Sixteenth—Releasing or extinguishing, in whole or in part, the indebtedness, liability, or obligation of any corporation or person to this state, or to any municipal corporation therein.

Seventeenth—Declaring any person of age or authorizing any minor to sell, lease, or encumber his or her property.

Eighteenth—Legalizing, except as against the state, the unauthorized or invalid act of any officer.

Nineteenth—Granting to any corporation, association, or individual any special or exclusive right, privilege, or immunity.

Twentieth—Exempting property from taxation.

Twenty-first—Changing county seats.

Twenty-second — Restoring to citizenship persons convicted of infamous crimes.

Twenty-third—Regulating the rate of interest on money.

Twenty-fourth—Authorizing the creation, extension, or impairing of liens.

Twenty-fifth—Chartering or licensing ferries, bridges, or roads.

Twenty-sixth—Remitting fines, penalties, or forfeitures.

Twenty-seventh—Providing for the management of common schools.

Twenty-eighth — Creating offices, or prescribing the powers and duties of officers in counties, cities, cities and counties, townships, election or school districts.

Twenty-ninth—Affecting the fees or salary of any officer.

Thirtieth—Changing the law of descent or succession.

Thirty-first—Authorizing the adoption or legitimation of children.

Thirty-second—For limitation of civil or criminal actions.

Thirty-third—In all other cases where a general law can be made applicable.

LOCAL AND SPECIAL LAWS—In general.—Under the former Constitution the legislature was not forbidden to pass local or special laws. (Wigmore v. Buell, 122 Cal. 144, 54 Pac. 600; People v. Twelfth District Court, 17 Cal. 547; Ex parte Burke, 59 Cal. 6, 43 Am. Rep. 231; Nevada School Dist. v. Shoecraft, 88 Cal. 372, 26 Pac. 211.)

The provisions of this section are prospective only, and do not affect statutes passed before its adoption. (Nevada School Dist. v. Shoecraft, 88 Cal. 372, 26 Pac. 211; Ex parte Burke, 59 Cal. 6, 43 Am. Rep. 231; Rollins v. Wright, 93 Cal. 395, 29 Pac. 58; Smith v. McDermott, 93 Cal. 421, 29 Pac. 34; Meade v. Watson, 67 Cal. 591, 8 Pac. 311; Ex parte Chin Yan, 60 Cal. 78.)

The provisions of this section are prospective only, and do not operate to destroy the force of existing special laws; such special laws or provisions in municipal charters became subject only to the general laws subsequently passed by the legislature touching the same subject matter. (Vallejo Ferry Co. v. Lang & McPherson, 161 Cal. 672, 120 Pac. 421.)

The legislature cannot make a special act general by a legislative declaration that it shall be considered a general act. (San Francisco v. Spring Valley W. W., 48 Cal. 493.)

A law which on its face is general and may be applied to all cities cannot be assailed on the ground that it was in fact passed to effect an improvement in one city only. (Davies v. Los Angeles, 86 Cal. 37, 24 Pac. 771.)

A special law is one relating to a selected class, as well as a particular object. (Smith v. McDermott, 93 Cal. 421, 29 Pac. 34.)

As to what is a general and what a special law, see Ex parte Burke, 59 Cal. 6, 43 Am. Rep. 231, per Morrison, C. J.

A general law must be as broad as the subject matter to which it relates. (Desmond v. Dunn, 55 Cal. 242.)

An act applying uniformly upon the whole of any single class of individuals or objects, when the classification is founded upon some

natural, intrinsic, or constitutional distinction, is a general law.
(Abeel v. Clark, 84 Cal. 226, 24 Pac. 383; Cody v. Murphey, 89 Cal.
522, 26 Pac. 1081; Foster v. Police Commrs., 102 Cal. 483, 41 Am. St.
Rep. 194, 37 Pac. 763; Rode v. Siebe, 119 Cal. 518, 39 L. R. A. 342, 51
Pac. 869; Ex parte Koser, 60 Cal. 177; Vail v. San Diego, 126 Cal. 35,
58 Pac. 392; People v. Central Pac. R. R. Co., 105 Cal. 576, 38 Pac. 905;
affirmed Central Pac. R. Co. v. California, 162 U. S. 91, 40 L. Ed. 903,
16 Sup. Ct. Rep. 766; Murphy v. Pacific Bank, 119 Cal. 334, 51 Pac. 317;
Murphy v. Pacific Bank, 130 Cal. 542, 62 Pac. 1059; Ruperich v. Baehr,
142 Cal. 190, 75 Pac. 782; In re Finley, 1 Cal. App. 198, 81 Pac. 1041;
In re Martin, 157 Cal. 51, 26 L. R. A. (N. S.) 242, 106 Pac. 235.)

In order to make the law general, the classification must not be
arbitrary, but must be founded upon some natural, intrinsic, or constitutional distinction, and some reason must appear why the act is
not made to apply generally to all classes. (Rauer v. Williams, 118
Cal. 401, 50 Pac. 691; Darcy v. Mayor, 104 Cal. 642, 38 Pac. 500.)

Although a law is general when it applies equally to all individuals
of a class founded upon a natural, intrinsic, or constitutional distinction, it is not general if it confers particular privileges or imposes
peculiar disabilities or burdensome conditions, in the exercise of a
common right, upon a class arbitrarily selected from the general body
of those who stand in precisely the same relation to the subject of
the law. (Pasadena v. Stimson, 91 Cal. 238, 27 Pac. 604; Bloss v.
Lewis, 109 Cal. 493, 41 Pac. 1081.)

A law which applies only to a part of a class—which relates not to
any genus, but only to species—is a special law. (People v. Central
Pac. R. R. Co., 83 Cal. 393, 23 Pac. 303.)

There is no reasonable foundation in the nature of things or such
intrinsic difference between corporations and natural persons that requires the application of a measure of jurisdiction of an offense committed by a corporation different from that to be invoked when an
individual is charged with the same offense. (People v. Palermo
L. & W. Co., 4 Cal. App. 717, 89 Pac. 723.)

As to when an entire act will not be affected by the fact that one
provision thereof is special, see Davidson v. Von Detten, 139 Cal.
467, 73 Pac. 189.

> What is special legislation forbidden by Constitution. See note,
> 21 Am. St. Rep. 780.

> Inhibition of local or special law where general law can be made
> applicable. See note, 93 Am. St. Rep. 106.

> Province of legislature to determine whether special law is neces-
> sary in given case. See note, 6 Ann. Cas. 926.

Acts held to be general.—The following acts have been held to be
general within the meaning of this section: An act relating to elections to elect boards of freeholders, and to adopt and amend charters
(Fragley v. Phelan, 126 Cal. 383, 58 Pac. 923); an act providing for
police courts in all cities of a designated population, and providing
that it shall go into effect upon the expiration of the term of office of
the present police judge of such cities (People v. Henshaw, 76 Cal.
436, 18 Pac. 413; Ex parte Halsted, 89 Cal. 471, 26 Pac. 961; In re
Mitchell, 120 Cal. 384, 52 Pac. 799); an act applying to all elections in

towns and cities (Vernon School Dist. v. Board of Education, **125**
Cal. 593, 58 Pac. 175); an act providing for an action by a reclamation district to determine the validity of an assessment (Lower Kings
River Reclamation Dist. No. 531 v. McCullah, 124 Cal. 175, 56 Pac.
887); the insanity law of 1897 (People v. King, 127 Cal. 570, 60 Pac.
35); section 1203 of the Code of Civil Procedure (Carpenter v. Furrey,
128 Cal. 665, 61 Pac. 369); an act providing a special method for
levying a tax for high schools, different from that provided for other
school districts (People v. Lodi High School Dist., 124 Cal. 694, 57
Pac. 660); an act providing for the refunding of indebtedness of
municipal corporations other than cities of the first class (Los Angeles
v. Teed, 112 Cal. 319, 44 Pac. 580; Waite v. Santa Cruz, 184 U. S.
302, 46 L. Ed. 552, 22 Sup. Ct. Rep. 327); an act providing for the
assessment of taxes upon railroads operating in more than one county
(People v. Central Pac. R. R. Co., 105 Cal. 576, 38 Pac. 905; affirmed,
Central Pac. R. Co. v. California, 162 U. S. 91, 40 L. Ed. 903, 16 Sup.
Ct. Rep. 766); a law making it a felony to sell intoxicating liquors
to Indians (People v. Bray, 105 Cal. 344, 27 L. R. A. 158, 38 Pac. 731);
an act providing for vaccination of all children attending public
schools (Abeel v. Clark, 84 Cal. 226, 24 Pac. 383; French v. Davidson,
143 Cal. 658, 77 Pac. 663); an act relating to the compensation of the
auditor and his clerk in all counties of the twentieth class (Farnum
v. Warner, 104 Cal. 677, 38 Pac. 421); an act forbidding the erection
of partition walls in cities and towns of a greater height than ten
feet, without the consent of the adjoining owner, except around public
gardens, etc. (Western etc. Co. v. Knickerbocker, 103 Cal. 111, 37
Pac. 192); the provisions of section 1001 of the Civil Code, providing for the acquisition of private property through the exercise of
the right of eminent domain (Santa Cruz v. Enright, 95 Cal. 105, 30
Pac. 197); a county ordinance providing a smaller license tax for the
sale of spirituous liquors at wayside inns and rural watering places,
outside of any city, than when sold in a city (Amador Co. v. Kennedy,
70 Cal. 458, 11 Pac. 757); an ordinance making it unlawful to conduct a laundry between 10 P. M. and 6 A. M., or on Sundays (Ex
parte Moynier, 65 Cal. 33, 2 Pac. 728); the provision of the Code of
Civil Procedure giving certain laborers preferred claims as against
other attaching creditors (Mohle v. Tschirch, 63 Cal. 381); a law requiring insane persons in state institutions to be supported out of
their estates (Estate of Yturburru, 134 Cal. 567, 66 Pac. 729); an act
relating to license taxes in cities of a particular class (Ex parte Jackson, 143 Cal. 564, 77 Pac. 457); the collateral inheritance tax act taxing brothers and sisters, and exempting the wife of a son, the widow
of a son, and the husband of a daughter, the classification being based
on a natural distinction (Estate of Campbell, 143 Cal. 623, 77 Pac.
674); an act providing that in divorce suits the final decree shall not
be entered until the expiration of one year from the filing of the
decision (Deyoe v. Superior Court, 140 Cal. 476, 98 Am. St. Rep. 73,
74 Pac. 28); the act providing for the application of the salaries of
public officers to the payment of their debts (Ruperich v. Baehr, 142
Cal. 190, 75 Pac. 782); section 1143 of the Penal Code relating to fees
of jurors in criminal actions (Jackson v. Baehr, 138 Cal. 266, 71 Pac.
167); the provision of section 1373 of the Political Code, making the

county in which the indictment was found chargeable with the support of insane criminals (Napa State Hospital v. Yuba County, 138 Cal. 378, 71 Pac. 450); the provisions of the Political Code in regard to road taxes, although cities and towns are exempted from their operation, since this does not exempt cities and towns from the tax, but compels cities and towns to maintain their streets under the street improvement act (Miller v. County of Kern, 137 Cal. 516, 70 Pac. 549); an act applying to all foreign corporations and providing for filing designation of agents, service of process and proof of corporate existence (Anglo-Californian Bank v. Field, 146 Cal. 644, 80 Pac. 1080); the act of 1901 authorizing suits against the state upon coyote bounty claims (Bickerdike v. State of California, 144 Cal. 681, 78 Pac. 270); the act of April 23, 1880 (Stats. 1880, p. 131), forbidding the acquisition or sale of mining ground by mining corporations without the assent of two-thirds of its stockholders (Lacy v. Gunn, 144 Cal. 511, 78 Pac. 30); the state dental law classifying those who may practice dentistry, as it does not discriminate between persons within the same class (Ex parte Whitley, 144 Cal. 167, 1 Ann. Cas. 13, 77 Pac. 879); section 3443 of the Political Code requiring the complaint to set forth certain papers, such provision being justified by the nature and object of the act (Boggs v. Gaueard, 148 Cal. 711, 84 Pac. 195); acts providing two independent schemes, to either of which a municipality may have resort as it shall deem expedient in the acquisition of land for park purposes (Oakland v. Thompson, 151 Cal. 572, 91 Pac. 387); a law forbidding the employment of children under the age of sixteen years in dangerous or immoral places (In re Weber, 149 Cal. 392, 86 Pac. 809); the provision of the child labor law permitting the employment of children whose parents are unable to labor from sickness (In re Spencer, 149 Cal. 396, 117 Am. St. Rep. 137, 9 Ann. Cas. 1105, 86 Pac. 896); the provision of the child labor law permitting the employment of children during vacations upon the permit of the school principal (In re Spencer, 149 Cal. 396, 117 Am. St. Rep. 137, 9 Ann. Cas. 1105, 86 Pac. 896); an act forbidding the employment of children in singing or playing on musical instruments, except in churches, schools or academies (In re Weber, 149 Cal. 392, 86 Pac. 809); the act providing for the establishment of titles to land when the records were destroyed by fire, though it makes provisions regulating practice which are not found in other judicial proceedings (Title etc. Restoration Co. v. Kerrigan, 150 Cal. 289, 119 Am. St. Rep. 199, 8 L. R. A. (N. S.) 682, 88 Pac. 356); the act providing for the establishment of titles when the records are destroyed by earthquake, fire, or flood and not covering destruction by other agencies (Title etc. Restoration Co. v. Kerrigan, 150 Cal. 289, 119 Am. St. Rep. 199, 8 L. R. A. (N. S.) 682, 88 Pac. 356); a curative act as to all tax deeds defective in not stating the time allowed for redemption (Baird v. Monroe, 150 Cal. 560, 89 Pac. 352); the law requiring electors to declare their party affiliation when registering which does not apply to persons who registered before its enactment (Schostay v. Cator, 151 Cal. 600, 91 Pac. 502); an act granting power to cities of a particular class to acquire waterworks (Cary v. Blodgett, 10 Cal. App. 463, 102 Pac. 668); an ordinance forbidding the

maintenance of public billiard and pool rooms, but permitting private billiard-rooms, and billiard-rooms in hotels for bona fide guests only (Ex parte Murphy, 8 Cal. App. 440, 97 Pac. 199); section 710 of the Code of Civil Procedure, providing for the garnishment of the salaries of certain public officers at the instance of their judgment creditors (Lawson v. Lawson, 158 Cal. 446, 111 Pac. 354); an act to provide for laying out, opening, etc., any street, etc. (Stats. 1889, p. 70), (Clute v. Turner, 157 Cal. 73, 106 Pac. 240); an act regulating the hours of employment in underground mines and in smelting and reduction works (In re Martin, 157 Cal. 51, 26 L. R. A. (N. S.) 242, 106 Pac. 235); an act forbidding the employment of women for more than eight hours a day in certain places (In re Miller, 162 Cal. 687, 124 Pac. 427; affirmed in Miller v. Wilson, 236 U. S. 373, 59 L. Ed. 628, 35 Sup. Ct. Rep. 342; the amendment of 1911 to section 395 of the Code of Civil Procedure regulating the place of trial of actions (Gridley v. Fellows, 166 Cal. 765, 138 Pac. 355); an act providing for the improvement of public streets in municipalities in cases where any damage to private property would result from such improvement, and for the assessment of the costs, damages and expenses thereof upon the property benefited thereby (Title Ins. & Trust Co. v. Lusk, 15 Cal. App. 358, 115 Pac. 53); "An act to prohibit the formation and existence of secret oath-bound fraternities in the public schools" (Bradford v. Board of Education, 18 Cal. App. 19, 121 Pac. 929); an act regulating the care of dependent and delinquent children until twenty-one years of age (Moore v. Williams, 19 Cal. App. 600, 127 Pac. 509); an act concerning actions for libel and slander which allows either party prevailing in such actions to recover as costs one hundred dollars to cover counsel fees (Engel v. Ehret, 21 Cal. App. 112, 130 Pac. 1197).

The proviso in the amendment of June 9, 1911, to section 1249 of the Code of Civil Procedure, which provided that nothing in the section, which affected the date with respect to which compensation in condemnation suits should be assessed, should be held to affect pending litigation. (Vallejo etc. R. R. Co. v. Reed Orchard Co., 169 Cal. 545, 147 Pac. 238.)

What are general statutes. See note, 21 Am. St. Rep. 780.

See, also, cases cited below under the particular subdivisions of this section.

Acts held to be special.—On the other hand, the following acts have been held to be special within the meaning of this section: An act providing for boards of election commissioners in cities and counties having one hundred and fifty thousand or more inhabitants, that being an arbitrary classification without reference to the existing classification by general law (Denman v. Broderick, 111 Cal. 96, 43 Pac. 516); the "McClure Charter," because it only applied to consolidated city and county governments of a designated population (Desmond v. Dunn, 55 Cal. 242); a provision of the County Government Act providing for salaries in addition to fees of constables in townships numbered one to ten in counties of one particular class (Lougher v. Soto, 129 Cal. 610, 62 Pac. 184); an act giving laborers employed by corporations by the week or month a lien for wages (Slocum v. Bear Valley Irr. Co., 122 Cal. 555, 68 Am. St. Rep. 68, 55 Pac. 403); a law

depriving certain persons arbitrarily of the right to participate in an election (Spier v. Baker, 120 Cal. 370, 41 L. R. A. 196, 52 Pac. 659); an act directed at and applicable to one particular named municipal corporation, and taking away a large part of its territory (People v. Common Council, 85 Cal. 369, 24 Pac. 727; Fisher v. Police Court, 86 Cal. 158, 24 Pac. 1000); an act to remedy the failure on the part of the tax collector to publish the names of the owners, etc. (Moore v. Patch, 12 Cal. 265); the provision of section 1203 of the Code of Civil Procedure, requiring contractors for the erection of buildings to secure their contracts by bonds (Shaughnessy v. American Surety Co., 138 Cal. 543, 69 Pac. 250, 71 Pac. 701); a law regulating the rate of interest on chattel mortgages on certain classes of property only. (Ex parte Sohncke, 148 Cal. 262, 113 Am. St. Rep. 236, 7 Ann. Cas. 475, 2 L. R. A. (N. S.), 813, 82 Pac. 956); the provision of the mechanic's lien law allowing the plaintiff, but not the defendant, an attorney's fee (Builders' Supply Depot v. O'Connor, 150 Cal. 265, 119 Am. St. Rep. 193, 11 Ann. Cas. 712, 17 L. R. A. (N. S.) 909, 88 Pac. 982); the amendment of 1911 to section 4256 of the Political Code fixing the compensation of justices of the peace and providing that a stenographer shall be appointed by the judge of the superior court, with the duties to report the proceedings at preliminary examinations and coroner's inquests, at a certain salary to be paid out of the county treasury, in the same manner and at the same time as other salaries are paid (Payne v. Murphy, 18 Cal. App. 446, 123 Pac. 350); section 1349 of the Code of Civil Procedure, as amended in 1907, providing that in the order admitting the will to probate "the court must ascertain and determine whether said estate is worth more or less than ten thousand dollars, which determination is conclusive for the purpose of giving notice to creditors" (Estate of Becker, 20 Cal. App. 513, 129 Pac. 795).

See, also, cases cited below under particular subdivisions of this section.

Subdivision 1.—An act establishing an additional police court in San Francisco, with the same jurisdiction, and to be governed by the same rules as the court already existing, is not a special law. (Ex parte Jordan, 62 Cal. 464.)

This subdivision does not apply to the terms of office of justices of the peace. (Kahn v. Sutro, 114 Cal. 316, 33 L. R. A. 620, 46 Pac. 87.)

An act creating a justice's court for one particular named town and fixing its jurisdiction is a special law. (Minor v. Justice's Court, 121 Cal. 264, 53 Pac. 795.)

An act creating a police court for cities of one class is constitutional. (Union etc. Co. v. Rose, 11 Cal. App. 357, 104 Pac. 1006.)

Subdivision 2.—An act making it a misdemeanor "for any person engaged in the business of baking to engage, or to permit others in his employ to engage, in the business of baking for the purpose of sale, between the hours of 6 o'clock P. M. on Saturday and 6 o'clock P. M. on Sunday," is a special law. (Ex parte Westerfield, 55 Cal. 550, 36 Am. Rep. 47.)

An act making it unlawful to keep open any place of business on Sunday, but exempting hotels, boarding-houses, barber-shops, baths,

markets, restaurants, taverns, livery-stables, and retail drug-stores, held not to be a special law. (Ex parte Koser, 60 Cal. 117.)

This section does not prohibit the legislature from authorizing by general laws ordinances which would be special laws if enacted by the legislature directly. (Ex parte Chin Yan, 60 Cal. 78.)

An act allowing certain convicts in the city and county of San Francisco to be imprisoned in the house of correction instead of the county jail or state prison does not violate this subdivision. (Ex parte Williams, 87 Cal. 78, 24 Pac. 602, 25 Pac. 248.)

An act establishing an additional police court in San Francisco, with the same jurisdiction and to be governed by the same rules as the court already existing, is not a special law. (Ex parte Jordan, 62 Cal. 464.)

An act making it a misdemeanor to keep open a barber-shop on Sundays and other holidays is special legislation. (Ex parte Jentzsch, 112 Cal. 468, 32 L. R. A. 664, 44 Pac. 803.)

Section 636½ of the Penal Code, which prohibits the use of certain kinds of nets in fishing, is not a special law in its application to the sixth fish and game district. (Matter of Application of Mascolo, 25 Cal. App. 92, 142 Pac. 903.)

Section 636½ of the Penal Code is not invalid because of this section of the Constitution, since it is qualified and limited by section 25½ of article IV subsequently adopted. (Matter of Application of Mascolo, 25 Cal. App. 92, 142 Pac. 903.)

Subdivision 3.—A provision in the municipal corporation act that in cities of one class it shall not be necessary to plead or prove the existence or validity of any ordinance thereof, and that courts shall take judicial notice thereof, is special legislation. (City of Tulare v. Hevren, 126 Cal. 226, 58 Pac. 530.)

A provision in the act supplemental to the "Wright Act," that in a proceeding to confirm the organization and bonds of an irrigation district "a motion for a new trial must be made upon the minutes of the court," is repugnant to this provision. (Cullen v. Glendora Water Co., 113 Cal. 503, 39 Pac. 769, 45 Pac. 822.)

The "Banking Commissioners' Act," providing for the winding up of banking corporations, and to that extent superseding the provisions of the general Insolvent Act, is constitutional. (People v. Superior Court, 100 Cal. 105, 34 Pac. 492.)

An act providing the form of a complaint in an action to condemn land is valid. (San Francisco v. Kiernan, 98 Cal. 614, 33 Pac. 720.)

An act requiring an undertaking on the part of the plaintiff in actions of libel and slander is not a special law. (Smith v. McDermott, 93 Cal. 421, 29 Pac. 34.)

The word "practice" includes all "pleadings." (People v. Central Pac. R. R. Co., 83 Cal. 393, 23 Pac. 303.)

Section 437a of the Code of Civil Procedure, providing that when an insurance company claims exemption from liability on the ground that, although the loss was proximately caused by a peril insured against, still it would not have occurred but for a peril excepted in the contract, it must set forth the facts constituting this defense, in detail, in its answer, is in violation of this section. (Board of Education v. Alliance Assur. Co., 159 Fed. 994.)

A law providing for a special form of complaint in an action to recover an assessment of taxes against a railroad situated in more than one county is in violation of this section. (People v. Central Pac. R. R. Co., 83 Cal. 393, 23 Pac. 303. But see People v. Central Pac. R. R. Co., 105 Cal. 576, 38 Pac. 905; affirmed, Central Pac. R. Co. v. California, 162 U. S. 91, 40 L. Ed. 903, 16 Sup. Ct. Rep. 766.)

An act allowing certain convicts in the city and county of San Francisco to be imprisoned in the house of correction instead of the county jail or state prison does not violate this subdivision. (Ex parte Williams, 87 Cal. 78, 24 Pac. 602, 25 Pac. 248.)

An act establishing an additional police court in San Francisco, with the same jurisdiction and to be governed by the same rules as the court already existing, is not a special law. (Ex parte Jordan, 62 Cal. 464.)

A provision of the act of March 6, 1905, providing for the levy of assessments upon a district to pay for lighting the streets therein, which provides that any appeal from a final judgment in an action or proceeding contesting the validity of an assessment to light public streets must be perfected within thirty days after entry of judgment, is constitutional. (Cohen v. City of Alameda, 168 Cal. 265, 142 Pac. 885.)

Under this section, section 682 of the Penal Code cannot be construed as authorizing the prosecution and trial of a person charged with causing and contributing to the dependency of a female under 21, on a verified complaint filed in the superior court. (People v. Budd, 24 Cal. App. 176, 140 Pac. 714.)

Subdivision 6.—Under this subdivision the legislature cannot by special law change the name of a corporation, but may by general law provide for such change by the superior court upon application of the incorporators. (Matter of La Societe Francaise, etc., 123 Cal. 525, 56 Pac. 458.)

Subdivision 7.—The act of 1891 supplemental to the Vrooman Act, relating to street work in all municipalities, is a general law. (Hellman v. Shoulters, 114 Cal. 136, 44 Pac. 915, 45 Pac. 1057.)

Subdivision 9.—A law providing that, in counties of one particular class only, witnesses in criminal cases shall be entitled to the same fees as jurors, in the discretion of the court, is special. (Turner v. Siskiyou Co., 109 Cal. 332, 42 Pac. 434.)

A provision of the County Government Act, that in counties of a certain class county licenses collected in cities shall be paid into the treasuries of such cities for street improvements, is in violation of this subdivision. (San Luis Obispo v. Graves, 84 Cal. 71, 23 Pac. 1032.)

The provisions of the County Government Act of 1893 empowering certain of the county officers in counties of one class to appoint a certain number of deputies, whose salaries are fixed by the act and made payable out of the county treasury, is valid, although in other counties the principals must pay the salaries of their deputies. (Tulare Co. v. May, 118 Cal. 303, 50 Pac. 427; Freeman v. Barnum, 131 Cal. 386, 82 Am. St. Rep. 355, 63 Pac. 691. Welsh v. Bramlet, 98

Cal. 219, 33 Pac. 66, and Walser v. Austin, 104 Cal. 128, 37 Pac. 869, overruled.)

An act directing the municipality to pay a particular claim against it is in violation of this provision. (Conlin v. Supervisors, 114 Cal. 404, 33 L. R. A. 752, 46 Pac. 279.)

A law providing for the payment by the state, county or city of the premium on official bonds of all state, county or city officers (except notaries public) when given by surety companies is not in violation of this section. (County of San Luis Obispo v. Murphy, 162 Cal. 588, Ann. Cas. 1913D, 712, 123 Pac. 808.)

The act of March 18, 1911, authorizing the respective counties and municipalities of the state to appoint sealers of weights and measures, is not a special law within the meaning of this section. (Scott v. Boyle, 164 Cal. 321, 128 Pac. 941.)

Subdivision 10.—A law providing that taxes upon personal property unsecured by real estate shall be collected at the time of the assessment, and before the time provided for the collection of taxes upon other property, is valid. (Rode v. Siebe, 119 Cal. 518, 39 L. R. A. 342, 51 Pac. 869, Van Fleet, J., and Harrison, J., dissenting; Pacific Postal etc. Co. v. Dalton, 119 Cal. 604, 51 Pac. 1072.)

Section 10 of article XIII of the Constitution is not "a local or special law" passed by the legislature. (San Francisco etc. R. R. Co. v. State Board, 60 Cal. 12.)

A law providing a special method of assessment and collection of taxes against railroads situated in more than one county is special legislation. (People v. Central Pac. R. R. Co., 83 Cal. 393, 23 Pac. 303. But see People v. Central Pac. R. R. Co., 105 Cal. 576, 38 Pac. 905; affirmed, Central Pac. R. Co. v. California, 162 U. S. 91, 40 L. Ed. 903, 16 Sup. Ct. Rep. 766.)

The Motor Vehicle Act of 1913, which includes San Francisco as a county for the purposes of the act and excludes all other cities, is valid. (In re Schuler, 167 Cal. 282, Ann. Cas. 1915C, 706, 139 Pac. 685.)

Subdivision 11.—In forming a new county the legislature may make special provisions as to the first election to be held in it, and as to all things which must be done in order to complete the organization and preserve the orderly and harmonious administration of the laws therein. (People v. McFadden, 81 Cal. 489, 15 Am. St. Rep. 66, 22 Pac. 851.)

A law creating and providing for the organization of a new county is not within the prohibition against special and local legislation. (People v. Glenn Co., 100 Cal. 419, 38 Am. St. Rep. 305, 35 Pac. 302.)

An act creating a new county may provide for the collection of taxes levied before the formation of the county, but collected afterward. (Kings County v. Johnson, 104 Cal. 198, 37 Pac. 870.)

The Primary Election Law of 1896, being expressly confined in its operation to counties of the first and second class, is local and special. (Marsh v. Supervisors, 111 Cal. 368, 43 Pac. 975.)

Subdivision 13.—A law providing a special method of assessment and collection of taxes against railroads situated in more than one county is special legislation. (People v. Central Pac. R. R. Co., 83

Cal. 393, 23 Pac. 303. But see People v. Central Pac. R. R. Co., 105 Cal. 576, 38 Pac. 905; affirmed, Central Pac. R. Co. v. California, 162 U. S. 91, 40 L. Ed. 903, 16 Sup. Ct. Rep. 766.)

Subdivision 14.—An act validating bonds of municipalities when authorized by two-thirds of the inhabitants of the county is not a special law. (Redlands v. Brook, 151 Cal. 474, 91 Pac. 150.)

Subdivision 16.—An act attempting retroactively to exempt resident nephews and nieces from the payment of unpaid taxes upon collateral inheritances is in violation of this provision. (Estate of Stanford, 126 Cal. 112, 45 L. R. A. 788, 54 Pac. 259, 58 Pac. 462.)

Subdivision 19.—Tulare Co. v. May, 118 Cal. 303, 50 Pac. 427; People v. Superior Court, 100 Cal. 105, 34 Pac. 492.

Subdivision 20.—A law providing a special method of assessment and collection of taxes against railroads situated in more than one county is special legislation. (People v. Central Pac. R. R. Co., 83 Cal. 393, 23 Pac. 303. But see People v. Central Pac. R. R. Co., 105 Cal. 576, 38 Pac. 905; affirmed, Central Pac. R. Co. v. California, 162 U. S. 91, 40 L. Ed. 903, 16 Sup. Ct. Rep. 766.

Sections 1670 and 1671 of the Political Code, as they existed prior to the amendments of 1909, exempting the property in a union high school district from taxation for the support of a county high school, were not in violation of this section. (Wood v. County of Calaveras, 164 Cal. 398, 129 Pac. 283.)

Subdivision 23.—An act making it a misdemeanor for a pawnbroker to charge or receive more than two per cent per month interest is not a special law. (Ex parte Lichenstein, 67 Cal. 359, 56 Am. Rep. 713, 7 Pac. 728.)

Subdivision 24.—People v. Central Pac. R. R. Co., 83 Cal. 393, 23 Pac. 303; People v. Central Pac. R. R. Co., 105 Cal. 576, 38 Pac. 905, affirmed, Central Pac. R. Co. v. California, 162 U. S. 91, 40 L. Ed. 903, 16 Sup. Ct. Rep. 766.

Subdivision 27.—The fixing of salaries of teachers is part of the "management of the common schools." (Earle v. Board of Education, 55 Cal. 489.)

An act relating to salaries of school teachers in cities having one hundred thousand inhabitants or more is local and unconstitutional. (Earle v. Board of Education, 55 Cal. 489.)

An act providing that in cities having a board of education the city treasurer is to have the custody of the state and county school money appropriated to the city is a special law. (Bruch v. Colombet, 104 Cal. 347, 38 Pac. 45.)

Subdivision 28.—An act authorizing the police commissioners of Sacramento to appoint policemen not exceeding thirty in number is a special law, and creates officers within the meaning of this subdivision. (Farrell v. Board of Trustees, 85 Cal. 408, 24 Pac. 868.)

The word "officers" includes policemen in cities, and includes all officers who exercise their office and perform their duties within the limits of either political division mentioned. (Farrell v. Board of Trustees, 85 Cal. 408, 24 Pac. 868.)

An act directing the municipality to pay a particular claim against it is in violation of this subdivision. (Conlin v. Supervisors, 114 Cal. 404, 33 L. R. A. 752, 46 Pac. 279.)

An act creating officers in but one class of counties, arbitrarily created and designated by population, without reference to the classification contained in the general law, is in violation of this provision. (San Francisco v. Broderick, 125 Cal. 188, 57 Pac. 887.)

This subdivision does not prevent the passage of a special law as to a board of harbor commissioners for the bay of San Diego. (People v. Mullender, 132 Cal. 217, 64 Pac. 299.)

The act of March 18, 1911, authorizing the respective counties and municipalities of the state to appoint sealers of weights and measures, is not a special law within the meaning of this section. (Scott v. Boyle, 164 Cal. 321, 128 Pac. 941.)

The provision of the charter of the city of Berkeley providing for compensation of school directors is not a special law under this subdivision. (Stern v. City Council of Berkeley, 25 Cal. App. 685, 145 Pac. 167.)

See, also, Ex parte Jordan, 62 Cal. 464; Welsh v. Bramlet, 98 Cal. 219, 33 Pac. 66; Tulare Co. v. May, 118 Cal. 303, 50 Pac. 427.

Subdivision 29.—An act making an appropriation to pay the salary of an officer during a certain period before the amount of the salary has been fixed is not in violation of this section. (Smith v. Dunn, 64 Cal. 164, 28 Pac. 232. Smith v. Kenfield, 57 Cal. 138, distinguished.)

The County Government Act is not in violation of this provision. (Longan v. Solano Co., 65 Cal. 122, 3 Pac. 463.)

An act fixing the salaries of county officers and providing that in all counties, except counties of three designated classes, it should not take effect until the expiration of the terms of the incumbents, and in those three it should take effect the first day of the month succeeding its passage, is a special law. (Miller v. Kister, 68 Cal. 142, 8 Pac. 813.)

An act readjusting the salaries of all county officers of counties of a particular class is a general law. (Cody v. Murphey, 89 Cal. 522, 26 Pac. 1081.)

An act making an appropriation to pay James W. Rankin for services in the state treasurer's office is not in violation of this section. (Rankin v. Colgan, 92 Cal. 605, 28 Pac. 673.)

An act providing that when the population of an existing county shall be reduced, by reason of the creation of any new county from the territory thereof, below the class first assumed by it under the act, it should be the duty of the supervisors of such county to designate the class to which such county has been reduced, is a general law. (Kumler v. Supervisors, 103 Cal. 393, 37 Pac. 383.)

A provision of the fee bill allowing justices of the peace a certain portion of the fees collected by them, without reference to the classification contained in the County Government Act, is a special law. (Dwyer v. Parker, 115 Cal. 544, 47 Pac. 372.)

The provision of the County Government Act of 1897, providing for salaries in certain counties in lieu of fees and per diem is valid. (Vail v. San Diego, 126 Cal. 35, 58 Pac. 392.)

The act of March 18, 1911, authorizing the respective counties and municipalities of the state to appoint sealers of weights and measures, is not a special law within the meaning of this section. (Scott v. Boyle, 164 Cal. 321, 128 Pac. 941.)

See, also, Ex parte Jordan, 62 Cal. 464; Tulare Co. v. May, 118 Cal. 303, 50 Pac. 427.

Subdivision 31.—Under this section of the Constitution of 1849 the legislature had the power to create municipal corporations at will, by special laws, and a given territory could be incorporated by it as a municipal corporation without the consent or the acceptance of the inhabitants thereof. (People v. California Fish Co., 166 Cal. 576, 138 Pac. 79.)

Subdivision 33.—In Earle v. Board of Education, 55 Cal. 489, it was suggested, but not decided, that the court may determine whether a general law can be made applicable in a given case.

As to whether the legislative determination of the question whether a general law can be made applicable is conclusive, discussed but not decided. (People v. Mullender, 132 Cal. 217, 64 Pac. 299.)

A law cannot be held invalid merely because, in the opinion of the court, it would have been possible to have framed a general law under which the purpose of the special law could have been accomplished. (People v. Mullender, 132 Cal. 217, 64 Pac. 299.)

It is impossible for the court to say that a general law could be made applicable to the subject of formation of new counties. (People v. McFadden, 81 Cal. 489, 15 Am. St. Rep. 66, 22 Pac. 851.)

A law requiring cities of two designated classes to make effort to agree with the owners of land sought to be condemned, before instituting condemnation proceedings, is special legislation. (Pasadena v. Stimson, 91 Cal. 238, 27 Pac. 604.)

A provision of the County Government Act that in all counties of one particular class certain additional fees shall be collected for filing the inventory in estates of deceased persons, is violative of this section. (Bloss v. Lewis, 109 Cal. 493, 41 Pac. 1081.)

The act of 1895, providing for the disincorporation of municipal corporations of the sixth class, is not a special law. (Mintzer v. Schilling, 117 Cal. 361, 49 Pac. 209.)

The act of 1893, providing a special method of collecting fees in cities and counties of over one hundred thousand inhabitants, is a special law. (Rauer v. Williams, 118 Cal. 401, 50 Pac. 691.)

An act providing a special mode of conducting the election of directors of mining corporations is a special law. (Krause v. Durbrow, 127 Cal. 681, 60 Pac. 438.)

An act providing that no misnomer of the owner shall affect any assessment by an irrigation district is a general law. (Escondido High School Dist. v. Escondido Seminary, 130 Cal. 128, 62 Pac. 401.)

The act of 1905 creating the "Sacramento Drainage District," while a special act, is not unconstitutional, as the subject matter necessitated a special law. Determination of the legislature as to necessity for special act will not be disturbed, except upon a clear showing that there was no such necessity. (People v. Sacramento Drainage District, 155 Cal. 373, 103 Pac. 207.)

A law prohibiting waste of water from artesian wells is not unconstitutional because not made applicable to surface water and pumps. (Ex parte Elam, 6 Cal. App. 233, 91 Pac. 811.)

An act appropriating money for the support of veterans of the Civil War at a particular home is not unconstitutional because not made applicable to all veterans of the Civil War. (Board v. Nye, 8 Cal. App. 527, 97 Pac. 208.)

The "Torrens Land Law" is not a special law, although it makes special provisions as to land which is brought under the act. (Robinson v. Kerrigan, 151 Cal. 40, 121 Am. St. Rep. 90, 12 Ann. Cas. 829, 90 Pac. 129.)

An act providing different qualifications for the electors who shall be allowed to vote at an election to be held in pursuance of such act is not a special law forbidden by this provision of the Constitution. (Wheeler v. Herbert, 152 Cal. 224, 92 Pac. 353.)

Section 172a of the Penal Code, prohibiting the sale of liquor near university grounds of any university of more than one thousand students, does not violate this section of the Constitution, merely because the class to which it applies consists of but one unit, individual or entity. (Matter of Petition of Burke, 160 Cal. 300, 116 Pac. 755.)

Under this section, section 682 of the Penal Code cannot be construed as authorizing the prosecution and trial of a person charged with causing and contributing to the dependency of a female under twenty-one, on a verified complaint filed in the superior court. (People v. Budd, 24 Cal. App. 176, 140 Pac. 714.)

See, also, Marsh v. Hanly, 111 Cal. 368, 43 Pac. 975; People v. Superior Court, 100 Cal. 105, 34 Pac. 492; Conlin v. Supervisors, 114 Cal. 404, 33 L. R. A. 752, 46 Pac. 279; Tulare Co. v. May, 118 Cal. 303, 50 Pac. 427; Ex parte Jentzsch, 112 Cal. 468, 32 L. R. A. 664, 44 Pac. 803.

Subdivision 37.—Under this section of the Constitution of 1849, the legislature had the power to create municipal corporations at will, by special laws, and a given territory could be incorporated by it as a municipal corporation without the consent or the acceptance of the inhabitants thereof. (People v. California Fish Co., 166 Cal. 576, 138 Pac. 79.)

Fish and game districts.

Sec. 25½. The legislature may provide for the division of the state into fish and game districts, and may enact such laws for the protection of fish and game therein as it may deem appropriate to the respective districts. (Amendment adopted November 4, 1902.)

FISH AND GAME.—The imposition of a license tax of ten dollars a year for the privilege of fishing for profit in the waters of the state tends to protect fish and this section expressly authorizes the legislature to enact laws for that purpose. (Matter of Application of Parra, 24 Cal. App. 339, 141 Pac. 393.)

Lotteries prohibited—Purchase and sale of shares of stock to be regulated.

Sec. 26. The legislature shall have no power to authorize lotteries or gift enterprises for any purpose and shall pass laws to prohibit the sale in this state of lottery or gift enterprise tickets or tickets in any scheme in the nature of a lottery. The legislature shall pass laws to prohibit the fictitious buying and selling of the shares of the capital stock of corporations in any stock board, stock exchange or stock market under the control of any corporation or association. All contracts for the purchase or sale of shares of the capital stock of any corporation or association without any intention on the part of one party to deliver and of the other party to receive the shares, and contemplating merely the payment of differences between the contract and market prices on divers days, shall be void, and neither party to any such contract shall be entitled to recover any damages for failure to perform the same, or any money paid thereon, in any court of this state. (Amendment adopted November 3, 1908.)

[ORIGINAL SECTION.]

Sec. 26. The legislature shall have no power to authorize lotteries or gift enterprises for any purpose, and shall pass laws to prohibit the sale in this state of lottery or gift enterprise tickets, or tickets in any scheme in the nature of a lottery. The legislature shall pass laws to regulate or prohibit the buying and selling of the shares of the capital stock of corporations in any stock board, stock exchange, or stock market under the control of any association. All contracts for the sale of shares of the capital stock of any corporation or association, on margin or to be delivered at a future day, shall be void, and any money paid on such contracts may be recovered by the party paying it by suit in any court of competent jurisdiction.

LOTTERIES.—Under this section an ordinance making the mere possession of a lottery ticket a misdemeanor is valid. (Collins v. Lean, 68 Cal. 284, 9 Pac. 173.)

Trading stamps and coupons are not a lottery. (Ex parte Drexel, 147 Cal. 763, 3 Ann. Cas. 878, 2 L. R. A. (N. S.) 588, 82 Pac. 429.)

What are lotteries. See notes, 16 Am. St. Rep. 42; 1 Ann. Cas. 91.

Chance as essential element of lottery. See notes, 1 Ann. Cas. 168; 12 Ann. Cas. 136.

Guessing contest or competition as lottery. See notes, 12 Ann. Cas. 321; 11 L. R. A. (N. S.) 609.

Distribution of parcels of land by chance as lottery. See notes, 18 Ann. Cas. 568; 23 L. R. A. (N. S.) 626; 27 L. R. A. (N. S.) 287.

Club formed by tailor for distributing clothes as lottery. See notes, 5 Ann. Cas. 837; 16 Ann. Cas. 846; 21 L. R. A. (N. S.) 876.

SALE OF STOCK ON MARGIN.—This provision is remedial, not penal. (Parker v. Otis, 130 Cal. 322, 92 Am. St. Rep. 56, 62 Pac. 571, 927.)

It is not in conflict with the federal Constitution. (Parker v. Otis, 130 Cal. 322, 92 Am. St. Rep. 56, 62 Pac. 571, 927; affirmed in Otis v. Parker, 187 U. S. 606, 47 L. Ed. 323, 23 Sup. Ct. Rep. 168.)

Whether or not a particular transaction is in violation of this provision is a question of fact. (Baldwin v. Zadig, 104 Cal. 594, 38 Pac. 363, 722.)

This provision will not be extended so as to forbid the delivery of stock as a conditional payment for the purchase of land, with a guaranty of cash value, and an agreement to take it back at the end of two years, upon request, and to make the payments in cash. (Maurer v. King, 127 Cal. 114, 59 Pac. 290.)

An undisclosed principal may recover money paid by his agent upon a contract in violation of this section. (Parker v. Otis, 130 Cal. 322, 92 Am. St. Rep. 56, 62 Pac. 571, 927; affirmed in Otis v. Parker, 187 U. S. 606, 47 L. Ed. 323, 23 Sup. Ct. Rep. 168.)

This provision is not to be confined to the particular person handing over the money. (Parker v. Otis, 130 Cal. 322, 92 Am. St. Rep. 56, 62 Pac. 571, 927; affirmed in Otis v. Parker, 187 U. S. 606, 47 L. Ed. 323, 23 Sup. Ct. Rep. 168.)

This provision will not be so construed as to permit an evasion of it. (Parker v. Otis, 130 Cal. 322, 92 Am. St. Rep. 56, 62 Pac. 571, 927; affirmed in Otis v. Parker, 187 U. S. 606, 47 L. Ed. 323, 23 Sup. Ct. Rep. 168.)

An agreement by which the broker is to purchase stock, charging the customer with commissions and the interest on the money advanced, and holding the stocks as security until their sale, the customer simply receiving and paying the difference between the buying and selling values of the stock, is in violation of this section. (Cashman v. Root, 89 Cal. 373, 23 Am. St. Rep. 482, 12 L. R. A. 511, 26 Pac. 883.)

The payment of a mere margin of the cost price of stock to brokers, under an agreement that the brokers were to make advances for the purchaser, and hold the stock purchased as security for their advances, with power to sell to protect their interest, without delivery to the purchaser of any particular shares of stock purchased, but with readiness of the brokers at any time on demand to deliver a like number of shares upon payment of all balance due, is within the prohibition of this section. (Parker v. Otis, 130 Cal. 322, 92 Am. St. Rep. 56, 62 Pac. 571, 927; affirmed in Otis v. Parker, 187 U. S. 606, 47 L. Ed. 323, 23 Sup. Ct. Rep. 168.)

A contract made with stock brokers for the purpose of speculating in stocks, to purchase a number of shares on margin, without know-

ing of whom or where they were to be bought, to be delivered at a
future day, if at all, with the understanding that in case of decline
margin was to be kept good, and brokers to retain shares as security
and sell when security should be endangered, violates this provision.
(Stillwell v. Cutter, 146 Cal. 657, 80 Pac. 1071.)

One who sues to recover money voluntarily paid for the purchase
of stocks on margins or to be delivered at a future day, in violation
of this provision, is not entitled to recover interest thereon. (Baldwin v. Zadig, 104 Cal. 594, 38 Pac. 363, 722.)

Evidence held to show a sale upon margins. (Pollitz v. Wickersham, 150 Cal. 238, 88 Pac. 911.)

The amendment of November 3, 1908, to this section did not validate previous contracts made in contravention of the repealed provision of this section, which invalidated all contracts for the sale of
stocks "on margin or to be delivered at a future day," the amendment not being retrospective in operation. (Willcox v. Edwards, 162
Cal. 455, Ann. Cas. 1913C, 1392, 123 Pac. 276.)

Sale of futures. See note, 1 Am. St. Rep. 752.

Illegality as gambling contract, of contract for sale of property
for future delivery when one party only intends delivery. See
note, 11 Ann. Cas. 440.

Congressional and senatorial districts.

Sec. 27.   When a congressional district shall be composed
of two or more counties, it shall not be separated by any
county belonging to another district. No county, or city
and county, shall be divided in forming a congressional district so as to attach one portion of a county, or city and
county, to another county, or city and county, except in
cases where one county, or city and county, has more population than the ratio required for one or more congressmen;
but the legislature may divide any county, or city and
county, into as many congressional districts as it may be
entitled to by law. Any county, or city and county, containing a population greater than the number required for
one congressional district, shall be formed into one or more
congressional districts, according to the population thereof,
and any residue, after forming such district or districts,
shall be attached by compact adjoining assembly districts,
to a contiguous county or counties, and form a congressional district. In dividing a county, or city and
county, into congressional districts, no assembly district
shall be divided so as to form a part of more than one congressional district, and every such congressional district
shall be composed of compact contiguous assembly districts.

CONGRESSIONAL DISTRICTS.—As to the apportionment of the state in general, see note to section 6 of this article.

Elections by legislature to be viva voce.

Sec. 28. In all elections by the legislature the members thereof shall vote viva voce, and the votes shall be entered on the journal.

General appropriation bill, what to contain.

Sec. 29. The general appropriation bill shall contain no item or items of appropriation other than such as are required to pay the salaries of the state officers, the expenses of the government, and of the institutions under the exclusive control and management of the state.

GENERAL APPROPRIATION BILL.—The general appropriation bill cannot create an office. (Lewis v. Colgan, 115 Cal. 529, 47 Pac. 357.)

Appropriations for claims for illegal taxes collected by the state treasurer cannot be embraced in the general appropriation bill. (Westinghouse Electric Co. v. Chambers, 169 Cal. 131, 145 Pac. 1025.)

Restriction on appropriations and grants of aid.

Sec. 30. Neither the legislature, nor any county, city and county, township, school district, or other municipal corporation, shall ever make an appropriation, or pay from any public fund whatever, or grant anything to or in aid of any religious sect, church, creed, or sectarian purpose, or help to support or sustain any school, college, university, hospital, or other institution controlled by any religious creed, church, or sectarian denomination whatever; nor shall any grant or donation of personal property or real estate ever be made by the state, or any city, city and county, town, or other municipal corporation for any religious creed, church, or sectarian purpose whatever; provided, that nothing in this section shall prevent the legislature granting aid pursuant to section twenty-two of this article.

Credit of state or municipalities not to be loaned.

Sec. 31. The legislature shall have no power to give or to lend, or to authorize the giving or lending, of the credit of the state, or of any county, city and county, city, township, or other political corporation or subdivision of the state now

existing, or that may be hereafter established, in aid of or to any person, association, or corporation, whether municipal or otherwise, or to pledge the credit thereof, in any manner whatever, for the payment of the liabilities of any individual, association, municipal or other corporation what·· ever; nor shall it have power to make any gift, or authorize the making of any gift, of any public money or thing of value to any individual, municipal or other corporation whatever; provided, that nothing in this section shall prevent the legislature granting aid pursuant to section twenty-two of this article; and it shall not have power to authorize the state or any political subdivision thereof, to subscribe for stock, or to become a stockholder in any corporation shall prevent the legislature granting aid pursuant to section twenty-two of this article; and it shall not have power to authorize the state, or any political subdivision thereof, to subscribe for stock, or to become a stockholder in any corporation whatever; provided, further, that irrigation districts for the purpose of acquiring the control of any entire international water system necessary for its use and purposes, a part of which is situated in the United States, and a part thereof in a foreign country, may in the manner authorized by law, acquire the stock of any foreign corporation which is the owner of, or which holds the title to the part of such system situated in a foreign country. (Amendment adopted November 3, 1914.)

[ORIGINAL SECTION.]

Sec. 31. The legislature shall have no power to give or to lend, or to authorize the giving or lending, of the credit of the state, or of any county, city and county, city, township, or other political corporation or subdivision of the state now existing, or that may be hereafter established, in aid of or to any person, association, or corporation, whether municipal or otherwise, or to pledge the credit thereof, in any manner whatever, for the payment of the liabilities of any individual, association, municipal or other corporation whatever; nor shall it have power to make any gift, or authorize the making of any gift, of any public money or thing of value to any individual, municipal or other corporation whatever; provided, that nothing in this section shall prevent the legislature granting aid pursuant to section twenty-two of this article; and it shall not have power to authorize the state, or any political subdivision thereof, to subscribe for stock, or to become a stockholder in any corporation whatever.

AID TO PRIVATE ENTERPRISE.—An appropriation to a railroad company to aid in building a railroad, in consideration of valuable services, is not a gift or loan of the credit of the state. (People v. Pacheco, 27 Cal. 175.)

Under the former Constitution, the legislature might compel a county to become a subscriber to a railroad, and the legislature was the sole judge of the question as to whether the railroad was a public benefit. (Napa Valley R. R. Co. v. Board of Suprs. of Napa Co., 30 Cal. 435.)

A promise by a municipality in a contract between it and a water company, for the supply of water in bulk to the municipality and its inhabitants for a term of years to pay for not less than a certain amount of water a day, does not amount to a loan of the credit of the municipality contrary to this section, in that the promise is based upon the covenants of the water company to construct a pipe-line extending its system to the municipality. (Marin Water etc. Co. v. Town of Sausalito, 168 Cal. 587, 143 Pac. 767.)

GIFTS.—A statute will not be held unconstitutional on the ground that it makes a gift, unless its invalidity appears upon its face or from facts of which the court takes judicial notice. (Conlin v. Board of Supervisors, 99 Cal. 17, 37 Am. St. Rep. 17, 21 L. R. A. 474, 33 Pac. 753; Stevenson v. Colgan, 91 Cal. 649, 25 Am. St. Rep. 230, 14 L. R. A. 459, 27 Pac. 1089; Rankin v. Colgan, 92 Cal. 605, 28 Pac. 673; Bourn v. Hart, 93 Cal. 321, 27 Am. St. Rep. 203, 15 L. R. A. 431, 28 Pac. 951.)

The courts will take judicial notice that in no case would a city be liable for any portion of the expense of street improvements; and, therefore, an act appropriating money for the same is unconstitutional. (Conlin v. Board of Supervisors, 99 Cal. 17, 37 Am. St. Rep. 17, 21 L. R. A. 474, 33 Pac. 753.)

A gift as used in this section includes all appropriations for which there is no authority or enforceable claim, or which rest alone upon some moral or equitable obligation, which in the mind of a generous or even just individual, dealing with his own money, might prompt him to recognize as worthy of reward. (Conlin v. Board of Supervisors, 99 Cal. 17, 37 Am. St. Rep. 17, 21 L. R. A. 474, 33 Pac. 753.)

A gift within the meaning of this section is a gratuitous transfer of the property of the state, made voluntarily and without consideration. (Yosemite Stage etc. Co. v. Dunn, 83 Cal. 264, 23 Pac. 369.)

Under the former Constitution the legislature might authorize the payment of claims invalid in law, but equitable and just in themselves. (Blanding v. Burr, 13 Cal. 343; Creighton v. Board of Suprs. of San Francisco, 42 Cal. 446.)

But a mere moral obligation will not make a transaction other than a gift. (Molineux v. California, 109 Cal. 378, 50 Am. St. Rep. 49, 42 Pac. 34.)

The legislature has no power to make gifts to its employees or to allow them extra compensation after service rendered. (Robinson v. Dunn, 77 Cal. 473, 11 Am. St. Rep. 297, 19 Pac. 878.)

The legislature has no power to create a liability against the state for any act of negligence on the part of its officers. (Chapman v. State, 104 Cal. 690, 43 Am. St. Rep. 158, 38 Pac. 457.)

The legislature has power to waive the statute of limitations in respect to a claim against the state. (Bickerdike v. State, 144 Cal. 681, 78 Pac. 270.)

A mere change in the remedy does not create a liability against the state. (Chapman v. State, 104 Cal. 690, 43 Am. St. Rep. 158, 38 Pac. 457.)

An act attempting retroactively to exempt resident nephews and nieces from the payment of unpaid taxes upon collateral inheritances is in violation of this provision. (Estate of Stanford, 126 Cal. 112, 45 L. R. A. 788, 54 Pac. 259, 58 Pac. 462.)

A purchase of an unexpired lease of the Yosemite and Wawona wagon road, made by the Yosemite commissioners, is not a gift. (Yosemite Stage etc. Co. v. Dunn, 83 Cal. 264, 23 Pac. 369.)

A law attempting to confer a right to recover interest on coupons upon which there was before no right to recover interest is a gift. (Molineux v. California, 109 Cal. 378, 50 Am. St. Rep. 49, 42 Pac. 34.)

An act creating an exempt firemen's relief fund, and requiring municipalities to aid exempt firemen who never rendered them any service, and thus creating a liability where none existed before, is in violation of this section. (Taylor v. Mott, 123 Cal. 497, 56 Pac. 256.)

As to whether a contract by a municipal corporation to pay money to any person or corporation to secure the construction of a railroad would be in violation of this section, see Higgins v. San Diego Water Co., 118 Cal. 524, 546, 45 Pac. 824, 50 Pac. 670.

An act providing a bounty on coyote scalps does not constitute a gift. (Ingram v. Colgan, 106 Cal. 113, 46 Am. St. Rep. 221, 28 L. R. A. 187, 38 Pac. 315, 39 Pac. 437.)

The mere fact that the city enjoyed the actual advantage of certain street improvements does not create any moral obligation, and cannot support a statute appropriating money for the same. (Conlin v. Board of Supervisors, 99 Cal. 17, 37 Am. St. Rep. 17, 21 L. R. A. 474, 33 Pac. 753.)

An act appropriating five thousand dollars for the benefit of the sufferers from the Tia Juana floods is clearly violative of this provision. (Patty v. Colgan, 97 Cal. 251, 18 L. R. A. 744, 31 Pac. 1133.)

An appropriation in payment of a claim for damages on account of personal injuries sustained while in the service of the state, and for which the state is not responsible, is a gift. (Bourn v. Hart, 93 Cal. 321, 27 Am. St. Rep. 203, 15 L. R. A. 431, 28 Pac. 951.)

An act creating a police life and health insurance fund, and providing for the payment into such fund of a certain portion of the salaries of police officers, does not make a gift of public money. (Pennie v. Reis, 80 Cal. 266, 22 Pac. 176.)

An act directing the payment of the salary of an officer of an irrigation district out of the funds of the county is in violation of this provision. (Knox v. Board of Suprs. of Los Angeles, 58 Cal. 59.)

The provision of the Political Code for the repayment to purchasers of swamp lands of the amounts which they had paid for their lands, being a part of the contract between them and the state, is not a gift of public money. (McCord v. Slavin, 143 Cal. 325, 76 Pac. 1104.)

An act providing for the payment of fees to jurors for past services, where there was no previous liability therefor, is in violation of this section. (Powell v. Phelan, 138 Cal. 271, 71 Pac. 335.)

After the right of the state to an inheritance tax has become vested by death, the legislature cannot, by repeal of the act creating it, affect the right of the state thereto. (Estate of Lander, 6 Cal. App. 744, 93 Pac. 202.)

The amendment of 1895 to the act providing for the formation of agricultural associations, authorizing the transfer of all the property of such an association to a private corporation formed within the association, to be used and disposed of for the benefit of such corporation and its stockholders (subject to certain limitations) is an attempted gift of public property. (Sixth District Agr. Assn. v. Wright, 154 Cal. 119, 97 Pac. 144.)

Under this section the legislature is without power, either by the repeal of the law in virtue of which the right to a tax under the inheritance tax law vested, or by any other means, to grant or donate it to the successor in estate, or to any other person. (Estate of Martin, 153 Cal. 225, 94 Pac. 1053.)

After the right of the state to a collateral inheritance tax has become vested by the death of the decedent, the legislature cannot surrender the same by any repeal or change in the law. (Trippet v. State, 149 Cal. 521, 8 L. R. A. (N. S.) 1210, 86 Pac. 1084.)

An appropriation for the support of the veterans of the Civil War at the Woman's Relief Corps Home Association is not a gift. (Board of Directors v. Nye, 8 Cal. App. 527, 97 Pac. 208.)

The appropriation for the transportation of veterans to Gettysburg and return is unconstitutional. (McClure v. Nye, 22 Cal. App. 248, 133 Pac. 1145.)

> What constitutes valid appropriation of public moneys. See note, 22 Am. St. Rep. 638.
>
> Appropriation of public moneys for private purposes. See note, 1 Ann. Cas. 935.
>
> Validity of statute appropriating public funds for fairs. See note, 9 Ann. Cas. 52.
>
> Appropriation in aid of charity as within constitutional provision against giving or loaning money or credit of state or municipality. See note, Ann. Cas. 1913C, 1234.

Extra compensation to officers forbidden.

Sec. 32. The legislature shall have no power to grant, or authorize any county or municipal authority to grant, any extra compensation or allowance to any public officer, agent, servant, or contractor, after service has been rendered, or a contract has been entered into and performed, in whole or in part, nor to pay, or to authorize the payment of, any claim hereafter created against the state, or any county or municipality of the state, under any agreement or

contract made without express authority of law; and all such unauthorized agreements or contracts shall be null and void.

EXTRA COMPENSATION.—The word "law" as used in this section is used in the same sense as the word "statute," and includes an unconstitutional statute. (Miller v. Dunn, 72 Cal. 462, 1 Am. St. Rep. 67, 14 Pac. 27.)

This section does not prevent the legislature from making an appropriation to pay a claim for work done on behalf of the state, in pursuance of an act of the legislature, which is judicially declared unconstitutional after the performance of the work. (Miller v. Dunn, 72 Cal. 462, 1 Am. St. Rep. 67, 14 Pac. 27.)

The legislature cannot retroactively give an officer increased compensation over that fixed by law when his term commenced, by ratifying the payment of such increased compensation. (County of Butte v. Merrill, 141 Cal. 396, 74 Pac. 1036.)

An act creating an exempt firemen's relief fund, and requiring municipalities to aid exempt firemen who never rendered them any service, and thus creating a liability where none existed before, is in violation of this section. (Taylor v. Mott, 123 Cal. 497, 56 Pac. 256.)

The legislature has no power to make gifts to its employees or to allow them extra compensation after service rendered. (Robinson v. Dunn, 77 Cal. 473, 11 Am. St. Rep. 297, 19 Pac. 878.)

A contract by a board of supervisors, employing the district attorney to try a suit in another county after the expiration of his term of office, does not increase his salary as district attorney, and is valid. (Jones v. Morgan, 67 Cal. 308, 7 Pac. 734.)

An act making an appropriation to pay the salary of an officer during a certain period before the amount of the salary has been fixed is not in violation of this section. (Smith v. Dunn, 64 Cal. 164, 28 Pac. 232.)

An act providing for a police life and health insurance fund does not grant an extra compensation in violation of this section. (Pennie v. Reis, 80 Cal. 266, 22 Pac. 176.)

A contract by the clerk of the board of supervisors to collect a claim against the state and divide the commission with the district attorney is in violation of this section. (Power v. May, 114 Cal. 207, 46 Pac. 6.)

Although there is no express authority of law for the board of examiners to appoint an expert, they have the power, since, in addition to its express powers, a board has such additional powers as are necessary for the due and efficient exercise of powers expressly granted, or as may be fairly implied. (Lewis v. Colgan, 115 Cal. 529, 47 Pac. 357.)

An act appropriating money for the salary of an expert to the board of examiners is valid, and the employment of such expert by the board is not void as being without express authority of law. (Lewis v. Colgan, 115 Cal. 529, 47 Pac. 357.)

> Validity of statute providing for payment by state, county, etc., of premium on bond of public officer. See note, Ann. Cas. 1913D, 715.

Constitutional provision against increasing compensation during
term of office as applicable where new duties are imposed on
officer after taking office. See note, 18 Ann. Cas. 403.

Applicability to nonconstitutional officer of constitutional provision against increase of salary of officer during his term of
office. See note, 26 L. R. A. (N. S.) 289.

Charges of gas and telegraph corporations to be regulated.

Sec. 33. The legislature shall pass laws for the regulation and limitation of the charges for services performed
and commodities furnished by telegraph and gas corporations, and the charges by corporations or individuals for
storage and wharfage, in which there is a public use; and
where laws shall provide for the selection of any person or
officer to regulate and limit such rates, no such person or
officer shall be selected by any corporation or individual interested in the business to be regulated, and no person shall
be selected who is an officer or stockholder in any such corporation.

WATER RATES.—As to water and gas rates, see note to section 1,
article XIV, and section 19, article XI.

This section does not make it necessary for the legislature to pass
laws regulating the manner in which the authority conferred by section 19, article XI, shall be exercised, before that section becomes
operative. (Denninger v. Recorder's Court, 145 Cal. 629, 79 Pac. 360.)

This section authorizes municipalities to regulate the charges for
services of telephone, telegraph, gas and certain other corporations.
(Home Telephone & Tel. Co. v. City of Los Angeles, 155 Fed. 554.)

Special appropriation bill, restriction as to.

Sec. 34. No bill making an appropriation of money, except the general appropriation bill, shall contain more than
one item of appropriation, and that for one single and certain purpose to be therein expressed.

APPROPRIATIONS.—The fact that an act making two or more
distinct appropriations has but one general purpose will not render it
consistent with this provision of the Constitution. (Murray v. Colgan, 94 Cal. 435, 29 Pac. 871.)

An act making an appropriation for a county for ramie fiber, and
also an appropriation for the salary of a state superintendent of
ramie culture, is in violation of this section. (Murray v. Colgan, 94
Cal. 435, 29 Pac. 871.)

An act appropriating money for the purchase of a site for a home
for feeble-minded children, and for the erection of buildings thereon,

is not in violation of this section. (People v. Dunn, 80 Cal. 211, 13 Am. St. Rep. 118, 22 Pac. 140.)

An act making an appropriation to pay the separate claims of five different persons for services rendered a receiver appointed at the suit of the state violates this section. (Sullivan v. Gage, 145 Cal. 759, 79 Pac. 537.)

See, also, People v. Counts, 89 Cal. 15, 19, 26 Pac. 612; State v. Sloan, 66 Ark. 575, 74 Am. St. Rep. 106, 53 S. W. 47.

Section 3669 of the Political Code, directing the state controller, in the event of a final judgment being recovered against the state treasurer for the amount of taxes illegally assessed by the state board of equalization and collected by the treasurer, to draw his warrant therefor upon the treasurer and directing the latter to pay it, is unconstitutional, since it is not a specific appropriation of the kind described in this section. (Westinghouse Electric Co. v. Chambers, 169 Cal. 131, 145 Pac. 1025.)

Lobbying defined—Punishment for.

Sec. 35. Any person who seeks to influence the vote of a member of the legislature by bribery, promise of reward, intimidation, or any other dishonest means, shall be guilty of lobbying, which is hereby declared a felony; and it shall be the duty of the legislature to provide, by law, for the punishment of this crime. Any member of the legislature, who shall be influenced in his vote or action upon any matter pending before the legislature by any reward, or promise of future reward, shall be deemed guilty of a felony, and upon conviction thereof, in addition to such punishment as may be provided by law, shall be disfranchised and forever disqualified from holding any office of public trust. Any person may be compelled to testify in any lawful investigation or judicial proceeding against any person who may be charged with having committed the offense of bribery or corrupt solicitation, or with having been influenced in his vote or action, as a member of the legislature, by reward, or promise of future reward, and shall not be permitted to withhold his testimony upon the ground that it may criminate himself or subject him to public infamy; but such testimony shall not afterward be used against him in any judicial proceeding, except for perjury in giving such testimony.

LOBBYING.—The term "lobbying" signifies to address or solicit members of a legislative body with the purpose of influencing their

votes. (Colusa Co. v. Welch, 122 Cal. 428, 55 Pac. 243; Le Tourneux v. Gilliss, 1 Cal. App. 546, 82 Pac. 627.)

Services rendered by an attorney in endeavoring to persuade the members of the legislature individually to act favorably upon a bill, in which no dishonest, secret, or unfair means were used, do not constitute "lobbying" within the meaning of this section. (Foltz v. Cogswell, 86 Cal. 542, 25 Pac. 60. Approved in Colusa Co. v. Welch, 122 Cal. 428, 55 Pac. 243.)

A contract to pay to secure, by means of personal solicitation, and by means of private interviews with members of the legislature, and by means of lobbying, the defeat of a bill pending in the legislature, is prohibited by this section. (Colusa Co. v. Welch, 122 Cal. 428, 55 Pac. 243.)

A contract, the object of which is to aid one of the parties to engage in the business of lobbying, will not be enforced. (Le Tourneux v. Gilliss, 1 Cal. App. 546, 82 Pac. 627.)

In order to show that certain acts constitute "lobbying," it is not necessary to show that any corrupt means were used to influence votes. (Le Tourneux v. Gilliss, 1 Cal. App. 546, 82 Pac. 627.)

This section does not take away the power of the legislature to define legislative bribery and to fix the punishment therefor. (In re Bunkers, 1 Cal. App. 61, 81 Pac. 748.)

Nor does it limit the power of the legislature itself to expel a member for bribery under section 9 of this article. (French v. Senate, 146 Cal. 604, 2 Ann. Cas. 756, 69 L. R. A. 556, 80 Pac. 1031.)

Validity of lobbying contracts. See note, 121 Am. St. Rep. 726.

Validity of contract for contingent compensation in procuring legislation. See note, 6 Ann. Cas. 218.

Contracts for services to procure legislation. See notes, 30 L. R. A. 737; 4 L. R. A. (N. S.) 213.

State highways.

Sec. 36. The legislature shall have power to establish a system of state highways or to declare any road a state highway, and to pass all laws necessary or proper to construct and maintain the same, and to extend aid for the construction and maintenance in whole or in part of any county highway.   (Amendment adopted November 4, 1902.)

ARTICLE V.

EXECUTIVE DEPARTMENT.

Executive power vested in governor.

Section 1. The supreme executive power of this state shall be vested in a chief magistrate who shall be styled the Governor of the state of California.

THE GOVERNOR.—When a ministerial duty, affecting a private right, is specially devolved on the governor by law, he may be compelled to perform the same by writ of mandate. (Middleton v. Low, 30 Cal. 596; Harpending v. Haight, 39 Cal. 189, 2 Am. Rep. 432.)

Whether mandamus may be issued against governor. See notes, 33 Am. Dec. 361; 31 Am. St. Rep. 294.

Election of governor and term of office.

Sec. 2. The governor shall be elected by the qualified electors at the time and places of voting for members of the assembly, and shall hold his office four years from and after the first Monday after the first day of January subsequent to his election, and until his successor is elected and qualified.

TERM.—The term is fixed at four years certain, with a contingent extension. When this contingency happens, this extension is as much a part of the entire term as any portion of the four years. (People v. Whitman, 10 Cal. 38.)

Eligibility and qualifications.

Sec. 3.   No person shall be eligible to the office of governor who has not been a citizen of the United States and a resident of this state five years next preceding his election, and attained the age of twenty-five years at the time of such election.

Returns of election—Counting votes.

Sec. 4.   The returns of every election for governor shall be sealed up and transmitted to the seat of government, directed to the speaker of the assembly, who shall, during the first week of the session, open and publish them in the presence of both houses of the legislature.   The person having the highest number of votes shall be governor; but, in case any two or more have an equal and the highest number of votes, the legislature shall, by joint vote of both houses, choose one of such persons so having an equal and the highest number of votes for governor.

Governor to be commander-in-chief of militia.

Sec. 5.   The governor shall be commander-in-chief of the militia, the army and navy of this state.

Executive business of.

Sec. 6.   He shall transact all executive business with the officers of government, civil and military, and may require information, in writing, from the officers of the executive department, upon any subject relating to the duties of their respective offices.

To see that laws are executed.

Sec. 7.   He shall see that the laws are faithfully executed.

EXECUTE LAWS.—In the absence of a provision in the "San Francisco Sea-Wall Act," for the publication required by article XVI, the duty to provide for the publication devolved upon the governor. (Spear v. Reeves, 148 Cal. 501, 83 Pac. 432.)

To fill vacancies in office.

Sec. 8.   When any office shall, from any cause, become vacant, and no mode is provided by the Constitution and

law for filling such vacancy, the governor shall have power to fill such vacancy by granting a commission, which shall expire at the end of the next session of the legislature, or at the next election by the people.

APPOINTMENT OF OFFICERS.—After the issuance of the commission, the governor cannot revoke the appointment. (People v. Cazneau, 20 Cal. 503.)

The words "Constitution and law" mean Constitution or law. (People v. Nye, 9 Cal. App. 148, 98 Pac. 241.)

Where an officer is to be appointed by the governor by and with the consent of the senate, and the governor makes an appointment during the recess of the legislature, he cannot, before such appointee is rejected by the senate, appoint another person to the office. (People v. Mizner, 7 Cal. 519.)

An appointment by the governor only lasts till the next election by the people. (People v. Melony, 15 Cal. 58.)

The words "next election by the people" do not mean the next general election, or the next election held by the people, but that the appointee shall hold until someone has been regularly elected to fill that office in the manner provided by law; and as applied to the lieutenant-governor it means the next gubernatorial election. (People v. Budd, 114 Cal. 168, 34 L. R. A. 46, 45 Pac. 1060.)

The words "next election by the people" mean the next election after the vacancy happens, and in cases of judges, does not mean the next general judicial election. (People v. Mott, 3 Cal. 502.)

This provision is to be read distributively, so that, if the office is elective, the appointee shall hold till the next election, and if not elective, till the end of the next session of the legislature, which shall either elect a successor or enact laws for his election. (People v. Mott, 3 Cal. 502.)

Officers.—The term "officer," as used in this section, is sufficiently comprehensive to include all persons in any public station or employment conferred by the government, and includes the clerks of the secretary of state. (Vaughn v. English, 8 Cal. 39.)

Vacancies.—This provision applies only to vacancies occurring under circumstances such that the original appointing or electing power cannot act. Such power is limited by the period when the people or the legislature can elect or appoint, on the arrival of which period his power ceases and the right of appointment returns to the original appointing power. (People v. Fitch, 1 Cal. 519.)

Before this section can apply two things must be shown: 1. That a vacancy exists; and 2. That no mode of filling it is provided by law. (People v. Mizner, 7 Cal. 519.)

This section has no application to the filling of a vacancy, the mode of filling which is provided by law. (People v. Cazneau, 20 Cal. 503; People v. Stratton, 28 Cal. 382.)

As to whether or not this section has any application to local officers, see People v. Hammond, 66 Cal. 654, 6 Pac. 741.

The power to fill an office carries with it, by implication, the power to fill a vacancy, and all necessary authority to carry out the original

power, and prevent it from becoming inoperative. (People v. Fitch, 1 Cal. 519.)

If an act creating an office provides that the incumbent of another office shall, ex officio, fill the office created, and the incumbent is prohibited by the Constitution from holding the office, there is no vacancy. (People v. Sanderson, 30 Cal. 160.)

When a district judge resigns during his term, there is a vacancy to be filled by the governor, and the appointee will hold until the next general election, or at most until the qualification of the person elected by the people. (People v. Rosborough, 14 Cal. 180.)

Where an officer continues to discharge the duties of the office after the expiration of his term, and before the qualification of his successor, there is no vacancy in the office within the meaning of this section. (People v. Edwards, 93 Cal. 153, 28 Pac. 831.)

Absence of a judge from the state does not create a vacancy within the meaning of this section. (People v. Wells, 2 Cal. 198, 610, Anderson, J., dissenting.)

The legislature has no power to determine when a vacancy exists within the meaning of this section. (People v. Wells, 2 Cal. 198, 610; People v. Mizner, 7 Cal. 519.)

When the Constitution clearly enumerates the events that shall constitute a vacancy in a particular office, all others must be excluded. (People v. Whitman, 10 Cal. 38.)

Failure of an elected officer to qualify does not create a vacancy in the office. (People v. Whitman, 10 Cal. 38.)

No vacancy occurs by the death, removal, or resignation of a sheriff, as the coroner, by operation of law, becomes sheriff upon the happening of such an event. (People v. Phoenix, 6 Cal. 92.)

As to whether a failure to elect a successor leaves an office vacant at the expiration of the term, see People v. Parker, 37 Cal. 639.

Particular cases.—If the office of lieutenant-governor becomes vacant during his term of office, the governor may fill the vacancy for the full remainder of the unexpired term. (People v. Budd, 114 Cal. 168, 34 L. R. A. 46, 45 Pac. 1060.)

Where a fire commissioner was appointed under the act of 1878 by the judge of the county court for the term of four years and until his successor is appointed and qualified, and the new Constitution superseded the appointing functions of such judge and did not vest them in any other person, such commissioner holds over, and there is no vacancy in the office. (People v. Edwards, 93 Cal. 153, 28 Pac. 831.)

Where the position of state printer becomes vacant during the session of the legislature, which was the appointing power, the governor has no power to appoint a successor. (People v. Fitch, 1 Cal. 519.)

Where the district judge was to be appointed by the legislature for the first term and thereafter elected by the people, and the legislature failed to appoint, and the governor appoints to fill the vacancy, the person so appointed only holds till the next election, and not till the next session of the legislature. (People v. Mott, 3 Cal. 502.)

Where an officer is appointed by the legislature to hold for two years, and until his successor is appointed and qualified, and the suc-

ceeding legislature fails to elect, the governor may appoint. (People v. Reid, 6 Cal. 288.)

Where the legislature fails to elect a successor to an officer at the expiration of the term, the governor may appoint. (People v. Baine, 6 Cal. 509; People v. Langdon, 8 Cal. 1.)

Where the appointment of an officer is vested in the governor, with the advice and consent of the senate, and the term expires during the recess of the senate, the governor may fill such vacancy for the full term, subject only to be defeated by nonconcurrence by the senate. (People v. Addison, 10 Cal. 1.)

When the legislature provides that in case of a vacancy in a particular office a board shall fill it until the next session of the legislature, the filling of the vacancy is provided for within the meaning of this section, and no vacancy is caused by the failure of the legislature to elect. (People v. Parker, 37 Cal. 639.)

> Power of appointing power to make appointment to office when term thereof does not begin until after expiration of term of appointing power. See note, 18 Ann. Cas. 142.
>
> Power of governor to appoint to office in absence of constitutional or statutory authority. See note, 19 Ann. Cas. 823.
>
> Term of office of person elected or appointed to fill vacancy in absence of constitutional or statutory provision. See notes, Ann. Cas. 1913D, 619; 12 Ann. Cas. 572.

When to convene special sessions.

Sec. 9.   He may, on extraordinary occasions, convene the legislature by proclamation, stating the purposes for which he has convened it, and when so convened it shall have no power to legislate on any subjects other than those specified in the proclamation, but may provide for the expenses of the session and other matters incidental thereto.

EXTRA SESSIONS.—The confirmation of appointments by the governor is not legislation within the meaning of this section. (People v. Blanding, 63 Cal. 333.)

But the proposing of constitutional amendments is such legislation. (People v. Curry, 130 Cal. 82, 62 Pac. 516.)

The governor is the sole judge of the existence of an extraordinary occasion for convening the legislature. (Whiteman v. Wilmington etc. R. R. Co., 2 Harr. (Del.) 514, 33 Am. Dec. 411.)

Messages to legislature.

Sec. 10.   He shall communicate by message to the legislature, at every session, the condition of the state, and recommend such matters as he shall deem expedient.

When to adjourn legislature.

Sec. 11. In case of a disagreement between the two houses with respect to the time of adjournment, the governor shall have power to adjourn the legislature to such time as he may think proper; provided, it be not beyond the time fixed for the meeting of the next legislature.

Disability to hold other offices.

Sec. 12. No person shall, while holding any office under the United States or this state, exercise the office of governor except as hereinafter expressly provided.

Keeper of seal of state.

Sec. 13. There shall be a seal of this state, which shall be kept by the governor, and used by him officially, and shall be called "The Great Seal of the State of California."

To sign and seal grants and commissions.

Sec. 14. All grants and commissions shall be in the name and by the authority of the people of the state of California, sealed with the great seal of the state, signed by the governor, and countersigned by the secretary of state.

TAX DEED.—The fact that a tax deed is not executed in the manner provided by this section does not affect its validity. (Schamblin v. Means, 6 Cal. App. 261, 91 Pac. 1020.)

Lands acquired by the state for nonpayment of taxes are not within the purview of this section, and the state may make the tax collector or any other person its agent and attorney in fact for the passing of the legal title to such lands. (Bank of Lemoore v. Fulgham, 151 Cal. 234, 90 Pac. 936.)

Lieutenant-governor—Election of, etc.

Sec. 15. A lieutenant-governor shall be elected at the same time and place, and in the same manner, as the governor, and his term of office and his qualifications shall be the same. He shall be president of the senate, but shall only have a casting vote therein. (Amendment adopted November 8, 1898.)

[ORIGINAL SECTION.]

Sec. 15. A lieutenant-governor shall be elected at the same time and place, and in the same manner, as the governor; and his term

of office and his qualifications of eligibility shall also be the same. He shall be president of the senate, but shall have only a casting vote therein. If, during a vacancy of the office of governor, the lieutenant-governor shall be impeached, displaced, resign, die, or become incapable of performing the duties of his office, or be absent from the state, the president pro tempore of the senate shall act as governor until the vacancy be filled or the disability shall cease. The lieutenant-governor shall be disqualified from holding any other office, except as specially provided in this Constitution, during the term for which he shall have been elected.

When powers of governor devolve on.

Sec. 16. In case of the impeachment of the governor, or his removal from office, death, inability to discharge the powers and duties of his office, resignation, or absence from the state, the powers and duties of the office shall devolve upon the lieutenant-governor for the residue of the term, or until the disability shall cease. And should the lieutenant-governor be impeached, displaced, resign, die, or become incapable of performing the duties of his office, or be absent from the state, the president pro tempore of the senate shall act as governor until the vacancy in the office of governor shall be filled at the next general election, when members of the legislature shall be chosen, or until such disability of the lieutenant-governor shall cease. In case of a vacancy in the office of governor for any of the reasons above named, and neither the lieutenant-governor nor the president pro tempore of the senate succeed to the powers and duties of governor, then the powers and duties of such office shall devolve upon the speaker of the assembly, until the office of governor shall be filled at such general election. (Amendment adopted November 8, 1898.)

[ORIGINAL SECTION.]

Sec. 16. In case of the impeachment of the governor, or his removal from office, death, inability to discharge the powers and duties of the said office, resignation, or absence from the state, the powers and duties of the office shall devolve upon the lieutenant-governor for the residue of the term, or until the disability shall cease. But when the governor shall, with the consent of the legislature, be out of the state in time of war, at the head of any military force thereof, he shall continue commander-in-chief of all the military force of the state.

State officers—Election and terms of office.

Sec. 17.   A secretary of state, a controller, a treasurer, an attorney general, and a surveyor-general shall be elected at the same time and places, and in the same manner as the governor and lieutenant-governor, and their terms of office shall be the same as that of the governor.

EXECUTIVE OFFICERS.—Neither an appointment by the governor, nor an election by the people, had before the election of governor, can deprive the people of their right to fill the office of controller at such election. (People v. Melony, 15 Cal. 58.)

The controller is a ministerial officer and has no discretion as to the issuance of warrants for appropriations. (People v. Brooks, 16 Cal. 11.)

Although the Constitution is wholly silent as to the duties of the attorney general, secretary of state, controller, and treasurer, and contains no express limitation on the power of the legislature as to the same, yet a limitation on their power is necessarily implied from the nature of these offices. (Love v. Baehr, 47 Cal. 364.)

The legislature may devolve on the secretary of state the performance of services foreign to the office, and may pay him a salary therefor in addition to his salary as secretary of state. (Melone v. State, 51 Cal. 549; Green v. State, 51 Cal. 577.)

In assigning duties to these officers, the legislature possesses a wide discretion, and while the legislature cannot compel the attorney general to perform the duties of a member of the board of examiners, it may compensate him for doing so voluntarily. (Love v. Baehr, 47 Cal. 364.)

The term of the controller begins on the first Monday after the first day of January. (People v. Nye, 9 Cal. App. 148, 98 Pac. 241.)

Where an incumbent of the office of controller dies after his election to a second term and before his qualification, an appointee for the balance of the unexpired term would hold only to the beginning of the second term. (People v. Nye, 9 Cal. App. 148, 98 Pac. 241.)

Secretary of state—Duties of.

Sec. 18.   The secretary of state shall keep a correct record of the official acts of the legislative and executive departments of the government, and shall, when required, lay the same, and all matters relative thereto, before either branch of the legislature, and shall perform such other duties as may be assigned him by law.

Compensation of state officers.

Sec. 19.   The governor, lieutenant-governor, secretary of state, controller, treasurer, attorney general, and surveyor-

general shall, at stated times during their continuance in office, receive for their services a compensation which shall not be increased or diminished during the term for which they shall have been elected, which compensation is hereby fixed for the following officers, as follows: Governor, ten thousand dollars per annum; lieutenant-governor, four thousand dollars, the secretary of state, controller, treasurer, and surveyor-general, five thousand dollars each per annum, and the attorney general, six thousand dollars per annum, such compensation to be in full for all services by them respectively rendered in any official capacity or employment whatsoever during their respective terms of office; provided, however, that the legislature may, by law, diminish the compensation of any or all of such officers, but in no case shall have the power to increase the same above the sums hereby fixed by this Constitution. No salary shall be authorized by law for clerical service, in any office provided for in this article, exceeding eighteen hundred dollars per annum for each clerk employed. The legislature may, in its discretion, abolish the office of surveyor-general; and none of the officers hereinbefore named shall receive for their own use any fees or perquisites for the performance of any official duty. (Amendment adopted November 3, 1908.)

[ORIGINAL SECTION.]

Sec. 19. The governor, lieutenant-governor, secretary of state, controller, treasurer, attorney general, and surveyor general shall, at stated times during their continuance in office, receive for their services a compensation which shall not be increased or diminished during the term for which they shall have been elected, which compensation is hereby fixed for the following officers for the two terms next ensuing the adoption of this Constitution, as follows: Governor, six thousand dollars per annum; lieutenant-governor, the same per diem as may be provided by law for the speaker of the assembly, to be allowed only during the session of the legislature; the secretary of state, controller, treasurer, attorney general, and surveyor general, three thousand dollars each per annum, such compensation to be in full for all services by them respectively rendered in any official capacity or employment whatsoever during their respective terms of office; provided, however, that the legislature, after the expiration of the terms hereinbefore mentioned, may, by law, diminish the compensation of any or all of such officers, but in no case shall have the power to increase the same

above the sums hereby fixed by this Constitution. No salary shall be authorized by law for clerical service, in any office provided for in this article, exceeding sixteen hundred dollars per annum for each clerk employed. The legislature may, in its discretion, abolish the office of surveyor general; and none of the officers hereinbefore named shall receive for their own use any fees or perquisites for the performance of any official duty.

SALARIES OF STATE OFFICERS.—The original provision of this section could not affect the power of the people to amend the same and increase the salaries of incumbents. (Kingsbury v. Nye, 9 Cal. App. 574, 99 Pac. 985.)

The amendment to this section in 1908 applied to, and increased the salaries of, the incumbents. (Kingsbury v. Nye, 9 Cal. App. 574, 99 Pac. 985.)

United States senators, how elected.

Sec. 20. United States senators shall be elected by the people of the state in the manner provided by law. (Amendment adopted November 3, 1914.)

[ORIGINAL SECTION.]

Sec. 20. The governor shall not, during his term of office, be elected a senator to the senate of the United States.

UNITED STATES SENATE.—The provision of the original section was invalid and not binding upon the United States senate. The qualification of members of that body being fixed by the United States Constitution, additional ones cannot be required by the states. (Barney v. McCreery, 1 Cong. El. Cas. 167; Turney v. Marshall, 2 Cong. El. Cas. 167; Trumbull's Case, 2 Cong. El. Cas. 618.)

ARTICLE VI.
JUDICIAL DEPARTMENT.

Judicial powers.

Section 1. The judicial power of the state shall be vested in the senate, sitting as a court of impeachment, in a supreme court, district courts of appeal, superior courts and such inferior courts as the legislature may establish in any incorporated city or town, township, county, or city and county. (Amendment approved October 10, 1911.)

[AMENDMENT OF 1904.]

Section 1. The judicial power of the state shall be vested in the senate, sitting as a court of impeachment, in a supreme court, district courts of appeal, superior courts, justices of the peace, and such inferior courts as the legislature may establish in any incorporated city or town, or city and county. (Amendment adopted November 8, 1904.)

[ORIGINAL SECTION.]

Section 1. The judicial power of the state shall be vested in the senate sitting as a court of impeachment, in a supreme court,

Constitution—19

superior courts, justices of the peace, and such inferior courts as the legislature may establish in any incorporated city or town, or city and county.

JUDICIAL DEPARTMENT—Preconstitutional courts.—The correctness of the proceedings of the courts exercising civil jurisdiction in California between the time of its acquisition by the United States and the establishment of a state government are not to be tested by the strict rules of the civil or common law. (Ryder v. Cohn, 37 Cal. 69.)

Judicial power.—It is the inherent authority not only to decide but to make binding orders or judgments which constitutes judicial power. (People v. Hayne, 83 Cal. 111, 17 Am. St. Rep. 217, 7 L. R. A. 348, 23 Pac. 1.)

The legislature cannot enjoin upon a private person the duty of settling a bill of exceptions, nor require a judge to continue to discharge judicial duties after his term of office has expired, though it may authorize him to settle such bill. (Leach v. Aitken, 91 Cal. 484, 28 Pac. 777.)

The matter of the adoption of children is not part of the judicial power within the meaning of this section, and may, therefore, be conferred upon a judge as distinguished from the court. (In re Stevens, 83 Cal. 322, 17 Am. St. Rep. 252, 23 Pac. 379.)

A tribunal presided over by a police judge is a court. (Boys' and Girls' Aid Soc. v. Reis, 71 Cal. 627, 12 Pac. 796.)

The proceeding to establish title to land in San Francisco when the records were destroyed by fire is judicial in its nature. (Title etc. Restoration Co. v. Kerrigan, 150 Cal. 289, 119 Am. St. Rep. 199, 8 L. R. A. (N. S.) 682, 88 Pac. 356.)

The legislature cannot confer jurisdiction of special cases upon a judge as distinguished from a court. (Spencer Creek etc. Co. v. Vallejo, 48 Cal. 70.)

An act creating supreme court commissioners to assist the court—which commissioners simply examine the record and report to the court their conclusions—is not unconstitutional as vesting judicial power in the commissioners. (People v. Hayne, 83 Cal. 111, 17 Am. St. Rep. 217, 7 L. R. A. 348, 23 Pac. 1.)

The legislature may provide that the city council shall be the final and exclusive judge of the election of all municipal officers. (Carter v. Superior Court, 138 Cal. 150, 70 Pac. 1067.)

The legislature cannot invest ministerial officers with the power to punish individuals by fine and imprisonment. (Burns v. Superior Court, 140 Cal. 1, 73 Pac. 597.)

The legislature may invest judicial officers with power to punish for contempt. (Crocker v. Conrey, 140 Cal. 213, 73 Pac. 1006.)

Inferior courts.—A freeholders' charter is not a law within the meaning of this section, and, therefore, an inferior court cannot be established by such charter. (People v. Toal, 85 Cal. 333, 24 Pac. 603; Miner v. Justice's Court, 121 Cal. 264, 53 Pac. 795; Ex parte Sparks, 120 Cal. 395, 52 Pac. 715.)

This section limits the power of the legislature to the establishment of municipal and inferior courts within the limits of an incorporated city or town. (Ex parte Stratman, 39 Cal. 517.)

The municipal criminal court of San Francisco is an inferior court within the meaning of this section. (Ex parte Stratman, 39 Cal. 517; People v. Nyland, 41 Cal. 129.)

The police court of San Francisco was not abolished by the constitutional amendments in 1862. (People v. Provines, 34 Cal. 520.)

The term "municipal courts" has a legal meaning and includes mayors' and recorders' courts. (Uridias v. Morrill, 22 Cal. 473.)

The legislature may vest in inferior courts jurisdiction of cases of which the courts established by the Constitution have jurisdiction. (Hickman v. O'Neal, 10 Cal. 292; Seale v. Mitchell, 5 Cal. 401; Vassault v. Austin, 36 Cal. 691; Curtis v. Richards, 9 Cal. 33.)

Under this section, the legislature has power to create police or other inferior courts in any incorporated city or town which has not taken advantage of the permission granted by section 8½ of article XI to include in its charter provision for the establishment of a police court. (Fleming v. Hance, 153 Cal. 162, 94 Pac. 620.)

The board of drainage commissioners created by the "Sacramento Drainage District" act, in equalizing assessments and correcting errors therein, is not exercising judicial functions in violation of the Constitution. (People v. Sacramento Drainage Dist., 155 Cal. 373, 103 Pac. 207.)

The legislature may authorize a municipal court to send its process beyond the territorial limits of the municipality. (Hickman v. O'Neal, 10 Cal. 292. Meyer v. Kalkmann, 6 Cal. 582, overruled.)

Judges of the police court of San Francisco are not affected by the provisions of the County Government Act, but derive their power from this section, and the act of 1893. (Kahn v. Sutro, 114 Cal. 316, 33 L. R. A. 620, 46 Pac. 87; In re Mitchell, 120 Cal. 384, 52 Pac. 799. But see People v. Cobb, 133 Cal. 74, 65 Pac. 325.)

An act creating police courts in cities having fifteen thousand, and under eighteen thousand, inhabitants, not being in conformity with the general classification of municipal corporations, is void. (Ex parte Giambonini, 117 Cal. 573, 49 Pac. 732.)

An act creating a justice's court for one particular named town, and fixing its jurisdiction, is not authorized by this section. (Miner v. Justice's Court, 121 Cal. 264, 53 Pac. 795.)

An act providing for a police judge necessarily presupposes a police court. (Ex parte Mauch, 134 Cal. 500, 66 Pac. 734.)

The late superior court of San Francisco was an inferior court, but its process ran outside of the city. (Chipman v. Bowman, 14 Cal. 157; McCauley v. Fulton, 44 Cal. 355.)

The legislature is vested with power to confer jurisdiction over all misdemeanors on inferior courts, unless jurisdiction over any of them is conferred upon some other court by the Constitution itself. (Matter of Application of Westenberg, 167 Cal. 309, 139 Pac. 674.)

The amendment of October 10, 1911, of this section does not abolish the justices' courts and other inferior courts which had been previously established by acts of the legislature. They remain in existence with the jurisdiction vested in them by the acts creating them, until the legislature shall, in the exercise of the power given by the section as amended, otherwise provide. (Matter of the Application of Woods, 161 Cal. 238, 118 Pac. 792.)

What is judicial power within constitutional theory as to separation of powers of government. See note, Ann. Cas. 1913E, 1097.

Power of legislature to create or abolish court of record. See note, Ann. Cas. 1913C, 1160.

Validity of statute concerning juvenile court. See notes, 120 Am. St. Rep. 952; Ann. Cas. 1914A, 1227.

Creation of courts by the Constitution. See 7 R. C. L., § 6, p. 977.

Supreme court, how constituted.

Sec. 2. The supreme court shall consist of a chief justice and six associate justices. The court may sit in departments and in bank, and shall always be open for the transaction of business. There shall be two departments, denominated, respectively, department one and department two. The chief justice shall assign three of the associate justices to each department, and such assignment may be changed by him from time to time. The associate justices shall be competent to sit in either department, and may interchange with each other by agreement among themselves or as ordered by the chief justice. Each of the departments shall have the power to hear and determine causes and all questions arising therein, subject to the provisions hereinafter contained in relation to the court in bank. The presence of three justices shall be necessary to transact any business in either of the departments, except such as may be done at chambers, and the concurrence of three justices shall be necessary to pronounce a judgment. The chief justice shall apportion the business to the departments, and may, in his discretion, order any cause pending before the court to be heard and decided by the court in bank. The order may be made before or after judgment pronounced by a department; but where a cause has been allotted to one of the departments, and a judgment pronounced thereon, the order must be made within thirty days after such judgment, and concurred in by two associate justices, and if so made it shall have the effect to vacate and set aside the judgment. Any four justices may, either before or after judgment by a department, order a case to be heard in bank. If the order be not made within the time above limited the judgment shall be final. No judgment by a department shall become final

until the expiration of the period of thirty days aforesaid, unless approved by the chief justice, in writing, with the concurrence of two associate justices. The chief justice may convene the court in bank at any time, and shall be the presiding justice of the court when so convened. The concurrence of four justices present at the argument shall be necessary to pronounce a judgment in bank; but if four justices, so present, do not concur in a judgment, then all the justices qualified to sit in the cause shall hear the argument; but to render a judgment a concurrence of four judges shall be necessary. In the determination of causes, all decisions of the court in bank or in departments shall be given in writing, and the grounds of the decision shall be stated. The chief justice may sit in either department, and shall preside when so sitting, but the justices assigned to each department shall select one of their number as presiding justice. In case of the absence of the chief justice from the place at which the court is held, or his inability to act, the associate justices shall select one of their own number to perform the duties and exercise the powers of the chief justice during such absence or inability to act.

SUPREME COURT.—This section by implication forbids the legislature to increase the number of justices of the supreme court. (People v. Wells, 2 Cal. 198, 610.)

In the absence of any provision on the subject, all the judges composing the court must sit. (People v. Ah Chung, 5 Cal. 103; People v. Barbour, 9 Cal. 230.)

The word "heard" means the consideration and determination of a cause by the court. (Niles v. Edwards, 95 Cal. 41, 30 Pac. 134.)

When a cause is submitted on briefs, all the justices are deemed to be present, and all of them are qualified to join in the decision. (Philbrook v. Newman, 148 Cal. 172, 82 Pac. 772.)

It is not necessary that four justices be physically present at an oral argument, nor that all of the justices qualified to "sit" shall literally "hear" an argument; but whenever there is an oral argument, only the justices who were present at such argument are authorized to take part in the decision of the court. (Niles v. Edwards, 95 Cal. 41, 30 Pac. 134.)

It is not necessary that four justices should concur in the judgment upon the same grounds. (Philbrook v. Newman, 148 Cal. 172, 82 Pac. 772.)

The fact that one of the judges who participated in a decision of the court did not hear the oral argument does not render the judgment absolutely void. It is an irregularity which may be waived by the parties. (Blanc v. Bowman, 22 Cal. 23.)

The Constitution requires the concurrence of four judges to pronounce a judgment, and a mere failure to agree cannot have the effect, ipso facto, of an affirmance; and where the personnel of the court is soon to be changed, a motion to affirm the judgment on account of an equal division of opinion will be denied. (Luco v. De Toro, 88 Cal. 26, 11 L. R. A. 543, 25 Pac. 983.)

But where there is no probability of an immediate change in the personnel of the court, the judgment will be affirmed. (Frankel v. Deidesheimer, 93 Cal. 73, 28 Pac. 794; Santa Rosa City R. R. v. Central St. Ry. Co., 112 Cal. 436, 44 Pac. 733.)

Judicial days.—The supreme court is always open for the transaction of business. (People v. Heacock, 10 Cal. App. 450, 102 Pac. 543.)

Opinions.—The legislature cannot require the supreme court to give in writing reasons for its decisions. (Houston v. Williams, 13 Cal. 24, 73 Am. Dec. 565.)

Rehearings.—In an original proceeding in the supreme court the proper practice is to move for a rehearing, and a motion for a new trial is not proper. (In re Philbrook, 108 Cal. 14, 40 Pac. 1061; Grangers' Bank v. Superior Court of San Francisco, 101 Cal. 198, 35 Pac. 642.)

There is only one supreme court, and the jurisdiction which is vested in it may be exercised either in bank or in department. The court in bank has power to correct an error in or modify a judgment rendered in a department, without application therefor, and without the case being argued in bank. (Niles v. Edwards, 95 Cal. 41, 30 Pac. 134.)

Although a petition for a rehearing by the court in bank is filed within thirty days after the judgment in department, if it does not reach the hands of the court until after the expiration of the period allowed by the Constitution for ordering a rehearing, the petition must be denied, irrespective of its merits. (Durgin v. Neal, 82 Cal. 595, 23 Pac. 133.)

The provision of this section as to the granting of rehearings in bank after the decision by a department does not create an implication against the constitutional power of the court in bank to grant rehearings in cases determined by it in bank. (In re Jessup, 81 Cal. 408, 6 L. R. A. 594, 21 Pac. 976, 22 Pac. 742, 1028.)

The supreme court, in bank, has power to grant rehearings by orders of the court entered upon its minutes, without the written signatures of five justices, and the legislature cannot take that power away. (In re Jessup, 81 Cal. 408, 6 L. R. A. 594, 21 Pac. 976, 22 Pac. 742, 1028.)

An order modifying a judgment is not rendered nugatory by reason of the failure of the clerk to enter it in the minutes until after the expiration of thirty days from the judgment in department. (Niles v. Edwards, 95 Cal. 41, 30 Pac. 134.)

The determination by the court on passing upon an application for a rehearing that the justice of that court, and not the justice of the court of appeals selected to act pro tempore on account of the illness of the former, was the proper one to act, becomes the law of the case, and will not be inquired into on a motion to set aside the rehearing. (Reeve v. Colusa Gas etc. Co., 151 Cal. 29, 91 Pac. 802.)

Remittitur.—The supreme court has no appellate jurisdiction over its own judgments. (Leese v. Clark, 20 Cal. 387.)

Therefore, after the issuance of the remittitur, the court loses jurisdiction of the cause. (Blanc v. Bowman, 22 Cal. 23; Grogan v. Ruckle, 1 Cal. 193; Mateer v. Brown, 1 Cal. 231; Davidson v. Dallas, 15 Cal. 75; Herrlich v. McDonald, 83 Cal. 505, 23 Pac. 710; In re Levinson, 108 Cal. 450, 41 Pac. 483, 42 Pac. 479; Martin v. Wagner, 124 Cal. 204, 56 Pac. 1023.)

After the remittitur has been duly and regularly issued without inadvertence, the court has no power to recall it, except in a case of mistake, fraud, or imposition. (In re Levinson, 108 Cal. 450, 41 Pac. 483, 42 Pac. 479.)

The mere pendency of a motion to modify the judgment is not sufficient ground for recalling the remittitur, when it was issued without inadvertence. (Herrlich v. McDonald, 83 Cal. 505, 23 Pac. 710.)

Nor is the fact that it was issued after the death of one of the parties ground for recalling it. (Martin v. Wagner, 124 Cal. 204, 56 Pac. 1023.)

But the remittitur may be recalled if issued by reason of fraud or imposition. (Trumpler v. Trumpler, 123 Cal. 248, 55 Pac. 1008.)

Election of supreme justices.

Sec. 3. The chief justice and the associate justices shall be elected by the qualified electors of the state at large at the general state elections, at the times and places at which state officers are elected; and the term of office shall be twelve years, from and after the first Monday after the first day of January next succeeding their election; provided, that the six associate judges elected at the first election shall, at their first meeting, so classify themselves, by lot, that two of them shall go out of office at the end of four years, two of them at the end of eight years, and two of them at the end of twelve years, and an entry of such classification shall be made in the minutes of the court in bank, signed by them, and a duplicate thereof shall be filed in the office of the secretary of state. If a vacancy occur in the office of a justice, the governor shall appoint a person to hold the office until the election and qualification of a justice to fill the vacancy, which election shall take place at the next succeeding general election, and the justice so elected shall hold the office for the remainder of the unexpired term. The first election of the justices shall be at the first general election after the adoption and ratification of this Constitution.

Jurisdiction of supreme court and courts of appeal.

Sec. 4. The supreme court shall have appellate jurisdiction on appeal from the superior courts in all cases in equity,
except such as arise in justices' courts; also, in all cases at
law which involve the title or possession of real estate, or the
legality of any tax, impost, assessment, toll, or municipal fine,
or in which the demand, exclusive of interest, or the value
of the property in controversy, amounts to two thousand
dollars; also, in all such probate matters as may be provided
by law; also, on questions of law alone, in all criminal cases
where judgment of death has been rendered; the said court
shall also have appellate jurisdiction in all cases, matters,
and proceedings pending before a district court of appeal
which shall be ordered by the supreme court to be transferred to itself for hearing and decision as hereinafter provided. The said court shall also have power to issue writs
of mandamus, certiorari, prohibition, and habeas corpus,
and all other writs necessary or proper to the complete
exercise of its appellate jurisdiction. Each of the justices
shall have power to issue writs of habeas corpus to any
part of the state, upon petition by or on behalf of any person held in actual custody, and may make such writs returnable before himself or the supreme court, or before any
district court of appeal, or before any judge thereof, or
before any superior court in the state, or before any judge
thereof.

The state is hereby divided into three appellate districts,
in each of which there shall be a district court of appeal
consisting of three justices. The first district shall embrace
the following counties: San Francisco, Marin, Contra Costa,
Alameda, San Mateo, Santa Clara, Fresno, Santa Cruz,
Monterey, and San Benito.

The second district shall embrace the following counties:
Tulare, Kings, San Luis Obispo, Kern, Inyo, Santa Barbara,

Ventura, Los Angeles, San Bernardino, Orange, Riverside, and San Diego.

The third district shall embrace the following counties: Del Norte, Siskiyou, Modoc, Humboldt, Trinity, Shasta, Lassen, Tehama, Plumas, Mendocino, Lake, Colusa, Glenn, Butte, Sierra, Sutter, Yuba, Nevada, Sonoma, Napa, Yolo, Placer, Solano, Sacramento, El Dorado, San Joaquin, Amador, Calaveras, Stanislaus, Mariposa, Madera, Merced, Tuolumne, Alpine, and Mono.

The supreme court, by orders entered in its minutes, may from time to time remove one or more counties from one appellate district to another, but no county not contiguous to another county of a district shall be added to such district.

Said district courts of appeal shall hold their regular sessions respectively at San Francisco, Los Angeles, and Sacramento, and they shall always be open for the transaction of business.

The district courts of appeal shall have appellate jurisdiction on appeal from the superior courts in all cases at law in which the demand, exclusive of interest, or the value of the property in controversy, amounts to three hundred dollars, and does not amount to two thousand dollars; also, in all cases of forcible and unlawful entry and detainer (except such as arise in justices' courts), in proceedings in insolvency, and in actions to prevent or abate a nuisance; in proceedings of mandamus, certiorari, and prohibition, usurpation of office, contesting elections and eminent domain, and in such other special proceedings as may be provided by law (excepting cases in which appellate jurisdiction is given to the supreme court); also, on questions of law alone, in all criminal cases prosecuted by indictment or information in a court of record, excepting criminal cases where judgment of death has been rendered. The said courts shall also have appellate jurisdiction in all cases, matters, and proceedings pending before the supreme court which shall be ordered by the supreme court to be transferred to a district court of appeal for hearing and decision. The said courts shall also have power to issue writs

of mandamus, certiorari, prohibition, and habeas corpus, and all other writs necessary or proper to the complete exercise of their appellate jurisdiction. Each of the justices thereof shall have power to issue writs of habeas corpus to any part of his appellate district upon petition by or on behalf of any person held in actual custody, and may make such writs returnable before himself or the district court of appeal of his district, or before any superior court within his district, or before any judge thereof.

The supreme court shall have power to order any cause pending before the supreme court to be heard and determined by a district court of appeal, and to order any cause pending before a district court of appeal to be heard and determined by the supreme court. The order last mentioned may be made before judgment has been pronounced by a district court of appeal, or within thirty days after such judgment shall have become final therein. The judgments of the district courts of appeal shall become final therein upon the expiration of thirty days after the same shall have been pronounced.

The supreme court shall have power to order causes pending before a district court of appeal for one district to be transferred to the district court of appeal of another district for hearing and decision.

The justices of the district courts of appeal shall be elected by the qualified electors within their respective districts at the general state elections at the times and places at which justices of the supreme court are elected. Their terms of office and salaries shall be the same as those of justices of the supreme court, and their salaries shall be paid by the state. Upon the ratification by the people of this amendment the governor shall appoint nine persons to serve as justices of the district courts of appeal until the first Monday after the first day of January in the year 1907, provided, that not more than six of said persons shall be members of the same political party. At the election in the year 1906 nine of such justices shall be elected as above provided, and the justices of each district court of appeal shall so classify themselves by lot that one of them shall go out

of office at the end of four years, one of them at the end of
eight years, and one of them at the end of twelve years; an
entry of such classification shall be made in the minutes of
the court, signed by the three justices thereof, and a duplicate thereof filed in the office of the secretary of state. If
any vacancy occur in the office of a justice of the district
courts of appeal, the governor shall appoint a person to
hold office until the election and qualification of a justice to
fill the vacancy; such election shall take place at the next
succeeding general state election as aforesaid; the justice
then elected shall hold the office for the unexpired term.

One of the justices of each of the district courts of appeal
shall be the presiding justice thereof, and as such shall be
appointed or elected as the case may be. The presence of
three justices shall be necessary for the transaction of any
business by such court, except such as may be done at chambers, and the concurrence of three justices shall be necessary to pronounce a judgment.

Whenever any justice of the supreme court is for any
reason disqualified or unable to act in a cause pending before it, the remaining justices may select one of the justices
of a district court of appeal to act pro tempore in the place
of the justice so disqualified or unable to act.

Whenever any justice of a district court of appeal is for
any reason disqualified or unable to act in any cause pending before it, the supreme court may appoint a justice of
the district court of appeal of another district, or a judge
of a superior court who has not acted in the cause in the
court below, to act pro tempore in the place of the justice so
disqualified or unable to act.

No appeal taken to the supreme court or to a district
court of appeal shall be dismissed for the reason only that
the same was not taken to the proper court, but the cause
shall be transferred to the proper court upon such terms
as to costs or otherwise as may be just, and shall be proceeded with therein as if regularly appealed thereto.

All statutes now in force allowing, providing for, or regulating appeals to the supreme court shall apply to appeals
to the district courts of appeal so far as such statutes are

not inconsistent with this article and until the legislature shall otherwise provide.

The supreme court shall make and adopt rules not inconsistent with law for the government of the supreme court and of the district courts of appeal and of the officers thereof, and for regulating the practice in said courts. (Amendment adopted November 8, 1904.)

[ORIGINAL SECTION.]

Sec. 4. The supreme court shall have appellate jurisdiction in all cases of equity, except such as arise in justices' courts; also, in all cases at law which involve the title or possession of real estate, or the legality of any tax, impost, assessment, toll or municipal fine, or in which the demand, exclusive of interest or the value of the property in controversy, amounts to three hundred dollars; also, in cases of forcible entry and detainer, and in proceedings in insolvency, and in actions to prevent or abate a nuisance, and in all such probate matters as may be provided by law; also, in all criminal cases prosecuted by indictment or information in a court of record on questions of law alone. The court shall also have power to issue writs of mandamus, certiorari, prohibition and habeas corpus, and all other writs necessary or proper to the complete exercise of its appellate jurisdiction. Each of the justices shall have power to issue writs of habeas corpus to any part of the state, upon petition by or on behalf of any person held in actual custody, and may make such writs returnable before himself or the supreme court, or before any superior court in the state or before any judge thereof.

JURISDICTION—In general.—The jurisdiction of the courts as established by the Constitution cannot be altered by the legislature. (Thompson v. Williams, 6 Cal. 88; Hicks v. Bell, 3 Cal. 219; Burgoyne v. Board of Supervisors, 5 Cal. 9; Parsons v. Tuolumne Co. Water Co., 5 Cal. 43, 63 Am. Dec. 76; People v. Applegate, 5 Cal. 295; Fitzgerald v. Urton, 4 Cal. 235; Wilson v. Roach, 4 Cal. 362; Zander v. Coe, 5 Cal. 230; Haight v. Gay, 8 Cal. 297, 68 Am. Dec. 323; People v. Peralta, 3 Cal. 379; Caulfield v. Hudson, 3 Cal. 389. But see Seale v. Mitchell, 5 Cal. 401; People v. Day, 15 Cal. 91.)

An affirmative grant of jurisdiction is negative of all others. (Burgoyne v. Board of Supervisors, 5 Cal. 9.)

But the grant of original jurisdiction to a particular court, of a particular class of cases, without any words excluding other courts from exercising jurisdiction in the same cases, does not deprive other courts of concurrent jurisdiction in such cases, when such courts are given jurisdiction in general terms broad enough to include such particular cases. (Courtwright v. Bear River etc. Min. Co., 30 Cal. 573; Zander v. Coe, 5 Cal. 230, distinguished.)

Where jurisdiction is given in all cases not otherwise provided for it is not exclusive. (People v. Fowler, 9 Cal. 85.)

Consent will not confer jurisdiction. (Feillett v. Engler, 8 Cal. 76.)

Supreme court.—The supreme court acquired its jurisdiction from the Constitution, and such jurisdiction can neither be enlarged nor abridged by the legislature. (In re Jessup, 81 Cal. 408, 6 L. R. A. 594, 21 Pac. 976, 22 Pac. 742, 1028; Ex parte Attorney General, 1 Cal. 85.)

The Constitution has not clothed the supreme court with the same powers and jurisdiction as the court of king's bench in England. (Ex parte Attorney General, 1 Cal. 85.)

District courts of appeal.—Under the plenary grant of power by this section and section 53 of the Code of Civil Procedure, the district courts of appeal have full authority to either affirm or reverse or modify the judgment or order of the trial court in any case before it. (Machado v. Machado, 26 Cal. App. 16, 145 Pac. 738.)

Procedure.—The right of appeal is conferred by the Constitution, and statutes and rules of procedure for its exercise are to be liberally construed; and no appeal will be dismissed on technical grounds, when there has been no violation or disregard of any express rules of procedure. (Estate of Nelson, 128 Cal. 242, 60 Pac. 772.)

The supreme court acquires jurisdiction upon the filing of the notice of appeal in the lower court, and the jurisdiction is not divested or suspended either on account of the failure to file a transcript on appeal, or by loss thereof. (Estate of Davis, 151 Cal. 318, 121 Am. St. Rep. 105, 86 Pac. 183, 90 Pac. 711.)

When jurisdiction is given to the supreme court of a particular case, it has jurisdiction of all appeals therein, whether or not they involve the merits. (Rickey Land etc. Co. v. Glader, 6 Cal. App. 113, 91 Pac. 414.)

The legislature cannot impair or take away the appellate jurisdiction of the supreme court, but it may prescribe the mode in which appeals may be taken. (Haight v. Gay, 8 Cal. 297, 68 Am. Dec. 323.)

It is the duty of the supreme court, whose jurisdiction is defined by the Constitution, to secure uniformity in the administration of justice, and the legislature, as a co-ordinate branch of the government, cannot interfere with that function, or control the use by the appellate court of the power and discretion vested in it. (San Jose Ranch Co. v. San Jose etc. Water Co., 126 Cal. 322, 58 Pac. 824.)

The supreme court cannot exercise appellate jurisdiction by means of a writ of prohibition, without any appeal, and in a case to which its appellate jurisdiction does not extend. (Powelson v. Lockwood, 82 Cal. 613, 23 Pac. 143.)

When the Constitution gives the supreme court jurisdiction, and the legislature fails to prescribe the means for taking the appeal, the supreme court has inherent power to establish any appropriate system of procedure. (People v. Jordan, 65 Cal. 644, 4 Pac. 683. But see Warner v. Hall, 1 Cal. 90; Warner v. Kelly, 1 Cal. 91; White v. Lighthall, 1 Cal. 347.)

If the legislature has not provided a mode of exercising the jurisdiction conferred by the Constitution, a case may be brought up from an inferior court to the supreme court by writ of error. (Ex parte Thistleton, 52 Cal. 220; Adams v. Town, 3 Cal. 247.)

The legislature may prescribe the procedure by which the jurisdiction conferred is to be exercised, provided the regulations adopted do

not substantially impair the constitutional power of the court, or practically defeat its exercise. (Ex parte Harker, 49 Cal. 465.)

Rules.—The supreme court has power to make rules having the force of positive law so far as the rights of the parties are concerned, if they do not conflict with any act of the legislature. (Brooks v. Union Trust etc. Co., 146 Cal. 134, 79 Pac. 843.)

Rule XXX of the supreme court, requiring a petition for rehearing to be served upon the adverse party within twenty days after judgment and allowing an answer thereto, is valid. (Brooks v. Union Trust etc. Co., 146 Cal. 134, 79 Pac. 843.)

Rules adopted by the supreme court for the government of appellate practice are as much part of our system of procedure as the rules promulgated by the legislature; and the consequence of a failure to observe them rests upon the lawyer and not the court. (Reclamation Dist. No. 70 v. Sherman, 11 Cal. App. 399, 105 Pac. 277.)

Rules of court. See notes, 41 Am. St. Rep. 639; 7 R. C. L., §§ 50-56, pp. 1023-1029.

Salaries.—The act fixing the salaries of justices of the supreme court at eight thousand dollars cannot affect the salaries of present incumbents of that court, and cannot be looked to as a measure of the salaries of justices of district courts of appeal. (Harrison v. Colgan, 148 Cal. 69, 82 Pac. 674.)

Removal before judgment.—The power to remove causes from the district court of appeal is entirely discretionary, and the parties have no right to insist upon the exercise of that power. (People v. Davis, 147 Cal. 346, 81 Pac. 718.)

A cause will not be transferred to the district court of appeal to accommodate the parties or to facilitate a decision. (Gates v. Green, 148 Cal. 728, 84 Pac. 37.)

Where a writ of prohibition is applied for from the supreme court to prevent the trial of a case of which the district court of appeal has jurisdiction, the proceeding will be transferred to that court. (Collins v. Superior Court, 147 Cal. 264, 81 Pac. 509.)

Where the appeal is erroneously taken to the district court of appeal, instead of to the supreme court, the proper practice is to file the record in the court to which the appeal was taken and to move in that court to transfer the cause to the supreme court. (In re Russell, 148 Cal. 768, 84 Pac. 155.)

Removal after judgment.—The supreme court will not exercise its power to remove a cause pending in a district court of appeal after decision for the purpose of revising its decision upon questions of fact. (People v. Davis, 147 Cal. 346, 81 Pac. 718.)

The supreme court will only remove a case pending in a district court of appeal after decision when it is necessary to secure uniformity of decision or to settle important questions of law. (People v. Davis, 147 Cal. 346, 81 Pac. 718.)

Where one of the justices signing an order transferring a cause to the supreme court, after a decision by the court of appeals, signed the order while in the state, but left the state before it received the signatures of the requisite number of judges to make it effective, such order is a nullity. (People v. Ruef, 14 Cal. App. 576, 114 Pac. 48, 54.)

Where the district court of appeal has issued an alternative writ of mandate which acts as a stay, the effect thereof is not affected by a judgment of the court denying the peremptory writ which has not become final by the expiration of thirty days. (Noel v. Smith, 2 Cal. App. 158, 83 Pac. 167.)

The supreme court has power, within thirty days after the decision of the district court of appeal has become final, to order the cause heard and determined by itself. (Noel v. Smith, 2 Cal. App. 158, 83 Pac. 167.)

The judgment of a district court of appeal is not final until the expiration of thirty days after the judgment is pronounced. (Noel v. Smith, 2 Cal. App. 158, 83 Pac. 167.)

An order of the district court of appeal denying a rehearing, but modifying the opinion theretofore rendered, is not a judgment, and the time within which the supreme court might order a transfer of the case runs from the original judgment. (National Bank v. Los Angeles Iron etc. Co., 2 Cal. App. 659, 84 Pac. 466, 468.)

The supreme court has no authority to order a transfer of a cause from the district court of appeal after the lapse of sixty days from the giving of the judgment of the district court. (National Bank v. Los Angeles Iron etc. Co., 2 Cal. App. 659, 84 Pac. 466, 468; People v. Ruef, 14 Cal. App. 576, 114 Pac. 48, 54.)

In cases going in the first instance to the court of appeal, a rehearing will be granted by the supreme court only when error appears upon the face of the opinion of the appellate court, or when a doubtful and important question is presented upon which further argument is desired by the court. (Burke v. Maze, 10 Cal. App. 206, 101 Pac. 438, 440.)

In causes referred to the court of appeal by the supreme court, the supreme court, in passing upon an application for rehearing, will look into the record to see whether anything deserving consideration has been overlooked in deciding the cause, or any of the facts misconceived in material particulars. (Burke v. Maze, 10 Cal. App. 206, 101 Pac. 438, 440.)

A justice may join in an order granting a rehearing apart from any consultation and from the presence of his associates. (People v. Ruef, 14 Cal. App. 576, 114 Pac. 48, 54.)

The court may exercise the power to grant a rehearing without any petition or application therefor. (People v. Ruef, 14 Cal. App. 576, 114 Pac. 48, 54.)

The supreme court has no power to transfer cases in habeas corpus. (Matter of Zany, 164 Cal. 724, 130 Pac. 710.)

Admission of attorneys.—The supreme court now has no authority to admit attorneys to practice, that power having been conferred by the legislature upon the district courts of appeal. (In re Mock, 146 Cal. 378, 80 Pac. 64.)

Cases at law.—The meaning of this section is that the supreme court shall have appellate jurisdiction in all cases at law; provided, that when the subject of litigation is capable of pecuniary compensation, the matter in dispute must exceed in value or amount the sum of three hundred dollars, unless a question of the legality of a tax,

etc., is drawn in question. (Conant v. Conant, 10 Cal. 249, 70 Am. Dec. 717.)

Therefore, the supreme court has jurisdiction of a case where the matter in dispute is incapable of pecuniary estimation. (Conant v. Conant, 10 Cal. 249, 70 Am. Dec. 717.)

The words "matter in dispute" mean the subject of litigation—the matter for which suit is brought—and do not include costs. (Dumphy v. Guindon, 13 Cal. 28; Maxfield v. Johnson, 30 Cal. 545; Zabriskie v. Torrey, 20 Cal. 173; Votan v. Reese, 20 Cal. 89; Bolton v. Landers, 27 Cal. 106; Henigan v. Ervin, 110 Cal. 37, 42 Pac. 457. Contra, Gordon v. Ross, 2 Cal. 156, overruled.)

But where the supreme court obtains jurisdiction of the appeal, it can correct the costs in the judgment. (Votan v. Reese, 20 Cal. 89.)

Neither is percentage allowed by statute any part of the matter in dispute. (Zabriskie v. Torrey, 20 Cal. 173.)

Under the former Constitution, before the amendments of 1862, it was held that the interest due forms part of the matter in dispute. (Skillman v. Lachman, 23 Cal. 198, 83 Am. Dec. 96; Malson v. Vaughn, 23 Cal. 61.)

But under the amendment of 1862 and under the present Constitution the demand must exceed three hundred dollars "exclusive of interest." (Dashiell v. Slingerland, 60 Cal. 653.)

In cases at law, when the demand in controversy, exclusive of interest, is less than three hundred dollars, the supreme court has no jurisdiction. (Sweet v. Tice, 45 Cal. 71; Votan v. Reese, 20 Cal. 89; Maxfield v. Johnson, 30 Cal. 545; Hopkins v. Cheeseman, 28 Cal. 180; Dungan v. Clark, 159 Cal. 30, 112 Pac. 718.)

The words "cases at law . . . which involve . . . the legality of any tax," etc., refer to civil, as distinguished from criminal, cases. (People v. Johnson, 30 Cal. 98.)

The record must affirmatively show that the case involves the constitutional amount, or the supreme court will not entertain jurisdiction. (Doyle v. Seawall, 12 Cal. 280.)

If the appeal is by the plaintiff and the verdict for the defendant, it is sufficient if the amount claimed by the complaint exceeds the jurisdictional amount. (Votan v. Reese, 20 Cal. 89; Skillman v. Lachman, 23 Cal. 198, 83 Am. Dec. 96.)

The ad damnum clause of the complaint is the test of jurisdiction of both the superior and supreme courts, and if the lower court had jurisdiction, the supreme court also has jurisdiction, whatever the amount recovered, and whether the appeal be taken by the plaintiff or the defendant. (Solomon v. Reese, 34 Cal. 28, overruling Votan v. Reese, 20 Cal. 89; Dashiell v. Slingerland, 60 Cal. 653; Lord v. Goldberg, 81 Cal. 596, 15 Am. St. Rep. 82, 22 Pac. 1126; Henigan v. Ervin, 110 Cal. 37, 42 Pac. 457.)

Where the plaintiff, having a judgment of more than the jurisdictional amount, sought to have a judgment against him for less than two hundred dollars set off against it, the supreme court has no jurisdiction of an appeal from an order denying the motion. (Crandall v. Blen, 15 Cal. 406.)

The fact that an offset is pleaded by the defendant which, together with the demand of the plaintiff, swells the amount to more than the

jurisdictional amount, does not give the court jurisdiction. (Simmons v. Brainard, 14 Cal. 278.)

Amount in controversy for purpose of appeal where defendant has filed counterclaim. See note, Ann. Cas. 1914A, 1041.

The appellate jurisdiction of the supreme court extends to an appeal from a judgment of a superior court dismissing a writ of certiorari, and affirming a judgment of a justice's court, which amounts to less than three hundred dollars. (Heinlen v. Phillips, 88 Cal. 557, 26 Pac. 366. Bienenfeld v. Fresno etc. Co., 82 Cal. 425, 22 Pac. 1113, overruled.)

. The supreme court has no jurisdiction of an appeal from the superior court in an action commenced in the justice's court under section 1206 of the Civil Code, whether the action be viewed as a suit in equity to enforce a lien upon personal property, or an action at law for wages due. (Edsall v. Short, 122 Cal. 533, 55 Pac. 327.)

The fact that the defendant in an action in a justice's court sets up a counterclaim in excess of three hundred dollars does not give the supreme court jurisdiction on appeal. (Maxfield v. Johnson, 30 Cal. 545.)

A proceeding in the nature of a quo warranto to try the title to a public office, where the court can impose a fine of five thousand dollars, is a case at law in which the demand amounts to three hundred dollars. (People v. Perry, 79 Cal. 105, 21 Pac. 423; People v. Bingham, 82 Cal. 238, 22 Pac. 1039.)

A writ of error will not lie to reverse the judgment of the superior court granting a nonsuit on appeal from a judgment of a justice's court. (Pool v. Superior Court, 2 Cal. App. 533, 84 Pac. 53.)

No appeal lies to the district court of appeal from any order or judgment of the superior court upon appeal from a justice's court. (Pool v. Superior Court, 2 Cal. App. 533, 84 Pac. 53.)

An appeal will not lie to the court of appeals from an order of the superior court dismissing an appeal from a judgment of a justice's court in an action at law involving less than three hundred dollars. (Willow Land Co. v. Goldschmidt, 11 Cal. App. 297, 104 Pac. 841.)

An action for damages exceeding two thousand dollars is within the jurisdiction of the supreme court. (Randall v. Freed, 7 Cal. App. 553, 94 Pac. 1056; Wright v. Sonoma Co., 7 Cal. App. 567, 96 Pac. 333; McAulay v. Tahoe Ice Co., 3 Cal. App. 642, 86 Pac. 912.)

Jurisdiction dependent on value, how to be determined. See note, 21 Am. St. Rep. 617.

The district court of appeals has appellate jurisdiction in cases at law where jurisdiction depends on the amount in controversy, only where the demand exclusive of interest, or the value of the property in controversy amounts to three hundred dollars, and does not amount to two thousand dollars. (Erving v. Napa Valley Brewing Co., 17 Cal. App. 367, 119 Pac. 940; Beswick v. Churchill Co., 21 Cal. App. 721, 132 Pac. 771.)

The original jurisdiction of the superior court and the appellate jurisdiction of the district courts of appeal are identical in "all cases at law, in which the demand, exclusive of interest, or the value of

the property in controversy, amounts to three hundred dollars." (J. Dewing Co. v. Thompson, 19 Cal. App. 85, 124 Pac. 1035.)

SUITS IN EQUITY.—An action to enforce a trust is a suit in equity. (Marston v. Kuhland, 2 Cal. App. 316, 84 Pac. 357.)

A suit to avoid a decree of foreclosure taken by default is within the equitable jurisdiction of the supreme court. (Litch v. O'Connor, 8 Cal. App. 489, 97 Pac. 207.)

An action for maintenance is a suit in equity. (Hiner v. Hiner, 5 Cal. App. 546, 90 Pac. 957.)

A suit to restrain a trespass is in equity and within the jurisdiction of the supreme court. (Barnes v. Daveck, 7 Cal. App. 220, 94 Pac. 779.)

Appellate jurisdiction of all cases in equity is given to the supreme court. (Rickey Land etc. Co. v. Glader, 6 Cal. App. 113, 91 Pac. 414.)

An action to enjoin the diversion of water is a suit in equity. (Rickey Land etc. Co. v. Glader, 6 Cal. App. 113, 91 Pac. 414.)

A suit to quiet title is equitable and within the jurisdiction of the supreme court. (Davey v. Mulroy, 7 Cal. App. 1, 93 Pac. 297.)

Under the general equity powers the superior court has power to remedy any wrong committed by election boards. (Cerini v. De Long, 7 Cal. App. 398, 94 Pac. 582.)

An action to foreclose a mechanic's lien is a case in equity, although the liens, by order of the court, are to be paid out of a fund deposited in court by the owner of the property. (Stockton L. Co. v. Schuler, 7 Cal. App. 257, 94 Pac. 399.)

A suit to foreclose a mortgage is within the equitable jurisdiction of the supreme court. (Aetna Indemnity Co. v. Altadena Mining etc. Co., 11 Cal. App. 26, 104 Pac. 470.)

Judgments in contempt cases are nonappealable. (Gale v. Tuolumne County Water Co., 169 Cal. 46, 145 Pac. 532.)

Real property.—Where a case is certified to the superior court from the justice's court on the ground that it involves the title or possession of real property, the supreme court has jurisdiction on appeal, although no question is raised on that subject on the appeal. (Baker v. Southern Cal. Ry. Co., 110 Cal. 455, 42 Pac. 975.)

A mere statement by counsel that a case involves the title or possession of real property is not sufficient to give the supreme court jurisdiction. (Raisch v. Sausalito Land etc. Co., 131 Cal. 215, 63 Pac. 346.)

The supreme court has jurisdiction of an action for the usurpation of a franchise for a toll road, since the right to the possession of real property is involved. (People v. Horsley, 65 Cal. 381, 4 Pac. 384.)

The supreme court has jurisdiction in actions for damages to real property, when the title thereto is involved, although the damages claimed are less than three hundred dollars. (Doherty v. Thayer, 31 Cal. 140.)

The district courts of appeal have appellate jurisdiction in all cases specifically mentioned as belonging to its jurisdiction, although they may incidentally involve the title to or possession of real estate, or the legality of a tax. (Keech v. Joplin, 157 Cal. 1, 106 Pac. 222.)

"Possession" under this section means such a possession of real property as has relation to title or is necessary to the enforcement or defeat of the cause of action asserted. (O'Meara v. Hables, 163 Cal. 240, 124 Pac. 1003.)

The supreme court has appellate jurisdiction on appeal from the superior courts in all cases at law which involve the title or possession of real estate, and the district court of appeals has no jurisdiction whatsoever of such a case. (Thomas v. Thomas, 22 Cal. App. 806, 136 Pac. 510.)

Fines.—A fine imposed by a county court for wrongfully demanding and collecting toll is not a municipal fine. (People v. Johnson, 30 Cal. 98.)

On the trial of a criminal action for wrongfully collecting toll, the legality of the fine to be imposed in case of a conviction is not involved. (People v. Johnson, 30 Cal. 98.)

The word assessment as used in the clause of this section conferring appellate jurisdiction on the supreme court of all cases involving "the legality of any . . . assessment," refers to assessments relating to public taxation or to raise funds for local public improvements. (Bottle Mining and Milling Co. v. Kern, 154 Cal. 96, 97 Pac. 25.)

Special cases.—The supreme court has jurisdiction of an appeal from an order discharging an insolvent. (Fisk v. His Creditors, 12 Cal. 281.)

An arbitration is a special proceeding. (Fairchild v. Doten, 42 Cal. 125.)

A proceeding to condemn land for the use of a railroad company is a "special case." (Stockton etc. Co. v. Galgiani, 49 Cal. 139.)

A contest of the right to purchase state lands is a special proceeding within the jurisdiction of the supreme court. (Risdon v. Prewett, 8 Cal. App. 434, 97 Pac. 73.)

Neither the supreme court nor the district courts of appeal have jurisdiction of an appeal from a judgment in a proceeding under section 772 of the Penal Code, for the removal of public officers. (People v. McKamy, 168 Cal. 531, 143 Pac. 752.)

Special orders.—The supreme court has appellate jurisdiction of all special orders made after final judgment in the superior court, without reference to the amount involved. (Southern Cal. Ry. Co. v. Superior Court, 127 Cal. 417, 59 Pac. 789; Harron v. Harron, 123 Cal. 508, 56 Pac. 334. Langan v. Langan, 83 Cal. 618, 23 Pac. 1084, and Fairbanks v. Lampkin, 99 Cal. 429, 34 Pac. 101, overruled.)

In all cases, legal or equitable, when the supreme court has appellate jurisdiction of the matter brought in controversy in the lower court, the appealability of an order made before or after final judgment is not controlled by the amount involved in such order. (Sierra Union etc. Min. Co. v. Wolff, 144 Cal. 430, 77 Pac. 1038.)

A special order after judgment, refusing to strike out a cost bill in the superior court in a case appealed from the justice's court, is not appealable to the supreme court, although the cost bill amounts to over three hundred dollars. (Henigan v. Ervin, 110 Cal. 37, 42 Pac. 457.)

An order for twenty-five dollars each month alimony, being a continuing order, may be reviewed upon appeal. (Langan v. Langan, 86 Cal. 132, 24 Pac. 852. See Harron v. Harron, 123 Cal. 508, 56 Pac. 334.)

Criminal cases.—The supreme court has jurisdiction in criminal cases upon questions of law alone. (People v. Logan, 123 Cal. 414, 56 Pac. 56; People v. Kuches, 120 Cal. 566, 52 Pac. 1002; People v. Smallman, 55 Cal. 185; People v. Williams, 133 Cal. 165, 65 Pac. 323.)

The propriety of a conviction on the evidence becomes a question of law only when there is a clear failure of proof. (People v. Kuches, 120 Cal. 566, 52 Pac. 1002; People v. Smallman, 55 Cal. 185.)

The supreme court has appellate jurisdiction of all misdemeanors prosecuted by indictment or information. (People v. Jordan, 65 Cal. 644, 4 Pac. 683, prescribing a method for taking such appeals.)

Under the former Constitution, the supreme court had no jurisdiction in criminal cases, except such as amount to felony. (People v. Apgar, 35 Cal. 389; People v. Johnson, 30 Cal. 98; People v. Shear, 7 Cal. 139; People v. Vick, 7 Cal. 165; People v. Applegate, 5 Cal. 295.)

The supreme court has jurisdiction of an appeal from a judgment sustaining a demurrer to an indictment for misconduct in office. (People v. Kalloch, 60 Cal. 113.)

The supreme court has jurisdiction of an appeal in a criminal case, although the lower court had no jurisdiction. (People v. Pingree, 61 Cal. 141.)

The supreme court has no jurisdiction of an appeal from a judgment of a superior court, affirming a judgment of the police court, adjudging a defendant guilty of a misdemeanor, and imposing a fine of fifty dollars, it not being "a criminal case prosecuted by indictment or information in a court of record." (People v. Meiggs' Wharf Co., 65 Cal. 99, 3 Pac. 491.)

Under the former Constitution the jurisdiction of the supreme court in criminal cases on defendant's appeal was not to be determined by the offense charged, but by the offense of which the defendant was convicted. (People v. Apgar, 35 Cal. 389.)

The "information" referred to is that named in section 8, article I, of the Constitution. (Larue v. Davies, 8 Cal. App. 750, 97 Pac. 903.)

A proceeding to remove an officer summarily for misdemeanor in office by accusation, not being presented by indictment or information, is not within the appellate jurisdiction of the supreme court or the court of appeals. (Larue v. Davies, 8 Cal. App. 750, 97 Pac. 903, arguendo.)

When there is ample evidence to support the verdict in a criminal case, the appellate court has no jurisdiction to disturb it. (People v. Meyers, 5 Cal. App. 674, 91 Pac. 167.)

The propriety of a conviction becomes a question of law only when there is a clear failure of proof. (People v. Caulfield, 7 Cal. App. 656, 95 Pac. 666.)

The supreme court has no jurisdiction of an appeal from a judgment of the superior court affirming a judgment of the police court imposing a fine for the violation of a city ordinance. (People v. Pacific Gas & Electric Co., 168 Cal. 496, 143 Pac. 727.)

The appellate courts cannot review questions of fact in criminal cases unless they have developed a character which converts them into questions of law. (People v. Lichtenstein, 22 Cal. App. 592, 135 Pac. 692.)

From this provision it follows that, unless the evidence upon which a verdict in a criminal case has been planted is, upon its face, incredible, or is inherently improbable, and it is in all other respects sufficient to support the verdict, a reversal of the judgment or an order refusing a new trial upon the ground that the evidence does not support the verdict is not allowable. (People v. Bonzani, 24 Cal. App. 549, 141 Pac. 1062.)

The district court of appeals has jurisdiction of an appeal by the people from an order made before judgment setting aside an information charging the crime of murder. (People v. White, 161 Cal. 310, 119 Pac. 79.)

Probate.—The supreme court has jurisdiction of only such appeals in probate matters as are provided by law. (Estate of Walkerly, 94 Cal. 352, 29 Pac. 719; Estate of Ohm, 82 Cal. 160, 22 Pac. 927; Estate of Moore, 86 Cal. 58, 24 Pac. 816; Estate of Winslow, 128 Cal. 311, 60 Pac. 931; Estate of Wittmeier, 118 Cal. 255, 50 Pac. 393; Estate of Cahill, 142 Cal. 628, 76 Pac. 383.)

An order compelling an administratrix to allow her name to be used by a creditor of the estate is a probate matter within the meaning of this section, and, not being one in which an appeal is provided by law, no appeal lies. (Estate of Ohm, 82 Cal. 160, 22 Pac. 927.)

Divorce.—An action for divorce is a case in equity within the meaning of this section. (Sharon v. Sharon, 67 Cal. 185, 7 Pac. 456, 635, 8 Pac. 709; Cassidy v. Sullivan, 64 Cal. 266, 28 Pac. 234; Stewart v. Torrance, 9 Cal. App. 209, 98 Pac. 396.)

The supreme court has jurisdiction of an appeal in an action for divorce. (Conant v. Conant, 10 Cal. 249, 70 Am. Dec. 717.)

Liens.—Under the former Constitution, prior to the amendments of 1862, the supreme court had no jurisdiction of an action to foreclose a mortgage or mechanic's lien when the amount involved did not exceed two hundred dollars. (Poland v. Carrigan, 20 Cal. 174.) Otherwise, since those amendments. (Willis v. Farley, 24 Cal. 490, 499.)

An action to foreclose a mechanic's lien or to reach the fund in the hands of the owner, being an equitable action, is within the appellate jurisdiction of the supreme court. (Weldon v. Superior Court, 138 Cal. 427, 71 Pac. 502.)

Writs.—The language of the present Constitution giving the supreme court power to "issue writs of mandamus, certiorari, prohibition, and habeas corpus, and all other writs necessary or proper to the complete exercise of the appellate jurisdiction," has the same meaning as the language in the former Constitution giving it power to "issue writs of mandamus, certiorari, prohibition, habeas corpus, and also all writs necessary or proper to the complete exercise of its appellate jurisdiction." Thus construed, the section gives the court original jurisdiction to issue the writs specially named. (Hyatt v. Allen, 54 Cal. 353.)

The writ of prohibition mentioned in this section is the writ of prohibition as known to the common law, and its office is to restrain subordinate courts and inferior judicial tribunals from exceeding their jurisdiction. (Maurer v. Mitchell, 53 Cal. 289.)

Courts which may issue prohibition. See note, 111 Am. St. Rep. 932.

The legislature cannot enlarge or extend the office of the writs mentioned in this section. (Camron v. Kenfield, 57 Cal. 550; Farmers' Union v. Thresher, 62 Cal. 407; Hobart v. Tillson, 66 Cal. 210, 5 Pac. 83.)

In issuing writs of mandamus or other prerogative writs, the su- preme court and the several superior courts are peers—each having original jurisdiction; and a determination thereon by a superior court is conclusive upon the supreme court, except on appeal. (Santa Cruz etc. Stock Co. v. Board of Suprs. of Santa Clara Co., 62 Cal. 40.)

The supreme court will not entertain an application for a writ of mandamus, or other prerogative writ, where the petition shows no sufficient reason why the application was not made to the superior court. (Menzies v. Board of Equalization, 62 Cal. 179.)

The supreme court has appellate jurisdiction in cases of mandamus. (Palache v. Hunt, 64 Cal. 473, 2 Pac. 245.)

The supreme court has appellate jurisdiction in a proceeding in the nature of a quo warranto. (People v. Perry, 79 Cal. 105, 21 Pac. 423.)

The supreme court may exercise its appellate jurisdiction by means of the writs mentioned in this section. (People v. Turner, 1 Cal. 143, 52 Am. Dec. 295.)

Mandamus is the proper remedy to compel the district court to restore an attorney whose name has been stricken from the rolls by the order of such court. (People v. Turner, 1 Cal. 143, 52 Am. Dec. 295.)

Prior to the amendment of 1862, the supreme court could issue writs of certiorari, etc., only in aid of its appellate jurisdiction. (Miliken v. Huber, 21 Cal. 166; Ex parte Attorney General, 1 Cal. 85.)

Under the amendment of 1862, the supreme court had jurisdiction to issue writs of mandamus, etc., without reference to its appellate jurisdiction. (Tyler v. Houghton, 25 Cal. 26; Miller v. Board of Su- pervisors, 25 Cal. 93.)

The district courts had jurisdiction to issue writs of mandate re- gardless of the amount involved. (Cariaga v. Dryden, 30 Cal. 244.)

The jurisdiction of the supreme court in cases of certiorari does not depend upon the amount in controversy. (Winter v. Fitzpatrick, 35 Cal. 269.)

The writ of certiorari can be rightfully issued only upon an order of the court, made upon application for that purpose, and not upon an order of the justices of the court as such, or any of them. (Smith v. Oakland, 40 Cal. 481.)

A mandamus proceeding involving the validity of the organization of a protection district and a tax thereof is within the jurisdiction of the supreme court. (Keech v. Joplin, 9 Cal. App. 217, 101 Pac. 417.)

When mandamus is sought in aid of the exercise of appellate juris- diction, as to compel the settlement of a bill of exceptions, the appli-

cation must be addressed to the court having appellate jurisdiction of the cause. (Stewart v. Torrance, 9 Cal. App. 209, 98 Pac. 396.)

The Constitution does not confine the jurisdiction of district courts to issue writs of mandamus within their respective districts, but, as a matter of comity, such writs should be invariably applied for to the court of the district in·which the cause for the writ arises, unless there are shown special circumstances which justify the issuance of the writ by the court of another district. (Older v. Superior Court, 10 Cal. App. 564, 102 Pac. 829.)

It is a sufficient ground for presenting a petition for writ of mandate to the district court of a district outside of which the cause for the writ arose that it would be impracticable to present it to the other court on account of loss of time. (Older v. Superior Court, 10 Cal. App. 564, 102 Pac. 829.)

Power of district court of appeals to issue writs in cases appealable to district court of appeals of another district discussed but not decided. (Older v. Superior Court, 157 Cal. 770, 109 Pac. 478.)

After judgment on appeal in a habeas corpus case there can be no rehearing of the case. (Matter of Application of Shoemaker, 25 Cal. App. 551, 144 Pac. 985.)

Sections 22 and 23 of article XII, as amended in 1911, enlarged the scope of the writ of certiorari, in proceedings before the supreme court to review orders and decisions of the railroad commission, beyond all former constitutional or statutory definitions, so that it now includes a determination of whether an order or decision of the commission violates any right of a party under the state or federal Constitution. (Pacific Tel. etc. Co. v. Eshleman, 166 Cal. 640, Ann. Cas. 1915C, 822, 50 L. R. A. (N. S.) 652, 137 Pac. 1119.)

Where, on a proceeding in certiorari in the superior court to obtain a review and an annulment of a judgment and orders subsequent thereto in a justice's court, an adverse judgment or order of dismissal is entered, an appeal may be taken to the district court of appeal. (Cohen v. Melrose, 167 Cal. 792, 141 Pac. 374.)

A stay of execution is not "necessary or proper to the complete exercise of its appellate jurisdiction" when such stay can be granted only at the risk of destroying rights which will unquestionably belong to the respondent if the judgment of the lower court shall be affirmed. (Hulbert v. California etc. Cement Co., 161 Cal. 239, 38 L. R. A. (N. S.) 436, 118 Pac. 928, concurring opinion by Sloss, J.)

Original jurisdiction of state court of last resort to issue writ of habeas corpus, see note, Ann. Cas. 1913A, 156.

Miscellaneous.—The supreme court has no jurisdiction of an appeal from a judgment in a proceeding under section 772 of the Penal Code, for the removal of public officers. (In re Curtis, 108 Cal. 661, 41 Pac. 793; Wheeler v. Donnell, 110 Cal. 655, 43 Pac. 1.)

The supreme court has appellate jurisdiction of an appeal in a civil proceeding to remove an officer. (Morton v. Broderick, 118 Cal. 474, 50 Pac. 644.)

The supreme court has no original jurisdiction to try the title to an office. (People v. Harvey, 62 Cal. 508.)

The supreme court has appellate jurisdiction of an election contest. (Lord v. Dunster, 79 Cal. 477, 21 Pac. 865.)

The supreme court has no jurisdiction to naturalize aliens. (Ex parte Knowles, 5 Cal. 300.)

The supreme court has no jurisdiction of an appeal from a judgment of the district court upon appeal from the court of sessions. (Webb v. Hanson, 3 Cal. 65.)

FAILURE TO AGREE.—When the judges of the district court of appeal fail to agree upon an application for a writ of mandate it is deemed denied. (Ex parte Sauer, 3 Cal. App. 237, 84 Pac. 995.)

The individual views expressed by one of the justices of a district court of appeal in an opinion rendered upon a reversal of a judgment in which the other justices fail to concur do not become the law of the case on a subsequent trial, or on a second appeal. (Matter of Coburn, 165 Cal. 202, 131 Pac. 352.)

PRESIDING JUSTICE.—The functions conferred on the chief justice by section 1174 of the Penal Code are to be performed by the presiding justices of the district courts of appeal, in cases in which appeals must be taken to such courts. (People v. Lapique, 154 Cal. 518, 98 Pac. 257.)

REMITTITUR.—The remittitur is the judgment of the appellate tribunal which is authenticated to the court from which the appeal is taken or over which its controlling influence is exercised, and applies to all judgments, whether rendered in the exercise of appellate or original jurisdiction. (Noel v. Smith, 2 Cal. App. 158, 83 Pac. 167.)

Under rule 34 of the supreme court a judgment of the district court of appeal does not become conclusive until the remittitur is issued thereon. (Noel v. Smith, 2 Cal. App. 158, 83 Pac. 167.)

APPEAL TO WRONG COURT.—Where an appeal is erroneously taken to the court of appeal instead of the supreme court, the case will be transferred to the latter court. (Marston v. Kuhland, 2 Cal. App. 316, 84 Pac. 357; Hiner v. Hiner, 5 Cal. App. 546, 90 Pac. 957; Rickey Land etc. Co. v. Glader, 6 Cal. App. 113, 91 Pac. 414; Barnes v. Daveck, 7 Cal. App. 220, 94 Pac. 779; Stockton L. Co. v. Schuler, 7 Cal. App. 257, 94 Pac. 399; Randall v. Freed, 7 Cal. App. 553, 94 Pac. 1056; Wright v. Sonoma, 7 Cal. App. 567, 96 Pac. 333; Aetna Indemnity Co. v. Altadena Mining etc. Co., 11 Cal. App. 26, 104 Pac. 470; Pacific Paving Co. v. Verso, 11 Cal. App. 383, 105 Pac. 136; Risdon v. Prewett, 8 Cal. App. 434, 97 Pac. 73; Litch v. O'Connor, 8 Cal. App. 489, 97 Pac. 207; Keech v. Joplin, 9 Cal. App. 217, 101 Pac. 417.)

When an appeal is taken to the supreme court, but the undertaking recites an appeal to the district court of appeal, it is ineffectual. (McAulay v. Tahoe Ice Co., 3 Cal. App. 642, 86 Pac. 912.)

When an appeal is properly taken to the supreme court, but the transcript and briefs are entitled in the district court of appeal, the latter court will not dismiss the appeal, but will order the record transmitted to the supreme court. (Davey v. Mulroy, 7 Cal. App. 1, 93 Pac. 297.)

An appeal bond erroneously reciting that the appeal was about to be taken to the supreme court instead of the court of appeal may be cured by a new bond. (Pacific Paving Co. v. Verso, 11 Cal. App. 383, 105 Pac. 136.)

Harmless errors to be disregarded.

Sec. 4½. No judgment shall be set aside, or new trial granted, in any case, on the ground of misdirection of the jury, or of the improper admission or rejection of evidence, or for any error as to any matter of pleading, or for any error as to any matter of procedure, unless, after an examination of the entire cause, including the evidence, the court shall be of the opinion that the error complained of has resulted in a miscarriage of justice. (Amendment adopted November 3, 1914.)

[ORIGINAL SECTION.]

Sec. 4½. No judgment shall be set aside, or new trial granted in any criminal case on the ground of misdirection of the jury or the improper admission or rejection of evidence, or for error as to any matter of pleading or procedure, unless, after an examination of the entire cause including the evidence, the court shall be of the opinion that the error complained of has resulted in a miscarriage of justice. (Amendment approved October 10, 1911.)

HARMLESS ERRORS.—This section abrogates the old rule that prejudice is presumed from any error of law, and that where error is shown it is the duty of the court to examine the evidence and ascertain whether the error did or did not in fact work any injury. This section does not repeal or abrogate the constitutional guaranties, accorded accused persons, but every invasion of even a constitutional right does not necessarily require a reversal. This section is applicable to offenses committed prior to its adoption and is not obnoxious to the provision of the federal Constitution against ex post facto laws. (People v. O'Bryan, 165 Cal. 55, 130 Pac. 1042.)

This section cannot sustain a conviction of a criminal offense, where there was no proof made of one of the essential elements of such offense. (People v. Frey, 165 Cal. 140, 131 Pac. 127.)

This section makes it the duty of any appellate court, in considering the questions of law presented on an appeal in a criminal case, to consider the entire cause including the evidence for the purpose of determining whether any error or erroneous procedure complained of has resulted in a miscarriage of justice, and if the court is of the opinion that such has been the effect, it must reverse the judgment. (People v. Fleming, 166 Cal. 357, Ann. Cas. 1915B, 881, 136 Pac. 291.)

"Miscarriage of justice" can only mean the conviction of a person who is probably innocent. (People v. Fleming, 166 Cal. 357, Ann. Cas. 1915B, 881, 136 Pac. 291, qualified concurrence by Beatty, C. J.)

Under this section substantial injury as well as error must be made affirmatively to appear for the setting aside of a judgment. (People v. Merritt, 18 Cal. App. 58, 122 Pac. 839.)

This section was not intended to change, nor did it change the rule that, in the exercise of their appellate jurisdiction, the appellate courts are restricted to the consideration of questions of law alone,

and a subject of review by those tribunals, except where there neces-. sarily arises from the evidence or is presented thereby, from its very nature, a question of law. (People v. Haydon, 18 Cal. App. 543, 123 Pac. 1102, 1114.)

This section is not confined to the review of cases in appellate courts, but was intended to apply as well to trial courts, in the review of records in criminal cases, on motions for new trial, and where the trial court sets aside a verdict or grants a new trial in contravention of this section, its action will be nullified upon appeal. (People v. Tomsky, 20 Cal. App. 672, 130 Pac. 184.)

Where the action of the trial court is up for review, the question whether the opinion of the trial court that the error complained of has or has not resulted in a "miscarriage of justice" presents a question of law to be determined from a review of the record. (People v. Tomsky, 20 Cal. App. 672, 130 Pac. 184.)

Reviewing courts are not permitted, even where matters prejudicial in their character appear in the record, to reverse such judgment, unless from the entire record it appears that there has been a miscarriage of justice. (People v. Kizer, 22 Cal. App. 10, 133 Pac. 516, 521.)

"Miscarriage of justice" is applicable to cases where the acquittal or conviction has resulted from some form of trial in which the essential rights of the people or of the defendant were disregarded or denied. (People v. Wilson, 23 Cal. App. 513, 138 Pac. 971.)

Since the adoption of this section, under which a defendant is without remedy, against errors of the trial court, on appeal, unless the appellate court can say upon the entire evidence that the errors resulted in a miscarriage of justice, a greater and larger responsibility rests upon the trial judge in seeing that a defendant is accorded every right to which he is entitled. (People v. Svendsen, 25 Cal. App. 1, 142 Pac. 861.)

Under this provision it is not sufficient to warrant a reversal to show that error was committed, but, after a review of the whole record, the error must be disregarded and the judgment affirmed unless the appellate court is of the opinion that the error resulted in a miscarriage of justice. (People v. Bartol, 24 Cal. App. 659, 142 Pac. 510.)

This provision was not designed to repeal or abrogate the guaranties accorded persons accused of crime by other parts of the Constitution or to overthrow all statutory rules of procedure and evidence in criminal cases. (People v. Ho Kim You, 24 Cal. App. 451, 141 Pac. 950.)

Where the appellate court is unable to determine whether a defendant would or would not have been convicted by the jury had erroneously admitted testimony been withdrawn from their consideration, this section cannot be applied to uphold a judgment. (People v. MacPhee, 26 Cal. App. 218, 146 Pac. 522.)

Under this section it is the duty of the appellate court to review conflicting evidence for the purpose of ascertaining whether or not an error "has resulted in a miscarriage of justice," and injury is no longer presumed from error but must be affirmatively shown. (Vallejo etc. R. R. Co. v. Reed Orchard Co., 169 Cal. 545, 147 Pac. 238.)

This section applies to pending appeals, although they may have been submitted prior to its adoption. (Vallejo etc. R. R. Co. v. Reed Orchard Co., 169 Cal. 545, 147 Pac. 238.)

Superior court, jurisdiction.

Sec. 5. The superior court shall have original jurisdiction in all cases in equity, and in all cases at law which involve the title or possession of real property, or the legality of any tax, impost, assessment, toll, or municipal fine, and in all other cases in which the demand, exclusive of interest or the value of the property in controversy amounts to three hundred dollars, and in all criminal cases amounting to felony, and cases of misdemeanor not otherwise provided for; of actions of forcible entry and detainer; of proceedings in insolvency; of actions to prevent or abate a nuisance; of all matters of probate; of divorce and for annulment of marriage; and of all such special cases and proceedings as are not otherwise provided for, and said courts shall have the power of naturalization, and to issue papers therefor. They shall have appellate jurisdiction in such cases arising in inferior courts in their respective counties as may be prescribed by law. They shall be always open (legal holidays and nonjudicial days excepted), and their process shall extend to all parts of the state; provided, that all actions for the recovery of the possession of, quieting the title to, or for the enforcement of liens upon real estate, shall be commenced in the county in which the real estate, or any part thereof, affected by such action or actions, is situated. Said courts, and their judges, shall have power to issue writs of mandamus, certiorari, prohibition, quo warranto, and habeas corpus, on petition by or on behalf of any person in actual custody, in their respective counties. Injunctions and writs of prohibition may be issued and served on legal holidays and nonjudicial days. (Amendment approved October 10, 1911.)

[ORIGINAL SECTION.]

Sec. 5. The superior court shall have original jurisdiction in all cases in equity, and in all cases at law which involve the title or possession of real property, or the legality of any tax, impost, assessment, toll, or municipal fine, and in all other cases in which the demand, exclusive of interest or the value of the property in

controversy, amounts to three hundred dollars, and in all criminal cases amounting to felony, and cases of misdemeanor not otherwise provided for; of actions of forcible entry and detainer; of proceedings in insolvency; of actions to prevent or abate a nuisance; of all matters of probate; of divorce and for annulment of marriage, and of all such special cases and proceedings as are not otherwise provided for. And said court shall have the power of naturalization, and to issue papers therefor. They shall have appellate jurisdiction in such cases arising in justices' and other inferior courts in their respective counties as may be prescribed by law. They shall be always open (legal holidays and nonjudicial days excepted), and their process shall extend to all parts of the state; provided, that all actions for the recovery of the possession of, quieting the title to, or for the enforcement of liens upon real estate, shall be commenced in the county in which the real estate, or any part thereof affected by such action or actions, is situated. Said courts, and their judges, shall have power to issue writs of mandamus, certiorari, prohibition, quo warranto, and habeas corpus, on petition by or on behalf of any person in actual custody in their respective counties. Injunctions and writs of prohibition may be issued and served on legal holidays and nonjudicial days.

JURISDICTION OF SUPERIOR COURT — In general. — The superior court is a court of general jurisdiction. (Bishop v. Superior Court, 87 Cal. 226, 25 Pac. 435; Campe v. Lassen, 67 Cal. 139, 7 Pac. 430.)

Its jurisdiction is conferred by the Constitution, and cannot be taken away by the legislature. (Tulare v. Hevren, 126 Cal. 226, 58 Pac. 530.)

The superior courts are state courts. (Pratt v. Browne, 135 Cal. 649, 67 Pac. 1082.)

There is only one superior court in each county. (Carter v. Lothian, 133 Cal. 451, 65 Pac. 962.)

This section was intended to be prospective only in its operation, and does not apply to actions pending when the Constitution went into effect. (Gurnee v. Superior Court, 58 Cal. 88; Watt v. Wright, 66 Cal. 202, 5 Pac. 91.)

This section does not prohibit the legislature from allowing judicial business to be transacted on a legal holiday or nonjudicial day. (People v. Soto, 65 Cal. 621, 4 Pac. 664.)

The fact that the Constitution gives the superior court jurisdiction in cases of equity does not prevent the legislature from regulating the practice of proceedings in such cases. (Wright v. Superior Court, 139 Cal. 469, 73 Pac. 145.)

A superior court is always in session. (County of San Luis Obispo v. Limas, 1 Cal. App. 175, 81 Pac. 972.)

As to jurisdiction in general, see note to last section.

HOLIDAYS.—There is an apparent conflict between this provision and section 134 of the Civil Code so far as holidays are concerned. (People v. Heacock, 10 Cal. App. 450, 102 Pac. 543.)

As to whether Saturday afternoon is a legal holiday so far as judicial business is concerned, see People v. Heacock, 10 Cal. App. 450, 102 Pac. 543.

This section does not forbid the legislature from permitting the transaction of business on legal holidays. (People v. Heacock, 10 Cal. App. 450, 102 Pac. 543.)

By this section it was never intended to prohibit all business in the superior courts on a legal holiday or nonjudicial day, except the issuance of injunctions and writs of prohibition, and the legislature is at liberty to allow or disallow the transaction of all or any class of judicial business on legal holidays. (Matter of Smith, 152 Cal. 566, 93 Pac. 191; Diepenbrock v. Superior Court, 153 Cal. 597, 95 Pac. 1121.)

> Power of court to sit and try cases on legal holiday other than Sunday. See notes, 5 Ann. Cas. 919; 11 Ann. Cas. 559.

Cases at law.—The ad damnum clause of the complaint determines the jurisdiction of the superior court. (Dashiell v. Slingerland, 60 Cal. 653; Jackson v. Whartenby, 5 Cal. 94; Maxfield v. Johnson, 30 Cal. 545; Greenbaum v. Martinez, 86 Cal. 459, 25 Pac. 12; Bailey v. Sloan, 65 Cal. 387, 4 Pac. 349; Derby v. Stevens, 64 Cal. 287, 30 Pac. 820; Rodley v. Curry, 120 Cal. 541, 52 Pac. 999; Tulare v. Hevren, 126 Cal. 226, 58 Pac. 530.)

The "demand" spoken of in this section is a demand for judgment evidenced by the prayer of the complaint, and a statement of facts which can uphold the judgment prayed for. (Derby v. Stevens, 64 Cal. 287, 30 Pac. 820, arguendo.)

It is the demand and not the finding of value which fixes the jurisdiction of the court. (Pratt v. Welcome, 6 Cal. App. 475, 92 Pac. 500.)

The jurisdiction of the court is not affected by the fact that the plaintiff does not succeed in establishing all that he claims. (Becker v. Superior Court, 151 Cal. 313, 90 Pac. 689.)

The jurisdiction depends upon the amount demanded in good faith in the complaint. (Jackson v. Whartenby, 5 Cal. 94, arguendo.)

In an action for conversion, where the value of the property sued for and the money expended in pursuit of it exceed three hundred dollars, the superior court has jurisdiction, although, separately considered, neither of them is equal to that sum. (Greenbaum v. Martinez, 86 Cal. 459, 25 Pac. 12.)

The superior court has no jurisdiction of a counterclaim, under subdivision 2 of section 438 of the Code of Civil Procedure, for less than three hundred dollars, where it is not pleaded as a defense, but merely as a ground for affirmative relief. (Griswold v. Pieratt, 110 Cal. 259, 42 Pac. 820.)

A counterclaim for less than three hundred dollars may be pleaded in an action in the superior court by way of defense, but no affirmative judgment can be rendered thereon. (Freeman v. Seitz, 126 Cal. 291, 58 Pac. 690.)

An action for less than the constitutional amount does not confer jurisdiction. (Page v. Ellis, 9 Cal. 248.)

But where the amount sued for exceeds the jurisdictional amount, the court has jurisdiction, although the amount recovered is less than that sum. (Solomon v. Reese, 34 Cal. 28; Pennybecker v. McDougal, 48 Cal. 160.)

Where several plaintiffs sue together on several distinct claims each for less than three hundred dollars, and the court enters a joint judgment for the entire amount of the claims, the judgment is void. (Winrod v. Wolters, 141 Cal. 399, 74 Pac. 1037.)

Costs are to be excluded in determining the jurisdictional amount. (Bradley v. Kent, 22 Cal. 169.)

The interest due is also to be excluded. (Arnold v. Van Brunt, 4 Cal. 89.)

This rule applies to compound as well as to simple interest. (Christian v. Superior Court, 122 Cal. 117, 54 Pac. 518.)

But a penalty of fifty per cent on the amount of principal and interest due on a promissory note, provided for in the note in case of a suit thereon, is to be included in determining the jurisdictional amount. (Reed v. Bernal, 40 Cal. 628.)

Also an attorney's fee provided for in a note. (De Jarnatt v. Marquez, 132 Cal. 700, 64 Pac. 1090.)

An action to recover funds in the hands of a receiver is an action at law. (Garniss v. Superior Court, 88 Cal. 413, 26 Pac. 351.)

The superior court has jurisdiction of an action to recover money, although the amount claimed in each count is less than three hundred dollars, when the aggregate amount sued for exceeds that sum. (Bailey v. Sloan, 65 Cal. 387, 4 Pac. 349; Ventura County v. Clay, 114 Cal. 242, 46 Pac. 9.)

The superior court has jurisdiction to enjoin an action in the justice's court for the price of goods sold, when the defendant has a counterclaim for breach of warranty of the goods in excess of the jurisdiction of the justice's court, and has brought an action for damages in the superior court. (Gregory v. Diggs, 113 Cal. 196, 45 Pac. 261.)

The superior court has no jurisdiction of an action to recover from one or more stockholders their several shares of a debt of a corporation, where the amount demanded from each is less than three hundred dollars, although the entire amount exceeds that sum. (Derby v. Stevens, 64 Cal. 287, 30 Pac. 820; Hyman v. Coleman, 82 Cal. 650, 16 Am. St. Rep. 178, 23 Pac. 62.)

The superior court has no jurisdiction of an action upon separate and distinct promises of several defendants, contained in one instrument, to pay respectively sums' less than three hundred dollars. (Thomas v. Anderson, 58 Cal. 99.)

An action to recover unpaid taxes is not a case in equity, but an action at law; and where the amount is less than three hundred dollars, the court has no jurisdiction; but an action to foreclose a lien for taxes is a case in equity, of which the superior court has jurisdiction regardless of the amount. (People v. Mier, 24 Cal. 61; Bell v. Crippen, 28 Cal. 327; People v. Olivera, 43 Cal. 492.)

An action for less than the constitutional amount does not confer jurisdiction. (Dungan v. Clark, 159 Cal. 30, 112 Pac. 718.)

The original jurisdiction of the superior court and the appellate jurisdiction of the district courts of appeal are identical in "all cases at law, in which the demand, exclusive of interest, or the value of the property in controversy, amounts to three hundred dollars." (J. Dewing Co. v. Thompson, 19 Cal. App. 85, 124 Pac. 1035.)

Cases in equity.—The legislature cannot take away the equity jurisdiction conferred by the Constitution. (Rosenberg v. Frank, 58 Cal. 387.)

But the constitutional grant of jurisdiction in all cases in equity was not intended as a limitation upon the power of the legislature to regulate the rights of persons; and the legislature may create new rights under which new cases in equity may arise, or cause some rights to cease to exist, so that certain cases which courts of equity once entertained can no longer arise. (Spreckels v. Hawaiian Com. etc. Co., 117 Cal. 377, 49 Pac. 353.)

The grant of jurisdiction in all cases in equity confers the same jurisdiction as that formerly exercised by a court of chancery. (Sanford v. Head, 5 Cal. 297.)

The superior court has jurisdiction of an action for an accounting between mortgagor and mortgagee, although the property is out of the state. (Peninsular etc. Co. v. Pacific etc. Co., 123 Cal. 689, 56 Pac. 604.)

Where an action in equity involves matters of probate jurisdiction, but no objection to the mode of exercising the jurisdiction is made in the trial court, it will be treated upon appeal as within the equity jurisdiction. (Simons v. Bedell, 122 Cal. 341, 68 Am. St. Rep. 35, 55 Pac. 3.)

An action against a county for less than three hundred dollars, claimed as compensation for services rendered by the plaintiff as a member of the county board of education, is not a suit in equity, and the superior court has no jurisdiction of it. (Wright v. Del Norte County, 115 Cal. 464, 47 Pac. 258.)

The same superior court has jurisdiction both in equity and in matters of probate; and in an action in equity for an accounting against the executor of a deceased administrator, it may administer full and entire relief according to the principles of equity, and also in accordance with the statutes with reference to matters of probate. (Pennie v. Roach, 94 Cal. 515, 29 Pac. 956, 30 Pac. 106.)

A court of equity has jurisdiction of an action to recover property intentionally and fraudulently concealed by a guardian from the court and the ward. (Lataillade v. Orena, 91 Cal. 565, 25 Am. St. Rep. 219, 27 Pac. 924.)

The superior court cannot enjoin the execution of a mandate of the supreme court. (Quan Wo Chung v. Laumeister, 83 Cal. 384, 17 Am. St. Rep. 261, 23 Pac. 320.)

An action to annul an ordinance of the board of supervisors fixing water rates is within the equitable jurisdiction of the superior court. (Spring Valley W. W. v. San Francisco, 82 Cal. 286, 16 Am. St. Rep. 116, 6 L. R. A. 756, 22 Pac. 910, 1046.)

The superior court, as a court of equity, has power in proper cases to hear and determine questions relating to the rights and duties of

executors and beneficiaries under wills which have been admitted to probate. (Williams v. Williams, 73 Cal. 99, 14 Pac. 394.)

The superior court has jurisdiction of a suit in equity against the administrator of a deceased person for the specific performance of a contract for the sale and purchase of lands. (Hall v. Rice, 64 Cal. 443, 1 Pac. 891, 2 Pac. 889.)

The superior courts are vested with the same chancery jurisdiction which was vested in the high courts of chancery in England, and the equity power is not curtailed by the code provisions regulating injunctions. (Pasadena v. Superior Court, 157 Cal. 781, 21 Ann. Cas. 1355, 109 Pac. 620.)

The superior court in an action brought in good faith to foreclose an asserted mechanic's lien has jurisdiction upon finding against the claim of lien to render a personal judgment. (Becker v. Superior Court, 151 Cal. 313, 90 Pac. 689.)

An action to foreclose a mechanic's lien is a suit in equity. (Becker v. Superior Court, 151 Cal. 313, 90 Pac. 689.)

The legislature cannot take away the equity jurisdiction conferred on the courts by the Constitution. (Bacon v. Bacon, 150 Cal. 477, 89 Pac. 317.)

The superior court has power to compel a discovery in all cases in which, under the established rules of chancery practice existing at the time of the adoption of the Constitution, a party would have been entitled to this relief. (Union etc. Co. v. Superior Court, 149 Cal. 790, 87 Pac. 1035.)

The district courts had power to appoint receivers in "cases where receivers had theretofore been appointed by the usages of the courts of equity." (Bateman v. Superior Court, 54 Cal. 285; La Societe Francaise v. District Court, 53 Cal. 495.)

In this state, the jurisdiction of courts of equity over questions of title to real estate has no existence. (Ritchie v. Dorland, 6 Cal. 33.)

Under the general grant of jurisdiction in all cases in equity, the court may issue writs of mandamus, certiorari, prohibition and habeas corpus. (Perry v. Ames, 26 Cal. 372.)

An action to abate a nuisance is a case in equity. (People v. Moore, 29 Cal. 427; Courtwright v. Bear River etc. Co., 30 Cal. 573; Yolo County v. Sacramento, 36 Cal. 193.)

In Rosenberg v. Frank, 58 Cal. 387, it was held that the corresponding section of the Constitution of 1849 conferred upon the district courts the same jurisdiction in equity as that administered by the high court of chancery in England, including the power to construe a will after it has been admitted to probate. But, under the present Constitution, it is held that the power to construe a will is vested exclusively in the superior court sitting as a court of probate. (Toland v. Earl, 129 Cal. 148, 79 Am. St. Rep. 100, 61 Pac. 914.)

Conceding that the superior court has jurisdiction of an action to construe a will, it is not bound to entertain such an action, and should not do so, except in case where there is some special reason for seeking its interpretation. (Siddall v. Harrison, 73 Cal. 560, 15 Pac. 130.)

Under the former Constitution it was held that an action in equity to compel an administrator to account would lie, although his account

had been settled by the probate court. (Clarke v. Perry, 5 Cal. 58, 63 Am. Dec. 82.)

Probate.—Prior to the organization of the state, there was no such a thing as the probate of a will; and the probate court has no jurisdiction to probate a will executed prior to that time by the death of the testator. (Grimes v. Norris, 6 Cal. 621, 65 Am. Dec. 545; Coppinger v. Rice, 33 Cal. 408; Castro v. Castro, 6 Cal. 158.)

The courts of first instance, between the acquisition of California by the United States and the passage of the probate act, had jurisdiction in matters of probate. (Ryder v. Cohn, 37 Cal. 69.)

The estates of deceased persons in this state, who died prior to the passage of the Probate Act of 1850, and subsequent to the organization of the state, can be administered on in accordance with the probate act. (People v. Senter, 28 Cal. 502.)

The probate court is a court of limited and inferior jurisdiction. (Grimes v. Norris, 6 Cal. 621, 65 Am. Dec. 545; Clarke v. Perry, 5 Cal. 58, 63 Am. Dec. 82; Smith v. Andrews, 6 Cal. 652; Smith v. Westerfield, 88 Cal. 374, 26 Pac. 206.)

No distinct "court of probate" has been created or recognized by the Constitution. (In re Burton, 93 Cal. 459, 29 Pac. 36.)

The superior court, when sitting as a court of probate, has power to hear and determine all questions of law and fact, the determination of which is ancillary to a proper judgment in such case. (In re Burton, 93 Cal. 459, 29 Pac. 36.)

The jurisdiction of the superior court over probate matters is conferred by the Constitution, and it is not a statutory tribunal when sitting in probate. (Heydenfeldt v. Superior Court, 117 Cal. 348, 49 Pac. 210.)

The probate court has exclusive jurisdiction of legacies. (Drinkhouse v. Merritt, 134 Cal. 580, 66 Pac. 785.)

The probate court has no jurisdiction to settle a disputed claim by a third person against the guardian or the estate of a ward. (Guardianship of Breslin, 135 Cal. 21, 66 Pac. 962.)

A court of equity cannot set aside a decree of distribution made by the probate court on the ground of fraud of the person securing it; but in case of extrinsic fraud it may declare such person a trustee of the defrauded parties. (Sohler v. Sohler, 135 Cal. 323, 87 Am. St. Rep. 98, 67 Pac. 282.)

Questions in regard to assignments made by an heir apparent are not within the scope of probate proceedings. (Estate of Ryder, 141 Cal. 366, 74 Pac. 993.)

The superior court sitting as a court of probate has no jurisdiction to annul an administration and compel the administrator to return all the property which has come into his hands, on the ground that the administration was granted on the estate of a living person. (Costa v. Superior Court, 137 Cal. 79, 69 Pac. 840.)

The determination of a judgment lien against a devisee is not a matter of probate. (Martinovich v. Marsicano, 137 Cal. 354, 70 Pac. 459.)

When a title by patent from the United States vested absolutely in the widow and two children of the deceased husband and father, free

Constitution—21

of any trust attaching to his estate, the superior court sitting in probate has no jurisdiction over it. (Southern Cal. M. T. Co. v. Lincoln University, 137 Cal. 508, 70 Pac. 1129.)

The former Constitution did not confer on the probate court jurisdiction of all matters relating to the estates of deceased persons, but of such matters only as the statutes direct it to exercise jurisdiction over. (Bush v. Lindsey, 44 Cal. 121.)

Probate courts have no jurisdiction to enforce a trust by compelling an administrator to convey property by him held in trust. (Haverstick v. Trudel, 51 Cal. 431.)

The probate court has no jurisdiction to compel an attorney of an executrix to return a fee paid him by her. (Tomaky v. Superior Court, 131 Cal. 620, 63 Pac. 1020.)

The probate courts had not exclusive jurisdiction in cases of guardianship of minors. (Wilson v. Roach, 4 Cal. 362.)

The district courts had the same control over the persons of minors, as well as their estates, that the court of chancery in England possesses. (Wilson v. Roach, 4 Cal. 362.)

Neither the probate court, nor the superior court when exercising probate jurisdiction, has power to set aside a decree of distribution on the ground of fraud, after the time mentioned in section 473 of the Code of Civil Procedure. (Estate of Hudson, 63 Cal. 454.)

The jurisdiction of the probate courts over the estates of deceased persons did not divest the district courts of their general jurisdiction as courts of chancery over actions for a settlement of the affairs of a partnership. (Griggs v. Clark, 23 Cal. 427.)

Where the executors named in the will are also appointed trustees to control and manage the residue of the estate and to distribute it among certain beneficiaries, a court of equity has no jurisdiction of a bill to enforce an accounting of the trust estate, pending administration of the estate in the probate court. (Dougherty v. Bartlett, 100 Cal. 496, 35 Pac. 431.)

The probate court cannot decide an adverse claim to property asked to be set aside as a homestead. (Estate of Kimberly, 97 Cal. 281, 32 Pac. 234.)

The superior court sitting as a court of probate may examine into the title to parcels of real estate, for the purpose of selecting a homestead, but has no jurisdiction to determine the title as between adverse claimants. (Estate of Burton, 64 Cal. 428, 1 Pac. 702.)

In probate proceedings the court has jurisdiction of the claims of assignees of the heir, but its jurisdiction does not extend to claims of an equitable nature against the legal owner, or, in other words, to trusts. (More v. More, 133 Cal. 489, 65 Pac. 1044.)

The probate court has no jurisdiction to settle the accounts of a deceased guardian. (In re Allgier, 65 Cal. 228, 3 Pac. 849.)

The probate court has no jurisdiction to determine whether or not certain property in the possession of the executor belongs to the estate or is held by him in some other capacity. (In re Haas, 97 Cal. 232, 31 Pac. 893, 32 Pac. 327.)

Sections 1458 to 1461 of the Code of Civil Procedure do not provide for a proceeding involving title to property of which the probate court

has no jurisdiction. (Levy v. Superior Court, 105 Cal. 600, 29 L. R. A. 811, 38 Pac. 965.)

Where property is devised, exonerated of the mortgage thereon, the probate court has jurisdiction to compel the executor to pay the mortgage debt from the assets of the estate. (In re Heydenfeldt, 106 Cal. 434, 39 Pac. 788.)

The probate court has inherent power to order the distributee to return to the executors the property distributed, when the decree of distribution is reversed upon appeal. (Heydenfeldt v. Superior Court, 117 Cal. 348, 49 Pac. 210.)

Under the former Constitution it was held that the jurisdiction of the probate court over testamentary and probate matters was not exclusive. The district court might take jurisdiction of the settlement of an estate when there were peculiar circumstances of embarrassment, and when the assuming jurisdiction would prevent waste, delay and expense, and thus conclude, by one action and decree, a protracted litigation. (Deck v. Gerke, 12 Cal. 433, 73 Am. Dec. 555.)

The probate court has exclusive jurisdiction of the following matters: Matters relating to the proof of wills (Castro v. Richardson, 18 Cal. 478); probate of wills, granting of letters, allowance of claims, settlement of accounts (In re Bowen, 34 Cal. 682); to adjust and enforce a claim for expenses of administration (Gurnee v. Maloney, 38 Cal. 85, 99 Am. Dec. 352); to compel an executor to account, and to distribute the estate (Anguisola v. Arnaz, 51 Cal. 435); to construe a will (Toland v. Earl, 129 Cal. 148, 79 Am. St. Rep. 100, 61 Pac. 914); to determine who is entitled to distribution (Simons v. Bedell, 122 Cal. 341, 68 Am. St. Rep. 35, 55 Pac. 3); to determine whether an attorney for absent or minor heirs shall be appointed, and to fix the amount of his compensation. (Dougherty v. Bartlett, 100 Cal. 496, 35 Pac. 431.)

The superior court, when sitting as a court of probate, has exclusive jurisdiction of the distribution of an estate, and is not bound by an adjudication by the same court, when sitting as a court of equity, as to the interest of an heir or devisee, where such interest was merely incidentally involved. (Estate of Freud, 134 Cal. 333, 66 Pac. 476.)

An action will not lie to recover from an executrix rents received by her after the settlement of her account, although she neglected to account for the same. (Washington v. Black, 83 Cal. 290, 23 Pac. 300.)

A court of equity has no power to establish a will, even though the will has been lost or destroyed, or has been fraudulently suppressed, and the relief is asked against a person who destroyed the will and is one of the witnesses necessary to prove its contents. (McDaniel v. Pattison, 98 Cal. 86, 27 Pac. 651, 32 Pac. 805.)

In an action of ejectment, the superior court has no power to set aside the land sought to be recovered as a homestead. This can only be done by the superior court sitting as a court of probate. (Richards v. Wetmore, 66 Cal. 365, 5 Pac. 620.)

Under the former Constitution, the district courts had power to decide issues of fact joined in the probate court and certified to the district courts. This provision, however, did not give such courts

any appellate jurisdiction from the probate courts. (Reed v. McCormick, 4 Cal. 342.)

An act providing for the transfer to the district courts of issues of fact already decided by the probate court is void as conferring appellate jurisdiction upon the district courts, which under the Constitution they cannot exercise. (Deck v. Gerke, 6 Cal. 666.)

After the amendment in 1862, district courts had no jurisdiction to try issues arising in the probate courts. (In re Bowen, 34 Cal. 682; Matter of Tomlinson, 35 Cal. 509.)

The probate court was not bound by a decision by the district court as to a fact certified to that court for decision. (Pond v. Pond, 10 Cal. 495.)

The probate court had jurisdiction to try and determine issues of fact arising in proceedings before it, and was only required to certify the issue to the district court when the evidence was conflicting, etc. (Keller v. Franklin, 5 Cal. 432.)

The supreme court sitting in probate has exclusive jurisdiction of accounts of executors and administrators. (Elizalde v. Murphy, 4 Cal. App. 114, 87 Pac. 245.)

The superior court sitting in probate has exclusive jurisdiction on allowance of administrator's fees, expenses and attorney's fees, whether claimed by the administrator or the representatives of a deceased administrator. (Elizalde v. Murphy, 4 Cal. App. 114, 87 Pac. 245.)

The superior court sitting in probate has such equitable jurisdiction as may be necessary to the exercise of its proper functions. (Elizalde v. Murphy, 4 Cal. App. 114, 87 Pac. 245.)

Under the former Constitution the probate court had such jurisdiction only as was conferred upon it by the legislature, while under the present Constitution the superior court has jurisdiction "of all matters of probate." (Elizalde v. Murphy, 4 Cal. App. 114, 87 Pac. 245.)

Section 1639 of the Code of Civil Procedure properly granted jurisdiction to a superior court sitting in probate to compel the personal representatives of a deceased executor or administrator to render an account of the administration of their testator or intestate, and to settle such account as in other cases. (King v. Chase, 159 Cal. 420, 115 Pac. 207.)

Divorce.—In a suit for divorce and a partition of the property acquired during coverture, the jurisdiction of the court does not depend upon the amount involved. (Deuprez v. Deuprez, 5 Cal. 387.)

The grant of jurisdiction in actions of divorce does not prevent the legislature from making reasonable regulations as to the proceedings by which such jurisdiction is exercised, or from taking away the right of divorce entirely. (Grannis v. Superior Court, 146 Cal. 245, 106 Am. St. Rep. 23, 79 Pac. 891.)

Insolvency.—The act creating the bank commissioners did not deprive the superior court of its power to hear and determine matters of insolvency. (People v. Superior Court, 100 Cal. 105, 34 Pac. 492.)

The legislature may pass an insolvency law while a United States bankruptcy law is in force, but its operation will be suspended until the repeal of the federal law. (Lewis v. County Clerk, 55 Cal. 604;

Seattle Coal etc. Co. v. Thomas, 57 Cal. 197; Boedefeld v. Reed, 55 Cal. 299.)

Since the new Constitution proceedings in insolvency are no longer special cases. (People v. Rosborough, 29 Cal. 415.)

The mere fact that jurisdiction in cases of insolvency is vested in the court does not prevent the legislature from authorizing the judge to make an order in chambers directing the clerk to give notice to creditors. (Flint v. Wilson, 36 Cal. 24.)

Tax, etc.—The term "assessment" as used in this section does not include assessments made by a private corporation upon its stockholders, but refers to such assessments as are authorized in relation to revenue and taxation, and such as may be made under the authority of a municipal or other corporation to meet the cost of a public improvement. (Arroyo Ditch etc. Co. v. Superior Court, 92 Cal. 47, 27 Am. St. Rep. 91, 28 Pac. 54.)

A forfeiture for issuing a certificate of relief in violation of section 596 of the Political Code is not a municipal fine, or a tax, impost, toll or assessment. (Thomas v. Justice's Court, 80 Cal. 40, 22 Pac. 80.)

An action against an assessor to recover damages for a wrongful and fraudulent assessment made by him does not involve "the legality of a tax." (Perkins v. Ralls, 71 Cal. 87, 11 Pac. 860.)

A proceeding to modify the grade of a street is a special one, and not a case at law involving the legality of an assessment. (Appeal of Houghton, 42 Cal. 35.)

A license fee or charge for the transaction of any business is a tax. (Santa Barbara v. Stearns, 51 Cal. 499.)

An action to recover a sum exacted by a toll gatherer, greater than he is permitted by law to collect, does not involve the legality of a toll. (Brown v. Rice, 52 Cal. 489.)

Special proceedings.—The county courts only had jurisdiction in such special cases as the legislature should determine. (Matter of Marks, 45 Cal. 199.)

A grant of jurisdiction in such special cases as the legislature may prescribe does not confer exclusive jurisdiction in special cases. (O'Callaghan v. Booth, 6 Cal. 63; Harper v. Freelon, 6 Cal. 76.)

As to whether the legislature may confer jurisdiction of special cases upon courts not established by the Constitution, see Spencer Creek Water Co. v. Vallejo, 48 Cal. 70.

The legislature cannot confer jurisdiction in "special cases" upon a judge. (Spencer Creek Water Co. v. Vallejo, 48 Cal. 70.)

Special cases are cases created by statute and the proceedings under which are unknown to the general framework of the courts of common law and equity. (Parsons v. Tuolumne Co. Water Co., 5 Cal. 43, 63 Am. Dec. 76; People v. Day, 15 Cal. 91; People v. Supervisors of Kern Co., 45 Cal. 679.)

An action to prevent or abate a nuisance is not a special case. (Parsons v. Tuolumne Co. Water Co., 5 Cal. 43, 63 Am. Dec. 76.)

Writs of mandate are not special cases. (People v. Supervisors of Kern Co., 45 Cal. 679.)

The incorporation of towns is not a special case. (People v. Nevada, 6 Cal. 143.)

The following matters are special cases within the meaning of the Constitution: Cases of insolvency (Harper v. Freelon, 6 Cal. 76); election contests (Dorsey v. Barry, 24 Cal. 449; Saunders v. Haynes, 13 Cal. 145); the examination of claims for public lands (Ricks v. Reed, 19 Cal. 551); proceedings to enforce mechanics' liens (McNiel v. Borland, 23 Cal. 144, distinguishing Brock v. Bruce, 5 Cal. 279); proceedings for the condemnation of water (Spencer Creek Water Co. v. Vallejo, 48 Cal. 70); proceedings under sections 312 and 315 of the Civil Code (Wickersham v. Brittan, 93 Cal. 34, 15 L. R. A. 106, 28 Pac. 792, 29 Pac. 51); proceedings to condemn land (Bishop v. Superior Court, 87 Cal. 226, 25 Pac. 435).

Section 4 of the act of 1897 for the formation of irrigation districts (Stats. 1897, p. 254), providing for an appeal directly to the superior court of the county from an order of the board of supervisors granting an application for the formation of a district, is unconstitutional and void. The legislature has no power to extend the jurisdiction, original or appellate, of the superior court. (Chinn v. Superior Court, 156 Cal. 478, 105 Pac. 580.)

The unconstitutionality of section 4 of the act of March 31, 1897, does not render the entire act void. (Imperial Water Co. v. Board of Supervisors, 162 Cal. 14, 120 Pac. 780.)

Real property.—The idea intended to be embodied in the phrase, "cases at law which involve the title or possession of real property," may be expressed by the paraphrase: Cases at law in which the title or possession of real property is a material fact in the case, upon which the plaintiff relies for a recovery or the defendant for a defense. (Holman v. Taylor, 31 Cal. 338; Copertini v. Oppermann, 76 Cal. 181, 18 Pac. 256.)

When the title to real property is involved, the amount sued for is not material in determining the jurisdiction. (Cullen v. Langridge, 17 Cal. 67; Holman v. Taylor, 31 Cal. 338.)

It is not enough that the possession is a fact in controversy, or incidentally in question, or that the fact of possession is in issue; but the right of possession must be involved. (Pollock v. Cummings, 38 Cal. 683; Cornett v. Bishop, 39 Cal. 319.)

An action to recover one-half of the value of a partition fence involves the title to real property. (Holman v. Taylor, 31 Cal. 338.)

An action brought in a justice's court against a railroad company by an owner of adjoining land, to recover for the killing of a colt alleged to have strayed upon the track by reason of the insufficiency of a division fence, necessarily involves the title to such land, although the answer raises no issue as to such ownership. (Boyd v. Southern Cal. Ry. Co., 126 Cal. 571, 58 Pac. 1046.)

An action to foreclose a vendor's lien upon premises contracted to be sold is an action for the enforcement of a lien upon real estate within the provisions of this section. (Southern Pac. R. R. Co. v. Pixley, 103 Cal. 118, 37 Pac. 194.)

An action by a vendee to a contract for the sale of land to recover a part payment made on the purchase price, because of a defect in the title of the vendor, involves the title to real property. (Copertini v. Oppermann, 76 Cal. 181, 18 Pac. 256.)

Where an action involving the title or possession of real property is brought in the justice's court, and the defendant appeals to the superior court, which renders judgment in favor of the plaintiff, the defendant may appeal to the supreme court. (Hart v. Carnall-Hopkins Co., 101 Cal. 160, 35 Pac. 633; Santa Barbara v. Eldred, 95 Cal. 378, 30 Pac. 562.)

Where an action to recover less than three hundred dollars is transferred from the justice's court to the superior court on the ground that it involves the title to real estate, and the plaintiff afterward amends his complaint and asks for damages to certain lands, the superior court has no jurisdiction of the action, as it does not appear that the action involves the title to real estate. (Gorton v. Ferdinando, 64 Cal. 11, 27 Pac. 941.)

An action for specific performance of a contract for the sale of land is not an action for the recovery of the possession of or quieting title to real estate. (Grocers' Fruit etc. Union v. Kern etc. Land Co., 150 Cal. 466, 89 Pac. 120.)

"Possession," under this section, means such a possession of real property as has relation to title or is necessary to the enforcement or defeat of the cause of action asserted. (O'Meara v. Hables, 163 Cal. 240, 124 Pac. 1003.)

Where plaintiff founds his right of action upon an allegation that title to land agreed to be purchased by him is invalid, and seeks the return of a purchase deposit upon the ground of such invalidity, original jurisdiction of the subject matter is in the superior court and not in the justice court. (Bates v. Ferrier, 19 Cal. App. 79, 124 Pac. 889.)

Where, in a proceeding under the McEnerney Act against "all persons," a person voluntarily appears as defendant and submits himself and his claim to the jurisdiction of the superior court, such court has jurisdiction of the subject matter of the controversy between the plaintiff and such person. (Faxon v. All Persons, 166 Cal. 707, 137 Pac. 919.)

Place of trial.—The proviso in this section is mandatory. (Fresno Nat. Bank v. Superior Court, 83 Cal. 491, 24 Pac. 157.)

The proviso to this section is to be strictly construed, and does not include an action to recover damages for interfering with an easement for a canal, where there is nothing in the complaint to indicate that the defendant claims any right or title to the easement of the canal. (Miller & Lux v. Kern Co. Land Co., 140 Cal. 132, 73 Pac. 836.)

An action may be brought under the proviso to this section to partition several distinct tracts of land situated in different counties. As to whether or not partition is an action "quieting title to" real estate not decided. (Murphy v. Superior Court, 138 Cal. 69, 70 Pac. 1070.)

An action to have it adjudged that plaintiff is the owner of an undivided third of a mining property, and to compel a conveyance thereof, must be brought in the county in which the mining property is located. (McFarland v. Martin, 144 Cal. 771, 78 Pac. 239.)

An action to establish a trust in land must be tried in the county where the land is situated. (Hannah v. Canty, 1 Cal. App. 225, 81 Pac. 1035.)

Where property situated in different counties is mortgaged to secure a debt, the superior court of either county has jurisdiction of a suit to foreclose. (Kent v. Williams, 146 Cal. 3, 79 Pac. 527.)

The superior court has no jurisdiction of an action to enforce a lien upon real property situated in another county. (Urton v. Woolsey, 87 Cal. 38, 25 Pac. 154.)

This section has no application to an action for the settlement of a trust in relation to real and personal property, and such an action is not required to be brought in the county where the real property is situated. (Le Breton v. Superior Court, 66 Cal. 27, 4 Pac. 777.)

If an action to quiet title to real estate is brought outside of the county in which the land is situated, the court has no jurisdiction, and such lack of jurisdiction cannot be waived. (Fritts v. Camp, 94 Cal. 393, 29 Pac. 867.)

An action to set aside a judgment procured by fraud is a suit in equity and need not be brought in the county in which the judgment was recovered. (Herd v. Tuohy, 133 Cal. 55, 65 Pac. 139.)

The creating of a new county does not affect an action pending in the superior court affecting real property in such new county. (Tolman v. Smith, 85 Cal. 280, 24 Pac. 743.)

This section does not provide that the actions referred to must be tried, but simply that they must be commenced in the county in which the land is situated. (Hancock v. Burton, 61 Cal. 70.)

If an action be for the determination, in any form, of a right or interest in real property, the action must be commenced and tried in the county where the land lies. (Bartley v. Fraser, 16 Cal. App. 560, 117 Pac. 683.)

Writs.—The legislature has no power to enlarge the office of the writs mentioned in this section. (Camron v. Kenfield, 57 Cal. 550; Farmers' etc. Union v. Thresher, 62 Cal. 407.)

The superior court may issue a writ of mandamus to run out of the county, or to be executed out of the county in which the court is held. (Kings County v. Johnson, 104 Cal. 198, 37 Pac. 870.)

If the provisions of this section reviving the writ of quo warranto repealed by implication the provisions of the code for an action against persons who usurp offices or franchises, it made little difference, as the power under a writ of quo warranto is quite as broad as under the statute. (People v. Dashaway Assn., 84 Cal. 114, 12 L. R. A. 117, 24 Pac. 277.)

The county court had no jurisdiction to issue the writ of certiorari, except in aid of its appellate jurisdiction. (Wilcox v. Oakland, 49 Cal. 29.)

Under the "power to issue writs of habeas corpus," a superior court has power to determine the legal effect of a judgment of conviction, and although its judgment holding a petition for a writ sufficient and a judgment of conviction void for insufficiency of the information, be erroneous, it cannot be annulled on certiorari. (Matter of Hughes, 159 Cal. 360, 113 Pac. 684.)

Criminal cases.—The superior court has jurisdiction of an offense punishable by imprisonment and fine, which may exceed one thousand dollars. (Ex parte Neustadt, 82 Cal. 273, 23 Pac. 124.)

Where the legislature confers upon police courts jurisdiction of certain misdemeanors, such jurisdiction is exclusive, and the superior court has no jurisdiction of such misdemeanors. (Green v. Superior Court, 78 Cal. 556, 21 Pac. 307, 541; People v. Joselyn, 80 Cal. 544, 22 Pac. 217; People v. Lawrence, 82 Cal. 182, 22 Pac. 1120; Ex parte Wallingford, 60 Cal. 103; Gafford v. Bush, 60 Cal. 149.)

If a defendant is charged with a felony of which the superior court has jurisdiction, he may be convicted of a lesser offense involved in such felony, although such lesser offense is not one of which the superior court is given jurisdiction. (Ex parte Donahue, 65 Cal. 474, 4 Pac. 449.)

The provision of the San Francisco charter giving the police court "concurrent jurisdiction with the superior court" of all other misdemeanors than those arising under the violation of ordinances is in violation of this section. (Robert v. Police Court, 148 Cal. 131, 82 Pac. 838.)

A newly created county has jurisdiction of a defendant charged with the commission of an offense prior to the creation of the county, upon territory within its boundaries; and a prosecution pending in the old county is no bar to the prosecution, if dismissed before the commencement of the prosecution in the new, and before jeopardy has attached. (People v. Stokes, 103 Cal. 193, 42 Am. St. Rep. 102, 37 Pac. 207.)

The superior court has no jurisdiction of a misdemeanor committed by a corporation punishable by fine not exceeding five hundred dollars or imprisonment not exceeding six months. (People v. Palermo Land & W. Co., 4 Cal. App. 717, 89 Pac. 723, 725.)

The superior court only has jurisdiction of cases of misdemeanor not otherwise provided for. (People v. Palermo Land & W. Co., 4 Cal. App. 717, 89 Pac. 723, 725.)

The legislature may repose exclusive jurisdiction in police courts of all classes of misdemeanors punishable by fine or imprisonment. (People v. Cory, 26 Cal. App. 735, 148 Pac. 532.)

Appellate jurisdiction.—The superior court has appellate jurisdiction only to the extent and in the mode which the legislature may prescribe. (Sherer v. Superior Court, 94 Cal. 354, 29 Pac. 716.)

The Constitution gives the superior court no appellate jurisdiction, but the legislature is permitted to give it such appellate jurisdiction as it may see fit. (Wells v. Torrance, 119 Cal. 437, 51 Pac. 626.)

By reason of the provisions of section 11, article XXII, of the Constitution, the superior court had jurisdiction of appeals from justices' courts before the legislature acted upon the subject. (California Fruit etc. Co. v. Superior Court, 60 Cal. 305.)

The superior courts only have jurisdiction of appeals from justices' courts in their respective counties, and therefore, after an appeal, the action cannot be transferred to another county for trial, although the defendant resides in another county. (Gross v. Superior Court, 71 Cal. 382, 12 Pac. 264; Luco v. Superior Court, 71 Cal. 555, 12 Pac. 677.)

The superior court has no jurisdiction of an appeal from an order of a justice's court, directing the judgment debtor to apply certain

property in satisfaction of the judgment. (Wells v. Torrance, 119 Cal. 437, 51 Pac. 626.)

Upon an appeal from a judgment of the justice's court vacating a former judgment, the superior court cannot affirm such former judgment, but, if it was erroneously set aside, it should reverse such judgment and order a new trial. (Sherer v. Superior Court, 94 Cal. 354, 29 Pac. 716.)

Although the county court was authorized to try cases on appeal de novo, such a trial was not an exercise of original jurisdiction. (Townsend v. Brooks, 5 Cal. 52.)

Where a case is appealed to the superior court on question of both law and fact, the superior court acquires jurisdiction of the cause, although it was not originally within the jurisdiction of the justice's court. (De Jarnatt v. Marquez, 132 Cal. 700, 64 Pac. 1090; Hart v. Carnall-Hopkins Co., 103 Cal. 132, 37 Pac. 196. But see Ballerino v. Bigelow, 90 Cal. 500, 27 Pac. 372.)

A judgment on appeal from a judgment of a justice's court, in which the amount is in excess of the jurisdiction of the justice, is not void, but merely erroneous. (Moore v. Martin, 38 Cal. 428.)

A judgment of a county court upon appeal for the sum of three hundred dollars is void, and will be annulled upon certiorari. (Will v. Sinkwitz, 39 Cal. 570.)

As to whether the provision of the Constitution of 1849 giving the county courts appellate jurisdiction in cases arising in inferior courts is self-executing, see People v. Nyland, 41 Cal. 129.

Forcible entry and detainer.—The words "forcible entry and detainer" include not only forcible entry and forcible detainer, but also unlawful detainer after the termination of or contrary to the terms of the lease. (Caulfield v. Stevens, 28 Cal. 118.)

Liens.—The superior court has concurrent jurisdiction with justices of the peace for the foreclosure of liens on personal property when the claim is for less than three hundred dollars, and the plaintiff is entitled to costs, whether he seeks relief in one jurisdiction or the other. (Clark v. Brown, 141 Cal. 93, 74 Pac. 548.)

Miscellaneous.—The county courts had common-law jurisdiction and might admit foreigners to citizenship. (In re Conner, 39 Cal. 98, 2 Am. Dec. 427.)

Granting to county judges power to issue injunctions did not trench upon the jurisdiction of the district courts. (Thompson v. Williams, 6 Cal. 88.)

An act providing for the confirmation of the organization and bonds of irrigation districts is not unconstitutional because it authorizes the court to determine the rights of the parties in advance of any controversy as to such rights. (Cullen v. Glendora Water Co., 113 Cal. 503, 39 Pac. 769, 45 Pac. 822, 1047.)

Superior court, how constituted.

Sec. 6.   There shall be in each of the organized counties, or cities and counties of the state, a superior court, for each of which at least one judge shall be elected by the qualified

electors of the county, or city and county, at the general state election; provided, that until otherwise ordered by the legislature, only one judge shall be elected for the counties of Yuba and Sutter, and that in the city and county of San Francisco there shall be elected twelve judges of the superior court, any one or more of whom may hold court. There may be as many sessions of said court, at the same time, as there are judges thereof. The said judges shall choose from their own number a presiding judge, who may be removed at their pleasure. He shall distribute the business of the court among the judges thereof, and prescribe the order of business. The judgments, orders, and proceedings of any session of the superior court, held by any one or more of the judges of said courts, respectively, shall be equally effectual as if all the judges of said respective courts presided at such session. In each of the counties of Sacramento, San Joaquin, Los Angeles, Sonoma, Santa Clara, and Alameda, there shall be elected two such judges. The term of office of judges of the superior courts shall be six years from and after the first Monday of January, next succeeding their election; provided, that the twelve judges of the superior court, elected in the city and county of San Francisco at the first election held under this Constitution, shall, at their first meeting, so classify themselves, by lot, that four of them shall go out of office at the end of two years, and four of them shall go out of office at the end of four years, and four of them shall go out of office at the end of six years, and an entry of such classification shall be made in the minutes of the court, signed by them, and a duplicate thereof filed in the office of the secretary of state. The first election of judges of the superior courts shall take place at the first general election held after the adoption and ratification of this Constitution. If a vacancy occur in the office of judge of a superior court, the governor shall appoint a person to hold the office until the election and qualification of a judge to fill the vacancy, which election shall take place at the next succeeding general election, and the judge so elected shall hold office for the remainder of the unexpired term.

SUPERIOR JUDGES.—There is only one superior court in the city and county of San Francisco. (Brown v. Campbell, 110 Cal. 644, 43 Pac. 12.)

The departments of the superior court of a single county, though theoretically one court, are practically as distinct, for the trial of causes, as other superior courts, and a jury drawn for one department cannot be used in another. (People v. Wong Bin, 139 Cal. 60, 72 Pac. 505.)

There is no probate court of the city and county of San Francisco, and there is no law authorizing the designation of any one department of said court for probate jurisdiction; but each of the twelve judges has jurisdiction in probate matters. (In re Pearsons, 113 Cal. 577, 45 Pac. 849, 1062.)

The legislature may fix the commencement of the term of a county judge as well as the time of election, but cannot fix the term. (People v. Rosborough, 14 Cal. 180.)

Though by the terms of this section the term of office of the superior judges appears to be exclusive of the first Monday in January after their election, yet this provision is controlled by section 20, article XX, making the terms of all officers elected under the Constitution commence on the first Monday after the first day of January next following their election. (Merced Bank v. Rosenthal, 99 Cal. 39, 31 Pac. 849, 33 Pac. 732.)

A judge elected under an act creating an additional judge holds for six years. (People v. Waterman, 86 Cal. 27, 24 Pac. 807.)

Under this section the commencement of the first regular full term of every newly created superior judgeship commences on the first Monday in January [first Monday after the first day of January] after the next ensuing general election, and the legislature has no power to extend the provisional term of office of a newly created judge beyond such date. (People v. Markham, 104 Cal. 232, 37 Pac. 918.)

The legislature may provide for the appointment of a judge of a newly created court to hold until the next election. (Brodie v. Campbell, 17 Cal. 11.)

The legislature has no power to increase or diminish the term of office of superior judges as fixed by the Constitution; and such judge, therefore, cannot hold after the expiration of such term and until his successor has been elected or appointed. (People v. Campbell, 138 Cal. 11, 70 Pac. 918.)

A district judge, elected on the occasion of a vacancy in the office caused by the resignation of the incumbent, holds, not merely for the unexpired term, but for the full six years. (People v. Burbank, 12 Cal. 378.)

A person elected judge of the district court is entitled to hold for six years, and it is not necessary that all district judges should be elected, or that their terms should expire, at the same time. (People v. Weller, 11 Cal. 77.)

Where, after the appointment of a judge to fill a vacancy caused by the death of the incumbent, the legislature passed an act reducing the number of judges of such county, and providing that the act should go into effect immediately in case of a vacancy in the term prior to January 1, 1897, the act did not go into effect by reason of

the election of a judge to fill the unexpired term. (Church v. Colgan, 117 Cal. 685, 50 Pac. 12.)

When the legislature provides for an additional superior judge, the governor may appoint a provisional judge to act until the next election, but the term of such judge ends absolutely with the beginning of the constitutional term of the additional judge and is not extended by the failure of the person elected to qualify. (Bush v. Nye, 6 Cal. App. 298, 92 Pac. 108.)

This section, with section 8, article VI, means that where a judge of a superior court of one county holds a superior court in another county upon the request of the governor, the court so held by him constitutes a session of the superior court, with the same jurisdiction as if one of the elected judges were sitting, and the amendment of November, 1910, did not change the rule, only having been adopted to remove all question of doubt. (Collins v. Johnston, 237 U. S. 502, 59 L. Ed. 1071, 35 Sup. Ct. Rep. 649.)

Superior judges, apportionment of business.

Sec. 7. In any county, or city and county, other than the city and county of San Francisco, in which there shall be more than one judge of the superior court, the judges of such court may hold as many sessions of said court at the same time as there are judges thereof, and shall apportion the business among themselves as equally as may be.

SESSIONS.—The rule is the same in the city and county of San Francisco, except that the business of the court is apportioned by the presiding judge. (See section 6 of this article.)

Judge may hold court in other county—Judge pro tempore.

Sec. 8. A judge of any superior court may hold a superior court in any county, at the request of a judge of the superior court thereof, and upon the request of the governor it shall be his duty so to do. But a cause in the superior court may be tried by a judge pro tempore, who must be a member of the bar, agreed upon in writing by the parties litigant, or their attorneys of record, and sworn to try the cause and the person so selected shall be empowered to act in such capacity in all further proceedings in any suit or proceedings tried before him until the final determination thereof. There may be as many sessions of a superior court at the same time as there are judges thereof, including any judge or judges acting upon request, or any judge or judges pro tempore. The judgments, orders, acts and

proceedings of any session of any superior court held by
one or more judges acting upon request, or judge or judges
pro tempore, shall be equally effective as if the judge or
all of the judges of such court presided at such session.
(Amendment adopted November 8, 1910.)

[ORIGINAL SECTION.]

Sec. 8. A judge of any superior court may hold a superior
court in any county, at the request of a judge of the superior court
thereof, and upon the request of the governor it shall be his duty
so to do. But a cause in a superior court may be tried by a judge
pro tempore, who must be a member of the bar, agreed upon in
writing by the parties litigant or their attorneys of record,
approved by the court, and sworn to try the cause.

JUDGE OF ONE COUNTY SITTING IN ANOTHER.—Where a
judge of one county acts in another, it must be presumed that he was
properly requested to do so. (In re Corralitos etc. Canning Co., 130
Cal. 570, 62 Pac. 1076.)

Under the Constitution of 1849 it was held that the legislature
might authorize a judge of one district to sit and act in another district, although no express provision was made in the Constitution on
the subject. (People v. McCauley, 1 Cal. 379.)

A statute authorizing a county judge of one county to hold court
for the county judge of another county is valid. (People v. Mellon.
40 Cal. 648.)

A judge who is disqualified has power to select a qualified judge to
try the case. (People v. Ebey, 6 Cal. App. 769, 93 Pac. 379.)

This section, with section 6, article VI, means that where a judge
of a superior court of one county holds a superior court in another
county upon the request of the governor, the court so held by him
constitutes a session of the superior court, with the same jurisdiction
as if one of the elected judges were sitting, and the amendment of
November, 1910, did not change the rule, only having been adopted to
remove all question of doubt. (Collins v. Johnston, 237 U. S. 502,
59 L. Ed. 1071, 35 Sup. Ct. Rep. 649.)

The majority of the judges of the superior court of a county may
request a judge of another county to preside over an extra session
of their court. (Williams v. Hawkins, 20 Cal. App. 161, 128 Pac.
754.)

Leave of absence—Limitation of time.

Sec. 9. The legislature shall have no power to grant
leave of absence to any judicial officer; and any such officer
who shall absent himself from the state for more than sixty
consecutive days shall be deemed to have forfeited his office.
The legislature of the state may at any time, two-thirds of
the members of the senate and two-thirds of the members

of the assembly voting therefor, increase or diminish the number of judges of the superior court in any county, or city and county, in the state; provided, that no such reduction shall affect any judge who has been elected.

ADDITIONAL JUDGES.—When the legislature provides for an additional judge, the governor may appoint a provisional judge to act until the next election, but the term of such judge ends absolutely with the beginning of the constitutional term of the additional judge and is not extended by the failure of the person elected to qualify. (Bush v. Nye, 6 Cal. App. 298, 92 Pac. 108.)

Justices and judges, how removed.

Sec. 10. Justices of the supreme court, and of the district courts of appeal, and judges of the superior courts may be removed by concurrent resolution of both houses of the legislature adopted by a two-thirds vote of each house. All other judicial officers, except justices of the peace, may be removed by the senate on the recommendation of the governor; but no removal shall be made by virtue of this section unless the cause thereof be entered on the journal, nor unless the party complained of has been served with a copy of the complaint against him and shall have had an opportunity of being heard in his defense. On the question of removal the ayes and noes shall be entered on the journal. (Amendment adopted November 8, 1904.)

[ORIGINAL SECTION.]

Sec. 10. Justices of the supreme court, and judges of the superior courts, may be removed by concurrent resolution of both houses of the legislature, adopted by a two-thirds vote of each house. All other judicial officers, except justices of the peace, may be removed by the senate on the recommendation of the governor, but no removal shall be made by virtue of this section, unless the cause thereof be entered on the journal, nor unless the party complained of has been served with a copy of the complaint against him, and shall have had an opportunity of being heard in his defense. On the question of removal, the ayes and noes shall be entered on the journal.

Justices of the peace, provision for.

Sec. 11. The legislature shall determine the number of each of the inferior courts in incorporated cities or towns, and in townships, counties, or cities and counties, according

to the population thereof and the number of judges or justices thereof, and shall fix by law the powers, duties and responsibilities of each of such courts and of the judges or justices thereof; provided, such powers shall not in any case, trench upon the jurisdiction of the several courts of record, except that the legislature shall provide that said courts shall have concurrent jurisdiction with the superior courts in cases of forcible entry and detainer, where the rental value does not exceed twenty-five dollars per month, and where the whole amount of damages claimed does not exceed two hundred dollars, and in cases to enforce and foreclose liens on personal property when neither the amount of liens nor the value of the property amounts to three hundred dollars. (Amendment approved October 10, 1911.)

[ORIGINAL SECTION.]

Sec. 11. The legislature shall determine the number of justices of the peace to be elected in townships, incorporated cities and towns, or cities and counties, and shall fix by law the powers, duties and responsibilities of justices of the peace; provided, such powers shall not in any case trench upon the jurisdiction of the several courts of record, except that said justices shall have concurrent jurisdiction with the superior courts in cases of forcible entry and detainer, where the rental value does not exceed twenty-five dollars per month, and where the whole amount of damages claimed does not exceed two hundred dollars, and in cases to enforce and foreclose liens on personal property when neither the amount of the liens nor the value of the property amounts to three hundred dollars.

JUSTICES OF THE PEACE—Creation of.—A justice's court cannot be created by a freeholders' charter. (People v. Toal, 85 Cal. 333, 24 Pac. 603; People v. Sands, 102 Cal. 12, 36 Pac. 404; Milner v. Reibenstein, 85 Cal. 593, 24 Pac. 935; Ex parte Reilly, 85 Cal. 632, 24 Pac. 807; Ex parte Giambonini, 117 Cal. 573, 49 Pac. 732.)

The laws relating to this portion of the judicial system need not be uniform throughout the state. (Kahn v. Sutro, 114 Cal. 316, 33 L. R. A. 620, 46 Pac. 87.)

The justice's court of Berkeley was not superseded by the Constitution. (Ex parte Armstrong, 84 Cal. 655, 24 Pac. 598.)

The provision of the County Government Act authorizing the supervisors to appoint a justice of the peace to fill a vacancy is not in conflict with this section making them elective. (People v. Chaves, 122 Cal. 134, 54 Pac. 596.)

Justices of the peace are judicial officers and must be elected at the general election. (McGrew v. Mayor etc. of San Jose, 55 Cal. 611.)

Justices of the peace are neither city nor county officers, but form part of the judicial system of the state. (People v. Cobb, 133 Cal. 74, 65 Pac. 325; Kahn v. Sutro, 114 Cal. 316, 33 L. R. A. 620, 46 Pac. 87.)

The board of supervisors of a county may by ordinance abolish two contiguous judicial townships having a justice's court in each, and may establish one new consolidated township, comprising the territory of both of them. (Proulx v. Graves, 143 Cal. 243, 76 Pac. 1025.)

The constitutional provision as to justice's courts operates specifically only by means of such local legislation as the state legislature has delegated to the supervisors under general laws, and automatically establishes a justice's court in each township established by the local body which continues while the township exists, and is merged in another justice's court when two townships are merged into one. (Proulx v. Graves, 143 Cal. 243, 76 Pac. 1025.)

Justices of the peace are part of the constitutional judicial system of the state. (Graham v. Fresno, 151 Cal. 465, 91 Pac. 147.)

The legislature, in creating justices' courts, is justified in classifying municipalities in accordance with population. (In re Johnson, 5 Cal. App. 734, 93 Pac. 199.)

As to whether it is necessary to classify justices' courts for the purpose of establishing them, as distinguished from prescribing their duties or jurisdiction, query? (In re Johnson, 6 Cal. App. 734, 93 Pac. 199.)

The amendment of October 10, 1911, of this section does not abolish the justices' courts and other inferior courts which had been previously established by acts of the legislature. They remain in existence with the jurisdiction vested in them by the acts creating them, until the legislature shall, in the exercise of the power given by the section as amended, otherwise provide. (Matter of the Application of Woods, 161 Cal. 238, 118 Pac. 792.)

Jurisdiction.—A justice's court is a court of limited and inferior jurisdiction, and its jurisdiction must be shown affirmatively by a party relying upon or claiming any right or title under its judgments. (Eltzroth v. Ryan, 89 Cal. 135, 26 Pac. 647; Jones v. Justice's Court, 97 Cal. 523, 32 Pac. 575; Keybers v. McComber, 67 Cal. 395, 7 Pac. 838.)

There can be no concurrent jurisdiction of any special proceeding other than the two mentioned in this section. (Edsall v. Short, 122 Cal. 533, 55 Pac. 327.)

No power can be conferred upon justices of the peace which has been by the Constitution conferred upon other courts. (Zander v. Coe, 5 Cal. 230; Small v. Gwinn, 6 Cal. 447.)

But where the jurisdiction conferred by the Constitution is not exclusive, the same may be conferred upon justices' courts. (People v. Fowler, 9 Cal. 85.)

Where the justice of the peace has no jurisdiction, the judgment should be reversed and the cause dismissed. (Ford v. Smith, 5 Cal. 331.)

It has been held that an appeal to the superior court upon questions of law and fact does not enlarge the jurisdiction of the justice's court, or confer jurisdiction upon the superior court, if the justice's court had no jurisdiction. (Ballerino v. Bigelow, 90 Cal. 500, 27 Pac. 372. But see De Jarnatt v. Marquez, 132 Cal. 700, 64 Pac. 1090; Hart v. Carnall-Hopkins Co., 103 Cal. 132, 37 Pac. 196.)

Where the verified answer in an action in a police court discloses that the action involves the legality of a tax, but, notwithstanding, the court proceeds with the case, and an appeal is taken to the superior court on questions of law and fact, the superior court acquires jurisdiction—not appellate, but original. (Santa Barbara v. Eldred, 95 Cal. 378, 30 Pac. 562.)

The parties to an action in the justice's court cannot confer jurisdiction upon the court of an action involving the title or possession of real estate by failing to plead such lack of jurisdiction by verified answer. (King v. Kutner-Goldstein Co., 135 Cal. 65, 67 Pac. 10.)

Cases at law.—A justice's court has no jurisdiction of an action upon a promissory note, where the amount of the principal sum and attorneys' fees demanded exceeds three hundred dollars. (De Jarnatt v. Marquez, 127 Cal. 558, 78 Am. St. Rep. 90, 60 Pac. 45.)

The justice's court has jurisdiction of an action upon a money demand of less than three hundred dollars for improving a street under a private contract, where there is nothing in the pleadings to show that the action involves the title or possession of real estate. (Raisch v. Sausalito Land etc. Co., 131 Cal. 215, 63 Pac. 346.)

Where several suits to recover the same property, the value of which is less than three hundred dollars, are consolidated, the justice's court has jurisdiction of the action as consolidated. (Cariaga v. Dryden, 29 Cal. 307.)

In an action for the recovery of specific property in a justice's court, the standard of jurisdiction is "the value of the property," and it would seem that the justice's jurisdiction for the incidental damages for detention is unlimited; and at all events, the demand for damages cannot oust the justice of jurisdiction, if the value of the property is less than three hundred dollars. (Astell v. Phillippi, 55 Cal. 265; Wratten v. Wilson, 22 Cal. 465.)

A justice's court has no jurisdiction of an action for the recovery of property alleged to exceed three hundred dollars in value, although the complaint prays judgment for a less sum in case possession cannot be had. (Shealor v. Superior Court, 70 Cal. 564, 11 Pac. 653.)

A justice's court has no jurisdiction of a counterclaim exceeding the jurisdictional amount. (Malson v. Vaughn, 23 Cal. 61; Maxfield v. Johnson, 30 Cal. 545.)

The justice's court has jurisdiction of an action for the recovery of property of the value of two hundred and fifty dollars and fifty dollars damages, where the plaintiff only prays for two hundred and ninety-nine dollars, since both the value of the property and the demand are less than three hundred dollars. (Sanborn v. Superior Court, 60 Cal. 425.)

Forcible entry and detainer.—The words "forcible entry and detainer" include unlawful detainer after the expiration of the term. (Caulfield v. Stevens, 28 Cal. 118; Brummagim v. Spencer, 29 Cal.

661; Mecham v. McKay, 37 Cal. 154; Norblett v. Farwell, 38 Cal. 155; Stoppelkamp v. Mangeot, 42 Cal. 316; Ivory v. Brown, 137 Cal. 603, 70 Pac. 657.)

The actual rental value, and not the value alleged in the complaint, is the test of jurisdiction. (Ballerino v. Bigelow, 90 Cal. 500, 27 Pac. 372.)

The justice's court has no jurisdiction of an action of unlawful detainer, when the amount of rent due is one hundred and twenty dollars, and the plaintiff asks to have it trebled, or of any such case when the amount of the rent when trebled exceeds two hundred dollars. (Hoban v. Ryan, 130 Cal. 96, 62 Pac. 296.)

Real property.—Where the proceedings do not show on their face that the title or possession of real property is involved, but only that it may contingently become involved, the justice has jurisdiction to try the case, unless it appears that the predicted contingency actually occurred during the trial. (Hart v. Carnall-Hopkins Co., 103 Cal. 132, 37 Pac. 196.)

Where a case involving the title or possession of real property is appealed from the justice's court on questions of law and fact, the superior court has jurisdiction to determine the case, and an appeal may be taken to the supreme court in the same manner as if the action had been originally brought in the superior court, or had been transferred to it by the justice. (Hart v. Carnall-Hopkins Co., 103 Cal. 132, 37 Pac. 196.)

A complaint to recover a sum paid upon a contract to locate the plaintiff on certain government land does not necessarily involve the title or possession of real property. (Hart v. Carnall-Hopkins Co., 103 Cal. 132, 37 Pac. 196.)

A justice of the peace has no jurisdiction to try a cause for an injury arising out of a diversion of water. (Hill v. Newman, 5 Cal. 445, 63 Am. Dec. 140.)

If the defendant's verified answer raises a question of title to real property, the cause must be transferred. (Doherty v. Thayer, 31 Cal. 140.)

An action for trespass on real property is within the jurisdiction of a justice of the peace, when the damages sued for are less than three hundred dollars. (Pollock v. Cummings, 38 Cal. 683.)

Fines, etc.—An act requiring actions to recover a penalty imposed upon a railroad company, for charging a passenger an excess of fare, to be brought in the justice's court, is valid. (Reed v. Omnibus R. R. Co., 33 Cal. 212; Smith v. Omnibus R. R. Co., 36 Cal. 281.)

The justice's court has jurisdiction of an action to recover two hundred dollars for a forfeiture for issuing a certificate of relief in violation of section 596 of the Political Code, the same being a penalty given by statute, and not a municipal fine. (Thomas v. Justice's Court, 80 Cal. 40, 22 Pac. 80.)

If, in an action to recover a money judgment for taxes, an answer is filed which puts in issue the legality of the tax, the justice of the peace is ousted of jurisdiction. (People v. Mier, 24 Cal. 61.)

Misdemeanors.—The jurisdiction of justices' courts of misdemeanors is exclusive of the jurisdiction of the superior court. (People v. Palermo Land & W. Co., 4 Cal. App. 717, 89 Pac. 723, 725.)

Miscellaneous.—A statute conferring equitable jurisdiction upon justices' courts is unconstitutional. (Young v. Wright, 52 Cal. 407; Sutherland v. Sweem, 53 Cal. 48.)

The county court had jurisdiction to try an indictment for misdemeanor, the jurisdiction of the justice of the peace being exclusive as to misdemeanors where no indictments had been found. (Ex parte McCarthy, 53 Cal. 412.)

Courts of record.

Sec. 12.   The supreme court, the district courts of appeal, the superior courts, and such other courts as the legislature shall prescribe, shall be courts of record. (Amendment adopted November 8, 1904.)

[ORIGINAL SECTION.]

Sec. 12.   The supreme court, the superior courts, and such other courts as the legislature shall prescribe, shall be courts of record.

Jurisdiction of inferior courts to be fixed by legislature.

Sec. 13.   The legislature shall fix by law the jurisdiction of any inferior courts which may be established in pursuance of section one of this article, and shall fix by law the powers, duties, and responsibilities of the judges thereof.

INFERIOR COURTS.—The jurisdiction, powers, duties and responsibilities of inferior courts cannot be fixed by a freeholders' charter. (People v. Toal, 85 Cal. 333, 24 Pac. 603; Ex parte Reilly, 85 Cal. 632, 24 Pac. 807; People v. Sands, 102 Cal. 12, 36 Pac. 404; Milner v. Reibenstein, 85 Cal. 593, 24 Pac. 935; Ex parte Giambonini, 117 Cal. 573, 49 Pac. 732.)

The municipal superior court of San Francisco had no authority to issue writs of quo warranto, it being an inferior court, and the jurisdiction not being expressly conferred by statute. (People v. Gillespie, 1 Cal. 342.)

As to the jurisdiction of the recorder's court, see Ex parte Soto, 88 Cal. 624, 26 Pac. 530.

The legislature may create a recorder's court with a dual jurisdiction—being a recorder as to some matters, and a justice of the peace as to others. (Prince v. Fresno, 88 Cal. 407, 26 Pac. 606.)

The act of 1889, creating the police court of the city and county of San Francisco, held constitutional. (Ex parte Lloyd, 78 Cal. 421, 20 Pac. 872.)

The legislature is vested with power to confer jurisdiction over all misdemeanors on inferior courts, unless jurisdiction over any of them is conferred upon some other court by the Constitution itself. (Matter of Application of Westenberg, 167 Cal. 309, 139 Pac. 674.)

Clerks of courts and court commissioners.

Sec. 14. The county clerks shall be ex-officio clerks of the courts of record in and for their respective counties or cities and counties. The legislature may also provide for the appointment, by the several superior courts, of one or more commissioners in their respective counties, or cities and counties, with authority to perform chamber business of the judges of the superior courts, to take depositions, and to perform such other business connected with the administration of justice as may be prescribed by law. (Amendment approved October 10, 1911.)

[ORIGINAL SECTION.]

Sec. 14. The legislature shall provide for the election of a clerk of the supreme court and shall fix by law his duties and compensation, which compensation shall not be increased or diminished during the term for which he shall have been elected. The county clerks shall be ex-officio clerks of the courts of record in and for their respective counties, or cities and counties. The legislature may also provide for the appointment, by the several superior courts, of one or more commissioners in their respective counties, or cities and counties, with authority to perform chamber business of the judges of the superior courts, to take depositions, and perform such other business connected with the administration of justice as may be prescribed by law.

Judicial officers not to receive fees and perquisites.

Sec. 15. No judicial officer, except court commissioners, shall receive to his own use any fees or perquisites of office; provided, that justices of the peace now holding office shall receive to their own use such fees as are now allowed by law during the terms for which they have been elected. (Amendment approved October 10, 1911.)

[ORIGINAL SECTION.]

Sec. 15. No judicial officer, except justices of the peace and court commissioners, shall receive to his own use any fees or perquisites of office.

FEES OF JUDICIAL OFFICERS.—The words "justices of the peace" as used in this section include those, by whatever name they are called, who are invested with the duties assigned by the law to those officers, and include a recorder of a city. (Curtis v. Sacramento, 13 Cal. 290.)

Right of justice of the peace to recover fees in separate action. See note, 9 Ann. Cas. 372.

The amendment of October 10, 1911, of this section does not abolish the justices' courts and other inferior courts which had been previously established by acts of the legislature. They remain in existence with the jurisdiction vested in them by the acts creating them, until the legislature shall, in the exercise of the power given by the section as amended, otherwise provide. (Matter of the Application of Woods, 161 Cal. 238, 118 Pac. 792.)

Supreme court opinions to be published.

Sec. 16. The legislature shall provide for the speedy publication of such opinions of the supreme court and of the district courts of appeal as the supreme court may deem expedient, and all opinions shall be free for publication by any person. (Amendment adopted November 8, 1904.)

[ORIGINAL SECTION.]

Sec. 16. The legislature shall provide for the speedy publication of such opinions of the supreme court as it may deem expedient, and all opinions shall be free for publication by any person.

Compensation of justices and judges.

Sec. 17. The justices of the supreme court and of the district courts of appeal, and the judges of the superior courts, shall severally, at stated times during their continuance in office, receive for their service such compensation as is or shall be provided by law. The salaries of the judges of the superior court, in all counties having but one judge, and in all counties in which the terms of the judges of the superior court expire at the same time, shall not hereafter be increased or diminished after their election, nor during the term for which they shall have been elected. Upon the adoption of this amendment the salaries then established by law shall be paid uniformly to the justices and judges then in office. The salaries of the justices of the supreme court and of the district courts of appeal shall be paid by the state. One-half of the salary of each superior court judge shall be paid by the state; and the other half thereof shall be paid by the county for which he is elected. On and after the first day of January, A. D. one thousand nine hundred and seven, the justices of the supreme court shall each receive an annual salary of eight thousand dollars, and the justices of the several district courts of appeal shall each

receive an annual salary of seven thousand dollars; the said salaries to be payable monthly. (Amendment adopted November 6, 1906.)

[AMENDMENT OF 1904.]

Sec. 17. The justices of the supreme court and of the district courts of appeal, and the judges of the superior court shall severally, at stated times during their continuance in office, receive for their services such compensation as is or shall be provided by law, which shall not be increased or diminished after their election, nor during the term for which they shall have been elected. The salaries of the justices of the supreme court and of the district courts of appeal shall be paid by the state. One-half of the salary of each superior court judge shall be paid by the state; the other half thereof shall be paid by the county for which he is elected. (Amendment adopted November 8, 1904.)

[ORIGINAL SECTION.]

Sec. 17. The justices of the supreme court and judges of the superior court shall severally, at stated times during their continuance in office, receive for their services a compensation which shall not be increased or diminished after their election, nor during the term for which they shall have been elected. The salaries of the justices of the supreme court shall be paid by the state. One-half of the salary of each superior court judge shall be paid by the state; the other half thereof shall be paid by the county for which he is elected. During the term of the first judges elected under this Constitution, the annual salaries of the justices of the supreme court shall be six thousand dollars each. Until otherwise changed by the legislature, the superior court judges shall receive an annual salary of three thousand dollars each, payable monthly, except the judges of the city and county of San Francisco, and the counties of Alameda, San Joaquin, Los Angeles, Santa Clara, Yuba and Sutter combined, Sacramento, Butte, Nevada, and Sonoma, which shall receive four thousand dollars each.

SALARIES OF JUDICIAL OFFICERS.—This provision does not exempt judges from the necessity of an appropriation for their salaries by the legislature. (Myers v. English, 9 Cal. 341.)

The law providing for an increase of salary of justices of the supreme court, though an existing statute, is not in force, because there is no subject upon which it can constitutionally operate until the expiration of the terms of the present justices. (Harrison v. Colgan, 148 Cal. 69, 82 Pac. 674.)

The terms of justices of the district court of appeal began to run as soon as that office was created, and not upon their appointment, and any increase in their salary cannot affect persons appointed for that term. (Harrison v. Colgan, 148 Cal. 69, 82 Pac. 674.)

An act which is approved before the beginning of a term, but does not go into effect until after the term commences, cannot affect the salary of officers during that term. (Harrison v. Colgan, 148 Cal. 69, 82 Pac. 674.)

Justices and judges ineligible to other offices.

Sec. 18.   The judges of the supreme court, and the district courts of appeal, and the judges of the superior courts shall be ineligible to any other office or public employment than a judicial office or employment during the term for which they shall have been elected.   (Amendment adopted November 8, 1904.)

[ORIGINAL SECTION.]

Sec. 18.   The justices of the supreme court and judges of the superior courts shall be ineligible to any other office or public employment than a judicial office or employment during the term for which they shall have been elected.

Charges to juries.

Sec. 19.   Judges shall not charge juries with respect to matters of fact, but may state the testimony and declare the law.

INSTRUCTIONS.—A mere statement of the evidence is not in violation of this section. (People v. Christensen, 85 Cal. 568, 24 Pac. 888.)

It is error for the judge to state his impressions of the substance and effect of the testimony without stating its contents, and to tell the jury that other witnesses corroborate certain statements of the prosecuting witness. (People v. Gordon, 88 Cal. 422, 26 Pac. 502.)

An instruction that "the testimony in the case shows" certain facts is violative of this section. (People v. Casey, 65 Cal. 260, 3 Pac. 874.)

A charge which assumes as proven a fact in issue is erroneous. (Caldwell v. Center, 30 Cal. 539, 89 Am. Dec. 131; People v. Dick, 32 Cal. 213.)

As to the effect of this provision on section 2061 of the Code of Civil Procedure, see People v. Paulsell, 115 Cal. 6, 14, 46 Pac. 734.

Improper instructions.—The following particular instructions have been held to violate this section: An instruction that possession of property recently stolen is a strong circumstance of guilt (People v. Cline, 74 Cal. 575, 16 Pac. 391; People v. Titherington, 59 Cal. 598; People v. Ah Sing, 59 Cal. 400); an instruction that the recent possession of stolen goods raises a presumption that the possessor is the thief (People v. Gutierrez, 74 Cal. 81, 15 Pac. 444; People v. Mitchell, 55 Cal. 236); an instruction that the flight of the defendant is strong presumptive evidence of his guilt (People v. Wong Ah Ngow, 54 Cal. 151, 35 Am. Rep. 69); a charge as to the relative value of direct and circumstantial evidence (People v. Vereneseneckockockhoff, 129 Cal. 497, 58 Pac. 156, 62 Pac. 111; People v. O'Brien, 130 Cal. 1, 62 Pac. 297); an instruction that "it may be impossible to show or establish a motive, for the reason that we cannot fathom the mind of the accused on trial, and ascertain if there is not a hidden desire of ven-

geance or some passion to be gratified" (People v. Vereneseneckockoekhoff, 129 Cal. 497, 58 Pac. 156, 62 Pac. 111; People v. Botkin, 132 Cal. 231, 84 Am. St. Rep. 39, 64 Pac. 286); an instruction that certain facts are proper to be taken into consideration by the jury, as throwing doubt upon a certain controverted fact (People v. Lee, 119 Cal. 84, 51 Pac. 22); an instruction that if the jury are satisfied that an attempt to commit rape was made, the evidence must also satisfy them that it was accomplished, and that in the opinion of the judge upon the evidence there could be no conviction of an attempt (People v. Baldwin, 117 Cal. 244, 49 Pac. 186); an instruction that if the prosecutrix committed lewd and immodest acts, she was not of chaste character (People v. Samonset, 97 Cal. 448, 32 Pac. 520); an instruction that the testimony of an accomplice ought to be viewed with distrust, and the evidence of the oral admissions of a party with caution (People v. O'Brien, 96 Cal. 171, 31 Pac. 45; Goss v. Steiger Terra Cotta etc. Works, 148 Cal. 155, 82 Pac. 681); an instruction that, if the testimony is believed, it would undoubtedly make out a case of murder in the first degree, and that it tended to show that the murder was willful (People v. Chew Sing Wing, 88 Cal. 268, 25 Pac. 1099); an instruction that, the testimony of the prosecuting witness not being disputed, the jury were bound to presume it to be true, where there is a conflict as to the facts testified to by such witness (People v. Murray, 86 Cal. 31, 24 Pac. 802); an instruction virtually assuming the testimony of a party to a material fact to be true (Vulicevich v. Skinner, 77 Cal. 239, 19 Pac. 424); an instruction that unless the dam had gates sufficient for certain named purposes, it was insufficiently and negligently constructed (Weiderkind v. Tuolumne County Water Co., 65 Cal. 431, 4 Pac. 415); an instruction that "under the case and proofs as here made no presumption of negligence arises against the defendant from the mere fact that an accident has occurred" (Sullivan v. Market St. Ry. Co., 136 Cal. 479, 69 Pac. 143); an instruction that the condemnation sought is not necessary (Santa Ana v. Gildmacher, 133 Cal. 395, 65 Pac. 883); an instruction that the testimony of an accomplice ought to be viewed with distrust and the evidence of the oral admission of a party with caution (People v. Wardrip, 141 Cal. 229, 74 Pac. 744); an instruction that if the jury believe a particular witness they shall render a verdict accordingly (People v. Barker, 137 Cal. 557, 70 Pac. 617); an instruction assuming that there may be an inference or definite presumption of guilt of the crime of burglary from the mere unexplained fact of possession of stolen property (People v. Boxer, 137 Cal. 562, 70 Pac. 671. See, also, Kerrigan v. Market Street Ry. Co., 138 Cal. 506, 71 Pac. 621); an instruction that to run an engine at a particular rate of speed is negligence (Wyckoff v. Southern Pac. Co., 4 Cal. App. 94, 87 Pac. 203); an instruction that there was no evidence of any conspiracy (People v. King, 4 Cal. App. 213, 87 Pac. 400); an instruction that it is negligence for a person to fail to have a trench (Ryan v. Oakland Gas etc. Co., 10 Cal. App. 484, 102 Pac. 558); an instruction that evidence of previous good character is to be considered "with great caution" (People v. Piner, 11 Cal. App. 542, 105 Pac. 780); an instruction that a person's confession is always admitted against him, for the law presumes that a person will not say anything untrue against himself

or his own interests (People v. Piner, 11 Cal. App. 542, 105 Pac. 780);
an instruction that the absence of motive is a circumstance in favor
of the accused (People v. McGee, 14 Cal. App. 99, 111 Pac. 264); an
instruction that a certain fact constitutes negligence (Manning v.
App Consol. Gold Min. Co., 149 Cal. 35, 84 Pac. 657); an instruction
that it is not negligence on the part of a motorman to assume that
a person will not attempt to cross the track in front of an approaching car, which is so near as to render a collision probable (Bresee v.
Los Angeles Traction Co., 149 Cal. 131, 5 L. R. A. (N. S.) 1059, 85
Pac. 152); an instruction that the defendant is permitted to show
"such circumstances by way of mitigation as would overcome the presumption raised by the law of malice" (Davis v. Hearst, 160 Cal.
143, 116 Pac. 530); an instruction that "You are hereby instructed
that if you entertain a reasonable doubt as to whether any particular witness in this case was or was not an accomplice, you are to give
the benefit of such doubt to the defendant, and for the purpose of
this case you must consider such person and such witness an accomplice" (People v. Brewer, 19 Cal. App. 742, 127 Pac. 808); an instruction cautioning the jury against the testimony of the plaintiff because of his interest in the event of the trial. (Dow v. City of
Oroville, 22 Cal. App. 215, 134 Pac. 197.)

Proper instructions.—On the other hand, the following instructions
have been held not to violate this provision: An instruction that the
jury may consider the circumstance that the defendant fled from arrest (People v. Ross, 115 Cal. 233, 46 Pac. 1059); an instruction that
there is no evidence which would reduce the crime charged to manslaughter (People v. King, 27 Cal. 507, 87 Am. Dec. 95); an instruction that there was evidence tending to show that the watch was
taken near the door, and that the defendant testified that he picked
it up near the counter (People v. Perry, 65 Cal. 568, 4 Pac. 572); an
instruction that possession of stolen goods soon after they were stolen,
unless satisfactorily explained, is a circumstance to be considered in
connection with other suspicious facts, in determining the guilt of the
defendant (People v. Hannon, 85 Cal. 374, 24 Pac. 706); an instruction that the jury might consider the relation of the defendant to
the case in considering his testimony, the consequences to him resulting from the verdict, etc. (People v. O'Brien, 96 Cal. 171, 31 Pac.
45); an instruction that a ratification may be found from an unreasonable delay to object (Hill v. Finigan, 77 Cal. 267, 11 Am. St. Rep. 279,
19 Pac. 494); an instruction as to the credibility of witnesses based
on section 1847 of the Code of Civil Procedure (People v. Matezuski,
11 Cal. App. 465, 105 Pac. 425); an instruction in a prosecution for
rape that the testimony of the prosecutrix need not be corroborated
and that it was sufficient if the jury believed beyond a reasonable
doubt from all the evidence in the case that the crime had been committed (People v. Akey, 163 Cal. 54, 124 Pac. 718); an instruction
that evidence had been introduced as to altercations with, threats
against and assaults upon the deceased by the defendant for the purpose of showing the relations existing between them and the motive,
and that it might be considered as a circumstance in determining
whether defendant was guilty (People v. Wilson, 23 Cal. App. 513, 138
Pac. 971); an instruction that the evidence or nonevidence of a mo-

tive for the commission of the crime was an important question of
fact, and that in criminal cases the proof of the motive is never essential (People v. Wilson, 26 Cal. App. 336, 146 Pac. 1048).

> What are proper subjects of instructions. See note, 72 Am. Dec.
> 538.
>
> Invasion of province of jury. See note, 14 Am. St. Rep. 36.
>
> Instructions on circumstantial evidence. See notes, 97 Am. St.
> Rep. 789, 69 L. R. A. 193.
>
> Instructions on reasonable doubt. See note, 48 Am. St. Rep. 566.
>
> Propriety of instructions containing technical terms. See note,
> 11 Ann. Cas. 622.

Style of process.

Sec. 20.   The style of all process shall be, "The People of
the State of California," and all prosecutions shall be conducted in their name and by their authority.

PROCESS.—The word "process" as used in this section does not
apply to the warrants by which prisoners are held and committed to
the state prison after conviction. (Ex parte Ahern, 103 Cal. 412, 37
Pac. 390.)

The notice to be given to creditors on filing a petition in insolvency
is not process; and even if it were process, the fact that it does not
run in the name of the people of the state of California is not a fatal
error going to the jurisdiction. (Brewster v. Ludekins 19 Cal. 162.)

An action to punish a defendant for the violation of an ordinance
is a criminal action, and must be prosecuted in the name of the
people. (Santa Barbara v. Sherman, 61 Cal. 57.)

An act authorizing the removal of a board of supervisors from office
for delay in fixing water rates "at the suit of any interested party"
is in conflict with this section. (Fitch v. Board of Supervisors, 122
Cal. 285, 54 Pac. 901.)

An order of arrest in a civil action is not "process" within the
meaning of this section. (Dusy v. Helm, 59 Cal. 188.)

If a contempt of the authority of the board of equalization were
a misdemeanor, it would have to be prosecuted in the name of the
people of the state of California and in the ordinary form of procedure, and subject to the common rights of defendants in criminal actions. (People v. Latimer, 160 Cal. 716, 117 Pac. 1051, concurring
opinion by Beatty, C. J.)

A proceeding by a municipal corporation, in its own name and in the
form and with the process of a civil action, to recover the penalty
for a sale of liquor in violation of an ordinance, which results in the
arrest and imprisonment of the defendant for default in payment of
the judgment recovered, violates this section. (Matter of Application of Clark, 24 Cal. App. 389, 141 Pac. 831.)

Clerk and reporter.

Sec. 21.   The supreme court shall appoint a clerk of the
supreme court; provided, however, that any person elected

to the office of clerk of the supreme court before the adoption hereof, shall continue to hold such office until the expiration of the term for which he may have been elected. Said court may also appoint a reporter and not more than three assistant reporters of the decisions of the supreme court and of the district courts of appeal.   Each of the district courts of appeal shall appoint its own clerk.   All the officers herein mentioned shall hold office and be removable at the pleasure of the courts by which they are severally appointed, and they shall receive such compensation as shall be prescribed by law, and discharge such duties as shall be prescribed by law, or by the rules or orders of the courts by which they are severally appointed. (Amendment approved October 10, 1911.)

[AMENDMENT OF 1904.]

Sec. 21. The supreme court may appoint a reporter and not more than three assistant reporters of the decisions of the supreme court and of the district courts of appeal. Each of the district courts of appeal shall appoint its own clerk. All of the officers herein mentioned shall hold office and be removable at the pleasure of the courts by which they are severally appointed, and they shall receive such compensation as shall be prescribed by law, and discharge such duties as shall be prescribed by law, or by the rules or orders of the courts by which they are severally appointed. (Amendment adopted November 8, 1904.)

[ORIGINAL SECTION.]

Sec. 21. The justices shall appoint a reporter of the decisions of the supreme court, who shall hold his office and be removable at their pleasure. He shall receive an annual salary not to exceed twenty-five hundred dollars, payable monthly.

REPORTER OF DECISIONS.—The provision of this section as to the salary of the reporter is prohibitory, and forbids a salary greater than two thousand five hundred dollars. (Smith v. Kenfield, 57 Cal. 138.)

Judges not to practice law.

Sec. 22. No judge of a court of record shall practice law in any court of this state during his continuance in office.

Eligibility of justices and judges.

Sec. 23. No one shall be eligible to the office of a justice of the supreme court, or of a district court of appeal, or of a judge of a superior court, unless he shall have been admit-

ted to practice before the supreme court of the state.
(Amendment adopted November 8, 1904.)

[ORIGINAL SECTION.]

> Sec. 23. No one shall be eligible to the office of justice of the supreme court, or to the office of judge of a superior court, unless he shall have been admitted to practice before the supreme court of the state.

Condition precedent to draft of salary.

Sec. 24. No judge of the supreme court nor of a district court of appeal, nor of a superior court, shall draw or receive any monthly salary unless he shall make and subscribe an affidavit before an officer entitled to administer oaths, that no cause in his court remains pending and undecided, that has been submitted for decision for a period of ninety days. In the determination of causes all decisions of the supreme court and of the district courts of appeal shall be given in writing, and the grounds of the decision shall be stated. When the justices of a district court of appeal are unable to concur in a judgment, they shall give their several opinions in writing and cause copies thereof to be forwarded to the supreme court. (Amendment adopted November 8, 1904.)

[ORIGINAL SECTION.]

> Sec. 24. No judge of a superior court nor of the supreme court shall, after the first day of July, one thousand eight hundred and eighty, be allowed to draw or receive any monthly salary unless he shall take and subscribe an affidavit before an officer entitled to administer oaths, that no cause in his court remains undecided that has been submitted for decision for the period of ninety days.

DECISIONS.—Failure to decide all cases within ninety days does not work a forfeiture of the salary of the judge. (Meyers v. Kenfield, 62 Cal. 512.)

The judge is liable to no penalty for failure to decide a case within the time specified except the penalty prescribed, and he cannot be answerable to an individual for damages for such delay. (Wyatt v. Arnot, 7 Cal. App. 221, 94 Pac. 86.)

Supreme court commission.

Sec. 25. The present supreme court commission shall be abolished at the expiration of its present term of office, and no supreme court commission shall be created or provided for after January 1st, A. D. 1905. (Amendment adopted November 8, 1904.)

ARTICLE VII.

PARDONING POWER.

Section 1. The governor shall have the power to grant reprieves, pardons, and commutations of sentence, after conviction, for all offenses except treason and cases of impeachment, upon such conditions, and with such restrictions and limitations, as he may think proper, subject to such regulations as may be provided by law relative to the manner of applying for pardons. Upon conviction for treason, the governor shall have power to suspend the execution of the sentence until the case shall be reported to the legislature at its next meeting, when the legislature shall either pardon, direct the execution of the sentence, or grant a further reprieve. The governor shall communicate to the legislature, at the beginning of every session, every case of reprieve or pardon granted, stating the name of the convict, the crime for which he was convicted, the sentence, its date, the date of the pardon or reprieve, and the reasons for granting the same. Neither the governor nor the legislature shall have power to grant pardons, or commutations of sentence, in any case where the convict has been twice convicted of felony, unless upon the written recommendation of a majority of the judges of the supreme court.

PARDONING POWER.—The pardoning power is the same as that exercised by the representatives of the English crown in this country in colonial times. (People v. Bowen, 43 Cal. 439, 13 Am. Rep. 148.)

A document signed by the governor releasing a prisoner before the expiration of his term for good behavior does not remove the disability to testify. (Blanc v. Rodgers, 49 Cal. 15.)

A pardon removes the disability to testify, and all disabilities which follow the conviction. (People v. Bowen, 43 Cal. 439, 13 Am. Rep. 148.)

An offender may be pardoned after he has suffered the punishment adjudged for his crime. (People v. Bowen, 43 Cal. 439, 13 Am. Rep. 148.)

An executive act restoring a convicted criminal to the right of citizenship is not a pardon and does not remove the legal infamy and disability. (People v. Bowen, 43 Cal. 439, 13 Am. Rep. 148.)

The pardoning power does not extend to the reinstatement of an attorney excluded from the practice by law or the order of a court. (Cohen v. Wright, 22 Cal. 293, 323.)

The governor may pardon as well before as after trial. (Hatzfield v. Gulden, 7 Watts (Pa.), 152, 32 Am. Dec. 750; York County v. Dalhousen, 45 Pa. 372; Commonwealth v. Hitchman, 46 Pa. 357.)

The pardon may be conditional as well as absolute. (Flavell's Case, 8 Watts & S. (Pa.), 197; People v. Potter, 1 Park. C. C. 47; Ex parte Wells, 18 How. 307, 314, 15 L. Ed. 421, 425.)

If a pardon be obtained by fraud it may be revoked before actual delivery. (Ex parte De Puy, 3 Ben. 307, Fed. Cas. No. 3814; Commonwealth v. Ahl, 43 Pa. 53.)

The pardoning power has no authority to decree a repayment of a fine. (Cook v. Board etc. of Middlesex, 27 N. J. L. 637.)

Delivery is essential to give effect to a pardon. (Matter of De Puy, 3 Ben. 307, 320, Fed. Cas. No. 3814.)

Definition and effect of pardons. See note, 59 Am. Dec. 572.

Conditional pardons. See notes, 111 Am. St. Rep. 108; 7 Ann. Cas. 92; 13 Ann. Cas. 1103; 14 L. R. A. 285.

Power of governor to pardon as confined to offenses against the state. See notes, 19 Ann. Cas. 115; Ann. Cas. 1914A, 484.

Necessity and sufficiency of recital of offense in pardon. See note, 3 Ann. Cas. 646.

Pardon as restoring forfeited office. See note, 19 Ann. Cas. 293.

Right to recall pardon. See note, 22 L. R. A. (N. S.) 238.

Power to impose in pardon conditions extending beyond term of sentence. See notes, 5 L. R. A. (N. S.) 1064; 20 L. R. A. (N. S.) 337; 26 L. R. A. (N. S.) 110.

Effect of pardon on right to disbar attorney convicted of felony. See note, 16 L. R. A. (N. S.) 272.

ARTICLE VIII.

MILITIA.

§ 1. Organization and calling forth of.
§ 2. Device, banner, or flag to be used.

Organization and calling forth of.

Section 1. The legislature shall provide, by law, for organizing and disciplining the militia, in such manner as it may deem expedient, not incompatible with the Constitution and laws of the United States. Officers of the militia shall be elected or appointed in such manner as the legislature shall from time to time direct, and shall be commissioned by the governor. The governor shall have power to call forth the militia to execute the laws of the state, to suppress insurrections, and repel invasions.

MILITIA.—As to the power of the governor to call out the militia, see Stimson's American Statute Law, sec. 298.

An act authorizing the governor to call out the militia when he deemed it necessary to suppress riots or mobs was held unconstitutional. (Green v. State, 15 Lea (Tenn.), 708.)

The mere refusal, by incumbents of offices, to surrender them is not an insurrection, and will not justify employment of the militia. (In re Fire etc. Commrs., 19 Colo. 482, 503, 36 Pac. 234.)

Martial law other than in time of war. See note, 98 Am. St. Rep. 772.

Martial law. See note, Ann. Cas. 1914C, 22.

Device, banner, or flag to be used.

Sec. 2. All military organizations provided for by this Constitution, or any law of this state, and receiving state support, shall, while under arms either for ceremony or duty, carry no device, banner, or flag of any state or nation, except that of the United States or the state of California.

ARTICLE IX.
EDUCATION.

Promotion of intellectual improvement.

Section 1. A general diffusion of knowledge and intelligence being essential to the preservation of the rights and liberties of the people, the legislature shall encourage by all suitable means the promotion of intellectual, scientific, moral, and agricultural improvement.

EDUCATION.—The act of 1880 establishing the state agricultural society, and providing for the exhibition of breeds of horses, etc., and of agricultural, mechanical, and domestic manufactures and productions, is authorized by this section. (Melvin v. State, 121 Cal. 16, 53 Pac. 416; People v. San Joaquin Valley Agr. Assn., 151 Cal. 797, 91 Pac. 740.)

Superintendent of public instruction.

Sec. 2. A superintendent of public instruction shall, at each gubernatorial election after the adoption of this Constitution, be elected by the qualified electors of the state. He shall receive a salary equal to that of the secretary of state, and shall enter upon the duties of his office on the first Monday after the first day of January next succeeding his election.

County superintendents of schools.

Sec. 3. A superintendent of schools for each county shall be elected by the qualified electors thereof at each gubernatorial election; provided, that the legislature may

authorize two or more counties to unite and elect one superintendent for the counties so uniting.

SUPERINTENDENT.—The superintendent of schools is a county
officer. (People v. Babcock, 114 Cal. 559, 46 Pac. 818.)

The superintendent of schools of San Francisco is not affected by
the provision of the County Government Act making the board of
supervisors the appointing power. (People v. Babcock, 114 Cal. 559,
46 Pac. 818.)

The election of superintendent of schools is governed by this constitutional provision, and not by the County Government Act. (Kahn
v. Sutro, 114 Cal. 316, 33 L. R. A. 620, 46 Pac. 87.)

Under a provision of the Consolidation Act providing that officers
appointed to fill vacancies should hold office "until the regular election then next following," a superintendent of schools thus appointed
will only hold till the next general election, and not till the next
gubernatorial election. (People v. Babcock, 123 Cal. 307, 55 Pac.
1017.)

School funds, source and origin, and how appropriated.

Sec. 4. The proceeds of all lands that have been or may
be granted by the United States to this state for the support
of common schools which may be, or may have been, sold
or disposed of, and the five hundred thousand acres of land
granted to the new states under an act of Congress distributing the proceeds of the public lands among the several
states of the Union, approved A. D. one thousand eight hundred and forty-one, and all estates of deceased persons who
may have died without leaving a will or heir, and also such
per cent as may be granted, or may have been granted, by
Congress on the sale of lands in this state, shall be and remain a perpetual fund, the interest of which, together with
all the rents of the unsold lands, and such other means as
the legislature may provide, shall be inviolably appropriated to the support of common schools through out the state.

SCHOOL FUND.—The word "means" includes any fund arising
from annual taxation for school purposes levied under general laws
passed for that purpose. (Crosby v. Lyon, 37 Cal. 242.)

Whenever the legislature raises a fund for the support of common
schools, any contemporaneous or subsequent legislation having for its
object the diversion of such fund to any other purpose is void.
(Crosby v. Lyon, 37 Cal. 242.)

This section does not limit the power of the legislature to declare
that aliens may be heirs. It contemplates some procedure in the nature of office found by which the right of the state shall be ascer-

tained and determined, and legislation providing for the sale of the land. (State v. Smith, 70 Cal. 153, 12 Pac. 121.)

Money raised for the support of the common schools does not become a part of the school fund of the county until it has been apportioned to the several counties by the superintendent of public instruction. (McCord v. Slavin, 143 Cal. 325, 76 Pac. 1104.)

> Power of legislature to authorize appropriation of school or other public lands of state for irrigation purposes. See note, Ann. Cas. 1914B, 338.

System of common schools to be provided.

Sec. 5. The legislature shall provide for a system of common schools by which a free school shall be kept up and supported in each district at least six months in every year, after the first year in which a school has been established.

SCHOOL SYSTEM. — The opportunity for instruction in public schools given by the statutes and Constitution is a legal right, as much as a vested right in property. (Ward v. Flood, 48 Cal. 36, 17 Am. Rep. 405.)

By the Constitution the educational department is made a state, as distinguished from a municipal, care, and the regulation of schools in San Francisco does not remain unchangeable under the Consolidation Act. The Consolidation Act may remain for municipal purposes, yet the educational department, as a state matter, be subject to general laws passed for that purpose. (Earle v. Board of Education, 55 Cal. 489.)

This provision requires the adoption of one system, which shall be applicable to all the common schools. (Kennedy v. Miller, 97 Cal. 429, 32 Pac. 558; San Diego v. Dauer, 97 Cal. 442, 32 Pac. 561; Bruch v. Colombet, 104 Cal. 347, 38 Pac. 45.)

It does not authorize one system for school districts having boards of education, and another system for school districts not having boards of education. (Bruch v. Colombet, 104 Cal. 347, 38 Pac. 45.)

It is within the constitutional power of the legislature to provide for the establishment of separate schools for colored children, and the exclusion of colored children from schools attended by white children. (Wysinger v. Crookshank, 82 Cal. 588, 23 Pac. 54; Ward v. Flood, 48 Cal. 36, 17 Am. Rep. 405.)

But the legislature cannot, while providing a system of education for the youth of the state, exclude from its benefits children merely because of their African descent. (Ward v. Flood, 48 Cal. 36, 17 Am. Rep. 405.)

The conference of the general power on the state board of education "to adopt rules and regulations not inconsistent with the laws of this state . . . for the government of public schools" is in harmony with this section requiring the adoption of one system of common schools which shall be applicable to all the common schools of the state, and the term "system" itself imports a unity of purpose, as well as an

entirety of operation. (San Francisco v. Hyatt, 163 Cal. 346, 125 Pac. 751.)

Separation of white and colored pupils for purposes of education. See note, 13 Ann. Cas. 342.

School system, what to include.

Sec. 6. The public school system shall include day and evening elementary schools, and such day and evening secondary schools, normal schools, and technical schools as may be established by the legislature, or by municipal or district authority. The entire revenue derived from the state school fund and from the general state school tax shall be applied exclusively to the support of day and evening elementary schools; but the legislature may authorize and cause to be levied a special state school tax for the support of day and evening secondary schools and technical schools, or either of such schools, included in the public school system, and all revenue derived from such special tax shall be applied exclusively to the support of the schools for which such special tax shall be levied. (Amendment adopted November 3, 1908.)

[AMENDMENT OF 1902.]

Sec. 6. The public school system shall include primary and grammar schools, and such high schools, evening schools, normal schools, and technical schools as may be established by the legislature, or by municipal or district authority. The entire revenue derived from the state school fund and from the general state school tax shall be applied exclusively to the support of primary and grammar schools; but the legislature may authorize and cause to be levied a special state school tax for the support of high schools and technical schools, or either of such schools, included in the public school system, and all revenue derived from such special tax shall be applied exclusively to the support of the schools for which such special tax shall be levied. (Amendment adopted November 4, 1902.)

[ORIGINAL SECTION.]

Sec. 6. The public school system shall include primary and grammar schools, and such high schools, evening schools, normal schools, and technical schools as may be established by the legislature, or by municipal or district authority; but the entire revenue derived from the state school fund, and the state school tax, shall be applied exclusively to the support of primary and grammar schools.

SCHOOLS AND FUNDS.—High schools are an integral part of our public school system. (Chico High School Board v. Board of Supervisors, 118 Cal. 115, 50 Pac. 275.)

A law providing a special method of levying a tax for high schools, differing from that provided for other school districts, is valid. (People v. Lodi High School Dist., 124 Cal. 694, 57 Pac. 660.)

A statute authorizing county assessors to retain, as their compensation in collecting, fifteen per cent of all poll taxes collected by them, is not in conflict with this section, since the word "exclusively" is directed to the point that the school funds must be applied to the support of primary and grammar schools, to the exclusion of other schools. (San Luis Obispo County v. Felts, 104 Cal. 60, 37 Pac. 780.)

The words "average daily attendance," used in subdivision 4 of section 1858 of the Political Code, in regard to apportionment of funds, mean average daily attendance in the common schools of the district, and do not include the high schools and evening schools. (Stockton School District v. Wright, 134 Cal. 64, 66 Pac. 34.)

All school funds must be applied exclusively to primary and grammar schools. (Stockton District v. Wright, 134 Cal. 64, 66 Pac. 34.)

The provision that the moneys derived from the sale of uncovered lands should be "paid into the school fund of the county where the land lies" was not an "appropriation" of these moneys. (McCord v. Slavin, 143 Cal. 325, 76 Pac. 1104.)

While high schools are part of the public school system, it was intended to make them entirely distinct from primary and grammar schools. (Brown v. City of Visalia, 141 Cal. 372, 74 Pac. 1042.)

The term "public schools" in section 798 of the Municipal Corporation Act does not embrace high schools. (Brown v. City of Visalia, 141 Cal. 372, 74 Pac. 1042.)

Kindergartens are not part of the "primary and grammar" schools, and attendance upon them cannot be considered in apportioning the state school fund. (Los Angeles v. Kirk, 148 Cal. 385, 83 Pac. 250.)

Evening schools having the status of a high school are authorized by the Constitution as a part of the public school system. (Board of Education v. Hyatt, 152 Cal. 515, 93 Pac. 117.)

State and local board of education—Text-books.

Sec. 7. The legislature shall provide for the appointment or election of a state board of education, and said board shall provide, compile, or cause to be compiled, and adopt, a uniform series of text-books for use in the day and evening elementary schools throughout the state. The state board may cause such text-books, when adopted, to be printed and published by the superintendent of state printing, at the state printing office; and wherever and however such text-books may be printed and published, they shall be furnished and distributed by the state free of cost or any charge whatever, to all children attending the day and

evening elementary schools of the state, under such conditions as the legislature shall prescribe. The text-books,
so adopted, shall continue in use not less than four years,
without any change or alteration whatsoever which will require or necessitate the furnishing of new books to such
pupils, and said state board shall perform such other duties
as may be prescribed by law. The legislature shall provide
for a board of education in each county in the state. The
county superintendents and the county boards of education
shall have control of the examination of teachers and the
granting of teachers' certificates within their respective
jurisdictions. (Amendment adopted November 5, 1912.)

[AMENDMENT OF 1911.]

Sec. 7. The governor, the superintehdent of public instruction,
the president of the University of California, and the professor of
pedagogy therein and the principals of the state normal schools,
shall constitute the state board of education, and shall compile, or
cause to be compiled, and adopt a uniform series of text-books for
use in the common schools throughout the state. The state board
may cause such text-books when adopted, to be printed, and published by the superintendent of state printing, at the state printing office; and when so printed and published, to be distributed
and sold at the cost price of printing, publishing and distributing
the same. The text-books, so adopted, shall continue in use not
less than four years, without any change or alteration whatsoever
which will require or necessitate the purchase of new books by
such pupils, and said state board shall perform such other duties
as may be prescribed by law. The legislature shall provide for a
board of education in each county in the state. The county superintendents and the county boards of education shall have control of the examination of teachers and the granting of teachers'
certificates within their respective jurisdictions. (Amendment approved October 10, 1911.)

[AMENDMENT OF 1894.]

Sec. 7. The governor, the superintendent of public instruction,
the president of the University of California, and the professor
of pedagogy therein, and the principals of the state normal schools
shall constitute the state board of education, and shall compile, or
cause to be compiled, and adopt, a uniform series of text-books
for use in the common schools throughout the state. The state
board may cause such text-books, when adopted, to be printed and
published by the superintendent of state printing, at the state
printing office, and, when so printed and published, to be distributed and sold at the cost price of printing, publishing, and distributing the same. The text-books so adopted shall continue in
use not less than four years; and said state board shall perform

such other duties as may be prescribed by law. The legislature
shall provide for a board of education in each county in the state.
The county superintendents and the county boards of education
shall have control of the examination of teachers and the granting
of teachers' certificates within their respective jurisdictions.
(Amendment adopted November 6, 1894.)

[AMENDMENT OF 1885.]

Sec. 7. The governor, superintendent of public instruction, and
the principals of the state normal schools, shall constitute the state
board of education, and shall compile, or cause to be compiled, and
adopt a uniform series of text-books for use in the common schools
throughout the state. The state board may cause such text-books,
when adopted, to be printed and published by the superintendent
of state printing, at the state printing office; and when so printed
and published, to be distributed and sold at the cost price of printing, publishing, and distributing the same. The text-books, so
adopted, shall continue in use not less than four years; and said
state board shall perform such other duties as may be prescribed
by law. The legislature shall provide for a board of education in
each county in the state. The county superintendents and the
county boards of education shall have control of the examination
of teachers and the granting of teachers' certificates within their
respective jurisdiction. (Ratification declared February 12, 1885.)

[ORIGINAL SECTION.]

Sec. 7. The local boards of education, and the boards of supervisors, and the county superintendents of the several counties
which may not have county boards of education, shall adopt a
series of text-books for the use of the common schools within their
respective jurisdictions; the text-books so adopted shall continue
in use for not less than four years; they shall also have control
of the examination of teachers and the granting of teachers' certificates within their several jurisdictions.

TEXT-BOOKS, ETC.—This section is self-executing in so far as it
provides for the selection of text-books by local boards, and operated
as a repeal of the act of 1875, which provided that the text-books in
use in the years 1873, 1874, 1875, should be continued in use until
otherwise provided by statute. (People v. Board of Education, 55
Cal. 331.)

The board of education is a legal body, capable of suing for lots
conveyed to them by the fund commissioners. (Board of Education
v. Fowler, 19 Cal. 11.)

The phrase "local board" applies to the territory over which it exercises jurisdiction as a board. Each board is local as to the territory
of its jurisdiction. The board in a city is local to the city; the board
of a township is local as to the township; and the board of a county
is local as to the county; and where portions of a county are subject
to local boards for such portions, the county board is local as to the
balance of the county. (People v. Board of Education, 55 Cal. 331.)

The provision of this section conferring upon county superintendents and the county board of education "control," etc., is not to be

construed as conferring unlimited or exclusive control, or power to legislate upon that subject, nor as taking away the power of the legislature to prescribe the rules by which the qualifications of teachers shall be determined, and to determine what shall entitle them to a certificate. (Mitchell v. Winnek, 117 Cal. 520, 49 Pac. 579.)

> Statutory regulation of text-books used in public schools. See note, Ann. Cas. 1912B, 476.

Sectarianism prohibited.

Sec. 8. No public money shall ever be appropriated for the support of any sectarian or denominational school, or any school not under the exclusive control of the officers of the public schools; nor shall any sectarian or denominational doctrine be taught or instruction thereon be permitted, directly or indirectly, in any of the common schools of this state.

> **SECTARIAN SCHOOLS.**—An act providing for the commitment of minor criminals to nonsectarian charitable corporations, the expense of maintenance to be paid by the county, is not in violation of this section, since it only applies to schools such as are provided for by the Constitution. (Boys' and Girls' Aid Soc. v. Reis, 71 Cal. 627, 12 Pac. 796.)
>
> > What are sectarian schools or institutions. See note, 8 Am. St. Rep. 411.
> >
> > Religious and sectarian teaching in schools. See notes, 105 Am. St. Rep. 151; 2 Ann. Cas. 522; 19 Ann. Cas. 234.
> >
> > Wearing of religious garb by teacher in public school. See notes, 6 Ann. Cas. 435; Ann. Cas. 1912A, 428.

University fund, creation, management, and application of.

Sec. 9. The University of California shall constitute a public trust, and its organization and government shall be perpetually continued in the form and character prescribed by the organic act creating the same, passed March twenty-third, eighteen hundred and sixty-eight (and the several acts amendatory thereof), subject only to such legislative control as may be necessary to insure compliance with the terms of its endowments, and the proper investment and security of its funds. It shall be entirely independent of all political or sectarian influence, and kept free therefrom in the appointment of its regents, and in the administration of its affairs; provided, that all the moneys derived from the sale of the public lands donated to this state by act of

Congress, approved July second, eighteen hundred and sixty-two (and the several acts amendatory thereof) shall be invested as provided by said acts of Congress, and the interest of said moneys shall be inviolably appropriated to the endowment, support, and maintenance of at least one college of agriculture, where the leading objects shall be (without excluding other scientific and classical studies, and including military tactics), to teach such branches of learning as are related to scientific and practical agriculture and the mechanic arts, in accordance with the requirements and conditions of said acts of Congress; and the legislature shall provide that if, through neglect, misappropriation, or any other contingency, any portion of the funds so set apart shall be diminished or lost, the state shall replace such portion so lost or misappropriated, so that the principal thereof shall remain forever undiminished. No person shall be debarred admission to any of the collegiate departments of the university on account of sex.

UNIVERSITY OF CALIFORNIA.—The University of California is a public corporation. (Estate of Royer, 123 Cal. 614, 44 L. R. A. 364, 56 Pac. 461.)

The regents of the university are not public officers. (Lundy v. Delmas, 104 Cal. 655, 26 L. R. A. 651, 38 Pac. 445.)

After the affiliation of the Hastings College of the Law with the University of California, the legislature had no power to change the form of the government of the college. (People v. Kewen, 69 Cal. 215, 10 Pac. 393.)

The present Constitution raised the University of California to the dignity of a constitutional department or function of the state government. (Williams v. Wheeler, 23 Cal. App. 619, 138 Pac. 937.)

The authorities of the university have the power to make reasonable rules and regulations relating to the health of its students. (Williams v. Wheeler, 23 Cal. App. 619, 138 Pac. 937.)

Leland Stanford Junior University.

Sec. 10. The trusts and estates created for the founding, endowment, and maintenance of the Leland Stanford Junior University, under and in accordance with "An act to advance learning, etc.," approved March ninth, eighteen hundred and eighty-five by the endowment grant executed by Leland Stanford and Jane Lathrop Stanford on the eleventh day of November, A. D. eighteen hundred and eighty-

five, and recorded in liber eighty-three of deeds, at page twenty-three et seq., records of Santa Clara county, and by the amendments of such grant, and by gifts, grants, bequests, and devises supplementary thereto, and by confirmatory grants, are permitted, approved, and confirmed. The board of trustees of the Leland Stanford Junior University, as such, or in the name of the institution, or by other intelligible designation of the trustees or of the institution may receive property, real or personal, and wherever situated, by gift, grant, devise, or bequest, for the benefit of the institution, or of any department thereof, and such property, unless otherwise provided, shall be held by the trustees of the Leland Stanford Junior University upon the trusts provided for in the grant founding the university, and amendments thereof, and grants, bequests, and devises supplementary thereto. The legislature, by special act, may grant to the trustees of the Leland Stanford Junior University corporate powers and privileges, but it shall not thereby alter their tenure, or limit their powers or obligations as trustees. All property now or hereafter held in trust for the founding, maintenance, or benefit of the Leland Stanford Junior University, or of any department thereof, may be exempted by special act from state taxation, and all personal property so held, the Palo Alto farm as described in the endowment grant to the trustees of the university, and all other real property so held and used by the university for educational purposes exclusively, may be similarly exempted from county and municipal taxation; provided, that residents of California shall be charged no fees for tuition unless such fees be authorized by act of the legislature. (Amendment adopted November 6, 1900.)

The California School of Mechanical Arts.

Sec. 11. All property now or hereafter belonging to "The California School of Mechanical Arts," an institution founded and endowed by the late James Lick to educate males and females in the practical arts of life, and incorporated under the laws of the state of California, November twenty-third, eighteen hundred and eighty-five, having its

school buildings located in the city and county of San Francisco, shall be exempt from taxation. The trustees of said institution must annually report their proceedings and financial accounts to the governor. The legislature may modify, suspend, and revive at will the exemption from taxation herein given. (Amendment adopted November 6, 1900.)

The California Academy of Sciences.

Sec. 12. All property now or hereafter belonging to the "California Academy of Sciences," an institution for the advancement of science and maintenance of a free museum, and chiefly endowed by the late James Lick, and incorporated under the laws of the state of California, January sixteenth, eighteen hundred and seventy-one, having its buildings located in the city and county of San Francisco, shall be exempt from taxation. The trustees of said institution must annually report their proceedings and financial accounts to the governor. The legislature may modify, suspend, and revive at will the exemption from taxation herein given. (New section added by amendment approved November 8, 1904.)

Cogswell Polytechnical College.

Sec. 13. All property now or hereafter belonging to the Cogswell Polytechnical College, an institution for the advancement of learning, incorporated under the laws of the state of California, and having its building located in the city and county of San Francisco, shall be exempt from taxation. The trustees of said institution must annually report their proceedings and financial accounts to the governor. The legislature may modify, suspend, and revive at will the exemption from taxation herein given. (New section added by amendment adopted November 6, 1906.)

ARTICLE X.

STATE INSTITUTIONS AND PUBLIC BUILDINGS.

§ 1. State prison directors, appointment and term of office.
§ 2. Authority and duties of.
§ 3. Power of appointment of employees.
§ 4. Allowance for expenses.
§ 5. Powers and duties to be regulated by law.
§ 6. Convict labor to be regulated.

State prison directors, appointment and term of office.

Section 1. There shall be a state board of prison directors, to consist of five persons, to be appointed by the governor, with the advice and consent of the senate, who shall hold office for ten years, except that the first appointed shall, in such manner as the legislature may direct, be so classified that the term of one person so appointed shall expire at the end of each two years during the first ten years, and vacancies occurring shall be filled in like manner. The appointee to a vacancy, occurring before the expiration of a term, shall hold office only for the unexpired term of his predecessor. The governor shall have the power to remove either of the directors for misconduct, incompetency, or neglect of duty after an opportunity to be heard upon written charges.

PRISON DIRECTORS.—Under this section the governor has authority to make an investigation into the conduct of the state board of prison directors with a view of removing them from office. (Chapman v. Stoneman, 63 Cal. 490.)

Authority and duties of.

Sec. 2. The board of directors shall have the charge and superintendence of the state prisons, and shall possess such powers, and perform such duties, in respect to other penal and reformatory institutions of the state, as the legislature may prescribe.

Power of appointment of employees.

Sec. 3. The board shall appoint the warden and clerk, and determine the other necessary officers of the prisons. The board shall have power to remove the wardens and

clerks for misconduct, incompetency, or neglect of duty. All other officers and employees of the prisons shall be appointed by the warden thereof, and be removed at his pleasure.

Allowance for expenses.

Sec. 4. The members of the board shall receive no compensation other than reasonable traveling and other expenses incurred while engaged in the performance of official duties, to be audited as the legislature may direct.

COMPENSATION.—An act allowing the state prison directors mileage and "one hundred dollars for other expenses" is in conflict with this section, since the legislature is not authorized to audit the expenses, but is directed to provide how and before what tribunal or board the expenses shall be audited. (People v. Chapman, 61 Cal. 262.)

Powers and duties to be regulated by law.

Sec. 5. The legislature shall pass such laws as may be necessary to further define and regulate the powers and duties of the board, wardens, and clerks, and to carry into effect the provisions of this article.

Convict labor to be regulated.

Sec. 6. After the first day of January, eighteen hundred and eighty-two, the labor of convicts shall not be let out by contract to any person, copartnership, company, or corporation, and the legislature shall, by law, provide for the working of convicts for the benefit of the state.

ARTICLE XI.

CITIES, COUNTIES, AND TOWNS.

Counties as subdivisions of the state.

Section 1. The several counties, as they now exist, are hereby recognized as legal subdivisions of this state.

COUNTIES.—The people of a county are not a corporation, nor can they sue or be sued, but the county itself is a corporation and the proper party plaintiff. (People v. Myers, 15 Cal. 33.)

To constitute a county something more is required than a law defining its boundaries. A local government must be provided. (People v. McGuire, 32 Cal. 140.)

A county is a part of the state government, and cannot be sued without the consent of the state. (Sharp v. Contra Costa County, 34 Cal. 284.)

The consolidated city and county of San Francisco is included in the designation "county." (Kahn v. Sutro, 114 Cal. 316, 33 L. R. A. 620, 46 Pac. 87.)

At common law an action did not lie against a county; and this was the law of this state until the legislature gave that right in 1854. (Gilman v. Contra Costa County, 8 Cal. 52, 68 Am. Dec. 290.)

The board of supervisors of a county is not the proper party defendant in an action upon a claim against the county. (Hastings v. San Francisco, 18 Cal. 49.)

Counties as municipal corporations. See note, Ann. Cas. 1914C, 968.

Nature of counties. See 7 R. C. L., § 3, p. 923.

Distinction between counties and municipal corporations. See 7 R. C. L., § 5, p. 925.

Removal of county seats.

Sec. 2. No county seat shall be removed unless two-thirds of the qualified electors of the county, voting on the proposition at a general election, shall vote in favor of such removal. A proposition of removal shall not be submitted in the same county more than once in four years.

COUNTY SEATS.—The legislature may delegate the power to the voters of a county to select a county seat. (Upham v. Sutter County Supervisors, 8 Cal. 378.)

County seat. See 7 R. C. L., § 12, p. 934.

New counties, establishment of.

Sec. 3. The legislature, by general and uniform laws, may provide for the alteration of county boundary lines, and for the formation of new counties; provided, however, that no new county shall be established which shall reduce any county to a population of less than twenty thousand; nor shall a new county be formed containing a less population than eight thousand; nor shall any line thereof pass within five miles of the exterior boundary of the city or town in which the county seat of any county proposed to be divided is situated. Every county which shall be enlarged or created from territory taken from any other county or counties, shall be liable for a just proportion of the existing debts and liabilities of the county or counties from which such territory shall be taken. (Amendment adopted November 8, 1910.)

[AMENDMENT OF 1894.]

Sec. 3. The legislature, by general and uniform laws, may provide for the formation of new counties; provided, however, that no new county shall be established which shall reduce any county to a population of less than eight thousand; nor shall a new county be formed containing a less population than five thousand; nor shall any line thereof pass within five miles of the county seat of any county proposed to be divided. Every county which shall be enlarged or created from territory taken from any other county or

counties, shall be liable for a just proportion of the existing debts and liabilities of the county or counties from which such territory shall be taken. (Amendment adopted November 6, 1894.)

[ORIGINAL SECTION.]

Sec. 3. No new county shall be established which shall reduce any county to a population of less than eight thousand; nor shall a new county be formed containing a less population than five thousand; nor shall any line thereof pass within five miles of the county seat of any county proposed to be divided. Every county which shall be enlarged or created from territory taken from any other county or counties, shall be liable for a just proportion of existing debts and liabilities of the county or counties from which such territory shall be taken.

NEW COUNTIES.—The legislature, except as restrained by constitutional limitations, may change the boundaries of counties, consolidate two or more into one, or divide and create new counties out of the territory of one or more existing ones; and may make any provision it sees fit as to a division of the property and debts of such counties. (Los Angeles Co. v. Orange Co., 97 Cal. 329, 32 Pac. 316.)

A newly created county does not become a county until its organization is perfected by the election of its officers. (People v. McGuire, 32 Cal. 140.)

The legislature cannot, in organizing a new county, change the term of the judges as fixed by the Constitution. (People v. Templeton, 12 Cal. 394.)

The last clause of this section relates only to the indebtedness of the county, and does not require any division of the assets of the old county. (Los Angeles Co. v. Orange Co., 97 Cal. 329, 32 Pac. 316.)

The legislature may fix the time at which to properly determine what would be a "just proportion" of the debts and liabilities to be assumed by the new county. (Los Angeles Co. v. Orange Co., 97 Cal. 329, 32 Pac. 316.)

The question of the liability of the new and old counties is purely legislative. (Riverside Co. v. San Bernardino Co., 134 Cal. 517, 66 Pac. 788.)

In creating a new county, it is for the legislature to determine how the debts and property of the county shall be divided and apportioned, and if the commissioners fail by mistake to divide a claim existing in favor of a county against the state, the remedy for such failure is legislative, and not judicial, and the courts have no jurisdiction of an action by the new county to recover its proportion of such claim when paid by the state to the county from which the new county was formed. (Orange Co. v. Los Angeles Co., 114 Cal. 390, 46 Pac. 173.)

The courts have no power to determine what is a "just proportion" under this section. (Tulare Co. v. Kings Co., 117 Cal. 195, 49 Pac. 8.)

Upon the division of a county, if no provision is made by law for any change in the custody of the swamp-land fund, no action will lie on behalf of the new county to recover a share of such fund, but the legislature is the appropriate and only source of relief. (Kings Co. v. Tulare Co., 119 Cal. 509, 51 Pac. 866.)

Where no provision is made as to the property and assets, the old county will be entitled to retain all public property and assets, except such buildings and structures as lie within the limits of the new, and will be liable for its prior obligations. (County of Colusa v. Glenn Co., 124 Cal. 498, 57 Pac. 477.)

When a new county is organized out of a part of the territory before constituting another county, the claim of the old against the new county for payment of the new county's proportion of the debts of the old county is of an equitable nature only, and requires legislation to enable the old county to enforce it. (Beals v. Board of Supervisors, 28 Cal. 449.)

The legislature may require a new county to pay interest upon a debt due to the old. (Beals v. Board of Supervisors, 35 Cal. 624.)

If an equitable claim exists in favor of one county against another arising out of the erection of a new county out of territory taken in part from one county, the legislature may compel the board of supervisors of the county indebted to levy a special tax to pay the same. (People v. Board of Supervisors, 26 Cal. 641.)

Upon the division of a county, with an agreed basis of apportionment of assets, which did not include prior unpaid railroad taxes, the validity of which were disputed, and which were subsequently reassessed to each of the counties upon the basis of their respective railroad mileage, the original county may recover from the new county at least the difference between the amount received by the old county and the amount it would have received upon the agreed basis of apportionment. (San Diego Co. v. Riverside Co., 125 Cal. 495, 58 Pac. 81.)

The prohibition against uniting parts of different counties in forming any legislative district, contained in section 6 of article IV of the Constitution, limits the power of the legislature in framing the general law for the decennial apportionment, but does not affect its power, included in the general grant of legislative power contained in section 1 of article IV, to alter county boundaries from time to time as it may deem best. (Wheeler v. Herbert, 152 Cal. 224, 92 Pac. 353.)

The legislature is not prohibited from changing by special act the boundaries between two or more counties, leaving all of them existing as political subdivisions of the state as before. Such power was vested in the legislature before the amendment of 1894, and the amendment did not change the section in this respect. (Wheeler v. Herbert, 152 Cal. 224, 92 Pac. 353.)

New counties, their relation and that of their officers to old counties. See note, 20 Am. St. Rep. 676.

Legal results of a change of county boundaries and of the erection of a new county out of part of an old one. See note, 85 Am. Dec. 100.

Time of apportionment of assets and liabilities of counties, towns or municipalities in case of division of territory by legislature. See note, 18 Ann. Cas. 324.

Validity of statute creating new county only on ratification of voters within territory affected. See note, Ann. Cas. 1914C, 626.

Alteration and change of boundaries. See 7 R. C. L., §§ 7-10, pp. 928-933.

Apportionment of liabilities. See 7 R. C. L., § 10, p. 932.

County governments to be uniform, under general laws.

Sec. 4. The legislature shall establish a system of county governments which shall be uniform throughout the state; and by general laws shall provide for township organization, under which any county may organize whenever a majority of the qualified electors of such county, voting at a general general election, shall so determine; and, whenever a county shall adopt township organization, the assessment and collection of the revenue shall be made, and the business of such county and the local affairs of the several townships therein shall be managed and transacted in the manner prescribed by such general laws.

COUNTY GOVERNMENT.—The "system" or plan for the government of the several counties must be uniform so that its several parts shall be applicable to each county. (Welsh v. Bramlet, 98 Cal. 219, 33 Pac. 66.)

This section does not deprive the legislature of the power to pass an act requiring boards of supervisors of certain named counties to issue and sell county bonds for the improvement of roads. (People v. Board of Supervisors, 50 Cal. 561.)

A provision of a County Government Act that in counties of a certain class county licenses collected in cities shall be paid into the treasuries of such cities for street improvements is in violation of this section. (San Luis Obispo County v. Graves, 84 Cal. 71, 23 Pac. 1032.)

A provision of the County Goverment Act that in all counties of one particular class certain additional fees shall be collected for filing the inventory in estates of deceased persons is violative of this section. (Bloss v. Lewis, 109 Cal. 493, 41 Pac. 1081.)

The provisions of the County Government Act of 1893 empowering certain of the county officers in counties of one particular class to appoint a certain number of deputies, whose salaries are fixed by the act and made payable out of the county treasury, is valid, although in other counties the principals must pay the salaries of their deputies. (Tulare Co. v. May, 118 Cal. 303, 50 Pac. 427; Freeman v. Barnum, 131 Cal. 386, 82 Am. St. Rep. 355, 63 Pac. 691. Welsh v. Bramlet, 98 Cal. 219, 33 Pac. 66; Walser v. Austin, 104 Cal. 128, 37 Pac. 869, overruled.)

The location of county lines is a political question to be settled by the legislature, and subject to change from time to time as the legislature may direct. (Trinity County v. Mendocino Co., 151 Cal. 279, 90 Pac. 685.)

TOWNSHIP GOVERNMENT.—The provision of this section as to town governments is not self-executing, and the legislature cannot confer upon the inhabitants of a certain territory, who have no town organization, the power to make laws. (Ex parte Wall, 48 Cal. 279, 17 Am. Rep. 425.)

The township government established by the County Government Act is not the township government mentioned in this section. (Longan v. Solano Co., 65 Cal. 122, 3 Pac. 463; Ex parte Wall, 48 Cal. 279, 17 Am. Rep. 425.)

The legislature never has established towns within the meaning of the Constitution. (Ex parte Wall, 48 Cal. 279, 17 Am. Rep. 425.)

Boards of supervisors, election and appointment of.

Sec. 5. The legislature, by general and uniform laws, shall provide for the election or appointment, in the several counties, of boards of supervisors, sheriffs, county clerks, district attorneys, and such other county, township, and municipal officers as public convenience may require, and shall prescribe their duties and fix their terms of office. It shall regulate the compensation of all such officers, in proportion to duties, and may also establish fees to be charged and collected by such officers for services performed in their respective offices, in the manner and for the uses provided by law, and for this purpose may classify the counties by population; and it shall provide for the strict accountability of county and township officers for all fees which may be collected by them, and for all public and municipal moneys which may be paid to them, or officially come into their possession. It may regulate the compensation of grand and trial jurors in all courts within the classes of counties herein permitted to be made; such compensation, however, shall not, in any class, exceed the sum of three dollars per day and mileage. (Amendment adopted November 3, 1908.)

[ORIGINAL SECTION.]

Sec. 5. The legislature, by general and uniform laws, shall provide for the election or appointment, in the several counties, of boards of supervisors, sheriffs, county clerks, district attorneys, and such other county, township, and municipal officers as public convenience may require, and shall prescribe their duties, and fix their terms of office. It shall regulate the compensation of all such officers, in proportion to duties, and for this purpose may classify the counties by population; and it shall provide for the strict accountability of county and township officers for all fees which may be collected by them, and for all public and municipal moneys which may be paid to them, or officially come into their possession.

COUNTY OFFICERS.—Under the former Constitution it was held that the provision requiring a uniform system of county government was merely directory. (People v. Board of Supervisors, 33 Cal. 487.)

But the provision of the present Constitution is mandatory, gives to the legislature exclusive authority to provide for the officers in the several counties, and to fix their terms and duties, provides that this must be done "by general and uniform laws," and that such laws must be uniformly applicable to all the counties of the state. (Welsh v. Bramlet, 98 Cal. 219, 33 Pac. 66.)

The legislature cannot delegate the power given it by this section. (People v. Wheeler, 136 Cal. 652, 69 Pac. 435; City of Woodland v. Leech, 20 Cal. App. 15, 127 Pac. 1040.)

A statute providing for a system of county government, which in its terms is limited to a portion of the state, is in violation of this section. (Hale v. McGettigan, 114 Cal. 112, 45 Pac. 1049.)

Under this provision of the Constitution, and the general laws therein provided for, the burden of prosecuting offenses against state laws and county ordinances is to be borne by the state or county and cannot be imposed upon a city because such prosecutions are to be conducted within its limits. (Fleming v. Hance, 153 Cal. 162, 94 Pac. 620.)

The power of the legislature to prescribe the respective duties of the various classes of county, township and municipal officers, and to regulate their compensation, cannot be doubted. (County of San Luis Obispo v. Murphy, 162 Cal. 588, Ann. Cas. 1913D, 712, 123 Pac. 808.)

Election of officers.—It seems that under this section the legislature has power to provide that all county officers shall be appointed instead of elected. (Barton v. Kalloch, 56 Cal. 95.)

The Constitution does not fix the term of these officers, but merely directs that the legislature shall provide for their election by the people and shall fix by law the duties and compensation. (People v. Brown, 16 Cal. 441.)

When the Constitution declares an office to be elective it cannot be filled in any other mode, but when it has been filled by election, the legislature may extend the term of the incumbent. (Christy v. Board of Supervisors, 39 Cal. 3.)

There is nothing in the Constitution which requires that a person elected district attorney shall be admitted to the bar. (People v. Dorsey, 32 Cal. 296.)

The sheriff as such cannot perform the duties of tax collector. (Lathrop v. Brittain, 30 Cal. 680.)

The legislature is not prohibited from creating more than one revenue district in a county, and providing for the election of assessor and tax collector in each district. (People v. Central Pac. R. R. Co., 43 Cal. 398.)

An act authorizing the district attorney of a county to bring suit in the name of the people to recover delinquent taxes does not interfere with the constitutional duties of the tax collector. (People v. Central Pac. R. R. Co., 43 Cal. 398.)

The term "assessor" does not necessarily mean an officer whose valuations are final. (Savings & Loan Soc. v. Austin, 46 Cal. 415.)

Compensation.—This section only authorizes one mode of fixing the compensation of officers, and that is to adjust the compensation in accordance with their respective duties, under a classification of counties by population made for this purpose. (Knight v. Martin, 128 Cal. 245, 60 Pac. 849; Dwyer v. Parker, 115 Cal. 544, 47 Pac. 372.)

The legislature has power to provide for but one salary as an incident to a county office. (Tout v. Blair, 3 Cal. App. 180, 84 Pac. 671.)

The legislature has power to provide that the salary attached to a public office shall be an incident, not to the title of the office, but to its occupation and exercise. (Tout v. Blair, 3 Cal. App. 180, 84 Pac. 671; Merkley v. Williams, 3 Cal. App. 268, 84 Pac. 1015.)

The sole purpose of the classification provided for by this section is of regulating the compensation of the officers in proportion to their duties. A classification for any other purpose is void. (San Luis Obispo County v. Graves, 84 Cal. 71, 23 Pac. 1032; San Francisco v. Broderick, 125 Cal. 188, 57 Pac. 887; Turner v. Siskiyou Co., 109 Cal. 332, 42 Pac. 434.*)

The salaries and fees allowed by the County Government Act are in full compensation for all services, and the fees collected by the treasurer for collecting the collateral inheritance tax cannot be retained by him for his own use. (San Diego County v. Schwartz, 145 Cal. 49, 78 Pac. 231.)

An act creating a class of counties and designating it by population arbitrarily, and without reference to the classification contained in the general law, is in violation of this section. (San Francisco v. Broderick, 125 Cal. 188, 57 Pac. 887.)

A provision of the fee bill allowing justices of the peace a certain portion of the fees collected by them as their compensation, irrespective of the classification contained in the County Government Act, is invalid. (Dwyer v. Parker, 115 Cal. 544, 47 Pac. 372; Reid v. Groezinger, 115 Cal. 551, 47 Pac. 373.)

An act allowing justices of the peace different fees for the same services in townships classified according to population is in violation of this section. (Tucker v. Barnum, 144 Cal. 266, 77 Pac. 919.)

The act of 1893 providing a special method of collecting fees in cities and counties of over one hundred thousand inhabitants is in violation of this provision. (Rauer v. Williams, 118 Cal. 401, 50 Pac. 691.)

The legislature is not directed to regulate the compensation in accordance with the classification of the counties by population, but in proportion to duties, and as a means of doing that it is authorized to classify the counties according to population. (Longan v. Solano Co., 65 Cal. 122, 3 Pac. 463; Welsh v. Bramlet, 98 Cal. 219, 33 Pac. 66.)

What compensation of an officer should be deemed "in proportion to his duties" is a matter of fact to be ascertained and determined by the legislature, and not by the courts. (Green v. Fresno Co., 95 Cal. 329, 30 Pac. 544.)

---

*In considering the subject of classification, it must be remembered that, while counties can only be classified for the purpose above mentioned, cities and towns may be classified according to population for any purpose. (See note to next section.)

This section does not prevent the legislature from allowing county officers the fees collected in lieu of salaries. (San Luis Obispo County v. Darke, 76 Cal. 92, 18 Pac. 118; Green v. Fresno Co., 95 Cal. 329, 30 Pac. 544. But see Kern Co. v. Fay, 131 Cal. 547, 63 Pac. 857.)

The legislature may provide that some county officers shall receive fees or per diem, and that others shall receive regular salaries. (Vail v. San Diego Co., 126 Cal. 35, 58 Pac. 392.)

The legislature cannot change the measure of compensation of officers fixed by the County Government Act otherwise than by amendment of it, preserving the standard fixed by the Constitution of the classification of counties by population for the purpose of fixing the compensation of officers. (Kiernan v. Swan, 131 Cal. 410, 63 Pac. 768.)

A law fixing the compensation of officers in all counties of a certain class is valid. (Summerland v. Bicknell, 111 Cal. 567, 44 Pac. 232.)

The duty of regulating the compensation of all county officers in proportion to duties cannot be delegated to boards of supervisors. (Dougherty v. Austin, 94 Cal. 601, 16 L. R. A. 161, 28 Pac. 834, 29 Pac. 1092; People v. Johnson, 95 Cal. 471, 31 Pac. 611.)

The provision in this section requiring the legislature to regulate and fix the compensation of county officers in proportion to dues, does not apply to offices created by the legislature under section 14 of this article. (Scott v. Boyle, 164 Cal. 321, 128 Pac. 941.)

Classification.—There is no limit to the number of classes of counties that the legislature may make. (Longan v. Solano, 65 Cal. 122, 3 Pac. 463.)

The legislature can only classify counties for the purpose of fixing salaries of county officers. Official reporters of the superior courts are not such officers. (Pratt v. Browne, 135 Cal. 649, 67 Pac. 1082.)

The legislature may classify townships as well as counties by population for the purpose of regulating the compensation of township officers. (Tucker v. Barnum, 144 Cal. 266, 77 Pac. 919; McCauley v. Culbert, 144 Cal. 276, 77 Pac. 923. But see Sanchez v. Fordyce, 141 Cal. 427, 75 Pac. 56.)

The provision of the County Government Act that, when the population of an existing county shall be reduced by reason of the creation of a new county from the territory thereof, below the class first assumed under that act, it should be the duty of the supervisors of such county to designate the class to which such county has been reduced, is not in conflict with this section. (Kumler v. Board of Supervisors, 103 Cal. 393, 37 Pac. 383.)

The courts will take judicial notice of the population of cities and towns as shown by the United States census returns. (People v. Wong Wang, 92 Cal. 277, 28 Pac. 270; People v. Williams, 64 Cal. 87, 27 Pac. 939; Welsh v. Bramlet, 98 Cal. 219, 33 Pac. 66.)

A county of a particular class is not ipso facto made a county of another class merely by the effect of a new census, but it remains in its original class until reorganized by the board of supervisors. (Hull v. Superior Court, 63 Cal. 174, per McKinstry, J.)

As to when a city of one class passes from one class to another, see Ex parte Halsted, 89 Cal. 471, 26 Pac. 961.

The legislature has no power to arbitrarily place any particular county in any particular class. But where the legislature declares that a particular newly formed county shall belong to a particular class, it will be assumed that the legislature thereby determined the population of such county. (Sanders v. Sehorn, 98 Cal. 227, 33 Pac. 58; People v. McFadden, 81 Cal. 489, 15 Am. St. Rep. 66, 22 Pac. 851.)

The legislature may pass a law regulating the compensation of township officers in counties of any one class. (Johnson v. Gunn, 148 Cal. 745, 84 Pac. 665.)

Under the act of 1901, amending the County Government Act and classifying townships according to population as fixed by the last federal census, a township created after that census and whose population cannot be determined thereby is not governed by that classification. (Chinn v. Gunn, 148 Cal. 755, 84 Pac. 669.)

The adjustment of compensation of justices of the peace by salaries in large cities, and fees in smaller cities, towns and nonurban communities proceeds upon intrinsic differences and is constitutional. (Summerfield v. Dow, 5 Cal. App. 678, 91 Pac. 156.)

The power of the legislature to classify counties by population is a power to be exercised for the limited purpose of enabling the compensation of the various officers to be fixed and adjusted. (Payne v. Murphy, 18 Cal. App. 446, 123 Pac. 350.)

Particular acts.—A provision of the County Government Act conferring power upon the supervisors to authorize the district attorney of any county to appoint an assistant, who shall receive a compensation fixed by the act, is void. (Knight v. Martin, 128 Cal. 245, 60 Pac. 849.)

The provision of the County Government Act of 1893, empowering certain officers of counties of one class to appoint a certain number of deputies, whose salaries are fixed by the act, and made payable out of the county treasury, is valid, although in other counties the principals must pay the salaries of their deputies. (Tulare County v. May, 118 Cal. 303, 50 Pac. 427. Welsh v. Bramlet, 98 Cal. 219, 33 Pac. 66; Walser v. Austin, 104 Cal. 128, 37 Pac. 869, overruled.)

A provision of the County Government Act providing for biennial election of county officers in counties of one particular class is void. (Hale v. McGettigan, 114 Cal. 112, 45 Pac. 1049.)

This section does not authorize the Primary Election Law of 1895, which is expressly confined in its operation to counties of the first and second class. (Marsh v. Hanly, 111 Cal. 368, 43 Pac. 975.)

This section does not authorize the collection in counties of one particular class of a percentage upon the inventory value of the estate for filing the inventory. (Bloss v. Lewis, 109 Cal. 493, 41 Pac. 1081.)

Section 726 of the Code of Civil Procedure, conferring upon the court authority to appoint commissioners to sell mortgaged property, does not violate this provision. (McDermot v. Barton, 106 Cal. 194, 39 Pac. 538.)

The provision of section 1770 of the Political Code as to the compensation of members of county boards of education is valid. (Thom v. Los Angeles County, 136 Cal. 375, 69 Cal. 18.)

The board of supervisors of a county have no power to create the office of license tax collector for the county. (El Dorado Co. v. Meiss,

100 Cal. 268, 34 Pac. 716; Los Angeles Co. v. Lopez, 104 Cal. 257, 38 Pac. 42. People v. Ferguson, 65 Cal. 288, 4 Pac. 4, overruled.)

There is nothing in the Constitution prohibiting the legislature from conferring upon the boards of supervisors of one county the power to lay out, open, and maintain a road in another county. (People v. Board of Suprs., 33 Cal. 487.)

The provision of the County Government Act requiring assessors in counties of one particular class to pay all percentages for the collection of poll taxes into the county treasury is valid. (Summerland v. Bicknell, 111 Cal. 567, 44 Pac. 232.)

Liability of county for expenses of jurors during trial. See note, 17 Ann. Cas. 1232.

Municipal corporations to be formed under general laws.

Sec. 6. Corporations for municipal purposes shall not be created by special laws; but the legislature shall, by general laws, provide for the incorporation, organization, and classification, in proportion to population, of cities and towns, which laws may be altered, amended, or repealed; and the legislature may, by general laws, provide for the performance by county officers of certain of the municipal functions of cities and towns so incorporated, whenever a majority of the electors of any such city or town voting at a general or special election shall so determine. Cities and towns heretofore organized or incorporated may become organized under the general laws passed for that purpose, whenever a majority of the electors voting at a general election shall so determine, and shall organize in conformity therewith. Cities and towns hereafter organized under charters framed and adopted by authority of this Constitution are hereby empowered, and cities and towns heretofore organized by authority of this Constitution may amend their charters in the manner authorized by this Constitution so as to become likewise empowered hereunder, to make and enforce all laws and regulations in respect to municipal affairs, subject only to the restrictions and limitations provided in their several charters, and in respect to other matters they shall be subject to and controlled by general laws. Cities and towns heretofore or hereafter organized by authority of this Constitution may, by charter provision or amendment, provide for the performance by county officers of certain of their municipal functions, whenever the dis-

charge of such municipal functions by county officers is authorized by general laws or by the provisions of a county charter framed and adopted by authority of this Constitution. (Amendment adopted November 3, 1914.)

[AMENDMENT OF 1896.]

Sec. 6. Corporations for municipal purposes shall not be created by special laws; but the legislature, by general laws, shall provide for the incorporation, organization, and classification, in proportion to population, of cities and towns, which laws may be altered, amended, or repealed. Cities and towns heretofore organized or incorporated may become organized under such general laws whenever a majority of the electors voting at a general election shall so determine, and shall organize in conformity therewith; and cities and towns heretofore or hereafter organized, and all charters thereof framed or adopted by authority of this Constitution, except in municipal affairs, shall be subject to and controlled by general laws. (Amendment adopted November 3, 1896.)

[ORIGINAL SECTION.]

Sec. 6. Corporations for municipal purposes shall not be created by special laws; but the legislature, by general laws, shall provide for the incorporation, organization, and classification, in proportion to population, of cities and towns, which laws may be altered, amended, or repealed. Cities and towns heretofore organized or incorporated may become organized under such general laws whenever a majority of the electors voting at a general election shall so determine, and shall organize in conformity therewith; and cities and towns heretofore or hereafter organized, and all charters thereof framed or adopted by authority of this Constitution, shall be subject to and controlled by general laws.

MUNICIPAL CORPORATIONS.—The Constitution does not, ex proprio vigore, create or establish any local, county, or municipal governments. (People v. Provines, 34 Cal. 520.)

Neither does it abolish the municipalities of the state. (In re Guerrero, 69 Cal. 88, 10 Pac. 261.)

Under the Constitution of 1849 the legislature had power to create a municipal corporation by a special law. (People v. Levee Dist. No. 6, 131 Cal. 30, 63 Pac. 676.)

A county is not a corporation for municipal purposes within the meaning of this section. (People v. McFadden, 81 Cal. 489, 15 Am. St. Rep. 66, 22 Pac. 851.)

County as municipal corporation. See note, Ann. Cas. 1914C, 968.

Distinction between counties and municipal corporations. See 7 R. C. L., § 5, p. 925.

A levee district is not a municipal corporation. (People v. Levee Dist. No. 6, 131 Cal. 30, 63 Pac. 676.)

The Sacramento Drainage District organized under the act of 1905 is not a corporation organized for municipal purposes. (People v. Sacramento Drainage Dist., 155 Cal. 373, 103 Pac. 207.)

Reclamation districts are not municipal corporations within the meaning of this section. (Reclamation District No. 70 v. Sherman, 11 Cal. App. 399, 105 Pac. 277.)

An irrigation district is a public corporation. (People v. Selma Irr. Dist., 98 Cal. 206, 32 Pac. 1047.)

Corporations organized by virtue of the Wright Act for the purpose of irrigation are public municipal corporations. (Fallbrook Irr. Dist. v. Bradley, 164 U. S. 112, 41 L. Ed. 369, 17 Sup. Ct. Rep. 56.)

Municipal corporations are not limited to cities and towns; but the legislature may by general laws classify and provide for as many species of municipal corporations as, in its judgment, are demanded by the welfare of the state. (In re Madera Irr. Dist., 92 Cal. 296, 27 Am. St. Rep. 106, 14 L. R. A. 755, 28 Pac. 272, 675.)

Consolidated cities and counties are municipal corporations within the meaning of this section. (Denman v. Broderick, 111 Cal. 96, 43 Pac. 516.)

A reclamation district is a public corporation for municipal purposes, and under the old Constitution might be created by special act. (Swamp Land Dist. No. 150 v. Silver, 98 Cal. 51, 32 Pac. 866.)

The term "municipal" is limited to "governmental," and cannot be extended to commercial purposes. (Low v. Mayor etc. of Marysville, 5 Cal. 214.)

Municipal corporations are but subordinate subdivisions of the state, which may be created, altered, or abolished at the will of the legislature, which may enlarge or restrict their powers, direct the mode of their exercise, and define what acts they may or may not perform, subject to the limitation that the legislature cannot direct the performance of an act which will impair the obligations of a contract. (San Francisco v. Canavan, 42 Cal. 541.)

Under sections 1, 31, and 37 of article IV of the Constitution of 1849, the legislature had the power to create municipal corporations at will, by special laws, and a given territory could be incorporated by it as a municipal corporation without the consent or the acceptance of the inhabitants thereof. (People v. California Fish Co., 166 Cal. 576, 138 Pac. 79.)

Classification.—The object of classifying municipal corporations according to population, and in preventing their creation by special laws, was to avoid the necessity of special legislation. (People v. Henshaw, 76 Cal. 436, 18 Pac. 413.)

This section does not limit the power of classification to purposes of the incorporation and organization of municipalities, but empowers the legislature to classify for the purpose of supplying the general laws required by the varying needs of the municipalities so classified. (Rauer v. Williams, 118 Cal. 401, 50 Pac. 691.)

The power to classify conferred by this section is not limited strictly to purposes of incorporation and organization. (Union Ice Co. v. Rose, 11 Cal. App. 357, 104 Pac. 1006.)

But a law providing the conditions and mode of exercising the power of eminent domain in counties of one particular class is not authorized by this section. (City of Pasadena v. Stimson, 91 Cal. 238, 27 Pac. 604.)

Classification must be founded on some constitutional or natural distinction, and must not be arbitrary. (Darcy v. City of San Jose, 104 Cal. 642, 38 Pac. 500.)

The classification mentioned in this section is one that will include all cities and towns. (Desmond v. Dunn, 55 Cal. 242.)

The "McClure Charter" was, therefore, held unconstitutional, because it excluded from its operation all municipal corporations, except consolidated city and county governments, and because it was also limited to municipal corporations of over one hundred thousand inhabitants, making no provision for those having less population. (Desmond v. Dunn, 55 Cal. 242.)

An act classifying all municipal corporations in the state into six classes according to population is a general law. (Pritchett v. Stanislaus Co., 73 Cal. 310, 14 Pac. 795.)

An act directed at and applicable to one particular named municipal corporation, which takes away a large part of its territory, is special and local. (People v. Common Council, 85 Cal. 369, 24 Pac. 727.)

An act applying to the organization of one particular class of municipal corporations is valid. (Mintzer v. Schilling, 117 Cal. 361, 49 Pac. 209.)

While the legislature cannot pass laws touching the organization and incorporation of municipalities except by conforming to the requirements of the classification act, upon other matters it may pass general and uniform laws applicable either to municipal corporations of a given class or to all of a separate class created by and designated in the act itself, provided some plain reason appears for the limitation to a class, where the law does not apply to all municipalities within the same general category. (Rauer v. Williams, 118 Cal. 401, 50 Pac. 691.)

The act of 1893, providing a special method of collecting fees in cities and counties of over one hundred thousand inhabitants, although in accordance with the general classification of cities, is not authorized by this section, since it only applies to one class without reason why it should not apply to all. (Rauer v. Williams, 118 Cal. 401, 50 Pac. 691.)

The act of 1891 creating police courts in cities having fifteen thousand and under eighteen thousand inhabitants, not being in conformity with the general classification of municipal corporations, is void. (Ex parte Giambonini, 117 Cal. 573, 49 Pac. 732.)

Section 3678 of the Political Code, authorizing the board of supervisors to provide for additional clerical force to enable the recorder to assist the assessor in the performance of his duties, violates this section. (Agard v. Shaffer, 141 Cal. 725, 75 Pac. 343.)

An act providing for boards of election commissioners in cities and counties and counties having one hundred and fifty thousand or more inhabitants is void as an attempt to create a class of municipal corporations for a special purpose, without reference to the existing classification by general law. (Denman v. Broderick, 111 Cal. 96, 43 Pac. 516.)

The legislature cannot by a special act create a class of cities by population of between ten thousand and twenty-five thousand, for the

purpose of increasing the salaries of policemen in a particular city. (Darcy v. City of San Jose, 104 Cal. 642, 38 Pac. 500.)

As to when a city of one class passes from one class to another, see Ex parte Halsted, 89 Cal. 471, 26 Pac. 961.

Validity of statute classifying according to differences in population. See note, 15 Ann. Cas. 856.

Formation.—The provision requiring that a "majority of the electors voting at a general election" must determine the question of organization imports that a majority of all the electors voting at the election is necessary to carry the proposition, and not simply a majority of all the electors who vote upon the proposition. (People v. Berkeley, 102 Cal. 298, 23 L. R. A. 838, 36 Pac. 591.)

In the absence of statutory provisions as to the ownership of property belonging to a school district annexed to a city, real estate belongs to the municipality within which it is located as the result of the annexation. (Vernon School Dist. v. Board of Education, 125 Cal. 593, 58 Pac. 175.)

An act providing for the annexation of territory to a city upon petition of electors of the municipality, to the exclusion of the annexed territory, is valid, if the residents of the annexed territory are fully protected by requiring a majority of the voters thereof to authorize the annexation. (Vernon School Dist. v. Board of Education, 125 Cal. 593, 58 Pac. 175.)

The legislature may delegate to municipal boards the power and discretion to say whether a railroad shall be laid in the streets, and when and under what conditions. (Town of Arcata v. Arcata etc. R. R. Co., 92 Cal. 639, 28 Pac. 676.)

Where territory is excluded from a municipal corporation, the legislature may adjust the burden of the corporate debt. (Johnson v. San Diego, 109 Cal. 468, 30 L. R. A. 178, 42 Pac. 249.)

An act providing for the refunding of the indebtedness of municipal corporations other than cities of the first class is authorized by this section. (Los Angeles v. Teed, 112 Cal. 319, 44 Pac. 580.)

A city or town can be incorporated, although not organized, and the application of general laws should not extend to them until organization takes place, in case the general law for incorporation should make it possible for some period of time to intervene between the act of incorporation and that of organization. (People v. California Fish Co., 166 Cal. 576, 138 Pac. 79.)

Charters.—City charters, except as to municipal affairs, are subject to and controlled by general laws. (Kennedy v. Board of Education, 82 Cal. 483, 22 Pac. 1042; People v. Henshaw, 76 Cal. 436, 18 Pac. 413; Ex parte Halsted, 89 Cal. 471, 26 Pac. 961; Davies v. Los Angeles, 86 Cal. 37, 24 Pac. 771; Ex parte Ah You, 82 Cal. 339, 22 Pac. 929; In re Carrillo, 66 Cal. 3, 4 Pac. 695; Farmer v. Behmer, 9 Cal. App. 773, 100 Pac. 901.)

The legislature may pass general laws affecting municipal corporations without reference to whether such corporations were formed before or after the Constitution of 1879. (Marysville v. County of Yuba, 1 Cal. App. 628, 634, 82 Pac. 975.)

Prior to the amendment of 1896, the only exception to this rule was that such charters were not subject to general laws for the organization and incorporation of municipal corporations, such as the Municipal Corporation Act. (People v. Bagley, 85 Cal. 343, 24 Pac. 716.)

This provision does not apply where there is no general law on a given subject to which the charter relates. (People v. Howard, 94 Cal. 73, 29 Pac. 485.)

The charters of consolidated city and county governments are subject to the control of general laws. (People v. Babcock, 114 Cal. 559, 46 Pac. 818.)

This provision is not to be construed as providing that charter provisions shall be repealed by a general law upon the same subject matter, but only that the operation of the inconsistent charter provision shall be suspended during the paramount operation of the general law. (Byrne v. Drain, 127 Cal. 663, 60 Pac. 433.)

Cities and towns incorporated previously to the new Constitution are subject to and controlled by general laws enacted for the organization of such governments, but the charters of such cities and towns remain in force until a majority of the electors determine to become organized under general laws, or to frame a charter for their own government. (Desmond v. Dunn, 55 Cal. 242; People v. Hammond, 66 Cal. 654, 6 Pac. 741; People v. Pond, 89 Cal. 141, 26 Pac. 648; Ex parte Helm, 143 Cal. 553, 77 Pac. 453.)

A municipality by its charter in the erection of schoolhouses and the issuance of bonds therefor can only run current with, and never counter to, the general laws of the state touching the common school system. (Los Angeles City School Dist. v. Longden, 148 Cal. 380, 83 Pac. 246.)

General Laws.—The following have been held to be general laws within the meaning of this section, and to be superior to city charters: The Vrooman Act, providing for street work in municipalities (Thomason v. Ruggles, 69 Cal. 465, 11 Pac. 20; Thomason v. Ashworth, 73 Cal. 73, 14 Pac. 615; Anderson v. De Urioste, 96 Cal. 404, 31 Pac. 266); the Hartson Act, providing for the election of county, city and county, and township officers in the even-numbered years (Staude v. Board of Election Commrs., 61 Cal. 313); the provision of section 1001 of the Civil Code, providing for the acquisition of private property through the exercise of the right of eminent domain (Santa Cruz v. Enright, 95 Cal. 105, 30 Pac. 197); the provisions of the Political Code as to elections (Fragley v. Phelan, 126 Cal. 383, 58 Pac. 923); subdivision 6 of section 3617 of the Political Code (Security Sav. Bank etc. Co. v. Hinton, 97 Cal. 214, 32 Pac. 3); the provision of the Political Code that all money pertaining to the public school fund shall be paid into the county treasury (Kennedy v. Miller, 97 Cal. 429, 32 Pac. 558); the act of 1889, providing for changing the boundaries of cities (People v. Coronado, 100 Cal. 571, 35 Pac. 162); section 536 of the Civil Code, which allows telegraph and telephone corporations to use rights of way along waters, roads and highways (Van Ness v. Rooney, 160 Cal. 131, 139, 116 Pac. 392); the Whitney Act, which conferred jurisdiction upon the police court of the city of Oak-

land over all misdemeanors (Matter of Application of Westenberg, 167 Cal. 309, 139 Pac. 674). See, also, note to section 25, article IV.

A provision of a city charter fixing the time during which the polls are to be open during a municipal election is not in conflict with the general law, which only refers to state and county elections. (People v. Hill, 125 Cal. 16, 57 Pac. 669.)

The provision of the charter of Los Angeles requiring contracts with the city to be in writing is not subject to the provisions of the general law as to the execution of contracts in general. (Frick v. Los Angeles, 115 Cal. 512, 47 Pac. 250.)

Notwithstanding the general law has defined an obstruction to a sidewalk a public nuisance and punishable as such, a city may make it a misdemeanor to fail to remove an obstruction to a sidewalk, since the municipality might legalize a partial obstruction of a street. (Ex parte Taylor, 87 Cal. 91, 25 Pac. 258.)

A provision of a city charter prescribing the form of the complaint in all actions to recover city taxes, there being no provision of the general law on the subject, is valid. (Stockton v. Western Fire etc. Ins. Co., 73 Cal. 621, 15 Pac. 314.)

A provision of a city charter allowing an assessment of city taxes after the first Monday in March was not superseded by section 8 of article XIII of the Constitution, since that section only has reference to prospective assessments. (Stockton v. Western Fire etc. Ins. Co., 73 Cal. 621, 15 Pac. 314.)

Municipal affairs.—The amendment to this section in 1896 is retro-active and applies to all existing charters, and has the effect to re-move the paramount control of general laws in respect to municipal affairs, and to restore the operation of municipal charters in respect to such affairs. (Byrne v. Drain, 127 Cal. 663, 60 Pac. 433.)

But that amendment did not revive provisions of charters which were void when enacted. (Banaz v. Smith, 133 Cal. 102, 65 Pac. 309; German Sav. etc. Soc. v. Ramish, 138 Cal. 120, 69 Pac. 89, 70 Pac. 1067; Ex parte Sweetman, 5 Cal. App. 577, 90 Pac. 1069.)

In other words, if the charter when adopted treated of a municipal affair which was afterward provided for by the general laws, the char-ter provision was revived by the amendment (Byrne v. Drain, 127 Cal. 663, 60 Pac. 433); but if at the time of the adoption of the char-ter a provision thereof was inconsistent with the general laws, it was void and was not revived by the amendment. (Banaz v. Smith, 133 Cal. 102, 65 Pac. 309.)

Prior to the amendment to this section, the charter of the town of Berkeley was subject to general laws, and a provision therein pre-scribing a penalty for selling liquor in conflict with the Penal Code was void. (Ex parte Sweetman, 5 Cal. App. 577, 90 Pac. 1069.)

The exception of municipal affairs from general legislative control is to be construed as relating wholly to cities and towns exercising municipal functions. It only applies to San Francisco, so far as it exercises municipal functions as distinguished from a county, and the power of the legislature to enact general laws for the government of counties as such, including San Francisco. remains unaffected and unimpaired. (Nicholl v. Koster, 157 Cal. 416, 108 Pac. 302.)

A municipal affair is one which refers to the internal business affairs of the municipality. (Fragley v. Phelan, 126 Cal. 383, 58 Pac. 923.)

The election of a board of freeholders and the adoption of a charter is not a municipal affair. (Fragley v. Phelan, 126 Cal. 383, 58 Pac. 923.)

This provision does not prevent the annexation of additional territory to a city under an act of the legislature, with the consent of the municipality. (People v. Oakland, 123 Cal. 598, 56 Pac. 445.)

Salaries of officers of the police and fire department of a city are municipal affairs. (Popper v. Broderick, 123 Cal. 456, 56 Pac. 53.)

The control of the almshouse of San Francisco is a municipal affair. (Weaver v. Reddy, 135 Cal. 430, 67 Pac. 683.)

Municipal charters supersede the general law upon municipal affairs. (People v. Williamson, 135 Cal. 415, 67 Pac. 504.)

The functions of the board of health created by the charter of the city and county of San Francisco are municipal affairs. (People v. Williamson, 135 Cal. 415, 67 Pac. 504.)

Municipal corporations organized under special charters are not subject to general laws on "municipal affairs." (Ex parte Helm, 143 Cal. 553, 77 Pac. 453; Ex parte Lemon, 143 Cal. 558, 65 L. R. A. 946, 77 Pac. 455.)

The provision of section 3366 of the Political Code forbidding the imposition of a license tax for the purpose of revenue deals with a municipal affair. (Ex parte Helm, 143 Cal. 553, 77 Pac. 453; Ex parte Lemon, 143 Cal. 558, 65 L. R. A. 946, 77 Pac. 455.)

The matter of the registration of voters for a municipal election is a municipal affair. (People v. Worswick, 142 Cal. 71, 75 Pac. 663.)

The regulation of the charges of a public service corporation within the limits of a city is a municipal affair. (Home Tel. & Tel. Co. v. City of Los Angeles, 155 Fed. 554.)

The power to determine boundaries of a proposed town cannot be exercised by the legislature, but must be exercised by subordinate bodies. (Vernon v. Board of Supervisors, 142 Cal. 513, 76 Pac. 253.)

A provision in a city charter conferring upon it power to impose license taxes for the purpose of revenue relates to a "municipal affair" and is superior to the general law forbidding such taxes. (Ex parte Braun, 141 Cal. 204, 74 Pac. 780.)

The school system is a matter of general concern and not a municipal affair. (Hancock v. Board of Education, 140 Cal. 554, 74 Pac. 44.)

The payment of fees of jurors in criminal actions is a state affair. (Jackson v. Baehr, 138 Cal. 266, 71 Pac. 167.)

A county affair is not a "municipal affair." (Popper v. Broderick, 123 Cal. 456, 461, 56 Pac. 53.)

An act requiring the signature of the mayor to the tax levy deals with a municipal affair. (Morton v. Broderick, 118 Cal. 474, 50 Pac. 644.)

The opening of streets in a city is clearly a municipal purpose. (Sinton v. Ashbury, 41 Cal. 525; Byrne v. Drain, 137 Cal. 663, 60 Pac. 433.)

The charter of the city and county of San Francisco superseded the Park and Boulevard Act, as that act related to a municipal affair

and was inconsistent with the charter. (Fritz v. San Francisco, 132 Cal. 373, 64 Pac. 566.)

The municipality is governed by general laws as to municipal affairs as to which the charter is silent. (Fragley v. Phelan, 126 Cal. 383, 58 Pac. 923.)

Conceding that the removal of municipal officers is a municipal affair, that cannot affect the concurrent jurisdiction of the superior court conferred by the general law. (Coffey v. Superior Court, 147 Cal. 525, 82 Pac. 75.)

Where the jurisdiction under the charter in regard to a municipal affair is left untrammeled, unrestrained and uncontrolled by the general law, both may stand. (Coffey v. Superior Court, 147 Cal. 525, 82 Pac. 75.)

The issuance of bonds for the repair of existing schoolhouses and for new schoolhouses is a municipal affair. (Law v. San Francisco, 144 Cal. 384, 77 Pac. 1014.)

The authority given to a city by its charter to issue bonds for the erection of schoolhouses within the city as a "municipal affair" is not exclusive of the power conferred upon the trustees of the school district comprising the city. (Los Angeles City School Dist. v. Longden, 148 Cal. 380, 83 Pac. 246.)

The disposition of fines for misdemeanors punished by virtue of the state law is not a municipal affair. (Marysville v. County of Yuba, 1 Cal. App. 628, 634, 82 Pac. 975.)

The act of 1901 restricting the power of licensing by local legislative bodies for purposes of regulation, does not apply to chartered cities. (In re Diehl, 8 Cal. App. 51, 96 Pac. 98.)

Upon the adoption of the San Francisco charter the Police Pension Act of 1899 (Stats. 1899, p. 57) ceased to be operative in that city and county. (Burke v. Board of Trustees, 4 Cal. App. 235, 87 Pac. 421.)

The removal of a chief of police of a city is a municipal affair. (Dinan v. Superior Court, 6 Cal. App. 217, 91 Pac. 806.)

The acquisition of waterworks by a city is a municipal affair. (Cary v. Blodgett, 10 Cal. App. 463, 102 Pac. 668.)

The adoption of the initiative and referendum is a municipal affair. (In re Pfahler, 150 Cal. 71, 11 Ann. Cas. 911, 11 L. R. A. (N. S.) 1092, 88 Pac. 270.)

The manner of enacting municipal ordinances and resolutions is a municipal affair. (In re Pfahler, 150 Cal. 71, 11 Ann. Cas. 911, 11 L. R. A. (N. S.) 1092, 88 Pac. 270.)

The licensing of forms of vice and crime which are both mala in se and mala prohibita cannot be classed as "municipal affairs." (Farmer v. Behmer, 9 Cal. App. 773, 100 Pac. 901.)

The extension of the jurisdiction of the superior courts to include "probation" work (Juvenile Court Law, Stats. 1909, p. 213) is an exercise of the police powers of the state, through the judicial department; this is not a matter coming within "municipal affairs" within the meaning of that term in the Constitution. (Nicholl v. Koster, 157 Cal. 416, 108 Pac. 302.)

The provision of the section denying the power of the legislature to abrogate or annul the special charters of municipal corporations

antedating its adoption, applies only to organized municipalities, and has no application to a municipality which has never been actually organized. (People v. Wilmington, 151 Cal. 649, 91 Pac. 524.)

The act for the consolidation of municipalities (Stats. 1909, p. 282) is not in conflict with the Constitution. It is in no sense a special law, but its provisions are applicable in every case of contiguous municipalities desiring to consolidate into one municipality, and has a uniform operation in all cases. (Williams v. Board of Trustees, 157 Cal. 711, 109 Pac. 482.)

The annexation of territory to a city is not a municipal affair, but is a matter pertaining to the state at large and within its general powers and functions, and the general law upon that subject controls. (People v. City of Long Beach, 155 Cal. 604, 102 Pac. 664.)

Under its authority to provide by general laws for the incorporation of cities, the legislature can provide for the annexation of territory to existing municipalities. (People v. City of Los Angeles, 154 Cal. 220, 97 Pac. 311.)

The power of the legislature to provide for police and inferior courts in cities and towns is not abridged by this section, where a city having a freeholders' charter has not taken advantage of the permission granted by section 8½ of article XI to include in its charter provision for the establishment of a police court. (Fleming v. Hance, 153 Cal. 162, 94 Pac. 620.)

The fixing of the boundaries of the territory to be annexed to a city or town is not a municipal affair. (People v. Ontario, 148 Cal. 625, 84 Pac. 205.)

The trial and punishment of offenses defined by the laws of the state is not a municipal affair. (Robert v. Police Court, 148 Cal. 131, 82 Pac. 838. Per Beatty, C. J., and Henshaw, J.)

A provision of a charter providing for the removal of municipal officers does not supersede the provisions of the Penal Code conferring jurisdiction of such removal upon the superior court. (Coffey v. Superior Court, 147 Cal. 525, 82 Pac. 75.)

To be "subject to" is "to become subservient to," or "subordinate to," and to control is defined as "to exercise a diverting, restraining or governing influence or to direct, to counteract, to regulate." (Coffey v. Superior Court, 147 Cal. 525, 82 Pac. 75.)

The municipality is governed by general laws as to municipal affairs as to which the charter is silent. (Clouse v. City of San Diego, 159 Cal. 434, 114 Pac. 573.)

The Constitution neither expressly nor impliedly forbids a municipal corporation from engaging in the business of supplying electricity for motive power. (Clark v. Los Angeles, 160 Cal. 30, 116 Pac. 722.)

The question whether and to what extent the streets of a municipality shall be subjected to such secondary uses as the maintenance therein of telegraph and telephone poles and wires is a "municipal affair." (Sunset Tel. & Tel. Co. v. Pasadena, 161 Cal. 265, 118 Pac. 796.)

In the matter of compensation of municipal officers, the charter provisions are paramount and prevail over any general law in conflict therewith existing at the time of the adoption of the charter, or

subsequently enacted by the legislature. (Trefts v. McDougald, 15 Cal. App. 584, 115 Pac. 655.)

Section 751 of the municipal corporation bill, as amended in 1901, authorizing the board of trustees of a city in its discretion to make the city treasurer ex-officio license tax collector, is constitutional. (City of Woodland v. Leech, 20 Cal. App. 15, 127 Pac. 1040.)

Municipalities operating under municipal charters have power to legislate uncontrolled by general law concerning municipal affairs. (Matter of Application of Prentice, 24 Cal. App. 345, 141 Pac. 220.)

City and county governments may be consolidated.

Sec. 7.   City and county governments may be merged and consolidated into one municipal government, with one set of officers, and may be incorporated under general laws providing for the incorporation and organization of corporations for municipal purposes.   The provisions of this Constitution applicable to cities, and also those applicable to counties, so far as not inconsistent or prohibited to cities, shall be applicable to such consolidated government. (Amendment adopted November 6, 1894.)

[ORIGINAL SECTION.]

Sec. 7. City and county governments may be merged and consolidated into one municipal government, with one set of officers, and may be incorporated under general laws providing for the incorporation and organization of corporations for municipal purposes. The provisions of this Constitution applicable to cities, and also those applicable to counties, so far as not inconsistent or not prohibited to cities, shall be applicable to such consolidated government. In consolidated city and county governments, of more than one hundred thousand population, there shall be two boards of supervisors or houses of legislation—one of which, to consist of twelve persons, shall be elected by general ticket from the city and county at large, and shall hold office for the term of four years, but shall be so classified that after the first election only six shall be elected every two years; the other, to consist of twelve persons, shall be elected every two years, and shall hold office for the term of two years. Any vacancy occurring in the office of supervisor, in either board, shall be filled by the mayor or other chief executive officer.

CONSOLIDATED GOVERNMENTS.—There is no constitutional inhibition against incorporating a portion of the inhabitants of a county as a city, or creating a county out of the territory of a city. (People v. Hill, 7 Cal. 97.)

The act consolidating the city and county of San Francisco, commonly known as the Consolidation Act, is constitutional. (People v. Hill, 7 Cal. 97.)

The act to incorporate the city and county of Sacramento did not repeal the law by which the county of Sacramento was created. The

city and county constitute a corporation for some purposes, while they are distinct as to others. (People v. Mullins, 10 Cal. 20.)

The city and county of San Francisco is the successor of the city of San Francisco, which was not destroyed by the consolidation, but continued. (People v. Board of Supervisors, 21 Cal. 668.)

The body politic known as the city and county of San Francisco is a municipal corporation, and in matters of government is to be regarded as a city. But the territory over which that government is exercised, considered in its political and judicial relations to other portions of the state, is a county. (Kahn v. Sutro, 114 Cal. 316, 33 L. R. A. 620, 46 Pac. 87; Crowley v. Freud, 132 Cal. 440, 64 Pac. 696. But see Martin v. Board of Election Commrs., 126 Cal. 404, 58 Pac. 932.)

The word "city," when used in the Constitution, includes a consolidated city and county. (People v. Hoge, 55 Cal. 612; Morgan v. Menzies, 60 Cal. 341.)

The provisions of this section are prospective and apply only to governments merged after the Constitution went into effect. (Wood v. Board of Election Commrs., 58 Cal. 561.)

The provision of this section for two boards of supervisors applied only to general laws or charters passed subsequently to the adoption of the Constitution. (Desmond v. Dunn, 55 Cal. 242.)

Under the provision of this section that the provisions of the Constitution as to cities shall apply to consolidated cities and counties, the provisions of section 6 of this article apply to consolidated cities and counties. (Desmond v. Dunn, 55 Cal. 242.)

The provisions of section 11, article XI, are applicable to consolidated city and county governments. (Ex parte Keeney, 84 Cal. 304, 24 Pac. 34.)

Section 5, article XI, requiring the legislature to provide for the strict accountability of county officers for all fees which may be collected by them, is applicable to consolidated cities and counties. (Rauer v. Williams, 118 Cal. 401, 50 Pac. 691.)

Freeholders' charters for counties.

Sec. 7½. Any county may frame a charter for its own government consistent with and subject to the Constitution (or, having framed such a charter, may frame a new one), and relating to matters authorized by provisions of the Constitution, by causing a board of fifteen freeholders, who have been for at least five years qualified electors thereof, to be elected by the qualified electors of said county, at a general or special election. Said board of freeholders may be so elected in pursuance of an ordinance adopted by the vote of three-fifths of all the members of the board of supervisors of such county, declaring that the public interest requires the election of such board for the purpose of prepar-

ing and proposing a charter for said county, or in pursuance of a petition of qualified electors of said county as hereinafter provided. Such petition, signed by fifteen per centum of the qualified electors of said county, computed upon the total number of votes cast therein for all candidates for governor at the last preceding general election at which a governor was elected, praying for the election of a board of fifteen freeholders to prepare and propose a charter for said county, may be filed in the office of the county clerk. It shall be the duty of said county clerk, within twenty days after the filing of said petition, to examine the same, and to ascertain from the record of the registration of electors of the county, whether said petition is signed by the requisite number of qualified electors. If required by said clerk, the board of supervisors shall authorize him to employ persons specially to assist him in the work of examining such petition, and shall provide for their compensation. Upon the completion of such examination, said clerk shall forthwith attach to said petition his certificate, properly dated, showing the result thereof, and if, by said certificate, it shall appear that said petition is signed by the requisite number of qualified electors, said clerk shall immediately present said petition to the board of supervisors, if it be in session, otherwise at its next regular meeting after the date of such certificate. Upon the adoption of such ordinance, or the presentation of such petition, said board of supervisors shall order the holding of a special election for the purpose of electing such board of freeholders, which said special election shall be held not less than twenty days nor more than sixty days after the adoption of the ordinance aforesaid or the presentation of said petition to said board of supervisors; provided, that if a general election shall occur in said county not less than twenty days nor more than sixty days after the adoption of the ordinance aforesaid, or such presentation of said petition to said board of supervisors, said board of freeholders may be elected at such general election. Candidates for election as members of said board of freeholders shall be nominated by petition, substantially in the same manner as may be provided by general law for

the nomination, by petition of electors, of candidates for county offices, to be voted for at general elections. It shall be the duty of said board of freeholders, within one hundred and twenty days after the result of such election shall have been declared by said board of supervisors, to prepare and propose a charter for said county, which shall be signed in duplicate by the members of said board of freeholders, or a majority of them, and be filed, one copy in the office of the county clerk of said county and the other in the office of the county recorder thereof. Said board of supervisors shall thereupon cause said proposed charter to be published for at least ten times in a daily newspaper of general circulation, printed, published and circulated in said county; provided, that in any county where no such daily newspaper is printed, published and circulated, such proposed charter shall be published for at least three times in at least one weekly newspaper, of general circulation, printed, published and circulated in such county; and provided, that in any county where neither such daily nor such weekly newspaper is printed, published and circulated, a copy of such proposed charter shall be posted by the county clerk in three public places in said county, and on or near the entrance to at least one public schoolhouse in each school district in said county, and the first publication or the posting of such proposed charter shall be made within fifteen days after the filing of a copy thereof, as aforesaid, in the office of the county clerk. Said proposed charter shall be submitted by said board of supervisors to the qualified electors of said county at a special election held not less than thirty days nor more than sixty days after the completion of such publication, or after such posting; provided, that if a general election shall occur in said county not less than thirty days nor more than sixty days after the completion of such publication, or after such posting, then such proposed charter may be so submitted at such general election. If a majority of said qualified electors, voting thereon at such general or special election, shall vote in favor of such proposed charter, it shall be deemed to be ratified, and shall be forthwith submitted to the legislature, if it be in regular session,

otherwise at its next regular session, or it may be submitted
to the legislature in extraordinary session, for its approval
or rejection as a whole, without power of alteration or
amendment. Such approval may be made by concurrent
resolution, and if approved by a majority vote of the members elected to each house, such charter shall become the
charter of such county and shall become the organic law
thereof relative to the matters therein provided, and supersede any existing charter framed under the provisions of
this section, and all amendments thereof, and shall supersede all laws inconsistent with such charter relative to the
matters provided in such charter. A copy of such charter,
certified and authenticated by the chairman and clerk of the
board of supervisors under the seal of said board and attested by the county clerk of said county, setting forth the
submission of such charter to the electors of said county,
and its ratification by them, shall, after the approval of such
charter by the legislature, be made in duplicate, and filed,
one in the office of the secretary of state and the other, after
being recorded in the office of the recorder of said county,
shall be filed in the office of the county clerk thereof, and
thereafter all courts shall take judicial notice of said charter.

The charter, so ratified, may be amended by proposals
therefor submitted by the board of supervisors of the county
to the qualified electors thereof at a general or special election held not less than thirty days nor more than sixty days
after the publication of such proposals for ten times in a
daily newspaper of general circulation, printed, published
and circulated in said county; provided, that in any county
where no such daily newspaper is printed, published and
circulated, such proposed charter shall be published for at
least three times in at least one weekly newspaper, of general circulation, printed, published and circulated in such
county; provided, that in any county where neither such
daily nor such weekly newspaper is printed, published and
circulated, a copy of such proposed charter shall be posted
by the county clerk in three public places in said county,
and on or near the entrance to at least one public school-

house in each school district in said county. If a majority of such qualified electors voting thereon, at such general or special election, shall vote in favor of any such proposed amendment or amendments, or any amendment or amendments proposed by petition as hereinafter provided, such amendment or amendments shall be deemed to be ratified, and shall be forthwith submitted to the legislature, if it be in regular session, otherwise at its next regular session, or may be submitted to the legislature in extraordinary session, for approval or rejection as a whole, without power of alteration or amendment, and if approved by the legislature, as herein provided for the approval of the charter, such charter shall be amended accordingly. A copy of such amendment or amendments shall, after the approval thereof by the legislature, be made in duplicate, and shall be authenticated, certified, recorded and filed as herein provided for the charter, and with like force and effect. Whenever a petition signed by ten per centum of the qualified electors of any county, computed upon the total number of votes cast in said county for all candidates for governor at the last general election, at which a governor was elected, is filed in the office of the county clerk of said county, petitioning the board of supervisors thereof to submit any proposed amendment or amendments to the charter of such county, which amendment or amendments shall be set forth in full in such petition, to the qualified electors thereof, such petition shall forthwith be examined and certified by the county clerk, and if signed by the requisite number of qualified electors of such county, shall be presented to the said board of supervisors, by the said county clerk, as hereinbefore provided for petitions for the election of boards of freeholders. Upon the presentation of said petition to said board of supervisors, said board must submit the amendment or amendments set forth therein to the qualified electors of said county at a general or special election held not less than thirty days nor more than sixty days after the publication or posting of such proposed amendment or amendments in the same manner as hereinbefore provided in the case of the submission of any proposed amendment

or amendments to such charter, proposed and submitted by the board of supervisors. In submitting any such charter, or amendments thereto, any alternative article or proposition may be presented for the choice of the electors, and may be voted on separately without prejudice to others.

Every special election held under the provisions of this section, for the election of boards of freeholders or for the submission of proposed charters, or any amendment or amendments thereto, shall be called by the board of supervisors, by ordinance, which shall specify the purpose and time of such election and shall establish the election precincts and designate the polling places therein, and the names of the election officers for each such precinct. Such ordinance, prior to such election, shall be published five times in a daily newspaper, or twice in a weekly newspaper, if there be no such daily newspaper, printed, published and circulated in said county; provided, that if no such daily or weekly newspaper be printed or published in such county, then a copy of such ordinance shall be posted by the county clerk in three public places in such county and in or near the entrance to at least one public schoolhouse in each school district therein. In all other respects, every such election shall be held and conducted, the returns thereof canvassed and the result thereof declared by the board of supervisors in the same manner as provided by law for general elections. Whenever boards of freeholders shall be elected, or any such proposed charter, or amendment or amendments thereto, submitted, at a general election, the general laws applicable to the election of county officers and the submission of propositions to the vote of electors, shall be followed in so far as the same may be applicable thereto.

It shall be competent, in all charters, framed under the authority given by this section to provide, in addition to any other provisions allowable by this Constitution, and the same shall provide, for the following matters:

1. For boards of supervisors and for the constitution, regulation and government thereof, for the times at which and the terms for which the members of said board shall be elected, for the number of members, not less than three, that

shall constitute such boards, for their compensation and for their election, either by the electors of the counties at large or by districts; provided, that in any event said board shall consist of one member for each district, who must be a qualified elector thereof; and

2. For sheriffs, county clerks, treasurers, recorders, license collectors, tax collectors, public administrators, coroners, surveyors, district attorneys, auditors, assessors and superintendents of schools, for the election or appointment of said officers, or any of them, for the times at which and the terms for which, said officers shall be elected or appointed, and for their compensation, or for the fixing of such compensation by boards of supervisors, and, if appointed, for the manner of their appointments; and

3. For the number of justices of the peace and constables for each township, or for the number of such judges and other officers of such inferior courts as may be provided by the Constitution or general law, for the election or appointment of said officers, for the times at which and the terms for which said officers shall be elected or appointed, and for their compensation, or for the fixing of such compensation by boards of supervisors, and if appointed, for the manner of their appointment; and

4. For the powers and duties of boards of supervisors and all other county officers, for their removal and for the consolidation and segregation of county offices, and for the manner of filling all vacancies occurring therein; provided, that the provisions of such charters relating to the powers and duties of boards of supervisors and all other county officers shall be subject to and controlled by general laws; and

4½. For the assumption and discharge by county officers of certain of the municipal functions of the cities and towns within the county, whenever, in the case of cities and towns incorporated under general laws, the discharge by county officers of such municipal functions is authorized by general law, or whenever, in the case of cities and towns organized under section eight of this article, the discharge by county officers of such municipal functions is authorized by provi-

sions of the charters, or by amendments thereto, of such cities or towns.

5. For the fixing and regulation by boards of supervisors, by ordinance, of the appointment and number of assistants, deputies, clerks, attachés and other persons to be employed, from time to time, in the several offices of the county, and for the prescribing and regulating by such boards of the powers, duties, qualifications and compensation of such persons, the times at which, and terms for which they shall be appointed, and the manner of their appointment and removal; and

6. For the compensation of such fish and game wardens, probation and other officers as may be provided by general law, or for the fixing of such compensation by boards of supervisors.

All elective officers of counties, and of townships, of road districts and of highway construction divisions therein shall be nominated and elected in the manner provided by general laws for the nomination and election of such officers.

All charters framed under the authority given by this section, in addition to the matters herein above specified, may provide as follows:

For officers other than those required by the Constitution and laws of the state, or for the creation of any or all of such offices by boards of supervisors, for the election or appointment of persons to fill such offices, for the manner of such appointment, for the times at which and the terms for which such persons shall be so elected or appointed, and for their compensation, or for the fixing of such compensation by boards of supervisors.

For offices hereafter created by this Constitution or by general law, for the election or appointment of persons to fill such offices, for the manner of such appointment, for the times at which and the terms for which such persons shall be so elected or appointed, and for their compensation, or for the fixing of such compensation by boards of supervisors.

For the formation, in such counties, of road districts for the care, maintenance, repair, inspection and supervision

only of roads, highways and bridges; and for the formation, in such counties, of highway construction divisions for the construction only of roads, highways and bridges; for the inclusion in any such district or division, of the whole or any part of any incorporated city or town, upon ordinance passed by such incorporated city or town authorizing the same, and upon the assent to such inclusion by a majority of the qualified electors of such incorporated city or town, or portion thereof, proposed to be so included, at an election held for that purpose; for the organization, government, powers and jurisdiction of such districts and divisions, and for raising revenue therein, for such purposes, by taxation, upon the assent of a majority of the qualified electors of such districts or divisions, voting at an election to be held for that purpose; for the incurring of indebtedness therefor by such counties, districts or divisions for such purposes respectively, by the issuance and sale, by the counties, of bonds of such counties, districts or divisions, and the expenditure of the proceeds of the sale of such bonds, and for levying and collecting taxes against the property of the counties, districts or divisions, as the case may be, for the payment of the principal and interest of such indebtedness at maturity; provided, that any such indebtedness shall not be incurred without the assent of two-thirds of the qualified electors of the county, district or division, as the case may be, voting at an election to be held for that purpose, nor unless before or at the time of incurring such indebtedness provision shall be made for the collection of an annual tax sufficient to pay the interest on such indebtedness as it falls due, and also for a sinking fund for the payment of the principal thereof on or before maturity, which shall not exceed forty years from the time of contracting the same, and the procedure, for voting, issuing and selling such bonds shall, except in so far as the same shall be prescribed in such charters, conform to general laws for the authorizing and incurring by counties of bonded indebtedness, so far as applicable; provided, further, that provisions in such charters for the construction, care, maintenance, repair, inspection and supervision of roads, highways and bridges for which

aid from the state is granted, shall be subject to such regulations and conditions as may be imposed by the legislature.

Whenever any county has framed and adopted a charter, and the same shall have been approved by the legislature, as herein provided, the general laws adopted by the legislature in pursuance of sections four and five of this article, shall, as to such county, be superseded by said charter as to matters for which, under this section it is competent to make provision in such charter, and for which provision is made therein, except as herein otherwise expressly provided; and except that any such charter shall not affect the tenure of office of the elective officers of the county, or of any district, township or division thereof, in office at the time such charter goes into effect, and such officers shall continue to hold their respective offices until the expiration of the term for which they shall have been elected, unless sooner removed in the manner provided by law.

The charter of any county, adopted under the authority of this section, may be surrendered and annulled with the assent of two-thirds of the qualified electors of such county, voting at a special election, held for that purpose, and to be ordered and called by the board of supervisors of the county upon receiving a written petition, signed and certified as hereinabove provided for the purposes of the adoption of charters, requesting said board to submit the question of the surrender and annulment of such charter to the qualified electors of such county, and, in the event of the surrender and annulment of any such charter, such county shall thereafter be governed under general laws in force for the government of counties.

The provisions of this section shall not be applicable to any county that is consolidated with any city. (Amendment adopted November 3, 1914.)

[ORIGINAL SECTION.]

Sec. 7½. Any county may frame a charter for its own government consistent with and subject to the Constitution (or, having framed such a charter, may frame a new one,) relating to the matters hereinafter in this section specified, and none other, by causing a board of fifteen freeholders, who have been for at least five years qualified electors thereof, to be elected by the qualified

electors of said county, at a general or special election. Said board of freeholders may be so elected in pursuance of an ordinance adopted by the vote of three-fifths of all the members of the board of supervisors of such county, declaring that the public interest requires the election of such board for the purpose of preparing and proposing a charter for said county, or in pursuance of a petition of qualified electors of said county as hereinafter provided. Such petition, signed by fifteen per centum of the qualified electors of said county, computed upon the total number of votes cast therein for all candidates for governor at the last preceding general election at which a governor was elected, praying for the election of a board of fifteen freeholders to prepare and propose a charter for said county, may be filed in the office of the county clerk. It shall be the duty of said county clerk, within twenty days after the filing of said petition, to examine the same, and to ascertain from the record of the registration of electors of the county, whether said petition is signed by the requisite number of qualified electors. If required by said clerk, the board of supervisors shall authorize him to employ persons specially to assist him in the work of examining such petition, and shall provide for their compensation. Upon the completion of such examination, said clerk shall forthwith attach to said petition his certificate, properly dated, showing the result thereof, and if, by said certificate, it shall appear that said petition is signed by the requisite number of qualified electors, said clerk shall immediately present said petition to the board of supervisors, if it be in session, otherwise at its next regular meeting after the date of such certificate. Upon the adoption of such ordinance, or the presentation of such petition, said board of supervisors shall order the holding of a special election for the purpose of electing such board of freeholders, which said special election shall be held not less than twenty days nor more than sixty days after the adoption of the ordinance aforesaid or the presentation of said petition to said board of supervisors; provided, that if a general election shall occur in said county not less than twenty days nor more than sixty days after the adoption of the ordinance aforesaid, or such presentation of said petition to said board of supervisors, said board of freeholders may be elected at such general election. Candidates for election as members of said board of freeholders shall be nominated by petition, substantially in the same manner as may be provided by general law for the nomination, by petition of electors, of candidates for county offices, to be voted for at general elections.

It shall be the duty of said board of freeholders, within one hundred and twenty days after the result of such election shall have been declared by said board of supervisors, to prepare and propose a charter for said county, which shall be signed in duplicate by the members of said board of freeholders, or a majority of them, and be filed, one copy in the office of the county clerk of said county and the other in the office of the county recorder thereof. Said board of supervisors shall thereupon cause said proposed charter to be published for at least ten times in a daily

newspaper of general circulation, printed, published and circulated in said county; provided, that in any county where no such daily newspaper is printed, published and circulated, such proposed charter shall be published for at least three times in at least one weekly newspaper, of general circulation, printed, published and circulated in such county; and provided, that in any county where neither such daily nor such weekly newspaper is printed, published and circulated, a copy of such proposed charter shall be posted by the county clerk in three public places in said county, and on or near the entrance to at least one public schoolhouse in each school district in said county, and the first publication or the posting of such proposed charter shall be made within fifteen days after the filing of a copy thereof, as aforesaid, in the office of the county clerk. Said proposed charter shall be submitted by said board of supervisors to the qualified electors of said county at a special election held not less than thirty days nor more than sixty days after the completion of such publication, or after such posting; provided, that if a general election shall occur in said county not less than thirty days nor more than sixty days after the completion of such publication, or after such posting, then such proposed charter may be so submitted at such general election. If a majority of said qualified electors, voting thereon at such general or special election, shall vote in favor of such proposed charter, it shall be deemed to be ratified, and shall be forthwith submitted to the legislature, if it be in regular session, otherwise at its next regular session, or it may be submitted to the legislature in extraordinary session, for its approval or rejection as a whole, without power of alteration or amendment. Such approval may be made by concurrent resolution, and if approved by a majority vote of the members elected to each house, such charter shall become the charter of such county and shall become the organic law thereof relative to the matters therein provided, and supersede any existing charter framed under the provisions of this section, and all amendments thereof, and shall supersede all laws inconsistent with such charter relative to the matters provided in such charter. A copy of such charter, certified and authenticated by the chairman and clerk of the board of supervisors under the seal of said board and attested by the county clerk of said county, setting forth the submission of said charter to the electors of said county, and its ratification by them, shall, after the approval of such charter by the legislature, be made in duplicate, and filed, one in the office of the secretary of state and the other, after being recorded in the office of the recorder of said county, shall be filed in the office of the county clerk thereof, and thereafter all courts shall take judicial notice of said charter.

The charter, so ratified, may be amended by proposals therefor submitted by the board of supervisors of the county to the qualified electors thereof at a general or special election held not less than thirty days nor more than sixty days after the publication of such proposals for ten times in a daily newspaper of general circulation, printed, published and circulated in said county, provided that in any county where no such daily newspaper is printed,

published and circulated, such proposed charter shall be published for at least three times in at least one weekly newspaper, of general circulation, printed, published, and circulated in such county; provided, that in any county where neither such daily nor such weekly newspaper is printed, published and circulated, a copy of such proposed charter shall be posted by the county clerk in three public places in said county, and on or near the entrance to at least one public schoolhouse in each school district in said county. If a majority of such qualified electors voting thereon, at such general or special election, shall vote in favor of any such proposed amendment or amendments, or any amendment or amendments proposed by petition as hereinafter provided, such amendment or amendments shall be deemed to be ratified, and shall be forthwith submitted to the legislature, if it be in regular session, otherwise at its next regular session, or may be submitted to the legislature in extraordinary session, for approval or rejection as a whole, without power of alteration or amendment, and if approved by the legislature, as herein provided for the approval of the charter, such charter shall be amended accordingly. A copy of such amendment or amendments shall, after the approval thereof by the legislature, be made in duplicate, and shall be authenticated, certified, recorded and filed as herein provided for the charter, and with like force and effect. Whenever a petition signed by ten per centum of the qualified electors of any county, computed upon the total number of votes cast in said county for all candidates for governor at the last general election, at which a governor was elected, is filed in the office of the county clerk of said county, petitioning the board of supervisors thereof to submit any proposed amendment or amendments to the charter of such county, which amendment or amendments shall be set forth in full in such petition, to the qualified electors thereof, such petition shall forthwith be examined and certified by the county clerk, and if signed by the requisite number of qualified electors of such county, shall be presented to the said board of supervisors, by the said county clerk, as hereinbefore provided for petitions for the election of boards of freeholders. Upon the presentation of said petition to said board of supervisors, said board must submit the amendment or amendments set forth therein to the qualified electors of said county at a general or special election held not less than thirty days nor more than sixty days after the publication or posting of such proposed amendment or amendments in the same manner as hereinbefore provided in the case of the submission of any proposed amendment or amendments to such charter, proposed and submitted by the board of supervisors. In submitting any such charter, or amendments thereto, any alternative article or proposition may be presented for the choice of the electors, and may be voted on separately without prejudice to others.

Every special election held under the provisions of this section, for the election of boards of freeholders or for the submission of proposed charters, or any amendment or amendments thereto, shall be called by the board of supervisors, by ordinance, which shall specify the purpose and time of such election and shall establish

the election precincts and designate the polling places therein, and the names of the election officers for each such precinct. Such ordinance, prior to such election, shall be published five times in a daily newspaper, or twice in a weekly newspaper, if there be no such daily newspaper, printed, published and circulated in said county; provided that if no such daily or weekly newspaper be printed or published in such county, then a copy of such ordinance shall be posted by the county clerk in three public places in such county and in or near the entrance to at least one public schoolhouse in each school district therein. In all other respects, every such election shall be held and conducted, the returns thereof canvassed and the result thereof declared by the board of supervisors in the same manner as provided by law for general elections. Whenever boards of freeholders shall be elected, or any such proposed charter, or amendment or amendments thereto, submitted, at a general election, the general laws applicable to the election of county officers and the submission of propositions to the vote of electors, shall be followed in so far as the same may be applicable thereto.

It shall be competent, in all charters, framed under the authority given by this section to provide, in addition to any other provisions allowable by this Constitution, and the same shall provide, for the following matters:

1. For boards of supervisors and for the Constitution, regulation and government thereof, for the times at which and the terms for which the members of said board shall be elected, for the number of members, not less than three, that shall constitute such boards, for their compensation and for their election, either by the electors of the counties at large, or by districts; provided, that in any event said board shall consist of one member for each district, who must be a qualified elector thereof; and

2. For sheriffs, county clerks, treasurers, recorders, license collectors, tax collectors, public administrators, coroners, surveyors, district attorneys, auditors, assessors and superintendents of schools, for the election or appointment of said officers, or any of them, for the times at which, and the terms for which, said officers, shall be elected or appointed, and for their compensation, or for the fixing of such compensation by boards of supervisors, and, if appointed, for the manner of their appointment; and

3. For the number of justices of the peace and constables for each township, or for the number of such judges and other officers of such inferior courts as may be provided by the Constitution or general law, for the election or appointment of said officers, for the times at which and the terms for which said officers shall be elected or appointed, and for their compensation, or for the fixing of such compensation by boards of supervisors, and if appointed, for the manner of their appointment; and

4. For the powers and duties of boards of supervisors and all other county officers, for their removal and for the consolidation and segregation of county offices, and for the manner of filling all vacancies occurring therein; provided, that the provisions of such charters relating to the powers and duties of boards of super-

visors and all other county officers shall be subject to and controlled by general laws; and

5. For the fixing and regulation by boards of supervisors, by ordinance, of the appointment and number of assistants, deputies, clerks, attachés and other persons to be employed, from time to time, in the several offices of the county, and for the prescribing and regulating by such boards of the powers, duties, qualifications and compensation of such persons, the times at which, and terms for which they shall be appointed, and the manner of their appointment and removal; and

6. For the compensation of such fish and game wardens, probation and other officers as may be provided by general law, or for the fixing of such compensation by boards of supervisors.

All elective officers of counties, and of townships, of road districts and of highway construction divisions therein shall be nominated and elected in the manner provided by general laws for the nomination and election of such officers.

All charters framed under the authority given by this section, in addition to the matters hereinabove specified, may provide as follows:

For officers other than those required by the Constitution and laws of the state, or for the creation of any or all of such offices by boards of supervisors, for the election or appointment of persons to fill such offices, for the manner of such appointment, for the times at which and the terms for which such persons shall be so elected or appointed, and for their compensation, or for the fixing of such compensation by boards of supervisors.

For offices hereafter created by this Constitution or by general law, for the election or appointment of persons to fill such offices, for the manner of such appointment, for the times at which and the terms for which such persons shall be so elected or appointed, and for their compensation, or for the fixing of such compensation by boards of supervisors.

For the formation, in such counties, of road districts for the care, maintenance, repair, inspection and supervision only of roads, highways and bridges; and for the formation, in such counties, of highway construction divisions for the construction only of roads, highways and bridges; for the inclusion in any such district or division, of the whole or any part of any incorporated city or town, upon ordinance passed by such incorporated city or town authorizing the same, and upon the assent to such inclusion by a majority of the qualified electors of such incorporated city or town, or portion thereof, proposed to be so included, at an election held for that purpose; for the organization, government, powers and jurisdiction of such districts and divisions, and for raising revenue therein, for such purposes, by taxation, upon the assent of a majority of the qualified electors of such districts or divisions, voting at an election to be held for that purpose; for the incurring of indebtedness therefor by such counties, districts or divisions for such purposes respectively, by the issuance and sale, by the counties, of bonds of such counties, districts or divisions,

and the expenditure of the proceeds of the sale of such bonds, and
for levying and collecting taxes against the property of the counties, districts or divisions, as the case may be, for the payment of
the principal and interest of such indebtedness at maturity; provided, that any such indebtedness shall not be incurred without
the assent of two-thirds of the qualified electors of the county,
district or division, as the case may be, voting at an election to be
held for that purpose, nor unless before or at the time of incurring
such indebtedness provision shall be made for the collection of an
annual tax sufficient to pay the interest on such indebtedness as it
falls due, and also for a sinking fund for the payment of the principal thereof on or before maturity, which shall not exceed forty
years from the time of contracting the same, and the procedure
for voting, issuing and selling such bonds shall, except in so far
as the same shall be prescribed in such charters, conform to general laws for the authorizing and incurring by counties of bonded
indebtedness, so far as applicable; provided, further, that provisions in such charters for the construction, care, maintenance, repair, inspection and supervision of roads, highways and bridges
for which aid from the state is granted, shall be subject to such
regulations and conditions as may be imposed by the legislature.

Whenever any county has framed and adopted a charter, and
the same shall have been approved by the legislature, as herein
provided, the general laws adopted by the legislature in pursuance
of sections 4 and 5 of this article, shall, as to such county, be
superseded by said charter as to matters for which, under this section it is competent to make provision in such charter, and for
which provision is made therein, except as herein otherwise expressly provided, and except that any such charter shall not affect
the tenure of the office of the elective officers of the county, or of
any district, township or division thereof, in office at the time such
charter goes into effect, and such officers shall continue to hold
their respective offices until the expiration of the term for which
they shall have been elected, unless sooner removed in the manner
provided by law.

The charter of any county, adopted under the authority of this
section, may be surrendered and annulled with the assent of two-
thirds of the qualified electors of such county, voting at a special
election, held for that purpose, and to be ordered and called by the
board of supervisors of the county upon receiving a written petition, signed and certified as hereinabove provided for the purposes
of the adoption of charters, requesting said board to submit the
question of the surrender and annulment of such charter to the
qualified electors of such county, and, in the event of the surrender and annulment of any such charter, such county shall thereafter be governed under general laws in force for the government
of counties.

The provisions of this section shall not be applicable to any
county that is consolidated with any city. (New section added
by amendment approved October 10, 1911.)

City or city and county charters, how framed and ratified.

Sec. 8. Any city or city and county containing a population of more than three thousand five hundred inhabitants, as ascertained by the last preceding census taken under the authority of the Congress of the United States or of the legislature of California, may form a charter for its own government, consistent with and subject to this Constitution; and any city, or city and county having adopted a charter may adopt a new one. Any such charter shall be framed by a board of fifteen freeholders chosen by the electors of such city at any general or special election; but no person shall be eligible as a candidate for such board unless he shall have been, for the five years next preceding, an elector of said city. An election for choosing freeholders may be called by a two-thirds vote of the legislative body of such city, and, on presentation of a petition signed by not less than fifteen per cent of the registered electors of such city, the legislative body shall call such election at any time not less than thirty nor more than sixty days from date of the filing of the petition. Any such petition shall be verified by the authority having charge of the registration records of such city or city and county and the expenses of such verification shall be provided by the legislative body thereof. Candidates for the office of freeholders shall be nominated either in such manner as may be provided for the nomination of officers of the municipal government or by petition, substantially in the same manner as may be provided by general laws for the nomination by petition of electors of candidates for public offices to be voted for at general elections. The board of freeholders shall, within one hundred and twenty days after the result of the election is declared, prepare and propose a charter for the government of such city; but the said period of one hundred and twenty days may with the consent of the legislative body of such city be extended by such board not exceeding a total of sixty days. The charter so prepared shall be signed by a majority of the board of freeholders and filed, in the office of the clerk of the legislative body of said city. The legislative body of said city shall within fifteen

days after such filing cause such charter to be published
once in the official paper of said city; (or in case there be no
such paper, in a paper of general circulation); and shall
cause copies of such charter to be printed in convenient
pamphlet form, and shall, until the date fixed for the election upon such charter, advertise in one or more papers of
general circulation published in said city a notice that such
copies may be had upon application therefor. Such charter
shall be submitted to the electors of such city at a date to
be fixed by the board of freeholders, before such filing and
designated on such charter, either at a special election held
not less than sixty days from the completion of the publication of such charter as above provided, or at the general
election next following the expiration of said sixty days.
If a majority of the qualified voters voting thereon at such
general or special election shall vote in favor of such proposed charter, it shall be deemed to be ratified, and shall be
submitted to the legislature, if then in session, or at the next
regular or special session of the legislature. The legislature
shall by concurrent resolution approve or reject such charter as a whole, without power of alteration or amendment;
and if approved by a majority of the members elected to
each house it shall become the organic law of such city or
city and county, and supersede any existing charter and all
laws inconsistent therewith. One copy of the charter so
ratified and approved shall be filed with the secretary of
state, one with the recorder of the county in which such city
is located, and one in the archives of the city; and thereafter the courts shall take judicial notice of the provisions
of such charter. The charter of any city or city and county
may be amended by proposals therefor submitted by the
legislative body of the city on its own motion or on petition
signed by fifteen per cent of the registered electors, or both.
Such proposals shall be submitted to the electors only during the six months next preceding a regular session of the
legislature or thereafter and before the final adjournment of
that session and at either a special election called for that
purpose or at any general or special election. Petitions for
the submission of any amendment shall be filed with the

legislative body of the city or city and county not less than sixty days prior to the general election next preceding a regular session of the legislature. The signatures on such petitions shall be verified by the authority having charge of the registration records of such city or city and county, and the expenses of such verification shall be provided by the legislative body thereof. If such petitions have a sufficient number of signatures the legislative body of the city or city and county shall so submit the amendment or amendments so proposed to the electors. Amendments proposed by the legislative body and amendments proposed by petition of the electors may be submitted at the same election. The amendments so submitted shall be advertised in the same manner as herein provided for the advertisement of a proposed charter, and the election thereon held at a date to be fixed by the legislative body of such city, not less than forty and not more than sixty days after the completion of the advertising in the official paper. If a majority of the qualified voters voting on any such amendment vote in favor thereof it shall be deemed ratified, and shall be submitted to the legislature at the regular session next following such election; and approved or rejected without power of alteration in the same manner as herein provided for the approval or rejection of a charter. In submitting any such charter or amendment separate propositions, whether alternative or conflicting, or one included within the other, may be submitted at the same time to be voted on by the electors separately, and, as between those so related, if more than one receive a majority of the votes, the proposition receiving the larger number of votes shall control as to all matters in conflict. It shall be competent in any charter framed under the authority of this section to provide that the municipality governed thereunder may make and enforce all laws and regulations in respect to municipal affairs, subject only to the restrictions and limitations provided in their several charters and in respect to other matters they shall be subject to general laws. It shall be competent in any charter to provide for the division of the city or city and county governed thereby into boroughs or districts, and to provide

that each such borough or district may exercise such general or special municipal powers, and to be administered in such manner, as may be provided for each such borough or district in the charter of the city or city and county.

The percentages of the registered electors herein required for the election of freeholders or the submission of amendments to charters shall be calculated upon the total vote cast in the city or city and county at the last preceding general state election; and the qualified electors shall be those whose names appear upon the registration records of the same or preceding year. The election laws of such city or city and county shall, so far as applicable govern all elections held under the authority of this section. (Amendment adopted November 3, 1914.)

[AMENDMENT OF 1911.]

Sec. 8. Any city containing a population of more than three thousand five hundred inhabitants as ascertained and established by the last preceding census, taken under the direction of the Congress of the United States, or by a census of said city, taken, subsequent to the aforesaid census, under the direction of the legislative body thereof, under laws authorizing the taking of the census of cities, may frame a charter for its own government, consistent with, and subject to, the Constitution, (or, having framed such a charter, may frame a new one), by causing a board of fifteen freeholders, who shall have been, for at least five years, qualified electors thereof, to be elected by the qualified electors of said city, at a general or special municipal election. Said board of freeholders may be so elected in pursuance of an ordinance adopted by a vote of two-thirds of all the members of the council, or other legislative body, of such city, declaring that the public interest requires the election of such board for the purpose of preparing and proposing a charter for said city, or in pursuance of a petition of qualified electors of said city, as hereinafter provided. Such petition, signed by fifteen per centum of the qualified electors of said city computed upon the total number of votes cast therein for all candidates for governor at the last preceding general election at which a governor was elected, praying for the election of a board of fifteen freeholders to prepare and propose a charter for said city, may be filed in the office of the city clerk thereof. It shall be the duty of said city clerk, within twenty days after the filing of said petition, to examine the same and to ascertain from the record of the registration of electors of the county, showing the registration of electors of said city, whether the petition is signed by the requisite number of qualified electors of such city. If required by said clerk, the council, or other legislative body, of said city shall authorize him to employ persons

specially to assist him in the work of examining such petition, and shall provide for their compensation. Upon the completion of such examination, said clerk shall forthwith attach to said petition his certificate, properly dated, showing the result thereof, and if, by said certificate, it shall appear that said petition is signed by the requisite number of qualified electors, said clerk shall present the said petition to said council, or other legislative body, at its next regular meeting after the date of such certificate. Upon the adoption of such ordinance, or the presentation of such petition, said council, or other legislative body, shall order the holding of a special election for the purpose of electing such board of freeholders, which said special election shall be held not less than twenty days, nor more than sixty days after the adoption of the ordinance aforesaid, or the presentation of said petition to said council, or other legislative body; provided, that if a general municipal election shall occur in said city not less than twenty days, nor more than sixty days, after the adoption of the ordinance aforesaid, or the presentation of said petition to said council, or other legislative body, said board of freeholders may be elected at such general municipal election. Candidates for election as members of said board of freeholders shall be nominated by petition, substantially in the same manner as may be provided by general laws for the nomination by petition of electors of candidates for public offices to be voted for at general elections.

It shall be the duty of said board of freeholders, within one hundred and twenty days after the result of such election shall have been declared by said council, or other legislative body, to prepare and propose a charter for said city, which shall be signed in duplicate by the members of said board of freeholders, or a majority of them, and be filed, one copy in the office of the city clerk of said city, and the other in the office of the county recorder of the county in which said city is situated. Said council, or other legislative body, shall, thereupon, cause said proposed charter to be published for at least ten times, in a daily newspaper of general circulation, printed, published and circulated in said city; provided, that in any city where no such daily newspaper is printed, published and circulated, such proposed charter shall be published, for at least three times, in at least one weekly newspaper of general circulation, printed, published and circulated in said city, and, in any event, the first publication of such proposed charter shall be made within fifteen days after the filing of a copy thereof, as aforesaid, in the office of the city clerk. Such proposed charter shall be submitted by said council, or other legislative body, to the qualified electors of said city at a special election held not less than twenty days, nor more than forty days, after the completion of such publication; provided, that if a general municipal election shall occur in said city not less than twenty days, nor more than forty days, after the completion of such publication, then such proposed charter may be so submitted at such general election. If a majority of such qualified electors voting thereon at such general or special election shall vote in favor of such proposed charter, it shall be deemed to be ratified, and shall be submitted to the legisla-

ture, if it be in regular session, otherwise at its next regular session, or it may be submitted to the legislature in extraordinary session, for its approval or rejection as a whole, without power of alteration or amendment. Such approval may be made by concurrent resolution, and if approved by a majority vote of the members elected to each house, such charter shall become the charter of such city, or, if such city be consolidated with a county, then of such city and county, and shall become the organic law thereof, and supersede any existing charter, (whether framed under the provisions of this section of the Constitution or not,) and all amendments thereof, and all laws inconsistent with such charter. A copy of such charter, certified by the mayor, or other chief executive officer of said city, and authenticated under the seal of such city, setting forth the submission of such charter to the electors of said city, and its ratification by them, shall, after the approval of such charter by the legislature, be made in duplicate and deposited, one in the office of the secretary of state and the other, after being recorded in the office of the recorder of the county in which such city is situated, shall be deposited in the archives of the city, and thereafter all courts shall take judicial notice of said charter.

The charter, so ratified, may be amended by proposals therefor submitted by the council, or other legislative body of the city, to the qualified electors thereof at a general or special municipal election held at intervals of not less than two years (except that charter amendments may be submitted at a general municipal election at an interval of less than two years after the last election on charter amendments provided that no other election on charter amendments has been held since the beginning of the last regular session of the state legislature or shall be held prior to the next regular session of the state legislature), and held not less than twenty days, nor more than forty days after the completion of the publication of such proposals for ten times in a daily newspaper of general circulation, printed, published and circulated in said city, or for three times in at least one weekly newspaper of general circulation, printed, published and circulated in said city, if there be no such daily newspaper. If a majority of such qualified electors voting thereon at such general or special election shall vote in favor of any such proposed amendment or amendments, or any amendment or amendments proposed by petition, as hereinafter provided, such amendment or amendments shall be deemed to be ratified, and shall be forthwith submitted to the legislature, if it be in regular session, otherwise at its next regular session, or may be submitted to the legislature in extraordinary session, for approval or rejection as a whole, without power of alteration or amendment, and if approved by the legislature, as herein provided for the approval of the charter, such charter shall be amended accordingly. A copy of such amendment or amendments shall, after the approval thereof by the legislature, be made in duplicate, and shall be authenticated, certified, recorded and filed as herein provided for the charter, and with like force and effect. Whenever a petition signed by fifteen per centum of the qualified

electors of the city, computed upon the total number of votes cast therein for all candidates for governor at the last preceding general election at which a governor was elected, is filed in the office of the city clerk of said city, petitioning the council, or other legislative body thereof, to submit any proposed amendment or amendments to the charter of such city, which amendment or amendments shall be set forth in full in such petition, to the qualified electors thereof, such petition shall forthwith be examined and certified by the city clerk, and if signed by the requisite number of qualified electors of said city, it shall be presented to the said council, or other legislative body, by the said city clerk, as hereinbefore provided for petitions for the election of boards of freeholders. Upon the presentation of said petition to said council, or other legislative body, said council, or other legislative body, must submit the amendment or amendments set forth in said petition to the qualified electors of said city, at a general or special municipal election, held not less than twenty, nor more than forty, days after the completion of the publication of such proposed amendment or amendments, in the same manner as hereinbefore provided in the case of the submission of any proposed amendment or amendments to such charter, proposed and submitted by the council, or other legislative body. The first publication of any proposed amendment or amendments to such charter so proposed by petition shall be made within fifteen days after the aforesaid presentation of said petition to said council, or other legislative body. In submitting any such charter, amendment or amendments thereto, any alternative article or proposition may be presented for the choice of the electors, and may be voted on separately without prejudice to others.

Every special election held in any city under the provisions of this section, for the election of a board of freeholders, or for the submission of any proposed charter or any amendment or amendments thereto, shall be called by the council, or other legislative body thereof, by ordinance, which shall specify the purpose and time of such election, and shall establish the election precincts and designate the polling places therein, and the names of the election officers for each such precinct. Such ordinance shall, prior to such election, be published five times in a daily newspaper, or twice in a weekly newspaper, if there be no such daily newspaper printed, published and circulated in said city. Such election shall be held and conducted, the returns thereof canvassed, and the result thereof declared by the council, or other legislative body of such city in the manner that is now or may be hereafter provided by general law for such elections in the particulars wherein such provision is now or may hereafter be made therefor, and in all other respects in the manner provided by law for general municipal elections, in so far as the same may be applicable thereto.

Whenever any board of freeholders shall be elected, or any such proposed charter or amendment or amendments thereto shall be submitted at a general municipal election, the laws governing the election of city officers, or the submission of propositions to the vote of electors, shall be followed in so far as the same may be applicable thereto and not inconsistent herewith.

It shall be competent in any charter framed by any city under the authority given in this section, or by amendment to such charter, to provide, in addition to those provisions allowed by this Constitution and by the laws of the state, for the establishment of a borough system of government for the whole or any part of the territory of such city, by which one or more districts may be created therein, which districts shall be known as boroughs, and which shall exercise such special municipal powers as may be granted by such charter, and for the organization, regulation, government and jurisdiction of such boroughs.

All the provisions of this section relating to the city clerk shall, in any city and county, be deemed to relate to the clerk of the legislative body thereof. (Amendment approved October 10, 1911.)

[AMENDMENT OF 1906.]

Sec. 8. Any city containing a population of more than three thousand five hundred inhabitants may frame a charter for its own government, consistent with and subject to the Constitution, (or, having framed such a charter, may frame a new one), by causing a board of fifteen freeholders, who shall have been for at least five years qualified electors thereof, to be elected by the qualified voters of said city at any general or special election, whose duty it shall be, within ninety days after such election, to prepare and propose a charter for such city, which shall be signed in duplicate by the members of such board, or a majority of them, and returned, one copy to the mayor thereof, or other chief executive officer of such city, and the other to the recorder of the county. Such proposed charter shall then be published in two daily newspapers of general circulation in such city, for at least twenty days, and the first publication shall be made within twenty days after the completion of the charter; provided, that in cities containing a population of not more than ten thousand inhabitants, such proposed charter shall be published in one such daily newspaper; and within thirty days after such publication it shall be submitted to the qualified electors of said city at a general or special election, and if a majority of such qualified electors voting thereon shall ratify the same, it shall thereafter be submitted to the legislature for its approval or rejection as a whole, without power of alteration or amendment. Such approval may be made by concurrent resolution, and if approved by a majority vote of the members elected to each house, it shall become the charter of such city, or, if such city be consolidated with a county, then of such city and county, and shall become the organic law thereof, and supersede any existing charter, (whether framed under the provisions of this section of the Constitution or not), and all amendments thereof, and all laws inconsistent with such charter. A copy of such charter, certified by the mayor, or chief executive officer, and authenticated by the seal of such city, setting forth the submission of such charter to the electors, and its ratification by them, shall after the approval of such charter by the legislature, be made in duplicate, and deposited, one in the office of the secretary of state, and the other, after being recorded in said recorder's office shall be deposited in the archives

of the city, and thereafter all courts shall take judicial notice of said charter. The charter, so ratified, may be amended at intervals of not less than two years by proposals therefor, submitted by the legislative authority of the city to the qualified electors thereof at a general or special election held at least forty days after the publication of such proposals for twenty days in a daily newspaper of general circulation in such city, and ratified by a majority of the electors, voting thereon, and approved by the legislature as herein provided for the approval of the charter. Whenever fifteen per cent of the qualified voters of the city shall petition the legislative authority thereof to submit any proposed amendment or amendments to said charter to the qualified voters thereof for approval, the legislative authority thereof must submit the same. In submitting any such charter, or amendments thereto, any alternative article or proposition may be presented for the choice of the voters, and may be voted on separately without prejudice to others. (Amendment adopted November 6, 1906.)

[AMENDMENT OF 1902.]

Sec. 8. Any city containing a population of more than three thousand five hundred inhabitants may frame a charter for its own government, consistent with and subject to the Constitution and laws of this state, by causing a board of fifteen freeholders, who shall have been for at least five years qualified electors thereof, to be elected by the qualified voters of said city at any general or special election, whose duty it shall be, within ninety days after such election to prepare and propose a charter for such city, which shall be signed in duplicate by the members of such board, or a majority of them, and returned, one copy to the mayor thereof, or other chief executive officer of such city, and the other to the recorder of the county. Such proposed charter shall then be published in two daily newspapers of general circulation in such city, for at least twenty days, and the first publication shall be made within twenty days after the completion of the charter; provided, that in cities containing a population of not more than ten thousand inhabitants, such proposed charter shall be published in one such daily newspaper; and within not less than thirty days after such publication it shall be submitted to the qualified electors of said city at a general or special election, and if a majority of such qualified electors voting thereon shall ratify the same, it shall thereafter be submitted to the legislature for its approval or rejection as a whole, without power of alteration or amendment. Such approval may be made by concurrent resolution, and if approved by a majority vote of the members elected to each house, it shall become the charter of such city, or, if such city be consolidated with a county, then of such city and county, and shall become the organic law thereof, and supersede any existing charter and all amendments thereof, and all laws inconsistent with such charter. A copy of such charter, certified by the mayor, or chief executive officer, and authenticated by the seal of such city, setting forth the submission of such charter to the electors, and its ratification by them, shall after the approval of such charter by

the legislature, be made in duplicate, and deposited, one in the office of the secretary of state, and the other, after being recorded in said recorder's office, shall be deposited in the archives of the city, and thereafter all courts shall take judicial notice of said charter. The charter, so ratified, may be amended at intervals of not less than two years by proposals therefor, submitted by the legislative authority of the city to the qualified electors thereof at a general or special election, held at least forty days after the publication of such proposals for twenty days in a daily newspaper of general circulation in such city, and ratified by a majority of the electors voting thereon, and approved by the legislature as herein provided for the approval of the charter. Whenever fifteen per cent of the qualified voters of the city shall petition the legislative authority thereof to submit any proposed amendment or amendments to said charter to the qualified voters thereof for approval, the legislative authority thereof must submit the same. In submitting any such charter, or amendments thereto, any alternative article or proposition may be presented for the choice of the voters, and may be voted on separately without prejudice to others. (Amendment adopted November 4, 1902.)

[AMENDMENT OF 1892.]

Sec. 8. Any city containing a population of more than three thousand five hundred inhabitants may frame a charter for its own government, consistent with and subject to the Constitution and laws of this state, by causing a board of fifteen freeholders, who shall have been for at least five years qualified electors thereof, to be elected by the qualified voters of said city at any general or special election, whose duty it shall be, within ninety days after such election, to prepare and propose a charter for such city, which shall be signed, in duplicate, by the members of such board, or a majority of them, and returned, one copy to the mayor thereof, or other chief executive officer of such city, and the other to the recorder of the county. Such proposed charter shall then be published in two daily newspapers of general circulation in such city, for at least twenty days, and the first publication shall be made within twenty days after the completion of the charter; provided, that in cities containing a population of no more than ten thousand inhabitants such proposed charter shall be published in one such daily newspaper; and within not less than thirty days after such publication it shall be submitted to the qualified electors of said city at a general or special election, and if a majority of such qualified electors voting thereat shall ratify the same, it shall thereafter be submitted to the legislature for its approval or rejection as a whole, without power of alteration or amendment. Such approval may be made by concurrent resolution, and if approved by a majority vote of the members elected to each house, it shall become the charter of such city, or if such city be consolidated with a county, then of such city and county, and shall become the organic law thereof, and supersede any existing charter and all amendments thereof, and all laws inconsistent with such charter. A copy of such charter, certified by the mayor, or chief

executive officer, and authenticated by the seal of such city, setting forth the submission of such charter to the electors, and its ratification by them, shall, after the approval of such charter by the legislature, be made, in duplicate, and deposited, one in the office of the secretary of state, and the other, after being recorded in said recorder's office, shall be deposited in the archives of the city, and thereafter all courts shall take judicial notice of said charter. The charter, so ratified, may be amended at intervals of not less than two years by proposals therefor, submitted by the legislative authority of the city to the qualified electors thereof, at a general or special election, held at least forty days after the publication of such proposals for twenty days in a daily newspaper of general circulation in such city, and ratified by at least three-fifths of the qualified electors voting thereat, and approved by the legislature, as herein provided for the approval of the charter. In submitting any such charter, or amendments thereto, any alternative article or proposition may be presented for the choice of the voters, and may be voted on separately without prejudice to others. (Ratification declared December 30, 1892.)

[AMENDMENT OF 1887.]

Sec. 8. Any city or consolidated city and county, containing a population of more than one hundred thousand inhabitants, may frame a charter for its own government, consistent with and subject to the Constitution and laws of this state, by causing a board of fifteen freeholders, who shall have been for at least five years qualified electors thereof, to be elected by the qualified voters of such city, or city and county, at any general or special election, whose duty it shall be, within one hundred days after such election, to prepare and propose a charter for such city, or city and county, which shall be signed in duplicate by the members of such board, or a majority of them, and returned, one copy thereof to the mayor, or other chief executive officer of such city or city and county, and the other to the recorder of deeds of the county, or city and county. Such proposed charter shall then be published in two daily papers of general circulation in such city, or city and county, for at least twenty days, and such publication shall be commenced within twenty (20) days after the completion of the charter, and within not less than thirty days after the completion of such publication, it shall be submitted by the legislative authority of said city, or city and county, to the qualified electors thereof at a general or special election, and if a majority of such qualified electors voting thereat shall ratify the same, it shall thereafter be submitted to the legislature for its approval or rejection as a whole, without power of alteration or amendment; and if approved by a majority vote of the members elected to each house, it shall become the charter of such city, or if such city be consolidated with a county, then of such city and county, and shall become the organic law thereof, and supersede any existing charter and all amendments thereof, and all special laws inconsistent with such charter. A copy of such charter, certified by the mayor or other chief executive officer, and authenticated by the seal of such city,

or city and county, setting forth the submission of such charter to the electors, and its ratification by them, shall be made in duplicate, and deposited, one in the office of the secretary of state, the other, after being recorded in the office of the recorder of deeds of the county, or city and county, among the archives of the city, or city and county. All courts shall take judicial notice thereof. The charter so ratified may be amended at intervals of not less than two years, by proposals therefor submitted by legislative authority of this city, or city and county, to the qualified voters thereof at a general or special election held at least sixty days after the publication of such proposals, and ratified by at least three-fifths of the qualified electors voting thereat, and approved by the legislature as herein provided, for the approval of the charter. In submitting any such charter, or amendment thereto, any alternative article or proposition may be presented for the choice of the voters, and may be voted on separately without prejudice to others. Any city, or consolidated city or county, containing a population of more than ten thousand and not more than one hundred thousand inhabitants, may frame a charter for its own government, consistent with and subject to the Constitution and laws of the state, by causing a board of fifteen freeholders, who shall have been for at least five years qualified electors thereof, to be elected by the qualified voters of said city, or city and county, at any general or special election, whose duty it shall be, within ninety days after such election, to prepare and propose a charter for such city, or city and county, which shall be signed in duplicate by the members of such board, or a majority of them, and returned, one copy thereof to the mayor, or other chief executive officer of said city or city and county, and the other to the recorder of the county, or city and county. Such proposed charter shall then be published in two daily papers of general circulation in such city, or city and county, for at least twenty days, and publication shall be commenced within twenty days after the completion of the charter; and within not less than thirty days after the completion of such publication it shall be submitted by the legislative authority of said city, or city and county, to the qualified electors of said city, or city and county, at a general or special election, and if a majority of such qualified electors voting thereat shall ratify the same, it shall thereafter be submitted to the legislature for its approval or rejection as a whole, without power of alteration or amendment, and if approved by a majority vote of the members elected to each house, it shall become the charter of such city, or if such city be consolidated with a county, then of such city and county, and shall become the organic law thereof, and shall supersede any existing charter and all amendments thereof, and all special laws inconsistent with such charter. A copy of such charter, certified by the mayor, or other chief executive officer, and authenticated by the seal of such city, or city and county, setting forth the submission of such charter to the electors, and its ratification by them, shall be made in duplicate, and deposited, one in the office of the secretary of state, and the other, after being recorded in the office of the recorder of deeds of the county,

or city and county, among the archives of the city, or city and county; and thereafter all courts shall take judicial notice thereof. The charter so ratified may be amended, at intervals of not less than two years, by proposals therefor, submitted by the legislative authority of the city, or city and county, to the qualified electors thereof, at a general or special election held at least sixty days after the publication of such proposals, and ratified by at least three-fifths of the qualified electors voting thereat, and approved by the legislature as herein provided for the approval of the charter. In submitting any such charter, or amendment thereto, any alternative article or proposition may be presented for the choice of the voters, and may be voted on separately without prejudice to others.

[ORIGINAL SECTION.]

Sec. 8. Any city containing a population of more than one hundred thousand inhabitants may frame a charter for its own government, consistent with and subject to the Constitution and laws of this state, by causing a board of fifteen freeholders, who shall have been for at least five years qualified electors thereof, to be elected by the qualified voters of such city, at any general or special election, whose duty it shall be, within ninety days after such election, to prepare and propose a charter for such city, which shall be signed in duplicate by the members of such board, or a majority of them, and returned one copy thereof to the mayor, or other chief executive officer of such city, and the other to the recorder of deeds of the county. Such proposed charter shall then be published in two daily papers of general circulation in such city for at least twenty days, and within not less than thirty days after such publication it shall be submitted to the qualified electors of such city at a general or special election, and if a majority of such qualified electors voting thereat shall ratify the same, it shall thereafter be submitted to the legislature for its approval or rejection as a whole, without power of alteration or amendment, and if approved by a majority vote of the members elected to each house, it shall become the charter of such city, or if such city be consolidated with a county, then of such city and county, and shall become the organic law thereof, and supersede any existing charter and all amendments thereof, and all special laws inconsistent with such charter. A copy of such charter, certified by the mayor, or chief executive officer and authenticated by the seal of such city, setting forth the submission of such charter to the electors, and its ratification by them, shall be made in duplicate, and deposited, one in the office of the secretary of state, the other, after being recorded in the office of the recorder of deeds of the county, or city and county, among the archives of the city, all courts shall take judicial notice thereof. The charter so ratified may be amended at intervals of not less than two years, by proposals therefor submitted by legislative authority of the city, to the qualified voters thereof at a general or special election held at least sixty days after the publication of such proposals, and ratified by at least three-fifths of the qualified electors voting thereat, and approved

by the legislature as herein provided for the approval of the charter. In submitting any such charter, or amendment thereto, any alternative article or proposition may be presented for the choice of voters, and may be voted on separately without prejudice to others.

CHARTERS—In general.—This section is self-executing. (People v. Hoge, 55 Cal. 612.)

> Self-executing provisions of Constitution. See note, Ann. Cas. 1914C, 1116.

The provisions of this section as to the adoption of the charter are mandatory and prohibitory, and a failure to observe them will invalidate the charter. (People v. Gunn, 85 Cal. 238, 24 Pac. 718.)

The purpose of this section was to emancipate municipal governments from the authority and control formerly exercised over them by the legislature. (People v. Hoge, 55 Cal. 612.)

The right to frame a charter is not a continuing right, and after it has been once exercised by the adoption of a charter, the municipality cannot adopt another charter, but must amend the one already adopted. (Blanchard v. Hartwell, 131 Cal. 263, 63 Pac. 349.)

The legislature cannot abridge the right given by this section to cities to adopt charters. (People v. Bagley, 85 Cal. 343, 24 Pac. 716.)

A charter is a "statute" within the meaning of section 1622 of the Civil Code. It is also a "law,' and also written law. (Frick v. Los Angeles, 115 Cal. 512, 47 Pac. 250.)

The authority to adopt a charter is a part of the law-making power of the state. (Sheehan v. Scott, 145 Cal. 684, 79 Pac. 350.)

A charter must be consistent with the Constitution and general laws of the state. But the whole charter will not be held invalid because a few of its provisions may be inconsistent with general statutes in force at the time of its adoption. (Brooks v. Fischer, 79 Cal. 173, 4 L. R. A. 429, 21 Pac. 652.)

A charter unlawfully attempting to give a police court exclusive jurisdiction of certain misdemeanors is not inconsistent with the general law giving such jurisdiction to justices' courts. (Ex parte Dolan, 128 Cal. 460, 60 Pac. 1094.)

A city may provide in its charter for taxation for municipal purposes. (Security Sav. Bank etc. Co. v. Hinton, 97 Cal. 214, 32 Pac. 3.)

The charter cannot extend its authority outside of the territory of the city. (Kennedy v. Miller, 97 Cal. 429, 437, 32 Pac. 558.)

A reference in a special charter of a city to a particular title of the Political Code for its powers and provisions has the effect to make the appropriate title a part of the charter of the city. (Ex parte Lemon, 143 Cal. 558, 65 L. R. A. 946, 77 Pac. 455.)

The provisions of the Political Code as to the formation of the legislative body of municipalities is not such a general law that a charter must be consistent with it. (In re Pfahler, 150 Cal. 71, 11 L. R. A. (N. S.) 1092, 11 Ann. Cas. 911, 88 Pac. 270.)

There is no limitation in the Constitution on the right to include in a freeholders' charter power to acquire, own and operate public utilities. (Platt v. City and County of San Francisco, 158 Cal. 74, 110 Pac. 304.)

Freeholders.—The board of election commissioners of San Francisco have power to call an election of freeholders under this section. (People v. Hoge, 55 Cal. 612.)

The action of the board of election commissioners in ordering an election of freeholders under this section is not judicial in its nature. (People v. Board of Election Commrs., 54 Cal. 404.)

All that is necessary to the validity of an election of freeholders is that they may be chosen at a general or special election; and where there has been such an election, the voice of the people is not to be rejected for a defect or even want of notice, if they have in truth been called upon and have spoken. (People v. Hoge, 55 Cal. 612.)

As to whether or not irregularities in the election of freeholders can affect the validity of the charter, see People v. Gunn, 85 Cal. 238, 24 Pac. 718.

Where the person receiving the highest number of votes for freeholder is disqualified, the next highest person is not entitled to a certificate of election. (People v. Hecht, 105 Cal. 621, 45 Am. St. Rep. 96, 27 L. R. A. 203, 38 Pac. 941.)

The acts of de facto freeholders are valid. (People v. Hecht, 105 Cal. 621, 45 Am. St. Rep. 96, 27 L. R. A. 203, 38 Pac. 941.)

Where some of the freeholders elected are ineligible, the remainder of them may frame the charter. A majority of those qualified may act. (People v. Hecht, 105 Cal. 621, 45 Am. St. Rep. 96, 27 L. R. A. 203, 38 Pac. 941.)

A person who has not been for at least five years a qualified elector of the city is incligible to the office of freeholder. (People v. Hecht, 105 Cal. 621, 45 Am. St. Rep. 96, 27 L. R. A. 203, 38 Pac. 941.)

The clause authorizing the presentation at a charter or charter amendment election of an "alternative article or proposition" is simply permissive, and there is no duty to present an alternative article or proposition for submission. (Apple v. Zemansky, 166 Cal. 83, 134 Pac. 1149.)

Charter provisions have the force and effect of legislative enactments within their constitutional limitations, the same being the organic law or local Constitution of the city. (Dalton v. Lelande, 22 Cal. App. 481, 135 Pac. 54.)

Unless prohibited by some provision of the Constitution, expressed or implied, a municipal charter adopted as provided in this section may contain any provision not in conflict with or covered by general laws of the state. (Stern v. City Council of Berkeley, 25 Cal. App. 685, 689, 145 Pac. 167.)

Ratification.—The duty of calling an election to ratify a charter is one clearly enjoined by law, and may be enforced by mandamus; and it is no defense that there may not be sufficient funds in the treasury to defray the expenses of the election. (Gibbs v. Bartlett, 63 Cal. 117.)

A municipal charter must receive a majority of all the votes cast at the election, and not merely a majority of the votes cast thereupon. (Santa Rosa v. Bower, 142 Cal. 299, 75 Pac. 829.)

An election is invalid if no duplicate of the proposed charter was delivered to the mayor or recorder, or if held without sufficient pub-

lication of notice, or in less than the required number of days after completion of the publication. (People v. Gunn, 85 Cal. 238, 24 Pac. 718.)

A city charter may be approved by a majority of the members elected to each house of the legislature by joint resolution, without the approval of the governor. (Brooks v. Fischer, 79 Cal. 173, 4 L. R. A. 429, 21 Pac. 652.)

The legislature in approving a freeholders' charter does not exercise its law-making power. (People v. Toal, 85 Cal. 333, 24 Pac. 603; People v. Gunn, 85 Cal. 238, 24 Pac. 718.)

The legislature in approving a freeholders' charter cannot conclusively determine whether or not the municipal authorities and people of the city have proceeded regularly in its framing and adoption. (People v. Gunn, 85 Cal. 238, 24 Pac. 718.)

If, by the approval, under this section, of a charter or an amendment which vests in a local body authority to legislate concerning local matters, the legislature may be said to be delegating legislative power, such delegation is one that is expressly authorized by the Constitution. (Mardis v. McCarthy, 162 Cal. 94, 121 Pac. 389.)

Effect.—A new charter supersedes the old and all amendments thereto. (People v. Oakland, 92 Cal. 611, 28 Pac. 807.)

A description of the territory of a municipal corporation is an essential part of the charter, and is superseded by an entirely new charter containing a different description of territory from that contained in the original charter. (People v. Oakland, 92 Cal. 611, 28 Pac. 807.)

The adoption of a new charter operates, not ex proprio vigore, but by virtue of the provisions of the Constitution, to supersede the existing charter and all amendments thereto, and although such charter cannot establish a police court, it will abolish one established by the former charter. (Ex parte Sparks, 120 Cal. 395, 52 Pac. 715.)

A new charter supersedes the provision of an existing charter establishing a justice's court. (Miner v. Justice's Court, 121 Cal. 264, 53 Pac. 795.)

While the charter of the city of Eureka superseded the provisions of the former charter creating the office of harbormaster, without making any provision for such officer, it did not supersede the provisions of the Political Code providing for the duties of such harbormaster. (Quigg v. Evans, 121 Cal. 546, 53 Pac. 1093.)

The charter is the organic law of this city and supersedes all laws inconsistent therewith. (Dinan v. Superior Court, 6 Cal. App. 217, 91 Pac. 806.)

The charter of San Francisco, when approved by the legislature, became the organic law of the city and county, and superseded the existing charter and all laws inconsistent therewith, and thereafter the city and county was no longer subject to or controlled by general laws. (Burke v. Board of Trustees, 4 Cal. App. 235, 87 Pac. 421.)

Validity.—The municipality, real or pretended, is a necessary party to a proceeding to test the validity of a municipal charter. (People v. Gunn, 85 Cal. 238, 24 Pac. 718.)

Amendments.—After the adoption of a freeholders' charter a second board of freeholders cannot be elected to frame a second charter for

the city to be adopted by a majority vote, but the first charter must be amended. (Blanchard v. Hartwell, 131 Cal. 263, 63 Pac. 349.)

The provisions of the Constitution in regard to the adoption and amendment of freeholders' charters are mandatory and prohibitory; and the mode of amendment of such charters is exclusively commanded, and all others are prohibited. (Blanchard v. Hartwell, 131 Cal. 263, 63 Pac. 349.)

The amendment mentioned in this section relates only to amendments made by and at the instance of the officers and electors of the city, and does not inhibit the amendment or change of the charter within two years under general laws. (People v. Coronado, 100 Cal. 571, 35 Pac. 162.)

The annexation of additional territory to the city does not work an amendment to the charter. (People v. Oakland, 123 Cal. 598, 56 Pac. 445.)

The mayor of the city and county of San Francisco is not included in the term "legislative authority of the city," and a proposed amendment need not be approved by him. (Harrison v. Roberts, 145 Cal. 173, 78 Pac. 537.)

The use of the words legislative authority was not intended to define the powers of that body or place it in a position where it would be beyond restriction by the organic law of the city. (In re Pfahler, 150 Cal. 71, 11 L. R. A. (N. S.) 1092, 11 Ann. Cas. 911, 88 Pac. 270.)

The interval of two years refers to the time which must elapse between the elections at which the amendments are ratified and not to the action of the legislative authority of the city or the approval by the legislature. (Harrison v. Roberts, 145 Cal. 173, 78 Pac. 537.)

Where amendments are petitioned for by fifteen per cent of the voters, the legislative authority of city has discretion either to call a special election or to wait until the next general election to submit them to the people. (Lubliner v. Alpers, 145 Cal. 291, 78 Pac. 722.)

A provision in a freeholder's charter fixing the salaries of officers and providing that "the common council in the month of January, 1891, and every four years thereafter shall readjust and fix anew the amount of all official salaries provided for in this charter," is not an amendment to the charter. (Coyne v. Rennie, 97 Cal. 590, 32 Pac. 578.)

In Harrison v. Roberts, 145 Cal. 173, 78 Pac. 537, it was held that the limitation of two years referred to the time of the adoption of the amendment by the electors, and not to the time of the proposal thereof or the ratification thereof by the legislature. In doing so the court said: "The only effect of the limitation as to time is to prohibit a submission for ratification by the electors of any proposed amendment within two years from the submission for ratification of any prior amendment; in other words, that proposals for amendments may be submitted at elections, only at intervals of two years." In Migliavacca v. Napa, 10 Cal. App. 383, 102 Pac. 227, it was held that this language could not be construed to mean that if the amendments were rejected at the first election other amendments could not be submitted within two years.

Amendments may be submitted in less than two years after the rejection of other amendments. (Migliavacca v. Napa, 10 Cal. App. 383, 102 Pac. 227.)

The "special election" provided for by this section is an election held for the special purpose of voting upon the amendments to the charter. (People v. Davie, 114 Cal. 363, 46 Pac. 150.)

One resolution approving thirteen separate amendments to a city charter is sufficient. (In re Pfahler, 150 Cal. 71, 11 L. R. A. (N. S.) 1092, 11 Ann. Cas. 911, 88 Pac. 270.)

The effect of this provision is necessarily to make any proposed amendment which is regularly submitted in accordance with its provisions to the people, ratified by a majority of the electors voting thereon, and approved in the manner required by a majority of the members of each house of the legislature, a part of the charter, from the date of legislative approval. (Apple v. Zemansky, 166 Cal. 83, 134 Pac. 1149.)

> Amendments to charters are binding without acceptance. (See note, 53 Am. Dec. 470.

When charter takes effect.—When a newly adopted charter expressly provided for a preliminary election under it on a date prior to the date at which the charter is to take effect, the charter is to be construed as consistent with itself, and the general provision as to its taking effect merely means that the machinery of the new government shall not start until the later date and does not conflict with the provision for a preliminary election. (Trafton v. Quinn, 143 Cal. 469, 77 Pac. 164.)

> Validity of statute conferring on municipality power to adopt or amend new charter. See note, Ann. Cas. 1913C, 788.

> Right of municipality to adopt commission form of government. See notes, Ann. Cas. 1912C, 999; 35 L. R. A. (N. S.) 802; 41 L. R. A. (N. S.) 111.

City or city and county charters, to contain what.

Section 8½. It shall be competent, in all charters framed under the authority given by section eight of this article to provide, in addition to those provisions allowable by this Constitution and by the laws of the state, as follows:

1. For the constitution, regulation, government, and jurisdiction of police courts, and for the manner in which, the times at which, and the terms for which the judges of such courts shall be elected or appointed, and for the qualifications and compensation of said judges and of their clerks and attachés; and for the establishment, constitution, regulation, government and jurisdiction of municipal courts, with such civil and criminal jurisdiction as by law may be conferred upon inferior courts; and for the manner in which, the times at which, and the terms for which the judges of such courts shall be elected or appointed, and for

the qualifications and compensation of said judges and of their clerks and attachés; provided such municipal courts shall never be deprived of the jurisdiction given inferior courts created by general law.

In any city or any city and county, when such municipal court has been established, there shall be no other court inferior to the superior court; and pending actions, trials, and all pending business of inferior courts within the territory of such city or city and county, upon the establishment of any such municipal court, shall be and become pending in such municipal court, and all records of such inferior courts shall thereupon be and become the records of such municipal court.

2. For the manner in which, the times at which, and the terms for which the members of boards of education shall be elected or appointed, for their qualifications, compensation and removal, and for the number which shall constitute any one of such boards.

3. For the manner in which, the times at which, and the terms for which the members of the boards of police commissioners shall be elected or appointed; and for the constitution, regulation, compensation, and government of such boards and of the municipal police force.

4. For the manner in which and the times at which any municipal election shall be held and the result thereof determined; for the manner in which, the times at which, and the terms for which the members of all boards of election shall be elected or appointed, and for the constitution, regulation, compensation and government of such boards, and of their clerks and attachés, and for all expenses incident to the holding of any election.

It shall be competent in any charter framed in accordance with the provisions of this section, or section eight of this article, for any city or consolidated city and county, and plenary authority is hereby granted, subject only to the restrictions of this article, to provide therein or by amendment thereto, the manner in which, the method by which, the times at which, and the terms for which the several county and municipal officers and employees whose compen-

sation is paid by such city or city and county, excepting
judges of the superior court, shall be elected or appointed,
and for their recall and removal, and for their compensation, and for the number of deputies, clerks and other employees that each shall have, and for the compensation,
method of appointment, qualifications, tenure of office and
removal of such deputies, clerks and other employees. All
provisions of any charter of any such city or consolidated
city and county, heretofore adopted, and amendments thereto, which are in accordance herewith, are hereby confirmed
and declared valid.

5. It shall be competent in any charter or amendment
thereof, which shall hereafter be framed under the authority given by section eight of this article, by any city having
a population in excess of fifty thousand ascertained as prescribed by said section eight, to provide for the separation
of said city from the county of which it has theretofore been
a part and the formation of said city into a consolidated
city and county to be governed by such charter, and to have
combined powers of a city and county, as provided in this
Constitution for consolidated city and county government,
and further to prescribe in said charter the date for the beginning of the official existence of said consolidated city and
county.

It shall also be competent for any such city, not having
already consolidated as a city and county to hereafter
frame, in the manner prescribed in section eight of this
article, a charter providing for a city and county government, in which charter there shall be prescribed territorial
boundaries which may include contiguous territory not included in such city, which territory, however, must be included in the county within which such city is located.

If no additional territory is proposed to be added, then,
upon the consent to the separation of any such city from
the county in which it is located, being given by a majority
of the qualified electors voting thereon in such county and
upon the ratification of such charter by a majority of the
qualified electors voting thereon in such city, and the ap-.
proval thereof by the legislature, as prescribed in section

eight of this article, said charter shall be deemed adopted and upon the date fixed therein said city shall be and become a consolidated city and county.

If additional territory which consists wholly of only one incorporated city or town, or which consists wholly of unincorporated territory, is proposed to be added, then, upon the consent to such separation of such territory and of the city initiating the consolidation proposal being given by a majority of the qualified electors voting thereon in the county in which the city proposing such separation is located, and upon the ratification of such charter by a majority of the qualified electors voting thereon in such city so proposing the separation, and also upon the approval of the proposal hereinafter set forth, by a majority of the qualified electors voting thereon in the whole of such additional territory, and the approval of said charter by the legislature, as prescribed in section eight of this article, said charter shall be deemed adopted, the indebtedness hereinafter referred to shall be deemed to have been assumed, and upon the date fixed in said charter such territory and such city shall be and become one consolidated city and county.

The proposal to be submitted to the territory proposed to be added shall be substantially in the following form and submitted as one indivisible question:

"Shall the territory (herein designate in general terms the territory to be added) consolidate with the city of (herein insert name of the city initiating the proposition to form a city and county government) in a consolidated city and county government, and shall the charter as prepared by the city of (herein insert the name of the city initiating such proposition) be adopted as the charter of the consolidated city and county, and shall the said added territory become subject to taxation along with the entire territory of the proposed city and county, in accordance with the assessable valuation of the property of the said territory, for the following indebtedness of said city (herein insert name of the city initiating such proposition) to wit: (herein insert in general terms reference to any debts to be assumed, and if none insert 'none')."

If additional territory is proposed to be added, which includes unincorporated territory and one or more incorporated cities or towns, or which includes more than one incorporated city or town, the consent of any such incorporated city or town shall be obtained by a majority vote of the qualified electors thereof voting upon a proposal substantially as follows:

. "Shall (herein insert the name of the city or town to be included in such additional territory) be included in a district to be hereafter defined by the city of (herein insert the name of the city initiating the proposition to form a city and county government) which district shall, within two years from the date of this election, vote upon a proposal submitted as one indivisible question that such district to be then described and set forth shall consolidate with (herein insert name of the city initiating said consolidation proposition) in a consolidated city and county government, and also that a certain charter, to be prepared by the city of (herein insert name of the city initiating such proposition) be adopted as the charter of such consolidated city and county, and that such district become subject to taxation along with the entire territory of the proposed city and county in accordance with the assessable valuation of the property of said district for the following indebtedness of said city of (herein insert name of the city initiating such proposition) to wit: (herein insert in general terms, reference to any debts to be assumed and if none insert 'none')."

· Any and all incorporated cities or towns to which the foregoing proposal shall have been submitted and a majority of whose qualified electors voting thereon shall have voted in favor thereof, together with such unincorporated territory as the city initiating such consolidation proposal may desire to have included, the whole to form an area contiguous to said city, shall be created into a district by such city, and the proposal substantially as above prescribed to be used when the territory proposed to be added consists wholly of only one incorporated city or town, or wholly of unincorporated territory, shall, within two years, be sub-

mitted to the voters of said entire district as one indivisible question.

Upon consent to the separation of such district and of the city initiating the consolidation proposal being given by a majority of the qualified electors voting thereon in the county in which the city proposing such separation is located, and upon the ratification of such charter by a majority of the qualified electors voting thereon in such city, and upon the approval of the proposal hereinbefore set forth by a majority of the qualified electors voting thereon in the whole of the said district so proposed to be added, and upon the approval of said charter by the legislature, as prescribed in section eight of this article, said charter shall be deemed adopted, the said indebtedness referred to in said proposal shall be deemed to have been assumed, and upon the date fixed in said charter, such district and such city shall be and become one consolidated city and county.

6. It shall be competent for any consolidated city and county now existing, or which shall hereafter be organized, to annex territory contiguous to such consolidated city and county, unincorporated or otherwise, whether situated wholly in one county, or parts thereof be situate in different counties, said annexed territory to be an integral part of such city and county, provided that such annexation of territory shall only include any part of the territory which was at the time of the original consolidation of the annexing city and county, within the county from which such annexing city and county was formed, together with territory which was concurrently, or has since such consolidation been joined in a county government with the area of the original county not included in such consolidated city and county.

If additional territory, which consists wholly of only one incorporated city, city and county or town, or which consists wholly of unincorporated territory, is proposed to be annexed to any consolidated city and county now existing or which shall hereafter be organized, then, upon the consent to any such annexation being given by a majority of the qualified electors voting thereon in any county or coun-

ties in which any such additional territory is located, and upon the approval of such annexation proposal by a majority of the qualified electors voting thereon in such city and county, and also upon the approval of the proposal hereinafter set forth by a majority of the qualified electors voting thereon in the whole of such territory proposed to be annexed, the indebtedness hereinafter referred to shall be deemed to have been assumed, and at the time stated in such proposal, such additional territory and such city and county shall be and become one consolidated city and county, to be governed by the charter of the city and county proposing such annexation, and any subsequent amendment thereto.

The proposal to be submitted to the territory proposed to be annexed, shall be substantially in the following form and submitted as one indivisible question:

"Shall the territory (herein designate in general terms the territory to be annexed) consolidate with the city and county of (herein insert the name of the city and county initiating the annexation proposal) in a consolidated city and county government, said consolidation to take effect (herein insert date when such consolidation shall take effect) and shall the said annexed territory become subject to taxation, as an integral part of the city and county so formed, in accordance with the assessable valuation of property of said territory for the following indebtedness of said city and county of (herein insert name of the city and county) to wit: (herein insert in general terms, reference to any debts to be assumed and if none insert 'none')."

If additional territory including unincorporated territory and one or more incorporated cities, cities and counties, or towns, or including more than one incorporated city, city anl county, or town, is proposed to be annexed to any consolidated city and county now existing or which shall hereafter be organized, the consent of each such incorporated city, city and county, or town, shall be obtained by a majority vote of the qualified electors of any such incorporated city, city and county, or town, voting upon a proposal substantially as follows:

"Shall (herein insert name of the city, city and county, or town, to be included in such annexed territory) be included in a district to be hereafter defined by the city and county of (herein insert the name of the city and county initiating the annexation proposal) which district shall within two years from the date of this election vote upon a proposal submitted as one indivisible question, that such district to be then described and set forth shall consolidate with (herein insert name of the city and county initiating the annexation proposal) in a consolidated city and county government, and that such district become subject to taxation, along with the entire territory of the proposed city and county in accordance with the assessable valuation of the property of said district for the following indebtedness of said city and county of (herein insert name of the city and county initiating the annexation proposal) to wit: (herein insert in general terms, reference to any debts to be assumed and if none insert 'none')."

Any and all incorporated cities, cities and counties, or towns, to which the foregoing proposal shall have been submitted, and a majority of whose qualified electors voting thereon shall have voted in favor thereof, together with such unincorporated territory as the city and county initiating such annexation proposal may desire to have included, the whole to form an area contiguous to said city and county, shall be created into a district by said city and county, and the proposal substantially in the form above set forth to be used when the territory proposed to be added consists wholly of only one incorporated city, city and county, or town, or wholly of unincorporated territory, shall, within said two years, be submitted to the voters of said entire district as one indivisible question.

Upon consent to any such annexation being given by a majority of the qualified electors, voting thereon in any county or counties in which any such territory proposed to be annexed to said city and county is located, and upon the approval of any such annexation proposal by a majority of the qualified electors voting thereon in such city and county proposing such annexation, and also upon the approval of

the proposal hereinbefore set forth by a majority of the qualified electors voting thereon in the whole of the district so proposed to be annexed, then, the said indebtedness referred to in said proposal shall be deemed to have been assumed, and upon the date stated in such annexation proposal such district and such city and county shall be and become one consolidated city and county, to be governed by the charter of the city and county proposing such annexation, and any subsequent amendment thereto.

Whenever any proposal is submitted to the electors of any county, territory, district, city, city and county, or town, as above provided, there shall be published, for at least five successive publications in a newspaper of general circulation printed and published in any such county, territory, district, city, city and county, or town, the last publication to be not less than twenty days prior to any such election, a particular description of any territory or district to be separated, added, or annexed, together with a particular description of any debts to be assumed, as above referred to, unless such particular description is contained in the said proposal so submitted. In addition to said description, such territory shall also be designated in such notice by some appropriate name or other words of identification, by which such territory may be referred to and indicated upon the ballots to be used at any election at which the question of annexation or consolidation of additional territory is submitted as herein provided. If there be no such newspaper so printed and published in any such county, territory, district, city, city and county, or town, then such publication may be made in any newspaper of general circulation printed and published in the nearest county, city, city and county, or town where there may be such a newspaper so printed and published.

If, by the adoption of any charter, or by annexation, any incorporated municipality becomes a portion of a city and county, its property, debts and liabilities of every description shall be and become the property, debts and liabilities of such city and county.

Every city and county which shall be formed, or the territory of which shall be enlarged as herein provided from territory taken from any county or counties, shall be liable for a just proportion of the debts and liabilities and be entitled to a just proportion of the property and assets of such county or counties, existing at the time such territory is so taken:

The provisions of this Constitution applicable to cities, and cities and counties, and also those applicable to counties, so far as not inconsistent or prohibited to cities, or cities and counties, shall be applicable to such consolidated city and county government; and no provision of subdivision 5 or 6 of this section shall be construed as a restriction upon the plenary authority of any city or city and county having a freeholders' charter, as provided for in this Constitution, to determine in said charter any and all matters elsewhere in this Constitution authorized and not inconsistent herewith.

The legislature shall provide for the formation of one or more counties from the portion or portions of a county or counties remaining after the formation of or annexation to · a consolidated city and county, or for the transfer of such portion or portions of such original county or counties to adjoining counties. But such transfer to an adjoining county shall only be made after approval by a majority vote of the qualified electors voting thereon in such territory proposed to be so transferred.

The provisions of section two of this article, and also those provisions of section three of this article which refer to the passing of any county line within five miles of the exterior boundary of a city or town in which a county seat of any county proposed to be divided is situated, shall not apply to the formation of, nor to the extension of the territory of such consolidated cities and counties, nor to the formation of new counties, nor to the annexation of existing counties, as herein specified.

Any city and county formed under this section shall have the right, if it so desires, to be designated by the official name of the city initiating the consolidation as it existed immediately prior to its adoption of a charter providing for

a consolidated city and county government, except that such city and county shall be known under the style of a city and county.

It shall be competent in any charter framed for a consolidated city and county, or by amendment thereof, to provide for the establishment of a borough system of government for the whole or any part of the territory of said city and county, by which one or more districts may be created therein, which districts shall be known as boroughs and which shall exercise such municipal powers as may be granted thereto by such charter, and for the organization, regulation, government and jurisdiction of such boroughs.

No property in any territory hereafter consolidated with or annexed to any city or city and county shall be taxed for the payment of any indebtedness of such city or city and county outstanding at the date of such consolidation or annexation and for the payment of which the property in such territory was not, prior to such consolidation or annexation, subject to such taxation, unless there shall have been submitted to the qualified electors of such territory the proposition regarding the assumption of indebtedness as hereinbefore set forth and the same shall have been approved by a majority of such electors voting thereon.

7. In all cases of annexation of unincorporated territory to an incorporated city, or the consolidation of two or more incorporated cities, assumption of existing bonded indebtedness by such unincorporated territory or by either of the cities so consolidating may be made by a majority vote of the qualified electors voting thereon in the territory or city which shall assume an existing bonded indebtedness. This provision shall apply whether annexation or consolidation is effected under this section or any other section of this Constitution, and the provisions of section eighteen of this article shall not be a prohibition thereof.

The legislature shall enact such general laws as may be necessary to carry out the provisions of this section and such general or special laws as may be necessary to carry out the provisions of subdivisions 5 and 6 of this section, including any such general or special act as may be neces-

sary to permit a consolidated city and county to submit a new charter to take effect at the time that any consolidation, by reason of annexation to such consolidated city and county, takes effect, and also, any such general law or special act as may be necessary to provide for any period after such consolidation, by reason of such annexation, takes effect, and prior to the adoption and approval of any such new charter. (Amendment adopted November 3, 1914.)

[AMENDMENT OF 1911.]

Sec. 8½. It shall be competent, in all charters framed under the authority given by section eight of article eleven of this Constitution, to provide, in addition to those provisions allowable by this Constitution and by the laws of the state, as follows:

1. For the Constitution, regulation, government, and jurisdiction of police courts, and for the manner in which, the times at which, and the terms for which the judges of such courts shall be elected or appointed, and for the qualifications and compensation of said judges and of their clerks and attachés.

2. For the manner in which, the times at which, and the terms for which the members of boards of education shall be elected or appointed, for their qualifications, compensation and removal, and for the number which shall constitute any one of such boards.

3. For the manner in which, the times at which, and the terms for which the members of the boards of police commissioners shall be elected or appointed; and for the constitution, regulation, compensation, and government of such boards and of the municipal police force.

4. For the manner in which and the times at which any municipal election shall be held and the result thereof determined; for the manner in which, the times at which, and the terms for which the members of all boards of election shall be elected or appointed, and for the constitution, regulation, compensation and government of such boards, and of their clerks and attachés; and for all expenses incident to the holding of any election.

Where a city and county government has been merged and consolidated into one municipal government, it shall also be competent, in any charter framed under said section eight of said article eleven, or by amendment thereto, to provide for the manner in which, the times at which and the terms for which the several county and municipal officers and employees whose compensation is paid by such city and county, excepting judges of the superior court, shall be elected or appointed, and for their recall and removal, and for their compensation, and for the number of deputies, clerks and other employees that each shall have, and for the compensation, method of appointment, qualifications, tenure of office and removal of such deputies, clerks and other employees. All provisions of any charter of any such consolidated city and county heretofore adopted, and amendments thereto, which are in accord-

ance herewith, are hereby confirmed and declared valid. (Amendment approved October 10, 1911.)

[AMENDMENT OF 1896.]

Sec. 8½. It shall be competent, in all charters framed under the authority given by section eight of article eleven of this Constitution, to provide, in addition to those provisions allowable by this Constitution and by the laws of the state, as follows:

1. For the constitution, regulation, government, and jurisdiction of police courts, and for the manner in which, the times at which, and the terms for which the judges of such courts shall be elected or appointed, and for the compensation of said judges and of their clerks and attachés.

2. For the manner in which, the times at which, and the terms for which the members of boards of education shall be elected or appointed, and the number which shall constitute any one of such boards.

3. For the manner in which, the times at which, and the terms for which the members of the boards of police commissioners shall be elected or appointed; and for the constitution, regulation, compensation, and government of such boards and of the municipal police force.

4. For the manner in which, the times at which, and the terms for which the members of all boards of election shall be elected or appointed, and for the constitution, regulation, compensation, and government of such boards, and of their clerks and attachés; and for all expenses incident to the holding of any election.

Where a city and county government has been merged and consolidated into one municipal government, it shall also be competent in any charter framed under said section eight of said article eleven, to provide for the manner in which, the times at which, and the terms for which the several county officers shall be elected or appointed, for their compensation, and for the number of deputies that each shall have, and for the compensation payable to each of such deputies. (Amendment adopted November 3, 1896.)

PROVISIONS OF CHARTER.—This section is not retroactive, and has no application to charters previously adopted. (Ex parte Sparks, 120 Cal. 395, 52 Pac. 715.)

This section does not revive or validate a provision in the charter of a municipality, adopted and ratified before the Constitution was amended, providing for the establishment of a police court. (Fleming v. Hance, 153 Cal. 162, 94 Pac. 620.)

As to such matters as this section authorizes to be provided for in freeholders' charters, the provisions of the charter are supreme. (Graham v. Fresno, 151 Cal. 465, 91 Pac. 147.)

Where the charter of a consolidated city and county government is silent as to the election or appointment of special officers or their compensation, the general law prevails. (Nicholl v. Koster, 157 Cal. 416, 108 Pac. 302.)

Under this provision the freeholders' charter of San Francisco properly fixed the manner in which, the times at which, and the terms for

which the several county officers shall be elected or appointed. (Martin v. Board of Election Commrs., 126 Cal. 404, 58 Pac. 932.)

Under this section the charter cannot vest exclusive jurisdiction of certain misdemeanors in the police court, and thus oust the justices' courts of such jurisdiction. (Ex parte Dolan, 128 Cal. 460, 60 Pac. 1094.)

Under this provision it is competent for the charter of a city and county to provide that the salary of the assessor shall be in full compensation for his services, although the general law allowed him extra compensation for collecting poll taxes. (Dodge v. San Francisco, 135 Cal. 512, 67 Pac. 973.)

As to the meaning of the word "deputies" as used in this section, see Garnett v. Brooks, 136 Cal. 585, 69 Pac. 298.

This section confers no power upon the municipality to prescribe by a freeholders' charter the qualifications of the deputies mentioned in this section. (Crowley v. Freud, 132 Cal. 440, 64 Pac. 696.)

A provision of a freeholders' charter that officers of the city and county must have been electors of the city and county for at least five years before their election is valid. (Sheehan v. Scott, 145 Cal. 684, 79 Pac. 350.)

Stenographers of the police court are "attachés" of the court within the meaning of this section. (Elder v. McDougald, 145 Cal. 740, 79 Pac. 429.)

This section does not authorize the charter to confer on the police court concurrent jurisdiction with the superior courts of misdemeanors. (Robert v. Police Court, 148 Cal. 131, 82 Pac. 838.)

The power given by the charter to the police judges to appoint stenographers and fixing their compensation supersedes the provisions of the Penal Code on the subject. (Elder v. McDougald, 145 Cal. 740, 79 Pac. 429.)

The power conferred by this section includes the power to provide for the attachés not only of the police court, but also of the police judge when acting as a committing magistrate, and whether acting under the charter or under the general law. (Elder v. McDougald, 145 Cal. 740, 79 Pac. 429.)

The mere fact that this section only refers to "police courts" does not prevent the city from conferring the same jurisdiction upon a "recorder." (In re Baxter, 3 Cal. App. 716, 86 Pac. 998.)

This provision has no application to justices' courts. (In re Johnson, 6 Cal. App. 734, 93 Pac. 199.)

Since the adoption of this section the legislature has no power to establish a police court in a city maintaining a police court under its charter. (Graham v. Fresno, 151 Cal. 465, 91 Pac. 147.)

The term "police court" probably includes such inferior courts as may properly be held to be purely municipal, though given by the state certain jurisdiction in state as distinguished from municipal matters. (Graham v. Fresno, 151 Cal. 465, 91 Pac. 147.)

The term "police court" ordinarily refers to an inferior municipal court with a limited jurisdiction in criminal cases only, with the power to try certain misdemeanor cases arising from the violation of state law or municipal ordinance, and to conduct preliminary exami-

nation in cases of felony and certain misdemeanors, and does not in-clude justices' courts. (Graham v. Fresno, 151 Cal. 465, 91 Pac. 147.)

This section has no application to justices of the peace and did not restrict the power of the legislature to provide for justices' courts in cities and towns. (Graham v. Fresno, 151 Cal. 465, 91 Pac. 147.)

This section means that as to criminal offenses such as violations of municipal ordinances the framers of a charter have the exclusive right to provide for, but it is not to be construed as authorizing such char-ters to confer upon their police courts jurisdiction over offenses of every character. (Matter of Application of Westenberg, 167 Cal. 309, 139 Pac. 674.)

A section of a city charter providing for the compensation of school directors is not invalid under this section, as it existed prior to the amendment of October, 1911, which expressly authorized charters to provide for the compensation of members of boards of education. (Stern v. City Council of Berkeley, 25 Cal. App. 685, 145 Pac. 167.)

Panama-Pacific International Exposition.

Sec. 8a.   The charter of the city and county of San Fran-cisco may be amended, in addition to the method and the times provided in section 8 of article XI of the Constitution, in the following particulars:

(a) Authorizing the city and county of San Francisco, a municipal corporation, by its legislative authority, to in-cur a bonded indebtedness in an amount not exceeding five million dollars, and to issue municipal bonds therefor, and to grant and turn over to the Panama-Pacific International Exposition Company (a corporation organized under the laws of the state of California March 22, 1910) the proceeds of said bonds, the same to be used and disbursed by said exposition company for the purposes of an exposition to be held in the city and county of San Francisco to celebrate the completion of the Panama Canal; said bonds, so issued, to be of such form and to be redeemable, registered and converted in such manner and amounts, and at such times not later than forty years from the date of their issue, as such legislative authority shall determine; the interest on said bonds to not exceed five per centum per annum, and said bonds to be exempt from all taxes for state and munici-pal purposes, and to be sold for not less than par at such times and places, and in such manner, as shall be deter-mined by said legislative authority; the proceeds of said bonds, when sold, to be payable immediately by the treasurer

of said city and county to the treasurer of said Panama-Pacific International Exposition Company, upon the demand of said treasurer of said exposition company, without the necessity of the approval of such demand by other authority, the same to be used and disbursed by said Panama-Pacific International Exposition Company for the purposes of such exposition, under the direction and control of such exposition company;

(b) Providing that any bonded indebtedness incurred for the purposes aforesaid shall be exclusive of the bonded indebtedness of the said city and county limited by section 9 of article XII of said charter.

(c) Granting to said Panama-Pacific International Exposition Company the exclusive possession and use, together with the management and control, of that portion of Golden Gate Park in the city and county of San Francisco westerly from Twentieth avenue, as extended, for such exposition purposes, such possession and use, also management and control, to terminate not later than one year after the closing of such exposition;

(d) Granting to said Panama-Pacific International Exposition Company the exclusive possession and use, together with the management and control, for such exposition purposes, of any lands held by the board of education of the city and county of San Francisco, and by the city and county of San Francisco, not in actual use, such possession and use, also management and control, to terminate not later than one year after the closing of such exposition.

(e) Authorizing said Panama-Pacific International Exposition Company to temporarily close streets in the city and county of San Francisco westerly from Twentieth avenue, for such exposition purposes, and to have the exclusive possession and use, together with the management and control, of said streets for such exposition purposes, such possession and use, also management and control of said streets, to terminate not later than one year after the closing of such exposition.

Proposals to amend the charter of the city and county of San Francisco in the foregoing particulars may be sub-

mitted by the legislative authority of said city and county to the electors of said city and county, at any general or special election (and a special election may be called therefor) held in said city and county, after the publication of such proposals in a newspaper of general circulation in said city and county, for such time as shall be determined by such legislative authority. Upon the ratification of any such proposed amendment by a majority of the electors of said city and county .voting at such election on such proposed amendment, said proposed amendment receiving such majority vote shall become operative immediately as an amendment to said charter, without the necessity of approval thereof by the legislature.

Any act of the legislative authority of the city and county of San Francisco, in submitting to the electors of said city and county, at any general or special election, proposals to amend the charter of said city and county in the foregoing particulars, including any notice by publication or otherwise of such proposals, and of such election, and the holding of such election, in accordance with the provisions hereof, before the adoption of this amendment, are hereby validated in all respects as if performed subsequent to the adoption of this amendment. The disbursement of all funds obtained from said bonds shall be accounted for by said Panama-Pacific International Exposition Company by an itemized statement thereof to be filed with the auditor of the city and county of San Francisco. (New section added by amendment adopted November 8, 1910.)

Compensation of officers.

Sec. 9. The compensation of any county, city, town, or municipal officer shall not be increased after his election or during his term of office; nor shall the term of any such officer be extended beyond the period for which he is elected or appointed.

COMPENSATION OF OFFICERS.—The provision against altering the compensation of an officer during his term applies to those officers elected at the first election after the adoption of the Constitution, whose salaries were fixed by previous laws. (Gross v. Kenfield, 57 Cal. 626.)

This section does not apply to incidental expenses of the office, but only to the compensation for services. (Kirkwood v. Soto, 87 Cal. 394, 25 Pac. 488.)

Where a County Government Act increases the salaries of certain officers and provides that it "shall not affect the present incumbents," such increase does not accrue to a person appointed to fill a vacancy in an unexpired term of such incumbent. (Larew v. Newman, 81 Cal. 588, 23 Pac. 227.)

An order of the board of supervisors allowing a county clerk a deputy at a salary of fifty dollars a month, to be paid by the county, made after the election of the county clerk, is in conflict with this provision. (Dougherty v. Austin, 94 Cal. 601, 16 L. R. A. 161, 28 Pac. 834, 29 Pac. 1092.)

An ordinance of a board of supervisors diminishing the compensation of constables during their term is not in conflict with this provision. (People v. Johnson, 95 Cal. 471, 31 Pac. 611.)

Under the provisions of the County Government Act providing that the salaries provided for therein shall be in full compensation for all services rendered by the officers, the clerk of the board of supervisors is not entitled to receive any extra compensation for extra work done by him in preparing data for a claim of the county against the state, whether rendered in the line of his official duty or otherwise. (Humboldt County v. Stern, 136 Cal. 63, 68 Pac. 324.)

This section only applies to a "county, city, town, or municipal officer," for whose term of office the Constitution makes no provision, and does not apply to superior judges. (People v. Campbell, 138 Cal. 11, 70 Pac. 918.)

Where the term is fixed by the Constitution, the legislature has no power to extend or diminish it. (People v. Campbell, 138 Cal. 11, 70 Pac. 918.)

An act relieving county officers, who were elected prior to the passage of the act, from the payment of their own assistants, is void. (Welsh v. Bramlet, 98 Cal. 219, 33 Pac. 66.)

An act increasing the salary of a policeman during his term of office is void. (Darcy v. City of San Jose, 104 Cal. 642, 38 Pac. 500.)

A contract to pay a city attorney extra compensation for services rendered during his term of office is void; but he might recover for services performed under such contract after the expiration of his term of office. (Buck v. Eureka, 109 Cal. 504, 30 L. R. A. 409, 42 Pac. 243.)

An act increasing the compensation of county officers cannot constitutionally increase the salaries of incumbents. (Tulare Co. v. Jefferds, 118 Cal. 303, 50 Pac. 427.)

This prohibition applies to a person appointed to fill a vacancy caused by the death of the incumbent, after the passage of the law increasing the salary of the officer. (Storke v. Goux, 129 Cal. 526, 62 Pac. 68.)

Also to an officer holding over after the expiration of his term, by failure of his successor to qualify. (Rice v. National City, 132 Cal. 354, 64 Pac. 580.)

The legislature may change the form of compensation from fees to a salary, provided the compensation is not increased. (McCauley v. Culbert, 144 Cal. 276, 77 Pac. 923.)

For the board of supervisors to allow the district attorney a salary for a stenographer not provided for by the County Government Act at the time of his election is a violation of this section. (Humiston v. Shaffer, 145 Cal. 195, 78 Pac. 651.)

This provision was intended as well to avoid and prevent the abuses which may arise by reason of arrangements between candidates who are reasonably assured of election or appointment and the legislative power, to take effect after the election of such candidates regardless of the time of the enactment, as arrangements made after such election or appointment. (Woods v. Potter, 8 Cal. App. 41, 95 Pac. 1125.)

The validity of a law fixing compensation is not to be judged by the date of its adoption but by the date when it took effect. (Woods v. Potter, 8 Cal. App. 41, 95 Pac. 1125.)

In the absence of a provision in the charter providing a salary for members of the city council, that body has no power to provide such salary by ordinance. (Woods v. Potter, 8 Cal. App. 41, 95 Pac. 1125.)

The expression "term of office" applies only to officers who have a fixed and definite term, and does not apply to appointive officers who hold at the pleasure of the appointing power. (Harrold v. Barnum, 8 Cal. App. 21, 96 Pac. 104.)

An increase in a separate allowance for expenses of an officer serving under a fixed salary, or an increase in the number of deputies or their compensation, does not violate this provision. (Newman v. Lester, 11 Cal. App. 577, 105 Pac. 785.)

The prohibition of this section refers only to increase of compensation, and the legislature has the power to reduce the compensation of any county or township officer during his term of office, or to change the method of compensation, provided the compensation is not increased. (Crockett v. Mathews, 157 Cal. 153, 106 Pac. 575.)

> Who is officer within prohibition against change of salary during term. See note, Ann. Cas. 1914C, 214.
>
> Constitutional provision against change of salary during term of office as applicable to office held during pleasure of appointing power. See note, Ann. Cas. 1913A, 316.
>
> Constitutional provision against change of salary during term as applicable to person appointed or elected to fill balance of unexpired term. See note, 16 Ann. Cas. 1027.
>
> Constitutional provision against increasing compensation during term of office as applicable where new duties are imposed on officer after taking office. See note, 18 Ann. Cas. 403.

This section has no application to an automatic increase in official salary due to the passing of a city, not by legislative act, but by increased population, from one class to another. (Puterbaugh v. Wadham, 162 Cal. 611, 123 Pac. 804.)

This section has reference only to the compensation as fixed by law when the officers' terms of office begin and the legislature may lower the compensation and afterward raise it, provided the subsequent raise is not in excess of the compensation fixed when the official term began. (Puterbaugh v. Wadham, 162 Cal. 611, 123 Pac. 804.)

As the only constitutional limitation upon the legislature in fixing the compensation of officers is a prohibition against increasing their

salary or emoluments during the term for which the officers are elected, it is permissible for the legislature to make any such increase to apply to future terms. (County of Sacramento v. Pfund, 165 Cal. 84, 130 Pac. 1041.)

Where the result of an act, which is declared to take effect immediately, is to increase the compensation of certain county officers, such act cannot be operative as to them during their terms of office. (Applestill v. Gary, 18 Cal. App. 385, 123 Pac. 228.)

Where after an incumbent of an office assumed office on a fixed salary, under the obligation to perform all of the duties of the office and to pay any deputies therefrom, when the county concerned belonged to a certain class, the legislature changed its classification, and reduced the salary of the office, and provided for as many copyists as might be required who should be paid out of the county treasury, and the incumbent appointed copyists to be so paid, it must be presumed that an increase of compensation would thereby result, and that the legislature did not intend that such change should be put into operation prior to the commencement of a new term. (Williams v. Garey, 19 Cal. App. 769, 127 Pac. 824.)

Where the compensation of an officer at the time of his election is fixed at a lump sum, there being no provision for the appointment of deputies, then the allowance of a deputy during such term constitutes an increase of salary, and is obnoxious to the Constitution. (Elder v. Garey, 19 Cal. App. 775, 127 Pac. 826.)

Where at the beginning of an officer's term the statute allows him a gross sum to cover his compensation and all the expenses of his office, such emolument may not be indirectly increased by the creation of the office of a deputy to be paid by the county. (County of Calaveras v. Poe, 167 Cal. 519, 140 Pac. 23.)

TERM OF OFFICE.—An act changing the time of the election of certain officers so that no election will be held until after the expiration of the terms of the present incumbents is not violative of this section, although they are entitled to hold until their successors are appointed. (Treadwell v. Board of Suprs. of Yolo Co., 62 Cal. 563.)

State taxes, no release or discharge from.

Sec. 10. This section was repealed by amendment adopted November 8, 1910. This amendment was part of the same amendment by which section 14 of article XIII was added. The section repealed was as follows:

> Sec. 10. No county, city, town, or other public or municipal corporation, nor the inhabitants thereof, nor the property therein, shall be released or discharged from its or their proportionate share of taxes to be levied for state purposes, nor shall commutation for such taxes be authorized in any form whatsoever.

RELEASE OF INDEBTEDNESS.—This section was not intended to embrace a release of doubtful claims which the state may hold against a corporation. (Burr v. Carbondale, 76 Ill. 455.)

Local police, sanitary, and other regulations may be enforced.

Sec. 11. Any county, city, town, or township may make and enforce within its limits all such local, police, sanitary, and other regulations as are not in conflict with general laws.

NATURE OF GRANT OF POWER.—The grant is to the body politic and not to the city council, and may be exercised by the electors directly by the initiative and referendum. (In re Pfahler, 150 Cal. 71, 11 L. R. A. (N. S.) 1092, 11 Ann. Cas. 911, 88 Pac. 270.)

This section contains a direct grant of power. (Denton v. Vann, 8 Cal. App. 677, 97 Pac. 675.)

The legislature cannot limit the power conferred by this section so long as it does not conflict with any general law of the state. (In re Ackerman, 6 Cal. App. 5, 91 Pac. 429.)

This grant must be construed to mean counties in their organized condition as bodies politic, and is an authorization by the Constitution to the local legislative body as the representative of the county thus organized to exercise the powers thereby granted in enacting local laws. (Denton v. Vann, 8 Cal. App. 677, 97 Pac. 675.)

The enumeration in the freeholders' charter of Los Angeles of certain trades, callings and occupations which may be prohibited is not a limitation upon the general police power conferred on the city by this section. (In re Montgomery, 163 Cal. 457, Ann. Cas. 1914A, 130, 125 Pac. 1070.)

A municipal corporation is vested with authority to make any such reasonable local police regulations as its legislative body may deem advisable, controlled only by the limitation that they must not conflict with any general laws enacted by the legislature on the subject. (Pasadena School District v. Pasadena, 166 Cal. 7, Ann. Cas. 1915B, 1039, 47 L. R. A. (N. S.) 892, 134 Pac. 985.)

The board of supervisors may make and enforce within the county all such police and sanitary regulations as are not in conflict with general laws. (Ex parte John, 17 Cal. App. 58, 118 Pac. 722.)

This section does not confer power upon a municipality to regulate rates or service or in any other way to regulate the relationship between a utility and its customers and patrons, as distinguished from the city or its inhabitants in general. (Pratt v. Spring Valley Water Co., 4 C. R. C. 1077, 1082.)

LOCAL, POLICE AND SANITARY LAWS.—The police power is subordinate to the power of the federal government to regulate commerce. (Lin Sing v. Washburn, 20 Cal. 534.)

The "other regulations" mentioned in this section must be limited to objects similar to those denominated police and sanitary. (Ex parte Hodges, 87 Cal. 162, 25 Pac. 277.)

Any restriction of the rights of individuals to pursue a lawful avocation must extend to all individuals who might exercise that right within the same district. (County of Los Angeles v. Hollywood Cem. Assn., 124 Cal. 344, 71 Am. St. Rep. 75, 57 Pac. 153.)

Any practice or business the tendency of which, as shown by experience, is to weaken or corrupt the morals of those who follow it or to encourage idleness, instead of habits of industry, is a legitimate subject of police regulation. Gambling is such a practice. (Ex parte Tuttle, 91 Cal. 589, 27 Pac. 933.)

The question as to what measures are needful or appropriate to be taken in the exercise of the police power is primarily for the legislative body to determine; and such determination will not be disturbed by the courts, unless the fundamental rights of the citizen are assailed. (Ex parte Tuttle, 91 Cal. 589, 27 Pac. 933.)

It is not necessary to the exercise of the police power in regulating a business that it shall constitute a nuisance per se. (Ex parte Lacey, 108 Cal. 326, 49 Am. St. Rep. 93, 38 L. R. A. 640, 41 Pac. 411.)

The right to regulate is not confined to such interference with the public welfare and comfort as comes strictly within the common-law definition of nuisance. (In re Junqua, 10 Cal. App. 602, 103 Pac. 159.)

The legislative determination of what is a proper exercise of police powers is not final but is subject to supervision by the courts, which will interfere when the case is made plain, either upon the face of the measure or by extraneous evidence, that needless oppression is worked or that constitutional rights are invaded, or when the local ordinance is unreasonable and oppressive. (In re Junqua, 10 Cal. App. 602, 103 Pac. 159.)

Police power is limited to such measures as are reasonable in their application and which tend in some appreciable degree to promote, protect, or preserve the public health, morals, or safety, or the general welfare. (Ex parte Quarg, 149 Cal. 79, 117 Am. St. Rep. 115, 9 Ann. Cas. 747, 5 L. R. A. (N. S.) 183, 84 Pac. 766.)

The business of conducting a laundry is not unlawful, and cannot be made to depend upon the will of any number of citizens or property owners. (Ex parte Sing Lee, 96 Cal. 354, 31 Am. St. Rep. 218, 24 L. R. A. 195, 31 Pac. 245.)

Police power is exercised in the enforcement of a penalty prescribed for a noncompliance with law. (Merced County v. Helm, 102 Cal. 159, 36 Pac. 399.)

The legislature may delegate to boards of supervisors of counties power to pass local, police and sanitary regulations. (Ex parte Shrader, 33 Cal. 279.)

This provision does not authorize cities to change their charters, or to revolutionize the city government or abrogate a department thereof. (People v. Newman, 96 Cal. 605, 31 Pac. 564.)

Under the charter the supervisors have power to pass ordinances placing such restrictions upon the use of any property or the conduct of any business as may be necessary for the public health. (Laurel Hill Cemetery v. San Francisco, 152 Cal. 464, 27 L. R. A. (N. S.) 260, 14 Ann. Cas. 1080, 93 Pac. 70.)

This section includes the power to amend an existing ordinance upon the same subject. (Foster v. Board of Police Commrs., 102 Cal. 483, 41 Am. St. Rep. 194, 37 Pac. 763.)

So far as mere police regulations are concerned, if city and county ordinances conflict, the police regulations made by the city will control within the limits of the city. (Ex parte Roach, 104 Cal. 272, 37

Pac. 1044; Ex parte Mansfield, 106 Cal. 400, 39 Pac. 775; Los Angeles County v. Eikenberry, 131 Cal. 461, 63 Pac. 766; Ex parte Pfirrmann, 134 Cal. 143, 66 Pac. 205.)

But a county license upon the sale of liquor, collected not merely as a regulation but for revenue, may be collected within a city although the city has collected a license tax for the same business. (Los Angeles County v. Eikenberry, 131 Cal. 461, 63 Pac. 766.)

A city ordinance is not a general law within the meaning of this section. (Los Angeles County v. Eikenberry, 131 Cal. 461, 63 Pac. 766.)

A sanitary district is not a municipal corporation, and has none of the powers granted by this section, nor can the legislature confer such powers upon it. (In re Werner, 129 Cal. 567, 62 Pac. 97.)

Under this section the right of a water company to occupy a public street of a municipality with a ditch is subject to regulation by the municipality. (Santa Ana v. Santa Ana Valley Irr. Co., 163 Cal. 211, 124 Pac. 847.)

A county board of supervisors has authority to submit to the voters of the various precincts in the county questions relating to the issuance of liquor licenses in such precincts, and to select the subdivision in which the vote may be taken. (In re Coombs, 169 Cal. 484; 147 Pac. 131.)

The regulation of the ditch of a water company within a city, with a view to protecting the health and safety of the inhabitants of the city, is a police or sanitary regulation, and the power to make such regulations is vested exclusively in the municipal authorities. (Santa Paula v. Santa Clara Water & Irrigation Co., 3 C. R. C. 143, 144.)

Conflict with general laws.—An act which is violative of an express provision of the Constitution cannot be upheld as a police regulation. (San Francisco v. Liverpool etc. Ins. Co., 74 Cal. 113, 5 Am. St. Rep. 425, 15 Pac. 380.)

A county ordinance in conflict with a valid general law is void. (San Luis Obispo County v. Graves, 84 Cal. 71, 23 Pac. 1032; Ex parte Keeney, 84 Cal. 304, 24 Pac. 34.)

But this is not true of a conflict between a valid county ordinance and an unconstitutional general statute. (San Luis Obispo County v. Graves, 84 Cal. 71, 23 Pac. 1032.)

A provision of a city ordinance prohibiting the sale of spirituous liquors in a city is not in conflict with the general law, which shows a tendency simply to regulate the sale of liquors. (Ex parte Campbell, 74 Cal. 20, 5 Am. St. Rep. 418, 15 Pac. 318; Ex parte Noble, 96 Cal. 362, 31 Pac. 224.)

An ordinance making it unlawful to visit a gambling-house is not in conflict with a provision of the general law making it unlawful to bet at such house. (Ex parte Boswell, 86 Cal. 232, 24 Pac. 1060.)

An ordinance undertaking to punish precisely the same acts which are punishable under the general law of the state is to be deemed in conflict with such general law. (Ex parte Stephen, 114 Cal. 278, 46 Pac. 86; In re Sic, 73 Cal. 142, 14 Pac. 405.)

The mere fact that a certain provision of a city ordinance is in conflict with the general law will not invalidate the entire ordinance if

the provisions thereof are separable. (Ex parte Christensen, 85 Cal. 208, 24 Pac. 747.)

An ordinance containing certain regulations as to the burden of proof and the effect of certain acts as evidence is void. (Ex parte Christensen, 85 Cal. 208, 24 Pac. 747.)

A municipal ordinance making it a misdemeanor to fail to remove an obstruction of a sidewalk is not in conflict with the provisions of the general law declaring such an obstruction a nuisance and punishable as such, since the municipality might legalize a partial obstruction of a street. (Ex parte Taylor, 87 Cal. 91, 25 Pac. 258.)

When the state law provides a general and municipal scheme to prevent the adulteration and sale of milk and dairy products, a municipal ordinance establishing a different standard of purity is void (In re Desanta, 8 Cal. App. 295, 96 Pac. 1027.)

An ordinance imposing a fine not less than twenty-five dollars nor more than five hundred dollars, and imprisonment not less than ten nor more than one hundred days is in conflict with a general law imposing a fine of not less than twenty-five dollars nor more than two hundred dollars and imprisonment not less than ten nor more than one hundred days. (In re Desanta, 8 Cal. App. 295, 96 Pac. 1027.)

An ordinance in direct conflict with a subsequently enacted general law cannot be enforced. (In re Desanta, 8 Cal. App. 295, 96 Pac. 1027.)

A municipal ordinance licensing brothels is subject to the state law punishing the crime of keeping a house of prostitution. (Farmer v. Behmer, 9 Cal. App. 773, 100 Pac. 901.)

An ordinance imposing a less punishment than that imposed by the general law for the same offense is void. (Ex parte Sweetman, 5 Cal. App. 577, 90 Pac. 1069.)

A city ordinance imposing a penalty for having lottery tickets in one's possession, greater than the penalty provided by the general laws for kindred and more serious offenses, is in conflict with the general laws and void. (Ex parte Solomon, 91 Cal. 440, 27 Pac. 757.)

A city ordinance providing that no opium shall be sold without a prescription of a physician is not in conflict with the state law prohibiting the sale of opium unless a record be kept of the sale and the package marked "poison." (Ex parte Hong Shen, 98 Cal. 681, 33 Pac. 799.)

An ordinance is not inconsistent with the general law merely because it makes another and different regulation on the same subject, when there is no direct conflict between its terms and the provisions of the state law. (Ex parte Hong Shen, 98 Cal. 681, 33 Pac. 799.)

Where the penalty imposed for the violation of an ordinance conflicts with the provisions of the Penal Code, the penal clause of the ordinance is void. (Ex parte Mansfield, 106 Cal. 400, 39 Pac. 775.)

An ordinance declaring it unlawful for any person to have in his possession any lottery ticket, unless it be shown that such possession is innocent, is void as in conflict with the general presumption of innocence. (In re Wong Hane, 108 Cal. 680, 49 Am. St. Rep. 138, 41 Pac. 693.)

An ordinance forbidding further interment in the city cemetery is not in conflict with section 3035 of the Political Code. (La Societa etc. v. San Francisco, 131 Cal. 169, 53 L. R. A. 382, 63 Pac. 174.)

It is competent for a city ordinance to prohibit all games played for money which are not specifically denounced by the statute. (In re Murphy, 128 Cal. 29, 60 Pac. 465.)

The fact that an ordinance prohibiting games for money includes, by way of general description, games prohibited by statute, as well as those not so prohibited, does not affect the validity of the ordinance; but all games so prohibited by the general laws must be excluded from the operation of the ordinance. (In re Murphy, 128 Cal. 29, 60 Pac. 465.)

A city ordinance fixing the limit of speed for vehicles in all parts of the city at twelve miles per hour, regardless of crossings or intersecting streets or of obstructions to the view of the operator in approaching an intersecting way, is in conflict with the Motor Vehicle Act of 1913. (Matter of Application of Smith, 26 Cal. App. 116, 146 Pac. 82.)

Under this section, section 549 of the Civil Code, and subdivision 14 of section 862 of the Municipal Corporation Act, cities of the sixth class have power to make a regulation requiring water companies to make service connections and install meters free of charge in the city limits. (Title Guarantee etc. Co. v. Railroad Commission, 168 Cal. 295, 142 Pac. 878.)

Under this section any county, city, town or township has the right to wholly prohibit the carrying on of the retail liquor business, and this includes the power to determine in what places in a county, etc., such business may or may not be carried on. (McRae v. Pine, 25 Cal. App. 594, 144 Pac. 983.)

A county ordinance fixing the maximum penalty for the sale of liquor without a license, so as to bring an infraction of the ordinance within the jurisdiction of the superior court, is in conflict with section 435 of the Penal Code, and therefore void. (Arfsten v. Superior Court, 20 Cal. App. 269, 128 Pac. 949.)

A county ordinance regulating the liquor traffic within the county limits conflicts with the Local Option Act of 1911, allowing subdivisions of a county to vote on the liquor question, and is therefore void. (Matter of Zany, 20 Cal. App. 360, 129 Pac. 295.)

So far as any authority of counties, cities, and towns in the matter of "local, police, sanitary and other regulations" is based on this section, it is subject at all times to the general laws, and such local regulations must give way to the general laws so far as they are in conflict therewith. (Ex parte Beck, 162 Cal. 701, 124 Pac. 543.)

A county ordinance forbidding the sale of liquor except at a fixed place of business and unless a license has been obtained, and forbidding the soliciting or receiving any order for the sale or delivery of liquor, except in precincts where licenses can be obtained, and providing that no license shall be granted unless at the last preceding general election at which the question of granting liquor licenses was submitted to the people, the majority of the people in the precinct for which the license is asked voted in favor of granting such licenses, does not conflict with the so-called "Wyllie Law." (In re Coombs, 169 Cal. 484, 147 Pac. 131.)

Reasonableness, etc.—A municipal ordinance must be consistent with the general powers and purposes of the corporation, must har-

monize with the general laws, the municipal charter, and the princi-
ples of the common law, and can have no extraterritorial force unless
by express permission of the sovereign power. (South Pasadena v.
Los Angeles Terminal Ry. Co., 109 Cal. 315, 41 Pac. 1093; Ex parte
Green, 94 Cal. 387, 29 Pac. 783; In re Ah You, 88 Cal. 99, 22 Am. St.
Rep. 280, 11 L. R. A. 408, 25 Pac. 974; In re Application of Glendale
& Eagle Rock Ry. Co., 4 C. R. C. 320, 324.)

But where the legislature in terms confers upon a municipal corporation the power to pass ordinances of a specified character, an ordinance passed in pursuance thereof cannot be impeached as invalid because it would have been regarded as unreasonable if it had been
passed under the incidental powers of the corporation, or under a
grant of power general in its nature. But where the power to legislate on a given subject is conferred and the mode of its exercise is
not prescribed, then the ordinance passed in pursuance thereof must
be a reasonable exercise of the power, or it will be pronounced void.
(Ex parte Chin Yan, 60 Cal. 78.)

When the question as to the unreasonableness of a municipal ordinance is in doubt, the ordinance will be upheld; but when the ordinance is clearly unreasonable, it will be held void. (Ex parte Mc-
Kenna, 126 Cal. 429, 58 Pac. 916.)

The question of the reasonableness of an ordinance is to be determined by the court from the ordinance, and not by the jury from evidence of facts not appearing upon the face of the ordinance. (Merced County v. Fleming, 111 Cal. 46, 43 Pac. 392.)

In determining whether or not an ordinance regulating a lawful
business is reasonable the court may consider matters dehors the ordinance, but not the motives of the supervisors. (In re Smith, 143 Cal.
368, 77 Pac. 180.)

An ordinance may be reasonable as applied to the regulation of
cemeteries within a city or town, which would be unreasonable if applied to all parts of a county thinly populated in many of its parts.
(County of Los Angeles v. Holywood Cem. Assn., 124 Cal. 344, 71 Am.
St. Rep. 75, 57 Pac. 153.)

An ordinance restricting the use of private property in the interest
of the public health must bear a rational relation to the object sought
to be obtained and cannot be arbitrary or unreasonable, or made a
cloak for the arbitrary interference with or suppression of a lawful
business. But the courts will not interfere with the exercise of legislative discretion unless it clearly appears that such discretion has
been arbitrarily or unreasonably exercised. (Laurel Hill Cemetery v.
San Francisco, 152 Cal. 464, 14 Ann. Cas. 1080, 27 L. R. A. (N. S.)
260, 93 Pac. 70.)

An ordinance imposing a fine not exceeding one thousand dollars
and imprisonment not exceeding six months, for uttering profane and
abusive language in the presence of other persons, is not unreasonable.
(McDonald v. Taylor, 89 Cal. 42, 26 Pac. 595.)

A city ordinance prohibiting the carrying of concealed weapons by
any person other than public officers and travelers, without a permit
of the police commissioners, and prescribing a fine of not less than
two hundred and fifty and not exceeding five hundred dollars, or imprisonment not less than three and not exceeding six months, or both,

does not impose any excessive or unreasonable penalty. (Ex parte
Cheney, 90 Cal. 617, 27 Pac. 436.)

An ordinance making a violation thereof punishable by imprisonment for ten days and a fine of one hundred and fifty dollars, and
imprisonment in case of nonpayment of the fine at the rate of two
dollars a day, is not unreasonable. (Ex parte Green, 94 Cal. 387, 29
Pac. 783.)

A municipal ordinance permitting a fine of not less than twenty
and not more than one thousand dollars for visiting a house of ill-
fame is unreasonable, and not in harmony with the general law. (In
re Ah You, 88 Cal. 99, 22 Am. St. Rep. 280, 11 L. R. A. 408, 25 Pac.
974.)

A county ordinance prohibiting the maintenance of gasworks in a
sparsely settled rural district, and which has the effect to stop the
operation of the gasworks of the petitioner, in the immediate vicinity
of which there are no dwelling-houses, is unreasonable. (In re Smith,
143 Cal. 368, 77 Pac. 180.)

An ordinance making it a misdemeanor to sell gas at a higher rate
than that fixed by law is not unreasonable or contrary to the policy
of the state. (Denninger v. Recorder's Court, 145 Cal. 629, 79 Pac.
360.)

Valid ordinances.—In accordance with the foregoing general principles, the following ordinances have been held valid as police and
sanitary measures: An ordinance for the removal of shade trees growing in the sidewalks of public streets (Vanderhurst v. Tholcke, 113
Cal. 147, 35 L. R. A. 267, 45 Pac. 266); an ordinance providing for a
sewer farm outside of a city (McBean v. Fresno, 112 Cal. 159, 53 Am.
St. Rep. 191, 31 L. R. A. 794, 44 Pac. 358); an ordinance prohibiting
the conducting of any carpet-beating machine within one hundred
feet of any church, schoolhouse, residence, or dwelling-house (Ex
parte Lacey, 108 Cal. 326, 49 Am. St. Rep. 93, 38 L. R. A. 640, 41
Pac. 411); an ordinance providing for the improvement of the channel and banks of a river passing through the city (De Baker v. Southern Cal. Ry. Co., 106 Cal. 257, 46 Am. St. Rep. 237, 39 Pac. 610); a
city ordinance forbidding the beating of drums in the traveled streets
of a city, without the permission of the president of the board of
trustees (In re Flaherty, 105 Cal. 558, 27 L. R. A. 529, 38 Pac. 981);
an ordinance providing that no liquor license shall be granted to any
person who has conducted the business of selling liquors in any place
where females are employed (Foster v. Board of Police Commrs., 102
Cal. 483, 41 Am. St. Rep. 194, 37 Pac. 763); an ordinance providing
that no license shall be issued to persons engaged in the sale of
liquors in dance-cellars or dance-halls, or in places where musical,
theatrical, or other public exhibitions are given, and where females
attend as waitresses (Ex parte Hayes, 98 Cal. 555, 20 L. R. A. 701,
33 Pac. 337); an ordinance fixing the license for conducting a saloon
where females are employed and where intoxicating liquors are sold
in less quantities than one quart at a higher rate than a license for
conducting a saloon where females are not employed (Ex parte
Felchlin, 96 Cal. 360, 31 Am. St. Rep. 223, 31 Pac. 224, approving
opinion of McKinstry, J., in Matter of Maguire, 57 Cal. 604, 40 Am.
Rep. 125); a city ordinance prohibiting the selling of pools on horse-

races, except within the inclosure of a race-track where the race is to be run (Ex parte Tuttle, 91 Cal. 589, 27 Pac. 933); an ordinance making the issuance of a liquor license depend upon the permission of a majority of the police commissioners or the approval of twelve property owners in the block in which the business is carried on (Ex parte Christensen, 85 Cal. 208, 24 Pac. 747; affirmed in Crowley v. Christensen, 137 U. S. 86, 34 L. Ed. 620, 11 Sup. Ct. Rep. 13); an act providing for the exclusion of all unvaccinated children from the public schools (Abeel v. Clark, 84 Cal. 226, 24 Pac. 383); a city ordinance making it unlawful to visit a place for the practice of gambling (Ex parte Lane, 76 Cal. 587, 18 Pac. 677); an ordinance prohibiting the maintenance within the city limits of any tippling-house, dramshop, or barroom, where spirituous liquors are sold or given away (Ex parte Campbell, 74 Cal. 20, 5 Am. St. Rep. 418, 15 Pac. 318); an ordinance which prohibits any person, for the purpose of prostitution, to visit any building kept for the purpose of prostitution (Ex parte Johnson, 73 Cal. 228, 15 Pac. 43); an ordinance prohibiting the alteration or repair of any wooden building within certain designated fire limits, without permission of the fire wardens and approval of a majority of the committee on fire department and the mayor (Ex parte Fiske, 72 Cal. 125, 13 Pac. 310); an ordinance prohibiting the keeping of more than two cows within certain portions of a city (In re Linehan, 72 Cal. 114, 13 Pac. 170); an ordinance prohibiting the carrying on of a public laundry within the city limits, except within prescribed boundaries (In re Hang Kie, 69 Cal. 149, 10 Pac. 327); an ordinance prohibiting the carrying on of a laundry without the consent of the board of supervisors, except in a brick or stone building (In re Yick Wo, 68 Cal. 294, 58 Am. Rep. 12, 9 Pac. 139; reversed by the supreme court of the United States in Yick Wo v. Hopkins, 118 U. S. 356, 20 L. Ed. 220); an ordinance providing that all buildings used as laundries shall be constructed but one story in height, with brick or stone walls, and with metal roofs, doors, and window shutters (Ex parte White, 67 Cal. 102, 7 Pac. 186); a provision of a city charter prohibiting the slaughtering of animals and the maintenance of slaughter-houses within the city (Ex parte Heilbron, 65 Cal. 609, 4 Pac. 648); an ordinance making it unlawful for any person to conduct a laundry within certain limits, without a certificate from the health officer as to its sanitary condition, and a certificate from one of the fire wardens as to the condition of the heating appliances, and forbidding the operation of any laundry between 10 P. M. and 6 A. M., or on Sundays (Ex parte Moynier, 65 Cal. 33, 2 Pac. 728); an ordinance prohibiting the utterance of profane language in the hearing of two or more persons (Ex parte Delaney, 43 Cal. 478); an ordinance forbidding the sale of milk of cows fed upon still slops, etc. (Johnson v. Simonton, 43 Cal. 242); an ordinance making it unlawful to play upon any musical instrument, etc., in any saloon, etc., after midnight (Ex parte Smith & Keating, 38 Cal. 702); an ordinance making it unlawful for any female to be in any saloon, etc., after midnight (Ex parte Smith & Keating, 38 Cal. 702); an ordinance providing that no person shall establish or maintain any slaughter-house, keep herds of more than five swine, keep or cure hides, slaughter cattle, etc., in any part of the city and county (Ex parte Shrader, 33 Cal. 279); an ordinance

making it unlawful for any person to have in his possession any lottery ticket, etc. (Ex parte McClain, 134 Cal. 110, 86 Am. St. Rep. 243, 54 L. R. A. 779, 66 Pac. 69); an ordinance making it unlawful to exhibit in any barred or barricaded house or room or in any place built or protected in a manner to make it difficult of access to police officers, when three or more persons are present, any cards, etc. (Matter of Ah Cheung, 136 Cal. 678, 69 Pac. 492); an ordinance of the city and county of San Francisco prohibiting interments of dead bodies within the city limits (Odd Fellows' Cem. Assn. v. San Francisco, 140 Cal. 226, 73 Pac. 987); an act providing that any person excluded from a place of amusement may recover his actual damages and a penalty (Greenberg v. Western Turf Assn., 140 Cal. 357, 73 Pac. 1050); an ordinance making it unlawful to maintain gasworks within certain defined limits (Dobbins v. Los Angeles, 139 Cal. 179, 96 Am. St. Rep. 95, 72 Pac. 970; reversed by Dobbins v. Los Angeles, 195 U. S. 223, 49 L. Ed. 165, 25 Sup. Ct. Rep. 18; In re Daly, 139 Cal. 216, 72 Pac. 1097); an ordinance requiring the exclusive removal of all garbage by the city to be consumed at the city crematory (In re Zhizhuzza, 147 Cal. 328, 81 Pac. 955); an ordinance employing an expert medical employee as health officer (Valle v. Shaffer, 1 Cal. App. 183, 81 Pac. 1028); an ordinance suppressing public billiard and pool rooms (Ex parte Murphy, 8 Cal. App. 440, 97 Pac. 199); an ordinance forbidding or regulating the sale of poisons (Ex parte Hallawell, 8 Cal. App. 563, 97 Pac. 320); reasonable regulations governing the use of streets by holders of franchises (Merced Falls Gas etc. Co. v. Turner, 2 Cal. App. 720, 84 Pac. 239); an ordinance prohibiting the selling, storing or keeping for sale of intoxicating liquors, except at private residences or for medicinal, mechanical or scientific purposes (Selma v. Brewer, 9 Cal. App. 70, 98 Pac. 61); an ordinance forbidding the alcoholic liquor traffic (Ex parte Mogensen, 5 Cal. App. 596, 90 Pac. 1063, 91 Pac. 334); an ordinance forbidding the escape of soot from any furnace in which distillate or crude oil is consumed (In re Junqua, 10 Cal. App. 602, 103 Pac. 159); an ordinance forbidding the maintenance of a laundry in the city limits in any building used in part for a public store (In re San Chung, 11 Cal. App. 511, 105 Pac. 609); an ordinance regulating the laying of sewers in the public streets (Harter v. Barkley, 158 Cal. 742, 112 Pac. 556); an ordinance prohibiting the business of selling intoxicating liquors within the county of Orange, etc. (Ex parte Young, 154 Cal. 317, 22 L. R. A. (N. S.) 330, 97 Pac. 822); an ordinance limiting the liquor business to certain specified districts within a municipality (Grumbach v. Lelande, 154 Cal. 679, 98 Pac. 1059); an ordinance forbidding the interment of dead bodies within the limits of the city and county of San Francisco (Laurel Hill Cemetery v. San Francisco, 152 Cal. 464, 14 Ann. Cas. 1080, 27 L. R. A. (N. S.) 260, 93 Pac. 70); a law forbidding the employment of children under the age of fourteen years at any regular occupation (In re Spencer, 149 Cal. 396, 117 Am. St. Rep. 137, 9 Ann. Cas. 1105, 86 Pac. 896); an ordinance appointing a deputy sealer of weights and measures for the city of Los Angeles (Milliken v. Meyers, 25 Cal. App. 510, 144 Pac. 321); an ordinance authorizing the appointment of a sealer of weights and measures, and his deputies, and fixing their compensation, and since the amendment of October 10, 1911, of section 14 of this article

did not repeal this section, the counties and municipalities would still have the power to enact such an ordinance as the one above under this section (Scott v. Boyle, 164 Cal. 321, 128 Pac. 941); an ordinance regulating and licensing the business of selling liquor and giving the city council discretion as to the granting of liquor licenses (Guzzi v. McAlister, 21 Cal. App. 276, 131 Pac. 336); an ordinance of a town forbidding the soliciting or taking of orders for the delivery of intoxicating liquors, it not conflicting with the Wyllie Local Option Law (Matter of Application of Anixter, 22 Cal. App. 117, 134 Pac. 193); an ordinance prohibiting any person connected with a laundry from laundering clothes between 10 P. M. and 6 A. M. or upon any portion of Sunday (Soon Hing v. Crowley, 113 U. S. 703, 28 L. Ed. 1145, 5 Sup. Ct. Rep. 730); an ordinance granting an exclusive privilege for fifty years to dispose of garbage and refuse matter by cremation or reduction, and requiring the delivery of all such material at the crematory there to be destroyed at the expense of the person conveying the same (California Reduction Co. v. Sanitary Reduction Works, 199 U. S. 306, 50 L. Ed. 204, 26 Sup. Ct. Rep. 100).

Invalid ordinances.—On the other hand, the following ordinances have been held to be invalid as police and sanitary measures: A county ordinance forbidding the shipment of game from the county in which it has been lawfully killed (Ex parte Knapp, 127 Cal. 101, 59 Pac. 315); a county ordinance making it unlawful to establish, extend or enlarge any cemetery within the county, but permitting burials in cemeteries already established (County of Los Angeles v. Hollywood Cem. Assn., 124 Cal. 344, 71 Am. St. Rep. 75, 57 Pac. 153); a municipal ordinance, not prohibiting all burials within the city, but merely prohibiting further purchases of cemetery lots, and allowing burials in lots already purchased (Ex parte Bohen, 115 Cal. 372, 36 L. R. A. 618, 47 Pac. 55); an ordinance regulating rates of transportation of a street railway outside of the city limits (South Pasadena v. Los Angeles Terminal Ry. Co., 109 Cal. 315, 41 Pac. 1093); a county ordinance providing that all insane asylums shall be constructed of either brick, iron or stone, and surrounded by a brick or stone wall, that they shall not be within four hundred yards of any dwelling or school, that only one class of persons shall be treated in the same building, and that male and female patients shall not be cared for in the same building (Ex parte Whitwell, 98 Cal. 73, 35 Am. St. Rep. 152, 19 L. R. A. 727, 32 Pac. 870); an ordinance prohibiting the carrying on of a public laundry within the corporate limits of the town, except in certain specified blocks thereof, without a written permit from the board of trustees, and the written consent of a majority of the real property owners within the block in which the business is to be carried on, and also of the four blocks immediately surrounding the same (Ex parte Sing Lee, 96 Cal. 354, 31 Am. St. Rep. 218, 24 L. R. A. 195, 31 Pac. 245); an ordinance requiring all occupants of lands within ninety days to exterminate and destroy the ground-squirrels on their respective lands (Ex parte Hodges, 87 Cal. 162, 25 Pac. 277); an ordinance making it unlawful for any contractor performing work for the city to employ any person to work more than eight hours a day, or to employ Chinese labor (Ex parte Kuback, 85 Cal. 274, 20 Am. St. Rep. 226, 9 L. R. A. 482, 24 Pac. 737); an ordi-

nance intended to discriminate in favor of sportsmen and against all other persons in respect to the disposition of game lawfully killed (Ex parte Knapp, 127 Cal. 101, 59 Pac. 315); an ordinance prohibiting the employment of females in dance-halls, etc. (Matter of Maguire, 57 Cal. 604, 40 Am. St. Rep. 125. But see Ex parte Felchlin, 96 Cal. 360, 31 Am. St. Rep. 223, 31 Pac. 224) ; a municipal ordinance which undertakes to absolutely forbid the erection or maintenance of any billboard for advertising purposes. (Varney & Green v. Williams, 155 Cal. 318, 132 Am. St. Rep. 88, 21 L. R. A. (N. S.) 741, 100 Pac. 867); an ordinance making it unlawful to maintain gasworks within certain defined limits, where the limits were shifted in a sudden and unexplained manner just after the gasworks had purchased property within the new limits and while it was proceeding to erect a plant thereon (Dobbins v. Los Angeles, 195 U. S. 223, 49 L. Ed. 169, 25 Sup. Ct. Rep. 18; overruling Dobbins v. Los Angeles, 139 Cal. 179, 16 Am. St. Rep. 95, 72 Pac. 970); an act prohibiting any person from selling tickets to a theater or other place of amusement for a price higher than that originally charged by the management thereof. (Ex parte Quarg, 149 Cal. 79, 117 Am. St. Rep. 115, 9 Ann. Cas. 747, 5 L. R. A. (N. S.) 183, 84 Pac. 766); an act requiring the durable marking of packages of butter containing less than six pounds, and more than one-half pound, by figures or letters not less than one-fourth of an inch high, so as to advise the purchaser or others as to the exact weight of butter contained in such package. (Ex parte Dietrich, 149 Cal. 104, 5 L. R. A. (N. S.) 873, 84 Pac. 770.)

License regulations.—An ordinance requiring a license tax from all peddlers of meat, fish, vegetables, fruit, game, poultry, etc., is valid. (Ex parte Heylman, 92 Cal. 492, 28 Pac. 675.)

An ordinance requiring a license to be obtained by every person who at a fixed place of business sells any goods, etc., is authorized by this section. (Ex parte Mount, 66 Cal. 448, 6 Pac. 78; San Luis Obispo County v. Greenberg, 120 Cal. 300, 52 Pac. 797.)

An ordinance imposing upon traveling salesmen a license tax of fifty dollars per quarter is valid, although a less amount is imposed upon those who sell at a fixed place of business. (Ex parte Haskell, 112 Cal. 412, 32 L. R. A. 527, 44 Pac. 725.)

An ordinance requiring all persons engaged in the business of raising, grazing, herding, or pasturing sheep in the county to pay an annual license of fifty dollars for every thousand sheep is valid. (Ex parte Mirande, 73 Cal. 365, 14 Pac. 888.)

A governing body of a city or county in denying a liquor license is not limited to the terms of the ordinance, but in the exercise of the police power may refuse it upon sufficient grounds addressed to the unfitness of the applicant or the unsuitableness of the place at which the license is to be exercised. (Reed v. Collins, 5 Cal. App. 494, 90 Pac. 973.)

An ordinance requiring a license on dogs and requiring the owner to attach to the collar a tag as evidence of ownership, and payment of the tax, and providing for the destruction of dogs bearing no collar as required is valid. (In re Ackerman, 6 Cal. App. 5, 91 Pac. 429.)

A license imposed upon dogs is an exercise of the police, and not of the taxing power. (In re Ackerman, 6 Cal. App. 5, 91 Pac. 429.)

The power to regulate a business may be exercised by means of a license fee, provided the amount is not more than is reasonably necessary for the regulation of the business. (Plumas Co. v. Wheeler, 149 Cal. 758, 87 Pac. 909.)

A city has no power to impose a license tax upon the right to practice law. (Sonora v. Curtin, 137 Cal. 583, 70 Pac. 674.)

An ordinance levying a license tax upon all sheep which are pastured in the county, except sheep listed as taxable property in the county, and upon which taxes are paid, is not a valid police regulation. (Lassen Co. v. Cone, 72 Cal. 387, 14 Pac. 100.)

A municipal ordinance which, under the guise of a revenue measure, attempts to put an end to the issue of trading stamps, by levying an excessive tax upon that business, however small their monthly sales, assuming to exact from them a tax eight times that required of merchants doing the largest business, is unreasonable and void. (Ex parte McKenna, 126 Cal. 429, 58 Pac. 916.)

An ordinance requiring a license fee of fifty dollars a month for carrying on a saloon, where liquors are sold or given away in quantities less than a gallon, will not be presumed to be oppressive, unreasonable or prohibitory of trade. (In re Guerrero, 69 Cal. 88, 10 Pac. 261.)

A county may impose a license tax upon the sale of spirituous liquors. (Ex parte Wolters, 65 Cal. 269, 3 Pac. 894.)

An ordinance making it a misdemeanor to sell liquors without a license is a valid police regulation. (In re Stuart, 61 Cal. 374.)

An ordinance establishing a license tax of twenty-five dollars a month for the sale of spirituous and fermented liquors is not unreasonable, oppressive or in restraint of trade. (Ex parte Benninger, 64 Cal 291, 30 Pac. 846.)

A county ordinance providing a smaller license tax for the sale of spirituous liquors at wayside inns and rural watering places than when sold in a city is not unlawful as unreasonable, oppressive, or in restraint of trade. (Amador Co. v. Kennedy, 70 Cal. 458, 11 Pac. 757.)

The same is true of an ordinance imposing a higher tax upon such saloons. (Ex parte Stephen, 114 Cal. 278, 46 Pac. 86.)

An ordinance imposing an annual tax of two hundred dollars upon the business of selling spirituous liquors within the city limits is valid. (Ex parte McNally, 73 Cal. 632, 15 Pac. 368.)

An ordinance providing that a liquor license can only be obtained upon petition to the city council of the applicant accompanied by a certificate of five respectable citizens of the neighborhood in which the business is to be conducted as to his character, and upon a determination by the board that he is qualified to carry on the business, is valid. (In re Bickerstaff, 70 Cal. 35, 11 Pac. 393.)

An ordinance purporting to regulate the business of selling liquors, but in fact prohibiting the sale thereof, cannot be upheld. (Merced Co. v. Fleming, 111 Cal. 46, 43 Pac. 392.)

An ordinance imposing a license tax for carrying on the "business" or "occupation" of retail liquor dealer in a "retail liquor establishment," is a tax upon the business and not upon the articles sold. (Los Angeles County v. Eikenberry, 131 Cal. 461, 63 Pac. 766.)

A county ordinance imposing a liquor license of thirteen dollars per month is reasonable. (Los Angeles County v. Eikenberry, 131 Cal. 461, 63 Pac. 766.)

> Laws and regulation of health and their validity. See note, 47 Am. St. Rep. 541.
>
> Power to establish markets. See note, 43 Am. Rep. 473.
>
> Power to establish and regulate markets. See notes, 23 Am. St. Rep. 581; 85 Am. Dec. 286.
>
> Power to create monopolies in removal of garbage and noxious substances. See notes, Ann. Cas. 1913D, 61; 97 Am. St. Rep. 688.
>
> Power to make and enforce regulations respecting street railways for the protection of the public. See note, 104 Am. St. Rep. 636.
>
> Regulation of billboards. See notes, 132 Am. St. Rep. 92; Ann. Cas. 1913D, 958.
>
> Validity of legislation establishing building line. See notes, Ann. Cas. 1914B, 194; 19 Ann. Cas. 188.

Assessment and collection of taxes.

Sec. 12. The legislature shall have no power to impose taxes upon counties, cities, towns, or other public or municipal corporations, or upon the inhabitants · or property thereof, for county, city, town, or other municipal purposes, but may, by general laws, vest in the corporate authorities thereof the power to assess and collect taxes for such purposes.

TAXATION FOR MUNICIPAL PURPOSES.—Under this section the whole subject of county and municipal taxes for local purposes is relegated to the corporate authorities thereof, and the legislature has no power to impose any tax whatever within those territories for local purposes. (San Francisco v. Liverpool etc. Ins. Co., 74 Cal. 113, 5 Am. St. Rep. 425, 15 Pac. 380.)

The legislature cannot directly exercise the power of assessment within an incorporated city, but may empower the municipal authorities to do so. (People v. Lynch, 51 Cal. 15, 21 Am. Rep. 677.)

The legislature has power to direct and control the affairs and property of a municipal corporation for municipal purposes, and may for such purposes so control its affairs by appropriate legislation as ultimately to compel it, out of the funds of its treasury, or by taxation, to pay a demand which in good conscience it ought to pay. (Sinton v. Ashbury, 41 Cal. 525.)

The legislature may authorize the authorities of a city to purchase an agricultural park, to issue bonds in payment therefor, and to levy a tax for the payment of the same. (Bank of Sonoma Co. v. Fairbanks, 52 Cal. 196.)

The power of a county or other public corporation to impose taxes is only that which is granted by the legislature. (Hughes v. Ewing, 93 Cal. 414, 28 Pac. 1067.)

The legislature cannot impose a tax upon the property or inhabitants of a school district, without leaving any discretion in regard thereto to the local authorities. (McCabe v. Carpenter, 102 Cal. 469, 36 Pac. 836.)

A local board cannot be authorized to levy local taxes and assessments for a general public purpose. (People v. Parks, 58 Cal. 624.)

An ordinance imposing a license tax and distinguishing between hotels where meals are cooked and served by a proprietor or the members of his family and those where meals are not so cooked and served is valid. (Ex parte Lemon, 143 Cal. 558, 65 L. R. A. 946, 77 Pac. 455.)

License taxes for revenue are taxes within the meaning of this section. (Ex parte Jackson, 143 Cal. 564, 77 Pac. 457.)

The act of 1876, authorizing the construction of a bridge, and declaring that the cost should be assessed upon certain specified lands, and providing for a commission to apportion the cost, was held constitutional. (Pacific Bridge Co. v. Kirkham, 64 Cal. 519, 2 Pac. 409.)

An act providing for the completion of the city hall in San Francisco, and providing that the work should only be done after the board of supervisors declare that they deem the work expedient, is not violative of this section. (People v. Bartlett, 67 Cal. 156, 7 Pac. 417.)

This section does not prevent a city from providing in a freeholders' charter for taxation for municipal purposes. (Security Sav. Bank etc. Co. v. Hinton, 97 Cal. 214, 32 Pac. 3.)

The words "corporate authorities thereof" are to be construed distributively as referring to the governing body of each of the several municipalities and quasi municipalities referred to in the section, and as importing the legislative department of the municipality only. (Board of Education v. Board of Trustees, 129 Cal. 599, 62 Pac. 173.)

The provision of the fee bill of 1895, requiring the payment of one dollar for each one thousand dollars, in excess of three thousand dollars, of the appraised value of an estate, upon the filing of the inventory, is in violation of this section. (Fatjo v. Pfister, 117 Cal. 83, 48 Pac. 1012.)

An act requiring foreign insurance corporations to pay to the county treasury a certain proportion of premiums received by them, to constitute a firemen's relief fund, to be under the control of the fire commissioners, is in violation of this section. (San Francisco v. Liverpool etc. Ins. Co., 74 Cal. 113, 5 Am. St. Rep. 425, 15 Pac. 380.)

An act validating a void assessment is contrary to the provisions of this section. (Brady v. King, 53 Cal. 44; Taylor v. Palmer, 31 Cal. 240; People v. Lynch, 51 Cal. 15, 21 Am. Rep. 677; Schumaker v. Toberman, 56 Cal. 508; Fanning v. Schammel, 68 Cal. 428, 9 Pac. 427; Kelly v. Luning, 76 Cal. 309, 18 Pac. 335.)

An act requiring the trustees of a swamp-land reclamation district to make up a sworn statement of the cost of the reclamation work, "based upon the books and vouchers thereof," and requiring the amount so reported to be assessed upon the lands of the district, is violative of the provisions of this section. (People v. Houston, 54 Cal. 536.)

The act of 1891, permitting the organization and creation of sanitary districts, is not in violation of this section, since such districts do not necessarily include municipal corporations. (Woodward v. Fruitvale Sanitary Dist., 99 Cal. 554, 34 Pac. 239.)

An act authorizing the county superintendent of schools to furnish the board of supervisors an estimate of a tax, and making it the duty of the board to proceed to fix a rate which will realize the amount of the estimate, is void. (McCabe v. Carpenter, 102 Cal. 469, 36 Pac. 836.)

This section does not invalidate the provisions of the Political Code making the city of Eureka liable for the expense of work on Humboldt bay outside of the city—that provision having been enacted prior to the new Constitution. (Quigg v. Evans, 121 Cal. 546, 53 Pac. 1093.)

The general municipal corporation act authorizing the boards of trustees of cities to adopt a revenue system is valid. (Escondido v. Escondido Lumber etc. Co., 8 Cal. App. 435, 97 Pac. 197.)

Section 39 of the Wright Irrigation Act, providing that if the trustees of the district fail to levy a tax to pay the bonds of the district, the board of supervisors shall do so, is not unconstitutional. (Nevada Nat. Bank v. Board of Supervisors, 5 Cal. App. 638, 91 Pac. 122.)

The question of sanitation is not a "local" or "municipal" affair within the inhibition of this section. (Pixley v. Saunders, 168 Cal. 152, 141 Pac. 815.)

License taxes.—A license tax graduated according to the amount of the monthly sales of the merchant is valid, since it applies uniformly to all persons in the same category. (Sacramento v. Crocker, 16 Cal. 119.)

A law imposing upon a person residing in a given section of the state a license as a merchant without reference to his occupation would be void. (Ex parte Ah Pong, 19 Cal. 106.)

Under this section a municipality may impose a license tax for the purpose of revenue. (In re Guerrero, 69 Cal. 88, 10 Pac. 261.)

This section authorizes the imposition by a county of a license tax on the sale of spirituous liquors and the appointment of a suitable person to collect the same. (In re Lawrence, 69 Cal. 608, 11 Pac. 217.)

A license imposed by the legislature for carrying on the business of selling goods, etc., at a fixed place of business, is a "tax" within the meaning of this section, and, being for county purposes, is in violation of this section. (People v. Martin, 60 Cal. 153.)

A county ordinance imposing a license tax upon every person engaged in the business of raising, grazing, herding, or pasturing sheep, etc., within the county, is authorized by this section. (El Dorado County v. Meiss, 100 Cal. 268, 34 Pac. 716.)

The fact that such ordinance applies to nonresidents as well as residents, instead of being an objection to the validity of the tax, is essential to sustain its validity. (El Dorado County v. Meiss, 100 Cal. 268, 34 Pac. 716.)

A city ordinance regulating liquor licenses, and a section of the city charter giving the city a remedy by civil action in any case where a person, required by any ordinance to take out a license and to pay

therefor, shall fail to do so, are not in conflict with this section. (Sacramento v. Dillman, 102 Cal. 107, 36 Pac. 385.)

When the right to collect a license tax by suit is limited to instances in which the persons commenced some "business," no action can be maintained to recover a license tax for the sale of intoxicating liquors, since such sale is not a business. (Merced Co. v. Helm, 102 Cal. 159, 36 Pac. 399.)

But an ordinance requiring "every person who in any saloon, etc., sells or gives away" any intoxicating liquor to pay a license tax, should be construed as a tax upon the business. (Ex parte Mansfield, 106 Cal. 400, 39 Pac. 775. Merced Co. v. Helm, 102 Cal. 159, 36 Pac. 399, distinguished. See, also, Ex parte Seube, 115 Cal. 629, 47 Pac. 596.)

Where a county passed an ordinance requiring a high license tax for the sale of intoxicating liquors but fixing no penalty for engaging in the business, the ordinance is not to be regarded as the exercise of the police power, but as a revenue measure. (Merced Co. v. Helm, 102 Cal. 159, 36 Pac. 399.)

A county ordinance imposing a license for revenue on the business of liquor dealer is valid, and such license may be collected within cities. (Ex parte Mansfield, 106 Cal. 400, 39 Pac. 775; Ventura Co. v. Clay, 112 Cal. 65, 44 Pac. 488.)

This section does not prohibit the legislature from enacting a law preventing counties, cities, etc., from levying and collecting a license tax for revenue. (Ex parte Pfirrmann, 134 Cal. 143, 66 Pac. 205.)

Powers not to be delegated to special commission, etc.

Sec. 13. The legislature shall not delegate to any special commission, private corporation, company, association or individual any power to make, control, appropriate, supervise or in any way interfere with any county, city, town or municipal improvement, money, property, or effects, whether held in trust or otherwise, or to levy taxes or assessments or perform any municipal function whatever, except that the legislature shall have power to provide for the supervision, regulation and conduct, in such manner as it may determine, of the affairs of irrigation districts, reclamation districts or drainage districts, organized or existing under any law of this state. (Amendment adopted November 3, 1914.)

[ORIGINAL SECTION.]

Sec. 13. The legislature shall not delegate to any special commission, private corporation, company, association, or individual, any power to make, control, appropriate, supervise, or in any way interfere with, any county, city, town, or municipal improvement, money, property, or effects, whether held in trust or otherwise, or to levy taxes or assessments, or perform any municipal functions whatever.

MUNICIPAL FUNDS.—This section is prospective, and applies only to legislation enacted after its adoption. (Board of Commissioners v. Board of Trustees, 71 Cal. 310, 12 Pac. 224.)

The legislature may direct a municipality to audit and allow claims against the municipality. (People v. Board of Supervisors, 11 Cal. 206.)

This section equally forbids the legislature from delegating to a municipal corporation power to do what the legislature is itself forbidden from doing by this section. (Yarnell v. Los Angeles, 87 Cal. 603, 25 Pac. 767.)

The legislature has no control over funds of a municipality except to appropriate them for municipal purposes or in satisfaction of some valid claim against the municipality. (Conlin v. Board of Supervisors, 114 Cal. 404, 33 L. R. A. 752, 46 Pac. 279.)

An act creating a police life and health insurance fund does not create a "special commission" within the meaning of this section. (Pennie v. Reis, 80 Cal. 266, 22 Pac. 176.)

Where an act leaves it discretionary with the local legislative body whether or not the improvement shall be made, but provides that, if done, it shall be done by a commission created by the act, it is not in violation of this section. (Lent v. Tillson, 72 Cal. 404, 14 Pac. 71.)

An act providing for the commitment of minor criminals to nonsectarian charitable corporations, the expense of maintenance to be paid by the county, is not in violation of this section. (Boys' and Girls' Aid Soc. v. Reis, 71 Cal. 627, 12 Pac. 796.)

Where commissioners to open streets are simply made the agents of the municipality, and act under the direction of the city authorities, this section is not violated. (Davies v. Los Angeles, 86 Cal. 37, 24 Pac. 771.)

The act of 1891, permitting the organization and creation of sanitary districts, is not in conflict with this section, since such districts do not necessarily include municipal corporations. (Woodward v. Fruitvale Sanitary Dist., 99 Cal. 554, 34 Pac. 239.)

Legislative power is not delegated under the Wright Act, by enacting conditions upon the performance of which a public corporation, namely, an irrigation district, is organized within boundaries fixed by a board of supervisors after a hearing and a vote of electors. (Fallbrook Irr. Dist. v. Bradley, 164 U. S. 112, 41 L. Ed. 369, 17 Sup. Ct. Rep. 56.)

An ordinance providing that municipal bonds shall be payable outside of the state, at a bank in New York, is in violation of this section. (Los Angeles v. Teed, 112 Cal. 319, 44 Pac. 580.)

But a contract by the board of supervisors for the sale of bonds at par, to be made payable at a bank in another county, does not constitute such bank a custodian of county funds, or the agent of either party. (Mack v. Jastro, 126 Cal. 130, 58 Pac. 372.)

A statute conferring upon the supervisors power to license individuals to take tolls on a public road, as compensation for keeping the road in repair, is not in violation of this provision. (Blood v. McCarty, 112 Cal. 561, 44 Pac. 1025.)

An act allowing county officers to appoint deputies, whose salaries are fixed by the act and made payable out of the county treasury, is

not in violation of this section. (Tulare Co. v. May, 118 Cal. 303, 50 Pac. 427.)

An act permitting the county clerk to make the compensation of the number of deputies he may see fit to appoint a charge upon the county treasury violates this section. (San Francisco v. Broderick, 125 Cal. 188, 57 Pac. 887.)

The authority given by the Vrooman Act to the contractor to collect the assessment is not a delegation of a municipal function. (Banaz v. Smith, 133 Cal. 102, 65 Pac. 309.)

To convey to a mortgagee the statutory powers of the board of trustees of an irrigation district is in violation of this section. (Merchants' Nat. Bank v. Escondido Irr. Dist., 144 Cal. 329, 77 Pac. 937.)

This provision applies to public or municipal corporations, such as irrigation districts, as well as to ordinary municipalities or cities. (Merchants' Nat. Bank v. Escondido Irr. Dist., 144 Cal. 329, 77 Pac. 937.)

The fixing of the boundaries of the territory to be annexed to a city or town is not a municipal function. (People v. Ontario, 148 Cal. 625, 84 Pac. 205.)

The initiative and referendum is not in violation of this section, since the aggregate body of voters cannot be held to be a special commission. (In re Pfahler, 150 Cal. 71, 11 Ann. Cas. 911, 11 L. R. A. (N. S.) 1092, 88 Pac. 270.)

The object of this section was to emancipate municipal corporations from the authority and control formerly exercised over them by the legislature. (In re Pfahler, 150 Cal. 71, 11 Ann. Cas. 911, 11 L. R. A. (N. S.) 1092, 88 Pac. 270.)

The commission provided for in the act of 1907 to change the boundary between Fresno and Kings counties is not within the prohibition of this section. (Wheeler v. Herbert, 152 Cal. 224, 92 Pac. 353.)

The question of sanitation is not a "local" or "municipal" affair within the inhibition of this section. (Pixley v. Saunders, 168 Cal. 152, 141 Pac. 815.)

Payment of bonds.

Sec. 13½. Any county, city and county, city, town, municipality, irrigation district, or other public corporation, issuing bonds under the laws of the state, is hereby authorized and empowered to make said bonds and the interest thereon payable at any place or places within or outside of the United States, and in any money, domestic or foreign, designated in said bonds. (Amendment adopted November 3, 1914.)

[ORIGINAL SECTION.]

Sec. 13½. Nothing in this Constitution contained shall be construed as prohibiting the state or any county, city and county, city, town, municipality, or other public corporation, issuing bonds

under the laws of the state, to make said bonds payable at any place within the United States designated in said bonds. (New section added by amendment adopted November 6, 1906.)

Inspection officers, appointment of.

Sec. 14. The legislature may by general and uniform laws provide for the inspection, measurement and graduation of merchandise, manufactured articles and commodities, and may provide for the appointment of such officers as may be necessary for such inspection, measurement and graduation. (Amendment approved October 10, 1911.)

[ORIGINAL SECTION.]

Sec. 14. No state office shall be continued or created in any county, city, town or other municipality, for the inspection, measurement or graduation of any merchandise, manufacture, or commodity; but such county, city, town, or municipality may, when authorized by general law, appoint such officers.

WEIGHTS AND MEASURES.—Prior to its amendment on October 10, 1911, this section empowered the legislature to enact the statute of March 18, 1911, authorizing the respective counties and municipalities of the state to appoint sealers of weights and measures. Under this section as amended the legislature may provide either a state system for such purpose, administered by state officers, or a local system administered by the respective counties, cities or cities and counties, through officers which they may appoint under the authority of the general statute. There being no statute providing such state system, the above-mentioned statute remains fully in force, and until the repeal of this act or the establishment of a state system, the provisions of the act prevail. (Scott v. Boyle, 164 Cal. 321, 128 Pac. 941.)

This section abolished the office of inspector of gas-meters created by section 577 et seq. of the Political Code. (Condict v. Police Court, 59 Cal. 278.)

Validity of legislation for prevention of fraud in weights and measures. See note, Ann. Cas. 1912C, 251.

Private property not liable for corporate debt of municipality.

Sec. 15. Private property shall not be taken or sold for the payment of the corporate debt of any political or municipal corporation.

Moneys, etc., to be deposited with treasurer.

Sec. 16. All moneys, assessments, and taxes belonging to or collected for the use of any county, city, town, or other

public or municipal corporation, coming into the hands of any officer thereof, shall immediately be deposited with the treasurer, or other legal depositary, to the credit of such city, town, or other corporation respectively, for the benefit of the funds to which they respectively belong.

MUNICIPAL FUNDS.—This section only relates to those officers who rightfully or officially receive money for the county. (San Luis Obispo County v. Farnum, 108 Cal. 562, 41 Pac. 445.)

The words "legal depositary" do not include a private individual or corporation. (Yarnell v. Los Angeles, 87 Cal. 603, 25 Pac. 767.)

An ordinance providing that municipal bonds shall be payable outside of the state, at a bank in New York, is in violation of this provision. (Los Angeles v. Teed, 112 Cal. 319, 44 Pac. 580.)

Funds of a school district are not subject to the control of the county. (Pacific Mut. Life Ins. Co. v. San Diego County, 112 Cal. 314, 41 Pac. 423, 44 Pac. 571.)

A contract by a municipal corporation making the bank which will pay the highest rate of interest a depository of the public moneys of the city is in violation of this section. (Yarnell v. Los Angeles, 87 Cal. 603, 25 Pac. 767.)

It is the duty of the tax collector to pay all taxes collected by him into the county treasury, whether or not the tax is valid. (Craig v. Boone, 146 Cal. 718, 81 Pac. 22.)

Deposit of public moneys.

Sec. 16½. All moneys belonging to the state, or to any county or municipality within this state, may be deposited in any national bank or banks within this state, or in any bank or banks organized under the laws of this state, in such manner and under such conditions as may be provided by law; provided, that such bank or banks in which such moneys are deposited shall furnish as security for such deposits, bonds of the United States, or of this state or of any county, municipality or school district within this state, or of any irrigation district within this state, to be approved by the officer or officers designated by law, to an amount in value of at least ten per cent in excess of the amount of such deposit; and provided, that such bank or banks shall pay a reasonable rate of interest, not less than two per cent per annum on the daily balances therein deposited; and provided, that no deposit shall at any one time exceed fifty per cent of the paid-up capital stock of such depository bank or banks; and provided, further, that no officer shall deposit

at one time more than twenty per cent of such public moneys available for deposit in any bank while there are other qualified banks requesting such deposits. (Amendment adopted November 5, 1912.)

[ORIGINAL SECTION.]

Sec. 16½. All moneys belonging to the state, or to any county or municipality within this state, may be deposited in any national bank or banks within this state, or in any bank or banks organized under the laws of this state, in such manner and under such conditions as may be provided by law; provided, that such bank or banks in which such moneys are deposited shall furnish as security for such deposits, bonds of the United States, or of this state or of any county, municipality or school district within this state, to be approved by the officer or officers designated by law, to an amount in value of at least ten per cent in excess of the amount of such deposit; and provided, that such bank or banks shall pay a reasonable rate of interest, not less than two per cent per annum on the daily balances therein deposited, and provided, that no deposit shall at any one time exceed fifty per cent of the paid-up capital stock of such depositary bank or banks, and provided further, that no officer shall deposit at one time more than twenty per cent of such public moneys available for deposit in any bank while there are other qualified banks requesting such deposits. (New section added by amendment adopted November 6, 1906.)

DEPOSITS IN BANKS.—Section 16½ of article XI of the Constitution, added by amendment November 6, 1906, providing for the deposit in banks of state, county and municipal funds, "in such manner and under such conditions as may be provided by law," does not authorize the legislature to enact a law authorizing the officers of a municipality governed by a freeholders' charter to make such deposits of municipal moneys, contrary to the express provision of its charter in that regard. (Rothschild v. Bantel, 152 Cal. 5, 91 Pac. 803.)

Making profit out of public funds a felony.

Sec. 17. The making of profit out of county, city, town, or other public money, or using the same for any purpose not authorized by law, by any officer having the possession or control thereof, shall be a felony, and shall be prosecuted and punished as prescribed by law.

Restrictions on power to incur indebtedness.

Sec. 18. No county, city, town, township, board of education, or school district, shall incur any indebtedness or liability in any manner or for any purpose exceeding in any year the income and revenue provided for such year, with-

out the assent of two-thirds of the qualified electors thereof, voting at an election to be held for that purpose, nor unless before or at the time of incurring such indebtedness provision shall be made for the collection of an annual tax sufficient to pay the interest on such indebtedness as it falls due, and also provision to constitute a sinking fund for the payment of the principal thereof on or before maturity, which shall not exceed forty years from the time of contracting the same; provided, however, that the city and county of San Francisco may at any time pay the unpaid claims, with interest thereon at the rate of five per cent per annum, for materials furnished to and work done for said city and county during the forty-first, forty-second, forty-third, forty-fourth, and fiftieth fiscal years, and for unpaid teachers' salaries for the fiftieth fiscal year, out of the income and revenue of any succeeding year or years, the amount to be paid in full of said claims not to exceed in the aggregate the sum of five hundred thousand dollars, and that no statute of limitations shall apply in any manner to these claims; and provided, further, that the city of Vallejo, of Solano county, may pay its existing indebtedness, incurred in the construction of its waterworks, whenever two-thirds of the electors thereof, voting at an election held for that purpose, shall so decide, and that no statute of limitations shall apply in any manner. Any indebtedness or liability incurred contrary to this provision, with the exceptions hereinbefore recited, shall be void. The city and county of San Francisco, the city of San Jose, and the town of Santa Clara may make provision for a sinking fund, to pay the principal of any indebtedness incurred, or to be hereafter incurred by it, to commence at a time after the incurring of such indebtedness of no more than a period of one-fourth of the time of maturity of such indebtedness, which shall not exceed seventy-five years from the time of contracting the same. Any indebtedness incurred contrary to any provision of this section shall be void; and provided, further, that the county of Alameda may, upon the assent of two-thirds of the qualified electors thereof voting at an election to be held for that purpose, incur a bonded indebtedness of not to exceed one

million dollars, and the legislative authority of said county
of Alameda shall issue bonds therefor and grant and turn
over to the Panama-Pacific International Exposition company, a corporation organized under the laws of the state
of California, March 22, 1910, the proceeds of said bonds
for stock in said company or under such other terms and
conditions as said legislative authority may determine, the
same to be used and disbursed by said exposition company
for the purposes of an exposition to be held in the city and
county of San Francisco to celebrate the completion of the
Panama canal; said bonds, so issued, to be of such form and
to be redeemable, registered and converted in such manner
and amounts, and at such times not later than forty years
from the date of their issue as the legislative authority of
said county of Alameda shall determine; the interest on said
bonds not to exceed five per centum per annum, and said
bonds to be exempt from all taxes for state, county and
municipal purposes, and to be sold for not less than par at
such times and places, and in such manner, as shall be determined by said legislative authority; the proceeds of said
bonds, when sold, to be payable immediately upon such
terms or conditions as said legislative body may determine,
to the treasurer of said Panama-Pacific International Exposition company, upon demands of said treasurer of said
exposition company, without the necessity of the approval
of such demands by other authority, than said legislative
authority of Alameda county, the same to be used and disbursed by said Panama-Pacific International Exposition
company for the purposes of such exposition, under the direction and control of said exposition company; and, the
legislative authority of said county of Alameda is hereby
empowered and directed to levy a special tax on all taxable
property in said county each year after the issue of said
bonds to raise an amount to pay the interest on said bonds
as the same become due, and to create a sinking fund to pay
the principal thereof when the same shall become due.
(Amendment adopted November 3, 1914.)

[AMENDMENT OF 1900.]

Sec. 18. No county, city, town, township, board of education, or school districts, shall incur any indebtedness or liability in any manner or.for any purpose exceeding in any year the income and revenue provided for such year, without the assent of two-thirds of the qualified electors thereof, voting at an election to be held for that purpose, nor unless before or at the time of. incurring such indebtedness provision shall be made for the collection of an annual tax sufficient to pay the interest on such indebtedness as it falls due, and also provision to constitute a sinking fund for the payment of the principal thereof on or before maturity, which shall not exceed forty years from the time of contracting the same; provided, however, that the city and county of San Francisco may at any time pay the unpaid claims, with interest thereon at the rate of five per cent per annum, for materials furnished to and work done for said city and county during the forty-first, forty-second, forty-third, forty-fourth, and fiftieth fiscal years, and for unpaid teachers' salaries for the fiftieth fiscal year, out of the income and revenue of any succeeding year or years, the amount to be paid in full of said claims not to exceed in the aggregate the sum of five hundred thousand dollars, and that no statute of limitations shall apply in any manner to these claims; and provided further, that the city of Vallejo, of Solano county, may pay its existing indebtedness, incurred in the construction of its waterworks, whenever two-thirds of the electors thereof, voting at an election held for that purpose, shall so decide, and that no statute of limitations shall apply in any manner. Any indebtedness or liability incurred contrary to this provision, with the exceptions hereinbefore recited, shall be void. (Amendment adopted November 6, 1900.)

By amendment. adopted November 6, 1906, the following was added at the end of this section:

The city and county of San Francisco, the city of San Jose and the town of Santa Clara may make provision for a sinking fund, to pay the principal of any indebtedness incurred, or to be hereafter incurred by it, to commence at a time after the incurring of such indebtedness of no more than a period of one-fourth of the time of maturity of such indebtedness, which shall not exceed seventy-five years from the time of contracting the same. Any indebtedness incurred contrary to any provision of this section shall be void.

[AMENDMENT OF 1892.]

Sec. 18. No county, city, town, township, board of education, or school district, shall incur any indebtedness or liability, in any manner, or for any purpose, exceeding in any year the income and revenue provided for it for such year, without the assent of two-thirds of the qualified electors thereof voting at an election to be held for that purpose, nor unless, before or at the time of incurring such indebtedness, provision shall be made for the collection of an annual tax sufficient to pay the interest on such indebtedness as it falls due, and also provision to constitute a sinking fund for the

payment of the principal thereof on or before maturity, which shall not exceed forty years from the time of contracting the same. Any indebtedness or liability incurred contrary to this provision shall be void. (Ratification declared December 30, 1892.)

[ORIGINAL SECTION.]

Sec. 18. No county, city, town, township, board of education, or school district, shall incur any indebtedness or liability in any manner or for any purpose, exceeding in any year the income and revenue provided for it for such year, without the assent of two-thirds of the qualified electors thereof voting at an election to be held for that purpose, nor unless, before or at the time of incurring such indebtedness, provision shall be made for the collection of an annual tax sufficient to pay the interest on such indebtedness as it falls due and also to constitute a sinking fund for the payment of the principal thereof within twenty years from the time of contracting the same. Any indebtedness or liability incurred contrary to this provision shall be void.

MUNICIPAL INDEBTEDNESS.—This provision is to be naturally and reasonably construed as providing that all legitimate indebtedness of the municipality must not exceed all the revenues and income provided for that year. (Higgins v. San Diego, 131 Cal. 294, 63 Pac. 470.)

It refers only to the acts or contracts of the city and not to liabilities which the law may cast upon her. (McCracken v. San Francisco, 16 Cal. 591; Lewis v. Widber, 99 Cal. 412, 33 Pac. 1128.)

It does not apply to the payment of the salary of a public officer, whose office has been created and salary fixed by law. (Lewis v. Widber, 99 Cal. 412, 33 Pac. 1128; Harrison v. Horton, 5 Cal. App. 415, 90 Pac. 716.)

It does not apply to the obligation of a city to return money which she has received by mistake or without authority of law. (Argenti v. San Francisco, 16 Cal. 255.)

It does not apply to a board of trustees of a free public library of a city. (Robertson v. Board of Library Trustees, 136 Cal. 403, 69 Pac. 88.)

Under this section no indebtedness or liability can be incurred by a municipality (except in the manner therein provided), exceeding in any year the income and revenue actually received by it. Each year's income and revenue must pay each year's indebtedness and liability, and no indebtedness or liability incurred in any one year can be paid out of the income of any future year. (San Francisco Gas Co. v. Brickwedel, 62 Cal. 641; Schwartz v. Wilson, 75 Cal. 502, 17 Pac. 449; Smith v. Broderick, 107 Cal. 644, 48 Am. St. Rep. 167, 40 Pac. 1033; Weaver v. San Francisco, 111 Cal. 319, 43 Pac. 972; Montague & Co. v. English, 119 Cal. 225, 51 Pac. 327.)

This is an inhibition against which a municipality cannot incur any indebtedness exceeding in any year the income and revenue provided for it for such year except in the mode prescribed, and the mode prescribed, therefore, becomes the measure of the power of the

municipality to incur an indebtedness beyond the constitutional limit. (City of Santa Cruz v. Wykes, 202 Fed. 357, 120 C. C. A. 485.)

The power to create the excess municipal indebtedness, given by this section, does not abide with the municipality or its common council alone, but with the assent of two-thirds of its electors. (City of Santa Cruz v. Wykes, 202 Fed. 357, 120 C. C. A. 485.)

The fact that the obligation is reduced to judgment and a special tax levied and collected for its payment does not alter the case. (Smith v. Broderick, 107 Cal. 644, 48 Am. St. Rep. 167, 40 Pac. 1033; Goldsmith v. San Francisco, 115 Cal. 36, 46 Pac. 816.)

A creditor of the city does not acquire a right to be paid out of the income for any subsequent year on the ground that the funds were depleted by a large excess in the expenses of a general election over the estimate made by the supervisors. (Weaver v. San Francisco, 111 Cal. 319, 43 Pac. 972.)

The income provided for a county during a given fiscal year must be applied to the payment of the county indebtedness incurred during such year, before the payment of any indebtedness of a preceding year can be made therefrom. (Shaw v. Statler, 74 Cal. 258, 15 Pac. 833.)

Moneys of a previous fiscal year, remaining in the treasury in a subsequent year, are not part of the fund of the subsequent year, but they remain a part of the fund of the previous year, and a claimant of that fund cannot be robbed of his due by a technical transfer. (Bilby v. McKenzie, 112 Cal. 143, 44 Pac. 341.)

Where the revenue of one fiscal year has been exhausted, the city officers cannot, for the purpose of providing for the present needs of the municipality during the remainder of the year, incur debts to be met in a subsequent year, except in the manner provided in this section. (Bradford v. San Francisco, 112 Cal. 537, 44 Pac. 912.)

This section does not prohibit the auditing of demands for salaries, although the aggregate amount of the salaries for a given year would exceed the amount limited by the board of supervisors for the payment of such salaries during that year. (Welch v. Strother, 74 Cal. 413, 16 Pac. 22.)

This section does not apply to irrigation districts. (In re Madera Irr. Dist., 92 Cal. 296, 27 Am. St. Rep. 106, 14 L. R. A. 755, 28 Pac. 272, 675.)

A contract for future annual payments for a sewer farm is not a present liability. (McBean v. Fresno, 112 Cal. 159, 53 Am. St. Rep. 191, 31 L. R. A. 794, 44 Pac. 358; Smilie v. Fresno County, 112 Cal. 311, 44 Pac. 556; Higgins v. San Diego Water Co., 118 Cal. 524, 45 Pac. 824, 50 Pac. 670.)

Sections 4445 to 4449 of the Political Code are not in conflict with this section, since they only provide for a change in the form of the evidence of the indebtedness, and not for the creation of new indebtedness. (Los Angeles v. Teed, 112 Cal. 319, 44 Pac. 580.)

An action by a taxpayer will lie to enjoin the officers of a city from incurring any indebtedness in violation of this provision. (Bradford v. San Francisco, 112 Cal. 537, 44 Pac. 912.)

A claim arising under a contract for the burial of the indigent dead is within this provision. (Pacific Undertakers v. Widber, 113 Cal. 201, 45 Pac. 273.)

The fact that the indebtedness is incurred for an urgent necessity will not take the case out of this provision. (Buck v. Eureka, 119 Cal. 44, 50 Pac. 1065.)

Notwithstanding this provision, a judgment against a municipality should be in form a general judgment, although it and the liability on which it is based can only be paid out of the municipal revenues of the fiscal year in which the liability was incurred. (Buck v. Eureka, 119 Cal. 44, 50 Pac. 1065.)

A judgment upon a claim against a city, although payable only out of the funds of a particular fiscal year, should be general in form and should not direct out of what funds it should be paid. (Fresno Canal etc. Co. v. McKenzie, 135 Cal. 497, 67 Pac. 900.)

A sum payable upon a contingency is not a debt within the meaning of this section, and cannot become such until the contingency happens. (Doland v. Clark, 143 Cal. 176, 76 Pac. 958.)

A contract to continue for a series of years, and providing for payments thereunder at different times, is not in violation of this provision. (Doland v. Clark, 143 Cal. 176, 76 Pac. 958.)

An implied liability of a city is within the prohibition of this section. (Buck v. Eureka, 124 Cal. 61, 56 Pac. 612.)

An implied liability for services rendered by an attorney of the city is incurred when, from time to time, the services were fully rendered, and the city, with knowledge, accepted the benefit of them. (Buck v. Eureka, 124 Cal. 61, 56 Pac. 612.)

In an action concerning the validity of a municipal obligation, it is error to reject evidence of the condition of the treasury at the time it was incurred. (Buck v. Eureka, 124 Cal. 61, 56 Pac. 612.)

Although there may be no money in the fund out of which a liability is payable at the time it is created, still, if at the end of the fiscal year there is money in such fund, it may be applied to such liability. (Higgins v. San Diego, 131 Cal. 294, 63 Pac. 470.)

This section only requires the assent of two-thirds of such electors as vote on the proposition of incurring the indebtedness, and not two-thirds of those voting at the election. (Howland v. Board of Supervisors, 109 Cal. 152, 41 Pac. 864.)

The fact that the election is held at the same time and place as the general election does not affect the character of the election. (Howland v. Board of Supervisors, 109 Cal. 152, 41 Pac. 864.)

This section does not require that at the time of the sale or issuance of the bonds, or the incurring of the bonded indebtedness, a sinking fund or interest tax be levied, but only that provision shall be made for their collection. (Howland v. Board of Supervisors, 109 Cal. 152, 41 Pac. 864.)

Where the law provides that "at least two-thirds of the electors voting at such special election shall be necessary," two-thirds of all persons voting at the election, and not merely two-thirds of those voting upon the proposition, are necessary. (Law v. San Francisco, 144 Cal. 384, 77 Pac. 1014.)

An order by the supervisors annexing a school district to a high school district upon terms of agreement which essentially involve the assumption by the school district of a pro rata part of the bonded debt of the high school district, without the vote herein required, is-

void. (People v. Hanford Union High School District, 148 Cal. 705, 84 Pac. 193.)

The objection that the expense of an election under the initiative cr referendum law might exceed the indebtedness permitted by this section cannot prevail to make such law unconstitutional. (In re Pfahler, 150 Cal. 71, 11 Ann. Cas. 911, 11 L. R. A. (N. S.) 1092, 88 Pac. 270.)

A board of supervisors cannot during the fiscal year allow claims against the indigent fund in excess of the revenues provided for that year, and then, by a fictitious sale of county property, and the repurchase thereof after the commencement of the next fiscal year, draw a warrant on the next year's fund to pay the indebtedness incurred during the previous year. (County of Tehama v. Sisson, 152 Cal. 167, 92 Pac. 64.)

The object of this section was to insure that at the time of the general tax levy each year provision would be made for such money as would be necessary to pay interest and principal falling due before the time of the next general tax levy and to make up the necessary sinking fund. (Johnson v. Williams, 153 Cal. 368, 95 Pac. 655.)

Courts of equity have power to protect and enforce the will of the people in the issuance of bonds. (Cerini v. De Long, 7 Cal. App. 398, 94 Pac. 582.)

The amendment allowing the city and county of San Francisco to pay certain claims against it was permissive only and not compulsory. (Weaver v. San Francisco, 146 Cal. 728, 81 Pac. 119.)

An act would be void so far as it purported to authorize the issuance of bonds maturing more than forty years from the time of contracting the same, leaving it in full force with respect to an issue of bonds maturing within such period, if it was otherwise valid. (Brookes v. City of Oakland, 160 Cal. 423, 117 Pac. 433.)

This section is not applicable to a board of public service commissioners in purchasing ground and erecting thereon an administrative building for its uses. (Mesmer v. Board of Public Service, 23 Cal. App. 578, 138 Pac. 935.)

A notice of an election to authorize a bond issue which recites that the election is called to vote bonds in the sum of twenty thousand dollars for the construction of a sewer, and which declares that the estimated cost of the improvement is twenty thousand dollars, is not insufficient in failing to state the amount of the proposed indebtedness as required by this section. (City of Venice v. Lawrence, 24 Cal. App. 350, 141 Pac. 406.)

As to the sufficiency of the notice of the election, see Los Angeles v. Teed, 112 Cal. 319, 44 Pac. 580.

> What constitutes "indebtedness" prohibited by law. See notes, 44 Am. St. Rep. 230; 7 R. C. L., § 28, p. 953.

> Right of municipality to contract for periodical payments throughout term of years where aggregate payments exceed authorized debt limit. See notes, 7 Ann. Cas. 150; Ann. Cas. 1913B, 1177.

> Evasion of municipal debt limit by creation of holding corporation for future purchase. See note, 2 Ann. Cas. 986.

Recitals in municipal bond that debt limit has not been exceeded as affecting validity thereof in hands of purchaser. See note, 17 Ann. Cas. 1245.

Interest on municipal bonds as factor in determining whether municipality has exceeded constitutional debt limit. See note, 17 Ann. Cas. 1243.

Right of municipality to contract for public improvement with deferred payments where cost exceeds debt limit. See note, 17 Ann. Cas. 420.

Municipal ownership of public utilities.

Sec. 19. Any municipal corporation may establish and operate public works for supplying its inhabitants with light, water, power, heat, transportation, telephone service or other means of communication. Such works may be acquired by original construction or by the purchase of existing works, including their franchises, or both. Persons or corporations may establish and operate works for supplying the inhabitants with such services upon such conditions and under such regulations as the municipality may prescribe under its organic law, on condition that the municipal government shall have the right to regulate the charges thereof. A municipal corporation may furnish such services to inhabitants outside its boundaries; provided that it shall not furnish any service to the inhabitants of any other municipality owning or operating works supplying the same service to such inhabitants, without the consent of such other municipality, expressed by ordinance. (Amendment approved October 10, 1911.)

[AMENDMENT OF 1885.]

Sec. 19. In any city where there are no public works owned and controlled by the municipality for supplying the same with water or artificial light, any individual, or any company duly incorporated for such purpose, under and by authority of the laws of this state, shall, under the direction of the superintendent of streets, or other officer in control thereof, and under such general regulations as the municipality may prescribe, for damages and indemnity for damages, have the privilege of using the public streets and thoroughfares thereof, and of laying down pipes and conduits therein, and connections therewith, so far as may be necessary for introducing into and supplying such city and its inhabitants either with gaslight, or other illuminating light, or with fresh water for domestic and all other purposes, upon the condition that the municipal government shall have the right to regulate the charges thereof. (Ratification declared February 12, 1885.)

[ORIGINAL SECTION.]

Sec. 19. No public work or improvement of any description whatsoever shall be done or made, in any city, in, upon or about the streets thereof, or otherwise, the cost and expense of which is made chargeable or may be assessed upon private property by special assessment, unless an estimate of such cost and expense shall be made, and an assessment, in proportion to benefits, on the property to be affected or benefited, shall be levied, collected, and paid into the city treasury before such work or improvement shall be commenced, or any contract for letting or doing the same authorized or performed. In any city where there are no public works owned and controlled by the municipality, for supplying the same with water or artificial light, any individual, or any company duly incorporated for such purpose under and by authority of the laws of this state, shall, under the direction of the superintendent of streets, or other officer in control thereof, and under such general regulations as the municipality may prescribe for damages and indemnity for damages, have the privilege of using the public streets and thoroughfares thereof, and of laying down pipes and conduits therein, and connections therewith, so far as may be necessary for introducing into and supplying such city and its inhabitants either with gaslight or other illuminating light, or with fresh water for domestic and all other purposes, upon the condition that the municipal government shall have the right to regulate the charges thereof.

WATER AND LIGHT.—The word "city," used in this section, includes "town." (Pereria v. Wallace, 129 Cal. 397, 62 Pac. 61; People v. Stephens, 62 Cal. 209.)

The provisions of this section are self-executing. (Denninger v. Recorder's Court, 145 Cal. 629, 79 Pac. 360; Boca etc. R. R. Co. v. Sierra Valleys R. R. Co., 2 Cal. App. 546, 84 Pac. 298.)

Nothing is required to make the power granted by this provision completely operative except a law for the organization or municipal corporations and prescribing a mode of exercising legislative power. (Denninger v. Recorder's Court, 145 Cal. 629, 79 Pac. 360.)

The power conferred by this section is not dependent upon action by the legislature under section 33 of article IV. (Denninger v. Recorder's Court, 145 Cal. 629, 79 Pac. 360.)

The franchise to lay pipes and conduits or erect poles is real estate and is inseparably annexed to the soil, and has a local situation in the place where the right is exercised. (Stockton Gas etc. Co. v. San Joaquin County, 148 Cal. 313, 7 Ann. Cas. 511, 5 L. R. A. (N. S.) 174, 83 Pac. 54.)

The fact that the gas which furnishes light also serves for cooking and heating does not prevent the legislative authorities from fixing the rate thereof. (Denninger v. Recorder's Court, 145 Cal. 638, 79 Pac. 364.)

The provision of the act of 1858, requiring water companies to furnish water free of charge to cities and counties, was abrogated by this section. (Spring Valley W. W. v. San Francisco, 61 Cal. 18.)

The board of supervisors has no power to delegate to a commission the power to fix the rates to be paid by the county for gas. But

where the board afterward ratifies the rates fixed by the commission, the final determination with respect to the rates is exercised by the board, and is valid. (San Francisco Gas Light Co. v. Dunn, 62 Cal. 580.)

This section does not deprive the right to collect rates for water of its character of a franchise. (Spring Valley W. W. v. Schottler, 62 Cal. 69.)

Although a contract fixing the price of gas may be void, still if the gas is actually furnished to and used by the municipality, the board may allow for its payment such sum as it is reasonably worth. (San Francisco Gas Light Co. v. Dunn, 62 Cal. 580.)

In the absence of an express limitation, a contract by the board as to rates for the term of five years will not be held unreasonable. (San Francisco Gas Light Co. v. Dunn, 62 Cal. 580.)

The question of what is a reasonable rate is a question of fact. (Redlands etc. Co. v. Redlands, 121 Cal. 312, 53 Pac. 791.)

The water company is not entitled to be reimbursed from the income derived from the rates for interest upon its indebtedness, nor for depreciation of its plant, aside from the amount requisite for its maintenance and repairs during the year. (Redlands etc. Co. v. Redlands, 121 Cal. 312, 53 Pac. 791.)

The bonded or other indebtedness of the company is not to be considered; but the fair value of the property which is necessarily used in furnishing the water is the basis upon which to determine the amount of revenue, which should be the same whether the works are acquired or constructed by the company with its own resources, or with money borrowed from others. (Redlands etc. Co. v. Redlands, 121 Cal. 365, 53 Pac. 843.)

The company has no absolute right to receive a given per cent on its capital stock. (Redlands etc. Co. v. Redlands, 121 Cal. 365, 53 Pac. 843.)

The rights of the public, as well as those of the stockholders, are to be considered; and the public cannot be subjected to unreasonable rates in order simply that stockholders may have dividends. The company has the right to receive only what, under all the circumstances, is such compensation as will be just to it and to the public. (Redlands etc. Co. v. Redlands, 121 Cal. 365, 53 Pac. 843.)

An ordinance requiring a special permission to be obtained from the board of supervisors, before streets can be obstructed, is reasonable. (Mutual Electric etc. Co. v. Ashworth, 118 Cal. 1, 50 Pac. 10.)

Under this section the city may require special permission from the city before poles can be erected in the streets by an electric light company; and the mere fact that the permission is granted to one company and unjustly refused to another will not entitle the latter to enjoin the city authorities from interfering with the erection of such poles—the proper remedy being to compel the granting of the permit by mandamus. (Mutual Electric etc. Co. v. Ashworth, 118 Cal. 1, 50 Pac. 10.)

By this section the operation of gasworks is recognized as a lawful business. (In re Smith, 143 Cal. 368, 77 Pac. 180.)

A gas company does not forfeit its franchise by supplying gas for cooking and heating as well as for lighting purposes which does not

subject the streets to any additional burden. (People v. Los Angeles etc. Gas Co., 150 Cal. 557, 89 Pac. 108.)

This section only applies to cities in which there are no public works owned and controlled by the city for supplying the same with water. (Colegrove Water Co. v. Hollywood, 151 Cal. 425, 13 L. R. A. (N. S.) 904, 90 Pac. 1053.)

A municipal corporation upon which has devolved the duty of supplying water to another municipality is a "corporation duly incorporated for such purpose" within the meaning of the Constitution. (South Pasadena v. Pasadena Land etc. Co., 152 Cal. 579, 93 Pac. 490.)

The power of a municipality to acquire and control public utilities is recognized by the Constitution in the language "in any city where there are no public works owned and controlled by the municipality for supplying the same with water or artificial light." (Platt v. City and County of San Francisco, 158 Cal. 74, 110 Pac. 304.)

The mere fact that a regulation will work irreparable injury to the company and will work inconvenience and deprival of use in the manner theretofore enjoyed by the inhabitants of the city sufficiently show an arbitrary or unreasonable exercise of power. (Merced Falls Gas etc. Co. v. Turner, 2 Cal. App. 720, 84 Pac. 239.)

An electric light company by erecting poles by permission of the municipal authorities does not obtain an absolute, indefeasible right to have the poles remain at the particular spot for all time, and the city authorities have the power by reasonable regulations to compel the company to change their location. (Merced Falls Gas etc. Co. v. Turner, 2 Cal. App. 720, 84 Pac. 239.)

This section does not curtail the power of the municipality in making needful and reasonable regulations touching the use of the streets, but the municipality will not be permitted to enforce regulations which are tantamount to a denial of the right, or are arbitrary, capricious, unreasonable, or prohibitory in their nature or effect. (Merced Falls Gas etc. Co. v. Turner, 2 Cal. App. 720, 84 Pac. 239.)

An ordinance requiring persons who desire to lay pipes in the streets to make a verified application for a permit from the superintendent of streets is invalid and is not a regulation for "damages and indemnity for damages." (In re Johnston, 137 Cal. 115, 69 Pac. 973.)

A statute requiring municipalities to sell franchises for laying pipes, etc., to the highest bidder is void. (Pereria v. Wallace, 129 Cal. 397, 62 Pac. 61.)

This section gives to every person the right to use the public streets of a municipality for the purposes indicated, and it deprives not only the municipality from granting, but the legislature from authorizing the granting, of franchises upon conditions other than those specified in the Constitution. (Town of St. Helena v. Ewer, 26 Cal. App. 191, 146 Pac. 191.)

A municipality which cannot grant franchises by legislative act on conditions not authorized by this section cannot avoid the effect of this section by attempting to convert its legislative acts into private contracts. (Town of St. Helena v. Ewer, 26 Cal. App. 191, 146 Pac. 191.)

The grant made by this section (as amended in 1885) regarding the use of streets for water or gas-pipes would vest only when actually accepted by the exercise of the right granted, and would be assessable only in the place where such exercise is had. (Western Union Telegraph Co. v. Hopkins, 160 Cal. 106, 116 Pac. 557.)

Under this section, where a grant of a franchise by the state or some municipality thereof to a private person or corporation to operate a public utility is not by its terms made exclusive, and the city in which it is to be exercised is not, by the law or ordinance granting it, forbidden from competing, then a city may establish its own works for the same purpose and engage in the same public service within the city, although it may thereby injure or practically destroy the business of the holder of such franchise. (Clark v. Los Angeles, 160 Cal. 30, 116 Pac. 722.)

This section should not be construed to grant an exclusive franchise in the streets to any individual or corporation, or to prevent a city from establishing and operating public waterworks or lightworks, notwithstanding the fact that private persons or corporations are using the streets in operating works of the same kind. (Clark v. Los Angeles, 160 Cal. 30, 116 Pac. 722.)

That the provisions of the charter of 1901 of Pasadena purporting to give full control as to the use of streets for pipes and conduits for the furnishing of water and light are not effective, in view of the direct grant for those purposes made by this section, is not a sufficient warrant for holding that it was not intended to vest such control in the city. (Sunset Tel. & Tel. Co. v. Pasadena, 161 Cal. 265, 118 Pac. 796.)

A corporation which at the time of the amendment of this section in 1911 was supplying the inhabitants of San Francisco with gas and electric light, and for that purpose had laid pipes and conduits in various public streets of San Francisco, had on that date a vested right to occupy parts of the streets for the purposes specified in this section, subject to the limitations therein contained, which right was not and could not be impaired by the amendment of this section in 1911. (Matter of Application of Keppelmann, 166 Cal. 770, 138 Pac. 346.)

The franchise to lay pipes and conduits or erect poles is real estate, and is inseparably annexed to the soil, and has a local situation in the place where the right is exercised. (People v. Lawley, 17 Cal. App. 331, 119 Pac. 1089.)

Either gas or water companies possess the right, having a commodity for sale, to enter upon the streets of a city, lay their pipes and put themselves in position to supply any demand made upon them, regardless of any existing demand, and the restriction that the right to lay down pipes is given "so far as may be necessary for introducing into and supplying such city and its inhabitants either with gaslight or other illuminating light," means that they may not excavate the streets and lay down pipes therein in a manner other than that necessary to a complete and practical system for supplying gas or water to the entire city and its inhabitants. (Vernon v. Los Angeles Gas etc. Corp., 19 Cal. App. 364, 125 Pac. 1084.)

Section 548 of the Civil Code, in so far as it makes a street franchise necessary for a water company to supply a municipality with

water in bulk under a contract, which water the municipality distributes to its inhabitants, was abrogated by this section, as it existed between 1885 and 1911, giving any corporation the right to occupy the streets to supply water to the inhabitants or to the city itself. (Marin Water etc. Co. v. Town of Sausalito, 168 Cal. 587, 143 Pac. 767.)

The power conferred by this section upon a municipality to regulate the charges for gas sold by a gas company is not limited to the establishing of a maximum rate, but authorizes it to fix a rate and prohibit the lowering thereof, directly or indirectly, by any sort of device which the gas company may adopt. (Economic Gas Co. v. Los Angeles, 168 Cal. 448, 143 Pac. 717.)

This section confers upon the cities in this state the power to fix the rates at which water is to be delivered to the inhabitants of a city by any company engaged in that service. (Title Guarantee etc. Co. v. Railroad Commission, 168 Cal. 295, 142 Pac. 878.)

This section, coupled with the duties imposed by the California Constitution and statutes upon municipalities to fix water rates annually, and upon private water companies within municipalities to comply with the rates, does not constitute a contract that the city will not operate a competing plant. (Madera Waterworks v. Madera, 228 U. S. 454, 57 L. Ed. 915, 33 Sup. Ct. Rep. 571.)

The amendment of October 10, 1911, to this section granted no right to a telephone company to occupy the streets of a city without its consent. (City of Pomona v. Sunset Tel. & T. Co., 224 U. S. 330, 56 L. Ed. 788, 32 Sup. Ct. Rep. 477.)

A water or light company gained a contract right to extend its mains into unopened streets by establishing a water or light plant, which was an acceptance of the state's offer made under this section, as amended in 1885, of the privilege of laying pipes in streets in municipalities. (Russell v. Sebastian, 233 U. S. 195, 58 L. Ed. 912, 34 Sup. Ct. Rep. 517, reversing Matter of Russell, 163 Cal. 668, 126 Pac. 875; Lukrawka v. Spring Valley Water Co., 169 Cal. 318, 146 Pac. 641; Pratt v. Spring Valley Water Co., 4 C. R. C. 1077, 1083.)

The amendment of 1911, and ordinances adopted in pursuance thereof, requiring franchises for extensions by companies established in municipalities prior to the amendment of 1911, unconstitutionally impaired the contract rights of such companies. (Russell v. Sebastian, 233 U. S. 195, 58 L. Ed. 912, 34 Sup. Ct. Rep. 517; reversing Matter of Russell, 163 Cal. 668, 126 Pac. 875.)

This section does not constitute a grant of unlimited or specific power over the public utilities operating within its borders (except in the matter of rates) to any city whose organic law contains no provision for the exercise of such power, but it merely places the utilities under such control as may be provided for by the charter or other organic law of the city. (Oro Electric Corp. v. Railroad Commission, 169 Cal. 466, 147 Pac. 118.)

This section, as in force in 1889 and 1905, gave any individual or company incorporated for that purpose the privilege, in cities which had no public light or waterworks, of using the public streets, and of laying down pipes and conduits therein for the purpose of supply-

ing the city and its inhabitants with light and water. (Oro Electric Corp. v. R. R. Commission, 169 Cal. 466, 147 Pac. 118.)

This section, as it read prior to the amendment of October 10, 1911, only granted a franchise to use city streets for the purpose of laying pipes to supply gas for illumination, and the right to use streets for the supplying of gas for heat and power was not granted by this section as it then existed. (Hanford v. Hanford Gas. etc. Co., 169 Cal. 749, 147 Pac. 969.)

A city may, by virtue of this section, purchase and accept existing works of public utilities, and continue the service of such utilities. (In re Southern California Mountain Water Co. Lease, 1 C. R. C. 520, 528.)

This section as amended on October 10, 1911, giving to municipalities the right to regulate charges of public utilities, probably has no application to steam railroads, but does apply to street railroads. (Niven v. San Diego Electric Ry. Co., 3 C. R. C. 62, 64.)

No city or town has the power to establish the fare to be charged by a street railroad or any other railroad between a point within the city limits and a point outside of the city limits. (Ramos v. San Francisco-Oakland Terminal Rys., 3 C. R. C. 800, 802.)

The Railroad Commission has no jurisdiction to require street railway companies to exchange transfers for transportation between points within municipal limits, since this would be usurping the power to regulate the rates for such transportation, which power is vested exclusively in municipal authorities. (Thompson v. The San Diego Electric Ry. Co., 3 C. R. C. 935, 936.)

A municipality may not regulate charges for electric energy where it is sold to the municipality and not to its inhabitants. (Ukiah v. The Snow Mountain Water & Power Co., 4 C. R. C. 293, 297.)

Municipalities were given no power under this section over such matters as adequacy of service of water companies or the making of extensions by them. (Pratt v. Spring Valley Water Co., 4 C. R. C. 1077, 1083.)

See, further, as to water rates, note to section 33, article IV, and section 1, article XIV.

Power of municipalities to furnish light. See note, 30 Am. St. Rep. 225.

STREET ASSESSMENTS.—The "front-foot" method of assessment is valid. (Hadley v. Dague, 130 Cal. 207, 62 Pac. 500; Cohen v. Alameda, 124 Cal. 504, 57 Pac. 377; Chambers v. Satterlee, 40 Cal. 497; Emery v. San Francisco Gas Co., 28 Cal. 345; Emery v. Bradford, 29 Cal. 75; Taylor v. Palmer, 31 Cal. 240; Whiting v. Quackenbush, 54 Cal. 306; Whiting v. Townsend, 57 Cal. 515; Lent v. Tillson, 72 Cal. 404, 14 Pac. 71; Jennings v. Le Breton, 80 Cal. 8, 21 Pac. 1127; San Francisco Pav. Co. v. Bates, 134 Cal. 39, 66 Pac. 2; Banaz v. Smith, 133 Cal. 102, 65 Pac. 309.)

An assessment for improving a street is a tax, and must be levied with equality and uniformity. (Whiting v. Quackenbush, 54 Cal. 306.)

A contract for a street improvement, made before the new Constitution went into effect, is not affected by its provisions, and the grant-

ing of an extension of time for the performance of the same is not a new contract. (Oakland Pav. Co. v. Barstow, 79 Cal. 45, 21 Pac. 544; Ede v. Cogswell, 79 Cal. 278, 21 Pac. 767; Ede v. Knight, 93 Cal. 159, 28 Pac. 860.)

The provisions of this section in its original form were self-executing, and the provisions of the act of 1872, relating to street improvements in San Francisco, and authorizing the superintendent of streets to execute contracts for such improvements in advance of the levy and collection of the assessment, were inconsistent with it, and ceased to be operative when it went into effect. (McDonald v. Patterson, 54 Cal. 245; Donahue v. Graham, 61 Cal. 276.)

The act of 1863, providing for the widening of streets in San Francisco by agreement with the owners, was not in conflict with this section. (San Francisco v. Kiernan, 98 Cal. 614, 33 Pac. 720.)

The provision of the charter of San Francisco for making a contract for street work before an assessment had been levied and collected was repealed by this section, and was not revived by the constitutional amendment dispensing with the necessity of such levy and collection. (Thomason v. Ruggles, 69 Cal. 465, 11 Pac. 20; Thomason v. Ashworth, 73 Cal. 73, 14 Pac. 615.)

The amendment to this section in 1885 was legally adopted. (Oakland Pav. Co. v. Tompkins, 72 Cal. 5, 1 Am. St. Rep. 17, 12 Pac. 801; Thomason v. Ashworth, 73 Cal. 73, 14 Pac. 615; People v. Strother, 67 Cal. 624, 8 Pac. 383; Sacramento Pav. Co. v. Anderson, 1 Cal. App. 672, 82 Pac. 1069. But see Oakland Pav. Co. v. Hilton, 69 Cal. 479, 11 Pac. 3.)

ARTICLE XII.

CORPORATIONS.

Corporations to be formed under general laws.

Sec. 1. Corporations may be formed under general laws, but shall not be created by special act. All laws now in force in this state concerning corporations, and all laws that may be hereafter passed pursuant to this section, may be altered from time to time or repealed.

CORPORATIONS—What are.—A levee district is not a private corporation, neither is it a municipal corporation, but it belongs to a class by itself, the creation, organization, and control of which is not limited by the Constitution. (People v. Levee Dist. No. 6, 131 Cal. 30, 63 Pac. 676.)

Prior to the new Constitution, a reclamation district was held to be a public corporation, which could be created by special act. (Reclamation Dist. No. 124 v. Gray, 95 Cal. 601, 30 Pac. 779.)

Irrigation districts, with respect to their public functions, are to be classed with public corporations; but with regard to the private rights of the individual land owners, they are to be classed as private corporations. (Merchants' Nat. Bank v. Escondido Irr. Dist., 144 Cal. 329, 77 Pac. 937.)

This section refers to private corporations, and it has no application to the creation of public corporations under the control and government of the state, such as state hospitals. (Napa State Hospital v. Dasso, 153 Cal. 698, 15 Ann. Cas. 910, 18 L. R. A. (N. S.) 643, 96 Pac. 355.)

A district agricultural association is a public agency of the state, and is a public corporation. (People v. San Joaquin Valley Agricultural Assn., 151 Cal. 797, 91 Pac. 740.)

Reclamation districts do not come within the purview of this section. (Reclamation Dist. No. 70 v. Sherman, 11 Cal. App. 399, 105 Pac. 277.)

> Distinction between public and private corporation. See notes, 1 Ann. Cas. 371; 7 R. C. L., § 14, p. 39.

Creation of.—The legislature cannot confer upon corporations any powers or grant them any privileges by special act. (San Francisco v. Spring Valley W. W., 48 Cal. 493.)

This section does not authorize the legislature to enact general laws under which corporations might extend the term of their corporate existence. (The Boca Mill Co. v. Curry, 154 Cal. 326, 97 Pac. 1117.)

A corporation sole can be created only by compliance with the provisions of the Civil Code. (Blakeslee v. Hall, 94 Cal. 159, 29 Pac. 623.)

This section does not prohibit the assignment of a franchise to a legally organized corporation, by persons having the lawful right to exercise and transfer the same—this section referring only to power directly conferred upon corporations by the legislature. (People v. Stanford, 77 Cal. 360, 2 L. R. A. 92, 18 Pac. 85, 19 Pac. 693.)

A law providing a special method of assessment and collection of taxes against railroads situated in more than one county is not in violation of this section. (People v. Central Pac. R. R. Co., 105 Cal. 576, 38 Pac. 905; affirmed, Central Pacific R. R. Co. v. People, 162 U. S. 91, 40 L. Ed. 903, 16 Sup. Ct. Rep. 766; People v. Central Pac. R. R. Co., 83 Cal. 393, 23 Pac 303, overruled.)

An act "to establish water rates in the city and county of San Francisco," and a supplemental act, held unconstitutional in so far as they attempt to provide a mode of fixing rates to be charged by corporations in San Francisco differing from the mode provided for other corporations by general laws. (San Francisco v. Spring Valley W. W., 53 Cal. 608; Spring Valley W. W. v. Bryant, 52 Cal. 132; San Francisco v. Spring Valley W. W., 48 Cal. 493.)

An act which authorizes the board of supervisors of a county to grant certain privileges to a particular corporation is void. (Waterloo etc. Road Co. v. Cole, 51 Cal. 381.)

An act which grants to individuals powers and privileges, and provides that the act shall not take effect unless such persons incorporate within a given time, is a grant to the corporation, and void. (San Francisco v. Spring Valley W. W., 48 Cal. 493. California State Tel. Co. v. Alta Tel. Co., 22 Cal. 398, disapproved.)

Under this section the legislature cannot by special act change the name of a corporation, but may by general law provide for such change by the superior court upon application of the incorporators. (Matter of La Societe Francaise etc., 123 Cal. 525, 56 Pac. 458, 787. See, also, Pacific Bank v. De Ro, 37 Cal. 538.)

An act granting to certain individuals the exclusive right to a line of telegraph does not violate this section. (California State Tel. Co. v. Alta Tel. Co., 22 Cal. 398. But see San Francisco v. Spring Valley W. W., 48 Cal. 493.)

Where a franchise is conferred by the legislature to certain individuals to supply a town with water, and they afterward sell such franchise to a corporation, this section is not violated. (San Luis Water Co., v. Estrada, 117 Cal. 168, 48 Pac. 1075. San Francisco v. Spring Valley W. W., 48 Cal. 493, distinguished.)

An act conferring the power of appointing boards of examiners upon three named societies, which are said to be "existing corporations," held not to be in conflict with this section, as the power is not conferred upon them as corporations—the expression "existing corporations" being merely descriptio personarum. (Ex parte Frazer, 54 Cal. 94; Ex parte McNulty, 77 Cal. 164, 11 Am. St. Rep. 257, 19 Pac. 237; Ex parte Johnson, 62 Cal. 263.)

This provision continued in force section 359 of the Code of Civil Procedure, limiting the time within which an action can be brought to enforce the stockholders' personal liability. (Santa Rosa Nat. Bank v. Barnett, 125 Cal. 407, 58 Pac. 85.)

Rights vesting under section 536 of the Civil Code, which allows telegraph and telephone companies to use rights of way along waters, roads and highways, cannot be revoked under this section of the Constitution. (Western Union Tel. Co. v. Hopkins, 160 Cal. 106, 116 Pac. 557.)

Visitation.—The legislature has what may be termed a visitorial or supervisorial power over corporations, and may examine into their affairs, with a view to correct corporate abuses. (In re Bunkers, 1 Cal. App. 61, 81 Pac. 748.)

Alteration and repeal of charters.—The right to alter and repeal is not without limit; it must be reasonable. Sheer oppression and wrong cannot be inflicted under the guise of amendment or alteration. (Spring Valley W. W. v. Board of Suprs. of San Francisco, 61 Cal. 3.)

The power of the legislature to alter and amend under this section does not authorize the legislature, while the corporation exists, to deprive it of the rights, guaranteed to it by the federal Constitution, to due process of law, and to the equal protection of the laws, nor to alter the charter of foreign corporations doing business in this state. (Johnson v. Goodyear Min. Co., 127 Cal. 4, 78 Am. St. Rep. 17, 47 L. R. A. 338, 59 Pac. 304.)

A provision in the charter of a water company permitting it to name two out of five commissioners to fix water rates is simply a privilege, and not a contract with the company, and may be repealed at any time. (Spring Valley W. W. v. Board of Suprs. of San Francisco, 61 Cal. 3.)

The legislature may, under the reserved power, provide for the consolidation of corporations by a majority vote of the stockholders, without reference to the will of the dissenting stockholders. (Market Street Ry. Co. v. Hellman, 109 Cal. 571, 42 Pac. 225.)

Under this provision the people of the state have power to change the law as to the liability of stockholders. (McGowan v. McDonald, 111 Cal. 57, 52 Am. St. Rep. 149, 43 Pac. 418.)

Dues to be secured by individual liability, etc.

Sec. 2. Dues from corporations shall be secured by such individual liability of the corporators and other means as may be prescribed by law.

Stockholders to be individually liable.

Sec. 3. Each stockholder of a corporation, or joint-stock association, shall be individually and personally liable for such proportion of all its debts and liabilities contracted or incurred, during the time he was a stockholder, as the amount of stock or shares owned by him bears to the whole of the subscribed capital stock, or shares of the corporation or association. The directors or trustees of corporations and joint-stock associations shall be jointly and severally liable to the creditors and stockholders for all moneys embezzled or misappropriated by the officers of such corporation or joint-stock association, during the term of office of such director or trustee.

Nothing in the preceding paragraph of this section shall be held to apply to any exposition company organized to promote and carry on any international exposition or world's fair within the state of California, and the liability of stockholders in any such exposition company shall be and the same is hereby limited to an amount not exceeding the par value of the stock of said corporation subscribed for by such stockholders. (Amendment adopted November 3, 1908.)

[ORIGINAL SECTION.]

Sec. 3. Each stockholder of a corporation, or joint-stock association, shall be individually and personally liable for such proportion of all its debts and liabilities contracted or incurred, during the time he was a stockholder, as the amount of stock or shares owned by him bears to the whole of the subscribed capital stock, or shares of the corporation or association. The directors or trustees of corporations and joint-stock associations shall be jointly and severally liable to the creditors and stockholders for all moneys embezzled or misappropriated by the officers of such corporation, or joint-stock association, during the term of office of such director or trustee.

STOCKHOLDERS' LIABILITY—In general.—Under this section a stockholder cannot be exempted by law from his individual liability. (McGowan v. McDonald, 111 Cal. 57, 52 Am. St. Rep. 149, 43 Pac. 418.)

A somewhat similar provision of the former Constitution was held not to be self-executing. (French v. Teschemaker, 24 Cal. 518.)

This section is self-executing, and any attempt by the legislature to limit its effect would be beyond its constitutional power, and therefore void. (Western Pac. Ry. Co. v. Godfrey, 166 Cal. 346, Ann. Cas. 1915B, 825, 136 Pac. 284.)

The word "stockholder," as used in this section, is synonymous with the term "owner of shares" as used in section 298 of the Civil Code. (Western Pac. Ry. Co. v. Godfrey, 166 Cal. 346, Ann. Cas. 1915B, 825, 136 Pac. 284.)

The former Constitution left it to the legislature to prescribe the rule by which each stockholder's proportion should be ascertained. (Larrabee v. Baldwin, 35 Cal. 155.)

Under the former Constitution it was held that any one creditor, whose debt was sufficient, might collect from one particular stockholder the entire amount of his liability on all the corporate debts, leaving him to seek contribution out of his costockholders. (Larrabee v. Baldwin, 35 Cal. 155.)

Under the former Constitution it was held that a creditor could collect his whole claim from a single stockholder, provided it did not exceed in amount the said stockholder's proportion of the corporation's entire indebtedness. (Gardiner v. Bank of Napa, 160 Cal. 577, 117 Pac. 667.)

Under the present Constitution and section 322 of the Civil Code, a single stockholder is liable to a single creditor for his proportion only of that creditor's debt, and the creditor has no right to collect upon his individual claim a sum equal to the stockholder's entire liability upon the debts of the corporation. (Gardiner v. Bank of Napa, 160 Cal. 577, 117 Pac. 667.)

"All" the debts means every debt of the company; and therefore any creditor is entitled to sue any stockholder for his proportion of the indebtedness of the company to such creditor, without reference to the other debts of the corporation. (Morrow v. Superior Court, 64 Cal. 383, 1 Pac. 354.)

This provision does not apply to stockholders of a foreign corporation doing business in California, where its charter exempts its stockholders from liability for its debts. (Thomas v. Matthiessen, 192 Fed. 495, 113 C. C. A. 101; affirming 170 Fed. 362.)

Section 322 of the Civil Code, providing the manner for enforcing the rights of a creditor of a corporation against a stockholder, does not conflict with this section of the Constitution. (Gardiner v. Bank of Napa, 160 Cal. 577, 117 Pac. 667.)

An act authorizing the formation of corporations, without attaching to the stockholders an individual liability would be unconstitutional, and the persons organized under such an act would acquire none of the rights of a corporation. (French v. Teschemaker, 24 Cal. 518.)

A contract between a corporation and its stockholders embodied in its articles of incorporation and expressed in its certificate, that its capital stock shall not be assessed after it is paid in full, is not inconsistent with this provision. (Lum v. American Wheel etc. Co., 165 Cal. 657, Ann. Cas. 1915A, 816, 133 Pac. 303.)

But the creditors of a corporation may waive the personal liability of the stockholders at the time of contracting with the corporation. (French v. Teschemaker, 24 Cal. 518.)

A depositor in a savings bank does not waive the personal liability of the stockholders by an unsigned agreement printed in the book of each depositor, nor by a printed release of liability inserted in the signature-book, to which no special subscription was made by the depositors. (Wells v. Black, 117 Cal. 157, 59 Am. St. Rep. 162, 37 L. R. A. 619, 48 Pac. 1090.)

A by-law of a corporation that the stockholders shall not be personally liable for the debts of the corporation is void. (Wells v. Black, 117 Cal. 157, 59 Am. St. Rep. 162, 37 L. R. A. 619, 48 Pac. 1090.)

A law limiting the time within which an action can be brought under this section to three years from the creation of the liability is valid. (Santa Rosa Nat. Bank v. Barnett, 125 Cal. 407, 58 Pac. 85; Gardiner v. Royer, 167 Cal. 238, 139 Pac. 75; Royal Trust Co. v. Mac-Bean, 168 Cal. 642, 144 Pac. 139.)

An act authorizing a city to subscribe to the stock of a corporation, provided the corporation should make it a condition of all contracts entered into by it that the city should not be liable as a stockholder, is not invalid as taking away the liability fixed by the Constitution. (French v. Teschemaker, 24 Cal. 518.)

One stockholder may enforce the personal liability of other stockholders in the corporation for a debt due such stockholder from the corporation. (Brown v. Merrill, 107 Cal. 446, 48 Am. St. Rep. 145, 40 Pac. 557; Knowles v. Sandercock, 107 Cal. 629, 40 Pac. 1047.)

This provision applies to corporations formed before as well as after the adoption of the new Constitution. (McGowan v. McDonald, 111 Cal. 57, 52 Am. St. Rep. 149, 43 Pac. 418.)

Under a like provision in the Constitution of Kansas it was held that it was enforceable in this state against California stockholders in a Kansas corporation. (Ferguson v. Sherman, 116 Cal. 169, 37 L. R. A. 622, 47 Pac. 1023.)

> Liability of stockholders. See notes, 9 Am. Dec. 96; 49 Am. Dec. 308.
>
> Liability of stockholders to creditors of corporation. See note, 3 Am. St. Rep. 806.
>
> Liability of purchasers of stock from corporation at less than par to creditors of corporation. See note, 5 Ann. Cas. 667.
>
> Liability as stockholder of transferrer of stock where transfer is not entered on books. See note, 14 Ann. Cas. 898.
>
> Stockholder's liability. See 7 R. C. L., §§ 332–409, pp. 352–421.

When it attaches.—This section has no application to liabilities of stockholders which accrued prior to its adoption. (Harmon v. Page, 62 Cal. 448.)

A subscriber for shares is responsible as a stockholder, although he has not paid for his stock or received a certificate therefor. (Mitchell v. Beckman, 64 Cal. 117, 28 Pac. 110.)

The sale of stock by a stockholder would under no circumstances release his personal or individual liability for his proper proportion

of all its debts and liabilities contracted or incurred during the time
he was a stockholder. (People v. California Safe Deposit & T. Co.,
18 Cal. App. 732, 124 Pac. 558.)

A pledgee of stock is not a stockholder within the meaning of this
section. (Borland v. Nevada Bank, 99 Cal. 89, 37 Am. St. Rep. 32,
33 Pac. 737.)

> Liability of holders of stock as collateral for debts of corporation.
> See notes, 1 Am. St. Rep. 783; 68 Am. St. Rep. 542; 121 Am.
> St. Rep. 197; 10 Ann. Cas. 783.
>
> Liability of transferee of stock for corporate debts. See notes,
> 3 Ann. Cas. 1120; Ann. Cas. 1914B, 754.
>
> Liability for corporate debts of stockholder who transfers stock
> to escape liability. See notes, 6 Ann. Cas. 428; 18 Ann. Cas.
> 341.

As to who is a stockholder under this section, see Abbott v. Jack,
136 Cal. 510, 69 Pac. 257.

The liability of the stockholder is dependent upon the fact that he
is a stockholder at the time the debt is created, and such liability
cannot be extended by the corporation by a note given for an indebtedness not created while he was a stockholder, by suffering a judgment to be recovered on such indebtedness, or in any other manner.
(Winona Wagon Co. v. Bull, 108 Cal. 1, 40 Pac. 1077; Larrabee v.
Baldwin, 35 Cal. 155; Danielson v. Yoakum, 116 Cal. 382, 48 Pac. 322;
Partridge v. Butler, 113 Cal. 326, 45 Pac. 678; Santa Rosa Nat. Bank
v. Barnett, 125 Cal. 407, 58 Pac. 85.)

The liability of a stockholder in a savings bank accrues at the time
of the acceptance of the deposit. (Wells v. Black, 117 Cal. 157, 59
Am. St. Rep. 162, 37 L. R. A. 619, 48 Pac. 1090.)

A stockholder in a savings bank is liable for his proportion of a
deposit in such bank. (Wells v. Black, 117 Cal. 157, 59 Am. St. Rep.
162, 37 L. R. A. 619, 48 Pac. 1090.)

A liability for overdrafts to a bank is created upon the daily balances against the corporation shown by the account. (Santa Rosa
Nat. Bank v. Barnett, 125 Cal. 407, 58 Pac. 85.)

The liability of a corporation for the services of an attorney is not
created until the rendition of the services. (Johnson v. Bank of Lake,
125 Cal. 6, 73 Am. St. Rep. 17, 57 Pac. 664.)

Where an accommodation indorser of the note of a corporation pays
the same, the debt is extinguished and the stockholder's liability upon
the debt comes to an end, and neither under the doctrine of equitable
assignment nor of subrogation can it be transferred as a live and sub-
sisting obligation, but at the time of payment by the indorser a new
liability springs up against the corporation and its stockholders, a
liability upon an implied contract to reimburse what has been expended, including costs and expenses. (Yule v. Bishop, 133 Cal. 574,
65 Pac. 1094.)

The legatee of shares of stock in a corporation who, upon distribution of the estate, accepts such legacy, is answerable to the creditors
of the corporation upon a stockholder's liability for corporate debts
contracted after the death of the decedent, but before distribution of

the estate. (Western Pacific Ry. Co. v. Godfrey, 166 Cal. 346, Ann. Cas. 1915B, 825, 136 Pac. 284.)

Nature of.—An action to recover upon the liability of a stockholder is an action at law. (Morrow v. Superior Court, 64 Cal. 383, 1 Pac. 354.)

A stockholder's liability is a "liability created by law." (Moore v. Boyd, 74 Cal. 167, 15 Pac. 670; Hunt v. Ward, 99 Cal. 612, 37 Am. St. Rep. 87, 34 Pac. 335.)

It is also a liability created by statute. (Bank of San Luis Obispo v. Pacific Coast S. S. Co., 103 Cal. 594, 37 Pac. 499.)

It is also an obligation arising upon contract. (Dennis v. Superior Court, 91 Cal. 548, 27 Pac. 1031; Kennedy v. California Sav. Bank, 97 Cal. 93, 33 Am. St. Rep. 163, 31 Pac. 846.)

The liability of a stockholder of a corporation for his proportionate share of its debts is created by statute and barred within three years after the cause of action accrues. (Jones v. Goldtree Bros. Co., 142 Cal. 383, 77 Pac. 939.)

The obligation of stockholders is direct and primary. They are principal debtors, and not sureties of the corporation, and their liability is not contingent upon a recovery against the corporation, nor is it affected by a suspension or renewal as to the corporation. (Faymonville v. McCollough, 59 Cal. 285; Davidson v. Rankin, 34 Cal. 503; Hyman v. Coleman, 82 Cal. 650, 16 Am. St. Rep. 178, 23 Pac. 62; Mitchell v. Beckman, 64 Cal. 117, 28 Pac. 110; Dolbear v. Foreign Mines Development Co., 196 Fed. 646, 116 C. C. A. 338.)

Stockholders are not jointly and severally liable, but each stockholder is severally liable for his proportion of the indebtedness, and when he has paid his portion of any debt, or of all the debts of the corporation, he is freed from all liability, and has no cause of action against any other stockholder for money so paid. (Brown v. Merrill, 107 Cal. 446, 48 Am. St. Rep. 145, 40 Pac. 557; Derby v. Stevens, 64 Cal. 287, 30 Pac. 820.)

The mere fact that the corporation has pledged to the debtor certain property as security for the debt does not prevent the debtor from suing the stockholders. (Sonoma Valley Bank v. Hill, 59 Cal. 107.)

A judgment against the corporation does not extinguish, suspend or merge the liability of the stockholders. (Young v. Rosenbaum, 39 Cal. 646.)

Nor does such a judgment prolong the time within which an action may be maintained against the stockholders. (Stilphen v. Ware, 45 Cal. 110.)

An action may be maintained against the stockholders, although the debt is secured by a mortgage of the corporation which has not been foreclosed. (Knowles v. Sandercock, 107 Cal. 629, 40 Pac. 1047; Dolbear v. Foreign Mines Development Co., 196 Fed. 646, 116 C. C. A. 338.)

Stockholders are liable for interest as well as principal. (Wells, Fargo & Co. v. Enright, 127 Cal. 669, 49 L. R. A. 647, 60 Pac. 439.)

A stockholder of an insolvent bank has no right to share in the dividends of the bank by way of subrogation to the rights of a credi-

tor to whom he has paid his proportionate share of his claim. (Sacramento Bank v. Pacific Bank, 124 Cal. 147, 71 Am. St. Rep. 36, 45
L. R. A. 863, 56 Pac. 787.)

Nature of stockholder's liability for debts of corporation. See
note, 99 Am. Dec. 432.

Release of.—Whenever a debt of a corporation is satisfied in part,
there is also pro tanto a discharge of the liability of the stockholders.
(San Jose Sav. Bank v. Pharis, 58 Cal. 380.)

Where a creditor of a corporation releases a stockholder from all
personal liability, he thereby discharges the corporation and other
stockholders to the same extent as the one to whom the release is executed. If the release is for the releasee's proportion, the company
and other stockholders are only released pro tanto. (Prince v. Lynch,
38 Cal. 528, 99 Am. Dec. 427.)

Practice.—A complaint to recover on the stockholder's liability
must state the amount of the whole number of shares subscribed for.
(Bidwell v. Babcock, 87 Cal. 29, 25 Pac. 752; Roebling's Sons Co. v.
Butler, 112 Cal. 677, 45 Pac. 6.)

As to the form of the complaint generally, see Duke v. Huntington,
130 Cal. 272, 62 Pac. 510; Whitehurst v. Stuart, 129 Cal. 194, 61 Pac.
963.

The complaint must show affirmatively that the defendant was a
stockholder when the debt was incurred, and a mere allegation that
he was a stockholder when the note was executed is insufficient.
(Case Plow Works v. Montgomery, 115 Cal. 380, 47 Pac. 108.)

A complaint in an action against stockholders to recover their proportionate share of the debts of the corporation, which does not aver
the whole number of shares of the subscribed capital stock, is fatally
defective. (San Francisco etc. Agency v. Miller, 4 Cal. App. 291, 87
Pac. 630.)

An allegation of the number of shares issued is not sufficient to
show the amount subscribed. (San Francisco etc. Agency v. Miller,
4 Cal. App. 291, 87 Pac. 630.)

A creditor is not bound to exhaust the remedies against the corporation before proceeding against the stockholder. (Morrow v. Superior Court, 64 Cal. 383, 1 Pac. 354.)

Necessity of exhausting remedy against corporation before enforcing stockholder's liability. See notes, 2 Ann. Cas. 28; 16
Ann. Cas. 1152.

The provisions of this section do not oust a court of equity of jurisdiction to compel stockholders to pay for the benefit of creditors the
amount of the capital stock subscribed for by him. (Harmon v. Page,
62 Cal. 448.)

Although the liability of the stockholder is that of an original
debtor, it is proper to plead the debt as that of the corporation.
(Knowles v. Sandercock, 107 Cal. 629, 40 Pac. 1047.)

Where one stockholder pays a note of the corporation, and sues the
other stockholders for contribution, the superior court has no jurisdiction, if the several amounts asked against each stockholder are

less than three hundred dollars. (Myers v. Sierra Valley Stock etc. Co., 122 Cal. 669, 55 Pac. 689.)

> Enforcement of stockholder's liability in other states. See note, 37 Am. St. Rep. 168.

> Actions against stockholders for debts of corporation. See note, 43 Am. Dec. 694.

LIABILITY OF DIRECTORS.—This provision only applies to such misappropriations of moneys as are similar to embezzlement, consisting of the misappropriations of funds intrusted to an officer for a particular purpose, by devoting them to some unauthorized purpose, and does not apply to the payment of an extravagant price for services or materials properly appertaining to the business of the corporation, (Fox v. Hale & Norcross etc. Min. Co., 108 Cal. 369, 41 Pac. 308.)

Liability must be strictly limited to money misappropriated by the officer. (Hercules Oil etc. Co. v. Hocknell, 5 Cal. App. 702, 91 Pac. 341.)

An action at law on behalf of one or more of the creditors of a corporation cannot be sustained under the provision as to the liability of directors, but the only proper remedy is a bill in equity where all the creditors are parties, or are represented, and in which there can be an accounting after ascertainment of facts. (Winchester v. Mabury, 122 Cal. 522, 55 Pac. 393.)

The provision of this section as to the liability of directors and trustees is self-executing. (Winchester v. Howard, 136 Cal. 432, 89 Am. St. Rep. 153, 64 Pac. 692, 69 Pac. 77.)

The proper remedy for the enforcement of this provision against directors and trustees is by bill in equity. (Winchester v. Howard, 136 Cal. 432, 89 Am. St. Rep. 153, 64 Pac. 692, 69 Pac. 77.)

This provision is not in violation of the federal Constitution. (Winchester v. Howard, 136 Cal. 432, 89 Am. St. Rep. 153, 64 Pac. 692, 69 Pac. 77.)

An assignee of a depositor in a bank may maintain an action under this section. (Winchester v. Howard, 136 Cal. 432, 89 Am. St. Rep. 153, 64 Pac. 692, 69 Pac. 77.)

Depositors who became such after the misappropriation may maintain the action. (Winchester v. Howard, 136 Cal. 432, 89 Am. St. Rep. 153, 64 Pac. 692, 69 Pac. 77.)

The claim of the creditor need not be reduced to judgment before an action is brought under this provision. (Winchester v. Howard, 136 Cal. 432, 89 Am. St. Rep. 153, 64 Pac. 692, 69 Pac. 77.)

Nor need he make a specific demand for an accounting before bringing the action. (Winchester v. Howard, 136 Cal. 432, 89 Am. St. Rep. 153, 64 Pac. 692, 69 Pac. 77.)

When a creditor brings an action under this section on behalf of himself and all other creditors, he becomes a trustee for them as to any amount recovered or received in settlement. (Niccolls v. Rice, 147 Cal. 633, 82 Pac. 321.)

When a creditor brings an action under this section in his own behalf and in behalf of all other creditors who may join with him, he does not become a trustee as to a creditor who never did join. (Niccolls v. Rice, 147 Cal. 633, 82 Pac. 321.)

An action begun for the enforcement of the liability of a director of a corporation survives the death of said director. (Major v. Walker, 23 Cal. App. 465, 138 Pac. 360.)

An action at law on behalf of one or more of the creditors of a corporation cannot be sustained under the provision as to the liability of directors, but the only proper remedy is a bill in equity where all the creditors are parties, or are represented, and in which there can be an accounting after ascertainment of facts. (Gardiner v. Bank of Napa, 160 Cal. 577, 117 Pac. 667.)

Corporations construed.

Sec. 4. The term corporations, as used in this article, shall be construed to include all associations and joint-stock companies having any of the powers or privileges of corporations not possessed by individuals or partnerships; and all corporations shall have the right to sue and shall be subject to be sued, in all courts, in like cases as natural persons.

Banking prohibited.

Sec. 5. The legislature shall have no power to pass any act granting any charter for banking purposes, but corporations or associations may be formed for such purposes under general laws, and the legislature shall provide for the classification of cities and towns by population for the purpose of regulating the business of banking. No corporation, association, or individual shall issue or put in circulation, as money, anything but the lawful money of the United States. (Amendment adopted November 8, 1910.)

[ORIGINAL SECTION.]

Sec. 5. The legislature shall have no power to pass any act granting any charter for banking purposes, but corporations or associations may be formed for such purposes under general laws. No corporation, association, or individual shall issue or put in circulation, as money, anything but the lawful money of the United States.

BANKING CORPORATIONS.—A corporation may be formed for the purpose of receiving deposits and loaning money, and if it does not issue paper to circulate as money, it is not a bank, although it is called such. (Bank of Sonoma v. Fairbanks, 52 Cal. 196.)

Sections 34 and 35, article IV, of the Constitution of 1849 did not prohibit the formation of banking corporations for the purpose of deposit and loan, which do not issue paper to circulate as money. (Bank of Martinez v. Hemme etc. Land Co., 105 Cal. 376, 38 Pac. 963.)

Existing charters, when invalid.

Sec. 6. All existing charters, grants, franchises, special or exclusive privileges, under which an actual and bona fide organization shall not have taken place, and business been commenced in good faith, at the time of the adoption of this Constitution, shall thereafter have no validity.

EXISTING FRANCHISES.—This section in no way repeals or affects section 536 of the Civil Code, which allows telegraph and telephone companies to use rights of way along waters, roads and highways. (Western Union Tel. Co. v. Hopkins, 160 Cal. 106, 116 Pac. 557.)

Charters not to be extended, nor forfeiture remitted.

Sec. 7. The legislature shall not extend any franchise or charter, nor remit the forfeiture of any franchise or charter of any quasi-public corporation now existing or which shall hereafter exist under the laws of this state. The term of existence of any other corporation now or hereafter existing under the laws of this state, may be extended, at any time prior to the expiration of its corporate existence, for a period not exceeding fifty years from the date of such extension, by the vote or written consent of stockholders representing two-thirds of its capital stock or of two-thirds of the members thereof. A certificate of such vote or consent shall be signed and sworn to by the president and secretary, and by a majority of the directors of the corporation and filed and certified in the manner and upon payment of fees required by law for filing and certifying articles of incorporation, and thereupon the term of the corporation shall be extended for the period specified in such certificate, and such corporation shall thereafter pay all annual or other fees required by law to be paid by corporations. (Amendment adopted November 3, 1908.)

[ORIGINAL SECTION.]

Sec. 7. The legislature shall not extend any franchise or charter, nor remit the forfeiture of any franchise or charter of any corporation now existing, or which shall hereafter exist under the laws of this state.

CORPORATE FRANCHISES.—An act waiving a right to enforce a forfeiture does not "remit the forfeiture," since there is no forfeiture until the sovereignty which created the franchise, by proper pro-

ceeding in a proper court, procure an adjudication of forfeiture, and enforce it. (People v. Los Angeles etc. Ry, Co., 91 Cal. 338, 27 Pac. 673.)

The amendment of 1907 to section 401, Civil Code, allowing corporations to extend the term of their corporate existence not exceeding fifty years from the date of such extension, is in conflict with this section. (Boca Mill Co. v. Curry, 154 Cal. 326, 97 Pac. 1117.)

> Extension of life of corporation as continuation of old or creation of new corporation. See note, Ann. Cas. 1914B, 390.

All franchises subject to the right of eminent domain.

Sec. 8. The exercise of the right of eminent domain shall never be so abridged or construed as to prevent the legislature from taking the property and franchises of incorporated companies and subjecting them to public use the same as the property of individuals, and the exercise of the police power of the state shall never be so abridged or construed as to permit corporations to conduct their business in such a manner as to infringe the rights of individuals or the general well-being of the state.

Restrictions on powers of corporations.

Sec. 9. No corporation shall engage in any business other than that expressly authorized in its charter, or the law under which it may have been or may hereafter be organized; nor shall it hold for a longer period than five years any real estate except such as may be necessary for carrying on its business.

CORPORATE PURPOSES.—A corporation is forbidden to engage in any business other than is expressly authorized in its charter or the law under which it is organized. To hold stock in another corporation is to engage in the business of such corporation. (Knowles v. Sandercock, 107 Cal. 629, 643, 40 Pac. 1047.)

This section does not cause property held in violation of it to escheat to the state. (People v. Stockton Sav. etc. Soc., 133 Cal. 611, 85 Am. St. Rep. 225, 65 Pac. 1078.)

While this provision is mandatory and prohibitory, it is not so self-executing as to deny the power of the legislature to prescribe penalties for its violation. (People v. Stockton Sav. etc. Soc., 133 Cal. 611, 85 Am. St. Rep. 225, 65 Pac. 1078.)

The mere fact that a bank is forbidden to take an assignment of a certificate of redemption does not invalidate the assignment in favor of a third person. (Youd v. German Sav. & Loan Soc., 3 Cal. App. 706, 86 Pac. 991.)

Liabilities of franchise under lease or grant.

Sec. 10. The legislature shall not pass any laws permitting the leasing or alienation of any franchise, so as to relieve the franchise or property held thereunder from the liabilities of the lessor or grantor, lessee or grantee, contracted or incurred in the operation, use, or enjoyment of such franchise, or any of its privileges.

ALIENATION OF FRANCHISES.—This section does not give a personal action against the corporation which owned property for an injury which has resulted to an employee of a lessee of the owner in the use of the property in the hands of the lessee, but is designed to subject the franchise and property to liability incurred in its occupation, whether the franchise be exercised or the property be used by the original owner or the lessee or grantee. (Lee v. Southern Pac. R. R. Co., 116 Cal. 97, 58 Am. St. Rep. 140, 38 L. R. A. 71, 47 Pac. 932.)

The transfer of a franchise by a water company is not prohibited by this section, which only forbids the transfer of a franchise "so as to relieve the franchise or property held thereunder" from liabilities incurred in its operation. Validity of section 361a, Civil Code, upheld. (South Pasadena v. Pasadena Land etc. Co., 152 Cal. 579, 93 Pac. 490.)

Corporation stock, restriction on issue of.

Sec. 11. No corporation shall issue stock or bonds, except for money paid, labor done, or property actually received, and all fictitious increase of stock or indebtedness shall be void. The stock and bonded indebtedness of corporations shall not be increased except in pursuance of general law, nor without the consent of the persons holding the larger amount in value of the stock, at a meeting called for that purpose, giving sixty days' public notice, as may be provided by law.

CORPORATE STOCK.—An increase of the capital stock of a corporation and the issuing of additional shares, to be sold at a price less than the nominal par value of the stock, to supply a fund actually required for the use of the corporation, is not a fictitious issuance. (Stein v. Howard, 65 Cal. 616, 4 Pac. 662.)

Non-negotiable notes secured by mortgages executed by a corporation do not constitute "bonded indebtedness" within the meaning of this section. (Underhill v. Santa Barbara etc. Imp. Co., 93 Cal. 300, 28 Pac. 1049.)

This provision is mandatory and not merely directory. (Navajo Min. etc. Co. v. Curry, 147 Cal. 581, 109 Am. St. Rep. 176, 82 Pac. 247.)

The requirement of sixty days' notice of stockholders' meeting cannot be waived by the stockholders, and the fact that all the stockholders attended and voted for the increase is immaterial. (Navajo Min. etc. Co. v. Curry, 147 Cal. 581, 109 Am. St. Rep. 176, 82 Pac. 247.)

It is legitimate for a corporation to dispose of its stock for full value received in land, property or services. (Turner v. Fidelity Loan Concern, 2 Cal. App. 122, 83 Pac. 62, 70.)

When a corporation issues stock for property or services, the presumption is that the transaction was fair until the contrary is shown. (Turner v. Fidelity Loan Concern, 2 Cal. App. 122, 83 Pac. 62, 70.)

The issue of stock as fully paid up to the stockholders of a corporation formed to take over partnership assets and hold the same as trustee for the stockholders is not unlawful. (Baldwin v. Miller & Lux, 152 Cal. 454, 92 Pac. 1030.)

The procedure provided by the Constitution for an increase of the bonded indebtedness of a corporation is not applicable to the original creation of a bonded debt. (Merced River Electric Co. v. Curry, 157 Cal. 727, 109 Pac. 264.)

The procedure provided by the Constitution for an increase of the bonded indebtedness of a corporation is not applicable to the original creation of a bonded debt. (McKee v. Title Ins. etc. Co., 159 Cal. 206, 113 Pac. 140.)

The provision of this section declaring "all fictitious increase of stock or indebtedness" void does not forbid the sale of bonds at a discount. (McKee v. Title Ins. etc. Co., 159 Cal. 206, 113 Pac. 140.)

This section does not mean that the consideration expressed should be of equal value with the stock issued, so long as the transaction is a real one, based upon a present consideration, and having reference to legitimate corporate purposes. (California Trona Co. v. Wilkinson, 20 Cal. App. 694, 130 Pac. 190.)

Fraudulent and overissued stocks. See note, 87 Am. St. Rep. 847.

Election of directors—Cumulative or distributive votes.

Sec. 12. In all elections for directors or managers of corporations every stockholder shall have the right to vote, in person or by proxy, the number of shares of stock owned by him for as many persons as there are directors or managers to be elected, or to cumulate said shares and give one candidate as many votes as the number of directors multiplied by the number of his shares of stock shall equal, or to distribute them, on the same principle, among as many candidates as he shall think fit; and such directors or managers shall not be elected in any other manner, except that members of co-operative societies formed for agricultural, mercantile, and manufacturing purposes, may vote

on all questions affecting such societies in manner prescribed by law.

DIRECTORS.—Under this section all the directors must be elected on one ballot. (Wright v. Central etc. Water Co., 67 Cal. 532, 8 Pac. 70.)

Voting by proxy. See notes, 27 Am. Dec. 60; 7 R. C. L., §§ 320–323, pp. 341–344.

State not to loan its credit nor subscribe to stock of corporations.

Sec. 13. The state shall not in any manner loan its credit, nor shall it subscribe to, or be interested in the stock of any company, association, or corporation.

STATE CREDIT.—This section prohibits the loaning of public credit for private purposes under any circumstances. (Stockton etc. R. R. Co. v. Common Council of Stockton, 41 Cal. 147; Ramsey v. Hoeger, 76 Ill. 432.)

It does not prohibit the appropriation of public funds to aid a corporation in the construction of a railroad to be used for military purposes. (People v. Pacheco, 27 Cal. 175.)

Corporations to have office for transaction of business in stocks.

Sec. 14. Every corporation other than religious, educational, or benevolent, organized or doing business in this state, shall have and maintain an office or place in this state for the transaction of its business, where transfers of stock shall be made, and in which shall be kept, for inspection by every person having an interest therein, and legislative committees, books in which shall be recorded the amount of capital stock subscribed, and by whom; the names of the owners of its stock, and the amounts owned by them respectively; the amount of stock paid in, and by whom; the transfers of stock; the amount of its assets and liabilities, and the names and place of residence of its officers.

CORPORATION BOOKS.—A stockholder in a corporation has the right to inspect the books, records and journals of the corporation, and this right may be enforced by mandamus. The purpose for which the inspection is desired is immaterial. (Johnson v. Langdon, 135 Cal. 624, 87 Am. St. Rep. 156, 67 Pac. 1050.)

Mandamus will lie to compel an inspection of corporate books, records and journals. (Gavin v. Pacific Coast M. F. Union, 2 Cal. App. 638, 84 Pac. 270.)

A corporation seeking to avoid the right of a stockholder to an inspection on the ground that it is a benevolent or charitable corporation has the burden of showing that it is such a corporation. (Gavin v. Pacific Coast M. F. Union, 2 Cal. App. 638, 84 Pac. 270.)

> Right of stockholder to inspect books and remedies for its enforcement. See note, 107 Am. St. Rep. 674.
>
> Right of stockholder to inspect books of corporation as absolute or qualified. See notes, 10 Ann. Cas. 990; 20 Ann. Cas. 612; Ann. Cas. 1913E, 173.
>
> Remedy of stockholder to enforce right to inspect corporate books. See note, 19 Ann. Cas. 310.
>
> Stockholder's right to inspect books of national bank. See note, 1 Ann. Cas. 130.
>
> Inspection of books. See 7 R. C. L., §§ 298–307, pp. 322–331.

Foreign corporations, conditions.

Sec. 15.   No corporation organized outside the limits of this state shall be allowed to transact business within this state on more favorable conditions than are prescribed by law to similar corporations organized under the laws of this state.

FOREIGN CORPORATIONS.—The act of 1880, providing for a penalty for failure of the directors of a domestic mining corporation to post weekly reports, etc., is not in violation of this section, and does not relate to the business of the corporation. (Miles v. Woodward, 115 Cal. 308, 46 Pac. 1076.)

This section was not designed to limit the powers of the legislature when dealing with the organization and government of corporations which are created by its own will and act. (Miles v. Woodward, 115 Cal. 308, 46 Pac. 1076.)

The act of 1876, requiring banking corporations to publish and file statements of their assets and liabilities, applies to foreign corporations. (Bank of British North America v. Madison, 99 Cal. 125, 133, 33 Pac. 762.)

As to whether by reason of this section foreign corporations must comply with section 299 of the Civil Code, query. (Anglo-Californian Bank v. Field, 146 Cal. 644, 80 Pac. 1080.)

The sale of a parcel of real estate by a foreign corporation of similar character and purpose to corporations formed under section 593 of the Civil Code, being merely incidental to the main purposes of incorporation, is not the transacting of business, forbidden to foreign corporations on more favorable conditions than are prescribed for domestic corporations. (General Conference of Free Baptists v. Berkey, 156 Cal. 466, 105 Pac. 411.)

This section is not violated by the corporation license tax act of March 29, 1905, as the conditions prescribed upon which corporations are allowed to transact business within this state are absolutely the

same as to both domestic and foreign corporations. (Kaiser Land & Fruit Co. v. Curry, 155 Cal. 638, 103 Pac. 341.)

The stockholders' liability created by article XII, section 3, of this Constitution does not apply to stockholders of a foreign corporation doing business in California, where its charter exempts its stockholders from liability for its debts. (Thomas v. Matthiessen, 192 Fed. 495, 113 C. C. A. 101; affirming 170 Fed. 362.)

Under this provision a foreign corporation's right to do business in California is taxable. (London & San Francisco Bank v. Block, 117 Fed. 900.)

None of the sections of the Civil Code relative to the organization of domestic corporations can be considered in the construction of this section, nor can any foreign corporation be required to organize under the laws of this state, as a condition of transacting business therein, since this section only refers to the transaction of business after the corporation is brought into being as such. (Western Union Tel. Co. v. Superior Court, 15 Cal. App. 679, 115 Pac. 1091, 1100.)

If section 359 of the Civil Code could, under this section of the Constitution, be applied to foreign corporations, the failure to observe its requirements does not make bonds issued under it void at the option of creditors, or of one acting in their interest, where they were issued for a valuable consideration and without fraud. (McKee v. Title Ins. Co., 159 Cal. 206, 113 Pac. 140.)

Jurisdiction over foreign corporations. See note, 85 Am. Dec. 905.

Power of states to discriminate against foreign corporations. See note, 95 Am. Dec. 536.

What constitutes doing business in state by foreign corporation. See notes, Ann. Cas. 1912A, 553; Ann. Cas. 1913E, 1154; 2 Ann. Cas. 307; 11 Ann. Cas. 320.

Power of state to impose additional burden on foreign corporation which has complied with conditions for doing business in state. See notes, 9 Ann. Cas. 981; 17 Ann. Cas. 1251.

Imposition of license tax or fee on foreign corporation. See note, Ann. Cas. 1913C, 812.

Corporations, where to be sued.

Sec. 16. A corporation or association may be sued in the county where the contract is made or is to be performed, or where the obligation or liability arises, or the breach occurs; or in the county where the principal place of business of such corporation is situated, subject to the power of the court to change the place of trial as in other cases.

ACTIONS AGAINST CORPORATIONS.—This section is merely permissive, and not mandatory. (Fresno Nat. Bank v. Superior Court, 83 Cal. 491, 24 Pac. 157.)

It applies to actions of tort as well as matters of contract. (Lewis v. Southern Pac. R. R. Co., 66 Cal. 209, 5 Pac. 79; Tingley v. Times-Mirror Co., 144 Cal. 205, 77 Pac. 918.)

It gives to the plaintiff the right to elect either to sue the corporation in the county where the contract is made, or is to be performed, or where the obligation or liability arises, or the breach occurs, or in the county where the principal place of business of the corporation is situated. (Trezevant v. W. R. Strong Co., 102 Cal. 47, 36 Pac. 395.)

An action to recover damages for trespass upon real property may be brought in the county of the principal place of the corporation defendant. (Miller & Lux v. Kern County Land Co., 134 Cal. 586, 66 Pac. 856.)

An action may be commenced against a corporation in the county where the contract was made, or where it was to be performed. (Bank of Yolo v. Sperry Flour Co., 141 Cal. 314, 65 L. R. A. 90, 74 Pac. 855.)

The right to sue a corporation in the county where the contract was made only applies when the corporation is the sole defendant in the case. (Griffin etc. Co. v. Magnolia etc. Fruit Cannery Co., 107 Cal. 378, 40 Pac. 495.)

An association of persons organized for a particular purpose, although not formerly a corporation, is included in this section. The word "association" does not necessarily mean an association possessing corporate powers and privileges. (Kendrick v. Diamond etc. Min. Co., 94 Cal. 137, 29 Pac. 324.)

Where the plaintiff sues an association and joins the persons composing it as defendants, he waives the provisions of this section. (Nelson v. East Side Grocery Co., 26 Cal. App. 344, 146 Pac. 1055.)

Under this section an action for libel may be maintained in the county in which the plaintiff resides, when the newspaper is circulated in that county but published in another. (Brady v. Times-Mirror Co., 106 Cal. 56, 39 Pac. 209; Tingley v. Times-Mirror Co., 144 Cal. 205, 77 Pac. 918.)

But where the plaintiff sues other persons than the corporation publishing the paper, he waives the provisions of this section. (Brady v. Times-Mirror Co., 106 Cal. 56, 39 Pac. 209.)

An action against a corporation for leave to redeem real estate is properly brought in the county where the real property is situated. (Baker v. Fireman's Fund Ins. Co., 73 Cal. 182, 14 Pac. 686.)

In an action against a corporation for damages for breach of contract, the defendant is entitled to a change of place of trial to the county in which its principal place of business is situated, when the county in which the action is brought is not the one in which the contract was made, or was to be performed, or in which the obligation arose, or in which the principal place of business is situated. (Cohn v. Central Pac. R. R. Co., 71 Cal. 488, 12 Pac. 498.)

If this provision should be construed as denying a corporation the right to a change of venue in cases in which a natural person is given such right, it would be in violation of the fourteenth amendment to the Constitution of the United States. (Grocers' etc. Union v. Kern Co. etc. Co., 150 Cal. 466, 89 Pac. 120.)

When it cannot be said from the facts set forth in the complaint that the contract involved was made, or was to be performed, or that the liability arose or breach occurred in the county where the action was commenced, the corporation is entitled to a change of venue to the county of its principal place of business. (Krogh v. Pacific Gateway etc. Co., 11 Cal. App. 237, 104 Pac. 698.)

When an act of negligence is committed by a corporation, the action may be brought in the county where committed. (Pittman v. Carstenbrook, 11 Cal. App. 224, 104 Pac. 699.)

When an action is brought against a foreign corporation and individuals, the action may be transferred to the county of the residence of individuals, although the corporation did not join in the motion for a change of venue. (Pittman v. Carstenbrook, 11 Cal. App. 224, 104 Pac. 699.)

A corporation has an absolute right to have an action removed to its place of residence. (Eddy v. Houghton, 6 Cal. App. 85, 91 Pac. 397.)

This section only applies to domestic corporations, and has no application to foreign corporations. (Waechter v. Atchison etc. Ry. Co., 10 Cal. App. 70, 101 Pac. 41.)

An action against a corporation may be prosecuted to final judgment where commenced unless the defendant can allege and show some sufficient ground for a change of the place of trial distinct from the fact that the residence of the corporation is in another county. (Cook v. W. S. Ray Mfg. Co., 159 Cal. 694, 115 Pac. 318.)

This section denying to domestic corporations the right, conferred upon all natural persons resident of the state, of having personal actions against them tried in the county where the defendant resides does not violate the federal Constitution by depriving them of the equal protection of the laws. (Cook v. W. S. Ray Mfg. Co., 159 Cal. 694, 115 Pac. 318.)

This section is permissive in effect, and it is intended to give to a plaintiff the right to choose which of the counties he will prosecute his action in. If it happens to be one within which the principal place of business of the corporation is not located, the corporation sued cannot secure a change of place of trial on the ground that the action is not brought in the county of its residence. (Bond v. Karma-Ajax Consol. Min. Co., 15 Cal. App. 469, 115 Pac. 254.)

This section does not deprive the superior court of any county of the state of jurisdiction to hear and determine all classes of actions generally, within the limits of its jurisdiction as defined in section 5 of article VI of the state Constitution. (Bond v. Karma-Ajax Consol. Min. Co., 15 Cal. App. 469, 115 Pac. 254.)

When a corporation has shown that its principal place of business is in another county, to defeat the motion for a change of venue the burden of proof is upon plaintiff to show that the contract was made, or was to be performed, or that the obligation or liability arose or the breach occurred in the county where the action is brought. (Hammond v. Ocean Shore Dev. Co., 22 Cal. App. 167, 133 Pac. 978.)

Jurisdiction and venue of actions against corporations. See 7 R. C. L., §§ 697–699, pp. 695–697.

Transportation companies, rights and liabilities of.

Sec. 17. All railroad, canal, and other transportation companies are declared to be common carriers, and subject to legislative control. Any association or corporation, organized for the purpose, under the laws of this state, shall have the right to connect at the state line with railroads of other states. Every railroad company shall have the right with its road to intersect, connect with or cross any other railroad, and shall receive and transport each the other's passengers, tonnage, and cars, without delay or discrimination.

RAILROADS.—The legislature may regulate railroad crossings. (Pittsburg etc. R. R. Co. v. Southwest etc. Ry. Co., 77 Pa. 173.)

It may require railroad companies to ring a bell or sound a whistle at a crossing. (Galena etc. R. R. Co. v. Appleby, 28 Ill. 283; Galena etc. R. R. Co. v. Loomis, 13 Ill. 548, 56 Am. Dec. 471.)

It may regulate the speed of trains in a city. (Chicago etc. R. R. Co. v. Haggerty, 67 Ill. 113.)

It may require them to erect fences and cattle-guards. (Suydam v. Moore, 8 Barb. (N. Y.) 358; Waldron v. Rensselaer etc. R. R. Co., 8 Barb. (N. Y.) 390; New Albany etc. R. Co. v. Tilton, 12 Ind. 3, 74 Am. Dec. 195; Madison etc. R. R. Co. v. Whiteneck, 8 Ind. 217; Ohio etc. R. R. Co. v. McClelland, 25 Ill. 140; Kansas etc. Ry. Co. v. Mower, 16 Kan. 573; Jones v. Galena etc. R. R. Co., 16 Iowa, 6; Indianapolis etc. R. R. Co. v. Kercheval, 16 Ind. 84; Nichols v. Somerset etc. R. R. Co., 43 Me. 356; Winona etc. R. R. Co. v. Waldron, 11 Minn. 515, 88 Am. Dec. 100; Gorman v. Pacific R. Co., 26 Mo. 441, 72 Am. Dec. 220; Blair v. Milwaukee etc. R. R. Co., 20 Wis. 254; Pennsylvania R. R. Co. v. Riblet, 66 Pa. 164, 5 Am. Rep. 360.)

A railroad company can be compelled to exercise its assumed duties and powers. (Madera Ry. Co. v. Raymond Granite Co., 3 Cal. App. 668, 87 Pac. 27.)

This provision is not self-executing in the sense of authorizing the taking of land by a railroad corporation, regardless of its charter powers and of the statute providing for condemnation. (Boca etc. R. R. Co. v. Sierra Valleys R. R. Co., 2 Cal. App. 546, 84 Pac. 298.)

Distinction between common and private carriers. See notes, 130 Am. St. Rep. 34; 4 R. C. L., § 8, p. 549.

Officers of corporations, restriction as to interests.

Sec. 18. No president, director, officer, agent, or employee of any railroad or canal company shall be interested, directly or indirectly, in the furnishing of material or supplies to such company, nor in the business of transportation as a common carrier of freight or passengers over the

works owned, leased, controlled, or worked by such company, except such interest in the business of transportation as lawfully flows from the ownership of stock therein.

Free passes on railroads prohibited to state officials.

Sec. 19. No railroad or other transportation company shall grant free passes, or passes or tickets at a discount, to any person holding any office of honor, trust, or profit in this state; and the acceptance of any such pass or ticket, by a member of the legislature or any public officer, other than railroad commissioner, shall work a forfeiture of his office.

RAILROAD PASSES.—As to the nature of a proceeding to remove an officer for accepting a railroad pass, see People v. Superior Court, 114 Cal. 466, 46 Pac. 383.

> Constitutional or statutory provisions against gift or receipt of free railroad transportation. See note, 17 Ann. Cas. 662.
>
> Forbidding issuance of free passes. See 4 R. C. L., § 84, p. 613.

Fares and freights to be regulated by government.

Sec. 20. No railroad or other transportation company shall raise any rate of charge for the transportation of freight or passengers or any charge connected therewith or incidental thereto, under any circumstances whatsoever, except upon a showing before the railroad commission provided for in this Constitution, that such increase is justified, and the decision of the said commission upon the showing so made shall not be subject to review by any court except upon the question whether such decision of the commission will result in confiscation of property. (Amendment approved October 10, 1911.)

[ORIGINAL SECTION.]

Sec. 20. No railroad company or other common carrier shall combine or make any contract with the owners of any vessel that leaves port or makes port in this state, or with any common carrier, by which combination or contract the earnings of one doing the carrying are to be shared by the other not doing the carrying. And whenever a railroad corporation shall, for the purpose of competing with any other common carrier, lower its rates for transportation of passengers or freight from one point to another, such reduced rates shall not be again raised or increased from such

Constitution—32

standard without the consent of the governmental authority in which shall be vested the power to regulate fares and freights.

COMPETITION.—Where a railroad company lowers its passenger rates in order to compete with another road, and afterward raises them without the consent of the railroad commissioners, such commissioners have no jurisdiction to require a restoration of the lower rate. (Edson v. Southern Pac. Co., 133 Cal. 25, 65 Pac. 15.)

The object of this provision was to foster legitimate competition by preventing destructive competition. (Edson v. Southern Pacific R. R. Co., 144 Cal. 182, 77 Pac. 894.)

Rates are not lowered for the purpose of competing with any other common carrier within the meaning of this section, when they are merely lowered in self-defense to meet a lower destructive rate first inaugurated by a rival railroad company. (Edson v. Southern Pacific R. R. Co., 144 Cal. 182, 77 Pac. 894.)

A railroad lowers its rates within the meaning of this section by establishing limited tickets at reduced rates which are used by ninety-five per cent of its passengers, although no stop-over privileges are given and liability for baggage is limited, and unlimited tickets are still kept on sale. (Edson v. Southern Pacific R. R. Co., 144 Cal. 182, 77 Pac. 894.)

Rates and rate regulation. See 4 R. C. L., §§ 78–136, pp. 606–657.

Discrimination in charges by carriers forbidden.

Sec. 21. No discrimination in charges or facilities for transportation shall be made by any railroad or other transportation company between places or persons, or in the facilities for the transportation of the same classes of freight or passengers within this state. It shall be unlawful for any railroad or other transportation company to charge or receive any greater compensation in the aggregate for the transportation of passengers or of like kind of property for a shorter than for a longer distance over the same line or route in the same direction, the shorter being included within the longer distance, or to charge any greater compensation as a through rate than the aggregate of the intermediate rates. Provided, however, that upon application to the railroad commission provided for in this Constitution such company may, in special cases, after investigation, be authorized by such commission to charge less for longer than for shorter distances for the transportation of persons or property and the railroad commission may from time to time prescribe the extent to which such company may be relieved from the prohibition to charge

less for the longer than for the shorter haul. The railroad commission shall have power to authorize the issuance of excursion and commutation tickets at special rates. Nothing herein contained shall be construed to prevent the railroad commission from ordering and compelling any railroad or other transportation company to make reparation to any shipper on account of the rates charged to said shipper being excessive or discriminatory, provided no discrimination will result from such reparation. (Amendment approved October 10, 1911.)

[ORIGINAL SECTION.]

Sec. 21. No discrimination in charges or facilities for transportation shall be made by any railroad or other transportation company between places or persons, or in the facilities for the transportation of the same classes of freight or passengers within this state, or coming from or going to any other state. Persons and property transported over any railroad, or by any other transportation company or individual, shall be delivered at any station, landing, or port, at charges not exceeding the charges for the transportation of persons and property of the same class, in the same direction, to any more distant station, port, or landing. Excursion and commutation tickets may be issued at special rates.

FREIGHTS AND FARES.—The provision of this section as to excursion or commutation tickets is not intended to modify section 20 of this article; but is simply a qualification of the preceding clause of this section. (Edson v. Southern Pacific R. R. Co., 144 Cal. 182, 77 Pac. 894.)

The new remedy of a proceeding before the railroad commission, in cases of excessive or discriminatory rates charged by carriers, attached to any such right as had not been barred by the statute of limitations. (Scott, Magner & Miller v. Southern Pac. Co., 1 C. R. C. 68, 69; F. Cames Co. v. Southern Pac. Co., 1 C. R. C. 74, 75; Pioneer Box Co. v. Southern Pac. Co., 1 C. R. C. 568, 572.)

There was no offense under this section, as it existed prior to October 10, 1911, unless the carrier made a lesser charge for a transportation to a more distant station or port in the same direction, and it is not sufficient that the lower rate is from a more distant station or port. (Scott, Magner & Miller v. Western Pacific Ry. Co., 2 C. R. C. 626, 629; Scott, Magner & Miller v. Southern Pacific Co., 3 C. R. C. 339, 342; Livermore Warehouse Co. v. Southern Pacific Co., 3 C. R. C. 343, 344.)

This section was only intended to apply to one-way fares higher than the aggregate of the intermediate one-way fares, and does not make unlawful the charging of round-trip fares in excess of the aggregate of the intermediate round-trip fares. (In re Fares, Rules and Regulations of the Northwestern Pacific R. R. Co., 2 C. R. C. 910, 923.)

The long and short haul clauses found here and in the so-called "Wright Act" are only binding upon the carriers until the state establishes the rates as provided, and thereafter the long and short haul principle governs the railroad commission in establishing the rates. (Scott, Magner & Miller v. Western Pacific Ry. Co., 2 C. R. C. 626, 637; Scott, Magner & Miller v. Southern Pac. Co., 3 C. R. C. 339, 340.)

This section as amended in 1911 does not apply to the transportation by a baggage or transfer company from or to the railroad company's depot. (Red Line Tourists Agency v. Southern Pacific Co., 3 C. R. C. 526, 532.)

The provisions of this section relating to through rates in excess of the aggregate of intermediate rates are prohibitory, and the railroad commission is not vested with any discretionary power in the application of this provision, as in the case of the long and short haul provision. (In re Application of Southern Pacific Co., 4 C. R. C. 649, 650; In re Application of Atchison, Topeka & Santa Fe Ry. Co., 4 C. R. C. 964, 965, 969, 970, 971, 972.)

> What are unlawful and unreasonable discriminations. See notes, 44 Am. Rep. 568; 54 Am. Rep. 862; 11 Am. St. Rep. 647.
>
> Discrimination between shippers. See note, 1 Ann. Cas. 55.
>
> Requirement of prepayment of freight charges as unlawful discrimination by carrier. See note, 16 Ann. Cas. 621.
>
> Discrimination by carriers. See 4 R. C. L., §§ 35–77, pp. 565–606.

Railroad commission, organization of.

Sec. 22.   There is hereby created a railroad commission which shall consist of five members and which shall be known as the railroad commission of the state of California. The commission shall be appointed by the governor from the state at large; provided, that the legislature, in its discretion, may divide the state into districts for the purpose of such appointments, said districts to be as nearly equal in population as practicable; and provided further that the three commissioners in office at the time this section takes effect shall serve out the term for which they were elected, and that two additional commissioners shall be appointed by the governor immediately after the adoption of this section, to hold office during the same term. Upon the expiration of said term, the term of office of each commissioner thereafter shall be six years, except the commissioners first appointed hereunder after such expiration, one of whom shall be appointed to hold office until January 1, 1917, two until January 1, 1919, and two until January 1, 1921. Whenever a vacancy in the office of commissioner

shall occur, the governor shall forthwith appoint a qualified person to fill the same for the unexpired term. Commissioners appointed for regular terms shall, at the beginning of the term for which they are appointed and those appointed to fill vacancies, shall, immediately upon their appointment, enter upon the duties of their offices. The legislature shall fix the salaries of the commissioners, but pending such action the salaries of the commissioners, their officers and employees shall remain as now fixed by law. The legislature shall have the power, by a two-thirds vote of all members elected to each house, to remove any one or more of said commissioners from office for dereliction of duty or corruption or incompetency. All of said commissioners shall be qualified electors of this state, and no person in the employ of or holding any official relation to any person, firm or corporation, which said person, firm or corporation is subject to regulation by said railroad commission and no person owning stock or bonds of any such corporation or who is in any manner pecuniarily interested therein, shall be appointed to or hold the office of railroad commissioner. No vacancy in the commission shall impair the right of the remaining commissioners to exercise all the powers of the commission. The act of a majority of the commissioners when in session as a board shall be deemed to be the act of the commission; but any investigation, inquiry or hearing which the commission has power to undertake or to hold may be undertaken or held by or before any commissioner designated for the purpose by the commission, and every order made by a commissioner so designated, pursuant to such inquiry, investigation or hearing, when approved or confirmed by the commission ordered filed in its office, shall be deemed to be the order of the commission.

Said commission shall have the power to establish rates of charges for the transportation of passengers and freight by railroads and other transportation companies, and no railroad or other transportation company shall charge or demand or collect or receive a greater or less or different compensation for such transportation of passengers or

freight, or for any service in connection therewith, between the points named in any tariff of rates, established by said commission, than the rates, fares and charges which are specified in such tariff. The commission shall have the further power to examine books, records and papers of all railroad and other transportation companies; to hear and determine complaints against railroad and other transportation companies; to issue subpoenas and all necessary process and send for persons and papers; and the commission and each of the commissioners shall have the power to administer oaths, take testimony and punish for contempt in the same manner and to the same extent as courts of record; the commission may prescribe a uniform system of accounts to be kept by all railroad and other transportation companies.

No provision of this Constitution shall be construed as a limitation upon the authority of the legislature to confer upon the railroad commission additional powers of the same kind or different from those conferred herein which are not inconsistent with the powers conferred upon the railroad commission in this Constitution, and the authority of the legislature to confer such additional powers is expressly declared to be plenary and unlimited by any provision of this Constitution.

The provisions of this section shall not be construed to repeal in whole or in part any existing law not inconsistent herewith, and the "Railroad Commission Act" of this state approved February 10, 1911, shall be construed with reference to this constitutional provision and any other constitutional provision becoming operative concurrently herewith. And the said act shall have the same force and effect as if the same had been passed after the adoption of this provision of the Constitution and of all other provisions adopted concurrently herewith, except that the three commissioners referred to in said act shall be held and construed to be the five commissioners provided for herein. (Amendment approved October 10, 1911.)

[ORIGINAL SECTION.]

Sec. 22. The state shall be divided into three districts as nearly equal in population as practicable, in each of which one railroad commissioner shall be elected by the qualified electors thereof at the regular gubernatorial elections, whose salary shall be fixed by law, and whose term of office shall be four years, commencing on the first Monday after the first day of January next succeeding their election. Said commissioners shall be qualified electors of this state and of the district from which they are elected, and shall not be interested in any railroad corporation, or other transportation company, as stockholder, creditor, agent, attorney or employee; and the act of a majority of said commissioners shall be deemed the act of said commission. Said commissioners shall have the power, and it shall be their duty, to establish rates of charges for the transportation of passengers and freight by railroad or other transportation companies, and publish the same from time to time, with such changes as they may make; to examine the books, records, and papers of all railroad and other transportation companies, and for this purpose they shall have power to issue subpoenas and all other necessary process; to hear and determine complaints against railroad and other transportation companies, to send for persons and papers, to administer oaths, take testimony, and punish for contempt of their orders and processes, in the same manner and to the same extent as courts of record, and enforce their decisions and correct abuses through the medium of the courts. Said commissioners shall prescribe a uniform system of accounts to be kept by all such corporations and companies. Any railroad corporation or transportation company which shall fail or refuse to conform to such rates as shall be established by such commissioners, or shall charge rates in excess thereof, or shall fail to keep their accounts in accordance with the system prescribed by the commission, shall be fined not exceeding twenty thousand dollars for each offense, and every officer, agent, or employee of any such corporation or company, who shall demand or receive rates in excess thereof, or who shall in any manner violate the provisions of this section, shall be fined not exceeding five thousand dollars, or be imprisoned in the county jail not exceeding one year. In all controversies, civil or criminal, the rates of fares and freights established by said commission shall be deemed conclusively just and reasonable, and in any action against such corporation or company for damages sustained by charging excessive rates, the plaintiff, in addition to the actual damage, may, in the discretion of the judge or jury, recover exemplary damages. Said commission shall report to the governor, annually, their proceedings, and such other facts as may be deemed important. Nothing in this section shall prevent individuals from maintaining actions against any of such companies. The legislature may, in addition to any penalties herein prescribed, enforce this article by forfeiture of charter or otherwise, and may confer such further powers on the commissioners as shall be necessary to enable them to perform the duties enjoined on them in this and

the foregoing section. The legislature shall have power, by a two-thirds vote of all the members elected to each house, to remove any one or more of said commissioners from office, for dereliction of duty, or corruption, or incompetency; and whenever, from any cause, a vacancy in office shall occur in said commission, the governor shall fill the same by the appointment of a qualified person thereto, who shall hold office for the residue of the unexpired term, and until his successor shall have been elected and qualified.

RAILROAD COMMISSION.—This section should be construed to extend the supervision of the commission to all persons engaged in the business of transportation, whether as corporations, joint-stock companies, partnerships, or individuals. (Moran v. Ross, 79 Cal. 159, 21 Pac. 547.)

This section did not repeal section 490 of the Civil Code, although that section refers to section 489 of the same code, which was superseded by this section. (Robinson v. Southern Pac. R. R. Co., 105 Cal. 526, 28 L. R. A. 773, 38 Pac. 94, 722.)

A statute may authorize the appointment of commissioners to determine the duties and obligations of railroad companies. (Portland etc. R. R. Co. v. Grand Trunk Ry. Co., 46 Me. 69.)

The commission has no jurisdiction over a street railroad corporation operated in a municipality. (Board of Railroad Commrs. v. Market St. Ry. Co., 132 Cal. 677, 64 Pac. 1065.)

The commission has no jurisdiction, upon a complaint that a railroad company lowered its passenger rates in order to compete with another road, and afterward raised them without the consent of the commission, to require a restoration of the lower rate. (Edson v. Southern Pac. Co., 133 Cal. 25, 65 Pac. 15.)

Sections 22 and 23 as amended in 1911 created, in the state railroad commission, both a court and an administrative tribunal, and gave such commission control of the public utilities of the state. These sections also authorized the legislature to confer such additional and different powers upon the commission touching public utilities as it may see fit, unrestrained by other constitutional provisions, and the legality of such powers as the legislature has or may thus confer upon the commission, if cognate and germane to the subject of public utilities, may not be questioned under the state Constitution. (Pacific Tel. etc. Co. v. Eshleman, 166 Cal. 640, Ann. Cas. 1915C, 822, 50 L. R. A. (N. S.) 652, 137 Pac. 1119.)

The deprivation of jurisdiction of the courts of the state may not be questioned, and the reasonableness of the railroad commission's orders and decrees may not be inquired into by any court of this state, and consequently is of federal cognizance only. (Pacific Tel. etc. Co. v. Eshleman, 166 Cal. 640, Ann. Cas. 1915C, 822, 50 L. R. A. (N. S.) 652, 137 Pac. 1119.)

Sections 22 and 23 as amended in 1911 confer jurisdiction upon the railroad commission in the matter of fixing rates to be charged for transportation of passengers and freight between two ports in this state, notwithstanding that the vessels, in passing from one port to the other, must travel in part over the high seas, and outside of

the territorial jurisdiction of the state. (Wilmington Transp. Co. v. Railroad Commission, 166 Cal. 741, 137 Pac. 1153; affirmed in Wilmington Transp. Co. v. Railroad Commission, 236 U. S. 151, 59 L. Ed. 508, 35 Sup. Ct. Rep. 276.)

No city has any jurisdiction over any purely transportation service, since, by virtue of this section, that power has always been lodged in the railroad commission. (In re Southern Pacific Co. et al., Canceling Items, 1 C. R. C. 744, 752.)

The amendments to sections 22 and 23 of 1910 conferred all of the power over public utilities theretofore exercised by boards of supervisors, and additional important powers respecting both the service and rates of such liabilities, upon the railroad commission. (In re Application of James A. Murray, 2 C. R. C. 464, 477.)

The legislature had the power under this provision to confer upon the railroad commission all the powers which it purported to confer with reference to railroad crossings by section 43 of the Public Utilities Act. (In re Application of Board of Trustees of Alhambra, 2 C. R. C. 361, 364.)

Under this section, prior to October 10, 1911, it was made the duty of the railroad commission to establish freight and passenger rates, and the rates thus established were made conclusively just and reasonable. (Scott, Magner & Miller v. Western Pacific Ry. Co., 2 C. R. C. 626, 630.)

As the carriers now make and file their own rates, pursuant to the amendment of October 10, 1911, to this section, they should be liable to make reparation if these rates are unjust and unreasonable. (Scott, Magner & Miller v. Western Pacific Ry. Co., 2 C. R. C. 626, 637.)

Where the board of railroad commissioners prior to October 10, 1911, established rates, they were conclusively just and reasonable, and no right of action arose on the doctrine of discrimination against any railroad company which collected the rates actually established by the board of railroad commissioners. (Penoyar v. Southern Pacific Co., 3 C. R. C. 576, 580.)

When a wharf is used to perform a terminal service which the carrier must perform under its contract of carriage, it is purely transportation service over which the railroad commission and not a municipality has jurisdiction. (In re Southern Pacific Co. et al., Canceling Items, 1 C. R. C. 744, 752.)

Services of a carrier which are not performed as carrier, but performed otherwise than as carrier,—for instance, as warehouseman,—may be under the jurisdiction of municipalities, if their charters had, prior to March 23, 1912, given them such jurisdiction. (In re Southern Pacific Co. et al., Canceling Items, 1 C. R. C. 744, 752.)

Railroad commission, regulation of public utilities.

Sec. 23. Every private corporation, and every individual or association of individuals, owning, operating, managing, or controlling any commercial railroad, interurban railroad, street railroad, canal, pipe-line, plant, or equip-

ment, or any part of such railroad, canal, pipe-line, plant
or equipment within this state, for the transportation or
conveyance of passengers, or express matter, or freight of
any kind, including crude oil, or for the transmission of
telephone or telegraph messages, or for the production,
generation, transmission, delivery or furnishing of heat,
light, water or power or for the furnishing of storage or
wharfage facilities, either directly or indirectly, to or for
the public, and every common carrier, is hereby declared to
be a public utility subject to such control and regulation
by the railroad commission as may be provided by the legislature, and every class of private corporations, individuals,
or associations of individuals hereafter declared by the
legislature to be public utilities shall likewise be subject
to such control and regulation. The railroad commission
shall have and exercise such power and jurisdiction to
supervise and regulate public utilities, in the state of California, and to fix the rates to be charged for commodities
furnished, or services rendered by public utilities as shall
be conferred upon it by the legislature, and the right of the
legislature to confer powers upon the railroad commission
respecting public utilities is hereby declared to be plenary
and to be unlimited by any provision of this Constitution.
From and after the passage by the legislature of laws conferring powers upon the railroad commission respecting
public utilities, all powers respecting such public utilities
vested in boards of supervisors, or municipal councils, or
other governing bodies of the several counties, cities and
counties, cities and towns, in this state, or in any commission created by law and existing at the time of the passage
of such laws, shall cease so far as such powers shall conflict
with the powers so conferred upon the railroad commission; provided, however, that this section shall not affect
such powers of control over public utilities as relate to the
making and enforcement of local, police, sanitary and other
regulations, other than the fixing of rates, vested in any
city and county or incorporated city or town as, at an election to be held pursuant to law, a majority of the qualified
electors of such city and county, or incorporated city or

town, voting thereon, shall vote to retain, and until such election such powers shall continue unimpaired; but if the vote so taken shall not favor the continuation of such powers they shall thereafter vest in the railroad commission as provided by law; and provided, further, that where any such city and county or incorporated city or town shall have elected to continue any of its powers to make and enforce such local, police, sanitary and other regulations, other than the fixing of rates, it may, by vote of a majority of its qualified electors voting thereon, thereafter surrender such powers to the railroad commission in the manner prescribed by the legislature; and provided, further, that this section shall not affect the right of any city and county or incorporated city or town to grant franchises for public utilities upon the terms and conditions and in the manner prescribed by law. Nothing in this section shall be construed as a limitation upon any power conferred upon the railroad commission by any provision of this Constitution now existing or adopted concurrently herewith. (Amendment adopted November 3, 1914.)

[AMENDMENT OF 1911.]

Sec. 23. Every private corporation, and every individual or association of individuals, owning, operating, managing or controlling any commercial railroad, interurban railroad, street railroad, canal, pipe-line, plant, or equipment, or any part of such railroad, canal, pipe-line, plant or equipment within this state, for the transportation or conveyance of passengers or express matter, or freight of any kind, including crude oil, or for the transmission of telephone or telegraph messages, or for the production, generation, transmission, delivery or furnishing of heat, light, water or power or for the furnishing of storage or wharfage facilities, either directly or indirectly, to or for the public, and every common carrier, is hereby declared to be a public utility subject to such control and regulation by the railroad commission as may be provided by the legislature, and every class of private corporations, individuals, or associations of individuals hereafter declared by the legislature to be public utilities shall likewise be subject to such control and regulation. The railroad commission shall have and exercise such power and jurisdiction to supervise and regulate public utilities, in the state of California, and to fix the rates to be charged for commodities furnished, or services rendered by public utilities as shall be conferred upon it by the legislature, and the right of the legislature to confer powers upon the railroad commission respecting public utilities is hereby declared to

be plenary and to be unlimited by any provision of this Constitution.

From and after the passage by the legislature of laws conferring powers upon the railroad commission respecting public utilities, all powers respecting such public utilities vested in boards of supervisors, or municipal councils, or other governing bodies of the several counties, cities and counties, cities and towns, in this state, or in any commission created by law and existing at the time of the passage of such laws, shall cease so far as such powers shall conflict with the powers so conferred upon the railroad commission; provided, however, that this section shall not affect such powers of control over any public utility vested in any city and county, or incorporated city or town as, at an election to be held pursuant to laws to be passed hereafter by the legislature, a majority of the qualified electors voting thereon of such city and county, or incorporated city or town, shall vote to retain, and until such election such powers shall continue unimpaired; but if the vote so taken shall not favor the continuation of such powers they shall thereafter vest in the railroad commission as provided by law; and provided, further, that where any such city and county or incorporated city or town shall have elected to continue any powers respecting public utilities, it may, by vote of a majority of its qualified electors voting thereon, thereafter surrender such powers to the railroad commission in the manner to be prescribed by the legislature; or if such municipal corporation shall have surrendered any powers to the railroad commission, it may, by like vote, thereafter reinvest itself with such power. Nothing in this section shall be construed as a limitation upon any power conferred upon the railroad commission by any provision of this Constitution now existing or adopted concurrently herewith. (Amendment approved October 10, 1911.)

[ORIGINAL SECTION.]

Sec. 23. Until the legislature shall district the state, the following shall be the railroad districts: The first district shall be composed of the counties of Alpine, Amador, Butte, Calaveras, Colusa, Del Norte, El Dorado, Humboldt, Lake, Lassen, Mendocino, Modoc, Napa, Nevada, Placer, Plumas Sacramento, Shasta, Sierra, Siskiyou, Solano, Sonoma, Sutter, Tehama, Trinity, Yolo, and Yuba, from which one railroad commissioner shall be elected. The second district shall be composed of the counties of Marin, San Francisco, and San Mateo, from which one railroad commissioner shall be elected. The third district shall be composed of the counties of Alameda, Contra Costa, Fresno, Inyo, Kern, Los Angeles, Mariposa, Merced, Mono, Monterey, San Benito, San Bernardino, San Diego, San Joaquin, San Luis Obispo, Santa Barbara, Santa Clara, Santa Cruz, Stanislaus, Tulare, Tuolumne, and Ventura, from which one railroad commissioner shall be elected.

RAILROAD COMMISSION.—Under this section as amended in 1911 and section 82 of the Public Utilities Act of 1911, the powers of control over existing public utilities which were vested in any city

at the time of the adoption of the amendment and of the taking effect of said Public Utilities Act of 1911 are still retained by such city, and do not pass to the railroad commission until the city by an election surrenders these powers to the commission. (Title Guarantee etc. Co. v. Railroad Commission, 168 Cal. 295, 142 Pac. 878.)

Section 50 of the Public Utilities Act (Stats. (Ex. Sess.) 1911, p. 43), requiring public utilities to obtain a certificate of public convenience and necessity from the railroad commission before beginning any new construction, does not go beyond the powers of supervision and regulation which the legislature may, under this section, confer on the railroad commission, nor does it constitute an improper delegation of legislative functions to the commission. (Oro Electric Corp. v. Railroad Commission, 169 Cal. 466, 147 Pac. 118.)

Under this section and section 82 of the Public Utilities Act, the cities are limited to the power which they had on March 23, 1912, and no extension of this power may be had. (In re Application of James A. Murray, 2 C. R. C. 464, 502.)

The legislature having, pursuant to this section, provided (c. 40, Stats. 1911, Extra Session) a complete scheme for presenting to the voters the question of the retention or relinquishment of powers over utilities vested in municipalities, such powers cannot be divested through the adoption of a charter amendment, but must be brought about under the scheme provided by the legislature. (Long Beach Chamber of Commerce v. Pacific Electric Ry. Co., 2 C. R. C. 455, 458; 3 C. R. C. 611, 613.)

Under this section and subdivision X of section 2 of the Public Utilities Act, a water company is subject to the jurisdiction of the railroad commission, even though it is not serving the public with water, but is only serving water for use on lands owned or sold by it, and even though its articles of incorporation specifically limit it to such distribution of water, and even though it is only distributing water under contracts which fix the price to be paid. (In re Rates and Service of San Gorgonio Water Co., 2 C. R. C. 706, 711.)

Under the provisions of this section as amended on October 10, 1911, public utilities in municipalities incorporated after the effective date of the Public Utilities Act, March 23, 1912, are subject to the jurisdiction of the railroad commission. (In re Rates and Service of San Gorgonio Water Co., 2 C. R. C. 706, 709.)

The power of regulating the ditch of a water and irrigation company in a municipality which has not voted to transfer its powers over public utilities to the railroad commission is vested exclusively in the authorities of such municipality. (Santa Paula v. Santa Clara Water & Irr. Co., 3 C. R. C. 143, 144.)

The railroad commission under this section and the Public Utilities Act has jurisdiction to establish the fare to be charged by a street railroad or any other railroad between a point within the city limits and a point outside of the city limits. (Ramos v. San Francisco-Oakland Terminal Rys., 3 C. R. C. 800, 802.)

Under this section, the Public Utilities Act, and chapter 80 of the Laws of 1913, the railroad commission has the power, after notice and hearing, to compel a water utility to extend its mains at its

own expense in all territory in this state other than incorporated cities and towns in which this power may vest by virtue of specific provisions of their charters. (Dooley v. People's Water Co., 3 C. R. C. 948, 960.)

When a city supplies water to consumers outside of its limits, such service is subject to the jurisdiction of the railroad commission. (In re Application of San Diego, 4 C. R. C. 902, 905.)

A utility selling electric energy to everyone who desires it is a public utility subject to the jurisdiction of the railroad commission, even though it buys its electric energy from another company under a contract. (Calistoga Electric Co. v. Napa Valley Electric Co., 5 C. R. C. 84, 85.)

A company which has agreed by contract and otherwise to deliver water to mutual companies, corporations, municipalities and an individual, and has by these means publicly held itself out as serving a certain territory, and is such territory's only source of supply of water for domestic and irrigation purposes, is a public utility water company subject to the jurisdiction of the railroad commission. (Becker v. Holabird, 5 C. R. C. 153, 167.)

A water company whose by-laws do not limit the delivery of water to stockholders only or to specific districts, which owns a system of canals and ditches and operates same for compensation, and which, while not owning any water and distributing water simply as the agent of riparian owners, is acting as a common carrier for all land owners, and owns certain shares of stock of a water company and of the waters represented thereby, which waters it distributes for compensation, is a public utility subject to the jurisdiction of the railroad commission. (Ferrasci v. Empire Water Co., 6 C. R. C. 309, 321.)

Where only the safety and convenience of the public using the street where it crosses over a railroad is involved, and a municipality had jurisdiction over such matter prior to March 23, 1912, the railroad commission has no jurisdiction to compel a separation of grades at the crossing involved. (Daum v. Southern Pacific Co., 6 C. R. C. 946, 949.)

> Power of state or public service commission to compel public service corporations to make connections with each other. See note, Ann. Cas. 1915C, 850.

Railroad commission—Power in eminent domain.

Sec. 23a.   The railroad commission shall have and exercise such power and jurisdiction as shall be conferred upon it by the legislature to fix the just compensation to be paid for the taking of any property of a public utility in eminent domain proceedings by the state or any county, city and county, incorporated city or town, or municipal water district, and the right of the legislature to confer such powers upon the railroad commission is hereby declared to be

plenary and to be unlimited by any provision of this Constitution. All acts of the legislature heretofore adopted, which are in accordance herewith, are hereby confirmed and declared valid. (New section added by amendment adopted November 3, 1914.)

RAILROAD COMMISSION—Power in eminent domain.—The effect of this provision is to remove all possible doubt concerning the validity of sections 47 and 70 of the Public Utilities Act as far as the Constitution of California is concerned. (In re Application of Marin Municipal Water District, 6 C. R. C. 507, 509.)

The purpose of this section was to secure the services in the condemnation of the property of public utilities not only of commissioners, but also of the trained employees of the railroad commission, who might testify in cases of this character and give the commission the advantage of having testimony presented in behalf of the state. (In re Application of Marin Municipal Water District, 6 C. R. C. 507, 515.)

Legislature to pass laws to enforce this article.

Sec. 24. The legislature shall pass all laws necessary for the enforcement of the provisions of this article.

ARTICLE XIII.

REVENUE AND TAXATION.

Taxation to be in proportion to value.

Section 1. All property in the state except as otherwise in this Constitution provided, not exempt under the laws of the United States, shall be taxed in proportion to its value, to be ascertained as provided by law, or as hereinafter provided. The word "property," as used in this article and section, is hereby declared to include moneys, credits, bonds, stocks, dues, franchises, and all other matters and things, real, personal, and mixed, capable of private ownership; provided, that a mortgage, deed of trust, contract, or other obligation by which a debt is secured when land is pledged as security for the payment thereof, together with the money represented by such debt, shall not be considered property subject to taxation; and further provided, that property used for free public libraries and free museums, growing crops, property used exclusively for public schools, and such as may belong to the United States, this state, or to any county, city and county, or municipal corporation within this state shall be exempt from taxa-

tion, except such lands and the improvements thereon located outside of the county, city and county or municipal corporation owning the same as were subject to taxation at the time of the acquisition of the same by said county, city and county or municipal corporation; provided, that no improvements of any character whatever constructed by any county, city and county or municipal corporation shall be subject to taxation. All lands or improvements thereon, belonging to any county, city and county or municipal corporation, not exempt from taxation, shall be assessed by the assessor of the county, city and county or municipal corporation in which said lands or improvements are located, and said assessment shall be subject to review, equalization and adjustment by the state board of equalization. The legislature may provide, except in the case of credits secured by mortgage or trust deed, for a deduction from credits of debts due to bona fide residents of this state. (Amendment adopted November 3, 1914.)

[AMENDMENT OF 1910.]

Section 1. All property in the state except as otherwise in this Constitution provided, not exempt under the laws of the United States, shall be taxed in proportion to its value, to be ascertained as provided by law, or as hereinafter provided. The word "property," as used in this article and section, is hereby declared to include moneys, credits, bonds, stocks, dues, franchises, and all other matters and things, real, personal, and mixed, capable of private ownership; provided, that a mortgage, deed of trust, contract, or other obligation by which a debt is secured when land is pledged as security for the payment thereof, together with the money represented by such debt, shall not be considered property subject to taxation; and further provided, that property used for free public libraries and free museums, growing crops, property used exclusively for public schools, and such as may belong to the United States, this state, or to any county or municipal corporation within this state shall be exempt from taxation. The legislature may provide, except in the case of credits secured by mortgage or trust deed, for a deduction from credits of debts due to bona fide residents of this state. (Amendment adopted November 8, 1910.)

[AMENDMENT OF 1894.]

Section 1. All property in the state, not exempt under the laws of the United States shall be taxed in proportion to its value, to be ascertained as provided by law. The word "property," as used in this article and section, is hereby declared to include moneys,

Constitution—33

credits, bonds, stocks, dues, franchises, and all other matters and things, real, personal, and mixed, capable of private ownership; provided that property used for free public libraries and free museums, growing crops, property used exclusively for public schools, and such as may belong to the United States, this state, or to any county or municipal corporation within this state, shall be exempt from taxation. The legislature may provide, except in case of credits secured by mortgage or trust deed, for a deduction from credits of debts due to bona fide residents of this state. (Amendment adopted November 6, 1894.)

[ORIGINAL SECTION.]

Section 1. All property in the state, not exempt under the laws of the United States, shall be taxed in proportion to its value, to be ascertained as provided by law. The word "property," as used in this article and section, is hereby declared to include moneys, credits, bonds, stocks, dues, franchises, and all other matters and things, real, personal, and mixed, capable of private ownership; provided, that growing crops, property used exclusively for public schools, and such as may belong to the United States, this state, or to any county or municipal corporation within this state, shall be exempt from taxation. The legislature may provide, except in the case of credits secured by mortgage or trust deed, for a deduction from credits of debts due to bona fide residents of this state.

TAXATION—What is.—The provisions of this article are limitations upon the power of the legislature, and are mandatory. (People v. McCreery, 34 Cal. 432; People v. Gerke, 35 Cal. 677.)

What constitutes a tax. See note, 8 Am. St. Rep. 506.

Purposes for which taxes may be imposed. See note, 16 Am. St. Rep. 365.

Classification of subjects of taxation as affected by constitutional requirement of uniformity. See note, 1 Ann. Cas. 638.

This section is not self-executing, but merely fixes the liability of property to taxation, and the standard upon which it is based, but confides the duty of prescribing the machinery by which to ascertain the value to the legislature. (McHenry v. Downer, 116 Cal. 20, 45 L. R. A. 737, 47 Pac. 779; De Witt v. Hays, 2 Cal. 463, 56 Am. Dec. 352.)

To make an outlying school district a part of a city high school district to the extent of making it liable for taxes imposed by the municipality of which it was not a part and in the election of whose taxing officers it had no voice, would violate the cardinal rule that there shall be no taxation without representation. (Mooney v. Board of Supervisors, 2 Cal. App. 65, 83 Pac. 165.)

It is a cardinal principle that there shall be no taxation without representation. (Mooney v. Board of Supervisors, 2 Cal. App. 65, 83 Pac. 165.)

The power of the legislature in the matter of taxation is unlimited, except as restricted by constitutional provisions, and extends to proceedings for assessments for local improvements upon any basis of

apportionment which the legislature may select; and the apportionment does not depend upon any special benefit to the taxpayer. (In re Madera Irr. Dist., 92 Cal. 296, 27 Am. St. Rep. 106, 14 L. R. A. 755, 28 Pac. 272, 675.)

The provisions of this article have no application to assessments for local improvements. (Turlock Irr. Dist. v. Williams, 76 Cal. 360, 18 Pac. 379.)

This provision only applies to direct taxation on property as such. (People v. Coleman, 4 Cal. 46, 60 Am. Dec. 581.)

The taxing power is an incident of sovereignty, the exercise of which belongs exclusively to every state, and attaches alike upon everything which comes within its jurisdiction. (People v. Coleman, 4 Cal. 46, 60 Am. Dec. 581.)

A tax is a charge upon persons or property, to raise money for public purposes. It is not founded upon contract and does not establish the relation of debtor and creditor, between the taxpayer and the state. (Perry v. Washburn, 20 Cal. 318.)

The words "taxation" and "taxed" relate to such general taxes upon all property as are levied to defray the ordinary expenses of the state, county, town, and municipal governments, and not to assessments levied on lots fronting on a street to pay the expense of its improvement. (Emery v. San Francisco Gas Co., 28 Cal. 345.)

The words "taxation" and "assessments" do not have the same signification. (Taylor v. Palmer, 31 Cal. 240.)

"Taxation" is the power to impose taxes upon the property of the citizen for the support of the government. (Taylor v. Palmer, 31 Cal. 240; People v. McCreery, 34 Cal. 432.)

The rate of taxation for state purposes must be uniform throughout the state. (People v. McCreery, 34 Cal. 432. People v. Coleman, 4 Cal. 46, 60 Am. Dec. 581; High v. Shoemaker, 22 Cal. 363, overruled.)

A charge by the gauger of the port of San Francisco upon wine, for services as gauger, is not a tax. (Addison v. Saulnier, 19 Cal. 82.)

The provision of the fee bill of 1895, requiring the payment of one dollar for each one thousand dollars in excess of three thousand dollars of the appraised value of an estate imposes a tax, and is in violation of this section in imposing an extraordinary tax in addition to the equal and uniform tax to which alone property is liable. (Fatjo v. Pfister, 117 Cal. 83, 48 Pac. 1012.)

The act of 1893, imposing a tax of five dollars on every hundred dollars of the market value of property collaterally inherited, bequeathed, or devised, where its value exceeds five hundred dollars, is constitutional. (In re Wilmerding, 117 Cal. 281, 49 Pac. 181.)

The collateral inheritance tax is not subject to the provision that all property shall be taxed in proportion to its value, as it is in the nature of an excise tax. (In re Wilmerding, 117 Cal. 281, 49 Pac. 181.)

Where property is sold for taxes to the state and the owner does not redeem, there is no constitutional objection to the state acquiring the title free from all equities, which it can sell and convey to the highest bidder for cash and which will be good as against the former owner. (Chapman v. Zobelein, 19 Cal. App. 132, 124 Pac. 1021.)

Property.—Bonds of foreign corporations are assessable in the state of the owner's domicile. (Estate of Fair, 128 Cal. 607, 61 Pac. 184; Mackay v. San Francisco, 128 Cal. 678, 61 Pac. 382.)

A seat in a stock exchange board is not taxable property. (San Francisco v. Anderson, 103 Cal. 69, 42 Am. St. Rep. 98, 36 Pac. 1034.)

A mere right of way for a pipe-line of a water company, entirely unconnected with any privilege to take tolls, is not a franchise. (Spring Valley W. W. v. Barber, 99 Cal. 36, 21 L. R. A. 416, 33 Pac. 735.)

Fruit trees are not growing crops within the meaning of this section, and are subject to taxation. (Cottle v. Spitzer, 65 Cal. 456, 52 Am. Rep. 305, 4 Pac. 435.)

Stock of a California corporation, whose tangible property is situated in another state, is taxable in this state in the possession of a resident of this state. (City and County of San Francisco v. Flood, 64 Cal. 504, 2 Pac. 264; San Francisco v. Fry, 63 Cal. 470.)

Stock in a corporation whose property is situated out of the state is assessable in this state. The Constitution is not to be construed to mean that "stocks" are not to be taxed when they represent property situated out of the state. (Canfield v. County of Los Angeles, 157 Cal. 617, 108 Pac. 705.)

The assessment of the stock of a corporation must necessarily include every element of value of its property, including its goodwill, franchise, and dividend earning power. (Crocker v. Scott, 149 Cal. 575, 87 Pac. 102.)

The possessory right to a mining claim is properly assessed as real estate. (Bakersfield & Fresno Oil Co. v. Kern County, 144 Cal. 148, 77 Pac. 892.)

A vessel registered out of the state, and never here except transiently in the course of her voyages for the purpose of receiving and discharging cargo, is not "in the state" within the meaning of this section, although owned in part by residents of this state. (San Francisco v. Talbot, 63 Cal. 485.)

A vessel is taxable at its "home port" as defined in section 4141 of the United States Revised Statutes. (Olson v. San Francisco, 148 Cal. 80, 113 Am. St. Rep. 191, 7 Ann. Cas. 443, 2 L. R. A. (N. S.) 197, 82 Pac. 850.)

A franchise to collect rates for water is taxable under this section. (Spring Valley W. W. v. Schottler, 62 Cal. 69.)

The franchise of a railroad company is property subject to taxation and is not exempt by reason of its being a means or instrument employed by Congress to carry into operation the powers of the general government. (Central Pac. R. R. Co. v. State Board of Equalization, 60 Cal. 35.)

A franchise merely to be a corporation is property, which is assessable to the corporation. (Bank of California v. San Francisco, 142 Cal. 276, 100 Am. St. Rep. 130, 64 L. R. A. 918, 75 Pac. 832.)

As to the proper method of arriving at the value of a franchise to be a corporation for the purpose of taxation, see Bank of California v. San Francisco, 142 Cal. 276, 100 Am. St. Rep. 130, 64 L. R. A. 918, 75 Pac. 832.

The creative franchise to be a corporation is taxable. (San Joaquin etc. Irr. Co. v. Merced County, 2 Cal. App. 593, 84 Pac. 285.)

Franchises are properly subject to taxation. (San Joaquin etc. Irr. Co. v. Merced County, 2 Cal. App. 593, 84 Pac. 285.)

Taxation of franchises. See note, 131 Am. St. Rep. 867.

Checks drawn upon the treasurer of the United States, payable on demand, as a mode of paying an obligation of the United States, are taxable as solvent credits. (Hibernia etc. Soc. v. San Francisco, 139 Cal. 205, 96 Am. St. Rep. 100, 5 L. R. A. (N. S.) 608, 72 Pac. 920.)

The franchise of a foreign banking corporation to do business in the state of California is taxable. (London & San Francisco Bank v. Block, 117 Fed. 900.)

Where a foreign banking corporation with branches in other states has credits on the books of its office in California, consisting of sums paid to the other branches for their benefit, and charged to them as mere matter of bookkeeping, without any promise or obligation on the part of the debited agencies to return the money to the California office, such credits are not taxable in California. (London & San Francisco Bank v. Block, 136 Fed. 138, 69 C. C. A. 136.)

State taxation of national banks. See note, 69 Am. St. Rep. 38.

The capital or capital stock of a corporation is taxable against the corporation. (San Francisco v. Spring Valley W. W., 54 Cal. 571.)

Personal property in the state, owned by nonresidents, and upon which they pay taxes in the state of their domicile, is taxable in this state. (Minturn v. Hays, 2 Cal. 590, 56 Am. Dec. 366.)

A municipal corporation has no power to impose a license tax upon a railroad company engaged in interstate commerce, and the mere fact that the tax is imposed on a branch line does not render the tax valid, where the branch is a part of the transcontinental line. (San Bernardino v. Southern Pac. Co., 107 Cal. 524, 29 L. R. A. 327, 40 Pac. 796.)

The possession of and claim to public land is property. (People v. Black Diamond etc. Min. Co., 37 Cal. 54; People v. Cohen, 31 Cal. 210.)

The word "property" is used in its ordinary and popular sense, and includes not only visible and tangible property, but also choses in action, such as solvent debts secured by mortgage. (People v. Eddy, 43 Cal. 331, 13 Am. Rep. 143; Lick v. Austin, 43 Cal. 590; Savings etc. Soc. v. Austin, 46 Cal. 415; People v. Ashbury, 46 Cal. 523; San Francisco v. La Societe etc., 131 Cal. 612, 63 Pac. 1016. But see Bank of Mendocino v. Chalfant, 51 Cal. 369, 471; People v. Hibernia Bank, 51 Cal. 243, 21 Am. Rep. 704.)

This is true although the debts are secured by pledge of property exempt from taxation. (Security Sav. Bank v. San Francisco, 132 Cal. 599, 64 Pac. 898.)

Money is property subject to taxation. (People v. Dunn, 59 Cal. 328.)

The holder of solvent credits secured by collateral security of personal property is entitled to have his assessment upon such credits reduced by the amount of his indebtedness to bona fide residents of the state, contracts of security on personal property not being mort-

gages or deeds of trust within the meaning of those words in the clause excepting such credits from the deduction allowed of debts due bona fide residents of the state. (Bank of Willows v. County of Glenn, 155 Cal. 352, 101 Pac. 13.)

Bonds owned by a foreign insurance company doing business in this state and deposited with a banker in pursuance to law are taxable. (People v. Home Ins. Co., 29 Cal. 533.)

The estate of a lessee in lands overlying oil bearing strata, who has the right to the oil produced thereon upon paying a royalty to the lessor, may be separately assessed for purposes of taxation to the lessee, and the remainder of the entire estate in the land may be separately assessed to the lessor. (Graciosa Oil Co. v. Santa Barbara County, 155 Cal. 140, 20 L. R. A. (N. S.) 211, 99 Pac. 483.)

Public property.—Public property is not taxable. (People v. Austin, 47 Cal. 353; People v. McCreery, 34 Cal. 432; People v. Doe G. 1,034, 36 Cal. 220.)

A railroad corporation cannot claim an exemption of its property lying within the state from state taxation, because the corporation has been subsequently employed by the federal government in the carriage of mails, munitions of war, etc. (People v. Central Pac. R. R. Co., 43 Cal. 398.)

A railroad company organized under the laws of this state to construct and operate a railroad in this state, which has subsequently received from the United States a franchise for the same purpose, may be assessed upon its franchise derived from the state. (People v. Central Pac. R. R. Co., 105 Cal. 576, 38 Pac. 905; affirmed, Central Pac. R. R. Co. v. People, 162 U. S. 91, 40 L. Ed. 903, 16 Sup. Ct. Rep. 766; Colusa County v. Glenn County, 124 Cal. 498, 57 Pac. 477. But see People v. Central Pac. R. R. Co., 83 Cal. 393, 23 Pac. 303.)

An act exempting school land and lands of the United States from taxation does not render the tax unequal. (High v. Shoemaker, 22 Cal. 363.)

A mortgage of land, executed to the Regents of the University of California, to secure money due said body, and the interest which it thereby holds in the land, is the property of the state within the meaning of this provision. (Webster v. Board of Regents, 163 Cal. 705, 126 Pac. 974.)

Bonds of the United States are not subject to taxation. (People v. Home Ins. Co., 29 Cal. 533.)

State taxation of federal bonds and obligations. See notes, 4 Ann. Cas. 936.

The property of a reclamation district is public property exempt from taxation. (Reclamation Dist. No. 551 v. Sacramento County, 134 Cal. 477, 66 Pac. 668.)

The assessment of a portion of a street is void. (Warren v. San Francisco, 150 Cal. 167, 88 Pac. 712.)

A county ordinance imposing a license upon the Southern Pacific Railroad Company for carrying persons and freight for hire by means of railroad cars in the county, is void as a tax upon the use of the franchise granted by the United States government. Both the franchise and the use of it are beyond the taxing power of the state. (San Benito Co. v. Southern Pac. R. R. Co., 77 Cal. 518, 19 Pac. 827.)

The Western Union Telegraph Company is one of the instruments employed by the United States government for carrying into effect its sovereign powers, and a tax upon its franchise is void. (City and County of San Francisco v. Western Union Tel. Co., 96 Cal. 140, 17 L. R. A. 301, 31 Pac. 10; Western Union Tel. Co. v. Visalia, 149 Cal. 744, 87 Pac. 1023.)

Whether or not a federal franchise has been assessed is a question of fact, and conversations with members of the board of equalization on the subject are not admissible. (People v. Central Pac. R. R. Co., 105 Cal. 576, 38 Pac. 905; affirmed, Central Pac. R. R. Co. v. People, 162 U. S. 91, 40 L. Ed. 903, 16 Sup. Ct. Rep. 766.)

> Liability to state taxation of United States property granted or sold by the government but to which government still holds legal title. See note, 11 Ann. Cas. 391.

> Right of state to tax federal franchise. See note, 17 Ann. Cas. 722.

National banks are agencies of the federal government, and are not subject to the taxing power of the state. (McHenry v. Downer, 116 Cal. 20, 45 L. R. A. 737, 47 Pac. 779.)

Taxation of property of a national bank, except as permitted by the United States Revised Statutes, is void. (First Nat. Bank v. San Francisco, 129 Cal. 96, 61 Pac. 778; Miller v. Heilbron, 58 Cal. 133.)

The act for the assessment of the stock of national banks is valid. (Crocker v. Scott, 149 Cal. 575, 87 Pac. 102.)

> State taxation of national banks. See note, 69 Am. St. Rep. 38.

Commerce.—A tax upon every person selling consigned goods from any state in proportion to the amount sold is not an interference with the power of Congress to regulate commerce. (People v. Coleman, 4 Cal. 46, 60 Am. Dec. 581.)

An act imposing a tax upon bills of lading for the transportation of gold or silver from any point in this state to any point without the state is in conflict with the provision of the United States Constitution forbidding the states to levy any imposts or duties on imports or exports. (Brumagin v. Tillinghast, 18 Cal. 265, 79 Am. Dec. 176.)

An act requiring the payment of a gauger for inspecting goods arriving at ports of this state is not in violation of the United States Constitution forbidding the state to impose duties on imports. (Addison v. Saulnier, 19 Cal. 82.)

An act requiring a shipper to place certain stamps on all tickets sold to persons about to leave the state is in violation of the commerce clause of the United States Constitution, and is void. It is a tax and not a police regulation. (People v. Raymond, 34 Cal. 492.)

Exemptions.—The legislature has no power to exempt any property from taxation. (Mackay v. San Francisco, 113 Cal. 392, 45 Pac. 696; Minturn v. Hays, 2 Cal. 590, 56 Am. Dec. 366; People v. Mc-Creery, 34 Cal. 432; People v. Black Diamond etc. Min. Co., 37 Cal.

54; Crosby v. Lyon, 37 Cal. 242; People v. Eddy, 43 Cal. 331, 13 Am. Rep. 143; People v. Latham, 52 Cal. 598.)

An act authorizing the remission of a tax is void. (Wilson v. Supervisors of Sutter Co., 47 Cal. 91.)

An act taxing the property of a district for a local improvement, which exempts personal property from its operation, is unconstitutional, because not levied on all the property in the district. (People v. Whyler, 41 Cal. 351.)

Alfalfa is not included in the exemption of "growing crops." (Miller v. County of Kern, 137 Cal. 516, 70 Pac. 549.)

The provisions of the Political Code in regard to road taxes are not in violation of this section because cities and towns are exempted from their operation, since this does not exempt cities and towns from the tax, but compels cities and towns to maintain their own streets under the street improvement act. (Miller v. County of Kern, 137 Cal. 516, 70 Pac. 549.)

The crediting of taxes heretofore paid upon property under an invalid levy does not amount to an exemption from taxation of the property upon which such taxes were paid. (People v. Latham, 52 Cal. 598.)

The legislature cannot exempt from taxation a vessel having its legal situs in this state. (Olson v. San Francisco, 148 Cal. 80, 113 Am. St. Rep. 191, 7 Ann. Cas. 443, 2 L. R. A. (N. S.) 197, 82 Pac. 850.)

Under this section equal assessment of all property is necessary. (People v. Latimer, 160 Cal. 716, 117 Pac. 1051, Lorigan's dissenting opinion.)

Double taxation.—The Constitution forbids the double taxation of property. (People v. Badlam, 57 Cal. 594; Germania Trust Co. v. San Francisco, 128 Cal. 589, 61 Pac. 178; Estate of Fair, 128 Cal. 607, 61 Pac. 184.)

Double taxation does not necessarily consist in assessing the same property twice to the same person, but may consist in requiring a double contribution to the same tax on account of the same property, though the assessments are to different persons. (Germania Trust Co. v. San Francisco, 128 Cal. 589, 61 Pac. 178; Estate of Fair, 128 Cal. 607, 61 Pac. 184.)

The inhibition of double taxation only applies to such taxation by the same government. (San Francisco v. Fry, 63 Cal. 470.)

Because the same subject matter has been twice taxed, it by no means follows that both taxes are void, but to entitle a party to relief in the courts, it must appear that the tax has been once paid or tendered. (Savings etc. Soc. v. Austin, 46 Cal. 415.)

If land subject to a mortgage is taxed, and the debt secured by the mortgage is also taxed, and the tax on the debt is paid by the mortgagee, the mortgagor cannot complain of double taxation. (Lick v. Austin, 43 Cal. 590.)

The levying a tax upon money at interest, as well as upon the property mortgaged to secure it, does not present a case of double taxation against the mortgagee. (People v. Whartenby, 38 Cal. 461.)

It would be assessing the same property twice to assess money on deposit in a savings bank to the bank and also to the depositor. (People v. Badlam, 57 Cal. 594.)

It would be assessing the same property twice to assess to a corporation all of its corporate property, and also to assess to each of the stockholders the shares held by them. (People v. Badlam, 57 Cal. 594.)

A balance of a money account on general deposit in a bank outside of the state, held by a corporation having its principal place of business in this state, is taxable in this state as a solvent credit. (Pacific Coast Sav. Soc. v. San Francisco, 133 Cal. 14, 65 Pac. 16.)

It is not double taxation to tax the roadbed and roadway of a railroad, as they are quite different. (San Francisco etc. R. R. Co. v. State Board of Equalization, 60 Cal. 12.)

Where all the property of a corporation has been assessed and it owns none of its capital stock, an assessment of "capital" or "capital stock" is void. (San Francisco v. Spring Valley W. W., 63 Cal. 524.)

An attempt to tax a seat in a stock exchange board, in addition to the taxes levied upon all the property of the board, is void as an attempt at double taxation. (San Francisco v. Anderson, 103 Cal. 69, 42 Am. St. Rep. 98, 36 Pac. 1034.)

Since a mortgage is assessed as an interest in the land, to also assess the bonds which the mortgage secures is double taxation. (Germania Trust Co. v. San Francisco, 128 Cal. 589, 61 Pac. 178; Estate of Fair, 128 Cal. 607, 61 Pac. 184.)

The lender of money is not subjected to double taxation by reason of the payment of taxes on money loaned by him, and on solvent debts due him over his own indebtedness. (People v. McCreery, 34 Cal. 432.)

The legislature may impose a penalty on those who neglect to have their property assessed at the proper time; and a law providing for the double taxation of property which has escaped assessment in the previous year is valid. (Biddle v. Oaks, 59 Cal. 94.)

Double taxation of franchises. See note, 131 Am. St. Rep. 874.

Taxation of shares of stock and capital stock or property of corporation as constituting double taxation. See notes, 7 Ann. Cas. 1195; 13 Ann. Cas. 636.

Assessment.—Assessment of property is a function of the executive department of the government; and the judiciary has no power to inquire as to the actual value of property for the purpose of taxation, in order to determine whether there has been misrepresentations as to its value. (Clunie v. Siebe, 112 Cal. 593, 44 Pac. 1064.)

The provisions of this section are self-executing, and require the assessor to ascertain the value of the property in the manner now provided by law. (Hyatt v. Allen, 54 Cal. 353.)

The provision of the former Constitution as to the election of assessor and tax collector was held mandatory, and restrained the legislature to a particular mode of providing for such officers. (People v. Kelsey, 34 Cal. 470.)

Under the former Constitution an assessment not made by an assessor elected by the electors of the district was void. (Williams v. Corcoran, 46 Cal. 553.)

This section does not require the value of the property to be found after the rate of taxation is fixed. (People v. Latham, 52 Cal. 598.)

A tax for school purposes must be based upon an assessment made by an assessor elected by the qualified electors of the school district. (People v. Stockton etc. Co., 49 Cal. 414.)

The legislature cannot confer on a state board of equalization of taxes the power to add to or deduct from the assessed value of the property, as fixed by the assessor. (Houghton v. Austin, 47 Cal. 646.)

The payment of a tax cannot be resisted on the ground that the property on which it was levied was not assessed at its true value. One whose property is not assessed according to its true value must apply to the board of equalization for relief. (People v. Whyler, 41 Cal. 351.)

The only mode in which defective assessments may be cured by the legislature is to empower the assessor to correct the same. (People v. Hastings, 34 Cal. 571.)

The failure of the assessor to assess certain property, whether by reason of a void statute or by mistake, does not invalidate the assessment. (People v. McCreery, 34 Cal. 432.)

The value of a franchise of a corporation is properly fixed by taking the value of all tangible property of the corporation from the market value of the capital stock. (Spring Valley W. W. v. Schottler, 62 Cal. 69.)

A law providing that taxes upon personal property unsecured by real estate shall be collected at the time of the assessment is valid, although other taxes are not payable until several months later. (Rode v. Siebe, 119 Cal. 518, 39 L. R. A. 342, 51 Pac. 869, Van Fleet, J., and Harrison, J., dissenting; Pacific Postal Tel. etc. Co. v. Dalton, 119 Cal. 604, 51 Pac. 1072.)

Purposes.—The extent to which the power of taxation may be exercised is left unlimited, except by legislative discretion. (Stockton etc. R. R. Co. v. Common Council of Stockton, 41 Cal. 147; Blanding v. Burr, 13 Cal. 343.)

The taxing power, whether it be asserted in the form of general taxation or of local assessment, cannot be upheld when the purpose in view can be judicially seen to be other than public. (In re Market Street, 49 Cal. 546.)

The legislature may recognize a moral obligation as the sole basis for the imposition of taxes. (Beals v. Board of Suprs. of Amador County, 35 Cal. 624.)

Taxation cannot be justified for an object or for the benefit of a class in which the taxpayer is directly excluded from participating. (Hughes v. Ewing, 93 Cal. 414, 28 Pac. 1067.)

Licenses.—A license fee or charge for the transaction of any business is not a tax within the meaning of this section. (Santa Barbara v. Stearns, 51 Cal. 499.)

A license tax upon the right to carry on a particular trade or business, imposing the same rate or amount on all engaged in the same

business regardless of the amount of capital employed or profits earned, is a valid exercise of the taxing power, and is not a tax upon property within the meaning of this section. (Los Angeles v. Los Angeles etc. Gas Co., 152 Cal. 765, 93 Pac. 1006.)

The Constitution does not prohibit the legislature from authorizing municipal corporations to tax occupations for purpose of revenue. An ordinance requiring the annual license of twenty dollars for each street-car operated upheld, although the cars also ran in an adjoining town. (San Jose v. San Jose etc. R. R. Co., 53 Cal. 475; People v. Coleman, 4 Cal. 46, 60 Am. Dec. 581; Sacramento v. Crocker, 16 Cal. 119; Ex parte Hurl, 49 Cal. 557, approved.)

A municipality has no inherent power, by virtue of its existence as a municipality, to impose a license upon a business, but its power in this respect comes from the legislature, and must be found in the organic act, or necessarily inferred from the powers therein expressly granted. (Ex parte Newton, 53 Cal. 571.)

An act prohibiting foreigners from working the gold mines, except on condition of paying a certain sum each month for the privilege, imposes a license and not a tax and is valid. (People v. Naglee, 1 Cal. 232, 52 Am. Dec. 312.)

This provision applies only to direct taxation upon property, and does not prohibit the legislature from enacting license laws. (People v. Naglee, 1 Cal. 232, 52 Am. Dec. 312.)

Purposes for which taxes may be imposed. See note, 16 Am. St. Rep. 365.

Assessments.—The word "assessment" represents those local burdens imposed by municipal corporations upon property bordering upon an improved street, for the purpose of paying the cost of the improvement, and laid with reference to the benefit the property is supposed to receive from the expenditure of the money. (Taylor v. Palmer, 31 Cal. 240.)

An assessment is a special and local charge upon property in the immediate vicinity of municipal improvements, predicated upon the theory of benefits, and levied upon land or property specially benefited by such improvements, while a charge imposed by law upon the assessed value of all property in a district is a tax, although for a local improvement. (Holley v. Orange County, 106 Cal. 420, 39 Pac. 790.)

An assessment upon lots adjacent to a street to pay for improvements made on the street, if held to be a tax, cannot be upheld, because it lacks the constitutional requirement of equality and uniformity. (Creighton v. Monson, 27 Cal. 613. But see Walsh v. Mathews, 29 Cal. 123.)

An assessment by an irrigation district upon the public lands of a city, which are unoccupied and uncultivated lands, susceptible of cultivation by irrigation, and which would be benefited thereby, is not a tax within the meaning of this section. (San Diego v. Linda Vista Irr. Dist., 108 Cal. 189, 35 L. R. A. 33, 41 Pac. 291.)

An assessment levied by an irrigation district, although referable to the power of taxation, is distinct from a tax, and is not subject to the constitutional provisions respecting taxation, and may be

levied upon all real property, without deducting therefrom any mortgages thereon. (Tregea v. Owens, 94 Cal. 317, 29 Pac. 643.)

An assessment for a street improvement upon the front-foot system is an exercise of the power of taxation. (Emery v. San Francisco etc. Co., 28 Cal. 345.)

This section does not apply to an assessment for a street improvement. (Burnett v. Mayor etc. Sacramento, 12 Cal. 76, 73 Am. Dec. 518; People v. Austin, 47 Cal. 353; Hagar v. Board of Supervisors, 47 Cal. 222; Chambers v. Satterlee, 40 Cal. 497.)

A charge imposed on all property of a district, to be used in constructing levees to protect the district from overflow, is a tax and not an assessment. (People v. Whyler, 41 Cal. 351; Williams v. Corcoran, 46 Cal. 553; Smith v. Farrelly, 52 Cal. 77.)

An "assessment" for a local improvement is a "tax," and, while it need not be assessed on the ad valorem principle, it must be equal and uniform. (People v. Lynch, 51 Cal. 15, 21 Am. Rep. 677.)

The fact that a statute designates as a "tax" that which in its elements is an "assessment" does not make it a "tax." (People v. Austin, 47 Cal. 353.)

The legislature cannot levy an assessment not uniform and equal, nor can it validate an assessment void for want of uniformity and equality. (People v. Lynch, 51 Cal. 15, 21 Am. Rep. 677.)

An assessment cannot be laid upon lots for street work done under an abortive contract with the municipality. (In re Market Street, 49 Cal. 546.)

The "front-foot" method of assessment is valid. (Oakland etc. Co. v. Rier, 52 Cal. 270; People v. Lynch, 51 Cal. 15, 21 Am. Rep. 677; Walsh v. Mathews, 29 Cal. 123; Hadley v. Dague, 130 Cal. 207, 62 Pac. 500; Cohen v. Alameda, 124 Cal. 504, 57 Pac. 377; Chambers v. Satterlee, 40 Cal. 497; Emery v. San Francisco etc. Co., 28 Cal. 345; Emery v. Bradford, 29 Cal. 75; Taylor v. Palmer, 31 Cal. 240; Whiting v. Quackenbush, 54 Cal. 306; Whiting v. Townsend, 57 Cal. 515; Lent v. Tillson, 72 Cal. 404, 14 Pac. 71; Jennings v. Le Breton, 80 Cal. 8, 21 Pac. 1127; San Francisco Pav. Co. v. Bates, 134 Cal. 39, 66 Pac. 2; Banaz v. Smith, 133 Cal. 102, 65 Pac. 309.)

An act levying the cost of a street improvement upon the adjacent property, in accordance with the assessed value of the land, is valid. (Burnett v. Mayor etc. Sacramento, 12 Cal. 76, 73 Am. Dec. 518.)

The legislature may provide for a local public improvement for the benefit of a portion of the state, and may tax all land within a limited district, notwithstanding some of the property of the district will not receive any benefit, and some property outside of the district may be incidentally benefited. (In re Madera Irr. Dist., 92 Cal. 296, 27 Am. St. Rep. 106, 14 L. R. A. 755, 28 Pac. 272, 675.)

An assessment upon specified property can be supported only upon the ground that the property taxed is benefited by the improvement. (In re Market Street, 49 Cal. 546.)

The fact that levees built to protect the land of a district from overflow injure some of the land instead of benefiting it does not render the tax unequal or void for want of uniformity. (People v. Whyler, 41 Cal. 351.)

A tax levied on the property of a given district, to pay for a local improvement, which is assessed upon the parcels of property in the district in proportion to the benefit each parcel derives from the work, is unconstitutional. Such tax must be levied on all property according to its value. (People v. Whyler, 41 Cal. 351.)

An owner may be made personally liable for the expense of a street improvement. (Walsh v. Mathews, 29 Cal. 123. Creighton v. Manson, 27 Cal. 613, overruled.)

An act requiring the owner of a lot to keep the street in front of it in repair after it has been planked and graded is valid. (Hart v. Gaven, 12 Cal. 476.)

The fact that a town is included within an irrigation district does not invalidate the district, since even though the land is not susceptible of irrigation, it may be benefited by the improvement. (In re Madera Irr. Dist., 92 Cal. 296, 27 Am. St. Rep. 106, 14 L. R. A. 755, 28 Pac. 272, 675.)

Recovery of taxes.—An action to recover municipal taxes is an action upon a liability created by statute, and is barred in three years; and where it has the force of a judgment, it is barred in five years. (San Diego v. Higgins, 115 Cal. 170, 46 Pac. 923.)

Recovery of taxes paid. See note, 94 Am. St. Rep. 425.

Colleges exempt from taxation.

Sec. 1a. Any educational institution of collegiate grade, within the state of California, not conducted for profit, shall hold exempt from taxation its buildings and equipment, its grounds within which its buildings are located, not exceeding one hundred acres in area, its securities and income used exclusively for the purposes of education. (New section added by amendment adopted November 3, 1914.)

United States army, navy, marine and revenue service.

Sec. 1¼. The property to the amount of one thousand dollars of every resident in this state who has served in the army, navy, marine corps, or revenue marine service of the United States in time of war, and received an honorable discharge therefrom; or lacking such amount of property in his own name, so much of the property of the wife of any such person as shall be necessary to equal said amount; and property to the amount of one thousand dollars of the widow resident in this state, or if there be no such widow, of the widowed mother resident in this state, of every person who has so served and has died either during his term

of service or after receiving honorable discharge from said service; and the property to the amount of one thousand dollars of pensioned widows, fathers, and mothers, resident in this state, of soldiers, sailors, and marines who served in the army, navy, or marine corps, or revenue marine service of the United States, shall be exempt from taxation; provided, that this exemption shall not apply to any person named herein owning property of the value of five thousand dollars or more, or where the wife of such soldier or sailor owns property of the value of five thousand dollars or more. No exemption shall be made under the provisions of this act of the property of a person who is not a legal resident of the state. (Amendment approved October 10, 1911.)

Churches exempt from taxation.

Sec. 1½. All buildings, and so much of the real property on which they are situated as may be required for the convenient use and occupation of said buildings, when the same are used solely and exclusively for religious worship, shall be free from taxation; provided, that no building so used which may be rented for religious purposes and rent received by the owner therefor, shall be exempt from taxation. (Amendment adopted November 6, 1900.)

> What is included in exemption of religious institution from taxation. See note, Ann. Cas. 1912A, 354.
>
> Exemption from taxation of parsonage or residence of minister, priest, etc. See note, 11 Ann. Cas. 1102.

Bonds of state and municipalities exempt from taxation.

Sec. 1¾. All bonds hereafter issued by the state of California, or by any county, city and county, municipal corporation, or district (including school, reclamation, and irrigation districts) within said state, shall be free and exempt from taxation. (Amendment adopted November 4, 1902.)

Land and improvements to be separately assessed.

Sec. 2. Land, and the improvements thereon, shall be separately assessed. Cultivated and uncultivated land, of

the same quality, and similarly situated, shall be assessed at the same value.

ASSESSMENT OF LAND.—An assessment of land claimed and occupied by a railroad company as a right of way, together with the track and all superstructures and substructures, without any separate assessment of land and improvement, is void. (California etc. R. R. Co. v. Mecartney, 104 Cal. 616, 38 Pac. 448.)

The Constitution leaves it to the legislature to define "improvements," and alfalfa, not being included in the legislative definition, must be taxed as realty and not as improvements. (Miller v. County of Kern, 137 Cal. 516, 70 Pac. 549.)

This section requires that fences erected upon the roadway or roadbed of a railroad, even if owned by the railroad company, be separately assessed as improvements. (Santa Clara County v. Southern Pacific R. R. Co., 118 U. S. 394, 30 L. Ed. 118, 6 Sup. Ct. Rep. 1132.)

Sectionized and unsectionized land, how assessed.

Sec. 3. Every tract of land containing more than six hundred and forty acres, and which has been sectionized by the United States government, shall be assessed, for the purposes of taxation, by sections or fractions of sections. The legislature shall provide by law for the assessment, in small tracts, of all lands not sectionized by the United States government.

Securities, taxable. (Repealed.)

Sec. 4. This section was repealed by amendment adopted November 8, 1910. The section so repealed was as follows:

Sec. 4. A mortgage, deed of trust, contract, or other obligation by which a debt is secured, shall, for the purposes of assessment and taxation, be deemed and treated as an interest in the property affected thereby. Except as to railroad and other quasi public corporations, in case of debts so secured, the value of the property affected by such mortgage, deed of trust, contract, or obligation, less the value of such security, shall be assessed and taxed to the owner of the property, and the value of such security shall be assessed and taxed to the owner thereof, in the county, city, or district in which the property affected thereby is situate. The taxes so levied shall be a lien upon the property and security, and may be paid by either party to such security; if paid by the owner of the security, the tax so levied upon the property affected thereby shall become a part of the debt so secured; if the owner of the property shall pay the tax so levied on such security, it shall constitute a payment thereon, and to the extent of such payment a

full discharge thereof; provided, that if any such security or in-. debtedness shall be paid by any such debtor or debtors, after assessment and before the tax levy, the amount of such levy may likewise be retained by such debtor or debtors, and shall be computed according to the tax levy for the preceding year.

ASSESSMENT OF MORTGAGES.—A mortgage as such is not liable to be assessed, but the assessment should be made of the debt which the mortgage was given to secure. (People v. Eastman, 25 Cal. 601.)

The provisions of this section apply to mortgages executed prior to the adoption of the Constitution. (McCoppin v. McCartney, 60 Cal. 367.)

This section has exclusive reference to mortgages, deeds of trust, contracts, or other obligations affecting realty. (Bank of Willows v. County of Glenn, 155 Cal. 352, 101 Pac. 13.)

When no tax is assessed against the interest of the mortgagee, but the whole tax is assessed against the property and paid by the owner, it cannot be deducted from the mortgage debt. (John Brickell Co. v. Sutro, 11 Cal. App. 460, 105 Pac. 948, 949.)

Where a mortgage executed prior to the new Constitution made no provision as to who should pay the taxes, the mortgagee is made primarily liable for them by this section. (Hay v. Hill, 65 Cal. 383, 4 Pac. 378.)

An assessment levied by an irrigation district may be levied upon all lands, without deducting therefrom any mortgages thereon. (Tregea v. Owens, 94 Cal. 317, 29 Pac. 643.)

This section is to be construed as having reference only to taxation in case of liens upon land, and does not apply to personal property. (Bank of Woodland v. Pierce, 144 Cal. 434, 77 Pac. 1012.)

Solvent credits may be taxed by a city to the owner domiciled therein, though secured by a lien upon wheat situated and taxed elsewhere. (Bank of Woodland v. Pierce, 144 Cal. 434, 77 Pac. 1012.)

Whether the loan secured by the stocks and bonds is or is not an interest in the "property affected thereby" for the purpose of taxation within the meaning of this section, and conceding that the stocks and bonds may be exempt from taxation, the debt secured thereby for money loaned is not exempt, but may be taxed to the lender. (Savings etc. Soc. v. San Francisco, 131 Cal. 356, 63 Pac. 665.)

A mortgage is not "real estate," except for the purpose of taxation. The mortgagor is still the owner of the land, and it is subject to liens for taxes on personal property owned by the mortgagor. (California Loan etc. Co. v. Weis, 118 Cal. 489, 50 Pac. 697.)

An assessment of a "mortgage upon the following described property, to wit" (describing the mortgaged premises), is an assessment of the land and not merely the mortgage. (Doland v. Mooney, 72 Cal. 34, 13 Pac. 71.)

Bonds of a railroad company secured by mortgages of its property within the state are not assessable to the holder of the bonds. (Germania Trust Co. v. San Francisco, 128 Cal. 589, 61 Pac. 178; Estate of Fair, 128 Cal. 607, 61 Pac. 184.)

Receipts for taxes on mortgaged lands found in the possession of the deceased mortgagee raise a presumption that the taxes were paid by him, though they are in the name of the mortgagor. (Lloyd v. Davis, 123 Cal. 348, 55 Pac. 1003.)

The last clause of this section does not give the mortgagor an exclusive remedy, but, if he fails to retain the money, he may recover it from the mortgagee. (San Gabriel Valley etc. Co. v. Witmer Bros. Co., 96 Cal. 623, 18 L. R. A. 465, 29 Pac. 500, 31 Pac. 588.)

Where the mortgagor pays the interest on the mortgage he cannot recover it back on the ground that the mortgage provides that the mortgagor shall pay the interest on the mortgage. (Matthews v. Ormerd, 140 Cal. 578, 74 Pac. 136.)

A first mortgagee, having foreclosed his mortgage against a second mortgagee, cannot maintain an action against the latter to recover money paid by him to redeem the property from taxes assessed upon the second mortgage. (Canadian etc. Trust Co. v. Boas, 136 Cal. 419, 69 Pac. 18.)

The purchaser under a first mortgage is not a party to the security of the second mortgage within the meaning of this section, and cannot recover a tax paid by him on the second mortgage. (Henry v. Garden City Bank etc. Co., 145 Cal. 54, 78 Pac. 228.)

The property of railroad and other quasi-public corporations is subject to taxation, without deduction of any mortgage or other like lien thereon. (Central Pac. R. R. Co. v. State Board of Equalization, 60 Cal. 35.)

The provision of this section taxing property of quasi-public corporations, without deduction of liens thereon, is not in conflict with the provision of the United States Constitution that no state shall "deny any person within its jurisdiction the equal protection of the laws," since that provision does not apply to artificial persons. (Central Pac. R. R. Co. v. State Board of Equalization, 60 Cal. 35.)

This provision must be understood as referring wholly to the taxation of private property and to mortgages made to private persons and not to those belonging to the state. (Webster v. Board of Regents, 163 Cal. 705, 126 Pac. 974.)

Vessels exempt from taxation.

Sec. 4a. All vessels of more than fifty tons burden registered at any port in this state and engaged in the transportation of freight or passengers, shall be exempt from taxation except for state purposes, until and including the first day of January, nineteen hundred thirty-five. (New section added by amendment adopted November 3, 1914.)

Contract of borrower to pay tax on loan void.

Sec. 5. This section was repealed by amendment adopted November 6, 1906. The section repealed read as follows:

Constitution—84

Sec. 5. Every contract hereafter made, by which a debtor is obligated to pay any tax or assessment on money loaned, or on any mortgage, deed of trust, or other lien, shall, as to any interest specified therein, and as to such tax or assessment, be null and void.

PAYMENT OF TAXES ON MORTGAGES.—This section, only applies to contracts made after its adoption. (Beckman v. Skaggs, 59 Cal. 541.)

A provision in a mortgage that the mortgagee "may pay all taxes, etc., upon the property, and the same shall be repaid with interest thereon at the rate of one per cent per month," does not violate this section. (Bank of Ukiah v. Reed, 131 Cal. 597, 63 Pac. 921.)

A contemporaneous agreement between the mortgagor and mortgagee that if the mortgagor should present proper official receipts showing the payment of the mortgage tax, he should receive credit of two and one-half per cent upon the mortgage note, is not in violation of this section, as it is not enforceable against the mortgagor, but simply permissive. (Hewitt v. Dean, 91 Cal. 5, 27 Pac. 423.)

But where a mortgage provides for interest of one per cent per month, but the mortgagee, by a separate instrument agrees that he will only exact interest amounting to eight per cent per annum and agrees to refund all interest paid over and above this amount after he has paid out of said one per cent per month the mortgage tax, the two instruments must be construed together, and, so construed, they constitute an agreement for eight per cent per annum interest, with the mortgagors paying the tax, and under this section such a contract is void. (Matthews v. Ormerd, 134 Cal. 84, 66 Pac. 67, 210.)

A provision in a mortgage that, in case of foreclosure, the mortgagee may include all payments made by him for the taxes on the mortgage, is void, and renders void the mortgage as to the payment of interest; but if the mortgagor pays the interest he cannot recover it back. (Harralson v. Barrett, 99 Cal. 607, 34 Pac. 342; Garms v. Jensen, 103 Cal. 374, 37 Pac. 337.)

Evidence of a parol agreement between the parties to the mortgage, whereby the mortgagor undertook to pay the taxes which might be assessed and levied upon the mortgage, is inadmissible. (Daw v. Niles, 104 Cal. 106, 37 Pac. 876; Harrelson v. Tomich, 107 Cal. 627, 40 Pac. 1032; California State Bank v. Webber, 110 Cal. 538, 42 Pac. 1066.)

Where a conventional rate of interest is agreed upon, a verbal agreement that if the mortgagor should pay the taxes on the mortgage, a reduction should be allowed upon the agreed interest, is not in violation of this provision. (California State Bank v. Webber, 110 Cal. 538, 42 Pac. 1066.)

A contemporaneous agreement by the mortgagor to pay the tax on the mortgage is void. (Burbridge v. Lemmert, 99 Cal. 493, 32 Pac. 310.)

The provision of this section for a forfeiture of interest has no application to a contract by a purchaser to pay taxes on the land; nor does it refer to a possible equitable lien of the purchaser for purchase

money paid, which could arise, if at all, only when the vendor is in default. (Vance Redwood Lumber Co. v. Durphy, 8 Cal. App. 664, 97 Pac. 702.)

Power of taxation cannot be surrendered.

Sec. 6. The power of taxation shall never be surrendered or suspended by any grant or contract to which the state shall be a party.

Payment of taxes by installments.

Sec. 7. The legislature shall have the power to provide by law for the payment of all taxes on real property by installments.

Annual statement of property to be given.

Sec. 8. The legislature shall by law require each taxpayer in this state to make and deliver to the county assessor, annually, a statement, under oath, setting forth specifically all the real and personal property owned by such taxpayer, or in his possession, or under his control, at twelve o'clock meridian, on the first Monday of March.

ASSESSMENT.—A tax must rest upon an assessment made in the mode prescribed by law, by an assessor elected by the qualified electors of the district, county, or town in which the property is taxed. (People v. Hastings, 29 Cal. 449.)

An assessment made by an assessor of the city and county of Sacramento is not sufficient basis for the levy of a tax in the city of Sacramento for city purposes. (People v. Hastings, 29 Cal. 449.)

The sheriff, as such, cannot perform the duties of tax collector. (Lathrop v. Brittain, 30 Cal. 680.)

The assessment must be made by the assessor, and, if not so made, the legislature cannot supply the defect by a curative act; but, if the assessment is good in substance, any error in mode, form, etc., may be remedied by the legislature. (People v. McCreery, 34 Cal. 432.)

Although the legislature cannot by law transfer the duties of tax collector from a person elected as such to one not so elected, it may provide for the election of a person as tax collector who may enter upon the discharge of his duties before the expiration of the term of a tax collector elected under the law as it previously stood. (Mills v. Sargent, 36 Cal. 379.)

The provision of section 3633 of the Political Code, providing for an arbitrary assessment, is not in conflict with this section. (Orena v. Sherman, 61 Cal. 101.)

This section only has reference to prospective assessments, and does not supersede a provision of a city charter. (Stockton v. Western Fire etc. Ins. Co., 73 Cal. 621, 15 Pac. 314.)

This section has no application to the assessment of property in in-corporated cities for local purposes. (Escondido v. Escondido Lumber etc. Co., 8 Cal. App. 435, 97 Pac. 197.)

This section designates the time when the assessable character of property becomes fixed, namely, at twelve o'clock meridian on the first Monday in March, and property exempt from taxation on that day cannot be assessed later, nor is the owner of property required to include in his return to the assessor any property not subject to taxation on the first Monday in March. (Dodge v. Nevada Nat. Bank, 109 Fed. 726, 48 C. C. A. 626.)

State board of equalization.

Sec. 9. A state board of equalization, consisting of one member from each congressional district in this state, as the same existed in eighteen hundred and seventy-nine, shall be elected by the qualified electors of their respective districts, at the general election to be held in the year one thousand eight hundred and eighty-six, and at each guber-natorial election thereafter, whose term of office shall be for four years, whose duty it shall be to equalize the valua-tion of the taxable property in the several counties of the state for the purposes of taxation. The controller of state shall be ex officio a member of the board. The boards of supervisors of the several counties of the state shall consti-tute boards of equalization for their respective counties, whose duty it shall be to equalize the valuation of the tax-able property in the county for the purpose of taxation; provided, such state and county boards of equalization are hereby authorized and empowered, under such rules of notice as the county boards may prescribe as to the county assessments, and under such rules of notice as the state board may prescribe as to the action of the state board, to increase or lower the entire assessment-roll, or any assess-ment contained therein, so as to equalize the assessment of the property contained in said assessment-roll and make the assessment conform to the true value in money of the property contained in said roll; provided, that no board of equalization shall raise any mortgage, deed of trust, con-tract, or other obligation by which a debt is secured, money or solvent credits, above its face value. The present state board of equalization shall continue in office until their suc-

cessors, as herein provided for, shall be elected and shall qualify. The legislature shall have power to redistrict the state into four districts, as nearly equal in population as practicable, and to provide for the election of members of said board of equalization. (Ratification declared February 12, 1885.)

[ORIGINAL SECTION.]

Sec. 9. A state board of equalization, consisting of one member from each congressional district in this state, shall be elected by the qualified electors of their respective districts at the general election to be held in the year eighteen hundred and seventy-nine, whose term of office, after those first elected, shall be four years, whose duty it shall be to equalize the valuation of the taxable property of the several counties in the state for the purposes of taxation. The controller of state shall be ex officio a member of the board. The boards of supervisors of the several counties of the state shall constitute boards of equalization for their respective counties, whose duty it shall be to equalize the valuation of the taxable property in the county for the purpose of taxation; provided, such state and county boards of equalization are hereby authorized and empowered, under such rules of notice as the county board may prescribe as to the county assessments, and under such rules of notice as the state board may prescribe, as to the action of the state board, to increase or lower the entire assessment-roll, or any assessment contained therein, so as to equalize the assessment of the property contained in said assessment-roll, and make the assessment conform to the true value in money of the property contained in said roll.

[An amendment to this section was voted upon November 6, 1894, but, although it appears in some publications as having been ratified, it was defeated by a vote of 88,605 noes to 86,777 ayes.]

BOARD OF EQUALIZATION. — It is within the constitutional power of the legislature to create a state board of equalization. (Savings etc. Soc. v. Austin, 46 Cal. 415.)

Section 1666 of the Political Code is unconstitutional, in so far as it delegates to the state board of equalization the right to fix the rate of taxation "after allowing for delinquency in the collection of taxes," because it is a delegation of legislative power. (Houghton v. Austin, 47 Cal. 646. Savings etc. Soc. v. Austin, 46 Cal. 415, overruled on this point. See, also, Grimm v. O'Connell, 54 Cal. 522; Wills v. Austin, 53 Cal. 152; Harper v. Rowe, 53 Cal. 233.)

The state board of equalization has no power to make a reassessment and reapportionment of taxes upon a railroad for previous years, if the taxes for such years were originally validly assessed and apportioned. (Colusa County v. Glenn County, 124 Cal. 498, 57 Pac. 477.)

Mandamus will not lie to compel the assessor to assess property in excess of its value, upon the ground that it was greatly undervalued

in the previous fiscal year. (Clunie v. Siebe, 112 Cal. 593, 44 Pac. 1064.)

As to the notice to be given by the board to the taxpayer, see Allison Ranch etc. Co. v. Nevada Co., 104 Cal. 161, 37 Pac. 875.

Section 3861 of the Political Code, requiring the assessor, at the request of the board of equalization, to list and assess property which he has failed to assess, is not in conflict with this section, since it simply confers an additional power upon the board. (Farmers' etc. Bank v. Board of Equalization, 97 Cal. 318, 32 Pac. 312.)

An act authorizing an assessment of taxes, after the time within which the board of supervisors can meet for the purpose of equalization, is violative of this section. (People v. Pittsburg R. R. Co., 67 Cal. 625, 8 Pac. 381.)

The state board of equalization has power to increase or lower the assessment-roll of a county so as to affect taxes for county purposes. (Baldwin v. Ellis, 68 Cal. 495, 9 Pac. 652.)

The action of the state board of equalization in raising the assessment-roll of a county under this section operates upon mortgage assessments. (Schroeder v. Grady, 66 Cal. 212, 5 Pac. 81.)

The state board of equalization has no power to increase the assessment of money, where the money is already assessed at its face value. (People v. Dunn, 59 Cal. 328.)

A refusal of a state board of equalization to reduce an assessment does not preclude the board from afterward raising the same assessment. (Central Pac. R. R. Co. v. Board of Equalization, 46 Cal. 667.)

The board of equalization has no power to strike out from an assessment, made by an assessor, property assessed by him. (People v. Board of Supervisors, 50 Cal. 282.)

The board of equalization has no power to cancel an assessment for taxes placed by the assessor upon the assessment-roll. (People v. Board of Supervisors, 44 Cal. 613.)

The board of equalization, in passing on the question whether an assessment is too high or too low, acts in a judicial capacity. (People v. Goldtree, 44 Cal. 323.)

A board of equalization acts judicially in raising or lowering an assessment, and has no arbitrary power of assessment or reassessment. It cannot act without a hearing, upon notice given to the person assessed, nor change an assessment made by the assessor without evidence adduced authorizing such change. (City of Oakland v. Southern Pac. R. R. Co., 131 Cal. 226, 63 Pac. 371.)

In order to give the board of equalization jurisdiction to increase the valuation of property assessed, the filing of a complaint is necessary. (People v. Goldtree, 44 Cal. 323.)

The state board of equalization cannot delegate to its clerk authority to issue orders prolonging the time of the sessions of the county boards of equalization. (Buswell v. Board of Supervisors, 116 Cal. 351, 48 Pac. 226.)

The board of equalization may appoint a committee to take testimony as to the valuation of property. (People v. McCreery, 34 Cal. 432.)

The presumption of law is that a board of equalization perform their duty and correct any inequality in the assessment of taxes. (Guy v. Washburn, 23 Cal. 111.)

The proviso to this section is to be read distributively, that is to say, as authorizing the state board to increase or lower the entire assessment-roll of any county, and the county boards to increase or lower the individual assessments of their respective counties. The state board, therefore, has no power to increase or lower individual assessments; nor has a county board the power to increase or lower the entire assessment-roll. (Wells, Fargo & Co. v. Board of Equalization, 56 Cal. 194; San Francisco etc. R. R. Co. v. State Board of Equalization, 60 Cal. 12.)

This section does not make it necessary for a county board, in a return to a writ of certiorari, to set out general rules of notice adopted by the board. (Garretson v. Board of Supervisors, 61 Cal. 54.)

Property, where assessed.

Sec. 10. All property, except as otherwise in this Constitution provided, shall be assessed in the county, city, city and county, town or township, or district in which it is situated, in the manner prescribed by law. (Amendment adopted November 8, 1910. This amendment was adopted as a part of the same amendment by which section 14 of this article was added. See note to that section.)

[ORIGINAL SECTION.]

Sec. 10. All property, except as hereinafter in this section provided, shall be assessed in the county, city, city and county, town, township, or district in which it is situated, in the manner prescribed by law. The franchise, roadway, roadbed, rails and rolling stock of all railroads operated in more than one county in this state shall be assessed by the state board of equalization, at their actual value, and the same shall be apportioned to the counties, cities and counties, cities, towns, townships, and districts in which such railroads are located, in proportion to the number of miles of railway laid in such counties, cities and counties, cities, towns, townships, and districts.

SITUS OF PROPERTY. — This section is self-executing. (San Francisco etc. R. R. Co. v. State Board of Equalization, 60 Cal. 12.)

It has no relation to the assessment of the property of railroad corporations, operated in more than one county. (Central Pac. R. R. Co. v. Board of Equalization, 60 Cal. 35.)

Boards of supervisors of the several counties through which run railroads operated in more than one county have no jurisdiction to raise or lower the assessment placed upon the property of such roads by the board of equalization. (People v. Sacramento County Suprs., 59 Cal. 321.)

This provision has reference to the permanent situs of the property, as distinguished from the place of temporary sojourn, or transit. (Rosasco v. Tuolumne County, 143 Cal. 430, 77 Pac. 148.)

> Place of taxation of realty situate in more than one taxing district. See note, 18 Ann. Cas. 713.

> Situs of personal property for purposes of taxation. See notes, 56 Am. Dec. 522; 62 Am. St. Rep. 448.

Water ditches for irrigating purposes must be assessed the same as real estate in the county in which they are situated. (Kern Valley Water Co. v. County of Kern, 137 Cal. 511, 70 Pac. 476.)

Section 39 of the Wright Irrigation Act, providing that if the trustees of the district fail to levy a tax to pay the bonds of the district, the board of supervisors shall do so, is constitutional. (Nevada Nat. Bank v. Board of Supervisors, 5 Cal. App. 638, 91 Pac. 122.)

The franchise to collect water rates is taxable in the county where exercised. (San Joaquin etc. Irr. Co. v. Merced County, 2 Cal. App. 593, 84 Pac. 285.)

The franchise to be a corporation is taxable at the principal place of business of the corporation. (San Joaquin etc. Irr. Co. v. Merced County, 2 Cal. App. 593, 84 Pac. 285.)

> Place of taxation of corporate franchise. See note, 7 Ann. Cas. 518.

The franchise to lay pipes and conduits or erect poles is real estate, and is inseparably annexed to the soil, and has a local situation in the place where the right is exercised, and can only be assessed in the counties where it is situated. (Stockton Gas etc. Co. v. San Joaquin County, 148 Cal. 313, 7 Ann. Cas. 511, 5 L. R. A. (N. S.) 174, 83 Pac. 54.)

> Place of taxation of tangible personalty of corporation as dependent upon location of principal office. See note, 19 Ann. Cas. 958.

Steamers used by a railroad company in transporting its freight-cars across the bay of San Francisco are not included in the property mentioned in this section, and should be assessed by the local assessor, and not by the state board of equalization. (San Francisco v. Central Pac. R. R. Co., 63 Cal. 467, 49 Am. Rep. 98; State of California v. Central Pacific R. Co., 127 U. S. 1, 32 L. Ed. 150, 8 Sup. Ct. Rep. 1073.)

Vessels not having any actual situs are properly assessed at the domicile of the owner when registered. (California Shipping Co. v. San Francisco, 150 Cal. 145, 88 Pac. 704.)

> Situs of vessels for purpose of taxation. See notes, 3 Ann. Cas. 1103; 20 Ann. Cas. 966.

For the purpose of taxation, the situs of money belonging to the estate of a decedent is in the county where the decedent resided at the time of his death, and the situs is not changed by placing the money on general deposit in a bank of another county. (City and County of San Francisco v. Lux, 64 Cal. 481, 2 Pac. 254.)

Situs of personal property of decedent for purpose of taxation.
See notes, 1 Ann. Cas. 438; 20 Ann. Cas. 729.

Situs of interest of deceased partner in partnership for purposes
of taxation. See note, 9 Ann. Cas. 692.

Debts are taxable at the domicile of the creditor. (Pacific Coast
etc. Soc. v. San Francisco, 133 Cal. 14, 65 Pac. 16.)

ASSESSMENT OF RAILROADS.—This section does not in terms
require the assessed value of the franchise, roadway, roadbed, rails,
and rolling stock, to be separately apportioned. (San Francisco etc.
R. R. Co. v. State Board of Equalization, 60 Cal. 12.)

Situs for taxation of rolling stock. See note, 10 Ann. Cas. 355.

The provisions of this section do not apply to "street" railroads,
though operating in more than one county. (San Francisco etc. Ry.
Co. v. Scott, 142 Cal. 222, 75 Pac. 575; Huntington v. Curry, 14 Cal.
App. 468, 112 Pac. 583.)

A county has no authority to collect taxes upon a railroad operated
in more than one county, which are due to a school district. (San
Bernardino County v. Southern Pac. R. R. Co., 137 Cal. 659, 70 Pac.
782.)

A law providing for the assessment and collection of taxes upon
railroads operating in more than one county is valid. (People v. Central Pac. R. R. Co., 105 Cal. 576, 38 Pac. 905; affirmed, Central Pac.
R. R. Co. v. People, 162 U. S. 91, 40 L. Ed. 903, 16 Sup. Ct. Rep. 766;
People v. Central Pac. R. R. Co., 83 Cal. 393, 23 Pac. 303, overruled.)

In making a reassessment of railroad taxes, to take the place of an
invalid assessment of a previous year, it is the duty of the board to
make the apportionment to the counties as they existed at the time
of the invalid assessment, and not at the time of the reassessment.
(San Diego County v. Riverside County, 125 Cal. 495, 58 Pac. 81.)

The power of the board of equalization to assess railroad property
depends wholly upon the constitutional grant of powers thereto, and
constitutes an express exception to the general rule which requires
all property to be assessed locally. It is only where the property
comes under the head of "franchise, roadway, roadbed, rails and rolling stock" of a railroad operated in more than one county, that it
can be assessed by the state board of equalization. (Atchison etc.
Ry. Co. v. Los Angeles County, 158 Cal. 437, 111 Pac. 250.)

The state board can only assess the franchise, roadway, roadbed
and rolling stock of railroads. All improvements situated on or off
the right of way are to be assessed by the local authorities. (San
Francisco & S. J. Ry. Co. v. Stockton, 149 Cal. 83, 84 Pac. 771.)

Fences along the line of a railway are not a part of the roadbed or
roadway of such railroad, and are not assessable by the state board
under this section. (Santa Clara County v. Southern Pacific R. R.
Co., 118 U. S. 394, 30 L. Ed. 118, 6 Sup. Ct. Rep. 1132.)

Railroad property consisting of blocks of land adjoining the right
of way, acquired and used for station purposes, for a passenger
depot, for a freight-house, with spur tracks and sidings, for a round-
house, for machine-shops, for a storehouse, with materials for construction purposes, with tracks for switching and repairing purposes,

for a water-tank and for a cattle-yard, and also a right of way and roadbed never used or operated for railroad purposes, are to be assessed exclusively by the city assessor. (San Francisco & S. J. V. Ry. Co. v. Stockton, 149 Cal. 83, 84 Pac. 771.)

It is constitutional to assess a franchise of an electric light and power company to use county highways, in each school district, by valuing it according to the number of miles of transmission lines in that district, without reference to the extent of the public highways over which the lines were erected. (Kern River Co. v. County of Los Angeles, 164 Cal. 751, 130 Pac. 714.)

Personal property to extent of one hundred dollars exempt.

Sec. 10½. The personal property of every householder to the amount of one hundred dollars, the articles to be selected by each householder, shall be exempt from taxation. (New section added by amendment approved November 8, 1904.)

Income taxes.

Sec. 11. Income taxes may be assessed to and collected from persons, corporations, joint-stock associations, or companies resident or doing business in this state, or any one or more of them, in such cases and amounts, and in such manner, as shall be prescribed by law.

Poll tax.

Sec. 12. No poll tax or head tax for any purpose whatsoever shall be levied or collected in the state of California. (Amendment adopted November 3, 1914.)

[ORIGINAL SECTION.]

Sec. 12. The legislature shall provide for the levy and collection of an annual poll tax of not less than two dollars on every male inhabitant of this state, over twenty-one and under sixty years of age, except paupers, idiots, insane persons, and Indians not taxed. Said tax shall be paid into the state school fund.

POLL TAXES.—A statute authorizing county assessors to retain, as their compensation in collecting, fifteen per cent of all poll taxes collected by them, is not in conflict with this section. (San Luis Obispo County v. Felts, 104 Cal. 60, 37 Pac. 780.)

The poll tax levied under this section is a state tax. (Alameda County v. Dalton, 148 Cal. 246, 82 Pac. 1050.)

Young trees and vines exempt from taxation.

Sec. 12¾. Fruit and nut-bearing trees under the age of four years from the time of planting in orchard form, and

grapevines under the age of three years from the time of planting in vineyard form, shall be exempt from taxation, and nothing in this article shall be construed as subjecting such trees and grapevines to taxation. (Amendment adopted November 6, 1894.)

Laws to be passed by legislature.

Sec. 13. The legislature shall pass all laws necessary to carry out the provisions of this article.

Legislation.—Under this provision the legislature may define the words "improvements" and "property." (Miller v. County of Kern, 137 Cal. 516, 70 Pac. 549.)

Taxes for state purposes.

Sec. 14. Taxes levied, assessed and collected as hereinafter provided upon railroads, including street railways, whether operated in one or more counties; sleeping-car, dining-car, drawing-room car and palace-car companies, refrigerator, oil, stock, fruit, and other car-loaning and other car companies operating upon railroads in this state; companies doing express business on any railroad, steamboat, vessel or stage line in this state; telegraph companies; telephone companies; companies engaged in the transmission or sale of gas or electricity; insurance companies; banks, banking associations, savings and loan societies, and trust companies; and taxes upon all franchises of every kind and nature, shall be entirely and exclusively for state purposes, and shall be levied, assessed and collected in the manner hereinafter provided. The word "companies" as used in this section shall include persons, partnerships, joint-stock associations, companies, and corporations.

*Taxes on railroads, express companies, telegraph and telephone companies, gas and electric companies.

(a) All railroad companies, including street railways, whether operated in one or more counties; all sleeping-car, dining-car, drawing-room car, and palace-car companies, all refrigerator, oil, stock, fruit and other car-loaning and

---

*The headings found in this section are not part of the enactment but are inserted for convenience of reference.

other car companies, operating upon the railroads in this state; all companies doing express business on any railroad, steamboat, vessel or stage line, in this state; all telegraph and telephone companies; and all companies engaged in the transmission or sale of gas or electricity shall annually pay to the state a tax upon their franchises, roadways, roadbeds, rails, rolling stock, poles, wires, pipes, canals, conduits, rights of way, and other property, or any part thereof, used exclusively in the operation of their business in this state, computed as follows: Said tax shall be equal to the percentages hereinafter fixed upon the gross receipts from operation of such companies and each thereof within this state. When such companies are operating partly within and partly without this state, the gross receipts within this state shall be deemed to be all receipts on business beginning and ending within this state, and a proportion, based upon the proportion of the mileage within this state to the entire mileage over which such business is done, of receipts on all business passing through, into, or out of this state.

*The percentages above mentioned shall be as follows: On all railroad companies, including street railways, four per cent; on all sleeping-car, dining-car, drawing-room car, palace-car companies, refrigerator, oil, stock, fruit and other car-loaning and other car companies, three per cent; on all companies doing express business on any railroad, steamboat, vessel or stage line, two per cent; on all telegraph and telephone companies, three and one-half per cent; on all companies engaged in the transmission or sale of gas or electricity, four per cent. Such taxes shall be in lieu of all other taxes and licenses, state, county and municipal, upon the property above enumerated of such companies except as otherwise in this section provided; provided, that nothing herein shall be construed to release any such company from the payment of any amount agreed to be paid or required by law to be paid for any special privilege

---

*These percentages have been twice changed by the legislature under the authority given by subdivision (f) of this section. See Statutes, 1913, p. 3, and 1915, p. 3.

or franchise granted by any of the municipal authorities of this state.

Taxes on insurance companies.

(b) Every insurance company or association doing business in this state shall annually pay to the state a tax of one and one-half per cent upon the amount of the gross premiums received upon its business done in this state, less return premiums and reinsurance in companies or associations authorized to do business in this state; provided, that there shall be deducted from said one and one-half per cent upon the gross premiums the amount of any county and municipal taxes paid by such companies on real estate owned by them in this state. This tax shall be in lieu of all other taxes and licenses, state, county and municipal, upon the property of such companies, except county and municipal taxes on real estate, and except as otherwise in this section provided; provided, that when by the laws of any other state or country, any taxes, fines, penalties, licenses, fees, deposits of money, or of securities, or other obligations or prohibitions are imposed on insurance companies of this state, doing business in such other state or country, or upon their agents therein, in excess of such taxes, fines, penalties, licenses, fees, deposits of money, or of securities, or other obligations or prohibitions, imposed upon insurance companies of such other state or country, so long as such laws continue in force, the same obligations and prohibitions of whatsoever kind may be imposed by the legislature upon insurance companies of such other state or country doing business in this state.

Taxes on bank stock.

(c) The shares of capital stock of all banks, organized under the laws of this state, or of the United States, or of any other state and located in this state, shall be assessed and taxed to the owners or holders thereof by the state board of equalization, in the manner to be prescribed by law, in the city or town where the bank is located and not elsewhere. There shall be levied and assessed upon such shares of capital stock an annual tax, payable to the state,

of one per centum upon the value thereof. The value of each share of stock in each bank, except such as are in liquidation, shall be taken to be the amount paid in thereon, together with its pro rata of the accumulated surplus and undivided profits. The value of each share of stock in each bank which is in liquidation shall be taken to be its pro rata of the actual assets of such bank. This tax shall be in lieu of all other taxes and licenses, state, county and municipal, upon such shares of stock and upon the property of such banks, except county and municipal taxes on real estate and except as otherwise in this section provided. In determining the value of the capital stock of any bank there shall be deducted from the value, as defined above, the value, as assessed for county taxes, of any real estate, other than mortgage interests therein, owned by such bank and taxed for county purposes. The banks shall be liable to the state for this tax and the same shall be paid to the state by them on behalf of the stockholders in the manner and at the time prescribed by law, and they shall have a lien upon the shares of stock and upon any dividends declared thereon to secure the amount so paid.

Taxes on unincorporated banks.

The moneyed capital, reserve, surplus, undivided profits and all other property belonging to unincorporated banks or bankers of this state, or held by any bank located in this state which has no shares of capital stock, or employed in this state by any branches, agencies, or other representatives of any banks doing business outside of the state of California, shall be likewise assessed and taxed to such banks or bankers by the said board of equalization, in the manner to be provided by law, and taxed at the same rate that is levied upon the shares of capital stock of incorporated banks, as provided in the first paragraph of this subdivision. The value of said property shall be determined by taking the entire property invested in such business, together with all the reserve, surplus, and undivided profits, at their full cash value, and deducting therefrom the value as assessed for county taxes of any

real estate, other than mortgage interests therein, owned
by such bank and taxed for county purposes.   Such taxes
shall be in lieu of all other taxes and licenses, state, county
and municipal, upon the property of the banks and bankers mentioned in this paragraph, except county and municipal taxes on real estate and except as otherwise in this
section provided.   It is the intention of this paragraph
that all moneyed capital and property of the banks and
bankers mentioned in this paragraph shall be assessed and
taxed at the same rate as an incorporated bank, provided
for in the first paragraph of this subdivision.   In determining the value of the moneyed capital and property of
the banks and bankers mentioned in this subdivision, the
said state board of equalization shall include and assess
to such banks all property and everything of value owned
or held by them, which go to make up the value of the
capital stock of such banks and bankers, if the same were
incorporated and had shares of capital stock.

The word "banks" as used in this subdivision shall include banking associations, savings and loan societies and
trust companies, but shall not include building and loan
associations.

Taxes on franchises.

(d) All franchises, other than those expressly provided
for in this section, shall be assessed at their actual cash
value, in the manner to be provided by law, and shall be
taxed at the rate of one per centum each year, and the
taxes collected thereon shall be exclusively for the benefit
of the state.

School and university funds.

(e) Out of the revenues from the taxes provided for in
this section, together with all other state revenues, there
shall be first set apart the moneys to be applied by the
state to the support of the public school system and the
state university.   In the event that the above-named revenues are at any time deemed insufficient to meet the annual
expenditures of the state, including the above-named expenditures for educational purposes, there may be levied,

in the manner to be provided by law, a tax, for state purposes, on all the property in the state, including the classes of property enumerated in this section, sufficient to meet the deficiency. All property enumerated in subdivisions a, b, and d of this section shall be subject to taxation, in the manner provided by law to pay the principal and interest of any bonded indebtedness created and outstanding by any city, city and county, county, town, township or district, before the adoption of this section. The taxes so paid for principal and interest on such bonded indebtedness shall be deducted from the total amount paid in taxes for state purposes.

Provisions self-executing, etc.

(f) All the provisions of this section shall be self-executing, and the legislature shall pass all laws necessary to carry this section into effect, and shall provide for a valuation and assessment of the property enumerated in this section, and shall prescribe the duties of the state board of equalization and any other officers in connection with the administration thereof. The rates of taxation fixed by this section shall remain in force until changed by the legislature, two-thirds of all the members elected to each of the two houses voting in favor thereof. The taxes herein provided for shall become a lien on the first Monday in March of each year after the adoption of this section and shall become due and payable on the first Monday in July thereafter. The gross receipts and gross premiums herein mentioned shall be computed for the year ending the thirty-first day of December prior to the levy of such taxes and the value of any property mentioned herein shall be fixed as of the first Monday in March. Nothing herein contained shall affect any tax levied or assessed prior to the adoption of this section; and all laws in relation to such taxes in force at the time of the adoption of this section shall remain in force until changed by the legislature. Until the year 1918 the state shall reimburse any and all counties which sustain loss of revenue by the withdrawal of railroad property from county taxation for the net loss

in county revenue occasioned by the withdrawal of railroad property from county taxation. The legislature shall provide for reimbursement from the general funds of any county to districts therein where loss is occasioned in such districts by the withdrawal from local taxation of property taxed for state purposes only.

Suits to recover or enjoin tax.

(g) No injunction shall ever issue in any suit, action or proceeding in any court against this state or against any officer thereof to prevent or enjoin the collection of any tax levied under the provisions of this section; but after payment action may be maintained to recover any tax illegally collected in such manner and at such time as may now or hereafter be provided by law. (New section added by amendment adopted November 8, 1910.)

TAXATION FOR STATE PURPOSES.—Section 468 of the Civil Code, defining when a railroad is to be deemed in full operation, has no application to the determination of the question whether or not the property of a railroad or other public service corporation is "operative" within the meaning of this section and the act of April 1, 1911 (Stats. 1911, p. 530), providing for the separation of state from local taxation and for the taxation of public service and other corporations. (San Diego etc. Ry. Co. v. State Board, 165 Cal. 560, 132 Pac. 1044.)

Where a railroad operates part of its line and runs a mixed train for freight and passengers daily except Sunday, such part is "operative property" within the meaning of the act of April 1, 1911, providing for the separation of state from local taxation, and for the taxation of public service and other corporations, and within the meaning of this section, and is taxable only for state purposes. (San Diego etc. Ry. Co. v. State Board, 165 Cal. 560, 132 Pac. 1044.)

The amendment of 1910 exempts a telephone company from liability for a license imposed by a pre-existing municipal ordinance, for purposes of revenue only, upon persons or corporations supplying telephone service to the inhabitants of the municipality, and it exempts them from the payment of such license for the first two quarters of 1911. (San Francisco v. Pacific Tel. & Tel. Co., 166 Cal. 244, 135 Pac. 971.)

Under this section steamboats belonging to and operated by a railroad company on a lake at which its railroad line terminates, for the purpose of carrying goods and passengers between many different points thereon both within and without the state, are not taxable under this section if such steamboats are not used exclusively in the operation of its railroad business. (Lake Tahoe Ry. etc. Co. v. Roberts, 168 Cal. 551, 143 Pac. 786.)

Constitution—35

The taxes imposed on public service companies by this section are in lieu of all other taxes and licenses, state, county and municipal upon the property enumerated in this section. (Pacific Gas & El. Co. v. Roberts, 168 Cal. 420, 143 Pac. 700.)

This section exempts a public service corporation transmitting and selling gas and electricity in the state from the payment of the license tax imposed by the Motor Vehicle Act on motor vehicles owned by it and used exclusively in its business in the state. (Pacific Gas & El. Co. v. Roberts, 168 Cal. 420, 143 Pac. 700.)

A revenue tax, imposed by a municipal ordinance, upon agents of insurance companies for the right to do business is in violation of this section. (Hughes v. Los Angeles, 168 Cal. 764, 145 Pac. 94.)

The amendment of 1910 taxing the franchises of insurance companies for state purposes exempted these corporations from the payment of the corporation license tax of March 20, 1905. (Hartford Fire Ins. Co. v. Jordan, 168 Cal. 270, 142 Pac. 839.)

This section renders invalid an excise or occupation tax attempted to be imposed by a municipal ordinance upon the right of banks, subject to the tax imposed by this section, to conduct their business. (Southern Trust Co. v. Los Angeles, 168 Cal. 762, 145 Pac. 94.)

This subdivision does not supersede or override sections 22 and 34 of article IV of the Constitution, in so far as they involve limitations upon the appropriations of money to satisfy final judgments against the state treasurer for state taxes illegally collected by him. (Westinghouse Electric Co. v. Chambers, 169 Cal. 131, 145 Pac. 1025.)

The action authorized by this subdivision would be complete when final judgment was obtained, and nothing in it provides for the actual payment of the money sued for, or the satisfaction of the judgment obtained in the action. (Westinghouse Electric Co. v. Chambers, 169 Cal. 131, 145 Pac. 1025.)

This section does not adopt section 3669 of the Political Code, and declare that final judgments against the state treasurer for state taxes illegally collected by him shall be paid out of the treasury on warrant drawn thereon by the controller. (Westinghouse Electric Co. v. Chambers, 169 Cal. 131, 145 Pac. 1025.)

An assessment on deposits in a bank, made pursuant to order of court in pending suits, is not an assessment against the bank or its shares or other property, within the meaning of this section, but is an assessment against funds in the hands of the bank acting as receiver. (Spring Valley Water Co. v. City and County of San Francisco, 225 Fed. 728.)

HISTORY OF SECTION.—This section was the result of a movement inaugurated in 1905 to separate the system of state and local taxation. To that end an act was passed on the twentieth day of March, 1905, authorizing the appointment of a commission on revenue and taxation. (Stats. 1905, p. 390.) Pursuant to that act the commission was appointed, consisting of Governor George C. Pardee, Professor Carl C. Plehn, expert on taxation and public finance, Senators J. B. Curtin and M. L. Ward, and Assemblymen H. S. G. McCartney and Edward F. Treadwell. That commission made an elaborate report to the governor in 1906 and recommended a constitutional

amendment for the purpose of carrying out its recommendations, which was adopted as Senate Constitutional Amendment No. 1, on March 9, 1907 (Stats. 1907, p. 1353). This amendment was voted upon at the election held in November, 1908, and failed of adoption, and thereupon the commission recommended a new amendment correcting the defects in the prior amendment, which was again adopted as Senate Constitutional Amendment No. 1, on March 19, 1909 (Stats. 1909, p. 1332). This amendment consisted of this new section 14, and the amendment to section 10 of this article, and the repeal of section 10 of article XI. This amendment was submitted to a vote of the people and adopted at the general election in November, 1910.

The general purpose and object of the amendment is fully discussed in the two reports of the commission above referred to. In the first report the question of the constitutionality of a gross earnings tax is discussed in some detail, and as that discussion is applicable to the validity of this section, it is here inserted:

"Is a gross earnings tax constitutional?

"The opinion is often expressed in tax commission reports and elsewhere that a tax on the gross earnings of railroads, in so far as those earnings are derived from interstate commerce, is of doubtful validity under provisions of the Federal Constitution. This view is very forcibly expressed by the Ontario Commission on Railway Taxation, 1905, which, however, brought in a very strong report in favor of the gross earnings tax on broad general grounds. Their recommendation applied, of course, to Canada, where the constitutional difficulties referred to could not apply. The Ontario Commission, after saying that 'The earning power is the only reliable and satisfactory basis of taxation,' alleged:

" 'In the United States, however, owing to the wording and interpretation of the Constitution, it is held by the courts that taxation by any State of the earnings of a railroad derived from interstate traffic is illegal. Consequently, even where the earnings of a railroad are made the basis of taxation, the tax laws are careful to state that the tax is a license tax or a franchise tax, merely measured by gross earnings; and it is often further guarded by some such qualifying clause as, "derived entirely from traffic within the State." In several states where the gross earnings tax is accepted by both the people and the railways, it is thought that the law is not really constitutional, but, as neither party cares to bring the matter to a test, it is permitted to stand. In Wisconsin, the gross earnings tax, lately abolished, was declared by several judges to be unconstitutional, but they refused to give judgments adverse to the state on account of the confusion which would be introduced into the State revenue.

" 'When such states as Michigan and Wisconsin, which had previously taxed the railroads on the gross earnings basis, reached the conviction that the railroads were not paying as much as they might be made to pay, we find that, instead of simply raising the rate of the existing tax from, say four, to say five or six per cent, they found it expedient to change the basis of taxation. This was obviously done because they knew that the raising of the rate would meet with the opposition of the railroads and would probably result in the tax law

being declared unconstitutional, thereby paralyzing a large section
of the revenue of the state until a new method of taxation should be
adopted. Yet, as already indicated, and as an examination of its
operation will show, the so-called ad valorem system of these and
other states is really a roundabout method of getting at earnings once
more on a higher rate of taxation.' (Report of Ontario Commission
on Railway Taxation, 1905, pp. 16–17.)

"This view, as forcibly expressed by the Ontario Commission, has
been sedulously spread by certain railroad attorneys and is somewhat
extensively held in the United States, but it does not accord with the
decisions of the Supreme Court. The following analysis of the long
series of interesting decisions upon this point will show at once where
the erroneous opinion arose and what the Supreme Court now holds:

"The constitutionality of a tax on the gross receipts of corporations
    engaged in interstate commerce.

"In writing the following synopsis of the decisions of the Supreme
Court as to the power of the states to tax interstate carriers we have
worked directly from the United States Reports. Much assistance
was, however, found in the admirable treatise by Frederick N. Judson, of the St. Louis Bar, on The Power of Taxation, State and Federal, in the United States: St. Louis, 1903, especially Chapters III,
VII and VIII.

"Mr. Treadwell went over the cases first and formulated the conclusions reached.

"Of the several provisions of the Federal Constitution intended
jointly to safeguard 'the freest interchange of commodities among
the people of the different states' (Justice Miller in Cook v. Pennsylvania, 97 U. S. 566, 574, 24 L. Ed. 1015, 1018), the one chiefly relied
upon in connection with the taxation of carriers engaged in interstate
commerce is paragraph 3, of Section 8, of Article I, which confers
upon Congress the power: 'To regulate commerce with foreign
nations, and among the several states, and with the Indian tribes.'

"The dictum of Chief Justice Marshall in McCulloch v. Maryland,
'that the power to tax involves the power to destroy, etc.,' was delivered solely with reference to the taxation of the 'instruments employed by the Government in the execution of its powers,' and no
attempts to apply it as a prohibition of state taxation of interstate
carriers, even when they are incorporated by the United States, have
been successful. (Thomson v. Pacific Railroad, 9 Wall. 579, 19 L. Ed.
792; Union Pac. R. R. Co. v. Peniston, 18 Wall. 5, 21 L. Ed. 787.)

"The difficulty of drawing a sharp line between the Federal powers
and the State powers in the matter of the taxation and regulation of
those great agencies of interstate commerce, like the railroads and
the telegraph, which extend from one end of the country to the other,
has troubled the courts since 1872. It is only recently that the problem has been definitely solved.

"While the greater part of each of the two fields, in which each of
the two great divisions of our Government may respectively exercise its powers, is clear enough, yet the boundary of one seems to
merge almost imperceptibly into that of the other at places. This
has resulted in much litigation, and the decisions of the Supreme

Court on some of the most vital points have occasionally seemed contradictory. In not a few instances the Court has apparently reversed itself.

"However, the following points seem now to have been conclusively settled:

"A. As to the taxation of interstate carriers on an ad valorem basis:

"1. A State may tax the property, within its bounds, of railroad companies and other persons or corporations engaged in interstate commerce. (Union Pac. R. R. Co. v. Peniston, 18 Wall. 5, 21 L. Ed. 787, and later cases based thereon.)

"2. It may tax both the tangible and the intangible property of the carriers, provided only, that it may not tax a Federal franchise. (Central Pacific R. R. Co. v. People of California, 162 U. S. 91, 40 L. Ed. 903, 16 Sup. Ct. Rep. 766.)

"3. A State may value that property by the 'unit rule,' i. e., make a valuation of the entire property of the 'system' of a given corporation engaged in interstate business, and tax that proportion of the entire property which the mileage in the State bears to the total mileage operated. Or, what is the same thing, may make the apportionment on the basis of business done. (State Railroad Tax Cases, 92 U. S. 575, 23 L. Ed. 663; Western Union Telegraph Co. v. Taggart, 163 U. S. 1, 41 L. Ed. 49, 16 Sup. Ct. Rep. 1054; Adams Express Co. v. Ohio, 165 U. S. 194.)

"4. It may arrive at a valuation by the following methods:

"(a) By adding the market, or fair cash, value of the shares of capital stock and the market, or par, value of the various kinds of funded indebtedness.

"Justice Miller, in rendering an oft-quoted decision on this point, said: 'It is therefore obvious that, when you have ascertained the current cash value of the whole funded debt, and the current cash value of the entire number of shares, you have, by the action of those who above all others can best estimate it, ascertained the true value of the road, all its property, its capital stock, and its franchises; for these are all represented by the value of its bonded debt and of the shares of its capital stock.'

"He added that this would be perhaps the fairest basis of taxation for the State at large, if all railroads were solvent and paid the interest promptly on their funded debt; but that this was not the case. The system adopted by the statute of Illinois and the rule of the board preserved the principle of taxing all the tangible property at its value, and then taxing the capital stock and franchise at their value, if there was any, after deducting the value of the tangible property. (State Railroad Tax Cases, 92 U. S. 575, 23 L. Ed. 663.)

"(b) By considering one or more of several elements, or evidences of value, as: the cost of construction or equipment, the market value of the outstanding securities, the gross earnings and the net earnings, and all other matters appertaining thereto. (Pittsburgh etc. Ry. Co. v. Backus (Indiana Railroad Cases), 154 U. S. 421 and 439, 38 L. Ed. 1031, 14 Sup. Ct. Rep. 1114.)

"5. The court has recognized the fact that the value of property of this class depends largely on the earnings. In some of the deci-

sions already referred to this is made clear. Thus in the Indiana Railroad Tax Cases (p. 445) it was said:

" 'The rule of property taxation is that the value of the property is the basis of taxation. It does not mean a tax upon the earnings which the property makes, nor for the privilege of using the property, but rests solely upon the value. But the value of property results from the use to which it is put and varies with the profitableness of that use, present and prospective, actual and anticipated. There is no pecuniary value outside of that which results from such use. The amount and profitable character of such use determines the value, and if property is taxed at its actual cash value, it is taxed upon something which is created by the uses to which it is put. In the nature of things it is practically impossible—at least in respect to railroad property—to divide its value, and determine how much is caused by one use to which it is put and how much by another. Take the case before us; it is impossible to disintegrate the value of that portion of the road within Indiana and determine how much of that value springs from its use in doing interstate business, and how much from its use in doing business wholly within the State. An attempt to do so would be entering upon a mere field of uncertainty and speculation. And because of this fact it is something which an assessing board is not required to attempt.'

"B. As to the taxation of carriers or of interstate business by methods other than the property or ad valorem tax:

"1. A State may not levy a license tax as a prerequisite in carrying on interstate business.

"In Osborne v. Mobile, 16 Wall. (U. S.) 479, 21 L. Ed. 470, decided in 1872, the Supreme Court decided that this could be done. But fifteen years later that case was overruled in Leloup v. Port of Mobile, 127 U. S. 640, 32 L. Ed. 311, 8 Sup. Ct. Rep. 1380. The trenchant part of this decision reads:

" 'A great number and variety of cases involving the commercial power of Congress have been brought to the attention of this court during the past fifteen years which have frequently made it necessary to re-examine the whole subject with care; and the result has sometimes been that in order to give full and fair effect to the different clauses of the Constitution, the court has felt constrained to refer to the fundamental principles stated and illustrated with so much clearness and force by Chief Justice Marshall and other members of the court in former times, and to modify in some degree certain dicta and decisions which have occasionally been made in the intervening period. This is always done, however, with great caution, and an anxious desire to place the final conclusion reached upon the fairest and most just constructions of the Constitution in all its parts.'

"The conclusion was, therefore (l. c., page 648), 'that no state has the right to lay a tax on interstate commerce in any form, whether by way of duties laid on the transportation of the subjects of that commerce, or on the receipts derived from that transportation, or on the occupation or business of carrying it on, and the reason is that such taxation is a burden on that commerce and amounts to a regulation of it, which belongs solely to Congress.' (See, also, Webster

v. Bell, 68 Fed. 183, 15 C. C. A. 360; McCall v. California, 136 U. S. 104, 34 L. Ed. 392, 10 Sup. Ct. Rep. 881; Norfolk and Webster R. Co. v. Pennsylvania, 136 U. S. 114, 34 L. Ed. 394, 10 Sup. Ct. Rep. 958; Crutcher v. Kentucky, 141 U. S. 47, 35 L. Ed. 649, 11 Sup. Ct. Rep. 851.)

"2. A State may levy a license tax on local or interstate business performed by interstate carriers. (Osborne v. Florida, 164 U. S. 650, 41 L. Ed. 586, 17 Sup. Ct. Rep. 214; Postal Telegraph Cable Co. v. Adams, 155 U. S. 688, 39 L. Ed. 311, 15 Sup. Ct. Rep. 268.)

"3. A State may not tax freight, in interstate commerce, nor interstate telegraph messages. (State Freight Tax Case, 15 Wall. 232, 21 L. Ed. 146; Western Union Telegraph Co. v. Texas, 105 U. S. 460, 26 L. Ed. 1067.)

"4. A State may levy a tax in proportion to the gross receipts from interstate commerce under certain conditions and in certain forms. But may not tax the receipts as such.

"The earliest case involving this point seems to be one decided in 1872, at about the same time that the State Freight Tax case, above referred to, was decided. This is known as 'The State Tax on Railway Gross Receipts,' 15 Wall. 284, 21 L. Ed. 164.

"The State of Pennsylvania levied a three-fourths of one per cent tax on the gross earnings of every railroad incorporated under its laws, and the tax was held valid, even when it covered the earnings of a State railroad on coal carried out of the State.

"This case was distinguished from the State Freight Tax case on the ground that not everything which affects commerce amounts to a regulation of it within the meaning of the Constitution.

"The court said, in words that often reappear in the later decisions on the same point, after showing that the states have authority to tax the property, real and personal, of all corporations whether engaged in interstate commerce or not:

" 'We think also that such tax may be laid upon a valuation, or may be an excise, and that in exacting an excise tax from their corporations, the states are not obliged to impose a fixed sum upon the franchises or upon the value of them, but they may demand a graduated contribution, proportioned either to the value of the privileges granted, or to the extent of their exercise, or to the results of such exercise. There certainly is a line which separates that power of the Federal Government to regulate commerce among the states, which is exclusive, from the authority of the states to tax a person's property, business, or occupation, within their limits. The line is sometimes difficult to define with distinctness. It is so in the present case; but we think it may safely be laid down that the gross receipts of railroad or canal companies, after they have reached the treasury of the carriers, though they may have been derived in part from transportation of freight between states, have become subject to legitimate taxation.'

"In commenting on these decisions, Mr. Judson says:

" 'It seems to have been conceded that a State can levy a tax upon net earnings, and the court said that it is difficult to state any well-founded distinction between a State tax upon net earnings and one

upon gross earnings, that net earnings are a part of the gross receipts, and that the gross receipts are a measure of approximate value.

" 'Neither of these cases has been overruled; but the authority of the decision in the case of the State Tax on Gross Receipts was for a time seriously impaired by decisions of the court apparently inconsistent with the broad statement therein of the right to tax gross receipts, on the ground that they have passed into the treasury of the company and lost their distinctive character as freight.' (See Philadelphia & S. M. Steamship Co. v. Pennsylvania, 122 U. S. 326, 30 L. Ed. 1200, 7 Sup. Ct. Rep. 1118; Fargo v. Stevens, 121 U. S. 230, 30 L. Ed. 888, 7 Sup. Ct. Rep. 857.)

" 'It will be noticed that the mileage rule of apportionment of interstate properties was not suggested or considered in the case of the State Tax on Gross Receipts. The case presented was that of a railroad whose line was entirely within the State, but which did an interstate business through its connections with other lines leading out of the State.'

"We come now to a series of cases in which a State tax on gross receipts from interstate trade has been held invalid. The first is Fargo v. Stevens, 121 U. S. 230, 30 L. Ed. 888, 7 Sup. Ct. Rep. 857. The Merchants' Despatch Transportation Company, a New York corporation, owned certain cars which it leased to the railroad companies which operated them. The State of Michigan assessed a tax on the gross receipts of that company in the State measured by the unit rule and based on receipts from the transportation of freight from points without to points within the State and from points within to points without, but did not tax the receipts from business passing entirely through the State. This case was distinguished from the Railway Gross Receipts case (which it did not distinctly overrule) on the grounds (1) that the Merchants' Despatch was not a Michigan corporation, and (2) that in the Pennsylvania case the money was in the treasury of the company in that State, while in the Michigan case the money for the freight was probably never in that State and hence not property subject to taxation.

'In the next term of the court the theory that gross receipts could not be taxed was more fully developed in the case of the Philadelphia & S. M. Steamship Co. v. Pennsylvania, 122 U. S. 326, 30 L. Ed. 1200, 7 Sup. Ct. Rep. 1118. In this case Pennsylvania had attempted to impose a tax on the gross receipts of railroads, canal, steamboat, and other transportation companies. The steamship company in question was a Pennsylvania corporation running steamers between Philadelphia and Savannah and from New Orleans to foreign ports. The court held that interstate commerce carried on by ships at sea is national in character and must be covered by one general rule. The court said:

" 'If, then, the commerce carried on by the plaintiff in error in this case could not be constitutionally taxed by the State, could the fares and freights received for transportation in carrying on that commerce be constitutionally taxed? If the State cannot tax the transportation, may it, nevertheless, tax the fares and freights received therefor? Where is the difference? Looking at the substance of things,

and not at the mere forms, it is very difficult to see any difference. The one thing seems to be tantamount to the other. It would seem to be rather metaphysics than plain logic for the State officials to say to the company: "We will not tax you for the transportation you perform, but we will tax you for what you get for performing it." Such a position can hardly be said to be based on a sound method of reasoning.

" 'No doubt a ship-owner, like any other citizen, may be personally taxed for the amount of his property or estate, without regard to the source from which it was derived, whether from commerce, or banking, or any other employment. But that is an entirely different thing from laying a special tax upon his receipts in a particular employment. If such a tax is laid, and the receipts taxed are those derived from transporting goods and passengers in the way of interstate or foreign commerce, no matter when the tax is exacted, whether at the time of realizing the receipts, or at the end of every six months or a year, it is an exaction aimed at the commerce itself, and is a burden upon it, and seriously affects it. A review of the question convinces us that the first ground on which the decision in State Tax on Railway Gross Receipts was placed is not tenable; that it is not supported by anything decided in Brown v. Maryland; but on the contrary, that the reasoning in that case is decidedly against it.'

"On the basis of these decisions the State courts quite generally held that gross receipts of carriers in interstate commerce could not be taxed.

"But there is another line of decisions which seem to modify the effect of the line running from Fargo v. Michigan without expressly overruling them. These connect with the cases sanctioning the taxation of property. But so far as they affect the question of the actual measurement of a State tax by the gross receipts, including an equitable portion of the receipts from interstate commerce, they are more recent than the other line and have ended in such emphatic reassertion that they seem absolutely conclusive.

"In 1881 Maine inaugurated a tax on each railroad in the State entitled 'an annual excise tax, for the privilege of exercising its franchises, and the franchises of its leased roads in the State.' This tax 'is in place of all taxes upon such railroad, its property and stock.' The amount of this tax was calculated on the basis of the average gross receipts per mile of road. It is important to note that the tax was payable in April and was computed on the basis of gross receipts for the year ending June 30 in the preceding year. The following provisions covered interstate railroads:

" 'When a railroad lies partly within and partly without the State, or is operated as a part of a line or system extending beyond the State, the tax shall be equal to the same proportion of the gross receipts in the State, as herein provided, and its amount shall be determined as follows: the gross transportation receipts of such railroad, line or system, as the case may be, over its whole extent, within and without the State, shall be divided by the total number of miles operated to obtain the average gross receipts per mile, and the gross receipts in the State shall be taken to be the average gross receipts

per mile, multiplied by the number of miles operated within the State.'

"The Grand Trunk Railroad Company, a Canadian corporation, operated a road in Maine, which it leased, and became subject to this tax. The railroad opposed the tax on the ground that the case of the State tax on gross receipts had been overruled in Fargo v. Michigan, and this contention was sustained by the United States court. On appeal to the Supreme Court the decision of the lower court was reversed and the tax was held to be valid. The court said:

" 'The tax, for the collection of which this action is brought, is an excise tax upon the defendant corporation for the privilege of exercising its franchises within the State of Maine. It is so declared in the statute which imposes it; and that a tax of this character is within the power of the State to levy there can be no question. The designation does not always indicate merely an inland imposition o' duty on the consumption of commodities, but often denotes an impost for a license to pursue certain callings, or to deal in special commodities, or to exercise particular franchises. It is used more frequently, in this country, in the latter sense than in any other. The privilege of exercising the franchises of a corporation within a State is generally one of value, and often of great value, and the subject of earnest contention. It is natural, therefore, that the corporation should be made to bear some proportion of the burdens of government. As the granting of the privilege rests entirely in the discretion of the State, whether the corporation be of domestic or foreign origin, it may be conferred upon such conditions, pecuniary or otherwise, as the State in its judgment may deem most conducive to its interests or policy. It may require the payment into its treasury, each year, of a specific sum, or may apportion the amount exacted according to the value of the business permitted, as disclosed by its gains or receipts of the present or past years. The character of the tax, or its valid-ity is not determined by the mode adopted in fixing its amount for any specific period or the times of its payment. The whole field of inquiry into the extent of revenue from sources at the command of the corporation is open to the consideration of the State in determining what may be justly exacted for the privilege. The rule of apportioning the charge to the receipts of the business would seem to be eminently reasonable, and likely to produce the most satisfactory results, both to the State and the corporation taxed.

" 'The court below held that the imposition of the taxes was a regulation of commerce, interstate and foreign, and therefore in conflict with the exclusive power of Congress in that respect; and on that ground alone it ordered judgment for the defendant. This ruling was founded upon the assumption that a reference by the statute to the transportation receipts and to a certain percentage of the same in determining the amount of the excise tax, was in effect the imposition of the tax upon such receipts, and therefore an interference with interstate and foreign commerce. But a resort to those receipts was simply to ascertain the value of the business done by the corporation, and thus obtain a guide to a reasonable conclusion as to the amount of the excise tax which should be levied; and we are unable to perceive in that resort any interference with transportation, domestic

or foreign, over the road of the railroad company, or any regulation of commerce which consists in such transportation. If the amount ascertained were specifically imposed as the tax, no objection to its validity would be pretended. And if the inquiry of the State as to the value of the privilege were limited to receipts of certain past years instead of the year in which the tax is collected, it is conceded that the validity of the tax would not be affected; and if not, we do not see how a reference to the results of any other year could affect its character. There is no levy by the statute on the receipts themselves, either in form or fact; they constitute, as said above, simply the means of ascertaining the value of the privilege conferred.

"'The case of Philadelphia and Southern M. Steamship Co. v. Pennsylvania, 122 U. S. 326, 30 L. Ed. 1200, 7 Sup. Ct. Rep. 1118, in no way conflicts with this decision. That was the case of a tax, in terms, upon the gross receipts of a steamship company, incorporated under the laws of the State, derived from the transportation of persons and property between different states and to and from foreign countries. Such tax was held, without any dissent, to be a regulation of interstate and foreign commerce, and, therefore, invalid. We do not question the correctness of that decision, nor do the views we hold in this case in any way qualify or impair it.' (State of Maine v. Grand Trunk Ry. Co., 142 U. S. 217, 228, 35 L. Ed. 994, 996, 12 Sup. Ct. Rep. 121.)

"From the above decision four justices dissented, which was regarded as slightly impairing its authority. But in New York L. E. & W. R. R. Co. v. Pennsylvania, 158 U. S. 431, 39 L. Ed. 1043, 15 Sup. Ct. Rep. 896, the same principle was reaffirmed. (See, also, Lehigh Valley R. R. Co. v. Pennsylvania, 145 U. S. 192, 36 L. Ed. 672, 12 Sup. Ct. Rep. 806; Western Union Telegraph Co. v. Taggart, 163 U. S. 1, 41 L. Ed. 49, 16 Sup. Ct. Rep. 1054.)

"The most recent case on the subject is Wisconsin & Michigan Ry. Co. v. Powers, 191 U. S. 379, 48 L. Ed. 229, 24 Sup. Ct. Rep. 107.

"The right of the State to levy a tax on the gross earnings of an interstate carrier was involved in this case, together with one other point not connected with our question.

"On the point in which we are interested the court said:

"'We need say but a word in answer to the suggestion that the tax is an unconstitutional interference with interstate commerce. In form the tax is a tax on "the property and business of such railroad corporation operated within the State," computed upon certain percentages of gross income. The prima facie measure of the plaintiffs gross income is substantially that which was approved in Maine v. Grand Trunk Railway Co., 142 U. S. 217, 228, 35 L. Ed. 994, 996, 12 Sup. Ct. Rep. 121. See, also, Western Union Telegraph Co. v. Taggart, 163 U. S. 1, 41 L. Ed. 49, 16 Sup. Ct. Rep. 1054. Decree affirmed.'

"This was a unanimous decision, except that Mr. Justice White, not having heard the argument, took no part in the decision. He concurred, however, in the decision in Erie Railroad v. Pennsylvania, a case involving the same points.

"It appears, then, that a State tax on the property, or on the franchise, measured by the gross receipts is valid and is not a 'regulation

of interstate commerce,' in the sense in which the right to regulate commerce is prohibited to the states by the Constitution."

NATIONAL BANKS.—In regard to the taxation of national banks and the extent of the power of the state in that regard, the report contained the following:

Points decided by the courts in interpretation of section 5219 of the Revised Statutes, and bearing on the amendment proposed by the Commission.

In general.

The power of the state to tax national banks rests solely upon the permission of Congress. Congress has provided the method in which this power may be exercised, and no other method is legal.

U. S. Revised Statutes, sec. 5219: "Nothing herein shall prevent all the shares in any association from being included in the valuation of the personal property of the owner or holder of such shares, in assessing taxes imposed by the authority of the state in which the association is located; but the legislature of each state may determine and direct the manner and place of taxing all shares of national banking associations located within the state, subject only to the two restrictions, that the taxation shall not be at a greater rate than is assessed upon other moneyed capital in the hands of individual citizens of such state, and that the shares of any national banking association owned by nonresidents of any state shall be taxed in the city or town where the bank is located, and not elsewhere. Nothing herein shall be construed to exempt the real property of associations from either state, county, or municipal taxes to the same extent, according to its value as other real property is taxed."

This provision has been interpreted, (1) By definition of the terms; (2) By prohibition of certain powers claimed by the states; (3) By granting certain powers to the states.

A. Defining the terms. 1. "Other moneyed capital" positively defined:

(a) "Other moneyed capital" is other taxable moneyed capital. (People v. Commissioners, 4 Wall. 244, 18 L. Ed. 344; Lionberger v. Rowse, 9 Wall. 468, 19 L. Ed. 721.)

(b) If none other is taxable it may be bank shares only. In First Nat. Bank of Wilmington v. Herbert, 44 Fed. 158, it was held that "where the only subjects of taxation were real estate, livestock and bank shares, it was no ground for complaint" that "moneyed capital" other than bank shares was not taxed.

(c) The leading authority on "other moneyed capital" is Mercantile National Bank v. New York, 121 U. S. 138, 30 L. Ed. 895, 7 Sup. Ct. Rep. 826 (affirming 28 Fed. 776).

In this case, confirmed by subsequent cases, the meaning of "other moneyed capital" is restricted to capital competing with national banks. (First Nat. Bank of Garnett v. Ayers, 160 U. S. 660, 40 L. Ed. 573, 16 Sup. Ct. Rep. 412; Talbott v. Board of Commrs. of Silver Bow County, 139 U. S. 438, 35 L. Ed. 210, 11 Sup. Ct. Rep. 594; First National Bank v. Chapman, 173 U. S. 205, 43 L. Ed. 669, 19 Sup. Ct. Rep. 407; First National Bank v. Chehalis County, 166 U. S. 440,

41 L. Ed. 1069, 17 Sup. Ct. Rep. 629; Bank of Commerce v. Seattle, 166 U. S. 463, 41 L. Ed. 1079, 17 Sup. Ct. Rep. 996.)

The definitions in the New York case are:

"Of course it includes shares in national banks; the use of the word 'other' requires that. If bank shares were not moneyed capital, the word 'other' in this connection would be without significance. But 'moneyed capital' does not mean all capital, the value of which is measured in terms of money. In this sense, all kinds of real and personal property would be embraced by it, for they all have an estimated value as the subjects of sale. Neither does it necessarily include all forms of investments in which the interest of the owner is expressed in money. Shares of stock in railroad companies, mining companies, manufacturing companies, and other corporations, are represented by certificates showing that the owner is entitled to an interest, expressed in money value, in the entire capital and property of the corporation, but the property of the corporation which constitutes its invested capital may consist mainly of real and personal property, which, in the hands of individuals, no one would think of calling moneyed capital, and its business may not consist in any kind of dealing in money, or commercial representatives of money. . . .

"The terms of the act of Congress, therefore, include shares of stock or other interests owned by individuals in all enterprises, in which the capital employed in carrying on its business is money, where the object of the business is the making of profit by its use as money. The moneyed capital thus employed is invested for that purpose in securities by way of loan, discount, or otherwise, which are from time to time, according to the rules of the business, reduced again to money and reinvested. It includes money in the hands of individuals employed in a similar way, invested in loans or in securities, for the payment of money, either as an investment of a permanent character, or temporarily with a view to sale or repayment and reinvestment. In this way the moneyed capital in the hands of individuals is distinguished from what is known generally as personal property."

2. "Other moneyed capital" defined by exclusion.

(a) Trust companies under the New York statute were held not to be competing with national banks. (Jenkins v. Neff, 186 U. S. 230, 46 L. Ed. 1140, 22 Sup. Ct. Rep. 905.)

(b) Savings banks held not to be competing with national banks even when lending on personal security. (National Bank of Redemption v. Boston, 125 U. S. 60, 68, 31 L. Ed. 689, 693, 8 Sup. Ct. Rep. 772; Davenport Nat. Bank v. Davenport Bd. of Equalization, 123 U. S. 83, 31 L. Ed. 94, 8 Sup. Ct. Rep. 73.)

(c) Building and Loan Associations, ibid. (Mercantile Nat. Bank v. Hubbard, 98 Fed. 465.)

3. "Taxation shall not be at a greater rate."

(a) Equality requires equality in valuation as well as in rate of taxation.

"This valuation, then, is part of the assessment of taxes. It is a necessary part of every assessment of taxes which is governed by a ratio or percentage. There can be no ratio or percentage without a

valuation. This taxation, says the act, shall not be at a greater rate than is assessed on other moneyed capital. What is it that shall not be greater? The answer is, taxation. In what respect shall it be not greater than the rate assessed upon other capital? We see that Congress had in its mind as assessment, a rate of assessment, and a valuation, and, taking all these together, the taxation on these shares was not to be greater than on other moneyed capital." (People v. Weaver, 100 U. S. 539, l. c., p. 545, 25 L. Ed. 705, 707; Merchants and Manufacturers' Bank v. Pennsylvania, 167 U. S. 461, 42 L. Ed. 236, 17 Sup. Ct. Rep. 829.)

See, also, what has been held to be discriminations and what not, B 6 and C 9.

B. The states may not:

1. Exact a license, or analogous tax. (Second Nat. Bank of Titus-ville (Pa.) v. Caldwell, 13 Fed. 429.)

2. Tax any property of national banks other than real estate. (San Francisco v. Bank, 92 Fed. 273; Rosenblatt v. Johnston, 104 U. S. 462, 26 L. Ed. 832; First Nat. Bank v. San Francisco, 129 Cal. 96, 61 Pac. 778.)

3. Levy a tax on the franchise. (Owensboro Nat. Bank v. Owensboro, 173 U. S. 664, 43 L. Ed. 850, 19 Sup. Ct. Rep. 537.)

4. Tax the capital of the bank in solido against the bank. (Numerous state cases.)

5. Tax the shares of nonresident shareholders elsewhere than in the town or city where the bank is located.

(The real meaning of this has not been brought out in any cases, save that it prohibits the nonresident shareholders' home state from taxing the shares.)

6. Discriminate against national banks in any of the following ways:

(a) By allowing state banks only to deduct capital, etc., invested in exempt securities. (Bradley v. Illinois, 4 Wall. 459, 18 L. Ed. 433.)

(b) By levying a different rate on national banks than on state banks. (Merchants and Manufacturers' Bank v. Pennsylvania, 167 U. S. 461, 42 L. Ed. 236, 17 Sup. Ct. Rep. 829.)

(c) By exempting from local taxation a very material part, relatively, of other moneyed capital in the hands of individual citizens within the same jurisdiction or taxing district. (As railroad and other securities.) (Boyer v. Boyer, 113 U. S. 689, 28 L. Ed. 1089, 5 Sup. Ct. Rep. 706.)

But this has since been modified. (See definitions A 1 c.)

(d) By allowing owners of personal property in general to "swear off" debts from personal property and not extending the same privilege to shareholders in national banks. (People v. Weaver, 100 U. S. 539, 25 L. Ed. 705; Supervisors of Albany Co. v. Stanley, 105 U. S. 305, 26 L. Ed. 1044, 1120; Hills v. Nat. Albany Exchange Bank, 105 U. S. 319, 26 L. Ed. 1052.)

But this has been modified. (See C 9 f.)

(e) By allowing taxpayers in general to deduct their debts from the sum of their credits, moneys at interest, and demands against persons or corporations, and not allowing same from national bank

shares. (Whitbeck v. Mercantile Nat. Bank, 127 U. S. 193, 32 L. Ed. 118, 8 Sup. Ct. Rep. 1121; Evansville Nat. Bank v. Britton, 105 U. S. 322, 26 L. Ed. 1053.)

But this has been modified. (See C 9 f.)

(f) By intentional and habitual undervaluation of other moneyed capital. (Pelton v. Commercial National Bank, 101 U. S. 143, 25 L. Ed. 901; Whitbeck v. Mercantile National Bank, 127 U. S. 193, 32 L. Ed. 118, 8 Sup. Ct. Rep. 1121.)

But see C 9 j.

C. The states may:

1. Tax the real estate of national banks as other real estate is taxed. (See Revised Statutes, sec. 5219.)

There is no provision in the federal statute that the assessed valuation of the real estate must be deducted from the capital in determining the value of the shares, but if such deduction is allowed in any other cases, as of other corporations, it must be allowed to national banks. (City Nat. Bank v. Paducah, 2 Flip. 61, 1 Thomp. Nat. Bank Cas. 300, Fed. Cas. No. 2743.)

This view is generally held by state courts, but based on state statutes.

The federal courts have held that if the state allows double taxation of other moneyed capital invested in corporate shares, by the taxation of both the shares and the property, the national bank act does not prohibit the same thing in the case of national banks. (People's Nat. Bank v. Marye, 107 Fed. 570.)

2. Tax the shareholders on the value of the shares, subject to conditions imposed. 'See statute.

3. Require the bank to pay the taxes levied on shareholders, as agent for shareholders. (First Nat. Bank v. Commonwealth, 9 Wall. 353, 19 L. Ed. 701.)

4. Collect taxes levied on shares by distraint. (First Nat. Bank of Omaha v. Douglas County, 3 Dill. 298, Fed. Cas. No. 4809.)

Also enforce other pains and penalties for nonpayment. (Palmer v. McMahon, 133 U. S. 660, 33 L. Ed. 772, 10 Sup. Ct. Rep. 324.)

5. Require the bank to pay the taxes levied on shareholders, even though state banks are not required to do so. (Merchants & Manufacturers' Bank of Pennsylvania, 167 U. S. 461, 42 L. Ed. 236, 17 Sup. Ct. Rep. 829.)

6. Assess the shares at their fair cash value on the assumption that the bank will continue its business, and not at what they would be worth in case the bank should be wound up. (Nat. Bank of Commerce v. New Bedford, 155 Mass. 313, 29 N. E. 532.)

In Hepburn v. School Directors, 23 Wall. 480, 23 L. Ed. 112, the supreme court held that the par value of the stock does not indicate its value.

7. In the valuation of the shares, ignore the fact that the capital or surplus is invested in property itself exempt, even if in United States bonds. (Talbott v. Board of Commrs. of Silver Bow County, 139 U. S. 438, 35 L. Ed. 210, 11 Sup. Ct. Rep. 594.)

This principle extends to holding of bonds or stocks taxed in the state. (Pacific Nat. Bank of Tacoma v. Pierce Co., 20 Wash. 675, 56 Pac. 936.)

8. Include in the valuation of the shares, real estate located in other states and taxed there. (Commercial Nat. Bank v. Chambers, 182 U. S. 556, 45 L. Ed. 1227, 21 Sup. Ct. Rep. 863; American Coal Co. v. Allegany County Commissioners, 59 Md. 185, 194.)

Real estate within the state and taxed there must be deducted.

9. The following provisions of law have been held to make no discrimination against national banks.

(a) Exempting property held for charitable or religious uses.

(b) Exempting mortgages, judgments, recognizances, and money owing on agreements to sell real estate.

In Hepburn v. School Directors, 23 Wall. 480, 23 L. Ed. 112, the court said: "This is a partial exemption only. It was evidently intended to prevent a double burden by the taxation both of property and debts secured upon it. Necessarily there may be other moneyed capital, as such is not exempt. Some part of it only is. It could not have been the intention of Congress to exempt bank shares from taxation because some moneyed capital was exempt."

This was modified in Boyer v. Boyer, 113 U. S. 689, 28 L. Ed. 1089, 5 Sup. Ct. Rep. 706. See under discriminations prohibited, B 6 e, above.

(c) Exempting shares of either railroad, business, insurance or mining companies. (Mercantile Nat. Bank v. New York, 121 U. S. 138, 30 L. Ed. 895, 7 Sup. Ct. Rep. 826.)

(d) Exempting municipal bonds. (Case last above cited.)

(e) Exempting stocks of corporations organized under laws of other states. (National Newark Banking Co. v. Newark, 121 U. S. 163, 30 L. Ed. 904, 7 Sup. Ct. Rep. 839.)

(f) Allowing deductions of debts from solvent credits when the shares of state banks were taxed precisely as were shares in national banks. (First Nat. Bank of Wilmington v. Chapman, 173 U. S. 205, 43 L. Ed. 669, 19 Sup, Ct. Rep. 407.)

(g) Allowing unincorporated banks to deduct debts before determining the real value of capital employed. (Case last above cited.)

(h) Failure to assess other moneyed capital. (First National Bank v. Chehalis County, 166 U. S. 440, 41 L. Ed. 1069, 17 Sup. Ct. Rep. 629.)

(This seems contrary to the spirit of the decision in San Francisco Nat. Bank v. Dodge.)

(i) A difference in the rate of taxation, provided state banks and "competing moneyed capital" are treated in the same way. (Merchants' and Manufacturers' Bank v. Pennsylvania, 167 U. S. 461, 42 L. Ed. 236, 17 Sup. Ct. Rep. 829.)

(j) By unintentional differences in valuation or mere mistakes in judgment. (Stanley v. Board of Supervisors of Albany Co., 121 U. S. 535, 30 L. Ed. 1000, 7 Sup. Ct. Rep. 1234; German Nat. Bank v. Kimball, 103 U. S. 732, 26 L. Ed. 469; Exchange Nat. Bank v. Miller, 19 Fed. 372.)

But these rulings are shaken by San Francisco Nat. Bank v. Dodge.

(k) By differences in the violation of different classes of personalty. (Nat. Bank of Baltimore v. Baltimore, 100 Fed. 24, 40 C. C. A. 254.)

ARTICLE XIV.

WATER AND WATER RIGHTS.

Section 1. The use of all water now appropriated, or that may hereafter be appropriated, for sale, rental, or distribution, is hereby declared to be a public use, and subject to the regulation and control of the state, in the manner to be prescribed by law; provided, that the rates or compensation to be collected by any person, company, or corporation in this state for the use of water supplied to any city and county, or city or town, or the inhabitants thereof, shall be fixed, annually, by the board of supervisors, or city and county, or city or town council, or other governing body of such city and county, or city or town, by ordinance or otherwise, in the manner that other ordinances or legislative acts or resolutions are passed by such body, and shall continue in force for one year and no longer. Such ordinances or resolutions shall be passed in the month of February of each year, and take effect on the first day of July thereafter. Any board or body failing to pass the necessary ordinances or resolutions fixing water rates, where necessary, within such time, shall be subject to peremptory process to compel action at the suit of any party interested, and shall be liable to such further processes and penalties as the legislature may prescribe. Any person, company, or corporation collecting water rates in any city and county, or city or town in this state, otherwise than as so established, shall forfeit the franchises and waterworks of such person, company, or corporation to the city and county, or city or town where the same are collected, for the public use.

USE OF WATER.—The provisions of this section are both self-executing and mandatory. (Spring Valley W. W. v. San Francisco Board of Suprs., 61 Cal. 18.)

All the provisions of the Constitution in regard to water in municipalities must be taken and read together, and effect given to each of them. They must receive a practical common-sense construction, and be considered with reference to the prior state of the law, and the mischief intended to be remedied. (People v. Stephens, 62 Cal. 209.)

Constitution—36

Prior to the adoption of the Constitution of 1879, the right of laying pipes in the streets of any incorporated city or town for the purpose of supplying the inhabitants thereof with water lay only in grant from the legislature. (People v. Stephens, 62 Cal. 209.)

This section does not apply to a case of a corporation which acquires and holds water solely for the use of its stockholders. (McFadden v. Board of Suprs. of Los Angeles, 74 Cal. 571, 16 Pac. 397.)

The water right of a corporation which was in private ownership at the time the Constitution of 1879 was adopted did not become dedicated to the public use by the adoption of the Constitution without the consent, express or implied, of its owners. (Stanislaus Water Co. v. Bachman, 152 Cal. 716, 15 L. R. A. (N. S.) 359, 93 Pac. 858.)

This section has no reference to water furnished by a municipality itself, but refers to the rates to be collected for water authorized by section 19, article XI, of the Constitution, to be introduced into cities by individuals or companies incorporated for that purpose. (People v. Stephens, 62 Cal. 209.)

By this section water is declared to be a public use, subject to the control and regulation of the legislature in the manner prescribed by statute; such regulation, however, being subject to certain constitutional provisions, and among them the provision in respect to rates. (People v. Stephens, 62 Cal. 209.)

Under this section the use of water for sale is a public use, and the price at which it shall be sold is a matter within the power of the board of supervisors to determine. (Spring Valley W. W. v. San Francisco, 82 Cal. 286, 16 Am. St. Rep. 116, 6 L. R. A. 756, 22 Pac. 910, 1046; Fellows v. Los Angeles, 151 Cal. 52, 90 Pac. 137.)

This section was not intended to appropriate water for the use of the public without compensation. (People v. Elk River Mill etc. Co., 107 Cal. 221, 48 Am. St. Rep. 125, 40 Pac. 531.)

When water is designated, set apart, and devoted to purposes of sale, rental, or distribution, it is "appropriated" within the meaning of this section, without reference to the mode of its acquisition. (Merrill v. Southside Irr. Co., 112 Cal. 426, 44 Pac. 720.)

A land owner may, by contract with a corporation supplying water for irrigation, acquire and attach to his land a permanent right to the use of water for irrigation. (Stanislaus Water Co. v. Bachman, 152 Cal. 716, 15 L. R. A. (N. S.) 359, 93 Pac. 858.)

A public service water company which is appropriating water for sale, rental and distribution under the Constitution cannot confer upon a consumer any preferential right to the use of any part of its water. (Leavitt v. Lassen Irr. Co., 157 Cal. 82, 29 L. R. A. (N. S.) 213, 106 Pac. 404.)

The statutory provision (Stats. 1881, p. 54) that any person or corporation collecting higher rates for water than those fixed shall upon complaint of any water-rate payer and upon conviction therefor forfeit its franchise and waterworks to the city and county, city or town wherein the water is furnished, is unconstitutional because inconsistent with this section. (Hatfield v. People's Water Co., 25 Cal. App. 502, 144 Pac. 300; Hatfield v. People's Water Co., 25 Cal. App. 711, 145 Pac. 164.)

Under this section and sections 1410–1417, Civil Code, an irrigation company by appropriating water for use on unoccupied public lands, and in advance of the actual construction of works, does not acquire the water right appurtenant to such lands so as to be enabled to charge subsequent settlers for such naked right in addition to rates for the water furnished. (Imperial Water Co. No. 5 v. Holabird, 197 Fed. 4, 116 C. C. A. 526.)

That water appropriated for sale is appropriated to a public use only means that the few within reach of the supply may demand it for a reasonable price. (San Joaquin & K. R. etc. Irr. Co. v. Stanislaus County, 233 U. S. 454, 58 L. Ed. 1041, 34 Sup. Ct. Rep. 652.)

The Constitution does not impress the distribution of appropriated water with a public use. (Niehaus Bros. Co. v. Contra Costa Water Co., 159 Cal. 305, 36 L. R. A. (N. S.) 1045, 113 Pac. 375.)

The use of all water appropriated for sale, rental or distribution is a public use, subject to the regulation and control of the state, and the rates to be collected by any person, company or corporation in this state for the use of water supplied to any city or town, or the inhabitants thereof, must be fixed, annually, by the city or town council or other governing body of such city or town. (Contra Costa Water Co. v. Oakland, 159 Cal. 323, 113 Pac. 668.)

This section applies to cases where one has appropriated water generally, for sale, rental or distribution, and not to cases where sales are made to particular persons at a fixed price by ordinary contracts of purchase and sale. (Thayer v. California Development Co., 164 Cal. 117, 128 Pac. 21.)

When a municipality goes into the business of furnishing its inhabitants with water, itself purchasing water from a water company under a contract and then delivering it through its own system to its inhabitants, the contract price therefor does not constitute the "rates" for the "compensation" subject to the "regulation" mentioned in this section, and the section does not apply to such a municipality. (Marin Water etc. Co. v. Town of Sausalito, 168 Cal. 587, 143 Pac. 767.)

A contract between a municipality owning its own water system and a water company for a bulk supply of water for the use of the municipality and its inhabitants for a period of years is not a violation of this section. (Marin Water etc. Co. v. Town of Sausalito, 168 Cal. 587, 143 Pac. 767.)

A municipality does not violate this section, when it itself furnishes its inhabitants with water, buying the water from a water company under a contract, and agrees to establish for a period of years rates which will produce a sum sufficient to pay for all water furnished by the water company. (Marin Water etc. Co. v. Town of Sausalito, 168 Cal. 587, 143 Pac. 767.)

Under this section it is made the duty of a water company supplying water for distribution to furnish water upon tender of the established rates, and no other duty than such tender can be lawfully prescribed or imposed by such company as a condition for supplying water as required by law. (Crow v. San Joaquin etc. Irr. Co., 130 Cal. 309, 62 Pac. 562, 1058.)

An agreement by a consumer, upon being furnished water upon credit, that no water need be furnished him in succeeding years until

such water is paid for, is without consideration, it being the duty of the company to furnish him the water whether he made such agreement or not. (Crow v. San Joaquin etc. Irr. Co., 130 Cal. 309, 62 Pac. 562, 1058, Beatty, C. J., and McFarland, J., dissenting.)

It is the duty of a water company to furnish water upon tender of the established rates. (Lowe v. Yolo Co. etc. Water Co., 8 Cal. App. 167, 96 Pac. 379.)

The duty to furnish water arises from the Constitution itself (Lowe v. Yolo County etc. Water Co., 8 Cal. App. 167, 96 Pac. 379.)

For failure to deliver water, exemplary damages may be recovered in case of fraud, malice, or oppression. (Lowe v. Yolo County etc. Water Co., 8 Cal. App. 167, 96 Pac. 379.)

It is the duty of a canal company to supply water for irrigation under the following conditions: 1. The land for which water is sought to irrigate must lie within the flow of the ditch; 2. A showing that the corporation has the water in quantity required to supply the one demanding and all others equally entitled: 3. That notice be given the irrigating company of the amount of water required; 4. Payment of the rates or tender thereof when due, and an allegation of willingness to pay when due. (Cozzens v. North Fork Ditch Co., 2 Cal. App. 404, 84 Pac. 342.)

A petition for a writ of mandate to compel the furnishing of water which alleges that the company has a sufficient amount of water to supply plaintiff, but does not allege that the quantity is sufficient for plaintiff and others equally entitled thereto is insufficient. (Cozzens v. North Fork Ditch Co., 2 Cal. App. 404, 84 Pac. 342.)

A petition for mandamus alleging that defendant was incorporated for the purpose, and is engaged in the business of distributing water for compensation to the residents of a certain town, of which petitioner is a resident and freeholder, and has been supplied with water, and the company has a sufficient quantity to supply him, sufficiently shows that defendant is in control of a public use and that plaintiff is a beneficiary of that use. (Mahoney v. American Land etc. Co., 2 Cal. App. 185, 83 Pac. 267.)

A person engaged in furnishing water to the inhabitants of a city under a franchise permitting him to lay pipes through the streets, cannot without reasonable cause shut off the water from one of such inhabitants, who is using the same at a fixed rate. (McCrary v. Beaudry, 67 Cal. 120, 7 Pac. 264.)

It was the duty of the legislature to enact all needful laws to carry this section into effect; but the failure of the legislature to enact such laws could not prevent the establishment of the rates required to be established by the Constitution. (People v. Stephens, 62 Cal. 209.)

The provision of the act of 1858, requiring water companies to furnish water free of charge to cities and counties, was abrogated by this section. (Spring Valley W. W. v. Board of Suprs. of San Francisco, 61 Cal. 18.)

The act of 1858 providing for the fixing of water rates by a commission was superseded by this section of the Constitution. (Spring Valley W. W. v. Board of Suprs. of San Francisco, 61 Cal. 3.)

A water company has the right to shut off the water from a consumer who refuses to pay for the water supplied. (Sheward v. Citizens' Water Co., 90 Cal. 635, 27 Pac. 439.)

It is only the use of water appropriated for sale, rental or distribution which is a public use under this section, and the public use impressed upon any particular water supply may be abandoned. (Escondido Mut. Water Co. v. Escondido, 169 Cal. 772, 147 Pac. 1172.)

The use of water is a public use, and a water corporation having appropriated water for sale, rental and distribution, may be regulated as any other public utility. (In re Application of James A. Murray, 2 C. R. C. 464, 495.)

Sections 1 and 2 deal only with the power of the state to regulate agencies impressed with a public use, which power is entirely independent of the method of acquisition by them of water. (Palmer v. Southern Cal. Mt. Water Co., 2 C. R. C. 43, 54.)

The statutes passed pursuant to this article up to 1909 could not be construed to amount to a contract on the part of the state to waive its admitted right to regulate agencies furnishing water. (In re Application of James A. Murray, 2 C. R. C. 464, 499.)

The delegation of power in this section affects simply the establishment of rates or charges for water, and not adequacy of service or the making of extensions. (Pratt v. Spring Valley Water Co., 4 C. R. C. 1077, 1083.)

Liabilities of water companies. See note, 81 Am. St. Rep. 478.

Liability of water companies to citizens for nonperformance of contracts with municipalities. See note, 18 Am. St. Rep. 380.

Water rates.—By this section the power to fix water rates in San Francisco is granted solely to the board of supervisors, and the mayor has no power to veto an ordinance fixing such rates. (Jacobs v. Board of Supervisors, 100 Cal. 121, 34 Pac. 630.)

The supervisors are not bound to give notice to a water company of its intention to fix water rates; but they must make a proper effort to procure all necessary information, to enable them to act intelligently and fairly in fixing the rates. (Spring Valley W. W. v. San Francisco, 82 Cal. 286, 16 Am. St. Rep. 116, 6 L. R. A. 756, 22 Pac. 910, 1046.)

The proceeding to fix water rates is not adversary, but is conducted without notice to the rate payer or water company. (San Diego Water Co. v. San Diego, 118 Cal. 556, 62 Am. St. Rep. 261, 38 L. R. A. 460, 50 Pac. 633.)

This section is not opposed to the United States Constitution in not giving the water company notice. (San Diego Water Co. v. San Diego, 118 Cal. 556, 62 Am. St. Rep. 261, 38 L. R. A. 460, 50 Pac. 633.)

If the board acts arbitrarily, without investigation, or without the exercise of judgment and discretion, or fixes rates so palpably unreasonable and unjust as to amount to arbitrary action, it violates its duty and goes beyond the powers conferred upon it. (San Diego Water Co. v. San Diego, 118 Cal. 556, 62 Am. St. Rep. 261, 38 L. R. A. 460, 50 Pac. 633.)

Where an ordinance fixing rates does not show upon its face that the rates to be collected, where the amount of consumption is ascer-

tained by a meter, are different from those collected from persons who are rated by the use to which they apply the water, it will not be held invalid because that may be the result. (Sheward v. Citizens' Water Co., 90 Cal. 635, 27 Pac. 439.)

The action of the city council in fixing rates is legislative and it is to receive all the presumptions and sanctions which belong to acts of legislative bodies generally; and the rates must be assumed to have been so fixed as to be just both toward the rate payer and the company. (Sheward v. Citizens' Water Co., 90 Cal. 635, 27 Pac. 439.)

An ordinance fixing water rates, and providing for meter and house rates at the option of the consumer and providing that the meter shall be supplied at the expense of the water company, is valid. (Spring Valley W. W. v. San Francisco, 82 Cal. 286, 16 Am. St. Rep. 116, 6 L. R. A. 756, 22 Pac. 910, 1046.)

When the Constitution provides for the fixing of rates, or compensation for the use of water, it means reasonable rates and just compensation. (Spring Valley W. W. v. San Francisco, 82 Cal. 286, 16 Am. St. Rep. 116, 6 L. R. A. 756, 22 Pac. 910, 1046.)

The power of regulating rates is not a power of confiscation, or to take the property of the water company without just compensation; and, if the power is arbitrarily exercised, without a fair investigation, and the rates are so fixed as to render it impossible to furnish the water without loss, it is not above the control of the courts. (Spring Valley W. W. v. San Francisco, 82 Cal. 286, 16 Am. St. Rep. 116, 6 L. R. A. 756, 22 Pac. 910, 1046.)

If the board have fairly investigated and exercised their discretion in fixing the rates, the courts have no right to interfere on the sole ground that, in the judgment of the court, the rates fixed are not reasonable. (Spring Valley W. W. v. San Francisco, 82 Cal. 286, 16 Am. St. Rep. 116, 6 L. R. A. 756, 22 Pac. 910, 1046.)

The fixing of water rates is not judicial. (Spring Valley W. W. v. Bartlett, 63 Cal. 245.)

An ordinance establishing water rates, and fixing certain rates to be paid by individuals and certain rates to be paid by the city, and providing that, if the city pays its rates, the rates of the individual consumers shall be diminished twenty-five per cent, is void, as the city has no power to make such condition. (San Francisco etc. Factory v. Brickwedel, 60 Cal. 166.)

This section confers upon the cities in this state the power to fix the rates at which water is to be delivered to the inhabitants of a city by any company engaged in that service. (Title Guarantee etc. Co. v. Railroad Commission, 168 Cal. 295, 142 Pac. 878.)

Under this article and the statute of 1885 as amended, passed pursuant thereto, the boards of supervisors were empowered only to fix maximum rates, and until they had fixed such maximum rates the parties were free to contract, and after such maximum rates had been fixed the parties were free to contract within such maximum rates. (In re Application of James A. Murray, 2 C. R. C. 464, 486.)

Even as to a public utility water corporation, the right to fix a rate by contract is subject to the power of the state to substitute a rate fixed by the properly constituted authorities for the rate agreed

upon by contract. (In re Application of James A Murray, 2 C. R. C. 464, 494.)

See further as to water rates, notes to section 33, article IV and section 19, article XI.

Failure to fix rates.—This provision does not authorize the court by mandamus to compel the board to fix the rates, where their action fixing them has been vetoed by the mayor. (Jacobs v. Board of Supervisors, 100 Cal. 121, 34 Pac. 630.)

An ordinance fixing rates passed subsequently to the month of February, and prior to July 1st, when it is required to take effect, is equally valid, if passed voluntarily, as if passed under peremptory process. (Fitch v. Board of Supervisors, 122 Cal. 285, 54 Pac. 901.)

The provision of this section authorizing the legislature to prescribe "further processes and penalties" only authorizes such processes and penalties as are within the power of the legislature, in view of other limitations of the Constitution. (Fitch v. Board of Supervisors, 122 Cal. 285, 54 Pac. 901.)

A taxpayer is not an "interested party" within the meaning of this section. (Fitch v. Board of Supervisors, 122 Cal. 285, 54 Pac. 901.)

In view of section 20, article VI, the legislature cannot authorize the removal of a board of supervisors from office for delay in fixing water rates "at the suit of any interested party," or in the name of any individual. (Fitch v. Board of Supervisors, 122 Cal. 285, 54 Pac. 901.)

Where the owners of water unite in some joint method of distributing the water among them, such as the formation of a corporation, this does not make the water a public use. (Hildreth v. Montecito C. W. Co., 139 Cal. 22, 72 Pac. 395.)

Where the execution of an ordinance fixing water rates has been enjoined, the city may, pending such injunction, enter into an agreement with the water company fixing a price to be paid by the city for water furnished. (Contra Costa W. Co. v. Breed, 139 Cal. 432, 73 Pac. 189.)

The words "otherwise than as so established," mean in violation of or contrary to the established rates. (Contra Costa W. Co. v. Breed, 139 Cal. 432, 73 Pac. 189.)

As to the effect of an injunction forbidding the execution of an ordinance establishing water rates, see Contra Costa W. Co. v. Breed, 139 Cal. 432, 73 Pac. 189.

Sec. 2. The right to collect rates or compensation for the use of water supplied to any county, city and county, or town, or the inhabitants thereof, is a franchise, and cannot be exercised except by authority of and in the manner prescribed by law.

WATER RATES.—The right to collect rates for water is a franchise. (Spring Valley W. W. v. Schottler, 62 Cal. 69; People v. Stephens, 62 Cal. 209; San Joaquin etc. Co. v. Merced County, 2 Cal. App. 593, 84 Pac. 285.)

This section does not take away the right under the general law of the land to collect rates or compensation fixed by contract of the parties for the irrigation of lands, in the absence of a special statute, or authorized provision, regulating such rates. (Fresno Canal etc. Co. v. Park, 129 Cal. 437, 62 Pac. 87; San Diego Flume Co. v. Souther, 104 Fed. 706, 44 C. C. A. 143, on rehearing of 90 Fed. 164, 32 C. C. A. 548.)

Prior to March 23, 1912, the rental and distribution of water outside of municipalities was subject to regulation by county boards of supervisors under provisions of an act passed in 1885, and amended in 1897, pursuant to this section. (In re Application of James A. Murray, 2 C. R. C. 464, 477.)

ARTICLE XV.

HARBOR FRONTAGES, ETC.

Section 1. The right of eminent domain is hereby declared to exist in the state to all frontages on the navigable waters of this state.

Sec. 2. No individual, partnership, or corporation, claiming or possessing the frontage or tidal lands of a harbor, bay, inlet, estuary, or other navigable water in this state, shall be permitted to exclude the right of way to such water whenever it is required for any public purpose, nor to destroy or obstruct the free navigation of such water; and the legislature shall enact such laws as will give the most liberal construction to this provision, so that access to the navigable waters of this state shall be always attainable for the people thereof.

NAVIGABLE WATERS.—If dams upon tide-water sloughs, though the sloughs be not themselves navigable, result in the obstruction of a navigable stream, they constitute a public nuisance, and are forbidden by this section. (People v. Russ, 132 Cal. 102, 64 Pac. 111.)

Rights of the public upon the seashore. See note, 16 Am. Rep. 51.

What waters are navigable. See note, 126 Am. St. Rep. 710.

TIDE-LANDS.—The provisions of this section are mandatory and prohibitory, and operate as a limitation upon the power of the legislature in the matter of the disposition of tide-lands, and are to be considered as incorporated in any grant or patent of such lands, and as a result the grantee of such lands must leave the navigable waters open for public use. (Forestier v. Johnson, 164 Cal. 24, 127 Pac. 156.)

This section of the present Constitution deprives the legislature of power to dispose of the tide-lands fronting upon navigable water so as to entitle the grantee to destroy or interfere with the public easement for navigation, and it to that extent repeals all laws which theretofore may have purported to authorize such alienation. (People v. California Fish Co., 166 Cal. 576, 138 Pac. 79.)

This section makes the doctrine that the rights of the grantee of tide-lands are subject to the public right of navigation a part of the fundamental law of the state. (People v. Southern Pac. R. R. Co., 166 Cal. 614, 138 Pac. 94, concurring opinion by Beatty, C. J.)

The use of lands fronting on navigable water for wharves, used by a railroad in its own business, is not forbidden by this section. (Vallejo etc. R. R. Co. v. Reed Orchard Co., 169 Cal. 545, 147 Pac. 238.)

Sec. 3. All tide-lands within two miles of any incorporated city or town in this state, and fronting on the waters of any harbor, estuary, bay, or inlet used for the purposes of navigation, shall be withheld from grant or sale to private persons, partnerships, or corporations.

TIDE-LANDS.—The constitutional injunction against the grant or sale of "tide-lands within two miles of any incorporated city or town in this state, and fronting on the waters of any harbor, estuary, bay, or inlet," forbids the legislature from disposing of them in any manner, and the statute of limitations in respect to lands owned by the state is subordinate to this constitutional provision, and is thereby made inapplicable to such lands. (People v. Kerber, 152 Cal. 731, 125 Am. St. Rep. 93, 93 Pac. 878.)

The town of Wilmington as delimited by the act of February 20, 1872, purporting to create and incorporate it, notwithstanding a town government was never organized therein, became and remained an incorporated town from the date of the passage of the act until its repeal on March 12, 1887, within the meaning of this section, and of section 3488 of the Political Code as it existed prior to 1901, excluding from sale all tide-lands or swamp-lands within two miles of any incorporated city or town. (People v. California Fish Co., 166 Cal. 576, 138 Pac. 79.)

The legislature can lease reclaimed tide-lands or ratify a city lease of them. (San Pedro etc. R. R. Co. v. Hamilton, 161 Cal. 610, 37 L. R. A. (N. S.) 686, 119 Pac. 1073.)

The words "tide-lands" are to be construed to embrace lands properly described as submerged lands, and will be so construed to protect the harbors of cities and towns from falling into private monopolistic ownership. (San Pedro etc. R. R. Co. v. Hamilton, 161 Cal. 610, 616, 37 L. R. A. (N. S.) 686, 119 Pac. 1073.)

The words "grant and sale" convey the idea of parting with the fee for a monetary or other consideration, and do not embrace the concept of a lease. (San Pedro etc. R. R. Co. v. Hamilton, 161 Cal. 610, 37 L. R. A. (N. S.) 686, 119 Pac. 1073.)

This section does not prohibit the grant by the state of tide-lands to municipal corporations, and such a grant must be deemed to be within the general powers of the legislature. (Cimpher v. City of Oakland, 162 Cal. 87, 121 Pac. 374.)

Title to lands covered by navigable waters. See note, 53 Am. St. Rep. 289.

ARTICLE XVI.

STATE INDEBTEDNESS.

Section 1. The legislature shall not, in any manner create any debt or debts, liability or liabilities, which shall, singly or in the aggregate with any previous debts or liabilities, exceed the sum of three hundred thousand dollars, except in case of war to repel invasion or suppress insurrection, unless the same shall be authorized by law for some single object or work to be distinctly specified therein which law shall provide ways and means, exclusive of loans, for the payment of the interest of such debt or liability as it falls due, and also to pay and discharge the principal of such debt or liability within seventy-five years of the time of the contracting thereof, and shall be irrepealable until the principal and interest thereon shall be paid and discharged, and such law may make provision for a sinking fund to pay the principal of such debt or liability to commence at a time after the incurring of such debt or liability of not more than a period of one-fourth of the time of maturity of such debt or liability; but no such law shall take effect until, at a general election, it shall have been submitted to the people and shall have received a majority of all the votes cast for and against it at such election; and all moneys raised by authority of such law shall be applied only to the specific object therein stated or to the payment of the debt thereby created, and such law shall be published in at least one newspaper in each county, or city and county, if one be published therein throughout the state for three months next preceding the election at which it is submitted to the people. The legislature may, at any time after the approval of such law by the people, if no debt shall have been contracted in pursuance thereof, repeal the same. (Amendment adopted November 3, 1908.)

[ORIGINAL SECTION.]

Section 1. The legislature shall not, in any manner, create any debt or debts, liability or liabilities, which shall, singly or in the aggregate with any previous debts or liabilities, exceed the sum

of three hundred thousand dollars, except in case of war to repel invasion or suppress insurrection, unless the same shall be authorized by law for some single object or work to be distinctly specified therein, which law shall provide ways and means, exclusive of loans, for the payment of the interest of such debt or liability as it falls due, and also to pay and discharge the principal of such debt or liability within twenty years of the time of the contracting thereof, and shall be irrepealable until the principal and interest thereon shall be paid and discharged; but no such law shall take effect until, at a general election, it shall have been submitted to the people and shall have received a majority of all the votes cast for and against it at such election; and all moneys raised by authority of such law shall be applied only to the specific object therein stated, or to the payment of the debt thereby created and such law shall be published in at least one newspaper in each county, or city and county, if one be published therein, throughout the state, for three months next preceding the election at which it is submitted to the people. The legislature may at any time after the approval of such law by the people, if no debt shall have been contracted in pursuance thereof, repeal the same.

STATE INDEBTEDNESS.—The political department of the state government is the sole judge of the existence of war or insurrection. (Franklin v. State Board of Examiners, 23 Cal. 173; People v. Pacheco, 27 Cal. 175.)

An appropriation for the purpose of repelling an invasion or suppressing insurrection, reciting the existence of such war, is conclusive evidence of its existence. (People v. Pacheco, 27 Cal. 175; Reis v. State, 133 Cal. 593, 65 Pac. 1102.)

The Constitution does not impose any limitation upon the amount of state indebtedness in case of war, to repel invasion or suppress insurrection. (Franklin v. State Board of Examiners, 23 Cal. 173.)

This section was intended to prevent the state from running into debt, and to keep her expenditures, except in certain cases, within her revenues. These revenues may be appropriated in anticipation of their receipt as effectually as when actually in the treasury. The appropriation of the moneys when received meets the services as they are rendered, thus discharging the liabilities as they arise, or rather anticipating and preventing their existence. (State v. McCauley, 15 Cal. 429.)

This provision is an express restriction upon the power of the legislature, and there is no power in the judiciary to set it aside, whatever inconvenience may result from the legitimate application of it. It is not simply advisory to the legislature, but is mandatory. (Nougues v. Douglass, 7 Cal. 65.)

It includes the necessary and ordinary expenses of the state, and includes an expenditure for the erection of a state capitol. (Nougues v. Douglass, 7 Cal. 65.)

This provision expressly prohibits the legislature from creating a debt in any case which shall, in the aggregate with previous debts and liabilities of the state, exceed the sum of three hundred thousand

dollars, except for the purposes and in the manner herein provided. (People v. Johnson, 6 Cal. 499.)

This provision is not limited to the power to borrow money, but includes all kinds of indebtedness and an indebtedness for constructing a road. (People v. Johnson, 6 Cal. 499.)

It does not apply to counties or municipal corporations. (Pattison v. Board of Suprs. of Yuba County, 13 Cal. 175.)

This provision distinguished from the provision of the charter of San Francisco in Argenti v. San Francisco, 16 Cal. 255.

The act creating the board of state prison commissioners is not in violation of this section, since the sums to be paid were to be paid in the future, and upon the performance of future services, and until such services were performed there was no debt against the state. (State v. McCauley, 15 Cal. 429; People v. Brooks, 16 Cal. 11.)

An act providing for the construction of a state capitol, and only authorizing the commissioners to contract for one hundred thousand dollars is not in violation of this section. (Koppikus v. State Capitol Commrs., 16 Cal. 248.)

An act which appropriates a sum of money for the future and directs certain payments to be made out of the same at designated periods, from year to year, and which imposes a special tax to meet the same as they become payable, is valid. (People v. Pacheco, 27 Cal. 175.)

Indebtedness which has been authorized by the people, debts actually paid, and current liabilities of the state for which provision is made by appropriation from current revenue, cannot be considered in determining whether the legislature has exceeded the constitutional limitation. (Bickerdike v. State, 144 Cal. 681, 78 Pac. 270.)

The coyote bounty act did not create any debt within the meaning of this section. (Bickerdike v. State, 144 Cal. 681, 78 Pac. 270.)

Publication of act.—In the absence of a provision in the "San Francisco sea-wall act," for the publication required by this section, the duty to provide for the publication devolved upon the governor. (Spear v. Reeves, 148 Cal. 501, 83 Pac. 432.)

In discharging the duty of making the publication required by this section, it was not necessary for the governor to act personally; but it was sufficient that he directed the secretary of state to make it. (Spear v. Reeves, 148 Cal. 501, 83 Pac. 432.)

It is not necessary that the act as published should be officially attested. (Spear v. Reeves, 148 Cal. 501, 83 Pac. 432.)

ARTICLE XVII.

LAND AND HOMESTEAD EXEMPTION.

§ 1. Homesteads.
§ 2. Land monopoly.
§ 3. Lands granted only to actual settlers.

Homesteads.

Section 1. The legislature shall protect, by law, from forced sale a certain portion of the homestead and other property of all heads of families.

HOMESTEAD.—The word "homestead" is here used in the popular sense, and represents the dwelling-house at which the family resides, with the usual appurtenances, including outbuildings of every kind necessary and convenient for family use, and land used for the purposes thereof. (Gregg v. Bostwick, 33 Cal. 220, 91 Am. Dec. 637.)

This section does not of itself create, nor does it vest, homestead rights in persons falling within the general description. It is merely directory. An act making the failure to file a declaration of homestead a forfeiture of the homestead right is valid. (Noble v. Hook, 24 Cal. 638.)

The Constitution contemplates legislation to exempt the homestead from forced sale, but not to restrain voluntary alienation. (Gee v. Moore, 14 Cal. 472.)

This provision is inoperative in itself, and looks to legislation to determine how far and in what manner the homestead shall be protected from forced sale. (Carey v. Tice, 6 Cal. 625.)

It looks to the legislature to fix the extent of the right and the mode of its protection, with the limitation of the rights of creditors therein. (Beaton v. Reid, 111 Cal. 484, 44 Pac. 167.)

This provision does not restrict the power of the legislature to give homesteads to heads of families only. (Hohn v. Pauly, 11 Cal. App. 724, 106 Pac. 266.)

The Constitution is based upon the idea that the homestead is to be carved out of the property of the husband, or at least out of the common property. (Gee v. Moore, 14 Cal. 472.)

If in the country, the homestead may include a garden or farm; if in a town or city, it may include one or more lots or blocks. It need not be compact in form, and is not measured by fences merely. The only tests are use and value. (Gregg v. Bostwick, 33 Cal. 220, 91 Am. Dec. 637.)

Statutes for the purpose of carrying out the constitutional command as to the preservation of the homestead for the family are remedial, and should be liberally, or at least fairly and reasonably, and not strictly, construed. (Southwick v. Davis, 78 Cal. 504, 21 Pac. 121.)

As to what constitutes a homestead, see Estate of Gallagher, 134 Cal. 96, 66 Pac. 70.

What may be exempt as homestead. See note, 70 Am. Dec. 344.

Who is head of family and what constitutes a family. See notes, 61 Am. Dec. 586; 70 Am. St. Rep. 107.

For what claims and credits homestead is liable. See note, 45 Am. St. Rep. 383.

Homestead exemptions as extending to premises used for hotel or lodging-house. See note Ann. Cas. 1913E, 1256.

Land monopoly.

Sec. 2. The holding of large tracts of land, unculti-vated and unimproved, by individuals or corporations, is against the public interest, and should be discouraged by all means not inconsistent with the rights of private property.

TRACTS OF LAND.—This section declares a policy against the holding of large tracts of land uncultivated, and this policy should not be limited by a narrow construction of the Constitution. (Fulton v. Brannan, 88 Cal. 454, 26 Pac. 506.)

Lands granted only to actual settlers.

Sec. 3. Lands belonging to this state, which are suit-able for cultivation, shall be granted only to actual set-tlers, and in quantities not exceeding three hundred and twenty acres to each settler, under such conditions as shall be prescribed by law.

PUBLIC LANDS.—The provision of this section that "lands be-longing to the state which are suitable for cultivation, shall be granted only to actual settlers" operates on applications made before as well as those made after the Constitution took effect. (Johnson v. Squires, 55 Cal. 103; Mosely v. Torrence, 71 Cal. 318, 12 Pac. 430.)

This section speaks with reference to the condition of the land at the initiation of proceedings for purchase. (Boggs v. Ganeard, 148 Cal. 711, 84 Pac. 195.)

An application to purchase state lands made by one not an actual settler, before the adoption of the new Constitution, and who had made no payments thereon, conferred no right to purchase such lands after the adoption of the Constitution. (Urton v. Wilson, 65 Cal. 11, 2 Pac. 411.)

A certificate of purchase, obtained before the adoption of the new Constitution, is not impaired by this section. (Miller v. Byrd, 90 Cal. 150, 27 Pac. 51.)

"Suitable for cultivation."—The phrase, "lands belonging to the state which are suitable for cultivation," includes all of its lands which are ready for occupation, and which, by ordinary farming pro-cesses, are fit for agricultural purposes. Thus swamp-lands may be suitable for cultivation. (Fulton v. Brannan, 88 Cal. 454, 26 Pac.

506; Goldberg v. Thompson, 96 Cal. 117, 30 Pac. 1019; McNee v. Lynch, 88 Cal. 519, 26 Pac. 508; McDonald v. Taylor, 89 Cal. 42, 26 Pac. 595; Belcher v. Farren, 89 Cal. 73, 26 Pac. 791; Dewar v. Ruiz, 89 Cal. 385, 26 Pac. 832; Manley v. Cunningham, 72 Cal. 236, 13 Pac. 622.)

The words "suitable for cultivation" mean all lands ready for occupation and which by ordinary farm processes are fit for agricultural purposes. (Robinson v. Eberhart, 148 Cal. 495, 83 Pac. 452.)

It is a question of fact whether state land is suitable or unsuitable for cultivation. (Robinson v. Eberhart, 148 Cal. 495, 83 Pac. 452.)

Desert land is not suitable for cultivation, although it might be developed by boring artesian wells. (Robinson v. Eberhart, 148 Cal. 495, 83 Pac. 452.)

The fact that the land is in most places heavily covered with redwood timber and brush, that it would not, when cleared, produce ordinary agricultural crops in average quantities, and that it is more valuable for timber than for agriculture, does not render it unsuitable for cultivation. (Jacobs v. Walker, 90 Cal. 43, 27 Pac. 48.)

Where some portion of each subdivision is suitable for cultivation, the land cannot be purchased by one not a settler. (Sanford v. Maxwell, 3 Cal. App. 242, 84 Pac. 1000.)

The definition of lands suitable for cultivation contained in section 3495 of the Political Code cannot be deemed to be exclusive, as that would render the section unconstitutional. (Sanford v. Maxwell, 3 Cal. App. 242, 84 Pac. 1000.)

A tract of land one-third of which as a whole is suitable for cultivation can only be sold to an actual settler. (Sanford v. Maxwell, 3 Cal. App. 242, 84 Pac. 1000.)

The words "suitable for cultivation" mean all tracts of land on which there is arable or tillable land sufficient, with the use of other lands for pasture or otherwise, to furnish a permanent support for the settler. (Sanford v. Maxwell, 2 Cal. App. 242, 84 Pac. 1000.)

Actual settlers.—An actual settler is one who establishes himself upon the land, or fixes his residence upon it, to take possession for his exclusive occupancy and use, with a view of acquiring title to it by purchase from the state. (Gavitt v. Mohr, 68 Cal. 506, 10 Pac. 337.)

Under this section a claimant to purchase state lands which are suitable for cultivation must be at the time of his application an actual settler thereon. (Gavitt v. Mohr, 68 Cal. 506, 10 Pac. 337.)

The fact that an applicant living upon swamp-land suitable for cultivation removed his family therefrom temporarily, because of ill health of a member of his family, does not show nor tend to show that he was not an actual settler. (Maddux v. Brown, 91 Cal. 523, 27 Pac. 771.)

Intervention.—An actual settler has a right to intervene in a contest of the right to purchase before, but not after, judgment. (Smith v. Roberts, 1 Cal. App. 148, 81 Pac. 1026.)

A person who has made application to purchase land, and whose application has been rejected, cannot intervene in a contest between other claimants and raise the point that the parties had agreed to divide the land in order to evade the provision of this section. (Youle v. Thomas, 146 Cal. 537, 80 Pac. 714.)

ARTICLE XVIII.
AMENDING AND REVISING THE CONSTITUTION.

§ 1.   Proposal of amendments—Submission to vote.
§ 2.   Revision—Convention for.

Proposal of amendments—Submission to vote.

Section 1.   Any amendment or amendments to this Constitution may be proposed in the senate or assembly, and if two-thirds of all the members elected to each of the two houses shall vote in favor thereof, such proposed amendment or amendments shall be entered in their journals, with the yeas and nays taken thereon; and it shall be the duty of the legislature to submit such proposed amendment or amendments to the people in such manner, and at such time, and after such publication, as may be deemed expedient. Should more amendments than one be submitted at the same election they shall be so prepared and distinguished, by numbers or otherwise, that each can be voted on separately. If the people shall approve and ratify such amendment or amendments, or any of them, by a majority of the qualified electors voting thereon, such amendment or amendments shall become a part of this Constitution.

CONSTITUTIONAL AMENDMENTS.—A general act as to the submission of constitutional amendments is valid; and it is not necessary that an amendment be submitted specially by the legislature proposing it. (Martin v. Board of Election Commrs., 126 Cal. 404, 58 Pac. 932.)

When the Political Code provides for the certification of proposed constitutional amendments by the secretary of state to the county clerks "not less than twenty-five days before election," and provides for the printing of such amendments upon the ballots, it is to be presumed that they are to be voted upon at the next general election after the proposal of the amendment, and this section is sufficiently complied with. (People v. Curry, 130 Cal. 82, 62 Pac. 516, Temple, J., and Harrison J., dissenting.)

The Constitution does not permit the legislature to propose an amendment that will not upon its adoption by the people become an effective part of the Constitution; nor one which, if ratified will take effect only at the will of other persons, or upon the approval of such other persons, or on some specified act or condition. (Livermore v. Waite, 102 Cal. 113, 25 L. R. A. 312, 36 Pac. 424.)

The Constitution can neither be revised nor amended, except in the manner prescribed by itself, and the power conferred upon the legisla-

ture by this section must be strictly construed. (Livermore v. Waite, 102 Cal. 113, 25 L. R. A. 312, 36 Pac. 424.)

The time at which a proposed amendment to the Constitution is to be submitted to the people for ratification must be fixed by an act of the legislature, approved by the governor in the same manner as other acts. (Hatch v. Stoneman, 66 Cal. 632, 6 Pac. 734.)

An amendment need not be entered in the journals at length, but it is sufficient if entered by identifying reference to the title of the amendment. (Thomason v. Ruggles, 69 Cal. 465, 11 Pac. 20; Oakland Pav. Co. v. Tompkins, 72 Cal. 5, 1 Am. St. Rep. 17, 12 Pac. 801; Thomason v. Ashworth, 73 Cal. 73, 14 Pac. 615. But see Oakland Pav. Co. v. Hilton, 69 Cal. 479, 11 Pac. 3.)

The certificate of the secretary of state showing the adoption of an amendment to the Constitution is conclusive of the fact that the same has been duly ratified. (Kingsbury v. Nye, 9 Cal. App. 574, 99 Pac. 985.)

> Entry of amendments in journal of the legislature. See notes, 1 Am. St. Rep. 21; 6 R. C. L., § 20, p. 29.
>
> Mode of entering proposed constitutional amendments on legislative journals. See note, 3 Ann. Cas. 756.
>
> Necessity of approval by executive of proposed constitutional amendment. See notes, 4 Ann. Cas. 703; 6 R. C. L., § 21, p. 29.
>
> Provision of Constitution for amendment thereof as mandatory or directory. See note, 15 Ann. Cas. 786.

Revision—Convention for.

Sec. 2. Whenever two-thirds of the members elected to each branch of the legislature shall deem it necessary to revise this Constitution, they shall recommend to the electors to vote at the next general election for or against a convention for that purpose, and if a majority of the electors voting at such election on the proposition for a convention shall vote in favor thereof, the legislature shall, at its next session, provide by law for calling the same. The convention shall consist of a number of delegates not to exceed that of both branches of the legislature, who shall be chosen in the same manner, and have the same qualifications, as members of the legislature. The delegates so elected shall meet within three months after their election at such place as the legislature may direct. At a special election to be provided for by law, the Constitution that may be agreed upon by such convention shall be submitted to the people for their ratification or rejection, in such manner as the convention may determine. The returns of

such election shall, in such manner as the convention shall direct, be certified to the executive of the state, who shall call to his assistance the controller, treasurer, and secretary of state, and compare the returns so certified to him; and it shall be the duty of the executive to declare, by his proclamation, such Constitution, as may have been ratified by a majority of all the votes cast at such special election, to be the Constitution of the state of California.

ARTICLE XIX.

CHINESE.

§ 1. Protection from alien paupers, etc.
§ 2. Corporations prohibited from hiring Chinese.
§ 3. Public works, Chinese not to be employed on.
§ 4. Coolieism prohibited—Removal of Chinese.

Protection from alien paupers, etc.

Section 1. The legislature shall prescribe all necessary regulations for the protection of the state, and the counties, cities, and towns thereof, from the burdens and evils arising from the presence of aliens who are or may become vagrants, paupers, mendicants, criminals, or invalids afflicted with contagious or infectious diseases, and from aliens otherwise dangerous or detrimental to the well-being or peace of the state, and to impose conditions upon which such persons may reside in the state, and to provide the means and mode of their removal from the state, upon failure or refusal to comply with such conditions; provided, that nothing contained in this section shall be construed to impair or limit the power of the legislature to pass such police laws or other regulations as it may deem necessary.

POLICE REGULATIONS.—A state has the power to exclude from its limits paupers, vagabonds, and criminals, or sick, diseased, infirm, and disabled persons, who are liable to become a public charge, or to admit them only on such terms as will prevent the state from being burdened with their support. (State v. Steamship Constitution, 42 Cal. 578, 10 Am. Rep. 303.)

The power to exclude from the limits of a state persons not paupers, etc., is a regulation of commerce, and cannot be exercised by the state. (State v. Steamship Constitution, 42 Cal. 578, 10 Am. Rep. 303.)

An act giving the horticultural commissioners power to abate a nuisance caused by insect pests in orchards, etc., is authorized by this section. (Los Angeles Co. v. Spencer, 126 Cal. 670, 77 Am. St. Rep. 217, 59 Pac. 202; Riverside Co. v. Butcher, 133 Cal. 324, 65 Pac. 745.)

An act requiring all children attending the public schools to be vaccinated is authorized by this section. (Abeel v. Clark, 84 Cal. 226, 24 Pac. 383.)

An act levying upon each person of the Mongolian race a monthly license tax of two dollars and fifty cents for working the mines, or for prosecuting any business, is in violation of the commerce clause

of the United States Constitution. (Lin Sing v. Washburn, 20 Cal. 534.)

An act forbidding the landing of lewd or debauched women within the state is valid. (Ex parte Ah Fook, 49 Cal. 402.)

An act requiring all fruit shipped to be labeled with the locality in which it is grown is not a valid exercise of the power given by this section. (Ex parte Hayden, 147 Cal. 649, 109 Am. St. Rep. 183, 1 L. R. A. (N. S.) 184, 82 Pac. 315.)

Corporations prohibited from hiring Chinese.

Sec. 2. No corporation now existing or hereafter formed under the laws of this state shall, after the adoption of this Constitution, employ, directly or indirectly, in any capacity, any Chinese or Mongolian. The legislature shall pass such laws as may be necessary to enforce this provision.

CHINESE LABOR.—This provision of the Constitution is in conflict with the treaty between the United States and China, and is void. (In re Parrott, 6 Sawy. 349, 1 Fed. 481. See, also, Baker v. City of Portland, 5 Sawy. 566, Fed. Cas. No. 777, 3 Pac. Coast Law J. 469; Chapman v. Toy Long, 4 Sawy. 28, Fed. Cas. No. 2610, 1 Morr. Min. Rep. 497; Ex parte Ah Cue, 101 Cal. 197, 35 Pac. 556.)

Public works, Chinese not to be employed on.

Sec. 3. No Chinese shall be employed on any state, county, municipal, or other public work, except in punishment for crime.

CHINESE EMPLOYMENT.—As to the validity of this provision, see Baker v. City of Portland, 5 Sawy. 566, Fed. Cas. No. 777, 3 Pac. Coast Law J. 469.

Coolieism prohibited—Removal of Chinese.

Sec. 4. The presence of foreigners ineligible to become citizens of the United States is declared to be dangerous to the well-being of the state, and the legislature shall discourage their immigration by all the means within its power. Asiatic coolieism is a form of human slavery, and is forever prohibited in this state, and all contracts for coolie labor shall be void. All companies or corporations, whether formed in this country or any foreign country, for the importation of such labor, shall be subject to such penalties as the legislature may prescribe. The legisla-

ture shall delegate all necessary power to the incorporated cities and towns of this state for the removal of Chinese without the limits of such cities and towns, or for their location within prescribed portions of those limits, and it shall also provide the necessary legislation to prohibit the introduction into this state of Chinese after the adoption of this Constitution. This section shall be enforced by appropriate legislation.

IMMIGRATION. — As to the validity of legislation excluding foreigners, see State v. Steamship Constitution, 42 Cal. 578, 10 Am. Rep. 303; Lin Sing v. Washburn, 20 Cal. 534; Ex parte Ah Fook, 49 Cal. 402; In re Parrott, 6 Sawy. 349, 1 Fed. 481; Baker v. City of Portland, 5 Sawy. 566, Fed. Cas. No. 777, 3 Pac. Coast Law J. 469; Ho Ah Kow v. Nunan, 5 Sawy. 552, Fed. Cas. No 6546, 3 Pac. Coast Law J. 415.

ARTICLE XX.

MISCELLANEOUS SUBJECTS.

Seat of government.

Section 1. The city of Sacramento is hereby declared to be the seat of government of this state, and shall so remain until changed by law; but no law changing the seat of government shall be valid or binding unless the same be approved and ratified by a majority of the qualified electors of the state voting therefor at a general state election, under such regulations and provisions as the legislature, by a two-thirds vote of each house, may provide, submitting the question of change to the people.

SEAT OF GOVERNMENT.—This section is subject to amendment in the same manner as any other part of the Constitution. (Livermore v. Waite, 102 Cal. 113, 25 L. R. A. 312, 36 Pac. 424.)

The proposed constitutional amendment of 1893 to change the seat of government to San Jose was held invalid and ineffective, its operation being limited upon the uncertain conditions of the donation to the state of not less than ten acres of land, and one million dollars in money, and the approval by the governor, secretary of state, and attorney general of the site so donated. (Livermore v. Waite, 102 Cal. 113, 25 L. R. A. 312, 36 Pac. 424.)

An act making Vallejo the permanent seat of government, and providing that one Vallejo should give a bond for the performance of
the proposition which he had submitted to the legislature, and should
provide a statehouse, and failing to do so, "then this act to be void,"
is constitutional, and operated to change the seat of government and
cannot be defeated by the breach of the condition. (People v. Big·
ler, 5 Cal. 23.)

Dueling, disabilities arising from.

Sec. 2. Any citizen of this state who shall, after the
adoption of this Constitution, fight a duel with deadly weapons, or send or accept a challenge to fight a duel with deadly
weapons, either within this state or out of it, or who shall
act as second, or knowingly aid or assist in any manner
those thus offending, shall not be allowed to hold any
office of profit, or to enjoy the right of suffrage under this
Constitution.

Oath of office.

Sec. 3. Members of the legislature, and all officers, executive and judicial, except such inferior officers as may
be by law exempted, shall, before they ·enter upon the
duties of their respective offices, take and subscribe the
following oath or affirmation:

"I do solemnly swear (or affirm, as the case may be),
that I will support the Constitution of the United States
and the Constitution of the state of California, and that I
will faithfully discharge the duties of the office of ——,
according to the best of my ability."

And no other oath, declaration, or test shall be required
as a qualification for any office or public trust.

OATH OF OFFICE.—The terms "office" and "public trust" have relation to such duties and responsibilities as are of a public nature.
(Ex parte Yale, 24 Cal. 241, 85 Am. Dec. 62.)

An attorney at law does not hold an "office" or "public trust" with·
in the meaning of this section. (Ex parte Yale, 24 Cal. 241, 85 Am.
Dec. 62; Cohen v. Wright, 22 Cal. 293.)

This provision does not prohibit the legislature from prescribing
an oath to such officers in a different form of words from that herein
used, if the meaning, object, and intent of the section be not vio·
lated. (Cohen v. Wright, 22 Cal. 293.)

It is competent for the legislature to make the taking of the oath
of office a condition subsequent. (Ball v. Kenfield. 55 Cal. 320.)

The legislature can neither increase nor diminish the qualifications which the Constitution has prescribed for eligibility to any offices created by that instrument, but may prescribe any qualifications for offices created by the legislature. (Sheehan v. Scott, 145 Cal. 684, 79 Pac. 350.)

It is to be presumed that officers will qualify within a reasonable time consistent with their duties. (Brodie v. Campbell, 17 Cal. 11.)

The provisions of the Purity of Election Law requiring a success-ful candidate for office to support his statement of election expenses by his oath as a prerequisite to his right to take office, is in violation of this section, as they impose an oath or test substantially different from that made exclusive by the construction. (Bradley v. Clark, 133 Cal. 196, 65 Pac. 395.)

The requirement of the primary election law that a candidate file with his nomination papers an affidavit as to his party affiliations is not in violation of the section of the Constitution, which applies only to persons who have been elected or appointed to office; it is a reason-able test, authorized by section 2½ of article II. (Socialist Party v. Uhl, 155 Cal. 776, 103 Pac. 181.)

Election and appointment of officers and commissioners.

Sec. 4. All officers or commissioners whose election or appointment is not provided for by this Constitution, and all officers or commissioners whose offices or duties may hereafter be created by law, shall be elected by the people, or appointed, as the legislature may direct.

ELECTION AND APPOINTMENT OF OFFICERS.—This section does not prevent the legislature itself from electing an officer created by it. (People v. Langdon, 8 Cal. 1.)

The words "elect" and "appoint" are used synonymously in the Con-stitution. (People v. Langdon, 8 Cal. 1.)

This section does not authorize the legislature to exercise the power of appointment to office, if that is essentially an executive function, under section 1, article III, of the Constitution. (People v. Freeman, 80 Cal. 233, 13 Am. St. Rep. 122, 22 Pac. 173.)

The Constitution does not prohibit the legislature from conferring on a voluntary association of persons, who are not citizens of the United States, nor electors of the city, the power to elect a person to fill an office created by the legislature. (In re Bulger, 45 Cal. 553.)

The provision of the act regulating the practice of medicine and surgery, that the board of examiners shall be appointed by certain medical societies is authorized by this section. (Ex parte Gerino, 143 Cal. 412, 66 L. R. A. 249, 77 Pac. 166.)

Under this section officers may be appointed by the legislature it-self, or the duty of appointment may be delegated and imposed upon some other person or body. (Ex parte Gerino, 143 Cal. 412, 66 L. R. A. 249, 77 Pac. 166.)

Fiscal year.

Sec. 5. The fiscal year shall commence on the first day of July.

FISCAL YEAR.—The fiscal year ends with the thirtieth day of June. (Rollins v. Wright, 93 Cal. 395, 29 Pac. 58.)

An act legalizing assessments for taxes for the fiscal year ending on the first day of March is not void because the Constitution provides that the fiscal year shall commence on the first day of July, but the word "fiscal" in the act may be treated as surplusage. (People v. Todd, 23 Cal. 181.)

Suits against state.

Sec. 6. Suits may be brought against the state in such manner and in such courts as shall be directed by law.

SUITS AGAINST THE STATE.—Where an action is properly brought against the state the attorney general has power to appear, although the state has not been regularly summoned. (California & Northern Ry. v. State, 1 Cal. App. 142, 81 Pac. 971.)

Even prior to the amendment to section 1240 of the Code of Civil Procedure, a suit might be maintained against the state to condemn lands belonging to it. (California & Northern Ry. v. State, 1 Cal. App. 142, 81 Pac. 971.)

This provision does not extend to suits against municipalities. (Goldtree v. San Diego, 8 Cal. App. 505, 97 Pac. 216.)

Actions against states. See note, 12 Am. Dec. 517.

Marriage contracts, validity of.

Sec. 7. No contract of marriage, if otherwise duly made, shall be invalidated for want of conformity to the requirements of any religious sect.

Separate property of husband and wife.

Sec. 8. All property, real and personal, owned by either husband or wife before marriage, and that acquired by either of them afterward by gift, devise, or descent, shall be their separate property.

SEPARATE PROPERTY.—The word "separate" neither enlarges nor limits her right to the property mentioned, but merely distinguishes it from her common property. (Dow v. Gould & Curry etc. Min. Co., 31 Cal. 629.)

The last clause of the corresponding section of the old Constitution refers only to the disabilities under which the wife labored at common law by reason of coverture. (Dow v. Gould & Curry etc. Min. Co., 31 Cal. 629.)

In the absence of any agreement the husband acquires no interest in the separate property of the wife by bestowing labor upon it. (Lewis v. Johns, 24 Cal. 98, 85 Am. Dec. 49.)

All property which can be shown by satisfactory testimony to belong to the separate estate of the wife, whether real, personal, or mixed, and all the rents, issues and profits thereof, are sacred to the use and enjoyment of the wife, and cannot be held to answer for the debts of the husband. (Lewis v. Johns, 24 Cal. 98, 85 Am. Dec. 49.)

The term "separate property" is used in its common-law sense, and by that law, "separate property" means an estate held, both in its use and title, for the exclusive benefit of the wife. To give the husband or his creditors any claim upon the separate property of the wife is unconstitutional. (George v. Ransom, 15 Cal. 322, 76 Am. Dec. 490.)

An act requiring a deed conveying the separate property of the wife to be signed by the husband is not unconstitutional. (Dow v. Gould & Curry etc. Min. Co., 31 Cal. 629.)

As to whether property devised in pursuance of a contract is separate property, see Bell v. Wyman, 147 Cal. 514, 82 Pac. 39.

What words in a will vest estate in wife as separate property. See note, 39 Am. Dec. 773.

Lands given by the sovereign to either spouse as separate property. See notes, 16 Am. Dec. 186; 96 Am. St. Rep. 916.

Statutes designating separate property of wife. See note, 76 Am. Dec. 366.

Perpetuities not allowed.

Sec. 9.   No perpetuities shall be allowed except for eleemosynary purposes.

PERPETUITIES.—Trusts for perpetual charitable uses are not in conflict with this section. (Estate of Hinckley, 58 Cal. 457.)

The term "eleemosynary" is not confined to almsgiving or charity shown exclusively to the poor but includes all charitable purposes, including schools, as well as asylums, hospitals, and religious institutions. (People v. Cogswell, 113 Cal. 129, 35 L. R. A. 269, 45 Pac. 270.)

A trust for the perpetual care of a burial plot is in violation of this provision. (Estate of Gay, 138 Cal. 552, 94 Am. St. Rep. 70, 71 Pac. 707.)

"Eleemosynary" as used in the Constitution is synonymous with charitable, as the latter word is used and understood in treatises and decisions upon the subject of trusts. (Estate of Sutro, 155 Cal. 727, 102 Pac. 920.)

After the will has been merged in the decree of distribution, it is too late to urge that it creates an illegal perpetuity. (Kauffman v. Foster, 3 Cal. App. 741, 86 Pac. 1108.)

Rule against perpetuities. See note, 49 Am. St. Rep. 117.

Perpetuities which are forbidden in the United States. See note,
90 Am. Dec. 101.

Trust of indefinite duration for maintenance, repair, etc., of resi
dence or homestead as offending against the rule against per
petuities. See note, Ann. Cas. 1914B, 551.

Disqualification for office by giving or taking bribe.

Sec. 10.   Every person shall be disqualified from holding any office of profit in this state who shall have been
convicted of having given or offered a bribe to procure his
election or appointment.

Exclusion from office, jury, and right of suffrage of certain persons—Protection of right of suffrage.

Sec. 11.   Laws shall be made to exclude from office,
serving on juries, and from the right of suffrage, persons
convicted of bribery, perjury, forgery, malfeasance in
office, or other high crimes.   The privilege of free suffrage
shall be supported by laws regulating elections and prohibiting, under adequate penalties, all undue influence thereon
from power, bribery, tumult, or other improper practice.

BRIBERY.—Where a candidate for office publicly pledges himself
before the election to perform the duties of the office for less than
the compensation established by law, and by reason thereof a sufficient number of voters were induced to vote for him to secure him
the election, his election is void. (State v. Collier, 3 Pac. Coast Law
J. 394; State v. Purdy, 36 Wis. 213, 17 Am. Rep. 485.)

A vote given for a public officer, in consideration of his promise,
in case he should be elected, to donate a sum of money, or other valuable thing to a third party, is void. (Tucker v. Aiken, 7 N. H. 113;
Alvord v. Collin, 20 Pick. (Mass.) 418.)

See, further, State v. Dustin, 5 Or. 375, 20 Am. Rep. 746; Commonwealth v. Shaver, 3 Watts & S. (Pa.) 338.

SUFFRAGE.—This section does not authorize the passage of a law
curtailing the privilege of free suffrage. (Spier v. Baker, 120 Cal.
370, 41 L. R. A. 196, 52 Pac. 659.)

What constitutes conviction of crime within constitutional provision denying right to vote to convicted person. See note, 15
Ann. Cas. 103.

Residence, when absence not to affect.

Sec. 12.   Absence from this state, on business of the
state or of the United States, shall not affect the question
of residence of any person.

Plurality vote to elect.

Sec. 13. A plurality of the votes given at any election shall constitute a choice where not otherwise directed in this Constitution, provided that it shall be competent in all charters of cities, counties or cities and counties framed under the authority of this Constitution to provide the manner in which their respective elective officers may be elected and to prescribe a higher proportion of the vote therefor; and provided also, that it shall be competent for the legislature by general law to provide the manner in which officers of municipalities organized or incorporated under general laws may be elected and to prescribe a higher proportion of the vote therefor. (Amendment approved October 10, 1911.)

[ORIGINAL SECTION.]

Sec. 13. A plurality of the votes given at any election shall constitute a choice, where not otherwise directed in this Constitution.

PLURALITY OF VOTES.—If the person receiving the highest number of votes is ineligible, the person receiving the next highest number is not elected, but the election must be annulled. (Campbell v. Free, 7 Cal. App. 151, 93 Pac. 1060.)

In order to be elected a person must receive a plurality of the votes cast. (Campbell v. Free, 7 Cal. App. 151, 93 Pac. 1060; McGregor v. Board of Trustees, 159 Cal. 441, 114 Pac. 566.)

Election of ineligible candidate does not entitle person receiving next highest number of votes to the office. See note, 12 Am. Rep. 341.

Effect of ineligibility of person receiving highest number of votes. See note, 124 Am. St. Rep. 211.

State board of health.

Sec. 14. The legislature shall provide, by law, for the maintenance and efficiency of a state board of health.

Mechanic's lien.

Sec. 15. Mechanics, materialmen, artisans, and laborers of every class, shall have a lien upon the property upon which they have bestowed labor or furnished material for the value of such labor done and material furnished; and the legislature shall provide, by law, for the speedy and efficient enforcement of such liens.

MECHANICS' LIENS.—This section is not self-executing and is inoperative, except as supplemented by legislation. (Spinney v. Griffith, 98 Cal. 149, 32 Pac. 974.)

The Constitution by this section has left to the legislature the duty of providing for the enforcement of these liens. (Morse v. De Ardo, 107 Cal. 622, 40 Pac. 1018.)

This section is self-executing. (Miltimore v. Nofziger Bros. L Co., 150 Cal. 790, 90 Pac. 114.)

The mechanic's lien is created by the Constitution. (Goldtree v. San Diego, 8 Cal. App. 505, 97 Pac. 216.)

The mechanic's lien law should be construed so as to be in consonance with the constitutional provision granting the lien. (Los Angeles P. B. Co. v. Higgins, 8 Cal. App. 514, 97 Pac. 414, 420.)

This section places mechanics, materialmen, artisans, and laborers in one class, and the legislature cannot impair their rights by giving one a lien in preference to the other. (Miltimore v. Nofziger Bros. L. Co., 150 Cal. 790, 90 Pac. 114.)

The legislature has power to provide that the owner shall be liable to materialmen and laborers, unless he executes his contract in a certain form, and files it in the recorder's office. (Kellogg v. Howes, 81 Cal. 170, 6 L. R. A. 588, 22 Pac. 509.)   •

This section does not give a lien upon public buildings or property. (Mayrhofer v. Board of Education, 89 Cal. 110, 23 Am. St. Rep. 451, 26 Pac. 646; Goldtree v. San Diego, 8 Cal. App. 505, 97 Pac. 216.)

A mechanic's lien can be enforced against a fund in the city treasury to pay for the public work in connection with which the lien is claimed. (Goldtree v. San Diego, 8 Cal. App. 505, 97 Pac. 216.)

Sections 1183 to 1199 of the Code of Civil Procedure, not being inconsistent with this section, remained in force after its adoption. (Germania Bldg. etc. Assn. v. Wagner, 61 Cal. 349.)

The provision of this section respecting mechanics' liens is subordinate to the Declaration of Rights. (Stimson Mill Co. v. Braun, 136 Cal. 122, 89 Am. St. Rep. 116, 57 L. R. A. 726, 68 Pac. 481.)

The provision of section 1203 of the Code of Civil Procedure requiring contractors for the erection of buildings to secure their contracts by bonds is not authorized by this section. (Shaughnessy v. American Surety Co., 138 Cal. 543, 69 Pac. 250, 71 Pac. 701.)

This section only provides for a lien where the materials have actually been used upon the property upon which the lien is claimed. (Bennett v. Beadle, 142 Cal. 239, 75 Pac. 843.)

This section authorizes the legislature to allow counsel fees in actions to foreclose mechanics' liens. (Peckham v. Fox, 1 Cal. App. 307, 82 Pac. 91.)

The right of materialmen, artisans, and laborers to have a lien for the full value of labor or materials furnished is solemnly guaranteed by the Constitution, and legislation must be subordinate to and in consonance with this provision. (Hampton v. Christensen, 148 Cal. 729, 84 Pac. 200.)

This section did not repeal existing statutes providing for the enforcement of liens of mechanics. (Peckham v. Fox, 1 Cal. App. 307, 82 Pac. 91.)

The lien law is not unconstitutional because it takes property without due process of law, or abridges the right to contract in respect to one's property. (Stimson Mill Co. v. Nolan, 5 Cal. App. 754, 91 Pac. 262.)

A subcontractor is entitled to a lien for labor and materials although he did not personally perform the labor. (Barrett-Hicks Co. v. Glas, 14 Cal. App. 289, 111 Pac. 760.)

To construe section 1188 of the Code of Civil Procedure as requiring a separate statement of the amount due on each building, when it is impossible to do so, would render nugatory the lien provided for by the Constitution. (Southern Cal. Lumber Co. v. Peters, 3 Cal. App. 478, 86 Pac. 816.)

The lien provided for by this section attaches to a building resting upon land in which the person causing the building to be erected has no interest. (Linck v. Meikeljohn, 2 Cal. App. 506, 84 Pac. 309.)

> Who are laborers. See notes, 58 Am. St. Rep. 303; Ann. Cas. 1913B, 138.
>
> Validity of mechanic's lien laws. See notes, 4 Ann. Cas. 620; Ann. Cas. 1912C, 339.
>
> Validity of mechanic's lien laws providing for taxing attorneys' fees. See note, 11 Ann. Cas. 714.

The mechanic's or materialman's lien attaches to the structure as the material is furnished or the labor performed, and cannot be made subordinate to or dependent on any legislative act. (People v. Moxley, 17 Cal. App. 466, 120 Pac. 43.)

The right of the owner to deduct stipulated damages as against a contractor cannot be allowed as a deduction from the last payment to the injury of lien claimants, especially as regards payment of such liens out of the last payment which was required to be withheld to satisfy lien claimants, and that fund cannot be sequestered in the interest of the owner as against the contractor. (Mannix v. Wilson, 18 Cal. App. 595, 123 Pac. 981.)

Section 1183a of the Code of Civil Procedure, giving a lien to persons supplying power by means of teams, wagons, vehicles, implements or appliances, used in the construction, alteration, addition to or repair of any of the improvements or works mentioned in section 1183 of that code, is constitutional. (Mendenhall v. Gray, 167 Cal. 233, 139 Pac. 67.)

Term of office, duration of.

Sec. 16. When the term of any officer or commissioner is not provided for in this Constitution, the term of such officer or commissioner may be declared by law; and, if not so declared, such officer or commissioner shall hold his position as such officer or commissioner during the pleasure of the authority making the appointment; but in no case shall such term exceed four years; provided, however, that in

the case of any officer or employee of any municipality governed under a legally adopted charter, the provisions of
such charter with reference to the tenure of office or the
dismissal from office of any such officer or employee shall
control; and provided, further, that the term of office of
any person heretofore or hereafter appointed to hold office
or employment during good behavior under civil service
laws of the state or of any political division thereof shall
not be limited by this section. (Amendment approved
October 10, 1911.)

[AMENDMENT OF 1906.]

Sec. 16. When the term of any officer or commissioner is not
provided for in this Constitution, the term of such officer or commissioner may be declared by law; and, if not so declared, such
officer or commissioner shall hold his position as such officer or
commissioner during the pleasure of the authority making the appointment; but in no case shall such term exceed four years;
provided, however, that in the case of any officer or employee of
any municipality governed under a legally adopted charter, the
provisions of such charter with reference to the tenure of office or
the dismissal from office of any such officer or employee shall control. (Amendment adopted November 6, 1906.)

[ORIGINAL SECTION.]

Sec. 16. When the term of any officer or commissioner is not
provided for in this Constitution, the term of such officer or commissioner may be declared by law; and, if not so declared, such
officer or commissioner shall hold his position as such officer or
commissioner during the pleasure of the authority making the appointment; but in no case shall such term exceed four years.

TERM OF OFFICE.—This section, being a re-enactment of section
7, article XI, of the former Constitution, must be construed in the
same manner. (People v. Edwards, 93 Cal. 153, 28 Pac. 831.)

The word "duration" signifies extent, limit, or time. (People v.
Hill, 7 Cal. 97.)

A hospital physician of the county is not a public officer. (People
v. Wheeler, 136 Cal. 652, 69 Pac. 435.)

This section only applies to officers whose term is "not provided
for in the Constitution" and does not apply to superior judges. (People v. Campbell, 138 Cal. 11, 70 Pac. 918.)

"Good behavior" is not a term within the meaning of this section.
(Somers v. State, 5 S. D. 584, 59 N. W. 962.)

When an ineligible person receives the highest number of votes,
there is a vacancy which the board of supervisors has power to fill.
(Campbell v. Board of Supervisors, 7 Cal. App. 155, 93 Pac. 1061.)

The legislature may direct the time and mode of the election of an
officer whose term is prescribed by the Constitution, but cannot
change the tenure. (People v. Burbank, 12 Cal. 378.)

Where an officer is appointed for two years, he does not hold by the tenure of the approbation of the appointing power. (People v. Reid, 6 Cal. 288.)

An officer appointed to hold for one year, or until his successor should be appointed and qualified, has no fixed term, and he may be removed at any time by the appointing power. (Higgins v. Cole, 100 Cal. 260, 34 Pac. 678.)

This section refers to officers of statutory creation as well as to officers mentioned in the Constitution itself. (People v. Perry, 79 Cal. 105, 21 Pac. 423.)

The commissioners to manage the Yosemite Valley are officers of the state within the meaning of this section, and their terms expired four years after their appointment. (People v. Ashburner, 55 Cal. 517.)

The commissioners of the funded debt of San Francisco were not officers. (People v. Middleton, 28 Cal. 603.)

The members of the board of health of San Francisco are officers within the meaning of this section, and a statute fixing their term of office at five years is unconstitutional and leaves the duration of the term unfixed and subject to the pleasure of the governor. (People v. Perry, 79 Cal. 105, 21 Pac. 423.)

The health inspector of San Francisco is an officer. (Patton v. Board of Health, 127 Cal. 388, 78 Am. St. Rep. 66, 59 Pac. 702.)

As to who are officers generally, see Vaughn v. English, 8 Cal. 39; Crawford v. Dunbar, 52 Cal. 36; Farrell v. Board of Trustees of Sacramento, 85 Cal. 408, 24 Pac. 868; State v. Brandt, 41 Iowa, 593; Somers v. State, 5 S. D. 584, 59 N. W. 962; United States v. Hartwell, 6 Wall. 385, 18 L. Ed. 830; note, 72 Am. Dec. 179–189; Wright v. Langenour, 55 Cal. 280; Phelps v. Winchomb, 3 Bulst. 77.

The legislature cannot provide that officers appointed by a board shall not be removed without just cause, where the duration of their terms is not fixed. (People v. Hill, 7 Cal. 97; Smith v. Brown, 59 Cal. 672; People v. Shear, 15 Pac. 92; Patton v. Board of Health, 127 Cal. 388, 78 Am. St. Rep. 66, 59 Pac. 702; Sponogle v. Curnow, 136 Cal. 580, 69 Pac. 255.)

Policemen appointed without any definite term hold during the pleasure of the appointing power, and may be removed without charges, notice or trial. (Farrell v. Board of Police Commissioners, 1 Cal. App. 5, 81 Pac. 674.)

As to whether or not the Civil Service provisions of the San Francisco charter are in violation of this provision, see Cahen v. Wells, 132 Cal. 447, 64 Pac. 699.

This section must be construed to deny the right of removal in those cases where the tenure is defined by law. (People v. Jewett, 6 Cal. 291.)

The Constitution does not prohibit an office created by the legislature from continuing over four years, but merely limits the incumbent's term to four years. (People v. Stratton, 28 Cal. 382.)

This section does not forbid a holding over until a successor has been chosen and qualified. (People v. Edwards, 93 Cal. 153, 28 Pac. 831.)

Where the term of an officer is not fixed by the Constitution or by law, and the authority of the power making the appointment has ceased, there is no vacancy in the office, but the officer holds over. (People v. Hammond, 66 Cal. 654, 6 Pac. 741; People v. Gunst, 110 Cal. 447, 42 Pac. 963.)

When the charter provides a tribunal with power to remove municipal officers, such method of procedure is exclusive and supersedes the provision of the Penal Code giving jurisdiction to the superior court. (Dinan v. Superior Court, 6 Cal. App. 217, 91 Pac. 806.)

The amendment of 1906 was intended to make it clear that the provisions of a freeholders' charter should control in the matter of the dismissal from office of any officer or employee of the municipality. (Craig v. Superior Court, 157 Cal. 481, 108 Pac. 310.)

The power of amotion may be, notwithstanding the existence of the general laws, conferred by charter upon municipal corporations, and when so conferred will be construed, depending upon the nature of the language, as being either concurrent or exclusive. (Legault v. Board of Trustees, 161 Cal. 197, 39 L. R. A. (N. S.) 519, 118 Pac. 706.)

Eight hours a legal day's labor.

Sec. 17.   The time of service of all laborers or workmen or mechanics employed upon any public works of the state of California, or of any county, city and county, city, town, district, township, or any other political subdivision thereof, whether said work is done by contract or otherwise, shall be limited and restricted to eight hours in any one calendar day, except in cases of extraordinary emergency caused by fire, flood, or danger to life and property, or except to work upon public, military, or naval works or defenses in time of war, and the legislature shall provide by law that a stipulation to this effect shall be incorporated in all contracts for public work and prescribe proper penalties for the speedy and efficient enforcement of said law. (Amendment adopted November 4, 1902.)

[ORIGINAL SECTION.]

Sec. 17. Eight hours shall constitute a legal day's work on all public work.

Minimum wage.

Sec. 17½. The legislature may, by appropriate legislation, provide for the establishment of a minimum wage for women and minors and may provide for the comfort, health, safety and general welfare of any and all employees

No provision of this Constitution shall be construed as a limitation upon the authority of the legislature to confer upon any commission now or hereafter created, such power and authority as the legislature may deem requisite to carry out the provisions of this section. (New section added by amendment adopted November 3, 1914.)

Sex not a disqualification for business.

Sec. 18. No person shall, on account of sex, be disqualified from entering upon or pursuing any lawful business, vocation, or profession.

SEX.—This section is self-executing, and needs no legislation to put it in effect, and imposes a restraint on every law-making power of the state, whether an act of the legislature or an ordinance of a municipal corporation. (Matter of Maguire, 57 Cal. 604, 40 Am. Rep. 125.)

The word "qualified," as used in this section, is presumed to be used in its natural and ordinary sense. (Matter of Maguire, 57 Cal. 604, 40 Am. Rep. 125; Weill v. Kenfield, 54 Cal. 111.)

An ordinance prohibiting the employment of females in dance-halls, etc., is in violation of this section. (Matter of Maguire, 57 Cal. 604, 40 Am. Rep. 125. But see Ex parte Felchlin, 96 Cal. 360, 31 Am. St. Rep. 223, 31 Pac. 224.)

A city ordinance which fixes the license for the carrying on of a saloon where females are employed, and where intoxicating liquors are sold in less quantities than one quart, at a higher rate than a license for conducting a saloon where females are not employed, is valid. (Ex parte Felchlin, 96 Cal. 360, 31 Am. St. Rep. 223, 31 Pac. 224. Opinion of McKinstry, J., in Matter of Maguire, 57 Cal. 604, 40 Am. Rep. 125, approved.)

An ordinance providing that no license shall be issued to persons engaged in the sale of liquors in dance-halls, or dance-cellars, or in places where musical, theatrical, or other public exhibitions are given, and where females attend as waitresses, is valid. (Ex parte Hayes, 98 Cal. 555, 20 L. R. A. 701, 33 Pac. 337.)

This section does not forbid such reasonable restrictions upon the hours of labor of women as may be necessary for the protection and preservation of the public health. (Matter of Application of Miller, 162 Cal. 687, 124 Pac. 427; affirmed in Miller v. Wilson, 236 U. S. 373, 59 L. Ed. 628, 35 Sup. Ct. Rep. 342.)

Payment of expenses of convention.

Sec. 19. Nothing in this Constitution shall prevent the legislature from providing, by law, for the payment of the expenses of the convention framing this Constitution, in-

cluding the per diem of the delegates for the full term thereof.

Election of officers—Term, when commences.

Sec. 20. Elections of the officers provided for by this Constitution, except at the election in the year eighteen hundred and seventy-nine, shall be held on the even-numbered years next before the expiration of their respective terms. The terms of such officers shall commence on the first Monday after the first day of January next following their election.

TIME OF ELECTIONS.—This section controls all other provisions of the Constitution as to when the term of office of officers elected under it commences. (Merced Bank v. Rosenthal, 99 Cal. 39, 31 Pac. 849, 33 Pac. 732.)

The officers mentioned in this section are not the county, township and municipal officers who are distinctly mentioned in section 5, article XI, and the duration of whose terms the legislature is expressly directed to fix. (In re Stuart, 53 Cal. 745.)

The officers mentioned in this section are the same as those mentioned in section 10, article XXII. (Barton v. Kalloch, 56 Cal. 95.)

Under this section justices of the peace are to be elected in the even-numbered years. (People v. Ransom, 58 Cal. 558; Bishop v. Council of City of Oakland, 58 Cal. 572; Jenks v. Council of City of Oakland, 58 Cal. 576; Coggins v. Sacramento, 59 Cal. 599.)

The words "from and after" must be construed to mean "on and after" and the controller's term includes the first Monday. (People v. Nye, 9 Cal. App. 148, 98 Pac. 241.)

Laws to remain in force.

Sec. 21. The legislature may by appropriate legislation create and enforce a liability on the part of all employers to compensate their employees for any injury incurred by the said employees in the course of their employment irrespective of the fault of either party. The legislature may provide for the settlement of any disputes arising under the legislation contemplated by this section, by arbitration, or by an industrial accident board, by the courts, or by either, any or all of these agencies, anything in this Constitution to the contrary notwithstanding. (Amendment approved October 10, 1911.)

ARTICLE XXI.

BOUNDARY.

Section 1. The boundary of the state of California shall be as follows: Commencing at the point of intersection of the forty-second degree of north latitude with the one hundred and twentieth degree of longitude west from Greenwich, and running south on the line of said one hundred and twentieth degree of west longitude until it intersects the thirty-ninth degree of north latitude; thence running in a straight line, in a southeasterly direction, to the River Colorado, at a point where it intersects the thirty-fifth degree of north latitude; thence down the middle of the channel of said river to the boundary line between the United States and Mexico, as established by the treaty of May thirtieth, one thousand eight hundred and forty-eight; thence running west and along said boundary line to the Pacific Ocean, and extending therein three English miles; thence running in a northwesterly direction and following the direction of the Pacific Coast to the forty-second degree of north latitude; thence on the line of said forty-second degree of north latitude to the place of beginning. Also, including all the islands, harbors, and bays along and adjacent to the coast.

ARTICLE XXII.

SCHEDULE.

That no inconvenience may arise from the alterations and amendments in the Constitution of this state, and to carry the same into complete effect, it is hereby ordained and declared:

Laws to remain in force.

Section 1. That all laws in force at the adoption of this Constitution, not inconsistent therewith, shall remain in full force and effect until altered or repealed by the legislature; and all rights, actions, prosecutions, claims, and contracts of the state, counties, individuals, or bodies corporate, not inconsistent therewith, shall continue to be as valid as if this Constitution had not been adopted. The provisions of all laws which are inconsistent with this Constitution shall cease upon the adoption thereof, except that all laws which are inconsistent with such provisions of this Constitution as require legislation to enforce them shall remain in full force until the first day of July, eighteen hundred and eighty, unless sooner altered or repealed by the legislature.

LAWS CONTINUED IN FORCE.—The Constitution of 1879 did not, proprio vigore, repeal or displace all the statutes of the state theretofore in force, but only such as were inconsistent with those provisions of that Constitution which do not require legislation to put them in force. (In re Stuart, 53 Cal. 745.)

Section 25, article IV, being merely prospective, special laws passed before the adoption of the Constitution are not superseded. (Smith v. McDermott, 93 Cal. 421, 29 Pac. 34.)

The provisions of the Constitution giving the superior court jurisdiction of special proceedings, not requiring legislation to enforce it, the superior court has jurisdiction, as the successor of the district court, to entertain proceedings under sections 312 and 315 of the Civil Code, although those sections mention the district court. (Wickersham v. Brittan, 93 Cal. 34, 28 Pac. 792, 15 L. R. A. 106, 29 Pac. 51.)

A statute giving the district court jurisdiction of a special proceeding is not inconsistent with the Constitution, and did not cease upon its adoption. (Wickersham v. Brittan, 93 Cal. 34, 15 L. R. A. 106, 28 Pac. 792, 29 Pac. 51. Fraser v. Alexander, 75 Cal. 147, 16 Pac. 757. overruled.)

Section 13, article XI, being only prospective, an act passed prior to the Constitution which is inconsistent with it is not superseded. (Board of Commissioners v. Board of Trustees, 71 Cal. 310, 12 Pac. 224.)

Sections 1183 to 1199 of the Code of Civil Procedure, not being inconsistent with section 15, article XX, of the Constitution, remained in force after its adoption. (Germania Bldg. etc. Assn. v. Wagner, 61 Cal. 349.)

Any general law in conflict with the Civil Code and passed subsequent to its adoption supersedes the provisions thereof, and the Constitution does not require such a law to be passed as an amendment to the Civil Code in order to affect any rights or powers therein given to corporations. (People v. Bank of San Luis Obispo, 154 Cal. 194, 97 Pac. 306.)

Section 1033 of the Penal Code is not inconsistent with section 9, article I of the Constitution, and was continued in force. (Older v. Superior Court, 157 Cal. 770, 109 Pac. 478.)

The law providing for the election of a clerk of the supreme court was not superseded by the Constitution. (Gross v. Kenfield, 57 Cal. 626.)

Section 1, article XIII, which provides that "all property in the state, not exempt under the laws of the United States, shall be taxed in proportion to its value, to be ascertained as provided by law," is self-executing, and requires the assessor to ascertain such value in the manner now provided by law. (Hyatt v. Allen, 54 Cal. 353; McDonald v. Patterson, 54 Cal. 245.)

The Consolidation Act of the city and county of San Francisco remained in force notwithstanding section 7, article XI, requiring two boards of supervisors, since that section required legislation to put it in effect. (Desmond v. Dunn, 55 Cal. 242.)

The effect of the new Constitution in repealing the provision of the act of 1878, declaring how and by whom two of the fire commissioners should be appointed, did not necessarily destroy the two offices, nor affect the validity of the act, but the incumbents continued to hold after the appointing power was abolished. (People v. Newman, 96 Cal. 605, 31 Pac. 564.)

Where, at the adoption of the Constitution, the Political Code fixed the salary of county superintendent of schools, and in 1878 the legislature passed a special law on the subject to go into effect on the first Monday of March, 1880, the provision of the Political Code remained

in force and the special act never went into effect. (Peachey v. Board of Supervisors, 59 Cal. 548; Whiting v. Haggard, 60 Cal. 513.)

Where a special act was passed prior to the new Constitution, but it was provided that it should not affect the present incumbent, whose term did not expire until after the Constitution went into effect, the act was not superseded by the Constitution. (Los Angeles County v. Lamb, 61 Cal. 196. Peachey v. Board of Supervisors, 59 Cal. 548, distinguished.)

Section 322 of the Civil Code, not being inconsistent with section 3, article XII, of the Constitution, remained in force after its adoption, (Gardiner v. Bank of Napa, 160 Cal. 577, 117 Pac. 667.)

The act of 1877–78 reviving the common-law rule as to trespassing animals, not being inconsistent with the Constitution, remained in force after its adoption. (Blevins v. Mullally, 22 Cal. App. 519, 135 Pac. 307.)

LAWS SUPERSEDED.—The provision of the charter of San Francisco for the making a contract for street work before an assessment had been levied and collected, being inconsistent with section 19, article XI, of the Constitution, was superseded by it. (Thomason v. Ruggles, 69 Cal. 465, 11 Pac. 20; Oakland Pav. Co. v. Hilton, 69 Cal. 479, 11 Pac. 3; McDonald v. Patterson, 54 Cal. 245; Donahue v. Graham, 61 Cal. 276.)

The act of 1858 providing for the fixing of water rates by a commissioner, being inconsistent with section 1, article XIV, of the Constitution, was superseded by that section. (Spring Valley W. W. v. Board of Suprs. of San Francisco, 61 Cal. 3.)

The provision of the act of 1858, requiring water companies to furnish water free of charge to cities and counties, was abrogated by this section, because in conflict with section 19, article XI, and section 1, article XIV. (Spring Valley W. W. v. Board of Suprs. of San Francisco, 61 Cal. 18.)

The provision of the Political Code imposing a license upon the business of selling goods, etc., at a fixed place of business, being in conflict with section 12, article XI, of the Constitution, became inoperative upon the adoption of the Constitution. (People v. Martin, 60 Cal. 153.)

An ordinance prohibiting the employment of females in dance-halls, etc., being in conflict with section 18, article XX, ceased upon the adoption of the Constitution. (Matter of Maguire, 57 Cal. 604, 40 Am. Rep. 125.)

The act of 1875, which provided that the text-books in use in 1873, 1874, 1875, should be continued in use until otherwise provided by statute, was superseded by section 7, article IX, which provides that the local boards of education should adopt text-books within their respective jurisdictions. (People v. Board of Education, 55 Cal. 331.)

An act passed before the adoption of the Constitution, but which was not to go into effect until a later date, never went into effect. (Speegle v. Joy, 60 Cal. 278.)

Recognizances, obligations, etc., unaffected.

Sec. 2. That all recognizances, obligations, and all other instruments entered into or executed before the adoption of this Constitution, to this state, or to any subdivision thereof, or any municipality therein, and all fines, taxes, penalties, and forfeitures due or owing to this state, or any subdivision or municipality thereof, and all writs, prosecutions, actions, and causes of actions, except as herein otherwise provided, shall continue and remain unaffected by the adoption of this Constitution. All indictments or informations which shall have been found, or may hereafter be found, for any crime or offense committed before this Constitution takes effect, may be proceeded upon as if no change had taken place, except as otherwise provided in this Constitution.

Courts, save justices' and police courts, abolished—Transfer of records, books, etc.

Sec. 3. All courts now existing, save justices' and police courts, are hereby abolished; and all records, books, papers, and proceedings from such courts, as are abolished by this Constitution, shall be transferred on the first day of January, eighteen hundred and eighty, to the courts provided for in this Constitution; and the courts to which the same are thus transferred shall have the same power and jurisdiction over them as if they had been in the first instance commenced, filed or lodged therein.

COURTS.—When a trial was commenced and the testimony taken by a judge before his term expired under the old Constitution, and he was re-elected under the new, he may, as a judge under the new, decide the case on the evidence then taken, without a resubmission. (Seale v. Ford, 29 Cal. 104.)

The amendments to the Constitution in 1862 did not ipso facto supersede the existing courts, but such courts continued in existence until the new system should be in a condition to exercise its functions. (In re Oliverez, 21 Cal. 415.)

The justices of the peace of the city and county of San Francisco, provided for by the act of 1866, were continued in force by this section, and are not affected by the provisions of the County Government Act. (Kahn v. Sutro, 114 Cal. 316, 33 L. R. A. 620, 46 Pac. 87. But see People v. Cobb, 133 Cal. 74, 65 Pac. 325.)

The superior court of San Francisco is the successor of the municipal criminal court of that city and county. (Ex parte Williams, 87
Cal. 78, 24 Pac. 602, 25 Pac. 248.)

An action to abate a nuisance pending in the district court, being
held to be an action in equity under the former Constitution, is not
affected by the adoption of the new Constitution. (Learned v. Cas-
tle, 67 Cal. 41, 7 Pac. 34.)

The superior court of San Francisco acquired jurisdiction of an
action pending in the district court of San Francisco to recover real
estate in Sonoma county. (Gurnee v. Superior Court, 58 Cal. 88; San
Francisco Sav. Union v. Abbott, 59 Cal. 400.)

It would seem that it was intended that the superior judge should
succeed to the duty of the county judge in respect to the drawing of
jurors. (People v. Gallagher, 55 Cal. 462.)

The superior court is the successor of the county court, and may
issue all necessary writs to the execution of its judgment. (Ex parte
Toland, 54 Cal. 344.)

The superior court is the successor of the district court, and may
carry into execution a judgment of death rendered by the district
court. (People v. Colby, 54 Cal. 184.)

A violation in 1913 of a perpetual injunction granted by a district court in 1870, constituted contempt of the superior court, which,
by virtue of this section, is the successor of the district court.
(Gale v. Tuolumne County Water Co., 169 Cal. 46, 145 Pac. 532.)

State printing.

Sec. 4. The superintendent of printing of the state of
California shall, at least thirty days before the first
Wednesday in May, A. D. eighteen hundred and seventy-
nine, cause to be printed at the state printing office in pamphlet form, simply stitched, as many copies of this Constitution as there are registered voters in this state, and mail
one copy thereof to the postoffice address of each registered voter; provided, any copies not called for ten days
after reaching their delivery office, shall be subject to general distribution by the several postmasters of the state.
The governor shall issue his proclamation, giving notice
of the election for the adoption or rejection of this Constitution, at least thirty days before the said first Wednesday
of May, eighteen hundred and seventy-nine, and the boards
of supervisors of the several counties shall cause said proclamation to be made public in their respective counties, and
general notice of said election to be given at least fifteen
days next before said election.

Ballots to be printed.

Sec. 5. The superintendent of printing of the state of California shall, at least twenty days before said election, cause to be printed and delivered to the clerk of each county in this state five times the number of properly prepared ballots for said election that there are voters in said respective counties, with the words printed thereon: "For the new Constitution." He shall likewise cause to be so printed and delivered to said clerks five times the number of properly prepared ballots for said election that there are voters in said respective counties, with the words printed thereon: "Against the new Constitution." The secretary of state is hereby authorized and required to furnish the superintendent of state printing a sufficient quantity of legal ballot paper, now on hand, to carry out the provisions of this section.

Registers, poll-books, etc., to be furnished.

Sec. 6. The clerks of the several counties in the state shall, at least five days before said election, cause to be delivered to the inspectors of elections, at each election precinct or polling-place in their respective counties, suitable registers, poll-books, forms of return, and an equal number of the aforesaid ballots, which number, in the aggregate, must be ten times greater than the number of voters, in the said election precincts or polling-places. The returns of the number of votes cast at the presidential election in the year eighteen hundred and seventy-six shall serve as a basis of calculation for this and the preceding section; provided, that the duties in this and the preceding section imposed upon the clerk of the respective counties shall, in the city and county of San Francisco, be performed by the registrar of voters for said city and county.

Who entitled to vote for Constitution.

Sec. 7. Every citizen of the United States, entitled by law to vote for members of the assembly in this state, shall be entitled to vote for the adoption or rejection of this Constitution.

Canvass of returns of vote.

Sec. 8. The officers of the several counties of this state, whose duty it is, under the law, to receive and canvass the returns from the several precincts of their respective counties, as well as of the city and county of San Francisco, shall meet at the usual places of meeting for such purposes on the first Monday after said election. If, at the time of meeting, the returns from each precinct in the county in which the polls were opened have been received, the board must then and there proceed to canvass the returns; but if all the returns have not been received, the canvass must be postponed from time to time until all the returns are received, or until the second Monday after said election, when they shall proceed to make out returns of the votes cast for and against the new Constitution; and the proceedings of said boards shall be the same as those prescribed for like boards in the case of an election for governor. Upon the completion of said canvass and returns, the said board shall immediately certify the same, in the usual form, to the governor of the state of California.

Computing returns of vote.

Sec. 9. The governor of the state of California shall, as soon as the returns of said election shall be received by him, or within thirty days after said election, in the presence and with the assistance of the controller, treasurer, and secretary of state, open and compute all the returns received of votes cast for and against the new Constitution. If, by such examination and computation, it is ascertained that a majority of the whole number of votes cast at such election is in favor of such new Constitution, the executive of this state shall, by his proclamation, declare such new Constitution to be the Constitution of the state of California, and that it shall take effect and be in force on the days hereinafter specified.

Terms of officers first elected.

Sec. 10. In order that future elections in this state shall conform to the requirements of this Constitution, the

terms of all officers elected at the first election under the same shall be, respectively, one year shorter than the terms as fixed by law or by this Constitution; and the successors of all such officers shall be elected at the last election before the expiration of the terms as in this section provided. The first officers chosen, after the adoption of this Constitution, shall be elected at the time and in the manner now provided by law. Judicial officers and the superintendent of public instruction shall be elected at the time and in the manner that state officers are elected.

ELECTIONS.—Suggested but not decided that it may have been, and probably was, contemplated by the framers of the Constitution that, when the legislature should provide for the election of county, township, and municipal officers, it would require such election to be held in the even-numbered years; but whether the legislature must do so, not decided. (Barton v. Kalloch, 56 Cal. 95.)

This section refers only to the officers mentioned in section 20, article XX; that is, only to officers who derive their right to hold office immediately from the Constitution; and does not refer to municipal or county officers. (Barton v. Kalloch, 56 Cal. 95.)

Justices of the peace are judicial officers within the meaning of this section, and must be elected at the general election. (McGrew v. Mayor etc. of San Jose, 55 Cal. 611; People v. Ransom, 58 Cal. 558.)

A police judge, though a judicial officer, is also a municipal officer, and is not one of those mentioned in this section. (People v. Henry, 62 Cal. 557.)

This section does not require that the term of such judicial officers as the legislature may authorize to be elected shall be uniform throughout the state. (Kahn v. Sutro, 114 Cal. 316, 33 L. R. A. 620, 46 Pac. 87.)

Laws applicable to judicial system.

Sec. 11. All laws relative to the present judicial system of the state shall be applicable to the judicial system created by this Constitution until changed by legislation.

JUDICIAL SYSTEM.—The several courts of the state continued with their jurisdiction, notwithstanding the adoption of the amendments of 1862, until the organization of the new courts by which they were to be superseded. (Gillis v. Barnett, 38 Cal. 393.)

Section 204 of the Code of Civil Procedure as to grand juries was continued in force by this provision of the Constitution. (People v. Durrant, 116 Cal. 179, 48 Pac. 75.)

The justices of the peace of the city and county of San Francisco provided for by the act of 1866 were continued in force by this section, and are not affected by the County Government Act. (Kahn v.

Sutro, 114 Cal. 316, 33 L. R. A. 620, 46 Pac. 87. But see People v. Cobb, 133 Cal. 74, 65 Pac. 325.)

The provision of the fee bill of 1876, so far as it provided for the fees to be paid to the clerk of the district court, was a law relating to the judicial system of the state, and was kept in force by the new Constitution, and made applicable to the courts organized thereunder. (People v. Hamilton, 103 Cal. 488, 37 Pac. 627.)

This section continued in force the provision for the drawing of trial jurors. (People v. Richards, 1 Cal. App. 566, 82 Pac. 691.)

The superior court has jurisdiction, as the successor of the district court, to entertain proceedings under sections 312 and 315 of the Civil Code, although those sections mention the district court. (Wickersham v. Brittan, 93 Cal. 34, 15 L. R. A. 106, 28 Pac. 792, 29 Pac. 51.)

The power of appointing police commissioners, vested in the judges of certain district courts by the act of 1878, was not a judicial power, did not pertain to the judicial system of the state, and did not devolve upon the judges of the superior courts. (Heinlen v. Sullivan, 64 Cal. 378, 1 Pac. 158.)

Under this section, the law giving the district court power to fix the compensation of phonographic reporters was continued in force, and made applicable to superior courts. (Ex parte Reis, 64 Cal. 233, 30 Pac. 806.)

Under this section, the law regulating appeals from justices' courts to the county courts applied to appeals to the superior court. (California Fruit etc. Co. v. Superior Court, 60 Cal. 305.)

The clerk of the superior court succeeding to a district court has power, without a previous order of the court, to issue an execution upon a judgment of the district court. (Dorn v. Howe, 59 Cal. 129.)

The statute providing for the drawing of jurors in the presence of the county judge, clerk and sheriff was not superseded by the Constitution, since the superior judge would either succeed to the duty of the county judge, or, there being no county judge, the presence of the clerk and sheriff would be sufficient. (People v. Gallagher, 55 Cal. 462.)

Constitution, when to take effect.

Sec. 12. This Constitution shall take effect and be in force on and after the fourth day of July, eighteen hundred and seventy-nine, at twelve o'clock meridian, so far as the same relates to the election of all officers, the commencement of their terms of office, and the meeting of the legislature. In all other respects, and for all other purposes, this Constitution shall take effect on the first day of January, eighteen hundred and eighty, at twelve o'clock meridian.

ARTICLE XXIII.

RECALL OF OFFICERS.

Section 1. Every elective public officer of the state of California may be removed from office at any time by the electors entitled to vote for a successor of such incumbent, through the procedure and in the manner herein provided for, which procedure shall be known as the recall, and is in addition to any other method of removal provided by law.

The procedure hereunder to effect the removal of an incumbent of an elective public office shall be as follows: A petition signed by electors entitled to vote for a successor of the incumbent sought to be removed, equal in number to at least twelve per cent of the entire vote cast at the last preceding election for all candidates for the office which the incumbent sought to be removed occupies (provided that if the officer sought to be removed is a state officer who is elected in any political subdivision of the state, said petition shall be signed by electors entitled to vote for a successor to the incumbent sought to be removed, equal in number to at least twenty per cent of the entire vote cast at the last preceding election for all candidates for the office which the incumbent sought to be removed occupies) demanding an election of a successor to the officer named in said petition, shall be addressed to the secretary of state and filed with the clerk, or registrar of voters, of the county or city and county in which the petition was circulated; provided that if the officer sought to be removed was elected in the state at large such petition shall be circulated in not less than five counties of the state, and shall be signed in each of such counties by electors equal in number to not less than one per cent of the entire vote cast, in each of said counties, at said election, as above estimated. Such petition shall contain a general statement of the grounds on which the removal is sought, which statement is intended solely for the information of the electors, and the sufficiency of which shall not be open to review.

When such petition is certified as is herein provided to the secretary of state, he shall forthwith submit the said

petition, together with a certificate of its sufficiency, to the governor, who shall thereupon order and fix a date for holding the election, not less than sixty days nor more than eighty days from the date of such certificate of the secretary of state.

The governor shall make or cause to be made publication of notice for the holding of such election, and officers charged by law with duties concerning elections shall make all arrangements for such election and the same shall be conducted, returned, and the result thereof declared, in all respects as are other state elections. On the official ballot at such election shall be printed, in not more than two hundred words, the reasons set forth in the petition for demanding his recall. And in not more than three hundred words there shall also be printed, if desired by him, the officer's justification of his course in office. Proceedings for the recall of any officer shall be deemed to be pending from the date of the filing with any county, or city and county clerk, or registrar of voters, of any recall petition against such officer; and if such officer shall resign at any time subsequent to the filing thereof, the recall election shall be held notwithstanding such resignation, and the vacancy caused by such resignation, or from any other cause, shall be filled as provided by law, but the person appointed to fill such vacancy shall hold his office only until the person elected at the said recall election shall qualify.

Any person may be nominated for the office which is to be filled at any recall election by a petition signed by electors, qualified to vote at such recall election, equal in number to at least one per cent of the total number of votes cast at the last preceding election for all candidates for the office which the incumbent sought to be removed occupies. Each such nominating petition shall be filed with the secretary of state not less than twenty-five days before such recall election.

There shall be printed on the recall ballot, as to every officer whose recall is to be voted on thereat, the following question: "Shall (name of person against whom the recall petition is filed) be recalled from the office of (title of the

office) ?", following which question shall be the words "Yes" and "No" on separate lines, with a blank space at the right of each, in which the voter shall indicate, by stamping a cross (X), his vote for or against such recall. On such ballots, under each such question, there shall also be printed the names of those persons who have been nominated as candidates to succeed the person recalled, in case he shall be removed from office by said recall election; but no vote cast shall be counted for any candidate for said office unless the voter also voted on said question of the recall of the person sought to be recalled from said office. The name of the person against whom the petition is filed shall not appear on the ballot as a candidate for the office. If a majority of those voting on said question of the recall of any incumbent from office shall vote "No," said incumbent shall continue in said office. If a majority shall vote "Yes," said incumbent shall thereupon be deemed removed from such office, upon the qualification of his successor. The canvassers shall canvass all votes for candidates for said office and declare the result in like manner as in a regular election. If the vote at any such recall election shall recall the officer, then the candidate who has received the highest number of votes for the office shall be thereby declared elected for the remainder of the term. In case the person who received the highest number of votes shall fail to qualify within ten days after receiving the certificate of election, the office shall be deemed vacant and shall be filled according to law.

Any recall petition may be presented in sections, but each section shall contain a full and accurate copy of the title and text of the petition. Each signer shall add to his signature his place of residence, giving the street and number, if such exist. His election precinct shall also appear on the paper after his name. The number of signatures appended to each section shall be at the pleasure of the person soliciting signatures to the same. Any qualified elector of the state shall be competent to solicit such signatures within the county, or city and county, of which

he is an elector. Each section of the petition shall bear
the name of the county, or city and county in which it is
circulated, and only qualified electors of such county or
city and county shall be competent to sign such section.
Each section shall have attached thereto the affidavit of
the person soliciting signatures to the same stating his
qualifications and that all the signatures to the attached
section were made in his presence and that to the best of
his knowledge and belief each signature to the section is
the genuine signature of the person whose name it purports to be; and no other affidavit thereto shall be required.
The affidavit of any person soliciting signatures hereunder
shall be verified free of charge by any officer authorized
to administer an oath.   Such petition so verified shall be
prima facie evidence that the signatures thereto appended
are genuine and that the persons signing the same are
qualified electors.   Unless and until it is otherwise proven
upon official investigation, it shall be presumed that the
petition presented contains the signatures of the requisite
number of electors.   Each section of the petition shall be
filed with the clerk, or registrar of voters, of the county
or city and county in which it was circulated; but all such
sections circulated in any county or city and county shall
be filed at the same time.   Within twenty days after the
date of the filing of such petition, the clerk, or registrar
of voters, shall finally determine from the records of registration what number of qualified electors have signed the
same; and, if necessary, the board of supervisors shall allow
such clerk or registrar additional assistants for the purpose
of examining such petition and provide for their compensation.   The said clerk or registrar, upon the completion
of such examination, shall forthwith attach to such petition
his certificate, properly dated, showing the result of
such examination, and submit said petition, except as to
the signatures appended thereto, to the secretary of
state and file a copy of said certificate in his office.   Within
forty days from the transmission of the said petition
and certificate by the clerk or registrar of voters to
the secretary of state, a supplemental petition, identical

with the original as to the body of the petition but containing supplemental names, may be filed with the clerk
or registrar of voters, as aforesaid. The clerk or registrar
of voters shall within ten days after the filing of such supplemental petition make like examination thereof as of the
original petition, and upon the conclusion of such examination shall forthwith attach to such petition his certificate,
properly dated, showing the result of such examination,
and shall forthwith transmit such supplemental petition,
except as to the signatures thereon, together with his said
certificate, to the secretary of state.

When the secretary of state shall have received from one
or more county clerks, or registrars of voters, a petition
certified as herein provided to have been signed by the
requisite number of qualified electors, he shall forthwith
transmit to the county clerk or registrar of voters of every
county or city and county in the state a certificate showing
such fact; and such clerk or registrar of voters shall thereupon file said certificate for record in his office.

A petition shall be deemed to be filed with the secretary
of state upon the date of the receipt by him of a certificate
or certificates showing the said petition to be signed by the
requisite number of electors of the state.

No recall petition shall be circulated or filed against any
officer until he has actually held his office for at least six
months; save and except it may be filed against any member of the state legislature at any time after five days from
the convening and organizing of the legislature after his
election.

If at any recall election the incumbent whose removal is
sought is not recalled, he shall be repaid from the state
treasury any amount legally expended by him as expenses
of such election, and the legislature shall provide appropriation for such purpose, and no proceedings for another
recall election of such incumbent shall be initiated within
six months after such election.

If the governor is sought to be removed under the provisions of this article, the duties herein imposed upon him
shall be performed by the lieutenant-governor; and if the

secretary of state is sought to be removed, the duties herein imposed upon him shall be performed by the state controller; and the duties herein imposed upon the clerk or registrar of voters shall be performed by such registrar of voters in all cases where the office of registrar of voters exists.

The recall shall also be exercised by the electors of each county, city and county, city and town of the state, with reference to the elective officers thereof, under such procedure as shall be provided by law.

Until otherwise provided by law, the legislative body of any such county, city and county, city or town may provide for the manner of exercising such recall powers in such counties, cities and counties, cities and towns, but shall not require any such recall petition to be signed by electors more in number than twenty-five per cent of the entire vote cast at the last preceding election for all candidates for the office which the incumbent sought to be removed occupies. Nothing herein contained shall be construed as affecting or limiting the present or future powers of cities or counties or cities and counties having charters adopted under the authority given by the Constitution.

In the submission to the electors of any petition proposed under this article all officers shall be guided by the general laws of the state, except as otherwise herein provided.

This article is self-executing, but legislation may be enacted to facilitate its operation, but in no way limiting or restricting the provisions of this article or the powers herein reserved. (Amendment approved October 10, 1911.)

THE RECALL.—The fixing of the tenure of office of the officers of a municipality, subject to removal by the body that elected them, is comparatively new in our system of government, and the interpretive branch of the law is in rather an undeveloped state. (Good v. Common Council of San Diego, 5 Cal. App. 265, 90 Pac. 44.)

Where a municipal charter provides that the holder of any elective office may be removed at any time by the electors qualified to vote for a successor, the charter does not contemplate an ordinary "removal for cause," but by virtue of the charter provisions, every elective officer elected after the provision was adopted holds his office subject to the condition subsequent expressed therein. (Good v. Common Council of San Diego, 5 Cal. App. 265, 90 Pac. 44.)

The recall provision is valid. The appellant accepted the trust subject to this power in his constituency, and the duration of his term of office is dependent upon the wish of the majority as expressed at the polls. (Hilzinger v. Gillman, 56 Wash. 228, 21 Ann. Cas. 305, 105 Pac. 471.)

The provision in Statutes (Mass.) 1908, p. 542, c. 574, amending the charter of the city of Haverhill, which requires officers to accept office of uncertain terms, with liability to be recalled at any time without just cause, is not unconstitutional. (Graham v. Roberts, 200 Mass. 152, 85 N. E. 1009.)

"It is contended that the recall provision of the charter" of Dallas "seeks to substitute within the municipality a socialistic and communistic system of government in lieu of a republican form of government—we do not concur in this contention. It is neither socialistic, communistic, nor obnoxious to a republican form of government to require an elective officer of a municipal government to submit to the voters of the city the issue for their determination whether he shall longer continue in office." (Bonner v. Besterling (Tex. Civ.), 137 S. W. 1154.)

J. P. HOGE,
President.

Attest: EDWIN F. SMITH, Secretary.

A. R. Andrews.
James J. Ayers,
Clitus Barbour,
Edward Barry,
James N. Barton,
C. J. Beerstecher,
Isaac S. Belcher,
Peter Bell,
Marion Biggs,
E. T. Blackmer,
Joseph C. Brown,
Saml. B. Burt,
Josiah Boucher,
James Caples,
Aug. H. Chapman,
J. M. Charles,
John D. Condon,
C. W. Cross,
Hamlet Davis,
Jas E. Dean,
P. T. Dowling,

Luke D. Doyle,
W. L. Dudley,
Jonathan M. Dudley,
Presley Dunlap,
John Eagon,
Thomas H. Estey,
Henry Edgerton,
M. M. Estee,
Edward Evey,
J. A. Filcher,
Simon J. Farrell,
Abraham Clark Freeman,
Jacob Richard Freud,
J. B. Garvey,
B. B. Glasscock,
Joseph C. Gorman,
W. P. Grace,
William J. Graves,
V. A. Gregg,
Jno. S. Hager,
John B. Hall,

Thomas Harrison,
Joel A. Harvey,
T. D. Heiskell,
Conrad Herold,
D. W. Herrington,
S. G. Hilborn,
J. R. W. Hitchcock,
J. E. Hale,
Volney E. Howard,
Sam A. Holmes,
W. J. Howard,
Wm. Proctor Hughey,
W. F. Huestis,
G. W. Hunter,
Daniel Inman,
George A. Johnson,
L. F. Jones,
Peter J. Joyce,
J. M. Kelley,
James H. Keyes,
John J. Kenny,
C. R. Kleine,
T. H. Laine,
Henry Larkin,
R. M. Lampson,
R. Lavigne,
H. M. La Rue,
David Lewis,
J. F. Lindow,
Jno. Mansfield,
Edward Martin,
J. West Martin,
Rush McComas,
John G. McCallum,
Thomas McConnell,
John McCoy,
Thomas B. McFarland,
Hiram Mills,
Wm. S. Moffatt,

John Fleming McNutt,
W. W. Moreland,
L. D. Morse,
James E. Murphy,
Edmund Nason,
Thorwald Klaudius Nelson,
Henry Neunaber,
Chas. C. O'Donnell,
George Ohleyer,
James O'Sullivan,
James Martin Porter,
William H. Prouty,
M. R. C. Pulliam,
Chas. F. Reed,
Patrick Reddy,
Jno. M. Rhodes,
Jas. S. Reynolds,
Horace C. Rolfe,
Chas. S. Ringgold,
James McM. Shafter,
Geo. W. Schell,
J. Schomp,
Rufus Shoemaker,
E. O. Smith,
Benj. Shurtleff,
Geo. Venable Smith,
H. W. Smith,
John C. Stedman,
E. P. Soule,
D. C. Stevenson,
Geo. Steele,
Chas. V. Stuart,
W. J. Sweasey,
Charles Swenson,
R. S. Swing,
D. S. Terry,
S. B. Thompson,
F. O. Townsend,
W. J. Tinnin,

Daniel Tuttle,
P. B. Tully,
H. K. Turner,
A. P. Vacquerel,
Walter Van Dyke,
Wm. Van Voorhies,
Hugh Walker,
Jno. Walker,
Byron Waters,

Joseph R. Weller,
J. V. Webster,
John P. West,
Patrick M. Wellin,
John T. Wickes,
Wm. F. White,
H. C. Wilson,
Jos. W. Winans,
N. G. Wyatt.

TABLE OF STATUTES
DECLARED UNCONSTITUTIONAL
IN WHOLE OR IN PART.

Statutes	Page	Chapter	Case
1880	1	1	Weill v. Kenfield, 54 Cal. 111.
	20	26	San Francisco v. Broderick, 125 Cal. 188, 57 Pac. 887.
	55	63	Hutson v. Woodbridge Protection Dist., 79 Cal. 90, 16 Pac. 549, 21 Pac. 435.
	67	71	People v. Chapman, 61 Cal. 262.
	80	84	Ex parte Westerfield, 55 Cal. 550, 36 Am. Rep. 47.
	119	109	Bixler's Appeal, 59 Cal. 550; Bixler v. Board of Suprs. of Sacramento County, 59 Cal. 698. (Decision of Superior Court.)
	123	116	In re Ah Chong, 5 Pac. C. L. J. 451.
	123	117	Doane v. Weil, 58 Cal. 334; People v. Parks, 58 Cal. 624; Callahan v. Dunn, 78 Cal. 366, 20 Pac. 737.
	131	118	Krause v. Durbrow, 127 Cal. 681, 60 Pac. 438.
	137	124	Desmond v. Dunn, 55 Cal. 242.
	527 (Ban.)	244	Leonard v. January, 56 Cal. 1; Dillon v. Bicknell, 116 Cal. 111, 47 Pac. 937.
1881	15	21	Nickey v. Stearns Ranchos Co., 126 Cal. 156, 58 Pac. 459.
	51	51	Ex parte Cox, 63 Cal. 21.
	54	52	Fitch v. Board of Supervisors, 122 Cal. 285, 54 Pac. 901; Hatfield v. People's Water Co., 25 Cal. App. 502, 144 Pac. 300.
	81	71	People v. Chapman, 61 Cal. 262.
1883	54	30	People v. Kewen, 69 Cal. 215, 10 Pac. 393.
	93	49	Tulare v. Hevren, 126 Cal. 226, 58 Pac. 530.
	370	82	Los Angeles v. Teed, 112 Cal. 319, 44 Pac. 580.
1885	13	15	San Francisco v. Liverpool etc. Ins. Co., 74 Cal. 113, 5 Am. St. Rep. 425, 15 Pac. 380.
	45	39	Western Granite etc. Co. v. Knickerbocker, 103 Cal. 111, 37 Pac. 192.
	166	154	Miller v. Kister, 68 Cal. 142, 8 Pac. 813; People v. Henshaw, 76 Cal. 436, 18 Pac. 413.
	203	157	People v. Kewen, 69 Cal. 215, 10 Pac. 393.
1887	178	169	Dougherty v. Austin, 94 Cal. 601, 28 Pac. 834, 16 L. R. A. 161, 29 Pac. 1092.
1889	8	5	Schaezlein v. Cabaniss, 135 Cal. 466, 87 Am. St. Rep. 122, 56 L. R. A. 733, 67 Pac. 755.
	148	138	Farrell v. Board of Trustees, 85 Cal. 408, 24 Pac. 868.
	212	178	Cullen v. Glendora Water Co., 113 Cal. 503, 39 Pac. 769, 45 Pac. 822, 1047.
	232	206	San Luis Obispo County v. Graves, 84 Cal. 71, 23 Pac. 1032.
	302	207	People v. Common Council, 85 Cal. 369, 24 Pac. 727; Fisher v. Police Court, 86 Cal. 158, 24 Pac. 1000.
	455	1	People v. Toal, 85 Cal. 333, 24 Pac. 603.

Statutes	Page	Chapter	Case
1891	5	7	San Francisco v. Broderick, 125 Cal. 188, 57 Pac. 887.
	182	137	McCabe v. Carpenter, 102 Cal. 469, 36 Pac. 836.
	195	146	Slocum v. Bear Valley Irr. Co., 122 Cal. 555, 68 Am. St. Rep. 68, 55 Pac. 403; Keener v. Eagle Lake etc. Co., 110 Cal. 627, 43 Pac. 14; Ackley v. Black Hawk etc. Min. Co., 112 Cal. 42, 44 Pac. 330.
	283	205	Murray v. Colgan, 94 Cal. 435, 29 Pac. 871.
	295	216	People v. Johnson, 95 Cal. 471, 31 Pac. 611; Welsh v. Bramlet, 98 Cal. 219, 33 Pac. 66; Bloss v. Lewis, 109 Cal. 493, 41 Pac. 1081.
	433	226	Ex parte Giambonini, 117 Cal. 573, 49 Pac. 732
	450	231	Patty v. Colgan, 97 Cal. 251, 18 L. R. A. 744, 31 Pac. 1133.
	513	279	Bourn v. Hart, 93 Cal. 321, 27 Am. St. Rep. 203, 15 L. R. A. 431, 28 Pac. 951.
	513	280	Conlin v. Board of Supervisors, 99 Cal. 17, 37 Am. St. Rep. 17, 21 L. R. A. 474, 33 Pac. 753.
1893	12	16	Bradley v. Clark, 133 Cal. 196, 65 Pac. 395.
	33	21	Ramish v. Hartwell, 126 Cal. 443, 58 Pac. 920.
	57	45	Molineux v. State, 109 Cal. 378, 50 Am. St. Rep. 49, 42 Pac. 34.
	59	47	Los Angeles v. Teed, 112 Cal. 319, 44 Pac. 580.
	61	48	City of Los Angeles v. Hance, 122 Cal. 77, 54 Pac. 387.
	127	112	Rauer v. Williams, 118 Cal. 401, 50 Pac. 691.
	168	143	People v. Markham, 104 Cal. 232, 37 Pac. 918.
	175	148	Merchants' Nat. Bank v. Escondido Irr. Dist., 144 Cal. 329, 77 Pac. 937.
	229	188	Provident etc. Loan Assn. v. Davis, 143 Cal. 253, 76 Pac. 1034.
	280	197	Darcy v. Mayor of San Jose, 104 Cal. 642, 38 Pac. 500.
	346	234	Hale v. McGettigan, 114 Cal. 112, 45 Pac. 1049; Knight v. Martin, 128 Cal. 245, 60 Pac. 849.
1895	1	2	Dwyer v. Parker, 115 Cal. 544, 47 Pac. 372.
	14	8	Sixth Dist. Agr. Assn. v. Wright, 154 Cal. 119, 97 Pac. 144.
	107	115	Taylor v. Mott, 123 Cal. 497, 56 Pac. 256.
	164	160	Rauer v. Williams, 118 Cal. 401, 50 Pac. 691.
	205	178	Miner v. Justice's Court, 121 Cal. 264, 53 Pac. 795.
	207	181	Marsh v. Hanly, 111 Cal. 368, 43 Pac. 975; Gett v. Board of Supervisors, 111 Cal. 366, 43 Pac. 1122.
	238	193	Sullivan v. Gage, 145 Cal. 759, 79 Pac. 537.
	246	200	Ex parte Jentzsch, 112 Cal. 468, 32 L. R. A. 664, 44 Pac. 803.
	267	207	Fatjo v. Pfister, 117 Cal. 83, 48 Pac. 1012; Dwyer v. Parker, 115 Cal. 544, 47 Pac. 372;

Statutes	Page	Chapter	Case
1895	267	207.	Cooley v. Calaveras Co., 121 Cal. 482, 53 Pac. 1075; Kiernan v. Swan, 131 Cal. 410, 63 Pac. 768; Reid v. Groezinger, 115 Cal. 551, 47 Pac. 374.
	341	221	Denman v. Broderick, 111 Cal. 96, 43 Pac. 516.
	348	223	Conlin v. Board of Supervisors, 114 Cal. 404, 33 L. R. A. 752, 46 Pac. 279.
	409	12	Miner v. Justice's Court, 121 Cal. 264, 53 Pac. 795.
1897	54	60	Popper v. Broderick, 123 Cal. 456, 56 Pac. 53.
	72	78	Popper v. Broderick, 123 Cal. 456, 56 Pac. 53.
	75	82	City of Los Angeles v. Hance, 122 Cal. 77, 54 Pac. 387.
	77	83	Estate of Stanford, 126 Cal. 112, 54 Pac. 259, 45 L. R. A. 788, 58 Pac. 462; Estate of Mahoney, 133 Cal. 180, 85 Am. St. Rep. 155, 65 Pac. 389. Overruled in Estate of Johnson, 139 Cal. 532, 96 Am. St. Rep. 161, 73 Pac. 424.
	115	106	Spier v. Baker, 120 Cal. 370, 41 L. R. A. 196, 52 Pac. 659.
	135	107	Pereira v. Wallace, 129 Cal. 397, 62 Pac. 61.
	192	132	Popper v. Broderick, 123 Cal. 456, 56 Pac. 53.
	231	170	Johnson v. Goodyear Min. Co., 127 Cal. 4, 78 Am. St. Rep. 17, 47 L. R. A. 338, 59 Pac. 304.
	304	225	Sixth Dist. Agr. Assn. v. Wright, 154 Cal. 119, 97 Pac. 144.
	311	227	Matter of Lambert, 134 Cal. 626, 86 Am. St. Rep. 296, 55 L. R. A. 856, 66 Pac. 851.
	452	277	Lougher v. Soto, 129 Cal. 610, 62 Pac. 184; Van Harlingen v. Doyle, 134 Cal. 53, 54 L. R. A. 771, 66 Pac. 44; Ex parte Anderson, 134 Cal. 69, 86 Am. St. Rep. 236, 66 Pac. 194; Pratt v. Browne, 135 Cal. 649, 67 Pac. 1082; Ex parte Young, 154 Cal. 317, 22 L. R. A. (N. S.) 330, 97 Pac. 822.
1899	24	24	People v. Curry, 130 Cal. 82, 62 Pac. 516.
	47	46	Britton v. Board of Election Commrs., 129 Cal. 337, 51 L. R. A. 115, 61 Pac. 1115.
1901	56	51	Hewitt v. State Board, 148 Cal. 590, 113 Am. St. Rep. 315, 7 Ann. Cas. 750, 3 L. R. A. (N. S.) 896, 84 Pac. 39.
	117	102	Lewis v. Dunne, 134 Cal. 291, 86 Am. St. Rep. 257, 55 L. R. A. 833, 66 Pac. 478.
	332	157	Lewis v. Dunne, 134 Cal. 291, 86 Am. St. Rep. 257, 55 L. R. A. 833, 66 Pac. 478.
	433	158	Lewis v. Dunne, 134 Cal. 291, 86 Am. St. Rep. 257, 55 L. R. A. 833, 66 Pac. 478.
	685	233	Tucker v. Barnum, 144 Cal. 266, 77 Pac. 919.
1903	14	11	Ex parte Dickey, 144 Cal. 234, 103 Am. St. Rep. 82, 1 Ann. Cas. 428, 66 L. R. A. 928, 77 Pac. 924.

Statutes	Page	Chapter	Case
1905	67	69	Ex parte Drexel, 147 Cal. 763, 3 Ann. Cas. 878, 2 L. R. A. (N. S.) 588, 82 Pac. 429.
	140	140	Ex parte Quarg, 149 Cal. 79, 117 Am. St. Rep. 115, 9 Ann. Cas. 747, 5 L. R. A. (N. S.) 183, 84 Pac. 766.
	224	249	Harrison v. Colgan, 148 Cal. 69, 82 Pac. 674.
	316	302	Ex parte Dietrech, 149 Cal. 104, 5 L. R. A. (N. S.) 873, 84 Pac. 770.
	338	313	Ex parte Hayden, 147 Cal. 649, 109 Am. St. Rep. 183, 1 L. R. A. (N. S.) 184, 82 Pac. 315.
	422	354	Ex parte Sohncke, 148 Cal. 262, 113 Am. St. Rep. 236, 7 Ann. Cas. 475, 2 L. R. A. (N. S.) 813, 82 Pac. 956.
	493	386	H. K. Mulford Co. v. Curry, 163 Cal. 276, 125 Pac. 236.
	711	55	Ex parte Sohncke, 148 Cal. 262, 113 Am. St. Rep. 236, 7 Ann. Cas. 475, 2 L. R. A. (N. S.) 813, 82 Pac. 956.
1907	344		Boca Mill Co. v. Curry, 154 Cal. 326, 97 Pac. 1117.
1911	40	23	Brookes v. City of Oakland, 160 Cal. 423, 117 Pac. 433.
	1268	663	In re Crane, 26 Cal. App. 22, 145 Pac. 733.
1913	204	107	McClure v. Nye, 22 Cal. App. 248, 133 Pac. 1145.
	276	171	McClure v. Nye, 22 Cal. App. 248, 133 Pac. 1145.
	277	172	McClure v. Nye, 22 Cal. App. 248, 133 Pac. 1145.
	277	173	McClure v. Nye, 22 Cal. App. 248, 133 Pac. 1145.
	135	102	McClure v. Nye, 22 Cal. App. 248, 133 Pac. 1145.
	278	174	McClure v. Nye, 22 Cal. App. 248, 133 Pac. 1145.
	988	575	Matter of Application of Mascolo, 25 Cal. App. 92, 142 Pac. 903.

TABLE OF PARALLEL SECTIONS IN CONSTITUTIONS OF 1849 AND 1879.

Constitution 1879		Constitution 1849	
Art.	Sec.	Art.	Sec.
I	1	I	1
	2		2
	3		
	4		4
	5		5
	6		6
	6		7
	7		8
	8		
	9		9
	10		10
	11		11
	12		12
	12		13
	13		8
	14		
	15		15
	16		16
	17		17
	18		18
	19		19
	20		20
	21		
	22		
	23		21
	24		
II	1	II	1
	1		5
	2		2
	3		3
	4		4
	5		6
III	1	III	1
IV	1	IV	1
	2		2
	3		3
	4		4
	4		5
	5		6
			7
	6	I	14
	6	IV	28
	6		29
	6	Schedule	14
	7	IV	8
	8		9
	9		10
	10		11

Constitution 1879		Constitution 1849	
Art.	Sec.	Art.	Sec.
IV	11	IV	12
	12		13
	13		14
	14		15
	15		16
	16		17
	17		18
	18		19
	19		20
	20		21
	21		22
	22		23
	23		24
	24		25
	24	XI	21
	25	IV	26
	26		27
	27		30
	28		38
	29		
	30		
	31	XI	10
	32		
	33		
	34	I	22
	35		
V	1	V	1
	2		2
	3		3
	4		4
	5		5
	6		6
	7		7
	8		8
	9		9
	10		10
	11		11
	12		12
	13		14
	14		15
	15		16
	16		17
	17		18
	18		19
			20
	19		21
	19	Schedule	15
	20		

Constitution 1879		Constitution 1849		Constitution 1879		Constitution 1849	
Art.	Sec.	Art.	Sec.	Art.	Sec.	Art.	Sec.
VI	1	VI	1	XI	8		
	2		2		8½		
	3		3		9		
	4		4		10		
	5		6		11		
	5		8		12		
			5		13		
	6		7		14		
	7				15		
	8				16		
	9				17		
	10				18	IV	37
	11		9		19		
	12			XII	1	IV	31
			12		2		32
	13		10		3		36
	14		11		4		33
	15		13		5		34
	16		14		5		35
	17		15		6		
	18		16		7		
	19		17		8		
	20		18		9		
	21				10		
	22				11		
	23				12		
	24				13		
VII	1	VII	1		14		
VIII	1	VIII	1		15		
	1		2		16		
	1		3		17		
	2				18		
IX	1	IX	2		19		
	2		1		20		
	3				21		
	4				22		
	5		3		23		
	6				24		
	7			XIII	1	XI	13
	8				2		
	9		4		3		
X	1				4		
	2				5		
	3				6		
	4				7		
	5				8		
	6				9		
XI	1				10		
	2				11		
	3				12		
	4	XI	4		13		
	5		5	XIV	1		
	5		9		2		
	6			XV	1		
	7				2		

Constitution 1879		Constitution 1849	
Art.	Sec.	Art.	Sec.
XV	3		
XVI	1	VIII	1
	1	Schedule	16
XVII	1	XI	15
	2		
	3		
XVIII	1	X	1
	2		2
XIX	1		
	2		
	3		
	4		
XX	1	XI	1
	2		2
	3		3
	4		6
	5		8
	6		11
	7		12
	8		14
	9		16
	10		17
	11		18
	12		19
	12	Schedule	4
	13	XI	20

Constitution—40

Constitution 1879		Constitution 1849	
Art.	Sec.	Art.	Sec.
	14	XI	
XX	15		
	16		7
	17		
	18		
	19		
	20	Schedule	13
XXI	1	XII	1
XXII	1	Schedule	3
	2		1
	3	VI	19
	3	Schedule	2
	4		6
	5		6
	6		6
	7		5
	8		
	9		7
			8
			9
			10
			11
			12
	10	IV	39
	11		
	12		

TABLE OF CALIFORNIA CITATIONS TO CONSTITUTION OF 1849.

[Citations are to California Reports, Vols. 1 to 169, and California Appellate Reports, Vols. 1 to 26.]

Art. I Sec. 1.		Art. I Sec. 8 (Con.)		Art. I Sec. 17 (Con.)		Art. III Sec. 1 (Con.)	
Vol.	Page	Vol.	Page	Vol.	Page	Vol.	Page
7 Cal.	6	40 Cal.	513	30 Cal.	189	46 Cal.	514
9 Cal.	504	41 Cal.	168	36 Cal.	671	47 Cal.	653
18 Cal.	680	42 Cal.	168	65 Cal.	595	50 Cal.	403
22 Cal.	324	43 Cal.	79			151 Cal.	285
23 Cal.	464	48 Cal.	334				
32 Cal.	249	50 Cal.	403	**Art. I Sec. 21.**			
33 Cal.	281	51 Cal.	248	32 Cal.	249	**Art. IV Sec. 1.**	
36 Cal.	671	53 Cal.	45			5 Cal.	21
38 Cal.	703	53 Cal.	212			46 Cal.	514
		53 Cal.	412	**Art. II Sec.1.**		47 Cal.	652
Art. I Sec. 2.		59 Cal.	245	5 Cal.	25	166 Cal.	605
22 Cal.	324	66 Cal.	500	26 Cal.	178		
30 Cal.	189	69 Cal.	372			**Art. IV Sec. 3**	
69 Cal.	372	109 Cal.	449			26 Cal.	254
		109 Cal.	622	**Art. II Sec. 2.**			
		130 Cal.	495	26 Cal.	209		
Art. I Sec. 3.		167 Cal.	318			**Art. IV Sec. 5**	
16 Cal.	253					26 Cal.	253
22 Cal.	316	**Art. I Sec. 9.**		**Art. II Sec. 3.**			
		22 Cal.	316	26 Cal.	249	**Art. IV Sec. 7**	
						8 Cal.	415
Art. I Sec. 4.		**Art. I Sec. 11.**		**Art. II Sec. 4.**			
9 Cal.	504	17 Cal.	552	26 Cal.	211	**Art. IV Sec. 8**	
17 Cal.	612	24 Cal.	544	28 Cal.	140	34 Cal.	535
18 Cal.	680	26 Cal.	255	38 Cal.	93		
		36 Cal.	671				
Art. I Sec. 5.		37 Cal.	375			**Art. IV Sec. 10**	
11 Cal.	226	38 Cal.	703	**Art. II Sec. 6.**		34 Cal.	535
		43 Cal.	432	26 Cal.	186		
		52 Cal.	601				
Art. I Sec. 7.		58 Cal.	61			**Art. IV Sec. 17**	
19 Cal.	541			**Art. III Sec. 1.**		6 Cal.	660
41 Cal.	31	**Art. I Sec. 15.**		5 Cal.	19	9 Cal.	522
		1 Cal.	440	5 Cal.	112	39 Cal.	541
		6 Cal.	240	8 Cal.	15		
Art. I Sec. 8.		53 Cal.	207	10 Cal.	403	**Art. IV Sec. 18**	
12 Cal.	83			17 Cal.	557	34 Cal.	535
18 Cal.	251	**Art. I Sec. 16.**		20 Cal.	43		
22 Cal.	316	22 Cal.	316	22 Cal.	478	**Art. IV Sec. 19**	
23 Cal.	326			24 Cal.	126	2 Cal.	211
29 Cal.	256	**Art. I Sec. 17**		29 Cal.	452	22 Cal.	314
32 Cal.	250	6 Cal.	253	30 Cal.	167	45 Cal.	218
33 Cal.	281	13 Cal.	165	33 Cal.	281	118 Cal.	483
				34 Cal.	525		

(627)

Art. VI Sec. 7		Art. VI Sec. 15		Art. XI Sec. 1		Art. XI Sec. 13	
Vol.	Page	Vol.	Page	Vol.	Page	Vol.	Page
16 Cal.	442	2 Cal.	203	5 Cal.	32	1 Cal.	252
30 Cal.	683	9 Cal.	346	50 Cal.	572	2 Cal.	592
40 Cal.	654	12 Cal.	392			4 Cal.	49
						12 Cal.	83
Art. VI Sec. 8				**Art. XI Sec. 3**		13 Cal.	350
5 Cal.	22	**Art. VI Sec. 16**		17 Cal.	20	14 Cal.	16
5 Cal.	104	12 Cal.	392	22 Cal.	307	22 Cal.	369
6 Cal.	89	30 Cal.	163	24 Cal.	243	29 Cal.	451
9 Cal.	87	38 Cal.	395			30 Cal.	683
10 Cal.	403					34 Cal.	475
20 Cal.	44	**Art. VI Sec. 17**		**Art. XI Sec. 4**		34 Cal.	657
28 Cal.	119	27 Cal.	513	33 Cal.	494	37 Cal.	246
30 Cal.	575	55 Cal.	238	34 Cal.	532	40 Cal.	513
34 Cal.	689			47 Cal.	656	41 Cal.	354
36 Cal.	27	**Art. VI Sec. 18**		48 Cal.	318	43 Cal.	335
37 Cal.	161	59 Cal.	191	50 Cal.	564	43 Cal.	434
38 Cal.	157			58 Cal.	61	44 Cal.	326
39 Cal.	99			121 Cal.	551	46 Cal.	506
41 Cal.	131	**Art. VI Sec. 19**				46 Cal.	556
42 Cal.	56	21 Cal.	416			47 Cal.	92
44 Cal.	125			**Art. XI Sec. 5**		47 Cal.	648
45 Cal.	217			33 Cal.	404	51 Cal.	244
45 Cal.	679	**Art. VIII Sec. 1**		39 Cal.	9	51 Cal.	501
48 Cal.	72	6 Cal.	500	47 Cal.	656	52 Cal.	81
51 Cal.	433	7 Cal.	66			52 Cal.	601
52 Cal.	223	13 Cal.	182			58 Cal.	61
53 Cal.	413	15 Cal.	454	**Art. XI Sec. 6**			
58 Cal.	402	16 Cal.	253	8 Cal.	16	**Art. XI Sec. 14**	
4 " App.	119	23 Cal.	174	22 Cal.	314	153	362
		27 Cal.	206	34 Cal.	541		
Art. VI Sec. 9		112 Cal.	167	45 Cal.	558	**Art. XI Sec. 15**	
3 Cal.	389					14 Cal.	474
5 Cal.	279					24 Cal.	640
6 Cal.	66	**Art. IX Sec. 2**		**Art. XI Sec. 7**			
9 Cal.	88	37 Cal.	244	6 Cal.	289	**Art. XI Sec. 16**	
15 Cal.	92			7 Cal.	102	58 Cal.	472
19 Cal.	572			22 Cal.	314		
24 Cal.	66	**Art. IX Sec. 3**		79 Cal.	113		
24 Cal.	452	48 Cal.	50	128 Cal.	604	**Art. XI Sec. 18**	
28 Cal.	119			1 " App.	7	2 Cal.	211
42 Cal.	67					22 Cal.	316
53 Cal.	413	**Art. IX Sec. 4**					
157 Cal.	776	123 Cal.	616	**Art. XI Sec. 8**			
				23 Cal.	182	**Art. XI Sec. 19**	
Art. VI Sec. 10						26 Cal.	211
8 Cal.	382	**Art. IX Sec. 5**		**Art. XI Sec. 9**			
		5 Cal.	22	34 Cal.	533		
Art. VI Sec. 11				47 Cal.	657	**Art. XII Sec. 4**	
32 Cal.	299	**Art. X Sec. 2**		51 Cal.	29	27 Cal.	211
43 Cal.	435	26 Cal.	186				
Art. VI Sec. 14				**Art. XI Sec. 10**		**Art. XII Sec. 31**	
5 Cal.	232	**Art. X Sec. 7**		27 Cal.	207	61 Cal.	5
9 Cal.	87	55 Cal.	524				

TABLE OF CALIFORNIA CITATIONS TO CONSTITUTION OF 1879.

[Citations are to California Reports, Vols. 1 to 169, and California Appellate Reports, Vols. 1 to 26.]

Art. I Sec. 1

Vol.	Page
65 Cal.	35
112 Cal.	471
128 Cal.	434
133 Cal.	354
133 Cal.	377
136 Cal.	125
147 Cal.	650
147 Cal.	763
148 Cal.	127
149 Cal.	400
154 Cal.	322
157 Cal.	774
158 Cal.	325
162 Cal.	691
5 " App.	759
6 " App.	236

Art. I Sec. 2

92 Cal.	316
160 Cal.	302

Art. I Sec. 3

105 Cal.	606
144 Cal.	79

Art. I Sec. 4

59 Cal.	13
60 Cal.	201
79 Cal.	176

Art. I Sec. 6

54 Cal.	103
67 Cal.	257
156 Cal.	737
160 Cal.	383
1 " App.	199
8 " App.	469
8 " App.	566
11 " App.	575
18 " App.	4

Art. I Sec. 7

64 Cal.	266
87 Cal.	354

Art. I Sec. 7 (Con.)

Vol.	Page
122 Cal.	139
139 Cal.	589
164 Cal.	177
169 Cal.	167
169 Cal.	169
169 Cal.	556
5 " App.	623
8 " App.	233
9 " App.	250

Art. I Sec. 8

56 Cal.	233
59 Cal.	245
60 Cal.	104
65 Cal.	646
108 Cal.	663
111 Cal.	612
115 Cal.	53
152 Cal.	73
167 Cal.	317
5 " App.	465
5 " App.	468
8 " App.	219
8 " App.	755
9 " App.	283
9 " App.	543
19 " App.	551
20 " App.	589
24 " App.	181

Art. I Sec. 9

72 Cal.	466
73 Cal.	123
112 Cal.	97
139 Cal.	121
167 Cal.	317
25 " App.	782

Art. I Sec. 10

129 Cal.	343

Art. I Sec. 11

59 Cal.	12
60 Cal.	189

Art. I Sec. 11 (Con.)

Vol.	Page
65 Cal.	35
68 Cal.	145
69 Cal.	151
71 Cal.	631
73 Cal.	582
76 Cal.	442
84 Cal.	76
89 Cal.	523
90 Cal.	558
91 Cal.	249
94 Cal.	603
104 Cal.	351
109 Cal.	334
109 Cal.	497
111 Cal.	371
111 Cal.	569
113 Cal.	646
114 Cal.	146
118 Cal.	305
119 Cal.	241
122 Cal.	147
126 Cal.	37
127 Cal.	7
129 Cal.	343
134 Cal.	55
136 Cal.	528
137 Cal.	481
138 Cal.	381
140 Cal.	487
143 Cal.	414
144 Cal.	269
147 Cal.	334
148 Cal.	265
148 Cal.	748
149 Cal.	400
151 Cal.	334
153 Cal.	61
155 Cal.	381
155 Cal.	657
157 Cal.	55
157 Cal.	75
157 Cal.	158
157 Cal.	163
162 Cal.	590
162 Cal.	691
164 Cal.	326

Art. I Sec. 11 (Con.)

Vol.	Page
164 Cal.	400
164 Cal.	568
1 " App.	199
6 " App.	240
11 " App.	407
12 " App.	405
17 " App.	425
18 " App.	33
24 " App.	89
24 " App.	218
25 " App.	95

Art. I Sec. 12

5 " App.	649

Art. I Sec. 13

65 Cal.	223
66 Cal.	102
68 Cal.	630
69 Cal.	372
70 Cal.	18
70 Cal.	177
82 Cal.	459
100 Cal.	153
103 Cal.	354
104 Cal.	527
107 Cal.	288
115 Cal.	61
116 Cal.	250
127 Cal.	7
130 Cal.	123
133 Cal.	351
136 Cal.	125
144 Cal.	56
145 Cal.	90
146 Cal.	315
150 Cal.	34
150 Cal.	550
151 Cal.	204
152 Cal.	617
154 Cal.	308
154 Cal.	322
154 Cal.	390
160 Cal.	338

Art. I Sec. 13 (Con.)		Art. I Sec. 14 (Con.)		Art. I Sec. 21 (Con.)		Art. II Sec. 1	
Vol.	Page	Vol.	Page	Vol.	Page	Vol.	Page
160 Cal.	427	169 Cal.	555	143 Cal.	414	92 Cal.	321
165 Cal.	61	169 Cal.	557	143 Cal.	573	117 Cal.	123
168 Cal.	781	1 " App.	444	148 Cal.	265	120 Cal.	374
1 " App.	199	2 " App.	560	149 Cal.	400	127 Cal.	88
2 " App.	204	5 " App.	730	151 Cal.	334	136 Cal.	451
5 " App.	214	10 " App.	381	152 Cal.	233	145 Cal.	341
5 " App.	590	19 " App.	134	154 Cal.	330	146 Cal.	513
5 " App.	750	23 " App.	273	156 Cal.	74	151 Cal.	603
6 " App.	236	24 " App.	266	157 Cal.	55	152 Cal.	231
7 " App.	753			162 Cal.	590	165 Cal.	778
8 " App.	117			162 Cal.	691	7 " App.	413
9 " App.	200	Art. I Sec. 15		164 Cal.	568	23 " App.	471
9 " App.	250	134 Cal.	661	6 " App.	237		
11 " App.	472	26 " App.	25	8 " App.	535	Art. II Sec. 2½	
13 " App.	545			12 " App.	405	146 Cal.	316
14 " App.	114			18 " App.	25	151 Cal.	602
17 " App.	6	Art. I Sec. 16		24 " App.	89	152 Cal.	434
18 " App.	65	72 Cal.	466	25 " App.	539	155 Cal.	780
24 " App.	800	116 Cal.	523			168 Cal.	322
26 " App.	337	146 Cal.	624				
		162 Cal.	233	Art. I Sec. 22		Art. II Sec. 4	
		166 Cal.	638	54 Cal.	247	105 Cal.	462
Art. I Sec. 14				57 Cal.	609	7 " App.	553
59 Cal.	265			69 Cal.	485		
66 Cal.	501			83 Cal.	403	Art. II Sec. 5	
68 Cal.	65	Art. I Sec. 17		83 Cal.	494	146 Cal.	316
74 Cal.	262	65 Cal.	594	86 Cal.	50	154 Cal.	282
79 Cal.	551	67 Cal.	382	92 Cal.	316	20 " App.	20
91 Cal.	456	70 Cal.	155	115 Cal.	548		
94 Cal.	492	158 Cal.	325	128 Cal.	247	Art. II Sec. 6	
94 Cal.	608			129 Cal.	403	20 " App.	19
95 Cal.	223			132 Cal.	219		
98 Cal.	262	Art. I Sec. 19		144 Cal.	387	Art. III Sec. 1	
98 Cal.	617	68 Cal.	288	147 Cal.	582	58 Cal.	643
103 Cal.	616	105 Cal.	606	160 Cal.	40	61 Cal.	322
106 Cal.	284	155 Cal.	546	164 Cal.	710	68 Cal.	196
109 Cal.	622	15 " App.	285	166 Cal.	587	80 Cal.	234
111 Cal.	563	23 " App.	665	9 " App.	159	102 Cal.	470
118 Cal.	287					106 Cal.	422
118 Cal.	572					123 Cal.	527
126 Cal.	153	Art. I Sec. 20		Art. I Sec. 23		126 Cal.	672
130 Cal.	495	144 Cal.	173	129 Cal.	347	127 Cal.	159
130 Cal.	634					129 Cal.	604
133 Cal.	105					140 Cal.	1
137 Cal.	579	Art. I Sec. 21		Art. I Sec. 24		146 Cal.	607
137 Cal.	621	60 Cal.	189	117 Cal.	123	148 Cal.	631
144 Cal.	212	65 Cal.	35	155 Cal.	389	150 Cal.	318
151 Cal.	273	69 Cal.	151	155 Cal.	789	151 Cal.	43
154 Cal.	322	73 Cal.	371	160 Cal.	355	155 Cal.	656
155 Cal.	320	112 Cal.	471			156 Cal.	501
157 Cal.	75	118 Cal.	5			157 Cal.	422
160 Cal.	299	129 Cal.	343			1 " App.	67
162 Cal.	717	134 Cal.	55	Art. I Sec. 25		11 " App.	572
166 Cal.	658	137 Cal.	181	24 " App.	340		
166 Cal.	688						

Art. IV Sec. 1		Art. IV Sec. 7		Art. IV Sec. 22		Art. IV Sec. 24 (Con.)	
Vol.	Page	Vol.	Page	Vol.	Page	Vol.	Page
56 Cal.	100	164 Cal.	57	61 Cal.	267	142 Cal.	13
63 Cal.	21			69 Cal.	77	143 Cal.	258
72 Cal.	466			71 Cal.	630	143 Cal.	627
92 Cal.	307	Art. IV Sec. 9		77 Cal.	134	144 Cal.	387
96 Cal.	291	146 Cal.	606	84 Cal.	58	146 Cal.	650
139 Cal.	28			92 Cal.	55	150 Cal.	326
145 Cal.	686			106 Cal.	116	151 Cal.	50
151 Cal.	803	Art. IV Sec. 10		121 Cal.	19	154 Cal.	202
152 Cal.	236	80 Cal.	213	123 Cal.	151	154 Cal.	388
164 Cal.	325	160 Cal.	760	126 Cal.	118	155 Cal.	113
167 Cal.	236	167 Cal.	319	144 Cal.	684	155 Cal.	384
167 Cal.	319			151 Cal.	800	155 Cal.	658
168 Cal.	709			154 Cal.	129	157 Cal.	58
9 " App.	159	Art. IV Sec. 15		156 Cal.	504	157 Cal.	75
22 " App.	249	54 Cal.	112	169 Cal.	137	159 Cal.	511
22 " App.	483	72 Cal.	467	169 Cal.	139	161 Cal.	348
		80 Cal.	213	8 " App.	531	162 Cal.	202
		85 Cal.	336	19 " App.	570	162 Cal.	232
Art. IV Sec. 2		100 Cal.	421	25 " App.	538	162 Cal.	691
56 Cal.	101	121 Cal.	267			164 Cal.	567
96 Cal.	291	145 Cal.	688			165 Cal.	210
114 Cal.	114	158 Cal.	84	Art. IV Sec. 23		165 Cal.	344
130 Cal.	88	23 " App.	581	15 " App.	302	165 Cal.	747
144 Cal.	173					167 Cal.	293
146 Cal.	607					1 " App.	64
		Art. IV Sec. 16				2 " App.	252
		72 Cal.	467	Art. IV Sec. 24		11 " App.	306
Art. IV Sec. 3		80 Cal.	213	55 Cal.	496	12 " App.	29
55 Cal.	622	83 Cal.	494	57 Cal.	618	18 " App.	27
56 Cal.	100	85 Cal.	337	58 Cal.	635	18 " App.	61
96 Cal.	291	121 Cal.	267	60 Cal.	30	19 " App.	602
114 Cal.	169	156 Cal.	501	74 Cal.	41	20 " App.	154
		160 Cal.	760	74 Cal.	552	20 " App.	515
				80 Cal.	270	22 " App.	27
Art. IV Sec. 4				84 Cal.	228	22 " App.	431
55 Cal.	622	Art. IV Sec. 18		88 Cal.	534	24 " App.	46
56 Cal.	100	85 Cal.	645	93 Cal.	635	25 " App.	95
96 Cal.	264	108 Cal.	662	102 Cal.	31		
119 Cal.	438	122 Cal.	293	102 Cal.	418		
154 Cal.	281	145 Cal.	37	114 Cal.	149	Art. IV Sec. 25	
168 Cal.	497	147 Cal.	533	117 Cal.	86	55 Cal.	490
168 Cal.	533	154 Cal.	281	120 Cal.	373	55 Cal.	618
		161 Cal.	174	122 Cal.	79	57 Cal.	613
Art. IV Sec. 5		168 Cal.	535	125 Cal.	414	59 Cal.	8
65 Cal.	578			128 Cal.	668	60 Cal.	32
66 Cal.	29			129 Cal.	570	61 Cal.	38
96 Cal.	291	Art. IV Sec. 20		129 Cal.	606	61 Cal.	267
145 Cal.	425	61 Cal.	267	130 Cal.	91	63 Cal.	382
		73 Cal.	231	132 Cal.	219	72 Cal.	466
		154 Cal.	281	133 Cal.	76	73 Cal.	77
Art. IV Sec. 6		2 " App.	55	134 Cal.	478	81 Cal.	499
65 Cal.	577			135 Cal.	652	84 Cal.	229
96 Cal.	290	Art. IV Sec. 21		139 Cal.	463	87 Cal.	79
152 Cal.	233	136 Cal.	445	140 Cal.	487	93 Cal.	400
156 Cal.	474	154 Cal.	28	141 Cal.	334	105 Cal.	616

Art. IV Sec. 25 (Con.)

Vol.	Page
124 Cal.	696
135 Cal.	518
137 Cal.	518
138 Cal.	381
140 Cal.	480
142 Cal.	195
143 Cal.	414
149 Cal.	399
150 Cal.	322
150 Cal.	566
151 Cal.	478
152 Cal.	231
154 Cal.	330
155 Cal.	381
156 Cal.	74
157 Cal.	55
160 Cal.	302
162 Cal.	590
162 Cal.	691
164 Cal.	326
164 Cal.	400
166 Cal.	768
167 Cal.	291
168 Cal.	267
6 " App.	240
8 " App.	533
11 " App.	361
11 " App.	407
12 " App.	227
12 " App.	291
12 " App.	292
17 " App.	425
18 " App.	25
18 " App.	449
19 " App.	549
20 " App.	515
22 " App.	442
24 " App.	179
25 " App.	95

Sub. 1.

62 Cal.	465
120 Cal.	401
121 Cal.	267

Sub. 2.

55 Cal.	551
60 Cal.	81
60 Cal.	189
62 Cal.	465
67 Cal.	360
112 Cal.	471
1 " App.	149

Sub. 3

Vol.	Page
62 Cal.	465
83 Cal.	402
93 Cal.	424
100 Cal.	120
113 Cal.	512
117 Cal.	363
120 Cal.	304
126 Cal.	230
127 Cal.	7
1 " App.	573

Sub. 4

62 Cal.	465

Sub. 6

123 Cal.	527

Sub. 7

114 Cal.	146

Sub. 9

55 Cal.	622
65 Cal.	123
84 Cal.	76
94 Cal.	620
98 Cal.	224
109 Cal.	335
111 Cal.	102
113 Cal.	646
114 Cal.	410
118 Cal.	306
148 Cal.	748

Sub. 10

60 Cal.	28
83 Cal.	402
105 Cal.	583
119 Cal.	521
124 Cal.	698

Sub. 11

55 Cal.	622
81 Cal.	501
100 Cal.	425
111 Cal.	102
111 Cal.	371
124 Cal.	698

Sub. 13

83 Cal.	402

Sub. 15

126 Cal.	117

Sub. 17

Vol.	Page
126 Cal.	117

Sub. 19

100 Cal.	120
118 Cal.	306
124 Cal.	698

Sub. 20

55 Cal.	495
83 Cal.	402

Sub. 23

67 Cal.	360

Sub. 24

83 Cal.	402
127 Cal.	7

Sub. 25.

161 Cal.	674

Sub. 27

55 Cal.	402
104 Cal.	351
124 Cal.	698
148 Cal.	384

Sub. 28

62 Cal.	465
65 Cal.	123
65 Cal.	291
85 Cal.	413
98 Cal.	224
111 Cal.	102
113 Cal.	646
114 Cal.	410
118 Cal.	305
124 Cal.	698
125 Cal.	192
132 Cal.	221
25 " App.	690

Sub. 29

62 Cal.	465
65 Cal.	123
68 Cal.	145
85 Cal.	496
89 Cal.	523
92 Cal.	606
103 Cal.	395
104 Cal.	644
113 Cal.	645
115 Cal.	549

Sub. 29 (Con.)

Vol.	Page
118 Cal.	306
126 Cal.	37
144 Cal.	269

Sub. 33

81 Cal.	498
84 Cal.	76
91 Cal.	249
94 Cal.	620
100 Cal.	120
109 Cal.	497
111 Cal.	371
112 Cal.	471
114 Cal.	410
118 Cal.	306
118 Cal.	404
119 Cal.	523
124 Cal.	698
126 Cal.	230
127 Cal.	7
127 Cal.	684
130 Cal.	134
132 Cal.	221
144 Cal.	269
148 Cal.	148
1 " App.	573

Art. IV Sec. 25½

24 " App.	341
24 " App.	342
25 " App.	94

Art. IV Sec. 26

68 Cal.	289
87 Cal.	607
89 Cal.	378
104 Cal.	599
127 Cal.	118
130 Cal.	326
146 Cal.	658
150 Cal.	241
154 Cal.	336
162 Cal.	457
12 " App.	647
24 " App.	69

Art. IV Sec. 28

80 Cal.	213

Art. IV Sec. 29

61 Cal.	267
115 Cal.	532

Art. IV Sec. 29 (Con.)

Vol.	Page
151 Cal.	800
156 Cal.	504
169 Cal.	137

Art. IV Sec. 30

115 Cal.	532
156 Cal.	504

Art. IV Sec. 31

72 Cal.	473
74 Cal.	125
77 Cal.	475
80 Cal.	270
83 Cal.	265
92 Cal.	606
93 Cal.	326
97 Cal.	252
99 Cal.	21
109 Cal.	380
112 Cal.	315
115 Cal.	532
117 Cal.	176
118 Cal.	546
123 Cal.	498
126 Cal.	118
138 Cal.	273
143 Cal.	331
144 Cal.	692
149 Cal.	528
151 Cal.	800
152 Cal.	735
153 Cal.	228
154 Cal.	129
156 Cal.	475
156 Cal.	504
157 Cal.	527
166 Cal.	605
168 Cal.	602
6 " App.	747
8 " App.	535
15 " App.	303
22 " App.	255

Art. IV Sec. 32

72 Cal.	465
74 Cal.	125
77 Cal.	475
80 Cal.	270
92 Cal.	606
93 Cal.	326

Art. IV Sec. 32 (Con.)

Vol.	Page
115 Cal.	532
121 Cal.	21
123 Cal.	498
138 Cal.	275
156 Cal.	504
15 " App.	303

Art. IV Sec. 33

145 Cal.	633

Art. IV Sec. 34

94 Cal.	435
145 Cal.	771
156 Cal.	504
169 Cal.	137
169 Cal.	138
169 Cal.	139

Art. IV Sec. 35

86 Cal.	550
146 Cal.	610
1 " App.	55

Art. IV Sec. 36

167 Cal.	286
26 " App.	123

Art. IV Sec. 37

166 Cal.	605

Art. V Sec. 1

148 Cal.	504
1 " App.	64

Art. V Sec. 2

56 Cal.	101
62 Cal.	569
99 Cal.	45
114 Cal.	169
9 " App.	154

Art. V Sec. 7

148 Cal.	504

Art. V Sec. 8

Vol.	Page
62 Cal.	565
62 Cal.	568
66 Cal.	655
93 Cal.	155
114 Cal.	170
123 Cal.	309
127 Cal.	397
9 " App.	154

Art. V Sec. 9

130 Cal.	89
146 Cal.	607

Art. V Sec. 14

151 Cal.	240
156 Cal.	486
6 " App.	262

Art. V Sec. 15

56 Cal.	101
62 Cal.	569
114 Cal.	169

Art. V Sec. 16

62 Cal.	569
9 " App.	158

Art. V Sec. 17

56 Cal.	101
9 " App.	154

Art. V Sec. 19

9 " App.	575

Art. VI Sec. 1

54 Cal.	186
62 Cal.	465
66 Cal.	4
71 Cal.	633
78 Cal.	557
82 Cal.	344
83 Cal.	112
85 Cal.	335
97 Cal.	216
114 Cal.	330
119 Cal.	232

Art. VI Sec. 1 (Con.)

Vol.	Page
120 Cal.	401
121 Cal.	267
140 Cal.	12
143 Cal.	246
151 Cal.	468
153 Cal.	165
155 Cal.	386
156 Cal.	480
157 Cal.	419
158 Cal.	448
161 Cal.	239
167 Cal.	312
3 " App.	645
6 " App.	739
11 " App.	361
24 " App.	394

Art. VI Sec. 2

81 Cal.	460
82 Cal.	599
83 Cal.	112
83 Cal.	494
95 Cal.	43
148 Cal.	177
10 " App.	457
24 " App.	394

Art. VI Sec. 3

56 Cal.	101
81 Cal.	460
83 Cal.	112
99 Cal.	45

Art. VI Sec. 4

54 Cal.	103
55 Cal.	191
60 Cal.	115
60 Cal.	654
62 Cal.	41
65 Cal.	99
65 Cal.	382
65 Cal.	645
67 Cal.	187
79 Cal.	107
79 Cal.	486
82 Cal.	162
82 Cal.	426
83 Cal.	112
94 Cal.	353
95 Cal.	646
100 Cal.	120

Art. VI Sec. 4 (Con.)

Vol.	Page
108 Cal.	663
110 Cal.	39
120 Cal.	569
122 Cal.	534
138 Cal.	429
142 Cal.	628
146 Cal.	138
147 Cal.	265
147 Cal.	347
148 Cal.	70
148 Cal.	742
148 Cal.	773
149 Cal.	292
149 Cal.	296
149 Cal.	309
149 Cal.	324
149 Cal.	351
149 Cal.	456
149 Cal.	428
149 Cal.	482
149 Cal.	712
151 Cal.	30
151 Cal.	203
151 Cal.	518
152 Cal.	110
152 Cal.	603
155 Cal.	66
156 Cal.	84
157 Cal.	4
157 Cal.	773
159 Cal.	33
161 Cal.	241
161 Cal.	310
163 Cal.	242
164 Cal.	731
165 Cal.	63
165 Cal.	206
166 Cal.	370
166 Cal.	647
166 Cal.	693
167 Cal.	793
169 Cal.	51
169 Cal.	170
169 Cal.	579
169 Cal.	619
2 " App.	160
2 " App.	316
2 " App.	533
2 " App.	664
2 " App.	728
3 " App.	238
3 " App.	645
3 " App.	646
5 " App.	548

Art. VI Sec. 4 (Con.)

Vol.	Page
5 " App.	678
6 " App.	114
7 " App.	3
7 " App.	221
7 " App.	257
7 " App.	567
7 " App.	658
8 " App.	434
8 " App.	490
8 " App.	755
9 " App.	210
9 " App.	218
10 " App.	567
11 " App.	27
11 " App.	298
11 " App.	385
12 " App.	122
13 " App.	391
13 " App.	736
14 " App.	624
17 " App.	368
19 " App.	89
21 " App.	114
21 " App.	722
22 " App.	605
22 " App.	807
24 " App.	408
24 " App.	555
25 " App.	568
26 " App.	17

Art. VI Sec. 4½

165 Cal.	63
165 Cal.	147
166 Cal.	370
166 Cal.	575
168 Cal.	319
169 Cal.	396
169 Cal.	414
169 Cal.	553
169 Cal.	554
17 " App.	785
18 " App.	65
18 " App.	554
18 " App.	571
19 " App.	694
20 " App.	47
20 " App.	680
21 " App.	69
22 " App.	20
22 " App.	605
22 " App.	709
23 " App.	114

Art. VI Sec. 4½ (Con.)

Vol.	Page
23 " App.	381
23 " App.	452
23 " App.	524
24 " App.	466
24 " App.	666
24 " App.	759
24 " App.	798
25 " App.	6
25 " App.	8
25 " App.	165
25 " App.	322
26 " App.	225
26 " App.	326
26 " App.	741

Art. VI Sec. 5

54 Cal.	186
60 Cal.	103
60 Cal.	152
60 Cal.	307
60 Cal.	427
61 Cal.	71
62 Cal.	41
64 Cal.	444
65 Cal.	476
65 Cal.	641
66 Cal.	204
71 Cal.	383
71 Cal.	555
73 Cal.	183
76 Cal.	184
78 Cal.	557
80 Cal.	41
82 Cal.	305
83 Cal.	493
84 Cal.	120
87 Cal.	231
92 Cal.	50
93 Cal.	463
94 Cal.	355
94 Cal.	397
100 Cal.	120
103 Cal.	120
104 Cal.	203
110 Cal.	264
117 Cal.	381
122 Cal.	119
123 Cal.	695
130 Cal.	98
133 Cal.	59
134 Cal.	588
138 Cal.	70
138 Cal.	154

Art. VI Sec. 5 (Con.)

Vol.	Page
140 Cal.	133
144 Cal.	773
149 Cal.	793
150 Cal.	468
150 Cal.	481
152 Cal.	568
153 Cal.	598
154 Cal.	97
154 Cal.	98
154 Cal.	464
154 Cal.	519
155 Cal.	73
155 Cal.	386
156 Cal.	85
156 Cal.	480
156 Cal.	491
157 Cal.	788
159 Cal.	33
159 Cal.	364
159 Cal.	424
163 Cal.	242
166 Cal.	647
166 Cal.	712
167 Cal.	312
168 Cal.	498
168 Cal.	701
1 " App.	181
1 " App.	227
4 " App.	720
6 " App.	476
10 " App.	457
11 " App.	362
12 " App.	486
13 " App.	274
15 " App.	474
16 " App.	564
19 " App.	82
24 " App.	360
26 " App.	742

Art. VI Sec. 6

55 Cal.	266
56 Cal.	101
86 Cal.	28
99 Cal.	44
104 Cal.	234
133 Cal.	455
135 Cal.	653
138 Cal.	15
139 Cal.	477
146 Cal.	10
6 " App.	300

Art. IV Sec. 6 (Con.)		Art. VI Sec. 14		Art. VI Sec. 19 (Con.)		Art. IX Sec. 3	
Vol.	Page	Vol.	Page	Vol.	Page	Vol.	Page
9 " App.	165	56 Cal.	101	13 " App.	636	56 Cal.	102
10 " App.	211	94 Cal.	47	14 " App.	101	114 Cal.	335
		103 Cal.	491	19 " App.	744	114 Cal.	561
		155 Cal.	814	22 " App.	229	123 Cal.	308
Art. VI Sec. 7				23 " App.	522		
55 Cal.	266	**Art. VI Sec. 15**		24 " App.	648	**Art. IX Sec. 4**	
133 Cal.	455	158 Cal.	448	26 " App.	389	70 Cal.	157
		161 Cal.	239			97 Cal.	431
						104 Cal.	658
Art. VI Sec. 8				**Art. VI Sec. 20**		143 Cal.	331
130 Cal.	573	**Art. VI Sec. 16**		103 Cal.	413		
168 Cal.	22	80 Cal.	222	122 Cal.	288		
6 " App.	771			153 Cal.	167	**Art. IX Sec. 5**	
20 " App.	163			160 Cal.	722	55 Cal.	334
		Art. VI Sec. 17		24 " App.	392	55 Cal.	490
		87 Cal.	396			97 Cal.	431
Art. VI Sec. 9		138 Cal.	37			104 Cal.	350
86 Cal.	29	148 Cal.	70	**Art. VI Sec. 21**		117 Cal.	523
104 Cal.	234	160 Cal.	177	57 Cal.	138	124 Cal.	698
118 Cal.	483	9 " App.	578			134 Cal.	65
6 " App.	301					141 Cal.	376
15 " App.	428			**Art. VI Sec. 22**		148 Cal.	384
		Art. VI Sec. 18		80 Cal.	221	148 Cal.	753
		118 Cal.	483				
Art. VI Sec. 11		154 Cal.	281				
55 Cal.	611			**Art. VI Sec. 24**		**Art. IX Sec. 6**	
60 Cal.	103			62 Cal.	514	55 Cal.	334
60 Cal.	152			164 Cal.	732	97 Cal.	431
60 Cal.	427	**Art. VI Sec. 19**		7 " App.	228	104 Cal.	63
80 Cal.	40	55 Cal.	238			117 Cal.	523
90 Cal.	502	65 Cal.	261			118 Cal.	119
114 Cal.	331	65 Cal.	431	**Art. VI Sec. 29**		124 Cal.	698
121 Cal.	267	65 Cal.	569	80 Cal.	222	134 Cal.	65
122 Cal.	119	86 Cal.	33			141 Cal.	375
122 Cal.	534	88 Cal.	270			148 Cal.	388
130 Cal.	98	88 Cal.	426	**Art. VI Sec. 34**		152 Cal.	517
133 Cal.	76	96 Cal.	181	80 Cal.	222		
143 Cal.	246	97 Cal.	453				
151 Cal.	469	115 Cal.	14			**Art. IX Sec. 7**	
158 Cal.	448	129 Cal.	509			55 Cal.	333
161 Cal.	239	130 Cal.	8	**Art. VII Sec. 1**		117 Cal.	522
162 Cal.	288	133 Cal.	398	12 " App.	298	153 Cal.	778
4 " App.	720	149 Cal.	41				
6 " App.	739	156 Cal.	727				
		160 Cal.	176	**Art. IX Sec. 1**		**Art. IX Sec. 8**	
		163 Cal.	55	118 Cal.	120	55 Cal.	334
Art. VI Sec. 13		167 Cal.	550	121 Cal.	22	71 Cal.	630
78 Cal.	560	169 Cal.	170	124 Cal.	699		
85 Cal.	336	4 " App.	96	151 Cal.	802		
97 Cal.	216	4 " App.	218	163 Cal.	352	**Art. IX Sec. 9**	
120 Cal.	401	10 " App.	491			55 Cal.	334
151 Cal.	469	11 " App.	467			66 Cal.	508
167 Cal.	316	11 " App.	553	**Art. IX Sec. 2**		69 Cal.	216
11 " App.	361	13 " App.	367	87 Cal.	396		

Art. IX Sec. 9 (Con.)		Art. XI Sec. 4 (Con.)		Art. XI Sec. 5 (Con.)		Art. XI Sec. 6 (Con.)	
Vol.	Page	Vol.	Page	Vol.	Page	Vol.	Page
104 Cal.	658	65 Cal.	123	128 Cal.	247	104 Cal.	275
123 Cal.	619	73 Cal.	77	129 Cal.	574	104 Cal.	644
23 " App.	622	84 Cal.	76	131 Cal.	550	111 Cal.	103
		94 Cal.	624	134 Cal.	70	114 Cal.	147
		98 Cal.	224	135 Cal.	650	114 Cal.	321
Art. IX Sec. 11		109 Cal.	334	136 Cal.	376	115 Cal.	514
104 Cal.	658	109 Cal.	496	136 Cal.	655	118 Cal.	403
		114 Cal.	320	141 Cal.	429	123 Cal.	459
		114 Cal.	561	141 Cal.	726	123 Cal.	603
Art. IX Sec. 12		118 Cal.	308	144 Cal.	269	126 Cal.	386
56 Cal.	101	118 Cal.	404	148 Cal.	747	127 Cal.	666
		129 Cal.	574	153 Cal.	168	129 Cal.	514
		134 Cal.	70	154 Cal.	330	131 Cal.	33
Art. IX Sec. 18		154 Cal.	330	157 Cal.	160	132 Cal.	381
5 " App.	419			157 Cal.	421	132 Cal.	442
				162 Cal.	593	133 Cal.	104
		Art. XI Sec. 5		164 Cal.	326	135 Cal.	519
Art. X Sec. 1		53 Cal.	748	3 " App.	182	138 Cal.	131
63 Cal.	490	56 Cal.	103	3 " App.	274	138 Cal.	152
		58 Cal.	90	4 " App.	119	141 Cal.	207
		58 Cal.	569	5 " App.	467	142 Cal.	515
Art. X Sec. 4		60 Cal.	514	5 " App.	679	143 Cal.	553
61 Cal.	264	61 Cal.	277	15 " App.	580	143 Cal.	567
		65 Cal.	123	18 " App.	448	144 Cal.	391
		65 Cal.	288			145 Cal.	634
		66 Cal.	4			145 Cal.	688
Art. XI Sec. 1		73 Cal.	77			147 Cal.	535
56 Cal.	103	76 Cal.	95	Art. XI Sec. 6		148 Cal.	382
61 Cal.	277	81 Cal.	500	55 Cal.	246	148 Cal.	629
114 Cal.	320	84 Cal.	75	58 Cal.	566	148 Cal.	752
114 Cal.	561	88 Cal.	531	60 Cal.	81	150 Cal.	82
129 Cal.	574	94 Cal.	608	61 Cal.	277	151 Cal.	470
134 Cal.	70	95 Cal.	332	61 Cal.	319	151 Cal.	652
8 " App.	679	95 Cal.	473	64 Cal.	242	152 Cal.	7
		98 Cal.	222	66 Cal.	5	152 Cal.	230
		98 Cal.	228	69 Cal.	470	152 Cal.	594
Art. XI Sec. 2		100 Cal.	273	73 Cal.	76	153 Cal.	165
61 Cal.	277	103 Cal.	394	73 Cal.	312	154 Cal.	225
71 Cal.	313	104 Cal.	130	73 Cal.	622	154 Cal.	331
		105 Cal.	626	74 Cal.	26	155 Cal.	381
		106 Cal.	197	74 Cal.	125	155 Cal.	610
Art. XI Sec. 3		109 Cal.	334	76 Cal.	446	155 Cal.	788
61 Cal.	277	109 Cal.	497	81 Cal.	497	157 Cal.	418
97 Cal.	331	111 Cal.	103	82 Cal.	341	157 Cal.	716
117 Cal.	196	111 Cal.	370	85 Cal.	346	158 Cal.	85
134 Cal.	522	111 Cal.	569	86 Cal.	41	159 Cal.	437
152 Cal.	228	113 Cal.	516	87 Cal.	92	160 Cal.	37
154 Cal.	330	113 Cal.	645	87 Cal.	606	160 Cal.	131
		114 Cal.	327	91 Cal.	249	161 Cal.	280
		114 Cal.	561	92 Cal.	316	166 Cal.	608
		115 Cal.	548	94 Cal.	74	167 Cal.	312
Art. XI Sec. 4		118 Cal.	308	94 Cal.	621	1 " App.	633
56 Cal.	103	118 Cal.	404	95 Cal.	111	3 " App.	274
61 Cal.	277	125 Cal.	192	99 Cal.	560	4 " App.	238
				102 Cal.	304	5 " App.	578

Art. XI Sec. 6 (Con.)		Art. XI Sec. 8 (Con.)		Art. XI Sec. 8½ (Con.)		Art. XI Sec. 11	
Vol.	Page	Vol.	Page	Vol.	Page	Vol.	Page
5 " App.	581	114 Cal.	364	148 Cal.	133	57 Cal.	607
6 " App.	223	115 Cal.	516	151 Cal.	470	61 Cal.	277
8 " App.	55	119 Cal.	233	153 Cal.	164	61 Cal.	375
9 " App.	781	121 Cal.	265	157 Cal.	419	65 Cal.	35
10 " App.	468	121 Cal.	553	157 Cal.	484	65 Cal.	270
11 " App.	361	123 Cal.	605	160 Cal.	209	66 Cal.	450
11 " App.	406	126 Cal.	390	167 Cal.	312	67 Cal.	103
12 " App.	529	128 Cal.	463	3 " App.	719	68 Cal.	296
13 " App.	277	129 Cal.	574	6 " App.	224	69 Cal.	90
13 " App.	583	130 Cal.	89	6 " App.	738	69 Cal.	151
13 " App.	774	131 Cal.	264	13 " App.	773	72 Cal.	115
15 " App.	588	132 Cal.	375	15 " App.	588	73 Cal.	77
24 " App.	347	133 Cal.	104	25 " App.	688	73 Cal.	148
25 " App.	514	134 Cal.	52	26 " App.	743	73 Cal.	371
		138 Cal.	131			73 Cal.	633
		141 Cal.	207			74 Cal.	23
Art. XI Sec. 7		142 Cal.	300	**Art. XI Sec. 9**		84 Cal.	305
55 Cal.	247	143 Cal.	556	61 Cal.	277	87 Cal.	165
56 Cal.	104	143 Cal.	560	62 Cal.	563	90 Cal.	620
58 Cal.	566	143 Cal.	569	62 Cal.	566	91 Cal.	590
60 Cal.	81	145 Cal.	175	81 Cal.	590	94 Cal.	391
61 Cal.	37	145 Cal.	291	85 Cal.	596	96 Cal.	356
61 Cal.	277	145 Cal.	742	87 Cal.	396	96 Cal.	608
84 Cal.	306	147 Cal.	530	92 Cal.	319	98 Cal.	556
91 Cal.	590	148 Cal.	133	94 Cal.	603	98 Cal.	684
111 Cal.	103	150 Cal.	74	95 Cal.	473	99 Cal.	560
114 Cal.	320	151 Cal.	467	98 Cal.	221	102 Cal.	489
126 Cal.	409	152 Cal.	9	104 Cal.	644	103 Cal.	114
129 Cal.	574	153 Cal.	164	109 Cal.	508	104 Cal.	644
		155 Cal.	608	114 Cal.	123	105 Cal.	616
		157 Cal.	147	118 Cal.	309	106 Cal.	283
Art. XI Sec. 7½		158 Cal.	78	118 Cal.	362	108 Cal.	327
26 " App.	581	160 Cal.	46	129 Cal.	527	109 Cal.	321
		160 Cal.	131	136 Cal.	65	112 Cal.	70
		161 Cal.	280	138 Cal.	16	124 Cal.	348
Art. XI Sec. 8		162 Cal.	100	144 Cal.	277	129 Cal.	574
55 Cal.	253	166 Cal.	79	145 Cal.	197	131 Cal.	466
55 Cal.	613	4 " App.	238	155 Cal.	754	134 Cal.	70
56 Cal.	104	6 " App.	219	157 Cal.	157	134 Cal.	111
60 Cal.	81	8 " App.	235	162 Cal.	615	134 Cal.	145
61 Cal.	277	9 " App.	781	165 Cal.	87	139 Cal.	183
61 Cal.	231	10 " App.	384	167 Cal.	520	140 Cal.	230
69 Cal.	477	25 " App.	514	8 " App.	22	143 Cal.	371
73 Cal.	82	25 " App.	688	8 " App.	44	145 Cal.	631
79 Cal.	176			11 " App.	578	147 Cal.	334
82 Cal.	342			14 " App.	664	149 Cal.	761
85 Cal.	335	**Art. XI Sec. 8½**		18 " App.	387	150 Cal.	80
85 Cal.	345	120 Cal.	399	19 " App.	771	152 Cal.	470
86 Cal.	40	126 Cal.	406			154 Cal.	322
87 Cal.	606	128 Cal.	462			154 Cal.	682
92 Cal.	612	132 Cal.	441			155 Cal.	117
97 Cal.	593	135 Cal.	514	**Art. XI Sec. 10**		158 Cal.	745
105 Cal.	624	136 Cal.	586	61 Cal.	277	162 Cal.	711
114 Cal.	147	145 Cal.	53	92 Cal.	319	163 Cal.	220
		145 Cal.	742	104 Cal.	644	163 Cal.	459

Art. XI Sec. 11 (Con.)		Art. XI Sec. 12 (Con.)		Art. XI Sec. 16		Art. XI Sec. 18 (Con.)	
Vol.	Page	Vol.	Page	Vol.	Page	Vol.	Page
164 Cal.	324	124 Cal.	696	61 Cal.	277	160 Cal.	41
166 Cal.	9	129 Cal.	604	87 Cal.	607	160 Cal.	318
168 Cal.	303	134 Cal.	148	92 Cal.	319	160 Cal.	433
169 Cal.	492	143 Cal.	567	97 Cal.	219	168 Cal.	592
1 " App.	184	144 Cal.	333	103 Cal.	493	7 " App.	412
2 " App.	722	150 Cal.	90	108 Cal.	565	17 " App.	293
5 " App.	499	154 Cal.	335	112 Cal.	315	23 " App.	583
5 " App.	597	167 Cal.	286	112 Cal.	329	24 " App.	354
6 " App.	10	168 Cal.	155	113 Cal.	211		
8 " App.	297	5 " App.	648	146 Cal.	719		
8 " App.	443	8 " App.	439			**Art. XI Sec. 19**	
8 " App.	565					54 Cal.	246
8 " App.	679			**Art. XI Sec. 16½**		61 Cal.	24
9 " App.	74	**Art. XI Sec. 13**		152 Cal.	8	61 Cal.	277
9 " App.	781	55 Cal.	618			62 Cal.	108
10 " App.	604	59 Cal.	96			62 Cal.	232
11 " App.	514	60 Cal.	32	**Art. XI Sec. 17**		69 Cal.	466
12 " App.	259	61 Cal.	277	61 Cal.	277	69 Cal.	482
12 " App.	326	64 Cal.	507	87 Cal.	608	72 Cal.	6
17 " App.	60	71 Cal.	312	97 Cal.	219	73 Cal.	75
20 " App.	270	71 Cal.	313	113 Cal.	211	92 Cal.	342
20 " App.	363	71 Cal.	631	136 Cal.	445	93 Cal.	161
21 " App.	277	80 Cal.	270			98 Cal.	618
22 " App.	120	86 Cal.	48			118 Cal.	5
23 " App.	787	87 Cal.	607	**Art. XI Sec. 18**		118 Cal.	483
25 " App.	513	97 Cal.	219	61 Cal.	277	118 Cal.	584
25 " App.	597	99 Cal.	560	62 Cal.	642	129 Cal.	402
26 " App.	122	112 Cal.	329	74 Cal.	259	137 Cal.	118
		112 Cal.	564	74 Cal.	417	142 Cal.	287
		118 Cal.	308	75 Cal.	505	143 Cal.	371
Art. XI Sec. 12		125 Cal.	193	92 Cal.	342	145 Cal.	632
58 Cal.	644	126 Cal.	134	97 Cal.	219	148 Cal.	315
60 Cal.	32	133 Cal.	103	99 Cal.	413	150 Cal.	558
60 Cal.	155	144 Cal.	333	107 Cal.	648	151 Cal.	428
61 Cal.	277	148 Cal.	631	109 Cal.	153	152 Cal.	586
62 Cal.	643	150 Cal.	82	111 Cal.	322	153 Cal.	27
65 Cal.	270	152 Cal.	234	112 Cal.	163	155 Cal.	651
66 Cal.	451	168 Cal.	155	112 Cal.	313	158 Cal.	82
69 Cal.	90	23 " App.	580	112 Cal.	326	160 Cal.	38
69 Cal.	610			112 Cal.	540	160 Cal.	111
71 Cal.	313			113 Cal.	202	161 Cal.	281
73 Cal.	77			118 Cal.	530	163 Cal.	111
73 Cal.	371	**Art. XI Sec. 14**		119 Cal.	44	163 Cal.	671
74 Cal.	117	55 Cal.	618	119 Cal.	227	166 Cal.	773
87 Cal.	607	59 Cal.	279	124 Cal.	67	168 Cal.	301
92 Cal.	319	61 Cal.	277	131 Cal.	397	168 Cal.	450
97 Cal.	218	73 Cal.	77	135 Cal.	500	168 Cal.	601
99 Cal.	560	87 Cal.	607	136 Cal.	405	169 Cal.	323
100 Cal.	272	164 Cal.	324	143 Cal.	179	169 Cal.	326
102 Cal.	111	25 " App.	511	144 Cal.	395	169 Cal.	480
102 Cal.	471			146 Cal.	730	169 Cal.	481
104 Cal.	644			148 Cal.	709	169 Cal.	482
112 Cal.	70			150 Cal.	86	169 Cal.	750
117 Cal.	86	**Art. XI Sec. 15**		152 Cal.	172	169 Cal.	751
121 Cal.	551	61 Cal.	277	153 Cal.	374	169 Cal.	752

Art. XI Sec. 19 (Con.)

Vol.	Page
169 Cal.	753
1 " App.	673
2 " App.	560
2 " App.	722
17 " App.	342
18 " App.	34
19 " App.	366
25 " App.	504
26 " App.	195

Art. XI Sec. 21

72 Cal.	389

Art. XII Sec. 1

61 Cal.	38
73 Cal.	77
83 Cal.	413
92 Cal.	316
123 Cal.	527
125 Cal.	412
131 Cal.	33
153 Cal.	702
154 Cal.	331
155 Cal.	652
157 Cal.	598
160 Cal.	121
1 " App.	67
11 " App.	404

Art. XII Sec. 2

62 Cal.	460
125 Cal.	410
160 Cal.	585

Art. XII Sec. 3

62 Cal.	461
97 Cal.	95
108 Cal.	425
111 Cal.	63
116 Cal.	384
122 Cal.	523
124 Cal.	150
125 Cal.	410
136 Cal.	437
142 Cal.	384
147 Cal.	640
154 Cal.	353
154 Cal.	782
160 Cal.	578

Art. XII Sec. 3 (Con.)

Vol.	Page
165 Cal.	661
166 Cal.	349
167 Cal.	241
168 Cal.	646
4 " App.	292
5 " App.	705
12 " App.	695
13 " App.	27
18 " App.	738
23 " App.	466

Art. XII Sec. 4

153 Cal.	703

Art. XII Sec. 5

73 Cal.	77
154 Cal.	331

Art. XII Sec. 6

160 Cal.	122

Art. XII Sec. 7

91 Cal.	340
121 Cal.	19
154 Cal.	328
155 Cal.	650

Art. XII Sec. 9

107 Cal.	643
133 Cal.	612
3 " App.	710

Art. XII Sec. 10

72 Cal.	466
116 Cal.	100
152 Cal.	586
154 Cal.	274

Art. XII Sec. 11

59 Cal.	331
65 Cal.	617
73 Cal.	77
93 Cal.	308
135 Cal.	585
147 Cal.	582

Art. XII Sec. 11 (Con.)

Vol.	Page
152 Cal.	457
154 Cal.	75
157 Cal.	729
159 Cal.	216
165 Cal.	671
2 " App.	130
20 " App.	701

Art. XII Sec. 12

67 Cal.	535
93 Cal.	418

Art. XII Sec. 14

135 Cal.	584
135 Cal.	625
2 " App.	639
13 " App.	27

Art. XII Sec. 15

99 Cal.	133
115 Cal.	311
146 Cal.	651
155 Cal.	657
156 Cal.	468
158 Cal.	281
159 Cal.	221
163 Cal.	281
165 Cal.	660
15 " App.	683

Art. XII Sec. 16

66 Cal.	209
71 Cal.	488
73 Cal.	183
83 Cal.	493
94 Cal.	137
98 Cal.	167
102 Cal.	48
106 Cal.	58
107 Cal.	380
134 Cal.	587
136 Cal.	439
141 Cal.	315
144 Cal.	205
150 Cal.	468
151 Cal.	159
159 Cal.	696
4 " App.	370
6 " App.	87

Art. XII Sec. 16 (Con.)

Vol.	Page
10 " App.	72
11 " App.	226
11 " App.	239
12 " App.	227
15 " App.	473
22 " App.	169
26 " App.	346

Art. XII Sec. 17

132 Cal.	685
2 " App.	560
3 " App.	683

Art. XII Sec. 18

132 Cal.	686

Art. XII Sec. 19

132 Cal.	686
145 Cal.	639

Art. XII Sec. 20

132 Cal.	686
133 Cal.	26
144 Cal.	184

Art. XII Sec. 21

109 Cal.	322
132 Cal.	686
144 Cal.	193

Art. XII Sec. 22

79 Cal.	163
105 Cal.	544
132 Cal.	678
133 Cal.	26
142 Cal.	225
166 Cal.	650
166 Cal.	691
166 Cal.	743

Art. XII Sec. 23

142 Cal.	225
166 Cal.	650
166 Cal.	691
166 Cal.	743
167 Cal.	672
168 Cal.	298

Art. XII Sec. 23 (Con.)		Art. XIII Sec. 4 (Con.)		Art. XIII Sec. 10 (Con.)		Art. XIV Sec. 1 (Con.)	
Vol.	Page	Vol.	Page	Vol.	Page	Vol.	Page
169 Cal.	470	96 Cal.	625	128 Cal.	593	62 Cal.	232
169 Cal.	471	99 Cal.	609	137 Cal.	515	74 Cal.	573
169 Cal.	476	118 Cal.	492	137 Cal.	660	82 Cal.	303
		123 Cal.	355	142 Cal.	223	90 Cal.	640
Art. XIII Sec. 1		128 Cal.	592	143 Cal.	432	100 Cal.	125
56 Cal.	202	128 Cal.	610	148 Cal.	317	107 Cal.	225
57 Cal.	600	131 Cal.	361	149 Cal.	84	112 Cal.	433
59 Cal.	336	134 Cal.	86	153 Cal.	54	118 Cal.	565
62 Cal.	108	144 Cal.	435	158 Cal.	439	122 Cal.	286
65 Cal.	457	145 Cal.	55	164 Cal.	754	129 Cal.	441
66 Cal.	603	153 Cal.	615	167 Cal.	426	130 Cal.	313
97 Cal.	220	155 Cal.	353	169 Cal.	141	139 Cal.	434
97 Cal.	324	160 Cal.	74	2 " App.	595	142 Cal.	287
108 Cal.	192	163 Cal.	709	5 " App.	648	144 Cal.	593
111 Cal.	86	11 " App.	463	14 " App.	474	150 Cal.	89
113 Cal.	397			22 " App.	176	151 Cal.	57
116 Cal.	23					152 Cal.	588
119 Cal.	521	**Art. XIII Sec. 5**				152 Cal.	729
128 Cal.	592	59 Cal.	544	**Art. XIII Sec. 12**		157 Cal.	89
128 Cal.	612	91 Cal.	11	104 Cal.	63	159 Cal.	312
131 Cal.	613	96 Cal.	626	135 Cal.	517	159 Cal.	333
132 Cal.	268	99 Cal.	608	148 Cal.	248	164 Cal.	133
132 Cal.	600	103 Cal.	376			164 Cal.	134
134 Cal.	478	110 Cal.	541			168 Cal.	301
137 Cal.	518	131 Cal.	604	**Art. XIII Sec. 12½**		168 Cal.	593
139 Cal.	210	8 " App.	670	137 Cal.	524	169 Cal.	778
142 Cal.	225			**Art. XIII Sec. 13**		2 " App.	187
142 Cal.	284	**Art. XIII Sec. 8**		56 Cal.	202	2 " App.	413
148 Cal.	85	56 Cal.	206	83 Cal.	402	2 " App.	417
149 Cal.	583	61 Cal.	103	17 " App.	548	8 " App.	169
152 Cal.	767	73 Cal.	623			25 " App.	712
153 Cal.	778	8 " App.	439				
155 Cal.	146			**Art. XIII Sec. 14**		**Art. XIV Sec. 2**	
155 Cal.	353	**Art. XIII Sec. 9**		164 Cal.	42	61 Cal.	38
155 Cal.	650	56 Cal.	102	165 Cal.	561	62 Cal.	108
157 Cal.	621	56 Cal.	195	166 Cal.	246	62 Cal.	233
160 Cal.	723	59 Cal.	329	168 Cal.	276	82 Cal.	304
160 Cal.	801	61 Cal.	55	168 Cal.	422	118 Cal.	579
163 Cal.	708	67 Cal.	625	168 Cal.	553	129 Cal.	441
167 Cal.	426	97 Cal.	324	168 Cal.	763	2 " App.	600
2 " App.	68	17 " App.	548	169 Cal.	135	25 " App.	712
2 " App.	595			169 Cal.	139		
		Art. XIII Sec. 10		169 Cal.	141	**Art. XV Sec. 2**	
Art. XIII Sec. 2		56 Cal.	201	169 Cal.	142	132 Cal.	106
104 Cal.	621	59 Cal.	325			164 Cal.	34
137 Cal.	525	60 Cal.	28			166 Cal.	587
149 Cal.	87	60 Cal.	58	**Art. XIII Sec. 19**		169 Cal.	567
		62 Cal.	565	19 " App.	133		
Art. XIII Sec. 4		63 Cal.	469				
59 Cal.	543	64 Cal.	483	**Art. XIV Sec. 1**		**Art. XV Sec. 3**	
60 Cal.	58	83 Cal.	401	60 Cal.	169	152 Cal.	735
66 Cal.	213	105 Cal.	591	61 Cal.	4	153 Cal.	46
72 Cal.	36	125 Cal.	499	61 Cal.	25		
91 Cal.	11						

Art. XV Sec. 3 (Con.)		Art. XIX Sec. 1		Art. XX Sec. 15		Art. XX Sec. 20	
Vol.	Page	Vol.	Page	Vol.	Page	Vol.	Page
161 Cal.	613	84 Cal.	230	61 Cal.	353	53 Cal.	747
162 Cal.	90	126 Cal.	674	89 Cal.	111	62 Cal.	565
163 Cal.	544	147 Cal.	651	98 Cal.	151	96 Cal.	291
164 Cal.	408			107 Cal.	623	99 Cal.	44
166 Cal.	603			136 Cal.	125	9 " App.	163
167 Cal.	446	Art. XX Sec. 1		138 Cal.	545		
24 " App.	200	102 Cal.	119	142 Cal.	242	Art.XXII Sec. 1	
		154 Cal.	281	148 Cal.	737	53 Cal.	747
				150 Cal.	792	54 Cal.	247
Art. XVI Sec.1				167 Cal.	235	55 Cal.	249
144 Cal.	694	Art. XX Sec. 3		169 Cal.	316	55 Cal.	334
148 Cal.	502	133 Cal.	200	1 " App.	308	57 Cal.	627
		151 Cal.	804	2 " App.	507	60 Cal.	155
		155 Cal.	791	3 " App.	480	60 Cal.	278
Art.XVII Sec.1				5 " App.	759	60 Cal.	514
111 Cal.	487			8 " App.	509	61 Cal.	4
156 Cal.	369	Art. XX Sec. 4		8 " App.	518	61 Cal.	32
11 " App.	727	80 Cal.	234	10 " App.	92	61 Cal.	279
12 " App.	359	85 Cal.	416	13 " App.	624	61 Cal.	353
		110 Cal.	451	14 " App.	302	67 Cal.	382
Art. XVII Sec.2				18 " App.	599	69 Cal.	467
88 Cal.	455					69 Cal.	485
96 Cal.	118	Art. XX Sec. 5				71 Cal.	312
1 " App.	150	93 Cal.	400	Art. XX Sec. 16		75 Cal.	153
3 " App.	245			55 Cal.	524	93 Cal.	40
				66 Cal.	655	93 Cal.	424
		Art. XX Sec. 6		79 Cal.	113	114 Cal.	563
Art. XVII Sec. 3		1 " App.	144	82 Cal.	495	119 Cal.	428
55 Cal.	103	8 " App.	510	85 Cal.	416	121 Cal.	551
65 Cal.	13			93 Cal.	155	152 Cal.	736
68 Cal.	508			100 Cal.	264	154 Cal.	200
71 Cal.	321	Art. XX Sec. 8		110 Cal.	451	154 Cal.	339
72 Cal.	240	147 Cal.	515	127 Cal.	392	157 Cal.	779
88 Cal.	455			132 Cal.	450	160 Cal.	586
89 Cal.	44			136 Cal.	581	164 Cal.	325
90 Cal.	47	Art. XX Sec. 9		136 Cal.	654	166 Cal.	587
96 Cal.	118	58 Cal.	472	138 Cal.	16	1 " App.	64
146 Cal.	543	113 Cal.	139	145 Cal.	471	12 " App.	291
148 Cal.	496	138 Cal.	553	157 Cal.	483	13 " App.	624
148 Cal.	714	3 " App.	747	161 Cal.	202	22 " App.	528
158 Cal.	616			1 " App.	7		
164 Cal.	408			6 " App.	222	Art.XXII Sec. 2	
1 " App.	150	Art. XX Sec. 10				60 Cal.	515
3 " App.	244	154 Cal.	281	Art. XX Sec. 17			
				151 Cal.	804	Art.XXII Sec. 3	
Art.XVIII Sec.1		Art. XX Sec. 11				54 Cal.	186
66 Cal.	633	120 Cal.	375			54 Cal.	346
69 Cal.	468	154 Cal.	281			55 Cal.	463
72 Cal.	6			Art. XX Sec. 18		58 Cal.	90
80 Cal.	213			57 Cal.	605	60 Cal.	307
102 Cal.	117	Art. XX Sec. 13		60 Cal.	82	60 Cal.	515
166 Cal.	252	143 Cal.	549	96 Cal.	361	66 Cal.	204
1 " App.	677	159 Cal.	444	98 Cal.	556	114 Cal.	331
11 " App.	727	7 " App.	152	162 Cal.	691	169 Cal.	51

Art.XXII Sec. 9

Vol.	Page
155 Cal.	734

Art.XXIISec.10

55 Cal.	611
56 Cal.	99
57 Cal.	626
60 Cal.	307
62 Cal.	557
62 Cal.	566
114 Cal.	333

Art.XXII Sec.11

64 Cal.	235
64 Cal.	378
93 Cal.	40
103 Cal.	491
114 Cal.	331
116 Cal.	195
1 " App.	574

Art.XXIISec.12

56 Cal.	99
57 Cal.	627

TABLE OF UNITED STATES AND FEDERAL CITATIONS TO THE CONSTITUTION OF CALIFORNIA OF 1849.

Volumes 1 to and including 238 U. S. Reports.
Volumes 101 to and including 225 Federal Reporter.

Art. I,	Sec. 8.	Art. IV,	Sec. 31.	Art. VI,	Sec. 4.	Art. VI,	Sec. 9.
Vol.	Page	Vol.	Page	Vol.	Page	Vol.	Page
110 U. S.	557	99 U. S.	728	4 Wall.	426	128 U. S.	78
142 U. S.	568	99 U. S.	731			128 U. S.	79
		110 U. S.	348				
		192 U. S.	201	Art. VI,	Sec. 6.	Art. XII, Sec. 22.	
Art. I,	Sec. 17.			128 U. S.	78	167 U. S.	495
113 U. S.	96	Art. V,	Sec. 1.				
		21 Wall.	515			Art. XIV, Sec. 1.	
				Art. VI,	Sec. 8.	116 U. S.	362
				21 Wall.	515		
Art. IV,	Sec. 4.	Art. VI,	Sec. 1.	128 U. S.	79	Art. XIV, Sec. 2.	
110 U. S.	349	128 U. S.	78	128 U. S.	80	110 U. S.	351

(645)

TABLE OF UNITED STATES AND FEDERAL CITATIONS TO THE CONSTITUTION OF CALIFORNIA OF 1879.

Volumes 1 to and including 238 U. S. Reports.
Volumes 101 to and including 225 Federal Reporter.

Art. I, Sec. 2.

Vol.	Page
167 U. S.	176

Art. I, Sec. 8.

110 U. S.	516
191 U. S.	60

Art. I, Sec. 13.

167 U. S.	175

Art. I, Sec. 17.

113 U. S.	89
180 U. S.	333

Art. I, Sec. 19.

167 U. S.	175

Art. IV, Sec. 25.

159 Fed.	994

Art. IV, Sec. 26.

166 U. S.	486
166 U. S.	487
187 U. S.	606

Art. IV, Sec. 31.

177 U. S.	575

Art. VI. Sec. 1.

128 U. S.	53

Art. VI, Sec. 6.

Vol.	Page
128 U. S.	53
237 U. S.	502

Art. VI, Sec. 8.

Vol.	Page
128 U. S.	53
128 U. S.	82
237 U. S.	502

Art. VI, Sec. 9.

128 U. S.	53

Art. IX, Sec. 2.

112 U. S.	233

Art. IX, Sec. 10.

127 U. S.	34

Art. XI, Sec. 11.

113 U. S.	703
118 U. S.	356
137 U. S.	86
195 U. S.	223
199 U. S.	306
126 Fed.	30

Art. XI, Sec. 18.

184 U. S.	302
202 Fed.	357

Art. XI, Sec. 19.

195 U. S.	223
224 U. S.	330
228 U. S.	454
233 U. S.	195
185 Fed.	281

Art. XII, Sec. 3.

164 Fed.	680
170 Fed.	362
196 Fed.	646

Art. XII, Sec. 15.

Vol.	Page
183 U. S.	144
186 U. S.	165
117 Fed.	900
170 Fed.	362
192 Fed.	495

Art. XII, Sec. 17.

110 U. S.	679

Art. XII, Sec. 21.

226 Fed.	349
226 Fed.	351

Art. XII, Sec. 22.

167 U. S.	479
226 Fed.	349
226 Fed.	351

Art. XIII, Sec. 1.

118 U. S.	394
162 U. S.	91
197 U. S.	70
197 U. S.	146
117 Fed.	900
136 Fed.	138

Art. XIII, Sec. 2.

118 U. S.	412

Art. XIII, Sec. 4.

118 U. S.	404
149 U. S.	308
162 U. S.	91

Art. XIII, Sec. 8.

109 Fed.	726

Art. XIII, Sec. 9.

Vol.	Page
118 U. S.	394
118 U. S.	405
127 U. S.	1

Art. XIII, Sec. 10.

118 U. S.	394
118 U. S.	405
118 U. S.	411
127 U. S.	1
127 U. S.	28
127 U. S.	29
127 U. S.	33
162 U. S.	91

Art. XIII, Sec. 14.

225 Fed.	728

Art. XIV.

164 U. S.	159

Art. XIV, Sec. 1.

110 U. S.	347
164 U. S.	112
174 U. S.	739
228 U. S.	454
104 Fed.	706
197 Fed.	4

Art. XIV, Sec. 2.

110 U. S.	347
110 U. S.	350
228 U. S.	454

Art. XVII, Sec. 1.

198 U. S.	202

TABLE OF CALIFORNIA RAILROAD COMMISSION
CITATIONS TO CONSTITUTION OF 1879.

Art. I, Sec. 16: 4 C. R. C. 298.
Art. VI, Sec. 4a: 6 C. R. C. 512.
Art. XI, Sec. 8: 4 C. R. C. 1083.
Art. XI, Sec. 11: 3 C. R. C. 144,
                  4 C. R. C. 324, 1080, 1082, 1083.
Art. XI, Sec. 19: 3 C. R. C. 64, 801, 936, 956, 1170, 1172,
                  4 C. R. C. 297, 445, 1080, 1082, 1083.
                  5 C. R. C. 301.
                  6 C. R. C. 536, 848.
Art. XII, Sec. 11: 1 C. R. C. 318.
Art. XII, Sec. 17: 1 C. R. C. 630.
Art. XII, Sec. 20: 1 C. R. C. 97, 115.
Art. XII, Sec. 21: 1 C. R. C. 69, 70, 71, 75, 77, 97, 103, 104, 114,
                            115, 571, 572, 693.
                  2 C. R. C. 628, 635, 637, 967.
                  3 C. R. C. 33, 337, 340, 342, 344, 532, 872.
                  4 C. R. C. 413, 650, 653, 654, 656, 964, 966, 967,
                            969, 970, 972, 973, 974.
                  6 C. R. C. 453.
Art. XII, Sec. 22: 1 C. R. C. 752.
                  2 C. R. C. 364, 366, 477, 630, 631, 632, 636, 637.
                  3 C. R. C. 45, 579, 580, 802.
Art. XII, Sec. 23: 2 C. R. C. 364, 457, 477, 502, 708, 709, 712.
                  3 C. R. C. 45, 64, 144, 612, 613, 802, 953, 958.
                  4 C. R. C. 298, 905, 1079.
                  5 C. R. C. 85, 165, 302.
                  6 C. R. C. 319, 515, 948.
Art. XII, Sec. 23a: 6 C. R. C. 508, 515.
Art. XIV, Sec. 1: 2 C. R. C. 54, 55, 56, 60, 477, 485, 489, 501.
                  3 C. R. C. 419.
                  4 C. R. C. 1080, 1082, 1083.
Art. XIV, Sec. 2: 2 C. R. C. 54, 55, 56, 60, 477, 485, 501.
                  6 C. R. C. 536.
Art. XIX, Sec. 11: 1 C. R. C. 528, 529.
Art. XXII, Sec. 17: 3 C. R. C. 45.

APPENDIX.

CONSTITUTION

OF THE

STATE OF CALIFORNIA.

'ADOPTED BY THE CONVENTION, OCTOBER 10, 1849; RATIFIED BY
THE PEOPLE, NOVEMBER 13, 1849; PROCLAIMED,
DECEMBER 20, 1849; AND AMENDED
IN 1857, 1862, AND 1871.

PREAMBLE.

We, the people of California, grateful to Almighty God for our freedom, in order to secure its blessings, do establish this Constitution.

ARTICLE I.

DECLARATION OF RIGHTS.

Section 1. All men are by nature free and independent, and have certain inalienable rights, among which are those of enjoying and defending life and liberty; acquiring, possessing, and protecting property, and pursuing and obtaining safety and happiness.

Sec. 2. All political power is inherent in the people. Government is instituted for the protection, security, and benefit of the people, and they have the right to alter or reform the same whenever the public good may require it.

Sec. 3. The right of trial by jury shall be secured to all, and shall remain inviolate forever; but a jury trial may be waived by the parties, in all civil cases, in the manner to be prescribed by law.

Sec. 4. The free exercise and enjoyment of religious profession and worship, without discrimination or prefer-

ence, shall forever be allowed in this state; and no person shall be rendered incompetent to be a witness on account of his opinions on matters of religious belief, but the liberty of conscience hereby secured shall not be so construed as to excuse acts of licentiousness, or justify practices inconsistent with the peace or safety of this state.

Sec. 5. The privilege of the writ of habeas corpus shall not be suspended, unless when, in cases of rebellion or invasion, the public safety may require its suspension.

Sec. 6. Excessive bail shall not be required, nor excessive fines imposed; nor shall cruel or unusual punishments be inflicted; nor shall witnesses be unreasonably detained.

Sec. 7. All persons shall be bailable by sufficient sureties, unless for capital offenses when the proof is evident or the presumption great.

Sec. 8. No person shall be held to answer for a capital or otherwise infamous crime (except in cases of impeachment, and in cases of militia when in actual service, and the land and naval forces in time of war, or which this state may keep, with the consent of Congress, in time of peace, and in cases of petit larceny, under the regulation of the legislature) unless on presentment or indictment of a grand jury; and, in any trial in any court whatever, the party accused shall be allowed to appear and defend, in person and with counsel, as in civil actions. No person shall be subject to be twice put in jeopardy for the same offense; nor shall he be compelled, in any criminal case, to be a witness against himself; nor be deprived of life, liberty, or property without due process of law; nor shall private property be taken for public use without just compensation.

Sec. 9. Every citizen may freely speak, write, and publish his sentiments on all subjects, being responsible for the abuse of that right; and no law shall be passed to restrain or abridge the liberty of speech or of the press. In all criminal prosecutions on indictments for libels, the truth may be given in evidence to the jury; and if it shall appear to the jury that the matter charged as libelous is true, and

was published with good motives and for justifiable ends, the party shall be acquitted; and the jury shall have the right to determine the law and the fact.

Sec. 10. The people shall have the right freely to assemble together to consult for the common good, to instruct their representatives, and to petition the legislature for redress of grievances.

Sec. 11. All laws of a general nature shall have a uniform operation.

Sec. 12. The military shall be subordinate to the civil power. No standing army shall be kept up by this state in time of peace; and, in time of war, no appropriation for a standing army shall be for a longer time than two years.

Sec. 13. No soldier shall, in time of peace, be quartered in any house without the consent of the owner; nor in time of war, except in the manner to be prescribed by law.

Sec. 14. Representations shall be apportioned according to population.

Sec. 15. No person shall be imprisoned for debt in any civil action, on mesne or final process, unless in cases of fraud; and no person shall be imprisoned for a militia fine in time of peace.

Sec. 16. No bill of attainder, ex post facto law, or law impairing the obligation of contracts, shall ever be passed.

Sec. 17. Foreigners who are or who may hereafter become bona fide residents of this state, shall enjoy the same rights in respect to the possession, enjoyment, and inheritance of property as native-born citizens.

Sec. 18. Neither slavery nor involuntary servitude, unless for the punishment of crime, shall ever be tolerated in this state.

Sec. 19. The right of the people to be secure in their persons, houses, papers, and effects, against unreasonable seizures and searches, shall not be violated; and no warrant shall issue, but on probable cause, supported by oath or affirmation, particularly describing the place to be searched and the persons and things to be seized.

Sec. 20. Treason against the state shall consist only in levying war against it, adhering to its enemies, or giving them aid and comfort. No person shall be convicted of treason, unless on the evidence of two witnesses to the same overt act, or confession in open court.

Sec. 21. This enumeration of rights shall not be construed to impair or deny others retained by the people.

Sec. 22. The legislature shall have no power to make an appropriation, for any purpose whatever, for a longer period than two years. (Added by amendment, ratified September 6, 1871.)

ARTICLE II.
RIGHT OF SUFFRAGE.

Section 1. Every white male citizen of the United States, and every white male citizen of Mexico who shall have elected to become a citizen of the United States, under the treaty of peace exchanged and ratified at Queretaro, on the thirtieth day of May, eighteen hundred and forty-eight, of the age of twenty-one years, who shall have been a resident of the state six months next preceding the election, and the county or district in which he claims his vote thirty days, shall be entitled to vote at all elections which are now or hereafter may be authorized by law; provided, that nothing herein contained shall be construed to prevent the legislature, by a two-thirds concurrent vote, from admitting to the right of suffrage Indians, or the descendants of Indians, in such special cases as such a proportion of the legislative body may deem just and proper.

Sec. 2. Electors shall, in all cases except treason, felony, or breach of the peace, be privileged from arrest on the days of election, during their attendance at such election, going to and returning therefrom.

Sec. 3. No elector shall be obliged to perform militia duty on the day of election, except in time of war or public danger.

Sec. 4. For the purpose of voting, no person shall be deemed to have gained or lost a residence by reason of his

presence or absence while employed in the service of the United States, nor while engaged in the navigation of the waters of this state or of the United States, or of the high seas; nor while a student at any seminary of learning; nor while kept at any almshouse, or other asylum, at public expense; nor while confined in any public prison.

Sec. 5. No idiot or insane person, or person convicted of any infamous crime, shall be entitled to the privilege of an elector.

Sec. 6. All elections by the people shall be by ballot.

ARTICLE III.
DISTRIBUTION OF POWERS.

Section 1. The powers of the government of the state of California shall be divided into three separate departments: The legislative, the executive, and judicial; and no person charged with the exercise of powers properly belonging to one of these departments shall exercise any functions appertaining to either of the others, except in the cases hereinafter expressly directed or permitted.

ARTICLE IV.
LEGISLATIVE DEPARTMENT.

Section 1. The legislative power of this state shall be vested in a senate and assembly, which shall be designated the legislature of the state of California, and the enacting clause of every law shall be as follows: "The People of the State of California represented in Senate and Assembly, do enact as follows."

Sec. 2. The sessions of the legislature shall be biennial, and shall commence on the first Monday of December next ensuing the election of its members, unless the governor of the state shall, in the interim, convene the legislature by proclamation. No session shall continue longer than one hundred and twenty days. (Amended 1862. The original provided for annual sessions, beginning on first Monday of January.)

Constitution—42

Sec. 3. The members of the assembly shall be chosen biennially, by the qualified electors of their respective districts, on the first Wednesday in September, unless otherwise ordered by the legislature, and their term of office shall be two years. (Amendment ratified September 3, 1862. The original provided for annual elections on the first Tuesday after the first Monday in November.)

Sec. 4. Senators and members of assembly shall be duly qualified electors in the respective counties and districts which they represent.

Sec. 5. Senators shall be chosen for the term of four years, at the same time and places as members of the assembly; and no person shall be a member of the senate or assembly who has not been a citizen and inhabitant of the state and of the county or district for which he shall be chosen one year next before his election. (Amendment ratified September 3, 1862. Original made term of two years, and residence in county or district of six months.)

Sec. 6. The number of senators shall not be less than one-third, nor more than one-half, of that of the members of the assembly; and at the first session of the legislature after this section takes effect, the senators shall be divided by lot, as equally as may be, into two classes. The seats of the senators of the first class shall be vacated at the expiration of the second year, so that one-half shall be chosen biennially. (Amendment ratified September 3, 1862. Original provided for annual election.)

Sec. 7. When the number of senators is increased, they shall be apportioned by lot, so as to keep the two classes as nearly equal in number as possible.

Sec. 8. Each house shall choose its own officers, and judge of the qualifications, elections, and returns of its own members.

Sec. 9. A majority of each house shall constitute a quorum to do business; but a smaller number may adjourn from day to day, and may compel the attendance of absent members, in such manner and under such penalties as each house may provide.

Sec. 10. Each house shall determine the rules of its own proceedings, and may, with the concurrence of two-thirds of all the members elected, expel a member.

Sec. 11. Each house shall keep a journal of its own proceedings, and publish the same; and the yeas and nays of the members of either house on any question shall, at the desire of any three members present, be entered on the journal.

Sec. 12. Members of the legislature shall, in all cases except treason, felony, and breach of the peace, be privileged from arrest, and shall not be subject to any civil process during the session of the legislature, nor for fifteen days next before the commencement and after the termination of each session.

Sec. 13. When vacancies occur in either house, the governor, or the person exercising the functions of the governor, shall issue writs of election to fill such vacancies.

Sec. 14. The doors of each house shall be open, except on such occasions as, in the opinion of the house, may require secrecy.

Sec. 15. Neither house shall, without the consent of the other, adjourn for more than three days, nor to any other place than that in which they may be sitting.

Sec. 16. Any bill may originate in either house of the legislature, and all bills passed by one house may be amended in the other.

Sec. 17. Every bill which may have passed the legislature shall, before it becomes a law, be presented to the governor. If he approve it, he shall sign it, but if not he shall return it, with his objections, to the house in which it originated, which shall enter the same upon the journal, and proceed to reconsider it. If, after such reconsideration, it again pass both houses by yeas and nays, by a majority of two-thirds of the members of each house present, it shall become a law, notwithstanding the governor's objections. If any bill shall not be returned within ten days after it shall have been presented to him (Sundays excepted), the

same shall be a law, in like manner as if he had signed it, unless the legislature, by adjournment, prevent such return.

Sec. 18.   The assembly shall have the sole power of impeachment, and all impeachments shall be tried by the senate.   When sitting for that purpose, the senators shall be upon oath or affirmation; and no person shall be convicted without the concurrence of two-thirds of the members present.

Sec. 19.   The governor, lieutenant-governor, secretary of state, controller, treasurer, attorney general, surveyor-general, justices of the supreme court, and judges of the district courts, shall be liable to impeachment for any misdemeanor in office; but judgment in such cases shall extend only to removal from office and disqualification to hold any office of honor, trust, or profit under the state; but the party convicted or acquitted shall, nevertheless, be liable to indictment, trial, and punishment according to law.   All other civil officers shall be tried for misdemeanors in office in such a manner as the legislature may provide.

Sec. 20.   No senator or member of assembly shall, during the term for which he shall have been elected, be appointed to any civil office of profit under this state which shall have been created or the emoluments of which shall have been increased during such term, except such offices as may be filled by election by the people.

Sec. 21.   No person holding any lucrative office under the United States, or any other power, shall be eligible to any civil office of profit under this state; provided, that officers in the militia to which there is attached no annual salary, or local officers and postmasters, whose compensation does not exceed five hundred dollars per annum, shall not be deemed lucrative.

Sec. 22.   No person who shall be convicted of the embezzlement or defalcation of the public funds of this state shall ever be eligible to any office of honor, trust, or profit under this state; and the legislature shall, as soon as practicable, pass a law providing for the punishment of such embezzlement or defalcation as a felony.

Sec. 23.   No money shall be drawn from the treasury but in consequence of appropriations made by law.   An accurate statement of the receipts and expenditures of the public moneys shall be attached to and published with the laws at every regular session of the legislature.

Sec. 24.   The members of the legislature shall receive for their services a compensation to be fixed by law, and paid out of the public treasury; but no increase of the compensation shall take effect during the term for which the members of either house shall have been elected.

Sec. 25.   Every law enacted by the legislature shall embrace but one object, and that shall be expressed in the title; and no law shall be revised or amended by reference to its title; but in such case the act revised or section amended shall be re-enacted and published at length.

Sec. 26.   No divorce shall be granted by the legislature.

Sec. 27.   No lottery shall be authorized by this state, nor shall the sale of lottery tickets be allowed.

Sec. 28.   The enumeration of the inhabitants of this state shall be taken, under the direction of the legislature, in the year one thousand eight hundred and fifty-two and one thousand eight hundred and fifty-five, and at the end of every ten years thereafter; and these enumerations, together with the census that may be taken under the direction of the Congress of the United States, in the year one thousand eight hundred and fifty and every subsequent ten years, shall serve as the basis of representation in both houses of the legislature.

Sec. 29.   The number of senators and members of assembly shall, at the first session of the legislature holden after the enumerations herein provided for are made, be fixed by the legislature, and apportioned among the several counties and districts to be established by law, according to the number of white inhabitants.   The number of members of assembly shall not be less than twenty-four, nor more than thirty-six, until the number of inhabitants within this state shall amount to one hundred thousand; and, after that period, in such ratio that the whole number of members of

assembly shall never be less than thirty nor more than eighty.

Sec. 30.   When a congressional, senatorial, or assembly district shall be composed of two or more counties, it shall not be separated by any county belonging to another district.   No county shall be divided in forming a congressional, senatorial, or assembly district *so as to attach one portion of a county to another county; but the legislature may divide each county into as many congressional, senatorial, or assembly districts as such county may by apportionment be entitled to.   (Words following the * were added by amendment ratified September 3, 1862.)

Sec. 31.   Corporations may be formed under general laws, but shall not be created by special act, except for municipal purposes.   All general laws and special acts passed pursuant to this section may be altered from time to time, or repealed.

Sec. 32.   Dues from corporations shall be secured by such individual liability of the corporators and other means as may be prescribed by law.

Sec. 33.   The term corporations, as used in this article, shall be construed to include all associations and joint-stock companies having any of the powers or privileges of corporations not possessed by individuals or partnerships.   And all corporations shall have the right to sue and shall be subject to be sued in all courts, in like cases as natural persons.

Sec. 34.   The legislature shall have no power to pass any act granting any charter for banking purposes, but associations may be formed, under general laws, for the deposit of gold and silver; but no such associations shall make, issue, or put in circulation any bill, check, ticket, certificate, promissory note, or other paper, or the paper of any bank, to circulate as money.

Sec. 35.   The legislature of this state shall prohibit by law any person or persons, association, company, or corporation from exercising the privileges of banking or creating paper to circulate as money.

Sec. 36. Each stockholder of a corporation or joint-stock association shall be individually and personally liable for his proportion of all its debts and liabilities.

Sec. 37. It shall be the duty of the legislature to provide for the organization of cities and incorporated villages, and to restrict their power of taxation, assessment, borrowing money, contracting debts, and loaning their credit, so as to prevent abuses in assessments and in contracting debts by such municipal corporations.

Sec. 38. In all elections by the legislature the members thereof shall vote viva voce, and the votes shall be entered on the journal.

Sec. 39. In order that no inconvenience may result to the public service from the taking effect of the amendments proposed to article IV by the legislature of eighteen hundred and sixty-one, no officer shall be suspended or superseded thereby until the election and qualification of the several officers provided for in said amendments. (New section ratified September 3, 1862.)

ARTICLE V.

EXECUTIVE DEPARTMENT.

Section 1. The supreme executive power of this state shall be vested in a chief magistrate, who shall be styled the governor of the state of California.

Sec. 2. The governor shall be elected by the qualified electors, at the time and places of voting for members of the assembly, and shall hold his office four years from and after the first Monday in December subsequent to his election, and until his successor is elected and qualified. (Amendment ratified September 3, 1862. Original provided for term of two years.)

Sec. 3. No person shall be eligible to the office of governor (except at the first election) who has not been a citizen of the United States and a resident of this state two years next preceding the election, and attained the age of twenty-five years at the time of said election.

Sec. 4. The returns of every election for governor shall be sealed up and transmitted to the seat of government, directed to the speaker of the assembly, who shall, during the first week of the session, open and publish them in presence of both houses of the legislature. The person having the highest number of votes shall be governor; but, in case any two or more have an equal and the highest number of votes, the legislature shall, by joint vote of both houses, choose one of said persons so having an equal and the highest number of votes, for governor.

Sec. 5. The governor shall be commander in chief of the militia, the army, and navy of this state.

Sec. 6. He shall transact all executive business with the officers of government, civil and military, and may require information in writing from the officers of the executive department, upon any subject relating to the duties of their respective offices.

Sec. 7. He shall see that the laws are faithfully executed.

Sec. 8. When any office shall, from any cause, become vacant, and no mode is provided by the Constitution and law for filling such vacancy, the governor shall have power to fill such vacancy by granting a commission, which shall expire at the end of the next session of the legislature, or at the next election by the people.

Sec. 9. He may, on extraordinary occasions, convene the legislature by proclamation, and shall state to both houses, when assembled, the purpose for which they shall have been convened.

Sec. 10. He shall communicate by message to the legislature, at every session, the condition of the state, and recommend such matters as he shall deem expedient.

Sec. 11. In case of a disagreement between the two houses with respect to the time of adjournment, the governor shall have power to adjourn the legislature to such time as he may think proper; provided, it be not beyond the time fixed for the meeting of the next legislature.

Sec. 12.   No person shall, while holding any office under the United States, or this state, exercise the office of governor, except as hereinafter expressly provided.

Sec. 13.   The governor shall have the power to grant reprieves and pardons after conviction, for all offenses, except treason and cases of impeachment, upon such conditions and with such restrictions and limitations as he may think proper, subject to such regulations as may be provided by law relative to the manner of applying for pardons.   Upon conviction for treason, he shall have the power to suspend the execution of the sentence until the case shall be reported to the legislature at its next meeting, when the legislature shall either pardon, direct the execution of the sentence, or grant a further reprieve.   He shall communicate to the legislature, at the beginning of every session, every case of reprieve or pardon granted, stating the name of the convict, the crime of which he was convicted, the sentence and its date, and the date of the pardon or reprieve.

Sec. 14.   There shall be a seal of this state, which shall be kept by the governor, and used by him officially and shall be called "The Great Seal of the State of California."

Sec. 15.   All grants and commissions shall be in the name and by the authority of the people of the state of California, sealed with the great seal of the state, signed by the governor, and countersigned by the secretary of state.

Sec. 16.   A lieutenant-governor shall be elected at the same time and places, and in the same manner as the governor; and his term of office, and his qualifications of eligibility, shall also be the same.   He shall be president of the senate, but shall only have a casting vote therein.   If, during a vacancy of the office of governor, the lieutenant-governor shall be impeached, displaced, resign, die, or become incapable of performing the duties of his office, or be absent from the state, the president of the senate shall act as governor until the vacancy be filled or the disability shall cease.

Sec. 17.   In case of the impeachment of the governor, or his removal from office, death, inability to discharge the pow-

ers and duties of the said office, resignation, or absence from the state, the powers and duties of the office shall devolve upon the lieutenant-governor for the residue of the term, or until the disability shall cease. But when the governor shall, with the consent of the legislature, be out of the state in time of war, at the head of any military force thereof, he shall continue commander in chief of all the military force of the state.

Sec. 18. A secretary of state, a controller, a treasurer, an attorney general, and a surveyor-general shall be elected at the same time and places, and in the same manner as the governor and lieutenant-governor, and whose term of office shall be the same as the governor. (Amendment ratified September 3, 1862.)

[ORIGINAL SECTION.]

Sec. 18. A secretary of state, a controller, a treasurer, an attorney general and surveyor general shall be chosen in the manner provided in this Constitution; and the term of office and eligibility of each shall be the same as are prescribed for the governor and lieutenant-governor.

Sec. 19. The secretary of state shall keep a fair record of the official acts of the legislative and executive departments of the government, and shall, when required, lay the same, and all matters relative thereto, before either branch of the legislature, and shall perform such other duties as may be assigned him by law; and in order that no inconvenience may result to the public service from the taking effect of the amendments proposed to said article V by the legislature of eighteen hundred and sixty-one, no officer shall be superseded or suspended thereby, until the election and qualification of the several officers provided for in said amendments. (Amendment ratified September 3, 1862. Original provided for appointment of secretary of state by the governor.)

Sec. 20. The controller, treasurer, attorney general, and surveyor-general, shall be chosen by joint vote of the two houses of the legislature at their first session under this Constitution, and thereafter shall be elected at the same time

and places, and in the same manner, as the governor and
lieutenant-governor.

Sec. 21.   The governor, lieutenant-governor, secretary of
state, controller, treasurer, attorney general, and surveyor-
general, shall each, at stated times during their continuance
in office, receive for their services a compensation, which
shall not be increased or diminished during the term for
which they shall have been elected; but neither of these
officers shall receive for his own use any fees for the performance of his official duties.

ARTICLE VI.

[Before it was revised by amendments ratified September
3, 1862.   For revision, see page 670.]

JUDICIAL DEPARTMENT.

Section 1.   The judicial power of this state shall be
vested in a supreme court, in district courts, in county
courts and in justices of the peace.   The legislature may
also establish such municipal and other inferior courts as
may be deemed necessary.

Sec. 2.   The supreme court shall consist of a chief justice
and two associate justices, any two of whom shall constitute
a quorum.

Sec. 3.   The justices of the supreme court shall be elected
at the general election, by the qualified electors of the state,
and shall hold their office for the term of six years from the
first day of January, next after their election; provided,
that the legislature shall, at its first meeting, elect a chief
justice and two associate justices of the supreme court, by
joint vote of both houses, and so classify them that one shall
go out of office every two years.   After the first election,
the senior justice in commission shall be the chief justice.

Sec. 4.   The supreme court shall have appellate jurisdiction in all cases when the matter in dispute exceeds two
hundred dollars, when the legality of any tax, toll, or impost, or municipal fine is in question, and in all criminal
cases amounting to felony, on questions of law alone.   And

the said court, and each of the justices thereof, as well as all district and county judges, shall have power to issue writs of habeas corpus at the instance of any person held in actual custody. They shall also have power to issue all other writs and process necessary to the exercise of their appellate jurisdiction and shall be conservators of the peace throughout the state.

Sec. 5. The state shall be divided by the first legislature into a convenient number of districts, subject to such alteration from time to time as the public good may require, for each of which a district judge shall be appointed by the joint vote of the legislature, at its first meeting, who shall hold his office for two years from the first day of January next after his election; after which said judges shall be elected by the qualified electors of their respective districts, at the general election, and shall hold their office for the term of six years.

Sec. 6. The district courts shall have original jurisdiction, in law and equity, in all civil cases where the amount in dispute exceeds two hundred dollars, exclusive of interest. In all criminal cases not otherwise provided for, and in all issues of fact joined in the probate courts, their jurisdiction shall be unlimited.

Sec. 7. The legislature shall provide for the election, by the people, of a clerk of the supreme court, and county clerks, district attorneys, sheriffs, coroners and other necessary officers; and shall fix by law their duties and compensation. County clerks shall be ex-officio clerks of the district courts in and for their respective counties.

Sec. 8. There shall be elected in each of the organized counties of this state one county judge, who shall hold his office for four years. He shall hold the county court and perform the duties of surrogate or probate judge. The county judge, with two justices of the peace, to be designated according to law, shall hold courts of sessions, with such criminal jurisdiction as the legislature shall prescribe, and he shall perform such other duties as shall be required by law.

Sec. 9. The county courts shall have such jurisdiction, in cases arising in justices' courts, and in special cases, as the legislature may prescribe, but shall have no original civil jurisdiction, except in such special cases.

Sec. 10. The times and places of holding the terms of the supreme court, and the general and special terms of the district courts within the several districts, shall be provided for by law.

Sec. 11. No judicial officer, except a justice of the peace, shall receive to his own use, any fees or perquisites of office.

Sec. 12. The legislature shall provide for the speedy publication of all statute laws, and of such judicial decisions as it may deem expedient; and all laws and judicial decisions shall be free for publication by any person.

Sec. 13. Tribunals for conciliation may be established with such powers and duties as may be prescribed by law; but such tribunals shall have no power to render judgment to be obligatory on the parties, except they voluntarily submit their matters in difference, and agree to abide the judg-ment, or assent thereto in the presence of such tribunal, in such cases as shall be prescribed by law.

Sec. 14. The legislature shall determine the number of justices of the peace to be elected in each county, city, town, and incorporated village of the state, and fix by law their powers, duties and responsibilities. It shall also determine in what cases appeals may be made from justices' courts to the county court.

Sec. 15. The justices of the supreme court and judges of the district courts shall severally, at stated times during their continuance in office, receive for their services a compensation to be paid out of the treasury.

Sec. 16. The justices of the supreme court and district judges shall be ineligible to any other office during the term for which they shall have been elected.

Sec. 17. Judges shall not charge juries with respect to matters of fact, but may state the testimony and declare the law.

ARTICLE VI.

[As revised by amendments ratified September 3, 1862.]

JUDICIAL DEPARTMENT.

Section 1. The judicial power of this state shall be vested in a supreme court, in districts courts, in county courts, in probate courts, and in justices of the peace, and in such recorder's and other inferior courts as the legislature may establish in any incorporated city or town. (1862.)

Sec. 2. The supreme court shall consist of a chief justice and four associate justices. The presence of three justices shall be necessary for the transaction of business, excepting such business as may be done at chambers, and the concurrence of three justices shall be necessary to pronounce a judgment. (1862.)

Sec. 3. The justices of the supreme court shall be elected by the qualified electors of the state at special elections to be provided by law, at which elections no officer other than judicial shall be elected, except a superintendent of public instruction. The first election for justices of the supreme court shall be held in the year eighteen hundred and sixty-three. The justices shall hold their offices for the term of ten years from the first day of January next after their election, except those elected at the first election, who, at their first meeting, shall so classify themselves by lot that one justice shall go out of office every two years. The justice having the shortest term to serve shall be the chief justice. (1862.)

Sec. 4. The supreme court shall have appellate jurisdiction in all cases in equity; also in all cases at law which involve the title or possession of real estate, or the legality of any tax, impost, assessment, toll, or municipal fine, or in which the demand, exclusive of interest or the value of the property in controversy, amounts to three hundred dollars; also in all cases arising in the probate courts; and also in all criminal cases amounting to felony, on questions of law alone. The court shall also have power to issue writs of mandamus, certiorari, prohibition, and habeas corpus, and

also all writs necessary or proper to the complete exercise of its appellate jurisdiction. Each of the justices shall have power to issue writs of habeas corpus to any part of the state, upon petition on behalf of any person held in actual custody, and make such writs returnable before himself, or the supreme court, or before any district court, or any county court in the state, or before any judge of said courts. (1862.)

Sec. 5. The state shall be divided, by the legislature of eighteen hundred and sixty-three, into fourteen judicial districts, subject to such alteration, from time to time, by a two-thirds vote of all the members elected to both houses, as the public good may require, in each of which there shall be a district court, and for each of which a judge shall be elected by the qualified electors of the district at the special judicial elections to be held as provided for the election of justices of the supreme court, by section three of this article. The district judges shall hold their offices for the term of six years from the first day of January next after their election. The legislature shall have no power to grant leave of absence to a judicial officer; and any such officer who shall absent himself from the state for upward of thirty consecutive days shall be deemed to have forfeited his office. (1862.)

Sec. 6. The district courts shall have original jurisdiction in all cases in equity; also, in all cases at law which involve the title or possession of real property, or the legality of any tax, impost, assessment, toll, or municipal fine, and in all other cases in which the demand, exclusive of interest or the value of the property in controversy, amounts to three hundred dollars; and also in all criminal cases not otherwise provided for. The district courts and their judges shall have power to issue writs of habeas corpus, on petition by or on behalf of any person held in actual custody, in their respective districts. (1862.)

Sec. 7. There shall be in each of the organized counties of the state a county court, for each of which a county judge shall be elected by the qualified electors of the county,

at the special judicial election to be held as provided for the election of justices of the supreme court by section three of this article. The county judges shall hold their offices for the term of four years from the first day of January next after their election. Said courts shall also have power to issue naturalization papers. In the city and county of San Francisco the legislature may separate the office of probate judge from that of county judge, and may provide for the election of a probate judge, who shall hold his office for the term of four years. (1862.)

Sec. 8. The county court shall have original jurisdiction of actions of forcible entry and detainer, of proceedings in insolvency, of actions to prevent or abate a nuisance, and of all such special cases and proceedings as are not otherwise provided for; and also such criminal jurisdiction as the legislature may prescribe; they shall also have appellate jurisdiction in all cases arising in courts held by justices of the peace and recorders, and in such inferior courts as may be established in pursuance of section one of this article, in their respective counties. The county judges shall also hold, in their several counties, probate court, and perform such duties as probate judges as may be prescribed by law. The county courts and their judges shall also have power to issue writs of habeas corpus, on petition by or on behalf of any person in actual custody in their respective counties. (1862.)

Sec. 9. The legislature shall determine the number of justices of the peace to be elected in each city and township of the state, and fix by law their powers, duties, and responsibilities; provided, such powers shall not in any case trench upon the jurisdiction of the several courts of record. The supreme court, the district courts, county courts, the probate courts, and such other courts as the legislature shall prescribe, shall be courts of record. (1862.)

Sec. 10. The legislature shall fix by law the jurisdiction of any recorder's or other inferior municipal court which may be established in pursuance of section one of this article, and shall fix by law the powers, duties, and responsibilities of the judges thereof. (1862.)

Sec. 11. The legislature shall provide for the election of a clerk of the supreme court, county clerks, district attorneys, sheriffs, and other necessary officers, and shall fix by law their duties and compensation. County clerks shall be ex-officio clerks of the courts of record in and for their respective counties. The legislature may also provide for the appointment by the several district courts of one or more commissioners in the several counties of their respective districts, with authority to perform chamber business of the judges of the district courts and county courts, and also to take depositions, and to perform such other business connected with the adminstration of justice as may be prescribed by law. (1862.)

Sec. 12. The times and places of holding the terms of the several courts of record shall be provided for by law. (1862.)

Sec. 13. No judicial officer, except justices of the peace, recorders, and comimssioners shall receive to his own use any fees or perquisites of office. (1862.)

Sec. 14. The legislature shall provide for the speedy publication of such opinions of the supreme court as it may deem expedient; and all opinions shall be free for publication by any person. (1862.)

Sec. 15. The justices of the supreme court, district judges, and county judges, shall severally, at stated times during their continuance in office, receive for their services a compensation, which shall not be increased or diminished, during the term for which they shall have been elected; provided, that county judges shall be paid out of the county treasury of their respective counties. (1862.)

Sec. 16. The justices of the supreme court, and the district judges, and the county judges, shall be ineligible to any other office than a judicial office during the term for which they shall have been elected. (1862.)

Sec. 17. Judges shall not charge juries with respect to matters of fact, but may state the testimony and declare the law. (1862.)

Sec. 18. The style of all process shall be: "The People of the State of California," and all prosecutions shall be conducted in their name and by their authority. (1862.)

Sec. 19. In order that no inconvenience may result to the public service from the taking effect of the amendments proposed to said article VI, by the legislature of eighteen hundred and sixty-one, no officer shall be superseded thereby, nor shall the organization of the several courts be changed thereby, until the election and qualification of the several officers provided for in said amendment. (1862.)

ARTICLE VII.
MILITIA.

Section 1. The legislature shall provide by law for organizing and disciplining the militia, in such manner as they shall deem expedient, not incompatible with the Constitution and laws of the United States.

Sec. 2. Officers of the militia shall be elected or appointed in such manner as the legislature shall from time to time direct, and shall be commissioned by the governor.

Sec. 3. The governor shall have power to call forth the militia to execute the laws of the state, to suppress insurrections, and repel invasions.

ARTICLE VIII.
STATE DEBTS.

Section 1. The legislature shall not in any manner create any debt or debts, liability or liabilities, which shall, singly or in the aggregate with any previous debts or liabilities, exceed the sum of three hundred thousand dollars, except in case of war, to repel invasion, or suppress insurrection, unless the same shall be authorized by some law for some single object or work, to be distinctly specified therein, which law shall provide ways and means, exclusive of loans, for the payment of the interest of such debt or liability as it falls due, and also to pay and discharge the principal of such debt or liability within twenty years from the time of

the contracting thereof, and shall be irrepealable until the principal and interest thereon shall be paid and discharged; but no such law shall take effect until, at a general election, it shall have been submitted to the people and have received a majority of all the votes cast for and against it at such election; and all money raised by authority of such law shall be applied only to the specific object therein stated, or to the payment of the debt thereby created; and such law shall be published in at least one newspaper in each judicial district, if one be published therein, throughout the state, for three months next preceding the election at which it is submitted to the people.

ARTICLE IX.
EDUCATION.

Section 1. A superintendent of public instruction shall, at the special election for judicial officers to be held in the year eighteen hundred and sixty-three, and every four years thereafter, at such special elections, be elected by the qualified voters of the state, and shall enter upon the duties of his office on the first day of December next after his election. (Amendment ratified September 3, 1862. Original provided for term of three years and election at the general election.)

Sec. 2. The legislature shall encourage, by all suitable means, the promotion of intellectual, scientific, moral, and agricultural improvement. The proceeds of all lands that may be granted by the United States to this state for the support of schools, which may be sold or disposed of, and the five hundred thousand acres of land granted to the new states, under an act of Congress distributing the proceeds of the public lands among the several states of the Union, approved A. D. one thousand eight hundred and forty-one, and all estates of deceased persons who may have died without leaving a will or heir, and also such per cent as may be granted by Congress on the sale of lands in this state, shall be and remain a perpetual fund, the interest of which, together with all the rents of the unsold lands, and such other means as the legislature may provide, shall be inviolably

appropriated to the support of common schools throughout the state.

Sec. 3. The legislature shall provide for a system of common schools, by which a school shall be kept up and supported in each district at least three months in every year; and any school district neglecting to keep up and support such a school may be deprived of its proportion of the interest of the public fund during such neglect.

Sec. 4. The legislature shall take measures for the protection, improvement, or other disposition of such lands as have been or may hereafter be reserved or granted by the United States, or any person or persons, to this state, for the use of a university; and the funds accruing from the rents or sale of such lands, or from any other source, for the purpose aforesaid, shall be and remain a permanent fund, the interest of which shall be applied to the support of said university, with such branches as the public convenience may demand, for the promotion of literature, the arts and sciences, as may be authorized by the terms of such grant. And it shall be the duty of the legislature, as soon as may be, to provide effectual means for the improvement and permanent security of the funds of said university.

ARTICLE X.
MODE OF AMENDING AND REVISING THE CONSTITUTION.

Section 1. Any amendment or amendments to this Constitution may be proposed in the senate or assembly; and if the same shall be agreed to by a majority of the members elected to each of the two houses, such proposed amendment or amendments shall be entered on their journals, with the yeas and nays taken thereon, and referred to the legislature then next to be chosen, and shall be published for three months next preceding the time of making such choice. And if, in the legislature next chosen as aforesaid, such proposed amendment or amendments shall be agreed to by a majority of all the members elected to each house, then it shall be the duty of the legislature to submit such proposed amendment or amendments to the people, in such manner

and at such time as the legislature shall prescribe; and if the people shall approve and ratify such amendment or amendments, by a majority of the electors qualified to vote for members of the legislature voting thereon, such amendment or amendments shall become part of the Constitution.

Sec. 2. And if at any time two-thirds of the senate and assembly shall think it necessary to revise and change this entire Constitution, they shall recommend to the electors at the next election for members of the legislature to vote for or against a convention; and if it shall appear that a majority of the electors voting at such election have voted in favor of calling a convention, the legislature shall, at its next session, provide by law for calling a convention, to be holden within six months after the passage of such law; and such convention shall consist of a number of members not less than that of both branches of the legislature. The Constitution that may have been agreed upon and adopted by such convention shall be submitted to the people, at a special election to be provided for by law, for their ratification or rejection. Each voter shall express his opinion by depositing in the ballot box a ticket, whereon shall be written or printed the words "For the new Constitution," or "Against the new Constitution." The returns of such election shall, in such manner as the convention shall direct, be certified to the executive of the state, who shall call to his assistance the controller, treasurer, and secretary of state, and compare the votes so certified to him. If, by such examination, it be ascertained that a majority of the whole number of votes cast at such election be in favor of such new Constitution, the executive of this state shall, by his proclamation, declare such new Constitution to be the Constitution of the state of California. (Amendment ratified November 4, 1856.)

ARTICLE XI.
MISCELLANEOUS PROVISIONS.

Section 1. The first session of the legislature shall be held at the Pueblo de San Jose, which place shall be the permanent seat of government until removed by law; provided,

however, that two-thirds of all the members elected to each house of the legislature shall concur in the passage of such law.

Sec. 2. Any citizen of this state who shall, after the adoption of this Constitution, fight a duel with deadly weapons, or send or accept a challenge to fight a duel with deadly weapons, either within this state or out of it, or who shall act as second or knowingly aid or assist in any manner those thus offending, shall not be allowed to hold any office of profit or to enjoy the right of suffrage under this Constitution.

Sec. 3. Members of the legislature and all officers, executive and judicial, except such inferior officers as may be by law exempted, shall, before they enter on the duties of their respective offices, take and subscribe the following oath or affirmation:

"I do solemnly swear (or affirm, as the case may be) that I will support the Constitution of the United States and the Constitution of the state of California, and that I will faithfully discharge the duties of the office of ——, according to the best of my ability."

And no other oath, declaration, or test shall be required as a qualification for any office or public interest. .

Sec. 4. The legislature shall establish a system of county and town governments, which shall be as nearly uniform as practicable throughout the state.

Sec. 5. The legislature shall have the power to provide for the election of a board of supervisors in each county, and these supervisors shall jointly and individually perform such duties as may be prescribed by law.

Sec. 6. All officers whose election or appointment is not provided for by this Constitution, and all officers whose offices may hereafter be created by law, shall be elected by the people, or appointed, as the legislature may direct.

Sec. 7. When the duration of any office is not provided for by this Constitution, it may be declared by law; and if not so declared, such office shall be held during the pleasure

of the authority making the appointment; nor shall the duration of any office not fixed by this Constitution ever exceed four years.

Sec. 8. The fiscal year shall commence on the first day of July.

Sec. 9. Each county, town, city, and incorporated village shall make provision for the support of its own officers, subject to such restrictions and regulations as the legislature may prescribe.

Sec. 10. The credit of the state shall not in any manner be given or loaned to or in aid of any individual, association, or corporation; nor shall the state, directly or indirectly, become a stockholder in any association or corporation.

Sec. 11. Suits may be brought against the state in such manner and in such courts as shall be directed by law.

Sec. 12. No contract of marriage, if otherwise duly made, shall be invalidated for want of conformity to the requirements of any religious sect.

Sec. 13. Taxation shall be equal and uniform throughout the state. All property in this state shall be taxed in proportion to its value, to be ascertained as directed by law; but assessors and collectors of town, county, and state taxes shall be elected by the qualified electors of the district, county, or town in which the property taxed for state, county, or town purposes is situated.

Sec. 14. All property, both real and personal, of the wife, owned or claimed by her before marriage, and that acquired afterward by gift, devise, or descent, shall be her separate property, and laws shall be passed more clearly defining the rights of the wife in relation as well to her separate property as to that held in common with her husband. Laws shall also be passed providing for the registration of the wife's separate property.

Sec. 15. The legislature shall protect by law from forced sale a certain portion of the homestead and other property of all heads of families.

Sec. 16.   No perpetuities shall be allowed except for elee-mosynary purposes.

Sec. 17.   Every person shall be disqualified from holding any office of profit in this state who shall have been convicted of having been given or offered a bribe to procure his election or appointment.

Sec. 18.   Laws shall be made to exclude from office, serving on juries and from the right of suffrage, those who shall hereafter be convicted of bribery, perjury, forgery, or other high crimes.   The privilege of free suffrage shall be supported by laws regulating elections, and prohibiting, under adequate penalties all undue influence thereon from power, bribery, tumult, or other improper practice.

Sec. 19.   Absence from this state on business of the state or of the United States shall not affect the question of residence of any person.

Sec. 20.   A plurality of the votes given at any election shall constitute a choice, where not otherwise directed in this Constitution.

Sec. 21.   All laws, decrees, regulations, and provisions which from their nature require publication shall be published in English and Spanish.

ARTICLE XII.
BOUNDARY.

Section 1.   The boundary of the state of California shall be as follows:

Commencing at the point of intersection of forty-second degree of north latitude with the one hundred twentieth degree of longitude west from Greenwich, and running south on the line of said one hundred twentieth degree of west longitude until it intersects the thirty-ninth degree of north latitude; thence running in a straight line in a southeasterly direction to the River Colorado, at a point where it intersects the thirty-fifth degree of north latitude; thence down the middle of the channel of said river to the boundary line between the United States and Mexico, as estab-

lished by the treaty of May thirtieth, one thousand eight hundred and forty-eight; thence running west and along said boundary line, to the Pacific Ocean, and extending therein three English miles; thence, running in a northwesterly direction and following the direction of the Pacific Coast, to the forty-second degree of north latitude; thence, on the line of said forty-second degree of north latitude, to the place of beginning. Also all the islands, harbors, and bays along and adjacent to the coast.

SCHEDULE.

Section 1. All rights, prosecutions, claims, and contracts, as well of individuals as of bodies corporate, and all laws in force at the time of the adoption of this Constitution and not inconsistent therewith, until altered or repealed by the legislature, shall continue as if the same had not been adopted.

Sec. 2. The legislature shall provide for the removal of all causes which may be pending when this Constitution goes into effect to courts created by the same.

Sec. 3. In order that no inconvenience may result to the public service from the taking effect of this Constitution, no office shall be superseded thereby nor the laws relative to the duties of the several officers be changed until the entering into office of the new officers to be appointed under this Constitution.

Sec. 4. The provisions of this Constitution concerning the term of residence necessary to enable persons to hold certain offices therein mentioned, shall not be held to apply to officers chosen by the people at the first election, or by the legislature at its first session.

Sec. 5. Every citizen of California declared a legal voter by this Constitution, and every citizen of the United States a resident of this state on the day of election, shall be entitled to vote at the first general election under this Constitution, and on the question of the adoption thereof.

Sec. 6. This Constitution shall be submitted to the people for their ratification or rejection at the general election to

be held on Tuesday, the thirteenth day of November next. The executive of the existing government of California is hereby requested to issue a proclamation to the people, directing the prefects of the several districts, or, in case of vacancy, the subprefects or senior judge of first instance, to cause such election to be held on the day aforesaid in their respective districts. The election shall be conducted in the manner which was prescribed for the election of delegates to this convention, except that the prefects, subprefects, or senior judge of first instance ordering such election in each district shall have power to designate any additional number of places for opening the polls, and that in every place of holding the election a regular poll list shall be kept by the judges and inspectors of election. It shall also be the duty of these judges and inspectors of election, on the day aforesaid, to receive the votes of the electors qualified to vote at such election. Each voter shall express his opinion by depositing in the ballot-box a ticket whereon shall be written or printed "For the Constitution," or "Against the Constitution," or some such words as will distinctly convey the intention of the voter. These judges and inspectors shall also receive the votes for the several officers to be voted for at the said general election, as herein provided. At the close of the election the judges and inspectors shall carefully count each ballot, and forthwith make duplicate returns thereof to the prefect, subprefect or senior judge of first instance, as the case may be, of their respective districts; and said prefect, subprefect, or senior judge of first instance shall transmit one of the same, by the most safe and rapid conveyance, to the secretary of state. Upon the receipt of said returns, or on the tenth day of December next, if the returns be not sooner received, it shall be the duty of a board of canvassers, to consist of the secretary of state, one of the judges of the superior court, the prefect, judge of first instance, and an alcalde of the district of Monterey, or any three of the aforementioned officers, in the presence of all who shall choose to attend, to compare the votes given at said election, and to immediately publish an abstract of the same in one or more of the newspapers of

California. And the executive will also, immediately after ascertaining that the Constitution has been ratified by the people, make proclamation of the fact; and thenceforth this Constitution shall be ordained and established as the Constitution of California.

Sec. 7. If this Constitution shall be ratified by the people of California, the executive of the existing government is hereby requested, immediately after the same shall be ascertained, in the manner herein directed, to cause a fair copy thereof to be forwarded to the President of the United States, in order that he may lay it before the Congress of the United States.

Sec. 8. At the general election aforesaid, viz.: the thirteenth day of November next, there shall be elected a governor, lieutenant-governor, members of the legislature, and also two members of Congress.

Sec. 9. If this Constitution shall be ratified by the people of California, the legislature shall assemble at the seat of government on the fifteenth day of December next; and in order to complete the organization of that body the senate shall elect a president pro tempore, until the lieutenant-governor shall be installed into office.

Sec. 10. On the organization of the legislature, it shall be the duty of the secretary of state to lay before each house a copy of the abstract made by the board of canvassers, and, if called for, the original returns of election, in order that each house may judge of the correctness of the report of said board of canvassers.

Sec. 11. The legislature, at its first session, shall elect such officers as may be ordered by this Constitution to be elected by that body, and within four days after its organization, proceed to elect two senators to the Congress of the United States. But no law passed by this legislature shall take effect until signed by the governor after his installation into office.

Sec. 12. The senators and representatives of the Congress of the United States elected by the legislature and people of California, as herein directed, shall be furnished

·with certified copies of this Constitution, when ratified, which they shall lay before the Congress of the United States, requesting, in the name of the people of California, the admission of the state of California into the American Union.

Sec. 13.   All officers of this state, other than members of the legislature, shall be installed into office on the fifteenth day of December next, or as soon thereafter as practicable.

Sec. 14.   Until the legislature shall divide the state into counties and senatorial and assembly districts, as directed by this Constitution, the following shall be the apportionment of the two houses of the legislature, viz.: The districts of San Diego and Los Angeles shall jointly elect two senators; the districts of Santa Barbara and San Luis Obispo shall jointly elect one senator; the district of Monterey, one senator; the district of San Jose, one senator; the district of San Francisco, two senators; the district of Sonoma, one senator; the district of Sacramento, four senators; and the district of San Joaquin, four senators.   And the district of San Diego shall elect one member of the assembly; the district of Los Angeles, two members of assembly; the district of Santa Barbara, two members of assembly; the district of San Luis Obispo, one member of assembly; the district of Monterey, two members of assembly; the district of San Jose, three members of assembly; the district of San Francisco, five members of assembly; the district of Sonoma, two members of assembly; the district of Sacramento, nine members of assembly; the district of San Joaquin, nine members of assembly.

Sec. 15.   Until the legislature shall otherwise direct, in accordance with the provisions of this Constitution, the salary of the governor shall be ten thousand dollars per annum; and the salary of the lieutenant-governor shall be double the pay of a state senator; and the pay of members of the legislature shall be sixteen dollars per diem while in attendance, and sixteen dollars for every twenty miles traveled by the usual route from their residences to the place of holding the session of the legislature, and in returning

therefrom. And the legislature shall fix the salaries of all officers other than those elected by the people at the first election.

Sec. 16. The limitation of the powers of the legislature contained in article VIII of this Constitution shall not extend to the first legislature elected under the same, which is hereby authorized to negotiate for such amount as may be necessary to pay the expenses of the state government.

R. SEMPLE,
President, and Delegate from Benicia.

WM. G. MARCY, Secretary.

Joseph Aram,
Ch. T. Botts,
Elam Brown,
Elisha O. Crosby,
José M. Covarubias,
Stephen C. Foster,
Wm. M. Gwin,
Edw. Gilbert,
Henry Hill,
J. D. Hoppe,
Joseph Hobson,
Julian Hanks,
H. W. Halleck,
L. W. Hastings,
J. McHenry Hollinsworth,
Jas. McHall Jones,
Thomas O. Larkin,
Francis J. Lippitt,
Benj. S. Lippincott,
Benj. F. Moore,
Rodman M. Price,
Jno. McDougall,
Man'l Dominguez,
Myron Norton,

Pablo De La Guerra,
Lewis Dent,
Kimball H. Dimmick,
A. J. Ellis,
José Anto Carrillo,
Pacificus Ord,
Miguel D. Pedrorena,
M. M. McCarver,
Antonia Ma. Pico,
Jacinto Rodriguez,
Hugh Reid,
J. A. Sutter,
Jacob R. Snyder,
Winfield Scott Sherwood,
William E. Shannon,
Abel Stearns,
P. Sansevaine,
Wm. M. Steuart,
Henry A. Tefft,
M. G. Vallejo,
Thos. L. Vermeule,
J. P. Walker,
O. M. Wozencraft.

THE

CONSTITUTION

OF THE

UNITED STATES.

(667)

CONSTITUTION

OF THE

UNITED STATES.

WE THE PEOPLE of the United States, in Order to form a more perfect Union, establish Justice, insure domestic Tranquility, provide for the common defense, promote the general Welfare, and secure the Blessings of Liberty to ourselves and our Posterity, do ordain and establish this CONSTITUTION for the United States of America.

ARTICLE I.

SECTION 1. All legislative Powers herein granted shall be vested in a Congress of the United States, which shall consist of a Senate and House of Representatives.

SECTION 2. ¹The House of Representatives shall be composed of Members chosen every second Year by the People of the several States, and the Electors in each State shall have the Qualifications requisite for Electors of the most numerous Branch of the State Legislature.

²No Person shall be a Representative who shall not have attained to the Age of twenty-five Years, and been seven Years a Citizen of the United States, and who shall not, when elected, be an Inhabitant of that State in which he shall be chosen.

³[Representatives and direct Taxes shall be apportioned among the several States which may be included within this Union, according to their respective Numbers, which shall be determined by adding to the whole Number of free Persons, including those bound to Service for a Term of Years, and excluding Indians not taxed, three-fifths of all other Persons.] The actual Enumeration shall be made within three Years after the first Meeting of the Congress of the United States,

and within every subsequent Term of ten Years, in such Manner as they shall by Law direct.   The Number of Representatives shall not exceed one for every thirty Thousand, but each State shall have at Least one Representative; and until such enumeration shall be made, the State of New Hampshire shall be entitled to chuse three, Massachusetts eight, Rhode-Island and Providence Plantations one, Connecticut five, New York six, New Jersey four, Pennsylvania eight, Delaware one, Maryland six, Virginia ten, North Carolina five, South Carolina five, and Georgia three.

⁴When vacancies happen in the Representation from any State, the Executive Authority thereof shall issue Writs of Election to fill such Vacancies.

⁵The House of Representatives shall chuse their Speaker and other Officers; and shall have the sole Power of Impeachment.

SECTION 3.   ¹The Senate of the United States shall be composed of two Senators from each State, chosen by the Legislature thereof, for six Years; and each Senator shall have one Vote.

See amendment, Article XVII, post.

²Immediately after they shall be assembled in Consequence of the first Election, they shall be divided as equally as may be in three Classes.   The Seats of the Senators of the first Class shall be vacated at the Expiration of the second year, of the second Class at the Expiration of the fourth Year, and the third Class at the Expiration of the sixth Year, so that one-third may be chosen every second Year; and if Vacancies happen by Resignation, or otherwise, during the Recess of the Legislature of any State, the Executive thereof may make temporary Appointments until the next Meeting of the Legislature, which shall then fill such Vacancies.

³No Person shall be a Senator who shall not have attained to the Age of thirty Years, and been nine Years a Citizen of the United States, and who shall not, when elected, be an Inhabitant of that State for which he shall be chosen.

⁴The Vice President of the United States shall be President of the Senate, but shall have no Vote, unless they be equally divided.

⁵The Senate shall chuse their other Officers, and also a President pro tempore, in the Absence of the Vice President, or when he shall exercise the Office of President of the United States.

⁶The Senate shall have the sole Power to try all Impeachments. When sitting for that Purpose, they shall be on Oath or Affirmation. When the President of the United States is tried, the Chief Justice shall preside; And no Person shall be convicted without the Concurrence of two-thirds of the Members present.

⁷Judgment in Cases of Impeachment shall not extend further than to removal from Office, and disqualification to hold and enjoy any Office of honor, Trust or Profit under the United States; but the Party convicted shall nevertheless be liable and subject to Indictment, Trial, Judgment and Punishment, according to Law.

SECTION 4. ¹The Times, Places and Manner of holding Elections for Senators and Representatives, shall be prescribed in each State by the Legislature thereof; but the Congress may at any time by Law make or alter such Regulations, except as to the Places of chusing Senators.

²The Congress shall assemble at least once in every Year, and such Meeting shall be on the first Monday in December, unless they shall by Law appoint a different Day.

SECTION 5. ¹Each House shall be the Judge of the Elections, Returns and Qualifications of its own Members, and a Majority of each shall constitute a Quorum to do Business; but a smaller Number may adjourn from day to day, and may be authorized to compel the attendance of absent Members, in such Manner, and under such Penalties as each House may provide.

²Each House may determine the Rules of its proceedings, punish its Members for disorderly Behavior, and, with the Concurrence of two thirds, expel a Member.

³Each House shall keep a Journal of its Proceedings, and from time to time publish the same, excepting such Parts as may in their Judgment require Secrecy; and the Yeas and Nays of the Members of either House on any question shall,

at the Desire of one fifth of those present, be entered on the Journal.

⁴Neither House, during the Session of Congress, shall, without the Consent of the other, adjourn for more than three days, nor to any other Place than that in which the two Houses shall be sitting.

SECTION 6. ¹The Senators and Representatives shall receive a Compensation for their Services, to be ascertained by Law, and paid out of the Treasury of the United States. They shall in all Cases, except Treason, Felony and Breach of the Peace, be privileged from Arrest during their Attendance at the Session of their respective Houses, and in going to and returning from the same; and for any Speech or Debate in either House, they shall not be questioned in any other Place.

²No Senator or Representative shall, during the Time for which he was elected, be appointed to any civil Office under the Authority of the United States, which shall have been created, or the Emoluments whereof shall have been encreased during such time; and no Person holding any Office under the United States, shall be a Member of either House during his Continuance in Office.

SECTION 7. ¹All Bills for raising Revenue shall originate in the House of Representatives; but the Senate may propose or concur with Amendments as on other Bills.

²Every Bill which shall have passed the House of Representatives and the Senate, shall, before it becomes a Law, be presented to the President of the United States; If he approve he shall sign it, but if not he shall return it, with his Objections to that House in which it shall have originated, who shall enter the Objections at large on their Journal, and proceed to reconsider it. If after such Reconsideration two thirds of that House shall agree to pass the Bill, it shall be sent, together with the Objections, to the other House, by which it shall likewise be reconsidered, and if approved by two thirds of that House, it shall become a Law. But in all such Cases the Votes of both Houses shall be determined by Yeas and Nays, and the Names of the Persons voting for and

against the Bill shall be entered on the Journal of each House respectively. If any Bill shall not be returned by the President within ten days (Sundays excepted) after it shall have been presented to him, the Same shall be a Law, in like Manner as if he had signed it, unless the Congress by their Adjournment prevent its Return, in which case it shall not be a Law.

³Every Order, Resolution, or Vote to which the Concurrence of the Senate and House of Representatives may be necessary (except on a question of Adjournment) shall be presented to the President of the United States; and before the Same shall take Effect, shall be approved by him, or being disapproved by him, shall be repassed by two-thirds of the Senate and House of Representatives, according to the Rules and Limitations prescribed in the Case of a Bill.

SECTION 8. ¹The Congress shall have Power To lay and collect Taxes, Duties, Imposts and Excises, to pay the Debts and provide for the common Defence and general Welfare of the United States; but all Duties, Imposts and Excises shall be uniform throughout the United States;

²To borrow Money on the credit of the United States;

³To regulate Commerce with foreign Nations, and among the several States, and with the Indian Tribes;

⁴To establish an uniform Rule of Naturalization, and uniform Laws on the subject of Bankruptcies throughout the United States;

⁵To coin Money, regulate the Value thereof, and of foreign Coin, and fix the Standard of Weights and Measures;

⁶To provide for the Punishment of counterfeiting the Securities and current Coin of the United States;

⁷To establish Post Offices and post Roads;

⁸To promote the Progress of Science and useful Arts, by securing for limited Times to Authors and Inventors the exclusive Right to their respective Writings and Discoveries;

⁹To constitute Tribunals inferior to the supreme Court;

¹⁰To define and punish Piracies and Felonies committed on the high Seas, and Offences against the Law of Nations;

¹¹To declare War, grant Letters of Marque and Reprisal, and make Rules concerning Captures on Land and Water;

[12]To raise and support Armies, but no Appropriation of Money to that Use shall be for a longer Term than Two Years;

[13]To provide and maintain a Navy;

[14]To make Rules for the Government and Regulation of the land and naval Forces;

[15]To provide for calling forth the Militia to execute the Laws of the Union, suppress Insurrections and repel Invasions;

[16]To provide for organizing, arming, and disciplining, the Militia, and for governing such Part of them as may be employed in the Service of the United States, reserving to the States respectively, the Appointment of the Officers, and the Authority of training the Militia according to the discipline prescribed by Congress;

[17]To exercise exclusive Legislation in all Cases whatsoever, over such District (not exceeding ten Miles square) as may, by Cession of particular States, and the Acceptance of Congress, become the Seat of the Government of the United States, and to exercise like Authority over all Places purchased by the Consent of the Legislature of the State in which the Same shall be, for the Erection of Forts, Magazines, Arsenals, dock-Yards, and other needful Buildings;—And

[18]To make all Laws which shall be necessary and proper for carrying into Execution the foregoing Powers, and all other Powers vested by this Constitution in the Government of the United States, or in any Department or Officer thereof;

SECTION 9. [1]The Migration or Importation of such Persons as any of the States now existing shall think proper to admit, shall not be prohibited by the Congress prior to the Year one thousand eight hundred and eight, but a Tax or duty may be imposed on such Importation, not exceeding ten dollars for each Person.

[2]The Privilege of the Writ of Habeas Corpus shall not be suspended, unless when in Cases of Rebellion or Invasion the public Safety may require it.

[3]No Bill of Attainder or ex post facto Law shall be passed.

[4]No Capitation, or other direct, tax shall be laid, unless in Proportion to the Census or Enumeration herein before directed to be taken.

[5]No Tax or Duty shall be laid on Articles exported from any State.

[6]No Preference shall be given by any Regulation of Commerce or Revenue to the Ports of one State over those of another; nor shall Vessels bound to, or from, one State, be obliged to enter, clear, or pay Duties in another.

[7]No Money shall be drawn from the Treasury, but in Consequence of Appropriations made by Law; and a regular Statement and Account of the Receipts and Expenditures of all public Money shall be published from time to time.

[8]No Title of Nobility shall be granted by the United States; and no Person holding any Office of Profit or Trust under them, shall, without the Consent of Congress, accept of any present, Emolument, Office, or Title, of any kind whatever, from any King, Prince, or foreign State.

SECTION 10. [1]No State shall enter into any Treaty, Alliance, or Confederation; grant Letters of Marque and Reprisal; coin Money; emit Bills of Credit; make any Thing but gold and silver Coin a Tender in Payment of Debts; pass any Bill of Attainder, ex post facto Law, or Law impairing the Obigation of Contracts; or grant any Title of Nobility.

[2]No state shall, without the Consent of the Congress, lay any Imposts or Duties on Imports or Exports, except what may be absolutely necessary for executing its inspection Laws: and the net Produce of all Duties and Imposts, laid by any State on Imports or Exports, shall be for the Use of the Treasury of the United States; and all such Laws shall be subject to the Revision and Controul of the Congress.

[3]No State shall, without the Consent of Congress, lay any Duty or Tonnage, keep Troops, or Ships of War in time of Peace, enter into any Agreement or Compact with another State, or with a foreign Power, or engage in War, unless actually invaded, or in such imminent Danger as will not admit of delay.

ARTICLE II.

SECTION 1. ¹The executive Power shall be vested in a President of the United States of America. He shall hold his Office during the Term of four Years, and, together with the Vice President, chosen for the same Term, be elected, as follows:

²Each State shall appoint, in such Manner as the Legislature thereof may direct, a Number of Electors, equal to the whole number of Senators and Representatives to which the State may be entitled in the Congress; but no Senator or Representative, or Person holding an Office of Trust or Profit under the United States, shall be appointed an Elector.

³["The electors shall meet in their respective States, and vote by ballot for two Persons, of whom one at least shall not be an Inhabitant of the same State with themselves. And they shall make a List of all the persons voted for, and of the Number of Votes for each; which List they shall sign and certify, and transmit sealed to the Seat of the Government of the United States, directed to the President of the Senate. The President of the Senate shall, in the Presence of the Senate and House of Representatives, open all the Certificates, and the Votes shall then be counted. The Person having the greatest Number of Votes shall be the President, if such Number be a Majority of the whole Number of Electors appointed; and if there be more than one who have such Majority, and have an equal Number of Votes, then the House of Representatives shall immediately chuse by Ballot one of them for President; and if no Person have a Majority, then from the five highest on the List the said House shall in like Manner chuse the President. But in chusing the President, the Votes shall be taken by States, the Representation from each State having one Vote; A quorum for this Purpose shall consist of a Member or Members from two-thirds of the States, and a Majority of all the States shall be necessary to a Choice. In every Case, after the Choice of the President, the Person having the greatest Number of Votes of the Electors shall be the Vice-President. But if there should remain two or more who have equal Votes,

the Senate shall chuse from them by Ballot the Vice-President.'']

This Clause has been superseded by the twelfth amendment, p. 686.

⁴The Congress may determine the Time of chusing the Electors, and the Day on which they shall give their Votes; which Day shall be the same throughout the United States.

⁵No person except a natural born Citizen, or a Citizen of the United States, at the time of the adoption of this Constitution, shall be eligible to the Office of President; neither shall any Person be eligible to that Office who shall not have attained to the Age of thirty-five Years, and been fourteen Years a Resident within the United States.

⁶In case of the Removal of the President from Office, or of his Death, Resignation, or Inability to discharge the Powers and Duties of the said Office, the same shall devolve on the Vice President, and the Congress may by Law provide for the Case of Removal, Death, Resignation, or Inability, both of the President and Vice President, declaring what Officer shall then act as President, and such Officer shall act accordingly, until the Disability be removed, or a President shall be elected.

⁷The President shall, at stated Times, receive for his Services a Compensation, which shall neither be encreased nor diminished during the Period for which he shall have been elected, and he shall not receive within that Period any other Emolument from the United States, or any of them.

⁸Before he enter on the Execution of his Office, he shall take the following Oath or Affirmation:—''I do solemnly swear (or affirm) that I will faithfully execute the Office of President of the United States, and will to the best of my Ability, preserve, protect and defend the Constitution of the United States.''

SECTION 2.   ¹The President shall be Commander in Chief of the Army and Navy of the United States, and of the Militia of the several States, when called into the actual Service of the United States; he may require the Opinion, in writing, of the principal Officer in each of the executive Departments, upon any Subject relating to the Duties of

their respective Offices, and he shall have power to grant Reprieves and Pardons for Offenses against the United States, except in Cases of Impeachment.

²He shall have Power, by and with the Advice and Consent of the Senate, to make Treaties, provided two thirds of the Senators present concur; and he shall nominate, and by and with the Advice and Consent of the Senate, shall appoint Ambassadors, other public Ministers and Consuls, Judges of the supreme Court, and all other Officers of the United States, whose Appointments are not herein otherwise provided for, and which shall be established by Law: but the Congress may by Law vest the Appointment of such inferior Officers as they think proper, in the President alone, in the Courts of Law, or in the Heads of Departments.

³The President shall have Power to fill up all Vacancies that may happen during the Recess of the Senate, by granting Commissions which shall expire at the End of their next Session.

SECTION 3. He shall from time to time give to the Congress Information of the State of the Union, and recommend to their Consideration such Measures as he shall judge necessary and expedient; he may, on extraordinary Occasions, convene both Houses, or either of them, and in Case of Disagreement between them, with Respect to the Time of Adjournment, he may adjourn them to such Time as he shall think proper; he shall receive Ambassadors and other public Ministers; he shall take Care that the Laws be faithfully executed, and shall Commission all the Officers of the United States.

SECTION 4. The President, Vice President and all civil Officers of the United States, shall be removed from Office on Impeachment for, and Conviction of, Treason, Bribery, or other high Crimes and Misdemeanors.

ARTICLE III.

SECTION 1. The judicial Power of the United States, shall be vested in one supreme Court, and in such inferior Courts as the Congress may from time to time ordain and establish.

The Judges, both of the supreme and inferior Courts, shall hold their Offices during good Behaviour, and shall, at stated Times, receive for their Services, a Compensation, which shall not be diminished during their Continuance in Office.

SECTION 2.   ¹The judicial Power shall extend to all Cases, in Law and Equity, arising under this Constitution, the Laws of the United States, and Treaties made, or which shall be made, under their Authority;—to all Cases affecting Ambassadors, other public Ministers and Consuls;—to all Cases of admiralty and maritime Jurisdiction;—to Controversies to which the United States shall be a Party;—to Controversies between two or more States;—between a State and Citizens of another State;—between Citizens of different States,— between Citizens of the same State claiming Lands under Grants of different States, and between a State, or the Citizens thereof, and foreign States, Citizens or Subjects.

²In all Cases affecting Ambassadors, other public Ministers and Consuls, and those in which a State shall be Party, the Supreme Court shall have original Jurisdiction. In all the other Cases before mentioned, the supreme Court shall have appellate Jurisdiction, both as to Law and Fact, with such Exceptions, and under such Regulations as the Congress shall make.

³The Trial of all Crimes, except in Cases of Impeachment, shall be by Jury; and such Trial shall be held in the State where the said Crimes shall have been committed; but when not committed within any State, the Trial shall be at such Place or Places as the Congress may by Law have directed.

SECTION 3.   ¹Treason against the United States, shall consist only in levying War against them, or in adhering to their Enemies, giving them Aid and Comfort. No Person shall be convicted of Treason unless on the Testimony of two Witnesses to the same overt Act, or on Confession in open Court.

²The Congress shall have Power to declare the Punishment of Treason, but no Attainder of Treason shall work Corruption of Blood, or Forfeiture except during the Life of the Person attainted.

ARTICLE IV.

SECTION 1. Full Faith and Credit shall be given in each State to the public Acts, Records, and judicial Proceedings of every other State. And the Congress may by general Laws prescribe the Manner in which such Acts, Records and Proceedings shall be proved, and the Effect thereof.

SECTION 2. [1]The Citizens of each State shall be entitled to all Privileges and Immunities of Citizens in the several States.

[2]A Person charged in any State with Treason, Felony, or other Crime, who shall flee from Justice, and be found in another State, shall on Demand of the executive Authority of the State from which he fled, be delivered up to be removed to the State having Jurisdiction of the Crime.

[3]No Person held to Service or Labour in one State, under the Laws thereof, escaping into another, shall, in Consequence of any Law or Regulation therein, be discharged from such Service or Labour, but shall be delivered up on Claim of the Party to whom such Service or Labour may be due.

SECTION 3. [1]New States may be admitted by the Congress into this Union; but no new State shall be formed or erected within the Jurisdiction of any other State; nor any State be formed by the Junction of two or more States, or Parts of States, without the Consent of the Legislatures of the States concerned as well as of the Congress.

[2]The Congress shall have Power to dispose of and make all needful Rules and Regulations respecting the Territory or other Property belonging to the United States; and nothing in this Constitution shall be so construed as to Prejudice any Claims of the United States, or of any particular State.

SECTION 4. The United States shall guarantee to every State in this Union a Republican Form of Government, and shall protect each of them against Invasion; and on Application of the Legislature, or of the Executive (when the Legislature cannot be convened) against domestic Violence.

ARTICLE V.

The Congress, whenever two thirds of both Houses shall deem it necessary, shall propose Amendments to this Constitution, or, on the Application of the Legislatures of two thirds of the several States, shall call a Convention for proposing Amendments, which, in either Case, shall be valid to all Intents and Purposes, as Part of this Constitution, when ratified by the Legislatures of three fourths of the several States, or by Conventions in three fourths thereof, as the one or the other Mode of Ratification may be proposed by the Congress; Provided that no Amendment which may be made prior to the Year One thousand eight hundred and eight shall in any Manner affect the first and fourth Clauses in the Ninth Section of the first Article; and that no State, without its Consent, shall be deprived of its equal Suffrage in the Senate.

ARTICLE VI.

[1]All Debts contracted and Engagements entered into, before the Adoption of this Constitution, shall be as valid against the United States under this Constitution, as under the Confederation.

[2]This Constitution, and the Laws of the United States which shall be made in Pursuance thereof; and all Treaties made, or which shall be made, under the Authority of the United States, shall be the supreme Law of the Land; and the Judges in every State shall be bound thereby, any Thing in the Constitution or Laws of any State to the Contrary notwithstanding.

[3]The Senators and Representatives before mentioned, and the Members of the several State Legislatures, and all executive and judicial Officers, both of the United States and of the several States, shall be bound by Oath or Affirmation, to support this Constitution; but no religious Test shall ever be required as a Qualification to any Office or public Trust under the United States.

ARTICLE VII.

The Ratification of the Conventions of nine States, shall be sufficient for the establishment of this Constitution between the States so ratifying the Same.

Done in Convention by the Unanimous Consent of the States present the Seventeenth Day of September in the Year of our Lord one thousand seven hundred and Eighty seven, and of the Independence of the United States of America the Twelfth. In Witness whereof We have hereunto subscribed our Names,

G⁰ : WASHINGTON—
Presidt. and Deputy from Virginia

New Hampshire.

John Langdon   Nicholas Gilman

Massachusetts.

Nathaniel Gorham   Rufus King

Connecticut.

W. Saml. Johnson   Roger Sherman

New York.

Alexander Hamilton

New Jersey.

Wil : Livingston   Wm. Paterson
David Brearley   Jona : Dayton

Pennsylvania.

B. Franklin   Thos. Fitzsimons
Thomas Mifflin   Jared Ingersoll
Robt. Morris   James Wilson
Geo. Clymer   Gouv Morris

Delaware.

Geo : Read   Richard Bassett
Gunning Bedford Jun   Jaco : Broom
John Dickinson

Maryland.

James McHenry   Danl. Carroll
Dan of St Thos Jenifer

Virginia.

John Blair—   James Madison Jr.

North Carolina.

Wm. Blount   Hu Williamson
Richd. Dobbs Spaight

South Carolina.

J. Rutledge   Charles Pinckney
Charles Cotesworth Pinckney Pierce Butler

Georgia.

William Few   Abr Baldwin

Attest   **WILLIAM JACKSON,** *Secretary*

ARTICLES IN ADDITION TO, AND AMENDMENT OF, THE CONSTITU-
TION OF THE UNITED STATES OF AMERICA, PROPOSED BY CON-
GRESS, AND RATIFIED BY THE LEGISLATURES OF THE SEVERAL
STATES PURSUANT TO THE FIFTH ARTICLE OF THE ORIGINAL
CONSTITUTION.

[ARTICLE I.]

Congress shall make no law respecting an establishment of
religion, or prohibiting the free exercise thereof; or abridg-
ing the freedom of speech, or of the press; or the right of the
people peaceably to assemble, and to petition the Government
for a redress of grievances.

[ARTICLE II.]

A well regulated Militia, being necessary to the security of
a free State, the right of the people to keep and bear Arms,
shall not be infringed.

[ARTICLE III.]

No Soldier shall, in time of peace be quartered in any
house, without the consent of the Owner, nor in time of war,
but in a manner to be prescribed by law.

[ARTICLE IV.]

The right of the people to be secure in their persons,
houses, papers, and effects, against unreasonable searches and
seizures, shall not be violated, and no Warrants shall issue,
but upon probable cause, supported by Oath or affirmation,
and particularly describing the place to be searched, and the
persons or things to be seized.

[ARTICLE V.]

No person shall be held to answer for a capital, or otherwise infamous crime, unless on a presentment or indictment
of a Grand Jury, except in cases arising in the land or naval
forces, or in the Militia, when in actual service in time of
War or public danger; nor shall any person be subject for
the same offense to be twice put in jeopardy of life or limb;

nor shall be compelled in any Criminal Case to be a witness against himself, nor be deprived of life, liberty, or property, without due process of law; nor shall private property be taken for public use, without just compensation.

[ARTICLE VI.]

In all criminal prosecutions, the accused shall enjoy the right to a speedy and public trial, by an impartial jury of the State and district wherein the crime shall have been committed, which district shall have been previously ascertained by law, and to be informed of the nature and cause of the accusation; to be confronted with the witnesses against him; to have compulsory process for obtaining Witnesses in his favor, and to have the Assistance of Counsel for his defense.

[ARTICLE VII.]

In suits at common law, where the value in controversy shall exceed twenty dollars, the right of trial by jury shall be preserved, and no fact tried by a jury shall be otherwise re-examined in any Court of the United States, than according to the rules of the common law.

[ARTICLE VIII.]

Excessive bail shall not be required, nor excessive fines imposed, nor cruel and unusual punishments inflicted.

[ARTICLE IX.]

The enumeration in the Constitution, of certain rights, shall not be construed to deny or disparage others retained by the people.

[ARTICLE X.]

The powers not delegated to the United States by the Constitution, nor prohibited by it to the States, are reserved to the States respectively, or to the people.

[ARTICLE XI.]

The Judicial power of the United States shall not be construed to extend to any suit in law or equity, commenced or

prosecuted against one of the United States by Citizens of another State, or by Citizens or Subjects of any Foreign State.

[ARTICLE XII.]

The Electors shall meet in their respective states, and vote by ballot for President and Vice-President, one of whom, at least, shall not be an inhabitant of the same state with themselves; they shall name in their ballots the person voted for as President, and in distinct ballots the person voted for as Vice-President, and they shall make distinct lists of all persons voted for as President, and of all persons voted for as Vice-President, and of the number of votes for each, which lists they shall sign and certify, and transmit sealed to the seat of the government of the United States, directed to the President of the Senate;—The President of the Senate shall, in the presence of the Senate and House of Representatives, open all the certificates and the votes shall then be counted;—The person having the greatest number of votes for President, shall be the President, if such number be a majority of the whole number of Electors appointed; and if no person have such majority, then from the persons having the highest numbers not exceeding three on the list of those voted for as President, the House of Representatives shall choose immediately, by ballot, the President. But in choosing the President, the votes shall be taken by states, the representation from each state having one vote; a quorum for this purpose shall consist of a member or members from two-thirds of the states, and a majority of all the states shall be necessary to a choice. And if the House of Representatives shall not choose a President whenever the right of choice shall devolve upon them, before the fourth day of March next following, then the Vice-President shall act as President, as in the case of the death or other constitutional disability of the President. The person having the greatest number of votes as Vice-President, shall be the Vice-President, if such number be a majority of the whole number of Electors appointed, and if no person have a majority, then from the two highest numbers on the list, the Senate shall choose the Vice-

President; a quorum for the purpose shall consist of two-thirds of the whole number of Senators, and a majority of the whole number shall be necessary to a choice. But no person constitutionally ineligible to the office of President shall be eligible to that of Vice-President of the United States.

[ARTICLE XIII.]

SECTION 1. Neither slavery nor involuntary servitude, except as a punishment for crime whereof the party shall have been duly convicted, shall exist within the United States, or any place subject to their jurisdiction.

SECTION 2. Congress shall have power to enforce this article by appropriate legislation.

[ARTICLE XIV.]

SECTION 1. All persons born or naturalized in the United States, and subject to the jurisdiction thereof, are citizens of the United States and of the State wherein they reside. No State shall make or enforce any law which shall abridge the privileges or immunities of citizens of the United States; nor shall any State deprive any person of life, liberty, or property, without due process of law; nor deny to any person within its jurisdiction the equal protection of the laws.

SECTION 2. Representatives shall be apportioned among the several States according to their respective numbers, counting the whole number of persons in each State, excluding Indians not taxed. But when the right to vote at any election for the choice of electors for President and Vice-President of the United States, Representatives in Congress, the Executive and Judicial officers of a State, or the members of the Legislature, thereof, is denied to any of the male inhabitants of such State, being twenty-one years of age, and citizens of the United States, or in any way abridged, except for participation in rebellion, or other crime, the basis of representation therein shall be reduced in the proportion which the number of such male citizens shall bear to the whole number of male citizens twenty-one years of age in such State.

SECTION 3. No person shall be a Senator or Representative in Congress, or elector of President and Vice-President, or hold any office, civil or military, under the United States, or under any State, who, having previously taken an oath, as a member of Congress, or as an officer of the United States, or as a member of any State legislature, or as an executive or judicial officer of any State, to support the Constitution of the United States, shall have engaged in insurrection or rebellion against the same, or given aid or comfort to the enemies thereof. But Congress may by a vote of two-thirds of each House, remove such disability.

SECTION 4. The validity of the public debt of the United States, authorized by law, including debts incurred for payment of pensions and bounties for services in suppressing insurrection or rebellion, shall not be questioned. But neither the United States nor any State shall assume or pay any debt or obligation incurred in aid of insurrection or rebellion against the United States, or any claim for the loss or emancipation of any slave; but all such debts, obligations and claims shall be held illegal and void.

SECTION 5. The Congress shall have power to enforce, by appropriate legislation, the provisions of this article.

[ARTICLE XV.]

SECTION 1. The right of citizens of the United States to vote shall not be denied or abridged by the United States, or by any State on account of race, color, or previous condition of servitude.

SECTION 2. The Congress shall have power to enforce this article by appropriate legislation.

[ARTICLE XVI.]

The Congress shall have power to lay and collect taxes on incomes, from whatever source derived, without apportionment among the several states, and without regard to any census or enumeration. (Effective February 3, 1913.)

[ARTICLE XVII.]

(Amendment to Article I, section 3, subdivision 1.)

The Senate of the United States shall be composed of two Senators from each state, elected by the people thereof, for six years; and each Senator shall have one vote. The electors in each state shall have the qualifications requisite for electors of the most numerous branch of the state legislatures.

When vacancies happen in the representation of any state in the Senate, the executive authority of such state shall issue writs of election to fill such vacancies; Provided, that the legislature of any state may empower the executive thereof to make temporary appointment until the people fill the vacancies by election as the legislature may direct.

This amendment shall not be so construed as to effect the election or term of any Senator chosen before it becomes valid as part of the Constitution. (Effective May 31, 1913.)

TREATY OF PEACE, FRIENDSHIP, LIMITS, AND SETTLEMENT.

BETWEEN THE UNITED STATES OF AMERICA AND THE MEXICAN REPUBLIC.

Dated at Guadalupe Hidalgo, 2d February, 1848.
Exchanged at Queretaro, 30th May, 1848.
Ratified by the President U. S., 16th March, 1848.
Proclaimed by the President U. S., 4th July, 1848.

BY THE PRESIDENT OF THE UNITED STATES OF AMERICA.

A PROCLAMATION.

Whereas a Treaty of Peace, Friendship, Limits, and Settlement, between the United States of America and the Mexican Republic, was concluded and signed at the city of Guadalupe Hidalgo, on the second day of February, one thousand eight hundred and forty-eight, which Treaty, as amended by the senate of the United States, and being in the English and Spanish languages, is word for word as follows:

In the Name of Almighty God:

The United States of America and the United Mexican States, animated by a sincere desire to put an end to the calamities of the war which unhappily exists between the two republics, and to establish upon a solid basis relations of peace and friendship, which shall confer reciprocal benefits upon the citizens of both, and assure the concord, harmony, and mutual confidence, wherein the two people should live, as good neighbors, have for that purpose appointed their respective plenipotentiaries—that is to say, the President of the United States has appointed Nicholas P. Trist, a citizen of the United States, and the President of the Mexican Republic has appointed Don Luis Gonzaga Cuevas, Don Bernardo Couto, and Don Miguel Atristan, citizens of the said Republic, who, after a reciprocal communication of their respective full powers, have, under the protection of Almighty God, the author of peace, arranged, agreed upon, and signed the following:

(711)

Treaty of Peace, Friendship, Limits, and Settlement, be-
tween the United States of America and the Mexican
Republic.

ARTICLE I.

There shall be firm and universal peace between the United
States of America and the Mexican Republic, and between
their respective countries, territories, cities, towns, and
people, without exception of places or persons.

ARTICLE II.

Immediately upon the signature of this Treaty, a convention shall be entered into between a commissioner or commissioners appointed by the General-in-Chief of the forces
of the United States, and such as may be appointed by the
Mexican government, to the end that a provisional suspension
of hostilities shall take place, and that, in the places occupied
by the said forces, constitutional order may be re-established,
as regards the political, administrative, and judicial branches,
so far as this shall be permitted by the circumstances of military occupation.

ARTICLE III.

Immediately upon the ratification of the present Treaty by
the government of the United States, orders shall be transmitted to the commanders of their land and naval forces,
requiring the latter (provided this Treaty shall then have
been ratified by the government of the Mexican Republic,
and the ratifications exchanged) immediately to desist from
blockading any Mexican ports; and requiring the former
(under the same condition) to commence, at the earliest
moment practicable, withdrawing all troops of the United
States then in the interior of the Mexican Republic, to points
that shall be selected by common agreement, at a distance
from the seaports not exceeding thirty leagues; and such
evacuation of the interior of the Republic shall be completed
with the least possible delay; the Mexican government hereby
binding itself to afford every facility in its power for rendering the same convenient to the troops, on their march and in
their new positions, and for promoting a good understanding

between them and the inhabitants. In like manner, orders shall be despatched to the persons in charge of the custom-houses at all ports occupied by the forces of the United States, requiring them (under the same condition) immediately to deliver possession of the same to the persons authorized by the Mexican government to receive it, together with all bonds and evidences of debt for duties on importations and on exportations, not yet fallen due. Moreover, a faithful and exact account shall be made out, showing the entire amount of all duties on imports and on exports, collected at such custom-houses, or elsewhere in Mexico, by authority of the United States, from and after the day of the ratification of this Treaty by the government of the Mexican Republic; and also an account of the cost of collection; and such entire amount, deducting only the cost of collection, shall be delivered to the Mexican government, at the city of Mexico, within three months after the exchange of ratifications.

The evacuation of the capital of the Mexican Republic by the troops of the United States, in virtue of the above stipulation shall be completed in one month after the orders there stipulated for shall have been received by the commander of said troops, or sooner if possible.

ARTICLE IV.

Immediately after the exchange of ratifications of the present Treaty, all castles, forts, territories, places, and possessions, which have been taken or occupied by the forces of the United States during the present war, within the limits of the Mexican Republic, as about to be established by the following article, shall be definitely restored to the said republic, together with all the artillery, arms, apparatus of war, munitions, and other public property, which were in the said castles and forts when captured, and which shall remain there at the time when this Treaty shall be duly ratified by the government of the Mexican Republic. To this end, immediately upon the signature of this Treaty, orders shall be despatched to the American officers commanding such castles and forts, securing against the removal or destruction of any

such artillery, arms, apparatus of war, munitions, or other public property. The city of Mexico, within the inner line of intrenchments surrounding the said city, is comprehended in the above stipulations, as regards the restoration of artillery, apparatus of war, etc.

The final evacuation of the territory of the Mexican Republic, by the forces of the United States, shall be completed in three months from the said exchange of ratifications, or sooner if possible: the Mexican government hereby engaging, as in the foregoing article, to use all means in its power for facilitating such evacuation, and rendering it convenient to the troops, and for promoting a good understanding between them and the inhabitants.

If, however, the ratification of this Treaty by both parties should not take place in time to allow the embarcation of the troops of the United States to be completed before the commencement of the sickly season, at the Mexican ports on the Gulf of Mexico, in such case a friendly arrangement shall be entered into between the General-in-Chief of the said troops and the Mexican government, whereby healthy and otherwise suitable places, at a distance from the ports not exceeding thirty leagues, shall be designated for the residence of such troops as may not yet have embarked, until the return of the healthy season. And the space of time here referred to as comprehending the sickly season, shall be understood to extend from the first day of May to the first day of November.

All prisoners of war taken on either side, on land or on sea, shall be restored as soon as practicable after the exchange of ratifications of this Treaty. It is also agreed that if any Mexicans should now be held as captives by any savage tribe within the limits of the United States, as about to be established by the following article, the government of the said United States will exact the release of such captives, and cause them to be restored to their country.

ARTICLE V.

The boundary line between the two republics shall commence in the Gulf of Mexico, three leagues from land, opposite the mouth of the Rio Grande, otherwise called Rio Bravo

del Norte, or opposite the mouth of its deepest branch, if it should have more than one branch emptying directly into the sea; from thence up the middle of that river, following the deepest channel, where it has more than one, to the point where it strikes the southern boundary of New Mexico; thence, westwardly, along the whole southern boundary of New Mexico (which runs north of the town called *Paso*) to its western termination; thence, northward, along the western line of New Mexico, until it intersects the first branch of the river Gila (or if it should not intersect any branch of that river, then to the point on the said line nearest to such branch, and thence in a direct line to the same); thence down the middle of the said branch and of the said river, until it empties into the Rio Colorado; thence across the Rio Colorado, following the division line between Upper and Lower California, to the Pacific Ocean.

The southern and western limits of New Mexico, mentioned in this article, are those laid down in the map entitled ''Map of the United Mexican States, as organized and defined by various Acts of the Congress of said Republic, and constructed according to the best Authorities. Revised edition. Published at New York, in 1847, by J. Disturnell.'' Of which map a copy is added to this Treaty, bearing the signatures and seals of the undersigned plenipotentiaries. And, in order to preclude all difficulty in tracing upon the ground the limit separating Upper from Lower California, it is agreed that the said limit shall consist of a straight line drawn from the middle of the Rio Gila, where it unites with the Colorado, to a point on the coast of the Pacific Ocean distant one marine league due south of the southernmost point of the port of San Diego, according to the plan of said port made in the year 1782 by Don Juan Pantoja, second sailing-master of the Spanish fleet, and published at Madrid in the year 1802, in the Atlas to the voyage of the schooners *Sutil* and *Mexicana*, of which plan a copy is hereunto added, signed and sealed by the respective plenipotentiaries.

In order to designate the boundary line with due precision, upon authoritative maps, and to establish upon the ground landmarks which shall show the limits of both republics, as

described in the present article, the two governments shall each appoint a commissioner and a surveyor, who, before the expiration of one year from the date of the exchange of ratifications of this treaty, shall meet at the port of San Diego and proceed to run and mark the said boundary in its whole course to the mouth of the Rio Bravo del Norte. They shall keep journals and make out plans of their operations; and the result agreed upon by them shall be deemed a part of this Treaty, and shall have the same force as if it were inserted therein. The two governments will amicably agree regarding what may be necessary to these persons, and also as to their respective escorts, should such be necessary.

The boundary line established by this article shall be religiously respected by each of the two republics, and no change shall ever be made therein, except by the express and free consent of both nations, lawfully given by the general government of each, in conformity with its own constitution.

ARTICLE VI.

The vessels and citizens of the United States shall, in all time, have a free and uninterrupted passage by the Gulf of California, and by the river Colorado below its confluence with the Gila, to and from their possessions situated north of the boundary line defined in the preceding article; it being understood that this passage is to be by navigating the Gulf of California and the river Colorado, and not by land, without the express consent of the Mexican government.

If, by the examinations which may be made, it should be ascertained to be practicable and advantageous to construct a road, canal, or railway, which should in whole or part run upon the river Gila, or upon its right or its left bank, within the space of one marine league from either margin of the river, the governments of both republics will form an agreement regarding its construction, in order that it may serve equally for the use and advantage of both countries.

ARTICLE VII.

The river Gila, and the part of the Rio Bravo del Norte lying below the southern boundary of New Mexico being,

agreeably to the fifth article, divided in the middle between the two republics, the navigation of the Gila and of the Bravo below said boundary shall be free and common to the vessels and citizens of both countries; and neither shall, without the consent of the other, construct any work that may impede or interrupt, in whole or in part, the exercise of this right; not even for the purpose of favoring new methods of navigation. Nor shall any tax or contribution, under any denomination or title, be levied upon vessels or persons navigating the same, or upon merchandise or effects transported thereon, except in the case of landing upon one of their shores. If, for the purpose of making the said rivers navigable, or for maintaining them in such state, it should be necessary or advantageous to establish any tax or contribution, this shall not be done without the consent of both governments.

The stipulations contained in the present article shall not impair the territorial rights of either republic within its established limits.

ARTICLE VIII.

Mexicans now established in territories previously belonging to Mexico, and which remain for the future within the limits of the United States, as defined by the present Treaty, shall be free to continue where they now reside, or to remove at any time to the Mexican Republic, retaining the property which they possess in the said territories, or disposing thereof, and removing the proceeds wherever they please, without their being subjected, on this account, to any contribution, tax, or charge whatever.

Those who shall prefer to remain in the said territories, may either retain the title and rights of Mexican citizens, or acquire those of citizens of the United States. But they shall be under the obligation to make their election within one year from the date of the exchange of ratifications of this Treaty; and those who shall remain in the said territories after the expiration of that year, without having declared their intention to retain the character of Mexicans, shall be considered to have elected to become citizens of the United States.

In the said territories, property of every kind, now belonging to Mexicans not established there, shall be inviolably re-

spected. The present owners, the heirs of these, and all Mexicans who may hereafter acquire said property by contract, shall enjoy, with respect to it, guarantees equally ample as if the same belonged to citizens of the United States.

ARTICLE IX.

The Mexicans who, in the territories aforesaid, shall not preserve the character of citizens of the Mexican Republic, conformably with what is stipulated in the preceding article, shall be incorporated into the Union of the United States and be admitted at the proper time (to be judged of by the Congress of the United States) to the enjoyment of all the rights of citizens of the United States according to the principles of the constitution; and in the meantime shall be maintained and protected in the free enjoyment of their liberty and property, and secured in the free exercise of their religion without restriction.

ARTICLE X.

[Stricken out.]

ARTICLE XI.

Considering that a great part of the territories which, by the present treaty, are to be comprehended for the future within the limits of the United States, is now occupied by savage tribes, who will hereafter be under the exclusive control of the government of the United States, and whose incursions within the territory of Mexico would be prejudicial in the extreme, it is solemnly agreed that all such incursions shall be forcibly restrained by the government of the United States whensoever this may be necessary; and that, when they cannot be prevented, they shall be punished by the said government, and satisfaction for the same shall be exacted—all in the same way, and with equal diligence and energy, as if the same incursions were meditated or committed within its own territory against its own citizens.

It shall not be lawful, under any pretext whatever, for any inhabitant of the United States to purchase or acquire any Mexican, or any foreigner residing in Mexico, who may have been captured by Indians inhabiting the territory of either

of the two republics, nor to purchase or acquire horses, mules, cattle, or property of any kind, stolen within Mexican territory by such Indians.

And in the event of any person or persons, captured within Mexican territory by Indians, being carried into the territory of the United States, the government of the latter engages and binds itself in the most solemn manner, so soon as it shall know of such captives being within its territory, and shall be able so to do, through the faithful exercise of its influence and power, to rescue them, and return them to their country, or deliver them to the agent or representative of the Mexican government. The Mexican authorities will, as far as practicable, give to the government of the United States notice of such captures; and its agent shall pay the expenses incurred in the maintenance and transmission of the rescued captives; who, in the meantime, shall be treated with the utmost hospitality by the American authorities at the place where they may be. But if the government of the United States, before receiving such notice from Mexico, should obtain intelligence, through any other channel, of the existence of Mexican captives within its territory, it will proceed forthwith to effect their release and delivery to the Mexican agent as above stipulated.

For the purpose of giving to these stipulations the fullest possible efficacy, thereby affording the security and redress demanded by their true spirit and intent, the government of the United States will now and hereafter pass, without unnecessary delay, and always vigilantly enforce, such laws as the nature of the subject may require. And finally, the sacredness of this obligation shall never be lost sight of by the said government when providing for the removal of the Indians from any portion of the said territories, or for its being settled by citizens of the United States; but on the contrary, special care shall then be taken not to place its Indian occupants under the necessity of seeking new homes, by committing those invasions which the United States have solemnly obliged themselves to restrain.

ARTICLE XII.

In consideration of the extension acquired by the boundaries of the United States, as defined in the fifth article of the present Treaty, the government of the United States engages to pay to that of the Mexican Republic the sum of fifteen millions of dollars.

Immediately after this Treaty shall have been duly ratified by the government of the Mexican Republic, the sum of three millions of dollars shall be paid to the said government by that of the United States, at the city of Mexico, in the gold or silver coin of Mexico. The remaining twelve millions of dollars shall be paid at the same place, and in the same coin, in annual installments of three millions of dollars each, together with interest on the same at the rate of six per centum per annum. This interest shall begin to run upon the whole sum of twelve millions from the day of the ratification of the present Treaty by the Mexican government, and the first of the installments shall be paid at the expiration of one year from the same day. Together with each annual installment, as it falls due, the whole interest accruing on such installment from the beginning shall also be paid.

ARTICLE XIII.

The United States engage, moreover, to assume and pay to the claimants all the amounts now due them, and those hereafter to become due, by reason of the claims already liquidated, and decided against the Mexican Republic, under the conventions between the two republics severally concluded on the eleventh day of April, eighteen hundred and thirty-nine, and on the thirtieth day of January, eighteen hundred and forty-three; so that the Mexican Republic shall be absolutely exempt for the future from all expense whatever on account of the said claims.

ARTICLE XIV.

The United States do furthermore discharge the Mexican Republic from all claims of citizens of the United States, not heretofore decided against the Mexican government, which may have arisen previously to the date of the signature of

this Treaty; which discharge shall be final and perpetual, whether the said claims be rejected or be allowed by the board of commissioners provided for in the following article, and whatever shall be the total amount of those allowed.

ARTICLE XV.

The United States, exonerating Mexico from all demands on account of the claims of their citizens mentioned in the preceding article, and considering them entirely and forever cancelled, whatever their amount may be, undertake to make satisfaction for the same, to an amount not exceeding three and one quarter millions of dollars. To ascertain the validity and amount of those claims, a board of commissioners shall be established by the government of the United States, whose awards shall be final and conclusive; provided that, in deciding upon the validity of each claim, the board shall be guided and governed by the principles and rules of decision prescribed by the first and fifth articles of the unratified convention, concluded at the city of Mexico on the twentieth day of November, one thousand eight hundred and forty-three; and in no case shall an award be made in favor of any claim not embraced by these principles and rules.

If, in the opinion of the said board of commissioners, or of the claimants, any books, records, or documents in the possession or power of the government of the Mexican Republic, shall be deemed necessary to the just decision of any claim, the commissioners, or the claimants through them, shall, within such period as Congress may designate, make an application in writing for the same, addressed to the Mexican Minister for Foreign Affairs, to be transmitted by the Secretary of State of the United States; and the Mexican government engages, at the earliest possible moment after the receipt of such demand, to cause any of the books, records, or documents, so specified, which shall be in their possession or power (or authenticated copies or extracts of the same), to be transmitted to the said Secretary of State, who shall immediately deliver them over to the said board of commissioners; provided, that no such application shall be made by,

or at the instance of, any claimant, until the facts which it is expected to prove by such books, records, or documents, shall have been stated under oath or affirmation.

ARTICLE XVI.

Each of the contracting parties reserves to itself the entire right to fortify whatever point within its territory it may judge proper so to fortify, for its security.

ARTICLE XVII.

The Treaty of amity, commerce, and navigation, concluded at the city of Mexico on the fifth day of April, A. D. 1831, between the United States of America and the United Mexican States, except the additional article, and except so far as the stipulations of the said Treaty may be incompatible with any stipulation contained in the present Treaty, is hereby revived for the period of eight years from the day of the exchange of ratifications of this Treaty, with the same force and virtue as if incorporated therein; it being understood that each of the contracting parties reserves to itself the right, at any time after the said period of eight years shall have expired, to terminate the same by giving one year's notice of such intention to the other party.

ARTICLE XVIII.

All supplies whatever for troops of the United States in Mexico, arriving at ports in the occupation of such troops previous to the final evacuation thereof, although subsequently to the restoration of the custom-houses at such ports, shall be entirely exempt from duties and charges of any kind; the government of the United States hereby engaging and pledging its faith to establish, and vigilantly to enforce all possible guards for securing the revenue of Mexico, by preventing the importation, under cover of this stipulation, of any articles other than such, both in kind and in quantity, as shall really be wanted for the use and consumption of the forces of the United States during the time they may remain in Mexico. To this end, it shall be the duty of all officers

and agents of the United States to denounce to the Mexican
authorities at the respective ports any attempts at a fraudulent abuse of this stipulation which they may know of or
may have reason to suspect, and to give to such authorities
all the aid in their power with regard thereto; and every
such attempt, when duly proved and established by sentence
of a competent tribunal, shall be punished by the confiscation
of the property so attempted to be fraudulently introduced.

ARTICLE XIX.

With respect to all merchandise, effects, and property
whatsoever, imported into ports of Mexico whilst in the occupation of the forces of the United States, whether by citizens
of either republic, or by citizens or subjects of any neutral
nation, the following rules shall be observed:

1. All such merchandise, effects, and property, if imported
previously to the restoration of the custom-houses to the
Mexican authorities, as stipulated for in the third article of
this Treaty, shall be exempt from confiscation, although the
importation of the same be prohibited by the Mexican tariff.

2. The same perfect exemption shall be enjoyed by all such
merchandise, effects, and property, imported subsequently to
the restoration of the custom-houses, and previously to the
sixty days fixed in the following article for the coming into
force of the Mexican tariff at such ports respectively; the
said merchandise, effects, and property being, however, at
the time of their importation, subject to the payment of
duties, as provided for in the said following article.

3. All merchandise, effects, and property described in the
two rules foregoing shall, during their continuance at the
place of importation, and upon their leaving such place for
the interior, be exempt from all duty, tax, or impost of every
kind, under whatsoever title or denomination. Nor shall
they be there subjected to any charge whatsoever upon the
sale thereof.

4. All merchandise, effects, and property described in the
first and second rules, which shall have been removed to any
place in the interior whilst such place was in the occupation

of the forces of the United States, shall, during their continuance therein, be exempt from all tax upon the sale or consumption thereof, and from every kind of impost or contribution, under whatsoever title or denomination.

5. But if any merchandise, effects, or property described in the first and second rules, shall be removed to any place not occupied at the time by the forces of the United States, they shall, upon their introduction into such place, or upon their sale or consumption there, be subject to the same duties which, under the Mexican laws, they would be required to pay in such cases if they had been imported in time of peace, through the maritime custom-houses, and had there paid the duties conformably with the Mexican tariff.

6. The owners of all merchandise, effects, or property described in the first and second rules, and existing in any port of Mexico, shall have the right to reship the same, exempt from all tax, impost, or contribution whatever.

With respect to the metals, or other property, exported from any Mexican port whilst in the occupation of the forces of the United States, and previously to the restoration of the custom-house at such port, no person shall be required by the Mexican authorities, whether general or state, to pay any tax, duty, or contribution upon any such exportation, or in any manner to account for the same to the said authorities.

ARTICLE XX.

Through consideration for the interests of commerce generally, it is agreed, that if less than sixty days should elapse between the date of the signature of this Treaty and the restoration of the custom-houses conformably with the stipulation in the third article, in such case all merchandise, effects, and property whatsoever, arriving at the Mexican ports after the restoration of the said custom-houses, and previously to the expiration of sixty days after the signature of this Treaty, shall be admitted to entry; and no other duties shall be levied thereon than the duties established by the tariff found in force at such custom-houses at the time of the restoration of the same. And to all such merchandise, effects, and property, the rules established by the preceding article shall apply.

ARTICLE XXI.

If unhappily any disagreement should hereafter arise between the governments of the two republics, whether with respect to the interpretation of any stipulation in this Treaty, or with respect to any other particular concerning the political or commercial relations of the two nations, the said governments, in the name of those nations, do promise to each other that they will endeavor, in the most sincere and earnest manner, to settle the differences so arising, and to preserve the state of peace and friendship in which the two countries are now placing themselves; using, for this end, mutual representations and pacific negotiations. And if, by these means, they should not be enabled to come to an agreement, a resort shall not, on this account, be had to reprisals, aggression, or hostility of any kind, by the one republic against the other, until the government of that which deems itself aggrieved shall have maturely considered, in the spirit of peace and good neighborship, whether it would not be better that such difference should be settled by the arbitration of commissioners appointed on each side, or by that of a friendly nation. And should such course be proposed by either party, it shall be acceded to by the other, unless deemed by it altogether incompatible with the nature of the difference, or the circumstances of the case.

ARTICLE XXII.

If (which is not to be expected, and which God forbid!) war should unhappily break out between the two republics, they do now, with a view to such calamity, solemnly pledge themselves to each other and to the world, to observe the following rules, absolutely, where the nature of the subject permits, and as closely as possible in all cases where such absolute observance shall be impossible.

1. The merchants of either republic then residing in the other shall be allowed to remain twelve months (for those dwelling in the interior), and six months (for those dwelling at the seaports), to collect their debts and settle their affairs; during which periods, they shall enjoy the same protection,

and be on the same footing, in all respects, as the citizens or
subjects of the most friendly nations; and, at the expiration
thereof, or at any time before, they shall have full liberty
to depart, carrying off all their effects without molestation
or hindrance; conforming therein to the same laws which the
citizens or subjects of the most friendly nations are required
to conform to. Upon the entrance of the armies of either
nation into the territories of the other, women and children,
ecclesiastics, scholars of every faculty, cultivators of the
earth, merchants, artisans, manufacturers, and fishermen, un-
armed and inhabiting unfortified towns, villages, or places,
and in general all persons whose occupations are for the common subsistence and benefit of mankind, shall be allowed to
continue their respective employments unmolested in their
persons. Nor shall their houses or goods be burnt or otherwise destroyed, nor their cattle taken, nor their fields wasted
by the armed force into whose power, by the events of war,
they may happen to fall; but if the necessity arise to take
anything from them for the use of such armed force, the same
shall be paid for at an equitable price. All churches, hospitals, schools, colleges, libraries, and other establishments for
charitable and beneficent purposes, shall be respected, and all
persons connected with the same protected in the discharge
of their duties and the pursuit of their vocations.

2. In order that the fate of prisoners of war may be alle-
viated, all such practices as those of sending them into distant, inclement, or unwholesome districts, or crowding them
into close and noxious places, shall be studiously avoided.
They shall not be confined in dungeons, prison-ships, or prisons; nor be put in irons, or bound, or otherwise restrained in
the use of their limbs. The officers shall enjoy liberty on
their paroles, within convenient districts, and have comfort-
able quarters; and the common soldiers shall be disposed in
cantonments, open and extensive enough for air and exercise,
and lodged in barracks as roomy and good as are provided
by the party in whose power they are, for its own troops.
But if any officer shall break his parole by leaving the district so assigned him, or any other prisoner shall escape from
the limits of his cantonment, after they shall have been des-

ignated to him, such individuals, officer, or other prisoner, shall forfeit so much of the benefit of this article as provides for his liberty on parole or in cantonment. And if any officer so breaking his parole, or any common soldier so escaping from the limits assigned him, shall afterwards be found in arms, previously to his being regularly exchanged, the person so offending shall be dealt with according to the established laws of war. The officers shall be daily furnished by the party in whose power they are, with as many rations, and of the same articles, as are allowed, either in kind or by commutation, to officers of equal rank in its own army; and all others shall be daily furnished with such ration as is allowed to a common soldier in its own service: the value of all which supplies shall, at the close of the war, or at periods to be agreed upon between the respective commanders, be paid by the other party, on a mutual adjustment of accounts for the subsistence of prisoners; and such accounts shall not be mingled with or set off against any others, nor the balance due on them be withheld, as a compensation or reprisal for any cause whatever, real or pretended. Each party shall be allowed to keep a commissary of prisoners, appointed by itself, with every cantonment of prisoners, in possession of the other; which commissary shall see the prisoners as often as he pleases; shall be allowed to receive, exempt from all duties or taxes, and to distribute, whatever comforts may be sent to them by their friends; and shall be free to transmit his reports in open letters to the party by whom he is employed.

And it is declared that neither the pretense that war dissolves all treaties, nor any other whatever, shall be considered as annulling or suspending the solemn covenant contained in this article. On the contrary, the state of war is precisely that for which it is provided; and during which its stipulations are to be as sacredly observed as the most acknowledged obligations under the law of nature or nations.

ARTICLE XXIII.

This treaty shall be ratified by the President of the United States of America, by and with the advice and consent of the Senate thereof; and by the President of the Mexican Repub-

lic, with the previous approbation of its General Congress; and the ratifications shall be exchanged in the city of Washington, or at the seat of government of Mexico, in four months from the date of the signature hereof, or sooner if practicable.

In faith whereof, we, the respective plenipotentiaries, have signed this treaty of peace, friendship, limits, and settlement; and have hereunto affixed our seals respectively. Done in quintuplicate at the city of Guadalupe Hidalgo, on the second day of February in the year of our Lord one thousand eight hundred and forty-eight.

N. P. TRIST,	[L. S.]
LUIS G. CUEVAS,	[L. S.]
BERNARDO COUTO,	[L. S.]
MIGL. ATRISTAN,	[L. S.]

And whereas the said treaty, as amended, has been duly ratified on both parts, and the respective ratifications of the same were exchanged at Queretaro on the thirtieth day of May last, by Ambrose H. Sevier and Nathan Clifford, Commissioners on the part of the Government of the United States, and by Senor Don Luis de la Rosa, Minister of Relations of the Mexican Republic, on the part of that Government:

Now, therefore, be it known, that I, James K. Polk, President of the United States of America, have caused the said Treaty to be made public, to the end that the same and every clause and article thereof may be observed and fulfilled with good faith by the United States and the citizens thereof.

In witness whereof, I have hereunto set my hand and caused the seal of the United States to be affixed.

Done at the city of Washington, this fourth day of July, one thousand eight hundred and forty-eight, and of the Independence of the United States the seventy-third.

[L. S.]   JAMES K. POLK.

By the President:

JAMES BUCHANAN,
    Secretary of State.

ARTICLES REFERRED TO IN THE FIFTEENTH ARTICLE OF THE PRECEDING TREATY.

First and Fifth Articles of the unratified Convention between the United States and the Mexican Republic of the 20th Nov. 1843.

ARTICLE I.

All claims of citizens of the Mexican Republic against the government of the United States which shall be presented in the manner and time hereinafter expressed, and all claims of citizens of the United States against the government of the Mexican Republic, which for whatever cause were not submitted to, nor considered nor finally decided by, the commission, nor by the arbiter appointed by the convention of 1839, and which shall be presented in the manner and time hereinafter specified, shall be referred to four commissioners, who shall form a board, and shall be appointed in the following manner, that is to say: Two commissioners shall be appointed by the President of the Mexican Republic, and the other two by the President of the United States, with the approbation and consent of the senate. The said commissioners, thus appointed, shall, in presence of each other, take an oath to examine and decide impartially the claims submitted to them, and which may lawfully be considered, according to the proofs which shall be presented, the principles of right and justice, the law of nations, and the treaties between the two republics.

ARTICLE V.

All claims of citizens of the United States against the government of the Mexican Republic, which were considered by the commissioners, and referred to the umpire appointed under the convention of the eleventh April, 1839, and which were not decided by him, shall be referred to, and decided by, the umpire to be appointed, as provided by this convention, on the points submitted to the umpire under the late convention, and his decision shall be final and conclusive. It is also agreed, that, if the respective commissioners shall deem it expedient, they may submit to the said arbiter new arguments upon the said claims.

INDEX.

(731)

INDEX.

Constitution—47

Constitution—48

J

Constitution—49

S

T

U